D1274633

Hugh Borton, Ph.D., Leiden University, is Senior Lecturer and Senior Research Associate, East Asian Institute, Columbia University. Dr. Borton also holds the LL.D. from Temple University, Haverford College, and the University of Pennsylvania. He was formerly Research Associate and Chief, Division of Japanese Affairs, United States Department of State; Professor of Japanese and Director of the East Asian Institute, Columbia University; and President of Haverford College. He was Chief of the American Delegation for three of the United States–Japan Conferences on Cultural and Intellectual Interchange. In 1968 he was decorated by the Japanese government with the Second Order of the Sacred Treasure, First Class.

Courtesy of The Bettmann Archive

Landing of Commodore Perry at Kanagawa, March 8, 1854

JAPAN'S MODERN CENTURY

FROM PERRY TO 1970

HUGH BORTON
EAST ASIAN INSTITUTE
COLUMBIA UNIVERSITY

SECOND EDITION

THE RONALD PRESS COMPANY • NEW YORK

4MP

Library of Congress Catalog Card Number: 70–110544
PRINTED IN THE UNITED STATES OF AMERICA

To

SIR GEORGE B. SANSOM

whose inspiration and
kindly guidance made
this book possible

Books are expendable, like the man-hours that go to the making of them. . . . The one thing that matters is that inquiry shall go on; for, so long as it continues, there is hope that it may also get further.

ARNOLD J. TOYNBEE, Introduction, *A Study of History, Reconsiderations,* Vol. XII, 1961.

History is that by means of which one records events. On the basis of events the true history shows itself that good should be rewarded and evil punished. . . . Writings should be authenticated and events be made clear. If one deviates in any direction from this, how can one call this true history?

TOKUGAWA TSUNAEDA, Preface, *Dai Nihon Shi* (The History of Japan), 1715.

Writing history is hardly private enterprise; it is public business of the republic of learning and letters, whose citizens desire that any job undertaken shall be done well.

BERNARD DE VOTO, Preface, *The Course of Empire,* 1953.

Preface

Japan, the world's third largest industrial power, with the strongest and most stable democratic government in Asia, achieved this status in an incredibly short time. In December, 1941, it challenged the United States by attacking Pearl Harbor. After four and a half years of total war, it was completely defeated and devastated. Since their defeat, the Japanese, through a combination of foreign aid and of their own prodigious effort, have put their country back on its feet, and it is rapidly becoming, both literally and figuratively, a strong island bastion of democracy in East Asia.

These developments are all the more significant in view of the fact that a century ago Japan was a secluded, semifeudal, agrarian country of about thirty million persons. In 1970, it is a modern industrial state with a population of about a hundred million. This book endeavors to explain, therefore, Japan's phenomenal transformation, seeking answers to the twofold question: How did Japan get that way? Where is it likely to go?

In general this book presents Japan's modern transformation as a narrative, interpreting and analyzing the forces which brought about this change. Since the formative influences, whether political, economic, social, or international, varied in their intensity throughout the different periods, these forces are emphasized in proportion to their shifting importance. For example, in the years prior to the restoration to power of the Emperor Meiji in 1868, internal rivalries among those contending for power are the most important. In the next two decades, practical problems in establishing a constitutional monarchy were paramount. In the period beginning with the war against China in 1894, international considerations increasingly dominated the scene. In the decade before Pearl Harbor, the effects of the growth of nationalism and militarism prevailed. After the Peace Treaty of 1952, economic recovery and growth and close American–Japanese collaboration on security problems have overshadowed everything else.

The selection of facts to be included in this analysis of Japan's modern century, which in fact covers roughly one hundred and twenty years from about 1850 to 1970, was a different problem. Anyone who writes a history of a civilization which is not rooted in the Western tradition must perforce include much background material that is new to many readers. Also, the more recent the events, the more material there is from which to choose. It was decided that detailed facts would be included where they were necessary for a clear understanding of the narrative, where the significance of events has been lost or misinterpreted by previous writers, or where information has hitherto been scanty.

Through a provocative approach to certain fundamental questions, it is hoped that this book will stimulate both the general reader and Western and Japanese historians to reevaluate past events and to arrive at a more accurate assessment of historical developments. For example, on the basis of the record, it is questionable to what extent democratic, representative institutions existed or functioned prior to World War II. With this heritage will these new institutions prosper or decline? The record also shows clearly that a drive to dominate China was one of the basic determinants of Japanese foreign policy throughout the past century. The current prevalence in Japan of a desire for closer commercial contacts with Communist China is a natural outcome of this historical background. Will this materialize or will they continue estranged? In the past the necessity for economic survival was used as justification for strong state controls and for overseas expansion. Will the search for economic viability in the future or the intensive fervor of student opposition to the Establishment produce the same results if alternative solutions are not found?

As for some of the technical problems, because of the importance of economic forces in Japan's development, special effort has been made to try to obtain the most reliable statistical material. Biographical notes, supplementary remarks and references are relegated to notes at the end of each chapter to avoid interrupting the narrative. The bibliographical notes, referring to both Japanese and Western language sources, are suggestive rather than exhaustive but should be of assistance to the reader who wishes to pursue a particular subject further. Japanese personal names are given with the family name first. In a few cases, such as "Konoye" or "Tokyo," I have used the more popular romanization.

In conclusion, it is difficult to acknowledge adequately and impossible to list all those who assisted me with this revision. My initial thanks are due my wife for her keen criticisms and for her hours of labor preparing the manuscript. My students' criticism of the text helped to correct several errors. My colleagues in the East Asian Institute at Columbia University have been generous in their interest. With the assistance of the Institute's funds, I was able to devote a sabbatical year's research and study at Tokyo University in 1951–1952. More recently, another sabbatical year supported by Haverford College in 1967–1968 enabled me to learn at first hand about contemporary Japan and to become familiar with the most recent publications. Thanks to additional support from the East Asian Institute I have been able to prepare a completely enlarged and revised edition of a book which originally appeared in 1955.

I am eternally grateful to Sir George B. Sansom, who introduced me to the study of Japanese history at a private seminar which he conducted in Tokyo in the winter of 1928–1929. If this book has any special merit, it is due to his interest. We spent many hours discussing both its contents and the method of presentation. I am indebted to several scholars in Japan for their help, especially Dr. Takagi Yasaka and Mr. Narusawa Akira. I am most grateful to American colleagues for reading the new manuscript and making helpful corrections and suggestions. Professor Marius Jansen of Princeton University commented on Chapters 2–6 and the two final chapters of the book. Professor Ardath Burks of Rutgers University read Chapters 11–13 and 15–16. Professor James Nakamura of Columbia University not only advised me on the latest bibliographical sources for the economic sections but made very helpful comments on Chapters 7, 9, and 14. Finally, Professor James B. Crowley, Professor of History at Yale University, was most helpful in reference to Chapters 17 and 18. To Miss Miwa Kai of the East Asian Library of Columbia University, my warm thanks for her constant help, for pointing out several typographical errors in the first edition, and for writing the Chinese characters in the footnotes. The illustrations of Ii Naosuke, of his poem, and of the early cannon are gifts from his great grandson, Ii Naoyoshi. Thanks to Miss Elizabeth Scott Blair of the East Asian Institute and to Mrs. Mary Campbell, the manuscript was completed on time. Hopefully, together we have made an interesting and useful book.

Hugh Borton

New York, N. Y.
February, 1970

Contents

PART I

The Opening of Japan, 1850–1868

PART II

Formation of a Centralized Monarchy, 1868–1890

PART III

Establishment of the Japanese Empire, 1890–1915

PART IV

Leadership in Greater East Asia, 1915–1941

PART V

Japan Rebounds from War and Defeat, 1941–1970

APPENDIXES

PART I

THE OPENING OF JAPAN
1850-1868

He shall have the use of two oceans—the mighty Pacific and the turbulent Atlantic shall be his.

Speech at New Jersey Democratic State Convention, 1844

Chronology

1853–1868

1853	July	Perry arrives in Japan
	August	Shogun seeks opinion of barons on opening Japan
		Industrialization in western clans
1854		Treaty of Kanagawa with the United States
1855		Treaty of Shimoda with Russia
1856		Arrival of U. S. Consul-General Townsend Harris
1857	December	Consul-General Harris presents credentials to Shogun
1858		United States–Japan Commercial Treaty
1860		First Japanese Mission to the United States
1861		Antiforeign assassinations
1863		Extremists demand the expulsion of foreigners
		British bombardment of Satsuma
	September	Satsuma troops stage coup d'état in Kyoto and expel Chōshū army
1864		Foreign squadron opens Straits of Shimonoseki
1865–1866		Civil war in Chōshū; Shogun's army defeated
1866		Satsuma–Chōshū alliance supporting Emperor
1867	November	The Shogun resigns
1868	January	Emperor Meiji announces restoration of power
	April	Shogun surrenders in Edo (Tokyo)

1

Introduction

Flung across the great circle route from North America to the Asiatic continent lies the Empire of Japan. Its boundaries, as verified by the Treaty of Peace signed at San Francisco on September 8, 1951, were essentially the same as those of a century earlier when President Millard Fillmore and Secretary of State Daniel Webster were making plans to send a naval mission to open Japan to the West. In the mid-nineteenth century Japan was the only large Asiatic country to remain closed to the Western world. The British and the Dutch, who had already developed strong colonial empires, were anxious to expand their Far Eastern trade. Following the defeat of China by Great Britain in the Opium War, in 1842, China had been forced to relinquish important attributes of its sovereignty to the Western powers.

On the North American continent, Americans had been pressing toward the West—the sunset—until their territory had reached the Pacific. This basic urge emanated partly from fancy, partly from fact. Cabeza de Vaca, one of the first European explorers of the New World, wrote as early as 1535 that he was certain that he would find what he desired by going toward the sunset. This lure in America to follow the sun was intensified by tales of the fabulous wealth of the seven cities, of the riches of Quivira, of the "Island of California," and of the Western Sea. Even Coronado's failure to discover little more than the Pueblo Indians failed to diminish men's hopes of finding their fortune in the Orient. The myth was kept alive by the Jesuit missionaries in the Mississippi Valley, who claimed that Hudson Bay was separated from Japan by 3,500 miles of open water. At the beginning of the nineteenth century, as the continental ridge was conquered and its contours and sources examined at first hand by explorers such as Lewis and Clark, fancy turned into fact. There was no easy route across the continent to the shore of the Pacific Ocean. Nevertheless, America's concept of Manifest Destiny, the exuberance and energy of the young Republic, led to only one eventuality: the extension of the borders of the United States from the Atlantic to the Pacific.

But the adventurous American of the 1850's was not willing to stop at the eastern shores of the Pacific Ocean. The expansionist movement, stimulated by the growth of industrialization in both western Europe and the United States, focused the eyes of ambitious traders, merchants, and sailors on the mysterious and fabulous Orient. China was made all the more alluring by the special privileges for foreigners written into the "unequal treaties." Owners of sleek clipper ships had already profited from this trade. American whalers had found the Pacific their most lucrative region. The developments in steam navigation made shipowners keenly aware of the need for coaling stations at convenient intervals along the main sea routes. But Japan, which was the logical place for ports of refuge and for coaling stations, was closed to all foreign ships except a limited number of Dutch and Chinese boats. American seamen who had been shipwrecked on Japan's rugged and treacherous shores had been maltreated. Although Japan and the United States were separated by nearly five thousand miles of the Pacific Ocean, these factors and many others made it inevitable that it was only a matter of time before the United States would force Japan to renounce its self-imposed seclusion.

Japan's history during the past century, therefore, is the account of how it reacted to the world after its seclusion was shattered. It is the study of the response of an Oriental civilization to the challenge which faced it. It is an analysis of the effect of the stimulus from without and the struggle from within on the only Oriental country in the nineteenth century to accept the challenge of the West by westernization and to become one of the leading world powers. But Japan's sudden rise, its even more precipitous decline, and rapid postwar recuperation raise many important questions. Why did Japan react as it did to the stimulus of westernization? Why was its response in sharp contrast to the ineffectual reaction of India and China? Why was Japan able to resist colonization and carry through its own political, economic, and social metamorphosis? Why was it bold enough to challenge the United States in a life and death struggle in our own time? What is its future?

Some historians, especially the Japanese Marxists such as Tōyama Shigeki, would interpret Japan's modernization in terms of economic determinism and Marxist phraseology. He maintains, for example, that the uprisings of the Japanese peasants, which were not antiforeign as had been the case in China, were the first sprouts of the struggle against feudalism which made the development of absolutism inevitable. Having formed itself into an absolutist state, Japan was thus able to escape the same fate as China. Other historians naïvely attribute the difference between China and Japan to geographical and social factors and especially to what they call "the superior character of the Japanese people."

But the history of Japan's modernization is too complicated to be interpreted or explained by any single factor or theory. As Sir George Sansom has aptly noted, Japan's modern political development presents so many peculiar features that they cannot be reconciled with any theory, deterministic or otherwise.[1]

It will be found, for example, that Japan's ability to resist colonization and to carry through its own political, economic, and social metamorphosis was the result of a complex of factors. They included a combination of the casual coincidence of historical events, and geographical, social, and economic forces. It was comparatively easy, as Britain had also found, for Japan to industrialize a small island kingdom with protected harbors and landlocked lines of communications such as those afforded by the Inland Sea. Furthermore, the country was ruled by warriors or *samurai* who were eager to import western weapons and to build up a militarily strong, industrialized nation. Finally, the Japanese had long been blessed with a unique ability to adapt those aspects of foreign civilizations useful to them and to reject the rest. All these forces combined, therefore, to produce Japan's modernization: its rise to become the most powerful country in Asia; its final collapse and complete defeat; its reemergence as a potentially democratic and law-abiding member of the family of nations and the world's third industrial power.

In addition to attempting to answer the question of how Japan's modernization occurred and what brought it about, this book will analyze certain startling similarities between conditions confronting Japan at the middle of the nineteenth century, when this study begins, and by 1970. At both times, the Western powers had a higher standard of living and far greater military prowess than Japan. Most of the Western countries were larger in area and their national borders enclosed more varied and valuable resources.

On the other hand, the dissimilarities between the present time and over a century ago are even greater than the similarities. In the mid-nineteenth century, the West, and particularly the United States, took the initiative in forcing Japan out of seclusion. The latter had ignored and defied the Western powers. In fact, it had taken an attitude of indifference and aloofness toward them. In the mid-twentieth century, it had forced the issue and, due to ultranationalism and expansionism, had clashed directly with the national interests of the Soviet Union, China, the United States, the United Kingdom, and other Allies. Furthermore, a century ago the Tokugawa dictatorship was overthrown, the Emperor was restored to power, and feudalism was formally abolished without involving Japan in a foreign war or a nationwide internal revolution. Japan's capitulation in 1945 came only after an intensive, destructive, and costly war. In 1850, such nationalism as existed was directed toward the restoration of Imperial power and toward retention of territory which had been traditionally Japanese. In the decade prior to World War II, nationalism was aggressive and militant and was the inspiration for the acquisition of overseas territories and the establishment of Japanese hegemony throughout the entire Far East.

But one of the most important differences between conditions at the beginning and the end of this past century is the fact that, when the Emperor regained control of state power in 1868, he and his ministers could decide their own destiny. The small group of autocrats who actually ran the country were comparatively free to choose the course they wished to follow in the realm of politics, economics, finance, and international relations. For example, the treaties with the Western powers made no mention of Japan's future form of government, nor were the Occidental diplomats particularly concerned over the question of whether Japan should have a monarchy, a republic, or a military dictatorship. The main concern of the foreigners was whether the Japanese government was able to maintain law and order and to protect their rights established by the treaties.

There was no outside direction as to the structure of the new economy; there was no insistence that there be strict state control or free enterprise, or that land be owned privately or granted to warriors under a feudal contract. In the realm of finance, Japan was free to choose its own type of currency system, to select either the gold or silver standard for that currency, and to decide whether it would seek foreign loans. In the field of international relations, however, the foreign nations had forced Japan to make concessions. The new treaties opened certain ports to foreign trade, placed limitations on import and export tariffs, and granted foreigners extraterritorial rights. In other respects, the leaders of the new Japan made their own decisions.

In contrast to this earlier freedom, in the summer of 1945 the Allied Powers dictated the terms of surrender. General Douglas MacArthur, as Supreme Commander for the Allied Powers, had absolute authority and power, and all matters of policy were decided by the Allies independently of Japan's wishes. For all practical purposes, the Japanese had no choice as to the retention of the Imperial system, the deconcentration of economic power, and dissolution of the *zaibatsu* (financial magnates), agrarian reform, the purge, the capital levy, and, above all, the type of constitution they must sponsor.

But what of the future? Is the fear of Communism and Soviet aggression the main issue of common interest between Japan and the West? Will Japan's urge for independence, its allergy toward involvement in nuclear warfare, and the appeal of neutrality result in the 1970's in a strong movement to abrogate or change drastically the Japan–United

States Security Treaty? Will economic adversity, a new nationalism, and a propensity for a strong centralized government force it to the extreme right or left? Will Japan remain on the side of the democracies and develop new regional connections in the Pacific Basin or in Southeast Asia? An analysis of Japan's first century of modernization should go far toward helping to answer these questions.

Notes

1. One of the most representative works by a leftist historian is that by Tōyama Shigeki, entitled *Meiji Ishin* (A History of the Restoration; Tokyo: Iwanami, 1951). A general discussion of some of the other active members of the virile *Rekishi Gakkai* and of their historical studies, which have a strong flavor of economic determinism, will be found in John W. Hall's review of "Nihon Shakai no Shiteki Kyūmei," *Far Eastern Quarterly* (November, 1951), pp. 97–104; and in a note on the above by Sir George B. Sansom in *Far Eastern Quarterly* (August, 1952), p. 506.

2

The United States Challenges Japan's Seclusion

Manifest Destiny and Japan

By the mid-nineteenth century, Japan had been governed for over six and a half centuries by a series of military dictatorships which had exalted the warrior class at the expense of all others. One of the most successful and enduring of these dictatorships was that of the Tokugawa family which was created in 1603. For 250 years the Tokugawa generalissimos or *Shoguns* had ruled unchallenged throughout the entire country, but the evils inherent in their ruthless system of government were threatening the whole fabric of society. A dearth of capable leaders, an increase of financial indebtedness, the beginnings of nationalism and of an anti-Shogun alliance of some of the more progressive feudal barons, all contributed to the deterioration of the established order. International pressure was also increasing. *In fine,* the feudal government was in a precarious position and a marked increase in pressure from any of these forces could serve as the catalyst to precipitate the overthrow of the regime.

In another sense, Japan was a vacuum toward which the United States, Russia, and Great Britain were all being drawn. The rapid westward expansion of the United States, its belief in Manifest Destiny, and its desire to profit from a potentially lucrative Far Eastern trade, however, indicated that America was likely to play the decisive role in this drama. Even before their Constitution was ratified by the thirteen states, leading Americans had shown keen interest in trade with the Orient. John Jay, in the *Federalist Paper,* No. 4, warned that France, Great Britain, and other European nations would begrudge American advances in foreign trade. He reflected the deep interest of Robert Morris and other Federalists when he turned his attention on the Far East. He noted: "In the trade to China and India, we interfere with more than one nation, in as much as it enables us to partake in advantages which they had in a manner monopolized."

In the spring of 1792, three years after George Washington's inauguration as first President of the United States, a Boston captain, Robert Gray, was exploring the northwest coast of the American continent. He entered the Columbia River, gave it the name of his 212-ton ship, and claimed the river's watershed or the Oregon Territory for his country. Though England made a similar claim, which was not relinquished until 1846, Gray's voyage was the harbinger of momentous developments for an expansion-minded America.

By 1803 the threat of encirclement of the United States by Spain, England, or France, or by a combination of them, had vanished. In its stead, partly through the wisdom of Thomas Jefferson and partly through a combination of circumstances, the position had changed completely. Jefferson had long realized that whoever controlled New Orleans controlled the Mississippi watershed. He also recognized the significance of the British explorer MacKenzie having been the first to cross the American continent. Whoever was first to consolidate an empire from the Atlantic to the Pacific Oceans would control the continent in the future. Shortly after Jefferson became President, therefore, he moved to purchase New Orleans and to possess Louisiana. Napoleon Bonaparte, as part of his plan to weaken England after the defeat in his Haitian campaign, decided to give up his American colony of Louisiana. He confidently expected that if Louisiana were turned over to the United States, the increased strength of the latter, which would result from the transfer, would weaken Britain's position vis-à-vis France.

Thus the machinations of the French Emperor played into Jefferson's hands and accelerated events which led to the opening of Japan. On April 30, 1803, Louisiana—that vast territory from the mouth of the Mississippi to the sources of the Missouri River in the far northwest—became American territory. Henry Adams wrote that this event was "so portentous as to defy measurement." For Japan, as well as for America, Adams' statement proved to be correct. This expansion of American territory westward was one more event which made it inevitable that Manifest Destiny would force the United States to shatter Japan's seclusion.

Even before Napoleon had decided to sell the Louisiana Territory, Jefferson had planned an expedition to explore the northwest, to challenge British trade in that part of the American continent, and to reach the Pacific by an overland route. When Meriwether Lewis and William Clark started out on their famous expedition in 1804, their orders were to explore particularly the portage between the Missouri and the Columbia Rivers and the relationship of these rivers with the Rio Grande and Colorado Rivers. The success of their explorations substituted knowledge for fancy. It made possible the next phase of America's Manifest

Destiny, namely, the undisputed and inevitable acquisition of territory from the eastern to the western shores of the continent and the expansion of contacts with the Orient.[1]

Shortly thereafter, John Jacob Astor's dream of a profitable free trade between Astoria and the Orient was abruptly interrupted by British naval action in 1812. But the course of the American continental empire was not to be deflected. Senator Thomas Hart Benton was the most ardent advocate of the need to increase the country's knowledge of safe routes across the continental divide, to encourage western settlements, and to absorb Oregon and California as the western limits of the United States. At the same time he had visions of a great trade with the Orient and of the profits to be derived therefrom. Always arguing that American western expansion was the highroad to the riches of Asia and the Indies, Benton claimed that Jefferson believed that the Lewis and Clark expedition would result in overland commercial relations with Asia. He fought constantly for the development of the Oregon Territory and for wresting Oriental trade from the British. To him, the Arkansas, Platte, and Yellowstone Rivers, with sources interlocking with those of rivers draining into the Pacific, would become "the lines of communication for peoples of the United States with Eastern Asia." He saw one of his dreams realized when Great Britain relinquished to the United States its rights to the Oregon Territory in 1846 and the new American domain stretched from the Atlantic to the Pacific Oceans.

When his son-in-law, Captain John C. Frémont, explorer and cartographer of the West, declared the independence of the Republic of California the same year, Senator Benton's joy was unbounded. He boasted that the arrival of the Caucasian race on the shores of the Pacific Ocean was one of the most significant moments of world history. He believed that the possibilities of spiritual and economic gain from the fabulous and pagan Orient were limitless. It was easier than ever before for the advocates of Manifest Destiny to prove by historical events that America was destined to play a decisive role in the Pacific area basin.[2]

Early Attempts To Open Japan

Simultaneously with the extension of the American border to the Pacific Ocean, attempts were made to force Japan out of seclusion. For several years, a formidable fleet of American whalers, averaging over 200 annually, had roamed the Pacific Ocean in search of their prey. Clipper ships, bound for the lucrative Canton trade, skirted Japan's eastern coast. Some of them never reached their destination because they were wrecked on the rocky, typhoon-swept shore. The rough and inhumane treatment which these seamen received in Japan was well known to both the American government and people. It was questionable how long the United States would tolerate this situation. Furthermore, potential trade with the Orient had always fired America's imagination. The rapid growth of steam navigation, coupled with the fact that the shortest route to the Asian mainland passed close to Japan's shores, made both the navy and merchant marine anxious to have coaling stations there. It was not surprising, therefore, that suggestions came from various quarters for an expedition to open Japan to trade, to ensure humane treatment of foreign seamen, and to secure a port where coal and provisions could be obtained.

One of the persons to demand such an expedition was Charles W. King, a member of a firm in Canton which sponsored the unsuccessful trip of an American ship, the "Morrison." Hopeful of starting private trade, he had organized the voyage ostensibly to return seven Japanese castaways. In 1837, when the ship appeared a few miles south of modern Yokohama, Japan was in a helpless position. It had absolutely no navy, and coastal defenses were pitiably weak. The authorities relied, therefore, on a strict enforcement of an old decree which declared that any foreign ship which came close to shore should be destroyed and any persons who landed should be arrested or killed. The "Morrison" fell into this category. When it dropped anchor it was immediately surrounded with a flotilla of small boats. After the boarding party had ascertained that the ship was unarmed, it was fired upon by a coastal mortar which forced its withdrawal. As a passenger on that vessel, King was piqued by the firing on his ship and by a subsequent refusal of the representatives of one of the strongest fiefs in the southwest to negotiate with him. After his return to China, he recommended that a United States naval expedition be organized immediately, that it anchor off Japan's coast and issue an ultimatum demanding trade relations and proper treatment for castaways.

Another American merchant, Aaron Haight Palmer, after an examination in Holland of official reports on Dutch–Japanese trade, returned to the United States convinced that an expedition should be dispatched to Japan as soon as possible.[3] The immediate result of this interest and enthusiasm was authorization in June, 1845, to Commodore James Biddle, chief of the East India Squadron, to carry the American Commissioner to China and thence to Japan to negotiate a trade treaty. The instructions added that if the Commissioner did not get to Japan, Biddle was free to go himself if he thought it advisable. As the Commissioner never reached the Orient, Biddle decided to attempt to break down Japan's seclusion. Thus in July, 1846, two American warships under his command anchored off the coast south of Edo (present-day Tokyo).

Unfortunately, Biddle was hampered from the start by restricting instructions. He was ordered to use utmost caution in his dealing with the Japanese, to act so as not to excite a hostile feeling toward, or a distrust of, the government of the United States. Consequently, when a low-ranking Japanese seaman pushed him around when he entered a landing boat, he took no retaliatory action. Having allowed himself to be humiliated in this fashion, Biddle lost the respect of those with whom he had come to negotiate. The Japanese officials decided that he had little authority and that the United States was not capable of forcing its will on Japan. He was forced to leave empty-handed.

Events within America were contributing, however, to a wider acceptance of the concept of Manifest Destiny and of a desire to play a vital role in the Far East. In the short period between 1846 and 1851, the United States established the Oregon Territory, Mexico was defeated, gold was discovered in California, the great migration to the western seaboard had begun, and the State of California was admitted to the Union. These developments convinced many Americans that their country was destined to become not only great, but also the commercial leader in the Orient. George Wilkes of New York proposed the construction of a transcontinental railway to capitalize on the potential profits from trade with what he described as "the opulent empire of Japan." The founders of the Pacific Mail Steamship Company were advised by Commodore Glynn, who had just returned from repatriating several American seamen, that they should ask the government to take steps to permit them to make use of Japanese ports. Consequently, Secretary of State Daniel Webster was easily convinced in 1851 that the United States manifestly was destined to dispatch a special expedition to force Japan out of seclusion.

Commodore Perry: Sailor of Destiny

When Commodore Matthew Calbraith Perry (1794–1858) was first informed of his assignment to lead an expedition to force open the door of Japan, he protested. He believed that his outstanding career and seniority entitled him to a more important task. As he became immersed in his new undertaking, however, he was challenged by its enormous possibilities.

Actually, he was admirably suited to succeed where others—British, Dutch, French, Russian, and American—had failed. His training, experience, and personality all contributed to his success. He approached this assignment, the success or failure of which was to affect the whole course of history in the western Pacific, from the viewpoint of one of America's leading and most experienced naval officers. He devoted all his energies to planning the entire expedition, from the selection of personnel to the adoption of basic policies that should govern his action in Japan. He was a stern disciplinarian and expected complete obedience from his men. His birth and upbringing had instilled him with a strong belief in himself. Such arrogance and pomposity, though it might have been resented by some of his subordinates, made a deep and favorable impression on the Japanese.

He perused all available material in Washington on contemporary Japan. On the basis of this information, he insisted that he be given a flotilla strong enough to impress that nation with the prowess of America. As he had long advocated the adoption of the latest developments in steam navigation for naval craft, it was no mere coincidence that his squadron included two of the navy's best steamships. His flagship was the "Susquehanna," one of the new steam frigates. She was accompanied by the "Mississippi," which had already been under his command in 1847 and had performed creditably for him at Vera Cruz.

Long experience had also taught Perry that restrictive orders and directives were of questionable value in a situation in which former precedents could not be applied. He had complete confidence in his own ability to force a treaty on Japan providing he were given enough latitude of action and freedom to use his own discretion. Consequently, he persuaded Secretary of State Daniel Webster to allow him to decide the basic policies under which the expedition would operate. Webster supported this point of view and in an interview with Perry promised him that he could "write his own ticket." Consequently, the instructions which he received, parts of which he clearly wrote himself, were completely in accord with his own ideas. They took the form of a letter dated November 5, 1852, from the Acting Secretary of State to the Secretary of the Navy. According to these orders, the objectives of the United States in Japan were threefold:

1. To arrange for the protection of American seamen and property
2. To obtain permission for American ships to enter one or more ports for provisions and to establish a coal depot
3. To carry on trade by sale or barter

The instructions then emphasized the necessity of explaining to the Japanese, because of their distrust of the British and other European powers, that the United States had no connections with any European country. Rather, it was a country with large cities extending from the Atlantic to the Pacific Ocean and from which, with the aid of steam, Japan could be reached in twenty days. Furthermore, if during the negotiations the Japanese showed no signs of willingness either to relax the system of exclusion or to guarantee humane treatment of American shipwrecked seamen, Perry was empowered to take a firm position. He was instructed to inform the Japanese "in the most unequivocal terms that it is the determination of the United States government to insist that all United States citizens be treated with humanity." Finally, Perry covered every possible contingency and protected himself against failure. His instructions concluded, "It is proper that the commodore should be invested with large discretionary powers, and should feel assured that any departure from usage, or any error of judgment he may commit will be viewed with indulgence." [4]

He was less successful, however, in his plans to assemble an imposing squadron. The new screw ship, "Princeton," which he had hoped would be completed in time, had failed in its preliminary tests. Despite the fact that only four ships were available, Perry decided sometime in November, 1852, that further delay might jeopardize the success of the whole expedition. He was afraid that the new Democratic President-elect, Franklin Pierce, might change the instructions or cancel the whole project. There was also the real possibility that other powers, notably Holland and Russia, might force Japan open before the United States could negotiate a treaty and hence put America at a disadvantage and humiliate him. Consequently, he left Norfolk, Virginia, on November 24, 1852, on the "Mississippi" en route to Hong Kong where his small fleet was to rendezvous. When he reached Hong Kong four and a half months later he was chagrined and disgruntled to find that the "Susquehanna," which he would use as flagship, had gone to Shanghai with refugees from the Taiping Rebellion. He stopped long enough, however, to add his son, Oliver, to his staff as secretary, and Dr. S. Wells Williams, an American Board Missionary in China, as chief interpreter. Williams had accompanied the "Morrison" sixteen years earlier on its abortive voyage to the Japanese coast, had acquired a reputation as a thorough scholar through the publication of his *Chinese Repository,* and had a knowledge of both Chinese and Japanese.

The two steam frigates "Susquehanna" and "Mississippi" left Shanghai in May, 1853, for Naha, the capital city of the Ryūkyū (Liuchiu) Islands. Perry hoped to serve a double purpose by his visit to the islands. In the first place, he needed a base of operations free from the suspicious and jealous eyes of Europeans. For this purpose, Naha was far superior to either Shanghai or Hong Kong. In the second place, he knew that the Ryūkyū Islands were considered to be directly under Japanese suzerainty. Hence, any activity of foreigners in that region would immediately be reported to the Japanese government. Consequently, Perry acted in a manner which he was sure would impress the Japanese on the islands. He insisted that the Regent entertain him at the palace rather than in the Regent's residence in Naha. He came and went as he pleased and demanded a house for use of the seamen. Finally, he carried out landing-party maneuvers to prepare his forces for possible similar operations in Japan.

In June, 1853, nearly seven months after he left Norfolk, Perry's squadron of four ships was ready for the last lap of their voyage. The two steam frigates sailed for Japan, towing the sailing sloops "Saratoga" and "Plymouth." They steamed straight for the heart of the Empire, Edo Bay, at whose head was located the seat of the Tokugawa dictatorship. On July 8, 1853, they were sighted off the coast at Uraga, at the foot of the bay. Japanese guard boats were immediately launched to head off the flotilla. Since the oarsmen could not keep up with the speed of the steamships, Perry ignored their shoutings and gesticulations; the flotilla continued up the bay to an anchorage of Perry's choice.

Frantic attempts were made by the Japanese to determine the plans of the Americans but Perry had issued strict orders to prevent any boarding of the vessels except by duly authorized officials. The time for either negotiations or hostilities had arrived. Perry would soon know whether he had received the correct intelligence concerning his enemy and whether he had made a wise estimate of the situation. If his planning had been based on sound reasoning, his arrival would mark a turning point in Japanese and world history.

Japan in the Mid-Nineteenth Century

Before the reaction to the arrival of the American naval force can be understood, it is necessary to describe briefly conditions within Japan when Perry pierced the curtain of isolation. At the beginning of the seventeenth century, the entire country had been united through the shrewdness and military power of Tokugawa Ieyasu (1542–1616). He had established his seat of government at Edo (modern Tokyo), was appointed Barbarian Subduing Generalissimo or Shogun in 1603, and ruled with an iron hand from his impregnable castle within the city.[5] For two and a half centuries his family held undisputed sway over the land by means of a military dictatorship usually called the Tokugawa Shogunate. Main branches of the family were enfeoffed at strategic centers and protected their holdings by formidable castles. Approximately 250 feudal barons (*daimyō*) held their fiefs at the pleasure of the Shogun.

These feudal barons were divided into two classes. Those who were vassals of Ieyasu prior to the decisive battle of Sekigahara in 1600 were called "hereditary vassals." The barons who were not vassals of Ieyasu before this battle were termed "outside vassals." Those among this latter group who fought at Ieyasu's side were rewarded for their services.

On the other hand, the barons who fought against him were isolated from the strategic positions of the realm and their fiefs were reduced in strength. Toward the end of the period, however, their isolation helped them. Some of them were able to form the core of the opposition which caused the downfall of the Tokugawa Shogun in the nineteenth century. But in the seventeenth century, any indication of infidelity by a feudal baron resulted in confiscation or reduction in size of his domain, his transfer to an isolated region, or his death. All the barons, whether "hereditary" or "outside," swore allegiance to each new scion of the Tokugawa family and were required to spend half of their time in attendance at the Shogun's court.

Just as the Tokugawa family had its own retainers and vassals, each feudal baron had his own warriors who kept order within the boundaries of each fief and were subject to call for duty from the central government in time of national crisis. As further precaution against revolt, the barons were forbidden to form military or political alliances among themselves or with the Imperial court or to build or repair their castles without permission. Even the Emperor, with his small court in Kyōto, who had only ceremonial power, was dependent upon the will of the Shogun for the extent of his income.

Under this dictatorship, the country had been at peace since 1615 except for one Christian rebellion in the early seventeenth century and numerous peasant uprisings. This enforced peace had been acquired by methods which have been identified in the twentieth century with totalitarianism. Japanese society was rigidly stratified and harsh penalties restrained persons from shifting from one class to another. The warriors were the ruling class and all other classes in society were subservient to and dependent on them. Wealth was measured in terms of rice income and fiefs were assigned and incomes estimated on the basis of the productive capacity of the land. Consequently, the well-being and fortune of the warriors were dependent on the rice-producing class, the peasant or farmer.

The farmers, or second highest class in society, comprised about five-sixths of the total population of approximately thirty million. They were the economic base of feudalism and hence were recognized as an essential element in society. Nonetheless, most of them lived a primitive existence and were barely able to eke out enough to generate sufficient energy for themselves and their families to continue to cultivate the fields. They were taxed at least 50 per cent of their crop and were forbidden to sell their lands, divide their property, or leave their occupation. Since they frequently resorted to infanticide or abortion, their numbers remained static. The increasing frequency of their uprisings, despite the death penalty for every person so implicated, gave eloquent evidence that their economic plight was deteriorating.

The other two important groups in society were the artisans and the merchants. The former supplied the populace with daily necessities as well as luxuries, such as building supplies, clothing, household utensils, farming tools and simple machines, porcelain ware, lacquer, straw products, paper, silks and brocades, cotton cloth, footgear, and weapons. Until the importation in the 1850's of contemporary Western techniques of manufacturing guns and a few consumers' goods, practically all industry was in the handicraft stage. The merchants or townsmen, who were despised by the warriors, rose to power with the rapid increase in the size of the large cities centered around the castles. For example, Edo grew in two centuries from little more than a fishing village at the beginning of the seventeenth century to a busy metropolis of well over half a million bustling people. Money came to be used extensively as the medium of exchange. The townsmen became the shippers, wholesalers, storekeepers, and later business managers for the fiefs. As the bankers for the central government, for the feudal barons, and for individual warriors, the townsmen soon became creditors to the military class. Consequently, their actual power increased in proportion to their fortunes.

The dictatorship issued laws binding on all classes of society. It provided the death penalty for most crimes and for any act which could be construed as subversive, such as escaping to another fief, plotting an uprising, forgery, or counterfeiting. The laws were enforced by an elaborate system of secret police or spies who immediately reported any suspicious or irregular activity. The military power of the dictatorship was bolstered by financial and economic power. The Tokugawa family owned fiefs whose income totaled one-fourth of Japan's average annual rice crop of nearly 150 million bushels. It monopolized the mining of precious metals, taxed the merchants and guilds in the large cities, and held the feudal barons responsible for the construction and repair of its castles.

Finally, in the early seventeenth century, when the founders of the Tokugawa Shogunate believed that foreign trade could not be carried on without endangering the peace and security of the realm, Japan was sealed from the outside world. Except for limited, carefully regulated, and controlled trade with a few Chinese and Dutch merchants at Nagasaki, no foreigners were allowed within the country. No Japanese were permitted to go abroad or to return from abroad on pain of death. Christianity was interdicted and practically exterminated through ruthless persecutions. In its stead, orthodox Confucianism, which justified ab-

Ploughing and Planting the Seed Bed

Transplanting

RICE—THE BASIS OF

These prints from a late seventeenth-century treatise on agriculture, the *Nōgyō Zensho* by Miyazaki Yasusada, illustrate the various processes in growing rice, from preparing the ground in early spring to storing the harvest in the fall. Though they

Harvesting and Threshing

Hulling and Storing

Japanese Agriculture

depict farming methods that are centuries old, similar scenes were common in the early part of the twentieth century.

solutism, became the official philosophy of the state. Education based on this philosophy was restricted largely to members of the warrior class. Everything possible was done to keep life static and to preserve the traditions of the founders of the dictatorship. As the German physician Van Siebold observed after his residence in Japan in 1823, that country had "condemned itself to complete immobility in the midst of universal movement."

Forces Challenging the Immutable Shogunate

By 1850, the Shogunate still maintained undisputed and complete control throughout the country. In fact, there was no concerted effort on the part of any class or group to usurp its power or to bring about its overthrow. Nonetheless, even the most complacent official could not fail to see indications which presaged momentous changes. In the first place, the Shoguns had long since ceased to be leaders and men of outstanding ability. For example, the eleventh Shogun, Ienari, who reigned from 1786 to 1837, longer than any member of his family, took a personal interest in the affairs of state. He did not, however, let this interest interfere with his personal pleasures. He "was guilty of the most extreme debauchery among the Tokugawa Shoguns."[6] His son and successor, Ieyoshi, who ruled from 1837 to 1853, was little better than a nonentity and rarely attempted to exert his own will or influence his ministers. A band of selfish opportunistic subordinates surrounded the ruler and vied among themselves for his favor. The situation was further complicated by the large group of ladies in waiting and concubines at the court and by the comings and goings of the priests from temples which had found favor in the eyes of the Shogun. Everyone schemed for the supremacy of his own faction. Jealousy, corruption, and weakness had led to degeneration and intrigue.

Despite the harsh edicts which forbade a shift from one class in society to another or a change in one's profession, social and economic forces produced change. For example, money had come to replace rice as the accepted medium of exchange, and the warrior, who usually lived in the castle towns or cities, was in constant need of it. His unquenchable thirst for luxury soon put him in debt to the merchant. The latter, to improve his social status, would often cancel the debt in exchange for the privilege of becoming a warrior. The warriors, who were the mainstay of the military power of the country, had become soft and degenerate.

On the other hand, as the period progressed, there was a marked increase in education, primarily for the warriors but also for the commoners. By the mid-eighteenth century, most of the large fiefs had their own official schools while innumerable smaller private ones existed throughout the domains. The basis of education was Chinese Confucian writings and "its purpose was primarily to develop moral character both as an absolute human duty and in order the better to fulfill the samurai's function in society."[7] It stressed loyalty, selflessness, benevolence, and the need to put knowledge to the good of the group—excellent qualities to have instilled into Japan's future leaders. Through reading these Confucian books, together with some Japanese books on history and philosophy, these future warrior-statesmen obtained a knowledge of men and of the basic principles of government. Training in the military arts was a part of the students' daily routine. As some of the more enlightened feudal barons became aware of the superiority of European weapons and industrial development, they sent their young warriors to Nagasaki to study under the Dutch. Many of these men turned up later as leaders of the new Imperial government. They had already acquired a sufficiently sophisticated vocabulary to understand their own society and to conceive of new forms of organization.

The peasants, who were expected to remain docile and till the land regardless of hardships, occasionally revolted. In some instances, the central government was forced to accept their demands. Others were condemned for moving to the city to live or for adopting such luxurious habits as the use of perfumed hair oil, paper raincoats, and umbrellas. They were admonished to return to the simple ways and to make their own raincoats and broad-brimmed hats from home-grown straw. On the other hand, their lot had been improving considerably through the use of commercial fertilizers such as night soil and fish products, the extension of irrigation into new areas, and the shortening of working hours. The more prosperous peasants became village officials or accumulated enough money to carry on small business enterprises.[8]

Economic and social forces were creating changes among all groups which, in turn, stimulated the growth of new leadership. But change and new leaders are anathema to a dictatorship and were particularly intolerable to the Shogunate. While these changes could be kept to a minimum, they could not be controlled indefinitely. The economic and financial distress of the central government and of most of the ruling class was the most striking evidence, however, that the end of the dictatorship was near. In 1605 when Ieyasu had retired as first Shogun and turned the government over to his son, he had two million gold pieces (*ryō*) stored in his warehouse. A little more than a century later, there was an estimated average yearly excess of about 200,000 bushels of rice and 250,000 gold pieces.

In the early eighteenth century, expenses increased at such an alarming rate that the annual deficit had to be met by frequent debasement of the currency, borrowing from the rich merchants, special transportation taxes, or withdrawal from the cash reserves of the government. According to a memorial prepared in 1858 by the Commissioner of Finance, the years 1834–1836 saw an average annual deficit of 587,000 gold pieces which was offset by an excess of only 55,000 bushels of rice. Immediately thereafter, expenses suddenly jumped as a result of poor harvests, natural calamities, and the destruction by fire of one of the main castles. By 1854, the annual deficit was reported as 738,000 gold pieces.[9]

It is clear that the government was facing a financial crisis. Specific reforms had been inaugurated to decrease expenses and restrict luxuries. The monopolistic trade organizations had been temporarily abolished. Forced loans or requisitions from the rich merchants in the western cities had been increased. Half of the indebtedness of the feudal barons and the direct retainers of the Shogun had been canceled and the remainder was to be paid back without interest charges. But the basic financial weakness of the government was too fundamental to be cured by mere palliative measures. The whole feudal structure was rotten and was bound to collapse. As a leading scholar had predicted a half century earlier:

> The feudal barons have become impoverished and are unable to support those retainers who serve them. The Shogun's private retainers are luxurious in their habits and are unable to carry on their duties. If by chance there is a crisis, those in charge will be unable to cope with it.

The reactionary and conservative officials of the Shogunate were also confronted, in the philosophical and intellectual realm, with a new nationalism which was to challenge the right of the Tokugawa dictators to continue to usurp the power and authority of the Imperial throne. A small group of fearless scholars re-examined the oldest histories and discovered that Japan presumably had been produced by the Sun Goddess and that the Emperor was her direct descendant. Some scholars who hinted that the Shoguns were usurpers of the Imperial prerogatives were summarily banished from Edo. Since the middle of the seventeenth century, the cadet branch of the Tokugawa family at Mito, a castle town seventy-five miles north of Edo, had sponsored the writing of a huge history of Japan entitled *Dai Nihon Shi*. One of the members of this Mito school described its early objectives to be to define the legitimate dynasty of Japan and to describe the morality of its subjects. Thus, this new History of Japan, completed in the eighteenth century, whose sections on the "Chronicles of the Emperors" and "Biographies" were presented to the Emperor Kōkaku in 1810, subtly challenged the legitimacy of the Tokugawa Shogunate.[10]

Although for many centuries the Imperial Court at Kyōto had been shorn of its political and economic power by the warlords, and the Tokugawa government strictly controlled the activities of the Emperor and the Court through its representative in Kyōto, the Imperial Court still retained a limited amount of prestige. In return for the protection and income he received from the Shogun, the Emperor continued to act as the semisacred legitimizer of the right of every Shogun to rule. Each successive Shogun was appointed by the Emperor. The Imperial Court also gained in stature as the Mito school and other unorthodox writers maintained that the Shoguns were usurping the power of the Emperor. Thus the continuance of the Imperial Court as an institution remained a potential threat to the Tokugawa dictators.[11]

Particularly after the accession to the throne of Emperor Kōmei (reigned 1846–1866), the great-grandfather of Emperor Hirohito, members of the Imperial Court became aware of the potential power of the throne and used it to embarrass and challenge the Shogun. For example, when the American warships under Commodore Biddle appeared in 1846, Emperor Kōmei dispatched a letter to the Shogun reproving the government for not having sufficiently prepared the coastal defenses against foreign encroachments. The letter continued:

> We are therefore filled with anxiety and desire that henceforth our warriors . . . should perfect military strategy and devote themselves completely to their duty so that . . . the Imperial mind will be at ease.

Here then was the first official expression during the Tokugawa period (1603–1867) of the Imperial Court's opinion on a vital national issue: the danger from foreign encroachments on the "Land of the Gods." In view of the fact that the Regent of the Emperor, Takatsukasa Masamichi (1789–1868), was the brother-in-law of Tokugawa Nariaki, the feudal baron of Mito, and that the two had kept in close touch on how the prestige of the Imperial Court might be raised, it is quite likely Nariaki may have inspired the dispatch of this letter.[12]

Furthermore, the Emperor's courtiers began to show a new interest in improving the Court's status. New regulations for court behavior were issued by the youthful sovereign. They read in part as follows:

> The guards, both day and night, will cease their laziness and work together diligently.
>
> All of the officials, high and low, will be on duty and there shall not be any ignorance of the rules for ceremonies.
>
> There shall be no unauthorized goings and comings nor any arguments in a loud voice. If there is wrangling without cause, those responsible will receive heavy punishment.
>
> Drinking shall be limited to three cups full [of rice wine].
>
> Those who do not follow simplicity will be punished.

The court persisted in making requests to the Shogun for permission to expand its activities to include the reading of the Buddhist scriptures, the performance of classical plays, and the establishment of a school for the courtiers. Permission was finally granted in 1845 for a school which opened two years later under the name of Gakushūin. All courtiers under fifty years of age were required to attend the classes in reading the Chinese classics and were expected to apply Confucian ethics to their own personal conduct. By 1848, classes in the earliest Japanese laws and histories were added to the curriculum. It was a modest beginning but a first step toward preparing the Emperor's young advisers for their future leadership.

Progressive Feudal Domains

At the same time, there were important economic and political developments taking place within several of the fiefs which later were to be in the forefront of the successful movement to overthrow the Tokugawa dictatorship and re-establish the power and the position of the Emperor. (See Chapter 4.) This success would have been impossible, however, if the clan chieftains and their advisers had not sponsored modern technological advances and built some small Western industries. In other words, by the time Commodore Perry arrived in 1853 to open Japan's closed curtain, more effective progress toward modernization had been made in many of the outlying clans than within the Tokugawa domains. It was natural, therefore, that these clan leaders should be more enlightened and progressive than the ostentatious officials of the central government.

One of the most capable and powerful feudal barons of this period was Shimazu Nariakira (d. 1858) of Satsuma, in the southwest tip of the country. When he succeeded to his domain in 1851, many practical reforms had already been instigated. Animal husbandry had been fostered in each village where foreign-type cattle and horses were nurtured. A tremendous debt of five million gold pieces, accumulated partly as a result of supporting three mansions in Edo and a daughter at the Shogun's court, had been largely eliminated by the fief arbitrarily repudiating it. Future expenses were greatly augmented by the profits from a sugar monopoly in the northern Ryūkyū Islands. Sales of sugar from the decade 1830–1840 had equaled two and a half million gold pieces. When Admiral Cecille, commander of the French fleet in the Far East, sought a treaty of friendship in 1846 with the King of the Ryūkyū Islands, the Shogun granted Nariakira full responsibility over the islands, "to rule them as he saw fit." The profits which he made from continued trade were invested in industries which surpassed those of any other area. For example, a special institute, known as the Shūseikan, was established. Under its stimulus, medicine, sugar, glass, and glazed porcelain were manufactured. Smelting works were built in 1850 and two years later three small reverberatory furnaces and two blast furnaces for the production of cannon for coastal defense were completed. Translations were ordered to be made of Dutch books on naval construction and the central government had been requested to permit the fief to build a ship larger than the legal maximum tonnage, for use in foreign trade.

The fief of Hizen, which along with Satsuma was to become one of the four leaders of the Restoration movement, was also one of the most highly advanced industrially. Hizen surrounded the city of Nagasaki, the port of call for the Dutch and Chinese traders and for ships of other countries seeking foreign trade. Consequently the domain was given responsibility for the protection of that port. The feudal lord of the domain, Nabeshima Kansō (1814–1871) had realized that industrialization of his domain was essential to permit manufacture of the military installations necessary to protect the harbor. As the central government provided no funds for these coastal defenses, the fief was compelled to manufacture other goods which could be sold to help pay for the production of the military installations. Finally, contact of the clansmen with the Hollanders, who had been trading at Nagasaki for two centuries, had stimulated interest in European science and technological developments. Western techniques, including iron smelting, shipbuilding, and electricity, were officially sponsored, and by 1842 cannon had been manufactured with Dutch help.

After six years of procrastination, the Tokugawa authorities reluctantly agreed to give the fief a small loan and to permit 53 cannon to be placed around Nagasaki harbor. The first successful reverberatory furnace in Japan was completed in 1850 and cannon were produced as rapidly as possible. As a contemporary described them, "Although they were not yet equal to Occidental guns, still the difference is not appreciable." Even before the country was opened to Western intercourse, the clan had secretly asked the Dutch to bring with them on their next trip a model of a steamship. By 1853, although the Hizen clan was not openly hostile to the Tokugawa dictatorship, conditions within the clan were such that it could become a strong potential rival.

The same situation was true of the other two western clans, Chōshū and Tosa, which were to play such prominent roles in the Imperial Restoration. Chōshū on the western tip of the main island of Honshū, commanded the western entrance to the Inland Sea. In terms of actual income, it ranked among the five largest fiefs in Japan. Furthermore, it had the special privilege of being allowed to visit the Imperial Court. It was strong economically because of income derived from monopolies of salt, paper, and other products, from newly surveyed and previously untaxed land and from commerce. The establishment of a Bureau of

Savings and Investment made funds available to purchase rifles, cannon, and warships from Europe. The fourth of the great clans, Tosa, was located on the Pacific Ocean side of the island of Shikoku. Like the other three, it had extensive monopolies, especially salt, dried fish, lumber, and paper. It had a new head of the fief in 1848 who was quick to support a thorough administrative reform within the fief. Several upper middle-class warriors, who later became important figures in the Imperial government, received their training as a result of these reforms.

As already noted, another center of both potential and real subversive activity, from the point of view of the Shogunate, was the fief of Mito on the north edge of the fertile eastern plain. Ironically, it had been established in the early seventeenth century as one of the main branches of the Tokugawa family to help assure the continuance of the family's military dictatorship. It produced only one Shogun, the last; but, as illustrated by the nationalistic *Dai Nihon Shi* which it sponsored, it had been a hotbed of antigovernment activity and intrigue. As in the case of the western clans, such as Satsuma and Hizen, the Mito clan had championed military preparedness and industrialization.

When Tokugawa Nariaki succeeded to the fief at the age of thirty in 1829, he immediately ordered the various officials of the domain to give up their luxurious habits and to emphasize learning and the military arts. He set up village schools throughout the domain for the education of the people and appointed efficient officials who soon reduced the expenditures of the fief. He also established public granaries for famine relief and instituted public works projects such as dredging the rivers. The warriors were ordered to return to the villages and all their debts were canceled. Finally, Nariaki led his warriors on a hunting expedition in 1840 which was equivalent to military maneuvers and which became an annual affair. As he had disregarded the central government's prohibition against local fiefs building up their armament, he was forced into retirement for four years, and his program of industrialization lagged temporarily. Nevertheless, the coastal defenses were finally strengthened, Dutch books were borrowed from Satsuma, and Mito clansmen were sent to that fief to inspect the newly constructed furnaces. Subsequently, the Mito clan built its own model furnace with the help of engineers from Satsuma and elsewhere.

New Ideas and Leaders

In addition to the comparatively advanced economic development of several of the feudal domains which traditionally were the enemies of the military dictatorship of the Tokugawa family, there was a small but important group of intellectual leaders who advocated policies counter to those in force. As most of these persons had contacts with Western learning, they took a keen interest in the basic question of Japan's best defense against possible attack from abroad. Many of them devoted their lives to increasing their knowledge of Western military science. Others went a step further and argued that it was folly for Japan to remain secluded and that wealth and strength could be best attained by foreign trade. Their advocacy of a policy counter to that of the past was sufficient to make the government consider them subversive influences.

Two of the outstanding intellectuals in this group, who suffered severely because of their beliefs, were Watanabe Kazan (1793–1841) and Takano Chōei (1804–1850). Both men were ardent students of Occidental learning and especially military science; both were convinced that

Courtesy of The Bettmann Archive

Samurai Learn New Tactics

Japan should take a more lenient attitude toward the foreign demands that Japan be opened to the outside world. They were members of a group of scholars and government officials who opposed the forceful expulsion of the American ship "Morrison" in 1837 and were falsely accused by a jealous, conservative official. Takano, who had written a book critical of the government, was condemned to life imprisonment. After escaping from prison when it burnt and wandering "underground" for six years, he was finally betrayed. He killed one of the police who came to arrest him and then committed suicide. Watanabe had fared badly, too. Condemned to perpetual confinement in his own clan, he committed suicide.

Takashima Shūhan (1798–1866), an employee in the city magistrate's office in the city of Nagasaki, is another example of this group of "subversives." He had studied Dutch military drill and artillery methods, ordered guns and mortars from the Dutch, and instructed about 300 of his pupils in European-type drill formations. When he heard of China's defeat in the Opium War, he was convinced that Japan should reform its military system and use the newest weapons. Called to Edo in 1841 to give a demonstration of Dutch drill tactics and artillery practice, he made such a favorable impression that the government purchased his cannon and ordered him to start a new school for the instruction of military officers. He then became a victim of the reactionary and jealous attitude of conservative members of the government who feared any type of innovation. Imprisoned in 1842 by the same person who accused Watanabe and Takano, he was forced to remain in seclusion until after the arrival of Commodore Perry.

The fate of these men, who devoted their efforts to strengthening the military and economic position of their country, was eloquent evidence of the fact that there were persons courageous enough to oppose the government despite the consequences. It also showed that the military dictatorship was rapidly forcing its own capitulation by refusing to recognize the tremendous external and internal changes that were taking place. The end of the universal state of the Tokugawa Shogunate was in sight.[13]

Notes

1. As will be immediately apparent to anyone familiar with his work, I have relied heavily on DeVoto for the interpretation of the events from Gray's discovery of the Columbia to the exploration of the Missouri. Although somewhat of a digression from our main theme, the events cannot be ignored since they led directly to Perry's expedition and Japan's opening. See Bernard DeVoto, *The Course of Empire* (Boston: Houghton Mifflin Co., 1953), pp. 315 ff.

2. Senator Benton had been responsible for Congressional support for two expeditions led by Frémont, the first up the Oregon Trail and across the High Sierras in 1842 and the second into California.

3. Henry Graff, *Bluejackets with Perry in Japan* (New York: New York Public Library, 1952), pp. 62 ff.

4. In his excellent biography of Commodore Perry, Samuel E. Morison states there is no documentary proof that Perry wrote his own orders but quotes several paragraphs of his instructions which James Watson Webb, a close friend of both Webster and Perry, attributes to Perry. See Samuel Eliot Morison, *"Old Bruin" Commodore Matthew C. Perry, 1794–1858* (Boston: Little, Brown and Co., 1967), pp. 283 ff.; and Arthur Walworth, *Black Ships off Japan* (New York: Archon Books, 1966), pp. 35 ff.

5. The present Imperial Palace in Tokyo is on the site of the old Edo Castle. The watchtowers on the eastern moat, the gates, huge stone walls, and ramparts surrounding the palace grounds are all that remains of the original castle.

6. George Sansom, *A History of Japan 1615–1867* (Stanford: Stanford University Press, 1963), p. 208.

7. For a thorough and valuable account of education at this time, see R. D. Dore, *Education in Tokugawa Japan* (Berkeley: University of California Press, 1965), pp. 59 ff.

8. See Thomas C. Smith, *The Agrarian Origins of Modern Japan* (Stanford: Stanford University Press, 1959), and Hugh Borton, *Peasant Uprisings in Japan of the Tokugawa Period,* 2nd Ed. (New York: Paragon Reprints, 1968).

9. Unfortunately, it is extremely difficult to obtain accurate figures on the annual budget, and it is questionable whether complete figures were kept. In any case, only fragmentary information is available. The memorial referred to gives figures for only the years 1791–1793, 1811–1813, 1820–1822, 1834–1836, and 1854–1856. According to Takekoshi, who gives no sources for his data, the annual average deficit amounted to 545,000 gold pieces and the excess of rice was only 17,593 bushels for the years 1834–1836. He gives no figures for 1854. See Toki Tomomasa, "Tairō Ii Naosuke bakufu zaisei kyūbō no ken" (Memorial of eleventh month, 1858), in Nakamura Katsumaro (ed.), *Shigaku Kenkyū Roku,* pp. 317–29.

10. See Herschel Webb, *The Japanese Imperial Institution in the Tokugawa Period* (New York: Columbia University Press, 1968), pp. 146 and 176 ff.

11. In considering the role of the Imperial Court in the transformation of Japan from the feudal dictatorship of the Tokugawa period to a modern state under limited constitutional monarchy, the author agrees with Professor John W. Hall that postwar Japanese historians are at fault in arguing that the Imperial system had only a bad influence on Japan's development. While the Court was manipulated by the militants in the 1930's, resulting in Japan's defeat in 1945, it served as a rallying point for the overthrow of feudalism and the emergence of a constitutional monarchy. The monarchy *per se* was not responsible for the weakness in the operation of the Meiji Constitution. See John W. Hall, "A Monarch for Modern Japan," in Robert E. Ward (ed.), *Political Development in Modern Japan* (Princeton: Princeton University Press, 1968), pp. 11 ff. For a perceptive account of the position of the Emperor under the Tokugawa Shoguns see Webb, *op. cit.*, pp. 64 ff.

12. See Webb, *op. cit.*, pp. 231 ff.

13. For an account of the forerunners of the restoration see G. B. Sansom, *The Western World and Japan* (New York: Alfred A. Knopf, Inc., 1950), pp. 248–75.

3

Japan Is Opened to the West, 1853–1857

Fear and Dismay Within Japan in 1853

The arrival in July, 1853, of Perry's "black ships," as they were called, created an immediate furor among both the people and the officials. Many of the fishermen and coastal villagers were astonished at the sight of the paddle-wheelers which ejected black clouds of smoke. Rumors that the barbarians had harnessed volcanoes soon swept the countryside. In Edo, thirty-five miles to the north of Perry's anchorage, the populace was thrown into near panic and feared the worst. The reports from Chinese sea captains of China's defeat in the so-called Opium War by England (1840–1842) were still fresh in the minds of the intellectual leaders. Some of these reports, which had been published in Japan, were surprisingly accurate.[1] They stated that China had been forced to cede territory to Great Britain, to pay an indemnity, and to open its ports to trade.

People wondered, therefore, whether the arrival of this fleet of American warships signaled a fate for Japan similar to that of China. Unlike the ordinary citizens of Edo, the leading officials of the Tokugawa government knew full well the significance of the arrival of this flotilla of warships. They knew that they were American and that Perry had come to ask for a treaty. They also knew that several of the European countries, notably Russia, England, and France, were determined to break the Dutch monopoly of trade with Japan. Russian official requests for trade and attacks on Japanese outposts on the Kurile Islands had underlined the emergency. British warships had also appeared in Japanese waters in defiance of Japan's exclusion policy. Now that the Americans had arrived, even greater international pressure was added to the other forces working toward the overthrow of the dictatorship.

The central government, fearful lest its traditional policy of forceful expulsion of foreign ships lead to war, had modified its exclusion policy in the hope that the impending crisis might be postponed. As early as 1842, a new edict had been issued to all feudal barons responsible for coastal defenses. This decree ordered that foreign ships should be supplied with provisions and then advised to leave. Ships reconnoitering along the coast were not to be molested.

An unequivocal policy of exclusion gave way to a new policy of vacillation. The Tokugawa officials hoped that they could avoid a showdown with foreigners through threats, vacillation, and procrastination. They recognized that these objectives might be accomplished if the "red-headed barbarians" could be persuaded to carry on all their negotiations at Nagasaki. That city had special magistrates to deal with foreigners and the fortifications in the harbor were the best in the country. Furthermore, the movements of foreigners in Nagasaki could be kept from most of the country. As Perry was well aware, however, the American squadron's arrival at the entrance to Edo Bay meant that the problem must be faced immediately by the Japanese officials. There was always the possibility that the ships would proceed on toward Edo and there were no fortifications strong enough to stop them. A failure on the part of the local feudal barons or even of the forces of the Shogun, the Barbarian Subduing Generalissimo, to resist and overcome an attack would spell disaster for the Tokugawa dictatorship.

The Ministers of State had long struggled with the all-important security problem of how to protect Japan's shores. Some of the officials, such as Tsutsui Masanori, who later negotiated with the Russian Admiral Putiatin, argued in 1846 that the coastal defenses should be greatly strengthened, naval ships should be built, and provisions supplied to foreign ships to minimize the possibility of later attack. Those persons responsible for the country's defense realized, however, that protection from foreign invasion could come only if the various clans combined their efforts. On the other hand, if these clans were to give effective protection, they would have to be permitted to rearm. There was no assurance that a newly acquired strength would not be directed against the dictatorship itself. It was finally decided, nonetheless, to take a chance on the continued loyalty of the feudal barons and to encourage increased armaments in the different fiefs.

To assist in the implementation of this new policy, the Shogunate began to acquaint the feudal lords with the actual state of affairs. In a report of December, 1849, they were informed of the most recent encroachments of foreign ships into Japanese waters in both the north and the southwest. More specifically, a British ship had entered lower Edo Bay and its sailors had landed on the offshore island of Ōshima. In other cases, the "barbarians" had boarded the Japanese patrol boats. The report continued that if nothing were done to alleviate the situation, Japan's dangers would increase. Consequently, it recommended: "We have often ordered that you carry out the responsibilities of protecting the country. You should, despite the opinions you may hold, be prepared to supply soldiers and obey the instructions in reference to the expulsion of foreign ships." The smaller fiefs were ordered to be ready to join a general plan of defense. The report concluded:

> The only salvation from an attack by the foreign rebels is an alliance to defend the country and the exertion of the entire national strength. The barons (*daimyō*) are the bulwarks of defense. Their direct retainers are next who are followed by the merchants and farmers who should carry out their specific duties to the best of their ability.[2]

As one of the prerequisites for their privilege of continuing to trade, the Dutch had been required to make annual pilgrimages to the court at Edo and to present written reports on conditions abroad. Hence, they were on the alert for any foreign news which would be of special interest to the Shogun's court. Through reports from their embassy in Washington they were fully aware of the plans for an American expedition. Secretary of State Daniel Webster asked the Dutch Ambassador whether Japan intended to continue its policy of exclusion. The Netherlands government seized upon the American request as an opportunity to strengthen its position. In 1852, it appointed a new chief, Donker Curtius, to the Dutch trading outpost in Japan. He was instructed to promote, by every means in his power, the success of the American expedition and simultaneously to persuade the Japanese government to change its policy of exclusion not only toward Holland but toward America and other countries.

This plea, as well as a Dutch request for a commercial treaty, was categorically rejected. In the summer of 1852, the Dutch formally reported on the proposed American expedition and emphasized the fact that preparations were completed for landing a military force. The lethargic bureaucrats in Edo refused to give credence to the reports, but the Dutch insisted on their authenticity. When news reached the Edo government from the Ryūkyū Islands, through the *daimyō* of Satsuma, that Perry had arrived at Naha and would proceed to Japan, feverish efforts to bolster the coastal defenses were started.

The Japanese Stall for Time

When Perry finally appeared on July 8, 1853, he had already made important basic decisions on procedures which contributed greatly to the success of his expedition. In the first place, he would keep himself inaccessible except to the highest officials. Secondly, all Japanese would be treated with courtesy but firmness, and communications with nonofficials would not be tolerated. If they showed any signs of procrastination, he would take advantage of his instructions to survey Japanese waters to send ships up the bay closer to the capital city. Finally, he would brook no delay over minor matters but would deliver the letter from the President requesting a treaty, retrace his course to the Ryūkyūs and the China coast, strengthen his fleet, and return the next spring for an answer.

Consequently, when the Japanese began to bicker over where the American communication should be received, Perry was specific. He informed them that they had three days to agree to receive the letter on the shore opposite the anchorage of the squadron. From Perry's point of view, it was important to impress upon the Japanese at the start that he would not be intimidated but would carry out his own plans.

To underscore the seriousness of his demands he insisted that, "If the friendly letter of the President to the Emperor is not received and duly replied to, he will consider his country insulted and will not hold himself accountable for the consequences." Special parties from the expedition began surveying the bay for an anchorage nearer to Edo. This action had a magic effect on the Council of Elders, the chief governing body. Although the Americans were not aware of the fact, the largest Japanese shore batteries were one-fourth the size of the guns of the "Mississippi" and are reported to have had only ten rounds of ammunition. The government had little choice but to accede to Perry's wish.

Consequently, in less than a week after his arrival, he landed on shore in full dress with a strong guard and under the protective cover of the four naval ships. President Fillmore's letter was delivered. It was received by the specially appointed officials in silence. They handed the Americans a note which stated that the letter was received in opposition to Japanese law. It added tersely, "As the Uraga beach was not a place where negotiations or entertainment were authorized," and "as the letter has been received, you can depart."[3]

Perry realized that this final barb left him on the defensive and could be interpreted to mean that he had been forced to leave. Consequently, when the ceremonies were completed, the entire squadron was ordered underway, not down the bay but northeasterly toward Edo. A new anchorage was made ten miles nearer the city and later the "Mississippi" steamed close enough so that Perry could see the southern suburb of Shinagawa. That no guns were fired from the land fortifications, even though Perry approached within sight of the nerve center of the Tokugawa dictatorship, was clear proof that the Council of Elders had recognized the American squadron's superior strength and had decided that at all cost hostilities should be avoided at this time.

After the exchange of some presents, Perry headed his fleet for the open sea on July 17, having promised that he would return for an official reply to his government's request. He intimated that his squadron would be considerably augmented. He had accomplished exactly what he had intended to do. He had landed on shore at the place he, rather than the Japanese, had selected. He had officially communicated with the Japanese government and requested a formal reply. There was no question in his mind but that Japan's seclusion was near an end. He had hopes that it would come about without open hostilities. From his point of view, this would depend entirely on Japan's reply.

The Great Debate on Seclusion

Although there were many of the Councilors and lesser officials who gave a sigh of relief when the American ships disappeared over the horizon of lower Edo Bay, they knew that the basic question of whether to abolish the national policy of seclusion was still to be settled. President Fillmore's letter had stated that Perry was sent so that "the United States and Japan should live in friendship and have commercial intercourse with each other." It pointed out that the American Territory of Oregon and the State of California lay directly opposite the Shogun's dominions and that American steamships could cover the distance in eighteen days. It requested, just as Perry's instructions had stated, that (1) the two countries should trade for mutual benefit; (2) shipwrecked sailors should be treated kindly; (3) American steamers should be allowed to stop in Japan for supplies of coal and provisions and a convenient port be designated for this purpose.

Since all these requests were diametrically opposed to the traditional and accepted policy of seclusion, a real dilemma faced the Council of Elders. If the Councilors accepted the American demands, it would be a reversal of policy. Such action would be taken as a sign of weakness by the Dutch, British, Russian, and French. They would press for even greater concessions which would require even more humiliating capitulation. The government would be left open to direct or indirect attack by its enemies at home. On the other hand, if the demands were rejected, the Americans might open hostilities and force Japan to submit to demands such as those made on China by Great Britain. To make matters worse, though he had been little interested in state affairs, the Shogun had died only a few days after Perry withdrew. Much time had to be spent on ceremonials connected with his funeral.

The immediate danger from without, however, was too real to be ignored. The crumbling dictatorship had recourse to the only alternative left to it; it made such preparations as it could against an American invasion and simultaneously sought commitments from the feudal barons to support a common program. All coastal defenses, regardless of who governed the fief in which they were to be built, were ordered to be strengthened. Individual feudal barons were permitted to make purchases of cannon and ships directly from the Dutch or to build them in their own fiefs. The Imperial Court, for whose safety the Shogun was responsible, was notified of Perry's arrival and the purpose of his trip.

Finally, Chief Councilor Abe Masahiro (1819–1857), who hoped to be able to present a united front to the Americans when they returned, took an unprecedented and momentous step. In fact, it signified the dawn of the first day of Japan's modern century. On August 5, 1853, he had a translation of President Fillmore's letter sent to all the feudal barons, the leading government officials, the chief Confucian scholars, independent warriors, and merchants. The official communication read as follows:

> At this time, a great crisis faces the country. In fact, it is a time of danger. It is requested that you will all give serious consideration to the purport of the American President's letter and will express your opinions freely on the matter even though they may be contrary to established policy.[4]

Perry's arrival, his refusal to move to Nagasaki or to be intimidated, and his delivery of an official letter came as a shock to all classes of society living in the Edo area. The circulation of this communication from the United States came as an even greater shock. Few had realized that the Tokugawa government was so weak and frightened that it had to ask persons outside the inner circle of Councilors what policy should be adopted. As might be expected from such an unprecedented move, many of the replies were confused and some straddled the issue. Others, largely depending on the personal experiences of the feudal barons, took a strong position either pro or contra the rejection of the American demands and the continuation of seclusion.

When the opinions of fifty-nine of the most important *daimyō* are analyzed, it is found that they fall fairly evenly into three categories. The first group of replies supported some form of trade with the United States. The second group advocated avoiding hostilities to give the country time to increase its defenses. Finally, many persons categorically refused to consider any change in policy and demanded that America's requests be rejected. Twenty-two of the barons supported trade, eighteen wanted to avoid war, and nineteen were confident that the Americans could be driven away without the necessity of giving them any concessions.

Quite naturally Kuroda Narihiro, who had joint responsibility for the protection of Nagasaki, was one of those in the first group. He argued that any victory which might be achieved would be only temporary. Hence it would be better to accede graciously to the American demands. The Lord of Hikone, Ii Naosuke, was also among those who favored a conciliatory reply. In fact, he soon came to be the leading Councilor who supported greater contacts with foreigners. Some of the persons in this first group argued that the profit from trade should be used to buy necessary guns and ships for the country's defense. This position was eloquently presented by Takashima Shūhan, who had come out of disgrace after Perry's arrival (see page 28) and whose technical and military knowledge was avidly sought by the government. He noted that Japan's plight, in terms of its supply of modern firearms, was the same as that of China. He bemoaned the fact that while every Western soldier had a gun, there were only thirty guns for each 1,000 soldiers in Japan. The navy was completely undeveloped and hence the Japanese could not compete successfully with the Westerners who were equipped with warships. He concluded that trade would produce the necessary funds to pay for armaments and that it would be useless to begin a war until Japan was properly armed.[5]

Shimazu Nariakira, feudal baron of Satsuma in the extreme southwest and one of the most powerful warriors, was particularly well informed on foreign affairs because of his contacts and trade with the Ryūkyū Islands and his personal interest in the problem. Nearly a decade earlier he had pleaded for trade on his own behalf. His vassals in the Ryūkyūs had warned him of Perry's intentions. One of his advisers, who later acted as official interpreter at the conferences with Perry, had been to America and knew of its power and strength.

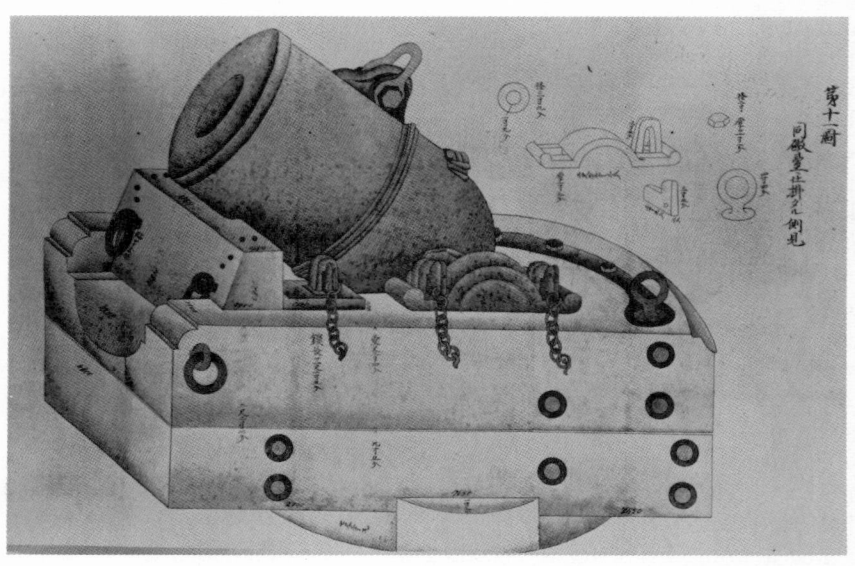

East Asian Library, Columbia University

EARLY TYPE CANNON FOR COASTAL DEFENSE

Nariakira's position on what to do with the American request carried special weight. It was, in fact, far more practical than the replies of most of the barons but falls between the first and second groups. He communicated privately with two other barons seeking their support for his proposal that the entire problem of coastal defense should be placed in the hands of a single individual, namely, Tokugawa Nariaki of Mito. He argued that it was impractical to refuse flatly the requests of the United States, England, and Russia; so Japan should play for time. Funds of the Tokugawa government, rather than those of the local feudal barons, should be used for building coastal defenses. Finally, he advocated limited trade, but not with America, to strengthen Japan. Specifically, he requested that he be permitted to build twelve large ships and a steamboat and that each feudal lord possess a ship for trading with India and China. Finally, all of the feudal barons should receive copies of the Dutch reports on conditions abroad so that they would be kept abreast of international developments.

Tokugawa Nariaki of Mito, who was nominated by Shimazu Nariakira for a position comparable to that of a minister of defense, wanted to avoid hostilities, improve the nation's defenses, and reject the demand for trade. It has already been observed how he had bent every effort to strengthen the defenses of his own fief. He was keenly aware, therefore, of the significance of Perry's visit. In his memorial he argued that the Shogun should decide the basic issue of war or peace. He believed that before this question was decided, all the feudal barons, the farmers, and the merchants should be ordered to live simply; all the people should strive for enlightenment; and the entire country of the gods should work together. He urged immediate use of the Dutch to augment Japan's defenses. They should be asked to import and to present to the government as a gift small and large guns and send steam warships from Europe. Shipbuilders, pilots, and mechanics should be collected and brought to Japan on the next Dutch ship. He pressed for military activities on a national scale similar to those which he had introduced into his own fief. The feudal barons should be ordered to build cannon and perfect the defenses in their respective fiefs and the warriors should be forced to take military exercises. Furthermore, all of them should study artillery. He even advocated the construction of fortresses along the seacoast with both private and public funds.

In direct opposition to customs and laws which placed the warrior class above all others and gave them special privileges, he recommended making fishermen into a coastal defense force. As he described it, "Fishermen should be intermingled with soldiers to protect the coast." Finally, he called upon the national and local divinities for help. He prayed that the spiritual power of the Sun Goddess enshrined at Ise would unify all the people of the land of the gods. In another memorial, Nariaki listed numerous reasons why Perry's request for a treaty should be turned down. He feared that acquiescence would result in the other powers making similar demands. He predicted that the foreigners would first ask for trade and then would proselytize the country. The result would be strife and contention. He concluded, "Seclusion has enervated the spirit of the people. The present moment is the most auspicious one to quicken their sinews of war." [6]

Finally, there were also many other important and influential barons who favored rejection of the American request and continuance of a tight seclusion. Significantly, these included three (Hizen, Chōshū, and Tosa) of the four powerful western clans, which were to rally around the Emperor and force the abdication of the Tokugawa Shogun. (See Chapter 4 below.) They were supported by most of the Confucian scholars, the royalists, and many of the leading political figures. As one of them tersely remarked, "There has been no attack by foreigners on the sacred soil of Japan since the Mongol invasion in the thirteenth century. If trade were granted, Japan's dignity would be lost and its unique national polity would be gone." The most ironical statement from this group was that made by the man who was to become the last Shogun and who had to capitulate in 1867 to the Imperial forces. He boasted that, "No matter how many vessels come from overseas, none of them will return—such is the strength and virtue of Japan."

The consensus seemed to support the view of this last group, namely, that Perry should be sent away without a treaty. The fact that this view was also strongly held by the Imperial Court made the situation even more difficult for the Tokugawa officials. Obviously, an ambiguous answer would receive the most support. Those officials who had already been in contact with Perry and his subordinates realized, however, that it would take more than prayers offered at seventeen-day intervals at the seven leading shrines to protect the country in its greatest crisis in history.

Perry's Return and the Treaty of Kanagawa of 1854

While Perry was wintering near Macao, replenishing his supplies, resting his crews, and awaiting reinforcements for his flotilla, he received two important reports. The first of these was an official request from the Japanese government through the Dutch that he postpone his return because of the death of the Shogun. He immediately recognized this request as a delaying tactic so that it had no effect on his plans. The second report was that a Russian naval expedition, under the command of Admiral Putiatin, had borrowed from the precious store of coal which Perry had reserved for himself in Shanghai; had proceeded to Nagasaki in

August, 1853; had returned to China for more coal; and had requested that the Americans join forces with the Russians in opening Japan. Distrustful of Russian designs and fearful lest they receive concessions prior to his obtaining a treaty, Perry advanced by several months the date of departure for his squadron.

Although Perry believed that the presence of the Russian fleet in Far Eastern waters endangered his chances of success, the timing of Putiatin's movements was actually a real advantage to him. The Russians had hoped to strengthen their East Asiatic empire by creating good relations with Japan. Admiral Putiatin had left Russia in August, 1852. His flagship sailed in October to join him in England a month before Perry departed from the United States. Both expeditions had been launched independently, but when Putiatin stopped at the Cape Verde Islands in February, 1853, he learned that Perry was ahead of him. The Russians reached Canton in the summer of 1853 only to hear that the American squadron was nearing the Japanese coast.

Four Russian warships entered Nagasaki two weeks after the feudal barons had been requested to submit their opinions regarding a treaty with the foreigners. Admiral Putiatin, the Russian commander, demanded the settlement of boundaries in the Kuriles and Sakhalin and the opening of a port for trade. By the time Perry reached the Japanese coast a second time, Putiatin had made two visits to Japan. In fact, one of the chief negotiators with Putiatin was returning from Nagasaki along the Eastern Seaboard Route just in time to see Perry's second flotilla cast anchor in lower Edo Bay. The Russian's request for a trade treaty had been denied but his visits made the Japanese officials keenly aware of the fact that they faced a threat from both Russia and the United States. The relentless pressure from overseas was becoming unbearable.

In the meantime, Commodore Perry had taken certain steps to protect his rear in the event that his final negotiations were unsuccessful. He proposed to his government that the United States should seize both the Ryūkyū and Bonin Islands and use them as a base of operations against Japan. He recommended that if his mission failed, the Island of Okinawa, the largest in the Ryūkyūs, should come under American control in repayment for insults and injuries to American citizens.

On his second trip, he stopped again at Okinawa but set up a small American outpost on the island before starting on the last lap of his voyage. This time, he was in command of an imposing squadron. Eight ships approached the familiar Japanese anchorage on February 12, 1854. They were later joined by two others. Their total complement of 1,600 men was equal to about one-fourth of the personnel in the American navy. The writings of the leading Japanese negotiators clearly indicate that they were overawed by this display of force. In fact, they grossly exaggerated the reserves which they believed were at Perry's disposal. Hayashi Noburō, the chief delegate, wrote:

> Perry said that he would enter into negotiations but if his proposals were rejected he was prepared to make war at once; that he would have 50 ships in nearby waters and 50 more in California.[7]

Believing that they were faced with an attack if they did not show a conciliatory attitude toward the American demands, the Japanese agreed to hold the negotiations at Kanagawa, a point nearer Edo than the old anchorage. The Shogun's answer to President Fillmore's letter was delivered on March 8, 1854. It agreed, subject to certain limitations, to comply with the American requests concerning coal and provisions and the proper treatment of ships and crews in distress. Coal and other supplies would be available only at Nagasaki after a year and no other form of trade would be permitted. Perry then countered unsuccessfully with a proposal that Japan sign a treaty permitting trade similar to that between the United States and China.

The remainder of the negotiations involved largely the question of suitable ports of call for American ships. Perry had rejected Nagasaki and substituted Kanagawa. Hayashi and his colleagues were without instructions. They hastened to Edo for consultations with the chief councilors including Nariaki of Mito. Obviously, from the Japanese point of view, Kanagawa was too near the seat of government. Consequently, isolated cities were substituted and finally accepted by both sides. These cities were Hakodate on the northern island of Hokkaidō, and Shimoda on the tip of Izu peninsula, some three days' journey from the capital. One point, which remained vague, concerned the right to appoint a consul in one of these ports. So long as the Japanese had refused to agree to carry on trade, Perry considered it imperative that the treaty provide for the appointment of an American consul who could negotiate a commercial treaty. Consequently, it was agreed that after eighteen months a consul could reside at Shimoda whenever either party decided such an arrangement was necessary. All these points were incorporated into the Treaty of Kanagawa, signed March 31, 1854.[8] Japan's protracted seclusion had finally come to an end. (See Frontispiece.)

As already intimated, the successful conclusion of these negotiations was enhanced by various factors. Perry had made thorough preparations and followed a policy which favorably impressed the Japanese negotiators. The requests of Russia for trade, which were made between Perry's two visits, only underlined the danger to Japan from abroad. The answers from the feudal barons concerning the advisability of abandoning the seclusion policy had shown that though a majority of persons agreed that

Japan should remain closed many had concluded that war would mean defeat. The government wished to avoid war at all costs.

Finally, the presents which the Americans gave to the Shogun and the lavish entertainment showered on the negotiators had a decidedly salutary influence. The model steam train, which circled the tracks at twenty miles an hour, and the telegraph sets, which sent instantaneous messages mysteriously through wires, were tangible evidence of the technological advancement of the United States. Many who saw them began to realize that there might be many advantages to be gained by trade with the Occident. For the sake of expediency, the Council of Elders had formally informed the barons that the Americans would be sent away without granting them concessions. Actually, the treaty had made numerous concessions. Furthermore, other Western powers were to make even greater demands. But for the moment, the Tokugawa government was preoccupied with meeting the criticism that arose when it became known that the new treaty had been signed.

Other Treaties and Conventions

As was to be expected, when the European powers interested in the Orient learned that the United States had ended Japan's seclusion, there was a rush by other powers to seek privileges for themselves. Admiral Sir James Stirling visited Nagasaki half a year after Perry had left. His purpose was twofold: to search for Russian ships as prizes in the Crimean War and to sign a treaty. He was unsuccessful in his search for the Russian Admiral Putiatin but obtained a treaty (October, 1854) which allowed British ships to call at Nagasaki or Hakodate for supplies.

Shortly after the British squadron had left Nagasaki, the Russians arrived in the east. This time, however, Admiral Putiatin had only one ship, the "Diana." His determination to obtain a favorable answer to his requests was clear from his decision to head for Ōsaka, the port nearest the Imperial capital of Kyōto. The Tokugawa officials were thrown into a frenzy. It seemed that their worst fears had been realized. The foreigners were even threatening to attack the Emperor's capital, which the Shogun was impotent to defend. The Japanese adamantly refused to negotiate with Putiatin at Ōsaka and ordered him to proceed elsewhere.

Although Putiatin was forced to move before he could renew negotiations, he had proved to his own satisfaction that another Japanese seaport was easily accessible to European-style ships and that the Ōsaka roadstead was not as shallow as had been rumored. Since he had realized the dangers of continued procrastination by the negotiators if he returned to Nagasaki, he headed eastward toward Shimoda, one of the two ports included in the Treaty of Kanagawa. At Shimoda, while negotiations were still proceeding, the "Diana" was severely damaged in the tidal wave and whirlpool created in the landlocked harbor by the devastating earthquake of December 23, 1854. The hapless ship was completely in the clutches of the elements. It rotated around its mooring forty-two times in a period of half an hour and was thrown about mercilessly by the tides. It was only by chance that it was not dashed upon the rocks. While being towed to safety to a nearby harbor a few days later, it finally sank.

Putiatin continued his negotiations while Japanese carpenters were building a new ship for his return voyage. The final results of his negotiations were incorporated into the Treaty of Shimoda of February, 1855. This treaty opened Nagasaki to Russian trade and allowed for a consul to be established either in Hakodate or Shimoda after 1856. In other respects, it went beyond either of the two other foreign treaties. In the first place, it contained territorial clauses which conceded all of the Kurile Islands south of Urup to Japan and that island and those north of it to Russia. Sakhalin was to remain unpartitioned as heretofore. Secondly, Russian subjects were not to be under the jurisdiction of Japanese law but were to be tried in Russian consular courts. In view of the most-favored-nation clause in the other treaties, this provision for extraterritorial rights in the Russian treaty meant that extraterritoriality would soon become a universal practice for all of the Western countries.[9]

The Netherlands and France were the next powers to obtain treaties with Japan and their demands included a request to start regular commercial activities. As pressure increased from the outside for the complete raising of the curtain of seclusion, a counter movement developed within Japan. The leaders of this movement capitalized on the potential strength and prestige of the Imperial Court in Kyōto and demanded that the barbarians be expelled from the sacred soil of Japan.

Internal Political Strife

In order to understand the intricate, and in many respects, unpredictable and apparently irrational reactions of the political leaders of Japan to the arrival of the foreigners, it is essential to realize that those statesmen were motivated by a strong sense of personal loyalty. This loyalty transcends all other beliefs of the leaders and makes Japan's history that much more fascinating yet difficult to understand. Some of the leaders, especially the responsible officials in the Tokugawa government, were primarily loyal to the Shogun. Others, particularly the feudal barons whose families had been traditional enemies of the Tokugawa dictators, were becoming conscious that their primary loyalty should be toward the Emperor. Still others paid their allegiance to one of the leaders of the numerous factions within the Shogun's government. In the decade and a half between the arrival of the foreigners in 1853 and the restoration of the Emperor to a position of supremacy in the state in 1868, there were two basic conflicts which interacted on each other. The first conflict was between the royalists and the foreigners; the second conflict was between the royalists and the Tokugawa supporters.

In the months immediately following the signing of the treaties with the foreigners, however, these two conflicts are difficult to isolate because of the struggle between two strong factions over the selection of the successor to the Shogun. As already noted, the twelfth Tokugawa Shogun had died in July, 1853, only a few days after Perry had sailed for the China coast with a promise to return. As the actual operation of the government was largely in the hands of the Council of Elders, the *Rōjū*, it made little practical difference in terms of basic policy as to who was Shogun. The office only became important when there was no direct heir to the generalissimo. Such an eventuality always presented a fertile ground for the growth of intrigues and feuds resulting from strong loyalties to the various contenders to the position of heir-apparent.

In 1853, when the thirteenth Shogun took office, he had no son nor was it considered likely that he would ever have one. Consequently, many of the feudal barons and chief Councilors of Elders aligned themselves on the side of one of two possible candidates. One contender was Tokugawa Iemochi, the first cousin of the incumbent and the closest in line of succession. The other was Tokugawa Keiki, the seventh son of the Lord of Mito, Tokugawa Nariaki. Since a final decision was not made on this question until 1858, many of the political events of this period can be understood only if it is remembered that this struggle continued in the background. Naturally, this conflict only complicated the problem of dealing with the foreigners.

More specifically, the history of the next few years is centered around the struggle for control of the Council of Elders and then shifts to the larger struggle between the Imperial Court, backed largely by the barons from the west and by Tokugawa Nariaki, and the old dictatorship. The struggle to dominate the Council was between Ii Naosuke, Lord of Hikone, and Tokugawa Nariaki, Lord of Mito. Ii had recommended that a conciliatory attitude be taken toward America's request. He was unquestionably loyal to the Tokugawa government and so was selected by it to protect the Emperor from foreign contamination. On the other hand, Tokugawa Nariaki was a royalist strongly opposed to making concessions to the foreigners and especially to the commercial treaty which the first American consul, Townsend Harris, proposed. In domestic affairs, he directed his efforts toward obtaining approval of a capable ruler and one friendly to him as successor to the weak Shogun. His choice for this post was his own son, Keiki (Hitotsubashi Yoshinobu). Nariaki was already under suspicion because of the independent military preparations he had made. Despite his connections at the Imperial Court in Kyōto and his prestige within the councils of the Shogunate, he was to fail in achieving either of his objectives.

Although neither Ii Naosuke nor Tokugawa Nariaki was a regular member of the Council of Elders, their views carried more weight than most of the Councilors. Even the President of the Council, Abe Masahiro, discovered that his tenure of office depended on the acquiescence of Nariaki. When Abe became fully aware of the crisis which faced the country, he prepared a reform program. It emphasized the need for the selection of able men to office, the reduction of expenditures, increased military preparations, and the formation of a single office for defense. He went still further and consulted Nariaki, together with several other officials, on the advisability of establishing some form of consultative body which would assist the authorities. It was to be composed of the leading Confucian scholars and students of Dutch learning, soldiers and artillerymen well versed in foreign affairs, and outstanding clan officials. He proposed that the group meet twelve times a month with officials from the office of defense to discuss problems of national preparedness.

Before this plan could be carried any further, however, Abe was involved in political intrigues. Nariaki, who had recommended the rejection of Abe's resignation in 1854, wrote to him in 1855 demanding the resignation of four of the Councilors who were jealous of Nariaki's power. A brief account of the ramification of these resignations will illustrate how closely loyalties and political events were related. Resignations of two of the Councilors were accepted. The officials in charge of the Castle guard were changed. In the far north, Hakodate, the largest city in Hokkaidō, was to be opened to foreigners. On the pretext of protecting the country from attack, the central government confiscated the fief in which Hakodate was located and placed it under the direct control of the Tokugawa family. Actually the confiscation was motivated by political reasons. Matsumae Takahiro, Lord of the fief, was a blood relative of one of the Councilors who had been jealous of Nariaki and who had been forced out of office.[10]

Just when one clique appeared to have gained the ascendancy in the Council, the opposition began to take over. Ii Naosuke was displeased with the apparent control that his rival Nariaki had over the President of the Council. In the early part of 1856, when Naosuke believed he had rallied enough support to force Abe out of office, the latter resigned and picked his own successor, Hotta Masayoshi. Although Ii's designs were temporarily stalled by these tactics, he was soon able to win Hotta over to the side of the proforeign forces. Hotta is described by Townsend

Harris, the first American consul in Japan, as about thirty-five years old, short in stature, of a pleasant and intelligent countenance and with a low, rather musical voice. He was to remain President of the Council for three years and to become the willing tool of Ii, especially during the latter's Regency which began on June 4, 1858.

During this period, Ii had two strong convictions. In the first place, he favored trade with the foreigners and hoped to strengthen the country through the profits from trade. In the second place, he believed that the constant crisis which faced Japan could be met successfully by an amalgamation of the Imperial Court and the warriors, an alliance of the crown with the Tokugawa and its most loyal feudal barons. This concept, known as *Kōbu gattai*, was given added impetus when the Emperor's approval was obtained for the earliest treaties—the Emperor even thanked the Shogun for his efforts.

With Hotta as President of the Council, and Ii as the most important figure behind the scenes, both in favor of closer relations with the foreigner, the central government encouraged the official translation of Western scientific and military books. A new school was established where lectures on foreign books were given to the most talented clan warriors and where English, French, and German were taught. But the proforeign officials soon discovered that the foreigners forced them to take a position far stronger than they would have taken voluntarily. This situation only stimulated criticism against the Tokugawa dictatorship. As the foreign pressure increased, resentment and hatred against the military and against Ii Naosuke increased.

Foreign Treaties Become a Political Issue

These political maneuvers and struggles between rival groups over the appointment of an heir to the Shogun, over control of the Council of Elders, and over foreign policy created an explosive political atmosphere. Consequently, when the American Consul, Townsend Harris, arrived at Shimoda on August 21, 1856, he found himself in an almost untenable position. Hotta had been President of the Council of State only a few months and Nariaki of Mito and other members of the pro-Imperial, antiforeign group still held considerable sway over the government's policies.

On the other hand, Harris was well prepared for these inconveniences and irritations which tried his patience. A wealthy New York banker and trader and former president of New York City's Board of Education, he had acquired early in life much firsthand experience and knowledge of the Orient through shipping as supercargo on his own boats and residing for several years in many of the cities east of Suez. He was well known by most of the leading foreigners in those ports. These facts, together with his patience and unshakable resolve to succeed, made him an admirable choice for the position. Harris' main task was to complete the work begun by Perry, namely, to place Japanese–American relations on a firm and lasting basis by the conclusion of a commercial treaty.

As is eloquently related in his *Journal*,[11] Harris was exposed to both major and minor inconveniences. The first foreign consul in Japan, he had to break down many barriers. He never relinquished his efforts, however, to be recognized and treated in a manner befitting a duly accredited representative of a foreign power and to obtain a new treaty. From his *Journal* it is clear that he fully expected his task to be a difficult one. For example, when he wrote President Pierce accepting his appointment as United States Consul General to Japan, he declared that he was prepared to endure the social banishment and mental isolation which such a mission entailed.

He was not prepared, however, for the fact that he was neither expected nor wanted by the Japanese government. This situation was the result of internal conditions and of a major difference between Japan and the United States in their interpretation of the Treaty of Kanagawa of 1854. Commodore Perry and his government had assumed that Article XI of the Treaty gave the United States the right to send a representative to Japan eighteen months after the Treaty went into effect. Hence, Townsend Harris had been dispatched as Consul General. On the other hand, the Japanese government had interpreted the Treaty to mean that a consul would be sent only if both countries considered it necessary.[12] It is also clear from the discussion which Perry had during the negotiations on the treaty that each of these interpretations reflected the desire of the respective countries. The United States wanted to obtain permission as soon as possible for Americans to reside in Japan and to begin to trade. For its part, Japan hoped to keep the foreigners out as long as possible and to postpone actual trade relations.

Harris found himself in a predicament from the start. When he first met with the Japanese officials in Shimoda, they had requested that he leave immediately and return in a year or two. He had insisted that the treaty gave him the right to remain but found it difficult to make headway on such matters as the removal of the guards from within the compound of his residence, the establishment of a fair rate of exchange for the dollar, and the right of his servants to make purchases in the public market. After six months of wrangling, he had made some progress. He had obtained permission to move about unmolested. The special guards posted around the old temple which served as a consulate were finally removed.

He then began negotiations for a new convention to expand the concessions obtained by Perry. Harris proposed four points: (1) Nagasaki should be included as a port of call for American ships; (2) American residents in Japan should be subject to American consular jurisdiction (extraterritoriality); (3) Americans should have the right to reside, lease property, and construct buildings; and (4) an equitable discount rate should be set for changing money. Although the first three points asked for no more than had already been granted to the Russians and the Dutch, the Japanese were adamant about granting Americans the right to reside permanently or to lease property. They also refused to budge on the currency issue, insisting that a 25 per cent discount, instead of 6 per cent asked by Harris, was necessary to cover coinage expenses. By persistence and patience, and with the passage of sufficient time to strengthen the position of the proforeign element headed by Hotta and Ii, Harris finally obtained a convention which contained all the points which he had demanded. It was signed in June, 1857.

He had been less successful, however, on another basic issue. He insisted from the start that he be permitted, as was the accepted international custom, to present in person his credentials and a letter from the President of the United States to the Shogun, the *de facto* head of the Japanese state. As all Harris' requests set a precedent, he discovered that the Shogun's government was most deliberate in reaching decisions on such a delicate problem. Ten months after he had first raised the issue, he had still received no definitive answer. In the meantime, the officials in charge of foreign affairs had told the feudal barons in attendance on the Generalissimo that Harris' demands were in accord with usual foreign procedure. They also reminded the Councilors and others that China was paying dearly for refusal to comply with the Treaty of Nanking. In fact, a British naval squadron had bombarded Canton in October, 1856, because of Chinese recalcitrance. It was intimated that refusal to grant Harris' request might result in a similar fate for Japan. Despite these warnings, "all of the barons attending the Shogun, with one accord, said that Harris should not be permitted to enter the capital."

Nevertheless, the government, through the Council of Elders, notified Harris in September, 1857, that he was to proceed to Edo where he would be officially received at court. His vivid description of the treatment he received during his week's trip along the main roadway is clear proof of the changed, official attitude toward him. He was given treatment accorded only the leading princes. The road was swept clean, bridges were repaired, traffic was halted, and arrangements were made to lodge him at the best inns. The final act in opening Japan's closed door occurred on December 7, 1857, when Harris stepped into the audience room of the Edo castle and personally presented his letter of credence to the Shogun. The precedent having been established, he stated, "My earnest wishes are to unite the two countries more closely in the ties of enduring friendship." To this the Shogun Iesada is reported to have replied:

Pleased with the letter sent with the Ambassador from a far distant country and likewise pleased with his discourse. Intercourse shall be continuous forever.[13]

The full impact of the shattering of the curtain of isolation was yet to come. From the point of view of the Tokugawa dictatorship, the policy of vacillation and procrastination had been most successful. While it had been necessary to sign treaties with the Western powers, such action had not seriously threatened the power or prestige of the government. Furthermore, by 1857, when Townsend Harris had his audience with the Shogun, there seemed no immediate danger of an attack from abroad. In view of the real weakness, militarily, economically, and politically, of the central regime, it was something of a victory to have been able to prevent a showdown with the foreigners. So long as the foreigners could be kept isolated and out of sight of the people, there was a possibility that the autocratic authority of the Shogun would not be challenged. But the arrival of Commodore Perry with President Fillmore's letter had forced the feudal barons to take sides on the vital issue of isolation or opening the country. It also aggravated the smoldering rivalry between the Imperial Court in Kyōto and the Shogunate in Edo. Those who opposed the foreigners were also those who questioned the authenticity of the Shogun's right to rule. As time passed, the increased demands of the foreigners created even greater antiforeign feeling. The Shogun's officials were accused of disloyalty to the Emperor, their orders and decrees were disregarded, and the royalists became strong enough to force the capitulation of the dictatorship.

Notes

1. For some of the books based on the war see Oka Yoshitake, *Kindai Nihon no Keisei* (Tokyo: Kōbun-dō, 1952), pp. 30 ff. As Sir George Sansom notes, some of the accounts were fantastically exaggerated. One rumor which persisted stated the English flotilla was composed of 25,860 vessels and a million men. See G. B. Sansom, *The Western World and Japan* (New York: Alfred A. Knopf, Inc., 1950), p. 250.
2. Ishin Shiryō Hensan Kakari (ed.), *Ishin Shi* (6 vols.; Tokyo: Meijishoin, 1939–1941), II, pp. 44 ff.
3. See Francis L. Hawks (ed.), *Narrative of the Expedition of an American Squadron . . . Under Commodore M. C. Perry* (3 vols.; Washington: Nicholson, 1856), I, pp. 244 and 261, for the texts of these communications.
4. *Ishin Shi*, II, *op. cit.*, p. 69.
5. See Tsuji Zennosuke, *Kaigai Kōtsu Shiwa* (Tokyo: Naigai Shoseki Kabushiki Kaisha), pp. 790 ff.

6. Memorials by Shimizu Nariaki, Tokugawa Nariaki, and others appear in the valuable collection of source materials in: W. G. Beasley, *Select Documents on Japanese Foreign Policy 1853–1868* (London: Oxford University Press, 1955), pp. 102–19.

7. "Diary," *Translations of Asiatic Society of Japan* (Tokyo: 2nd series, 1930), VII, p. 101.

8. For the text of the Treaty of Kanagawa see Hawks, *op. cit.*, II, final pages. It should be noted that this first treaty with a Western power did not contain a provision for extraterritoriality. On the insistence of Dr. Williams, this sign of Occidental superiority was omitted. As Article IX provided most-favored-nation treatment, however, the United States automatically received extraterritorial privileges after the other powers had received them in their treaties.

9. The Treaty of Shimoda was the culmination of numerous contacts and expeditions by the Russians to Japan. For an excellent account of these and later contacts see George A. Lensen, *The Russian Push toward Japan: Russo-Japanese Relations 1697–1875* (Princeton: Princeton University Press, 1959). Admiral Stirling had no authorization to negotiate a treaty but his actions were readily approved by the British government when it received his report. For an excellent, detailed account of British relations with Japan, see Grace Fox, *Britain and Japan 1858–1883* (Oxford: Clarendon Press, 1969).

10. *Ishin Shi*, II, *op. cit.*, p. 111.

11. See Mario Emilio Cosenza, *The Complete Journal of Townsend Harris, First American Consul to Japan* (Rutland, Vt.: Charles Tuttle Co., revised ed., 1959). Although Harris did not leave Japan until May 8, 1862, the *Journal* stops in February, 1858, without any explanation. It is supplemented by the *Journal* of his secretary and interpreter, Henry Heusken. Heusken's *Journal* has an unexplained gap of two and a half years from June 8, 1858. The last few entries describe the unrest in Edo and threats to foreigners, a grim prelude to the tragic assassination of Heusken which took place a week after his entry of January 8, 1861. See Henry Heusken, *Japan Journal 1855–1861*, Jeanne C. van der Corput and Robert C. Wilson (eds.) (New Brunswick, N. J.: Rutgers University Press, 1964).

12. To a certain extent both interpretations were possible. The English text read: "There shall be appointed by the government of the United States, consuls or agents to reside in Shimoda at any time after the expiration of eighteen months from the date of the signing of this treaty, provided that *either of the two governments deem such arrangement necessary.*" In the Japanese text, the subject of the clause, 無據儀有之候模様ニヨリ "If conditions make it necessary" is not given and could be assumed to be either Japan, or the United States, or both. Apparently Hayashi Noburō, the chief negotiator with Perry, had been persuaded by Perry to agree to an American Consul residing in Japan. By the time Harris arrived, however, the Japanese reverted to their original position of opposition to the establishment of an American Consulate for fear it would lead to the opening of trade. See Samuel Eliot Morison, *"Old Bruin" Commodore Matthew C. Perry, 1794–1858* (Boston: Little, Brown and Co., 1967), p. 384.

13. Cosenza, *op. cit.*, p. 475. Heusken, *op. cit.*, p. 149.

4

The Dictatorship Collapses 1857–1868

Embarrassment from the Foreigners

It was almost exactly a decade between December, 1857, when Harris had his audience with the Shogun, and November, 1867, when the last Tokugawa Generalissimo announced that he would resign. During that short period, each demand of the foreigners precipitated intrigues to control the Shogun's Council of Elders and increased rivalries between proforeign and antiforeign factions within the central government and among the feudal barons. This eventually led to an alliance of the powerful western clans in support of the Imperial Court with determination to overthrow the Tokugawa usurpers. The final results were the complete collapse of the old dictatorship; the restoration to power of the Emperor Meiji on January 3, 1868; and the emergence of a new group of leaders. No state can undergo such a transformation overnight, especially if the change is relatively peaceful. Vestiges of the old regime will still remain despite the formation of new institutions. The Meiji Restoration of 1868 can be understood, therefore, only if it is considered as a continuing process.

The reactionary and tradition-bound bureaucrats in the Edo government had done their best to postpone the interview of American Consul Townsend Harris with the Shogun Iesada lest the foreigner make even more embarrassing demands on them. These fears were well grounded, for Harris lost no time after his audience in 1857 in making the abolition of seclusion a reality. He pressed for the commercial treaty requested in the letter from the President of the United States. He asked for (1) permission for the American Minister to reside at Edo, the seat of government; (2) freedom of trade for Americans without interference from the Japanese government officials; and (3) the opening of additional harbors to foreigners.

Both Foreign Minister Hotta and the Governor of Shimoda informed Harris that as individuals they believed his requests to be reasonable and favored their acceptance. Since they were thoroughly cognizant of the influence exerted by antiforeign barons such as Tokugawa Nariaki of Mito and by the Emperor and his advisers, however, they were not certain that their views would prevail. They warned Harris that the Shogun and many of his Councilors were still opposed to foreign intercourse. On the other hand, fear of foreign retaliation for inaction caused Foreign Minister Hotta to set about the impossible task of trying to save the dictatorship from destruction from without by obtaining approval for a commercial treaty with the United States.

He attempted to explain to the barons at the Shogun's court the reasons for the inevitability of opening the country. His arguments failed to convince the opposition. Nariaki of Mito arrogantly declared that Harris' request should be refused and yet urged, quite illogically, that his fief be allowed to carry on trade. Even the most forward-looking intellectuals attached to the western clans also argued against a commercial treaty.

Having failed in his tactics in Edo and without informing Harris, Hotta then proceeded to Kyōto to consult the Emperor and his courtiers and to obtain Imperial sanction for the proposed treaty. If Imperial approval could be secured, all other objections could be ignored. Opposition in Kyōto was even stronger than in the east. The Emperor retorted:

> The Imperial mind is deeply concerned. Things having come to the present pass, public sentiment being what it is, and in view of the importance of matters of state, We desire that the opinions of the three families [Owari, Kii, and Mito] and of the *daimyō* be sought.[1]

In other words, the Imperial Court had sided with Nariaki of Mito and the other antiforeign elements, and it was fearful of the effect of having foreigners near Kyōto and the sacred shrine of Ise.

A smoldering opposition was beginning to take concrete form against the usurper in the east, the Tokugawa dictator. The courtiers who advised the Emperor intended to make the best possible use of any circumstances that would unbalance the opposition. They realized that the treaty issue could be a real cause of embarrassment to the government and hence opposed accepting the American commercial treaty.

For example, they were aware that Mōri Yoshiaki, the feudal baron of the powerful fief of Chōshū, strongly supported the Emperor's antiforeign position and rejection of the treaty. Mōri argued, "If the ports are opened and if the barbarians live among the Japanese and heathen churches are established, then the people's hearts will be deceived." Shortly thereafter, Chōshū formally adopted a clan policy of loyalty to the Imperial Court, trust in the Shogun's government, and filial piety to the ancestors of the fief.

When Hotta returned to Edo in June, 1858, he was defeated. Several months earlier he had written Harris that the treaty would be signed and

East Asian Library, Columbia University

II NAOSUKE, CHIEF COUNCILOR,
IN FORMAL DRESS

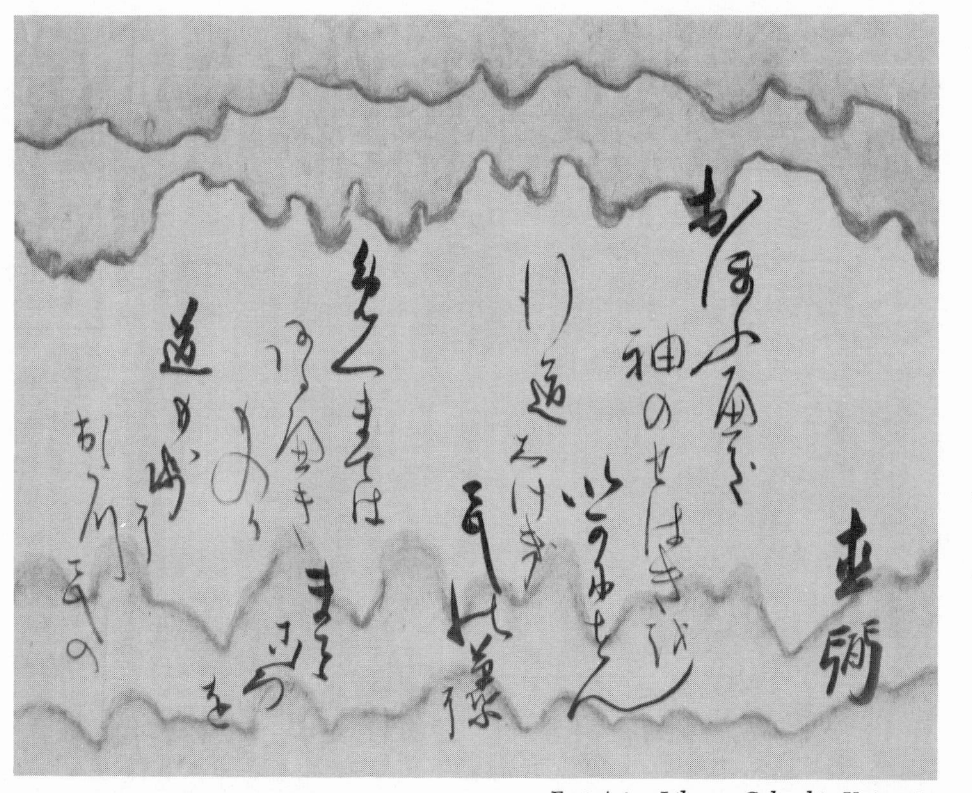

East Asian Library, Columbia University

AN EXAMPLE OF II'S CALLIGRAPHY

Famous as the statesman who urged the signing of the Treaty of Edo with the United States in 1858, Ii was also noted for his considerable artistic talents. The poem written to commemorate a recent public appearance, translates as follows: My sleeves are too narrow / To cover my embarrassed face / At the large number of persons / Who came to greet me. / I pray that my presence / Will bring some blessing / To the throngs / Who have shown their devotion / By filling the highway.

that the approval of the Imperial Court could be obtained. Now he realized this promise could not be fulfilled.

At this stage, Ii Naosuke saw an opportunity to enhance his own power and prestige. He became the central figure and took matters into his own hands. He was appointed President of the Councilors. He pushed for the signing of the United States–Japan Treaty of Commerce and Friendship on July 29, 1858, and planned to secure Imperial approval later. The new treaty opened four new ports to Americans, including Kanagawa south of Edo and Hyōgo on Osaka Bay. Both Edo and Osaka were open to foreign residents. Import and export duties were established. Extraterritoriality was permitted and freedom of worship was assured. Harris had achieved his objective. Ii Naosuke was more powerful than the antiforeign forces. In particular, Ii had gained the upper hand over his rival, Tokugawa Nariaki of Mito.

The political position of Ii Naosuke was also strengthened by his manipulations which resulted in his favorite candidate being selected as successor to the Shogun. Due to the strong campaign launched by Tokugawa Nariaki in support of his son, Keiki, no decision had been reached on the question. In early 1858, since most of the Imperial courtiers were in favor of Nariaki's son, efforts were made to get the Emperor to settle the issue. In fact, on July 1, 1858, the Emperor declared in favor of Keiki. But Ii Naosuke, who supported a rival candidate, the Shogun's first cousin, again challenged the wishes of the Imperial Court and of his arch rival Tokugawa Nariaki. Ii persuaded the Shogun to issue a proclamation naming his cousin as the heir-apparent.

Both the Imperial Court and Nariaki made no secret of their anger at Ii, even intimating that the Shogun's leading minister was disloyal to the throne. Ii struck back ruthlessly and quickly. On August 12 Nariaki and another son, who was feudal baron of the fief, were placed under house arrest. Keiki was prevented from entering the Shogun's castle. Members of those clans unfriendly toward the Shogun were forbidden to enter Kyōto or to confer with the Imperial Court.

Despite this ban, the Imperial Court became even more closely involved in politics than previously. In September, 1858, the Court told Chōshū that it was waiting for someone to champion its cause. Chōshū replied that it was already defending Hyōgo, the port nearest to the Imperial Palace in Kyōto and had resolved to protect the Imperial residence with all the strength of the fief.[2] Furthermore, the Chōshū representative in Kyōto informed one of the Imperial courtiers that his clan would send troops to defend the Emperor if hostilities developed as a result of the arbitrary action of Councilor Ii. In other words, if an incident could be manufactured, the excuse would be at hand for a coup d'état in which Chōshū troops would automatically become an Imperial army ready to fight against the Tokugawa forces.[3]

The Emperor also ordered Ii to appear in Kyōto to justify the signing of the American treaty. Ii refused to budge and sent one of his councilors, Manabe Akikatsu, as his representative. The latter arrived in mid-October and tried to strengthen the prestige of the Shogun by the dismissal of forty officials who held anti-Shogun sentiments. He was unable to dislodge the Emperor in his opposition to many of the provisions of the treaty. At the same time, he realized that an open break between the Imperial Court and the *Bakufu* (the Shogun's government) would be as disastrous for Japan as the penetration of the foreigners into the homeland.

In late December, 1858, Manabe submitted an extremely persuasive memorial to the Emperor. In it he argued that the only alternative to signing the treaties would be war with the foreign powers which would spell sure defeat for Japan. He noted, "This is not a question of America alone. Provisional treaties have also been concluded with Russia, England, France and Holland. . . . to rescind the treaties would be to invite both foreign and domestic dangers. To insist on abrogating them would be nothing less than to resolve on war." [4] Five weeks later the Emperor gave his consent to the treaties and enjoined the *Bakufu* to take every precaution to protect Kyōto and the great national shrine of Ise from foreign encroachments.

But the basic split over foreign policy continued and many of the young extremists among the warriors, especially in those feudal domains which opposed the treaties with the foreigners, used it as a rallying point for support of the Imperial cause. One of the best examples of this group is Yoshida Shōin (1830–1859), a Chōshū warrior. In 1855 he opened a school for his fellow clansmen, many of whom later became leaders of the Meiji Restoration. Yoshida was fiercely loyal to his feudal baron, his fief, and also to the Emperor. He was one of the key figures in the development of the new movement "to exalt the throne and expel the barbarians" (*Sonnō Jōi*). In his school, he had adopted the philosophy advocated by the Mito school with its stress on loyalty, especially toward the Emperor. In 1858, he urged the assassination of Manabe Akikatsu and an attack against Ii. He also tried to persuade his feudal lord to defy the Shogun by refusing to make the semiannual visit to Edo to attend the Shogun's Court.

Imprisoned by his clan's officials in 1859, he was sent to Edo for trial for treason. Determined to die for the cause of loyalty to the Emperor, he confessed to having plotted against Manabe and Ii, was found guilty and executed. His sincerity, simple and austere personal life, fanatical loyalty to the Emperor as a symbol of Japan's national superiority, and willingness to die for these beliefs created a tenaciously loyal group of followers. These discontented young warriors urged their feudal barons to shift their loyalty from the Tokugawa Shogun to the Emperor. Thus the stage was set for activist groups attempting to take matters into their own hands whenever their feudal lords followed too cautious a policy. This confused state of affairs, which was prevalent in such important fiefs as Mito, Chōshū, Satsuma, and Tosa, and in both Edo and Kyōto, made the history of the next few years both complicated and turbulent.

Assassination of Foreigners and Ii Naosuke

Japan's treaties with the Western Powers came into force in 1858. The subsequent arrival of the earliest foreign residents and consuls only aggravated the situation. Many Japanese, from their contacts with the foreigners, realized that there was a distinct possibility that the latter had come to stay. In fact, the presence of the official missions of several governments in the city of Edo gave the hot-headed antiforeign warriors added opportunities for violence. Murders and attacks followed one another. A Russian officer and two sailors were among the first to be killed. Other victims included a Chinese servant in the French Consulate, a Japanese linguist in the British Legation, two Hollanders, and Henry Heusken, the Dutch-born secretary and interpreter for Townsend Harris. Heusken, who had assisted several foreign envoys with their negotiations with the Japanese, was one of the most respected members of the foreign community. These assassinations and continued threats caused all the foreign representatives except Townsend Harris to leave Edo temporarily. Harris insisted on remaining at his post, thereby winning Japanese admiration for his courage.[5]

Even the highest of the Shogun's officials did not escape the wrath of the antiforeign extremists. By far the most significant assassination was that of Ii Naosuke. On the morning of March 24, 1860, while going to the castle in the middle of a snowstorm to consult with the Shogun, he was mortally wounded by a band of Mito warriors. Obviously they had considered him responsible for the temporary political demise of their feudal lord, Nariaki, and were violently opposed to Ii's foreign policy. His death was a serious blow to the government. In fact, it was kept secret for nearly a month. He was not officially removed from office until April 20 and his death was not announced until the next day. Furthermore, so long as the Lord of Mito, Nariaki, remained alive, the Shogun did not feel strong enough to arrest the culprits or take any action against them. When Nariaki died in August, 1860, the Mito clan was ordered to arrest those who had murdered Ii, the Shogun's chief Minister of State. A dictatorship which dared not take action for six months against political murders obviously had become a dictatorship in name only.

Direct action on the part of the various clansmen opposed to the foreigners continued. Mito and Chōshū men attacked the British legation on separate occasions. They declared that they were carrying out "a great deed to the honor of the sovereign." They had taken upon themselves the task of the expulsion of the foreigners since they considered it intolerable to stand by and see the sacred empire violated by the presence of the barbarians.

Sponsorship of Western Techniques

While the hot-headed clansmen who opposed the government's foreign policy were taking matters into their own hands and were doing their best to expel forcefully the hated barbarians, the more enlightened leaders sponsored the use of European technical knowledge. Even before Perry had left Japan after his first visit in 1853, orders had gone out from the central government to perfect the coastal defenses. While reliance was largely placed on the individual fiefs the Tokugawa government slowly began to support policies and practices which strengthened its own military power.

The western clans were permitted to build or purchase larger ships and the Dutch were asked to import a warship for the government. In the summer of 1855, the Dutch presented the Shogunate with its first steamship, the "Kankō Maru" (formerly the "Sunbeam"). The Dutch engineers, firemen, and seamen who brought the ship to Japan, totaling twenty-two persons, were used as instructors for the twenty ambitious warriors who were the first persons assigned to the study of naval science. Others followed, mostly from the strong western clans. Shortly thereafter, the first iron foundry was built under the government's auspices and the direction of a Hollander, M. H. Hardes. Other Dutch engineers remained in Japan after 1861 to provide technical guidance.[6]

Another Hollander who was influential in spreading technical information was Dr. J. C. L. Pompe van Meerdervoort. Assigned to Japan as a naval surgeon, when he arrived in Nagasaki in 1857 he was told the government wished him to teach medicine and surgical sciences. Lack of laboratory equipment and other necessary supplies and facilities hampered his efforts. For example, both custom and law forbade the use of cadavers in the study of anatomy, and Dr. Pompe had to wait a year for a papier mâché model of the human body to be sent from Paris before he could demonstrate his lectures. Because of the language barrier, his first lectures were little understood by his fourteen pupils, some of whom were from the Shogun's court, others from the feudal domains in Kyūshū. Although his physics classes were attended by ardent students, he regretted the fact that "their want of elementary instruction in arithmetic, algebra and mathematics" made it impossible for them to understand his explanations. His most successful course appears to have been in bandaging where the pupils jumped with alacrity at the chance to strap up their classmates. Before he left in 1862, he had established a medical school, planned and supervised a modern hospital, and taught 150 students. Inadequate though his medical school may have been, it was a beginning in the instruction of Western science. Other schools, directly under the support of the Tokugawa government, were started in Edo where the young warriors concentrated on foreign languages.[7]

One of the most important and dramatic events which impressed the Tokugawa authorities with the backwardness of Japan was the first official mission of the Shogunate to go to America. This mission was dispatched to the United States in 1860 at the insistence of Katsu Kaishū (1823–1890). Katsu had studied naval science under the Dutch naval officers at Nagasaki. He returned to Edo in 1859 and the next year persuaded the government to appoint him commander of the "Kanrin Maru," a gift from The Netherlands. This "propeller ship" then served as the escort of the Japanese Mission en route to Washington via San Francisco to exchange ratification of the new Treaty of Commerce. This was the first steamship manned by a Japanese crew to cross the Pacific.

When the embassy arrived in San Francisco, its members were naturally surprised at many of America's customs. The square lanterns on the carriages, the clocks in evidence in hotel rooms and lobbies, the long mirrors, fireplaces, and frame pictures on the walls all struck them as strange appurtenances of Western culture. Ballroom dancing was the most difficult custom for them to understand. For example, at a reception on May 18, 1860, given by Secretary of State Cass, members of the embassy found that they were expected to shake hands with everybody around them.

After dinner, when ushered into the ballroom, they were even more astonished. Vice-Ambassador Muragaki gave his impressions of the formal dance as follows:

> Immediately after we were seated, the music commenced and an officer in uniform with one arm around a lady's waist and the other hand holding one of hers, started moving round the room on his toes, many others following his example. . . . As for us, we had never seen or imagined anything like it before. It was, of course, with no small wonder that we witnessed this extraordinary sight of men and bareshouldered women hopping round the floor, arm in arm, and our wonder at the strange performance became so great that we began to doubt whether we were not on another planet.[8]

At a later party, they learned to enjoy themselves. They were amazed to learn, however, that the women danced for pleasure and were not paid entertainers but respectable members of society.

Their visit captivated the enthusiasm of the American people and left a lasting impression on them. In New York, the populace turned out in throngs to greet their triumphal procession up Broadway. Walt Whitman wrote of them:

> Over the Western sea hither from Niphon come,
> Courteous, the swart-cheek'd two-sworded envoys,
> Leaning back in their open barouches, bare-headed, impassive,
> Ride to-day through Manhattan.[9]

This adulation abruptly ended, however, when New Yorkers were distracted by the arrival from England of the gigantic steamship, "The Great Eastern," on its maiden voyage. Its appearance in New York was dramatic evidence to the Japanese of the material progress of America and Europe. They had already been intrigued with the railroads, the telegraph, the modern newspapers, and other examples of industrialization. They returned to convince many of the government officials at home that Japan was more backward militarily and economically than even the most sophisticated persons realized. They substantiated the belief of Hotta, Ii, and others that the presence in Japan of the foreigners must not only be tolerated and endured, but expected.

Civil War and Control of the Imperial Court

Nowhere was the real weakness of the Tokugawa regime more clearly apparent than in the desire of the strongest non-Tokugawa clans to obtain control over the Imperial Court and thus enhance their own power and prestige by obtaining Imperial sanction for their acts. Traditionally, Chōshū had been designated as the military guard for the Imperial family in Kyōto. For its part, Chōshū was resolved to protect the Imperial residence from outside threats with all the strength at its command. The situation was further complicated by the distrust and rivalry between the Chōshū and Satsuma clans and by the uncontrolled bands of warriors who murdered foreigners and leaders of the Tokugawa and of the clan governments alike. These loyalist extremists equated support for the Emperor with virtue, and conservative officials with evil.

In its role as protector of the Imperial residence in Kyōto, Chōshū was the first to receive the Imperial command to proceed to Edo and to act as official mediator between the two courts. In December, 1861, Mōri Takachika, feudal baron of Chōshū, was in Edo for this purpose. In the meantime, Shimazu Hisamitsu, head of the rival Satsuma clan and advocate of a more moderate policy of strengthening both the Imperial Court and the Tokugawa *Bakufu* through an alliance of the two (*Kōbu gattai*), arrived in Kyōto with a formidable armed force and a specific proposal for an Imperial Court–Tokugawa compromise and alliance.[10]

He then learned that a group of activist warriors from his own fief as well as from Chōshū had revolted in Fushimi, a small castle town just south of Kyōto, and threatened to attack. Hisamitsu immediately suppressed the revolt with the troops directly under his command and turned the participants in the revolt over to the officials of their respective fiefs.

In the summer of 1862, Hisamitsu received Imperial sanction to replace Mōri and to implement a policy of cooperation between the two courts. He was ordered to proceed with his troops to Edo and to deliver the Emperor's demands that the Shogun visit Kyōto to assure peace in the realm, to appoint leading feudal barons as councilors and Tokugawa Keiki of Mito as guardian of the Shogun. The Shogun assured Hisamitsu that he would come to Kyōto and that Keiki would be made his guardian.

On Hisamitsu's return from Edo to Kyōto, a notorious incident occurred which greatly intensified the foreign diplomatic and commercial communities' demands that their safety be guaranteed by the authorities. On September 14, 1862, while his retinue of Satsuma men was passing near the present city of Yokohama, within the prescribed area where foreigners were permitted to travel freely, it met a party of three British subjects on horseback. The fact that the British did not dismount and pay proper homage to Hisamitsu was taken by his retainers as an insult. They attacked the riders and C. L. Richardson, a merchant, was cut down. The foreign community was enraged and some persons demanded that Hisamitsu be arrested by the British military and naval forces in Yokohama. The British Consul refused to take military action without instructions from London so war was temporarily averted.

In the meantime, a strong loyalist faction was in control at the Imperial Court in Kyōto so Hisamitsu decided to retire to his domain in Satsuma to await developments. Furthermore, the Imperial Court had been persuaded to issue another command ordering the Tokugawa Shogun to expel the foreigners. An envoy was dispatched to Edo with the Imperial decree. In November, the Shogun agreed to comply with the Imperial order. Thus the supporters of the policy to "extol the Emperor and expel the barbarians" were temporarily in control of both the Chōshū clan and the Imperial Court and also had forced their wishes on the Shogun. Matters came to a head in the spring of 1863. The Shogun's officials were fully aware that it was physically impossible to force the foreigners to leave. Any attempt to do so would only mean retaliation by the Western Powers. In order to prevent such an eventuality, the Shogun went to Kyōto in early March. Later that month, the British government's demands for reparations for the Richardson murder arrived from London. They specified that the Tokugawa government and Satsuma were to apologize, and that the perpetrators of the crime should be apprehended and executed. The former was to pay £100,000 and the latter £25,000 in indemnity. Both the Shogun and Satsuma ignored these demands.

At the same time, the Shogun continued to be under strong pressure from the Imperial Court and the Chōshū leaders. When he tried to leave Kyōto, the Emperor forbade him to do so. The Chōshū warriors insisted that a specific date should be set for the expulsion of the foreigners from Japan's sacred soil. After weeks of evasion, on June 24 the Shogun paid the indemnity. At the same time it notified the British Consul that the foreigners would have to leave. Shortly thereafter, the Shogun reversed itself and told the British that the expulsion decree would not be applicable to them. Consequently, the extremists in power within the Chōshū fief decided to take upon themselves the responsibility to enforce the expulsion of the foreigners. The Shogun tried to stop such action by the dispatch of an emissary to Chōshū. The messenger's plea was disregarded and he was assassinated. As the American ship "Pembroke" neared the Shimonoseki Straits on June 24, 1863, she was fired on from Chōshū's shore batteries. During July, French and Dutch ships were also fired upon by Chōshū. The foreigners took matters into their own hands. American and French warships silenced the gun emplacements, but the Chōshū clansmen remained arrogant and insolent.

Although the Shogun had met its share of the British demands for the settlement of the Richardson affair, it was clear to the British authorities in Japan that the Shogun was either unwilling or unable to force Satsuma to accept responsibility for its actions. Consequently the British acted independently. In early August, a British naval squadron of seven ships headed for the Satsuma capital of Kagoshima. After their demands were formally rejected by representatives of the fief, on August 15 the British squadron seized three of Satsuma's Western-built ships in reprisal. The Japanese then opened fire on the British ships and hostilities continued for several hours. The captured ships were burned, many of the shore guns were silenced, and the city of Kagoshima was bombarded. The British squadron retired with the claim that it had inflicted property damage on Kagoshima of £1,000,000 and that 1,500 Satsuma soldiers had been killed. By mid-November, the views of the pro-British clique in Satsuma prevailed, an amicable settlement was reached, the indemnity was paid, a partial apology was tendered, and the murderers were executed. Satsuma then requested that Britain supply it with a ship and technical help. Thus began a close friendship between many of the future leaders of the Japanese navy, who came from Satsuma, and British naval officers.

Chōshū continued to defy the foreigners by keeping the Shimonoseki Straits closed. In the summer of 1864, two young Chōshū warriors, Itō Hirobumi and Inouye Kaoru, had returned from a secret trip to England

and rushed home to their native province in a vain attempt to persuade their fellow clansmen that resistance against the superior Western forces was useless. When these young warriors reported that their advice had gone unheeded, the consular representatives of Great Britain, Holland, France, and the United States agreed that the only effective way to open the Shimonoseki Straits was to mount a joint expedition against Chōshū. They notified the Shogun of their intended action and at the same time insisted that all aspects of the treaties be respected. In September, 1864, the joint foreign naval force silenced and dismantled the Chōshū shore batteries, and exacted a promise that the Straits would remain open in the future and that an indemnity would be paid.[11]

In the meantime, the influence of Chōshū in Kyōto and at the Imperial Court had suffered a severe setback and the strained relations between the two powerful fiefs of Chōshū and Satsuma nearly reached the breaking point. On September 30, 1863, the warriors from Satsuma and other anti-Chōshū fiefs carried out a successful coup d'état in Kyōto, surprising the Chōshū guard of the Imperial Palace. The Emperor then approved a new policy whereby no one was to be admitted into the Imperial Court without specific permission. The leaders of the policy advocating an Imperial Court–Shogun alliance were now in control. Chōshū troops were ordered out of the capital with some of the young courtiers, such as Sanjō Sanetomi, who had supported them. The Shogun's power was greatly restricted. He was forced to accept as his advisers those feudal barons who had the confidence of the Emperor, including the barons of Satsuma and Tosa. Nevertheless, his authority as the supreme generalissimo of the realm was reconfirmed by the Emperor.

Having suffered defeat both at the hands of the foreigners and by the rival clan of Satsuma in the struggle to control policies in Kyōto, the Chōshū warriors saw no alternative but to prepare for hostilities against their enemies. Kido Kōin, a young Chōshū loyalist, urged restraint and caution but his views were unheeded.[12] By mid-summer of 1864, Chōshū troops arrived at the outskirts of Kyōto, but their attack was decisively repulsed. Chōshū fortunes had reached a low ebb. Only one week after the news of their Kyōto defeat reached the fief, the Western powers started their second attack on the domain's capital to open the Straits of Shimonoseki.

United Policy Against the Shogun

To many of the leaders of the western clans, it was becoming obvious that if they were to achieve their common purpose of preserving the power of the Imperial throne against the threats of the foreigners, their fiefs should work together rather than fight each other. One of the most significant of these persons was Saigō Takamori of Satsuma, an antiforeign royalist who had been exiled by his feudal baron.[13] By 1864, he had been pardoned and was a leader of the Satsuma forces in Kyōto during the coup d'état. He realized that Chōshū's support for the restoration of power to the Emperor would be indispensable and hence worked with Kido Kōin of Chōshū to achieve this end.

From the point of view of both the Shogun and the Emperor, Chōshū was considered to be in revolt. In December, 1864, the former launched an expedition against the fief as an enemy of the Imperial court. While the Shogun's troops waited on Chōshū's borders, Saigō negotiated a compromise settlement with the moderate leaders of the fief.

Infuriated over this humiliation and the disarmament provisions of the compromise, some of the ardent loyalists in the fief, notably Takasugi Shinsaku (1839–1867) and Ōmura Masujirō, forced the moderates out of office in 1865 and prepared for battle. As early as 1859, several young Chōshū warriors had acquired considerable knowledge of western military science at the fief's school for western studies and medicine. Takasugi and his lieutenant, Ōmura, were among them. The former had developed an entirely new type of army for Japan. It was recruited from all classes of society within the fief and was well disciplined and supplied with 1,000 of the newest type of rifles imported from abroad. Takasugi's "modern army" was ready for the Shogun's second expedition.

The Shogun set out on his second expedition against Chōshū. Hoping to avoid hostilities he offered Chōshū various compromises which were firmly rejected. In the meantime, Shimazu Hisamitsu of Satsuma had shifted his basic position from that of advocating an Imperial Court–Shogun alliance to that of overthrowing the Shogun on behalf of the Emperor. This new situation made possible a firm alliance between Chōshū and Satsuma to overthrow the Tokugawa dictatorship and to restore power to the Emperor. The alliance, which was completed in March, 1866, provided that Satsuma would not become involved in the attack by the Shogun's army against Chōshū unless the Shogun or his armies tried to oust Satsuma from Kyōto. If Chōshū were to be victorious over the Shogun's forces, Satsuma promised to endeavor to have the former reinstated as a friend of the Imperial Court in Kyōto. If the Tokugawa forces were victorious then Satsuma and Chōshū would join forces at a later date to crush the old dictatorship.[14]

When the Shogun's forces finally entered the field of battle in the summer of 1866, they were easily defeated by the superior Chōshū army. The death of the Shogun on September 28, 1866, offered an excuse for a truce. Chōshū's excellent showing strengthened the movement for an anti-Tokugawa alliance advocated by Saigō of Satsuma and Kido of

Chōshū. Furthermore, the British Minister, Sir Harry Parkes, let it be known that he was losing confidence in the Shogun's government.

By the end of the summer of 1866, therefore, there was little left of the Tokugawa dictatorship. The Emperor had selected the advisers for the Shogun and deprived him of the right to allocate new domains. The powerful clans of Satsuma and Chōshū had openly defied the Shogun's policies. Civil war had broken out and the rebellious Chōshū forces were openly supporting the Emperor against the Shogun. There was increasing likelihood that the newly aroused loyalty for the Emperor would become the rallying force for a combined attack against the tottering dictatorship.

Economic and Financial Impotence of the Shogun

In the face of these overwhelming odds, the Shogunate had made a last-minute effort to salvage as much of its power as possible. It attempted to follow the difficult path of reliance on foreign help, both technical and financial, and of political independence from the country giving that assistance. Politically, France had shown the most interest in supporting the Shogun. Napoleon III had sent Leon Roches as his Minister to Japan in 1864 and had instructed him to give the Japanese as much assistance as possible. Ironworks, two docks, and three shipyards were planned to be built at Yokosuka over a period of four years with French assistance at a cost of $2,400,000. With the help of a $500,000 loan from France, work was begun in 1865. Japanese agents were sent to France to place the necessary orders for the machinery and to hire foreign experts. By 1866, forty-six such persons had begun to work on the project.

The French, again through their Minister Roches, offered military aid when the Shogun was engaged in the civil war in Chōshū. A treaty had been negotiated earlier with Napoleon III which included provision for military assistance. Since it was never ratified, the assistance was largely confined to French instructors in the Shogun's military school. When the government continued to be embarrassed by continued civil war in Chōshū, the brother of the Shogun was appointed head of the delegation to the Paris Exposition. Actually, he was instructed to obtain, if possible, a loan of $6,000,000, to defray the costs of the campaign in the west.

Although he failed in his mission, the French continued to be friendly to the Tokugawa cause. Leon Roches suggested certain administrative reforms. He proposed that the sincerity and loyalty of the western clans be challenged by throwing open three western ports to foreigners: Hyōgo near Ōsaka, Shimonoseki in Chōshū, and Kagoshima in Satsuma. His administrative reforms included a new system of taxation by which the merchants would be subject to a regular levy and all tax-free lands would be deprived of their exemptions. The restoration of power to the Emperor came too rapidly, however, to permit the implementation of any of these suggestions.

Foreign Trade

The Tokugawa government had also hoped to strengthen its financial position through profits from foreign trade. Heretofore, no new system of taxation had been adopted, no annual budget was prepared; revenues were derived largely from the income of government-owned land and "forced loans" imposed on the merchants. These sources were far from sufficient to meet the annual deficit of approximately 700,000 gold pieces (*ryō*). The opening of the ports and necessary preparations for the arrival of the foreigners had added noticeably to the annual expenses. For example, it was estimated that 300,000 *ryō* were needed for these purposes in Hokkaidō alone.

Consequently, it is not surprising that some government officers advocated official sponsorship of trade. Thus in April, 1859, the government-leased ship, the "Kamida Maru," sailed for Siberia with a Russian interpreter aboard. The silk, rice, soybeans, and sweet potatoes which it carried were not popular with the Siberian natives and the venture was a miserable failure.

In view of the reports which reached Edo through the foreign merchants in Yokohama and elsewhere of the fabulous profits to be obtained from trade with China, a second officially sponsored ship headed for Shanghai. Named the "Senzai Maru," it sailed with Dutch traders and a Japanese crew of fifty-one aboard. The cargo of coal, dried seafoods, lacquer, camphor, and textiles was treated as Dutch merchandise but the voyage likewise made no profit. A final attempt to trade in Shanghai, this time with the use of an American ship, resulted in the modest profit of 1,300 *ryō*. Obviously, therefore, the financial plight of the Tokugawa government was not to be alleviated through officially sponsored trade.

Turning to the foreign trade trends, the statistics in Table 1 reflect the internal political instability of the period from 1859–1867. For example, there was a tremendous increase in trade in 1860 after the Commercial Treaties were ratified. The drop in trade the next year indicates the growth of a strong antiforeign movement. The marked annual rise in imports after 1864 resulted from the costs of the military expeditions against the rebellious Chōshū fief as well as of the new naval yards and coastal defenses. The significantly greater exports were due to the government's efforts to develop new trade outlets, especially for raw silk. In 1860, silk accounted for seven-eighths of total exports and continued to

TABLE 1

VALUE (IN YEN) OF EXPORTS AND IMPORTS, 1859–1867[15]

Year	Exports	Imports	Balance
1859	¥ 570,927	¥ 543,005	¥ 35,902
1860	3,234,560	2,996,568	237,992
1861	2,343,755	2,198,406	145,349
1862	4,468,141	4,054,169	413,972
1863	4,751,631	4,336,840	384,791
1864	4,782,338	4,433,720	348,618
1865	6,058,718	5,950,231	135,487
1866	8,681,861	8,393,766	288,095
1867	8,575,822	10,445,888	−1,870,066

be one of the main items. A disease which practically wiped out the silk cocoons in Europe from 1866 to 1868 accounted for large exports of silkworm eggs from Japan and a consequent increase in exports for these years. Other important export items were tea and camphor.

In the early years, the heavy import demands for consumers' goods, such as cotton cloth, woolen cloth, and other fabrics, were evidence of the low state of industrialization throughout the country. For example, in 1860 cotton cloth accounted for one-half, and wool and other fabrics for one-third, of all imports into Yokohama. By 1867, infant industries had started to fill some of the demands of the domestic market so that imports of these products began to fall. They were replaced by new items which gave some indication of trends to come. For example, the purchase of foreign-style ships accounted for 20 per cent of Nagasaki's imports and guns and ammunition for 10 per cent of those of Yokohama. Rice and sugar, which were to be so important later when Japan began to feel the pressure of an accelerated increase in population, equaled 20 per cent of total imports. Finally, the small expenditure for military supplies indicates the precarious position of the Shogun. Although he had been faced with a civil war in 1865, military supplies were only a minor part of the total imports.

Despite a continuous favorable trade balance from 1859 to 1866, it should be remembered, however, that the benefits from this situation did not necessarily accrue to the Japanese government. Trade was not a government enterprise nor was it carried on by Japanese subjects. Foreign entrepreneurs and shippers handled practically all the trade and profited therefrom. Since most of these traders were British, over three-fourths of the total foreign trade at this time was with England. Furthermore, the treaties had originally permitted an import duty of 20 per cent. In 1865 the Western powers had forced the Shogun to reduce the duty to 5 per cent. Consequently, the revenue from 5 per cent of total imports and exports could hardly be expected to meet the new demands for national expenditures. Finally, the heavy unfavorable trade balance at the end of the period in 1867 reflected the precarious economic conditions.

Inflation and Loss of Bullion

Two other factors, both direct results of the opening of the ports, had a deleterious effect on Japan's economy. In the first place, the new demand for articles to be exported created a scarcity of goods and brought about an inflation in prices. For example, basic rice prices are reported to have risen from a unit price of 100 in 1862 to 530 in 1864 and 590 in 1866. Prices of other commodities are reported to have shown similar increases; those of tea doubled, silk tripled, and cotton quadrupled. A manifestation of the discontent resulting from these conditions was a steady increase in the number of peasant uprisings in the last years of the Tokugawa period. From an overall yearly average of 10.1 incidents throughout the period, the average of 1850 to 1860 was 14.6. For the seven years after 1860, the average was 32 uprisings with a peak of 71 recorded for 1866.[16]

The financial uncertainty was further aggravated by the debasement of the currency and the outflow of gold. Debasement had long been resorted to as a method of meeting increased financial needs until the standard coins equaled less than one-eighth their original value. This depreciation was also accompanied by a decrease in the metallic value of the silver and gold coins. In fact, after an analysis by the Philadelphia mint of the silver content of the *ichibu* silver coin, which Perry had stipulated should be equal to the Mexican dollar, it was discovered that it had a metallic value of about 33 cents. On the basis of the Japanese–American Commercial Treaty of 1858, which provided that metals should be exchanged weight for weight, the Mexican dollar came to be exchanged for three *ichibu* silver coins.

As soon as this exchange rate was settled and trade actually began, there was a sudden drain on Japanese gold coins which disturbed the financial market still further. For many centuries, silver had always been given a high value in Japan and was exchanged roughly in a ratio of one to six. As fifteen to twenty pieces of silver exchanged for one piece of gold on the Asiatic continent, the traders and sailors soon began to make a smart profit at the expense of Japan's supply of gold coins. During the last six months of 1859, a million gold pieces were exported from Japan and the Shogunate was forced to adjust the value of silver to that comparable to the rest of the world.[17]

Increased Strength of Western Clans

In contrast to this disorganization and deterioration of the national economy which adversely affected the Tokugawa government, the clans which were most active in the royalist movement were profiting from their progressive industrial policies. Many of the most powerful of the rival clans of the Shogunate, Mito in the north, Satsuma, Chōshū, Tosa, and Hizen in the west, were far more advanced economically than the rest of the clans or the fiefs of the central government. (See Chapter 2.) From the significant roles played in the turbulent 1860's by the Satsuma, Chōshū, and Tosa leaders, it is clear that the economic power of these clans had greatly augmented their potential military and political power. Before describing the final overthrow of the Shogun by a coalition of the four western clans, therefore, it is important to stop briefly to survey the most recent economic developments in a few of these fiefs.

For example, Satsuma in the extreme southwest, through its trade with the Ryūkyū Islands, had accumulated a limited amount of mercantilist capital which had been invested locally. After the completion of the blast and reverberatory furnaces in 1853, industrialization continued apace. Dutch patterns were followed to manufacture porcelain, glass, sulfuric acid, lacquers, farm implements, shipbuilding machinery, and oil extractors. A machine to produce static electricity had been built in Edo and both a telegraph line and gas lights were installed within the garden of the feudal mansion in the domain.

Pompe van Meerdervoort, when he visited the principality's capital city of Kagoshima in 1858, reported that he saw formidable coastal batteries with guns capable of firing cannon balls of 150-pound weight built by local foundries. But these cannon were no match for the fire power of the British flotilla which attacked the city in 1863. He also stated that 1,200 men were working in the fief's industrial development institute, the Shūseikan, and that one hundred more were melting, blowing, grinding, and using the latest coloring methods in the porcelain and glass factory. The clansmen were also working on a paddle-wheel steamer which they presented later to the Shogun. By 1867, a start had been made in spinning. Clansmen had been dispatched to Europe to purchase spinning machinery. It had been installed under British supervision and was operated by 200 Japanese employees under a British manager with six British assistants.

In the northwest corner of Kyūshū, surrounding the harbor of Nagasaki and center of foreign activity for nearly 300 years, the domain of Hizen had devoted much of its time and effort to the development of military industries. The iron foundry, which the Hollander Hardes had constructed, was busy on orders for the newly constructed forts at the head of Edo Bay at Shinagawa. By 1866 it was casting nearly forty cannon a month. At the same time, young technicians and engineers from neighboring clans were receiving technical training and instruction at the foundry.

Mention has already been made of the development of a new type of army in Chōshū and its decision to revolt against the Tokugawa regime. Chōshū was not a large fief, so it is surprising that it dared challenge the central authorities. While part of Chōshū's decision was the result of an almost fanatical loyalist movement, its actual economic strength was comparatively much stronger than its size. Its administration had been centralized; and, as its political crises increased in intensity, strict restrictions were placed on its subjects. Clan monopolies in paper, indigo, rice, silk, and lumber were encouraged. A moratorium was declared on all debts and henceforth the fief operated on a balanced budget.

Tosa, the third of the western clans which was to take a lead in the Restoration movement, had also made marked strides economically, commercially, and militarily. While the feudal baron Yamanouchi Yōdō (d. 1872) had originally advocated continuance of Japan's seclusion policy he was a strong advocate of Western methods of gunnery and naval construction. He used Manjirō, a waif returned from America, to assist in the modern industrialization of the fief. He sent many of his young warriors to other fiefs to study and learn the latest methods. As early as 1854, a people's army composed of unattached warriors (*rōnin*), farmers, and village officials, the first of its kind, was organized. Much of the new strength and vitality of Tosa after 1864 was due to the administrative skill and efforts of Gotō Shōjirō (1838–1897). As a member of the fief's central policy and control board, he formed a new bureau to centralize all of the fief's enterprises. Its financial problems were solved by stringent economies in fief expenditures and by forcing wealthy persons to make loans to the fief's treasury. Production of camphor, tea, sugar, gold, silver, copper, and iron (all clan monopolies) was encouraged. He also developed contacts with loyalist leaders such as Sakamoto Ryōma (1836–1867) and the young merchant, Iwasaki Yatarō (1834–1885), who was to become one of the nation's leading financiers and industrialists. Sakamoto had been sent to Nagasaki to develop a trading company for the fief which bought arms for Satsuma and Chōshū and sent trading ships to these fiefs. When some of Gotō's ventures failed, Iwasaki paid for the indebtedness.[18]

These industrial developments and the new types of armies which were recruited in Chōshū and Tosa were evidence that social mobility was an accepted fact. The townsmen, warriors, and farmers who had been stratified into separate classes by the Tokugawa dictatorship now worked together, making each feudal domain self-sufficient, strong, and independent of the Shogun's power. The townsmen were active in the management of the business affairs of the fief at home and at Ōsaka, including supervision of the various clan monopolies. The farmers were being recruited into the new local people's armies and thus attained the status of warriors. The most active and intellectually alert young warriors were busy advising their feudal lords on how to participate actively in the restoration of the Emperor to power and on ways to enhance the prestige of the fief. These men, especially those from the *Satchō Dohi* group (the abbreviated name given to Satsuma, Chōshū, Tosa, and Hizen) were obtaining invaluable practical experience which was to enable them to accomplish the herculean task of modernizing the entire country within a generation.

The growing need of the individual warrior to borrow cash to meet the bare essentials of living was an added incentive to shifts in social classes. Some of the warriors were so impoverished that they could not afford to sleep on a mattress in winter or under a mosquito net in summer. Many willingly sold their preferential social status and their annual stipend of 500 bushels of rice to merchants who were willing to lend them fifty gold pieces.

The clans also were in need of money to assure the successful conclusion of their political plans. Consequently, the local merchants and bankers found themselves inextricably entwined in the political movement to overthrow the Shogun. If they were to retrieve or salvage any of the heavy indebtedness owed them by the warriors and feudal barons, they could not afford to antagonize these warriors who planned to restore the Emperor as the actual ruler of Japan. Thus they acquiesced in the political changes that took place. In view of this debtor–creditor relationship, it was unlikely that the merchants would revolt against the class from which they hoped to continue to receive interest or capital payments on loans. For example, the Mitsui family, which had been bankers for the Shogunate, found it financially expedient and profitable to shift its allegiance from the Shogun to the Emperor after the former capitulated.[19]

Of equal if not greater importance for the restoration movement was the breakdown of the earliest restrictions forbidding travel between fiefs and to Kyōto. As already indicated, many of the young royalist clansmen in the west were traveling to Kyōto, to Nagasaki, and even to each other's fief. In fact, there are innumerable instances of clansmen from one fief being put up at the residence of another and of collusion to protect a fellow-royalist who was being sought by the authorities. In this way, these men from different feudal domains came to meet each other and to recognize that they all had a joint cause, the support of the Emperor and the overthrow of the Shogun. For example, Itō Hirobumi and

Inouye Kaoru of Chōshū had stayed at the Satsuma residence in Nagasaki. When the courtier Sanjō Sanetomi and some of the Chōshū leaders were forced out of Kyōto in 1864, they took refuge in northern Kyūshū also under Satsuma's protection. Sakamoto Ryōma of Tosa, who was so influential in acting as a mediator between Chōshū and Satsuma, making their alliance possible, was sheltered several times by Satsuma.

Consequently, the stage was set for a small body of political, military, and business leaders to form a new elite group. They concentrated first on amalgamating their strength to overthrow the Shogun and then tackled the innumerable practical problems which would make Japan strong and unified under the rule of the youthful Emperor Meiji. They were aided and abetted in their efforts at modernization by the existence of several important potentials for modern economic growth. These included a high level of education, a commercialized economy responsive to market stimuli, a low level of consumption among the populace, and a tradition of participation in industry by both the clan governments and the Tokugawa Shogunate.[20]

The Shogun Capitulates

When the Shogun died during the campaign against Chōshū in August, 1866, Keiki, the son of Tokugawa Nariaki of Mito, was selected as the next Shogun. The coalition of the western clans and the Emperor was developing rapidly but had not yet advanced to the point where it was strong enough to forestall Keiki's installation. Before he could take formal command of his army near Ōsaka it had been routed by the Chōshū forces. On February 3, 1867, the Emperor Kōmei died and was succeeded by his fifteen-year-old son, to be known as Emperor Meiji.

Following these events, the movement to restore the young Emperor as the *de facto* ruler of the country rapidly gained momentum. Contacts among the young loyalist warriors of the western clans with one another and with Imperial courtiers intensified. For example, Ōkubo Toshimichi, one of the young leaders of Satsuma, had been in close touch with Iwakura Tomomi, one of the courtiers who had been temporarily exiled.[21] When the young Emperor Meiji came to the throne, Iwakura was pardoned and placed in a key position to encourage the intrigues of the loyalists. During the summer of 1867, the *daimyō* of four of the most powerful domains, including Satsuma and Tosa, met with the Shogun to try to persuade him to pardon Chōshū for its recent revolt and also to meet the strong demands of the foreigners, underlined by the presence of foreign warships, to open the port of Hyōgo. Hyōgo was ordered open on June 26.

As the status of Chōshū remained unsettled, it was natural that the Chōshū leaders such as Kido Kōin urged Satsuma to implement the alliance of the two clans and to take a more belligerent attitude against the Shogun. To this the latter agreed by dispatching an army of 3,000 men to Ōsaka. Meanwhile, Yamanouchi Yōdō, the feudal baron of Tosa, agreed to go to Kyōto to endeavor to obtain the resignation of the new Shogun Keiki and his own appointment to some important post in the new government. On October 3, Imperial permission was granted to the Satsuma army to move to Kyōto, thus assuring the protection of the person of the Emperor. The Chōshū army was scheduled to arrive on October 23 so the feudal barons of both Satsuma and Tosa pressed Keiki to resign. By November 4, Iwakura received the Emperor's approval for Saigō Takamori to lead the Satsuma troops and those of other fiefs loyal to the throne in an attack against the Shogun's force. (In reality, Chōshū was again recognized by the Imperial Court as a staunch ally.) Keiki, who was virtually a prisoner in his own Nījō Palace in Kyōto had little choice. Realizing that his cause was lost, he resigned as Shogun on November 9, 1867.

The Emperor Meiji and his advisers had at their disposal the strongest feudal barons and armies in Japan. The first step had been taken in the Meiji Restoration. The second step was to follow within two months. In mid-December, Shimazu Hisamitsu, leader of Satsuma, arrived in Kyōto. He and other feudal lords were gathering for a secret meeting with the Emperor which courtier Iwakura had planned. On January 3, 1868, these barons pledged their personal loyalty to the Emperor Meiji who announced that all power was restored to him and that the office of Shogun was abolished.

Fortunately for the new Emperor and the new volunteer army placed at his disposal by the western feudal barons, the resistance of the Tokugawa forces was at a minimum. When Keiki decided a fortnight later to fight rather than to retire gracefully, he moved to Ōsaka. His forces were quickly defeated by the Imperial army and he escaped to the protection of his castle in Edo. Again the military leader of Satsuma, Saigō Takamori, came to the fore. His fellow clansmen had already reinforced the garrison of the Edo mansion of their feudal baron. They were more than ready for a fight to the finish but this eventuality was avoided in April, 1868, when Saigō obtained the Shogun's acceptance of the Emperor's terms of surrender. The Edo castle and all military and naval supplies were to be turned over to the Emperor. All the Shogun's vassals were to leave Edo and those who had conspired against the Emperor were to be punished. Keiki, the Shogun, who at one time had expected that at the very least he would be given an important post in the new government, was incarcerated in the family castle at Mito. Aside from a small group of his followers who escaped to the north by ship, the Tokugawa Shogunate had lost its support and the dictatorship had collapsed in the two hundred and sixty-fifth year of its existence.[22]

Notes

1. The three families were the chief branches of the Tokugawa family. The Emperor's reply was designed to embarrass Hotta, as the majority of the barons and Nariaki, head of the Mito family, were strongly opposed to any further concessions. Ishin Shiryō Hensan Kakari (ed.), *Ishin Shi* (6 vols.; Tokyo: Meijishoin, 1939–1941), II, p. 330.

2. See Albert M. Craig, *Chōshū in the Meiji Restoration* (Cambridge: Harvard University Press, 1961), p. 119. This is one of two excellent studies describing the struggles within two of the powerful western clans and the role which they and their neighbors played in the movement to restore the Emperor to power. The other study is Marius B. Jansen, *Sakamoto Ryōma and the Meiji Restoration* (Princeton: Princeton University Press, 1961).

3. *Ishin Shi,* II, *op. cit.,* p. 535.

4. For a translation of Manabe's complete letters as well as other key documents and a valuable commentary see W. G. Beasley (trans. and ed.), *Select Documents on Japanese Foreign Policy 1853–1868* (London: Oxford University Press, 1955), p. 191. Lord Elgin successfully negotiated the British–Japanese Treaty in Edo. Signed August 26, 1858, it provided that Nagasaki, Kanagawa, and Hakodate would be opened July 1, 1859, Niigata on January 1, 1860, and Hyōgo on January 1, 1863. See Grace Fox, *Britain and Japan 1858–1883* (Oxford: Clarendon Press, 1969), pp. 40 ff.

5. See Henry Heusken, *Japan Journal 1855–1861,* Jeanne C. van der Corput and Robert C. Wilson (eds.) (New Brunswick, N. J.: Rutgers University Press, 1964), p. 218. In contrast, the accounts of the sojourn of the crew of the damaged Russian frigate "Askold" in Nagasaki in 1858–1859 indicate that they received a warm reception and their neighbors were loath to see them leave. See George A. Lensen, *The Russian Push toward Japan: Russo-Japanese Relations 1697–1875* (Princeton: Princeton University Press, 1959), pp. 355 ff.

6. See *Ishin Shi,* II, *op. cit.,* pp. 142 ff. The largest proportion of the forty-seven persons assigned to training on the ship came from Hizen, the fief responsible for the protection of Nagasaki.

7. Thr. J. C. L. Pompe van Meerdevoort, "The Study of Natural Science in Japan," *Journal North China Branch Royal Asiatic Society I* (1859), pp. 213 ff., and Dr. John Z. Bowers, *Western Medical Pioneers in Feudal Japan* (Baltimore: Johns Hopkins University Press, 1969).

8. *The First Japanese Embassy to the United States of America* (Tokyo: The American–Japan Society, 1920), pp. 42–43.

9. "A Broadway Pageant," *The Poetry and Prose of Walt Whitman,* Louis Untermeyer (ed.) (New York: Simon and Schuster, Inc., 1949), p. 238.

10. Shimazu Hisamitsu (1817–1887) never inherited the domain but ran it after 1859 and soon became active in the coalition movement of warriors and the Imperial Court. He continuously cautioned his warriors against too rash or precipitate action and had the most recalcitrant of them killed when they persisted in their opposition to him. In 1864 he brought about a tem-

porary reconciliation between the Imperial Court and the Shogun. By the beginning of 1867, however, he realized that such a reconciliation was impossible and readily agreed to an alliance with the Chōshū fief to attack the Shogunate. He was appointed Minister of the Right in the new Imperial government but soon became disappointed in its policies and accomplishments. He frequently left Tokyo in disgust only to return to Satsuma. In 1876 he returned home to live in retirement until his death in 1887.

11. Itō Hirobumi (1841–1909). Itō was born of an extremely poor warrior family in the Chōshū fief. From this lowly beginning he became his country's most powerful figure. When about twelve, he was adopted by the Itō family which hired him out as a page to another warrior who was quick to observe his talents. In 1855 Itō studied for five months with the loyalist Yoshida Shōin. He then studied Dutch military science at Nagasaki and was in Edo at the height of the antiforeign movement. In 1861, he participated with Inouye Kaoru and other fellow clansmen in the attack on the British legation.

In 1863 he and Inouye were sent secretly to England, serving as forecastle hands on a small trading ship to London. In London Itō studied science for several months, but returned home immediately upon learning of the imminence of hostilities between Great Britain and Chōshū. When he reached home, he tried unsuccessfully to persuade his fellow clansmen to abandon their proposed attack on the foreigners. After Chōshū had been defeated, he worked out the treaty between Chōshū and the Dutch, American, and British commanders. In March, 1868, Itō received his first appointment in the new Imperial government in the Bureau of Foreign Affairs. He shifted to Finance, Industry, Prime Minister, President of the Privy Council, and Elder Statesman (*Genrō*). He was assassinated in Harbin in 1909.

On the issue of postponing the dates for the opening of the ports to foreigners as provided in the treaties, the Tokugawa government obtained important concessions from the British. Its threat to close Yokohama, however, was unsuccessful. See Fox, *op. cit.*, pp. 96–145.

12. Kido Kōin (1835–1877) was born in the Chōshū fief. A sickly youth, he studied Chinese classics, history, and fencing, and later took up Western military science. A few years later he was head of the clan's school in Edo for training its warriors.

When the cry, "Exalt the Emperor and expel the barbarians," arose, Kido advised his clan chieftain, Mōri Takachika, to prepare for war. In 1864, however, he advised against civil war but was overruled, and found himself later as leader of the army. After personal conferences with Saigō Takamori, leader of the rival Satsuma clan, Kido worked actively for their alliance against the Tokugawa. When the Shogun, Keiki, resigned, Kido recommended the complete destruction of his forces. He soon became one of the strongest and most active leaders in the new Imperial government.

13. Saigō Takamori (1828–1877) was born in Kagoshima, the capital of the Satsuma fief, of a low-rank warrior family. He was a boyhood friend and relation of Ōkubo. In February, 1854, he made a favorable impression on his feudal lord, Shimazu Nariakira. Several months later, he was appointed chief gardener of Nariakira's mansion, a position which brought him into close contact with his chief. He also served for several years in a rural tax office. During the next few years, Saigō's royalist and antiforeign feelings were stimulated by his contacts with Nariakira and other men of like mind and by visits on clan business in Kyōto and Edo. Like many other clan leaders he traveled widely.

In the fall of 1858, while Saigō was at Kyōto, he became known as an anti-Tokugawa warrior. Consequently, he was exiled for five years.

In April, 1864, he was again in Kyōto and was recognized as the effective leader of the Satsuma warriors. During the next three years, he was influential in keeping Satsuma from involvement in the civil war in Chōshū and in organizing the *rapprochement* of those two clans. In February, 1866, he and Kido of Chōshū hammered out the formal alliance between Satsuma and Chōshū. When the Imperial Restoration was proclaimed in January, 1868, Saigō was in charge of the Satsuma troops which formed the nucleus of the new Emperor's army.

14. For a valuable discussion of these key negotiations, as well as the role of Sakamoto Ryōma, a loyalist leader of Tosa fief, see Jansen, *op. cit.*, pp. 194 ff., and Craig, *op. cit.*, pp. 208 ff. The reader should not assume from the concentration on Chōshū and Satsuma that these were the only fiefs urging the overthrow of the Shogun. Aizu helped Satsuma with the coup of 1864; Mito and Tosa were also important. As the history of this struggle for power is extremely complicated, to simplify the narrative only the most important activities of the two strongest fiefs have been noted.

15. A word of caution is in order in reference to unreliability of Japanese statistics, especially those for the earlier years. The trends from figures available are, however, clear. See Horie Yasuzo, *Nihon Shihon Shūgi no Seiritsu* (Ōsaka: Daidō Shoin, 1938), pp. 108, 194.

16. Great Britain had the lion's share of foreign trade. In 1863, British merchants imported 80 per cent and exported 73 per cent of Japan's foreign trade. In 1865, the proportions were 87 and 81 per cent, respectively. The British firm of Glover and Co. was particularly active in trade with the western clans, especially with Satsuma. For example, by 1866, the Satsuma fief had purchased through Glover 16 ships, 6 saw mills, and other machinery. Itō and Inouye Kaoru ordered, in Satsuma's name, a warship and 7,300 rifles from Glover. British merchants, contrary to their government's stated policy of neutrality, had been active in supplying arms for both the Shogun and the Chōshū army during the civil war of 1865–1866. See Fox, *op. cit.*, pp. 153 ff., and Ishii Takashi, *Bakamatsu Bōeki Shi no Kenkyū* (Tokyo: Nihon Hyōron Sha, 1944), p. 80. For the importance of peasant uprisings at this time see Hugh Borton, *Peasant Uprisings in Japan of the Tokugawa Period*, 2nd Ed. (New York: Paragon Reprints, 1968), and Aoki Koji, *Hyakushō Ikki no Nenjiteki Kenkyū* (Tokyo: Shinseisha, 1966), p. 16.

17. For example, if a trader arrived in Yokohama with 60 silver Mexican dollars, he could trade them for 180 *ichibu* silver coins. These *ichibu* coins could then be exchanged for 45 *koban* gold pieces which could be sold in China for 90–150 silver dollars. The trader could make 150 per cent profit on a single trip.

18. Gotō Shōjirō (1838–1897). Born in Tosa, Gotō was a lifelong friend of Itagaki Taisuke, leader of the "liberals." After serving several months as a supervisor in the clan government, he went to Edo, entered the language school of the Tokugawa government, and studied navigation and "English studies." Always an advocate of the restoration of power to the Emperor, he was often used by his feudal baron as an emissary to important anti-Tokugawa fiefs such as Satsuma and Hizen. He was among those who urged the Shogun to resign in 1867, and in early 1868 he became Assistant Secretary of Foreign Affairs. While in that office, his quick action saved the life of the British

Minister, Sir Harry Parkes, when the latter was attacked in an antiforeign riot. Gotō, who had jumped from his horse and cut down Sir Harry's assailant, was later knighted by Queen Victoria for his bravery. He continued to be one of the chief leaders until his death. See Jansen, *op. cit.*, p. 243.

19. It has been suggested by Norman that this so-called merchant–warrior coalition was inevitable as a result of the large investment of the merchants in land rented to the peasantry. The debtor–creditor relationship appears, however, to be an even stronger cementing factor. The suppression of the peasants by the warriors was merely incidental to their effort to maintain their position of supremacy rather than a conscious effort to suppress the chief productive class. See E. Herbert Norman, *Japan's Emergence as a Modern State* (New York: American Institute of Pacific Relations, Inc., 1940), p. 54.

20. See E. Sydney Crawcour, "The Tokugawa Heritage," in *The State and Economic Enterprise in Japan,* William W. Lockwood (ed.) (Princeton: Princeton University Press, 1965), pp. 17–44.

21. Ōkubo Toshimichi (1830–1878) was born in Kagoshima in Satsuma. As the son of a warrior he entered the clan school where he studied Chinese literature and the Confucian classics and poetry. At a young age he became a clan official. In August, 1858, he was shocked to learn of the plan of his boyhood friend, Saigō Takamori, to commit suicide and of the death of Shimazu Nariakira, lord of the fief and advocate of a policy to revere the Emperor and expel the barbarians. Ōkubo then formed a small "League of Loyal Men" for the purpose of going to Edo to force drastic reforms on the *Bakufu* government. Ōkubo soon became one of the closest advisers of the *de facto* leader of the fief, Shimazu Hisamitsu, and advocate of a policy of compromise between the Imperial Court and the *Bakufu.* Until the Meiji Restoration in 1867, he played a key role within the clan, eventually shifting to a policy of strong anti-Tokugawa alliance.

On his various trips to Kyōto and Edo on behalf of Hisamitsu, he met the leaders of both the Imperial Court and the Shogun's government. In 1863, following the bombardment of Kagoshima by the British, he was entrusted with working out a three-cornered agreement among Great Britain, Satsuma, and the Shogun. In 1864 he advised Shimazu Hisamitsu of Satsuma to recall Saigō from exile for the good of the royalist cause. Two years later, in meetings in Kyōto with Saigō, Kido, and others, he helped to formalize the Satsuma–Chōshū alliance. After the Shogun surrendered, he became one of the strongest members of the new government. His biographer, Iwata, goes so far as to say, "Almost single-handedly, during the critical period from the spring of 1868 to 1871, he held the government together, coaxing and flattering jealous colleagues and suspicious feudal domains into devoting themselves to the national ideal." See Masakazu Iwata, *Ōkubo Toshimichi, the Bismarck of Japan* (Berkeley: University of California Press, 1964), p. 116.

22. For a detailed account of the events of the last weeks of the Shogun's government see Oka Yoshitake, *Kindai Nihon no Keisei* (Tokyo: Kōbun-dō, 1952), pp. 101 ff.; Jansen, *op. cit.*, pp. 313 ff., and Iwata, *op. cit.*, pp. 90 ff.

PART II

FORMATION OF A CENTRALIZED MONARCHY 1868-1890

We, sitting on the Throne which has been occupied by Our dynasty for over 2,500 years, and now exercising in Our name and right all authority and power transmitted to us by Our ancestors, have long had in view gradually to establish a constitutional form of government, to the end that Our successors on the Throne may be provided with a rule for their guidance.

Imperial decree promising the establishment of Parliament October 12, 1881

Chronology

1868–1890

1868	January 3	Imperial restoration of Emperor Meiji
	April 6	Imperial (Charter) Oath
1869	March	Four western clans (*Satchō Dohi*) petition Emperor to accept title to domain
1871	August	Imperial Decree formally abolishes clans
1872		Railroad opened between Tokyo and Yokohama
		Iwakura Mission tours United States and Europe
1873		Edict against Christianity removed
		Universal land tax in money instituted
		Creation of modern army based on conscription
	October	Split over question of Korean War
1874		Formosan Expedition
		Memorial requesting representative assembly
1875		Territorial settlement of Kuriles with Russia
		Ōsaka Conference
1876		Treaty of Kanghwa opens Korea
		Forced commutation of feudal pensions
1877		Saigō's Rebellion
1878		Expansion of Imperial Army
1879		Ryūkyū Islands incorporated into the Empire
1880		Law for sale of factories to private industry
1881	March	Ōkuma's Memorial demanding a Parliament
	July	Ōkuma exposes Hokkaidō scandal
		Iwakura establishes principles for Constitution
	October 11	Ōkuma ousted
		Parliament promised by 1890
		Retrenchment and currency stabilization by Finance Minister Matsukata
1885		Li–Itō Convention on Korea
		First Cabinet formed
1889	February 11	Meiji Constitution proclaimed

5

First Practical Steps of the Meiji Government 1868–1873

In a study of the factors and motive forces which molded and formed Japan during the past century, one is impressed with the fact that this development was the result, as is true of any historical event, of the interaction of various forces, national or international, economic, social, or political. At the same time, a more detailed analysis of the main events of any given period in history often reveals the preponderance of one set of forces over the others. This situation appears to be particularly true of the events of the first few years of the Meiji Restoration, and yet is often neglected by the historians of the period.

As will become apparent from the following analysis, economic problems were among the most important ones during the first few years of the Meiji Period, particularly from 1868 to 1873. In these early years of the Restoration the new leaders devoted their main strength and effort toward the solution of the economic dilemma in which Japan found itself and toward the development of a sound economic base for the new state. If the political and economic structure of modern Japan is to be understood clearly, therefore, it is important to recognize that the real problems which absorbed the actual rulers of the country during the early rule of the Emperor Meiji were practical problems. They were absorbed in questions such as lighthouses, stable currency, taxes, industrial production, a new army, a merchant marine, and the development of foreign markets. Political problems began to demand the dominant attention of these leaders only after many of the basic economic issues had been settled.

This point is made patently clear by Itō Hirobumi, who became the chief architect of the Constitution. In an article which he wrote some fifteen years after the Constitution was promulgated, he makes no mention of political developments from 1868, when the Emperor Meiji was restored to power, to 1880 when the law was issued which inaugurated the system of cities and prefectures. Apparently, in Itō's view, nothing important happened politically for the first twelve years of the Restoration.[1]

This interest of the officials in the new government in practical matters and Western techniques was partly due to their own beliefs and experiences. It was also bolstered by the writings of persons such as Fukuzawa Yukichi (1835–1901), an outstanding exponent of the need for a new "enlightenment." Prior to the Restoration, he had made two trips to the West, one to the United States and the other to Europe. These visits underlined his belief that Japan could only be saved from the restrictive and stifling influences of its old traditions by concentrating on Western techniques and by understanding certain basic laws and principles. His inquisitive mind and keen observations while abroad formed the basis for his famous *Seiyō Jijō* (Conditions of the West) in which he wrote about such practical things as schools, hospitals, banks, insurance companies, newspapers, workhouses, the election system, and taxation. Published in 1866, these descriptions of contemporary life and institutions in America and Western Europe fascinated the Japanese. A first edition of 150,000 copies was sold out and Fukuzawa thereby established his reputation as an authority on Western civilization.[2]

Temporary Form of Imperial Government

When the youthful Emperor Meiji issued the proclamation on January 3, 1868, of the "Restoration of Imperial Government," only very limited power had actually been restored to the throne.[3] The military campaigns against the Tokugawa forces, even though they were of a limited nature, had yet to be successfully concluded. There had been no revolution, no overthrow of one class by another. The warriors were still the most powerful element in society. The feudal barons of most of the strongest fiefs had shifted their allegiance from the Tokugawa generalissimo, the Shogun, to the Emperor. Though the sovereign had an army at his disposal far stronger than the combined forces of his potential enemies, this army was available to him only so long as the feudal barons willed it.

Furthermore, the new Imperial government had not yet acquired many of the basic attributes of a government. It did not have the power to tax the land. Its treasury was completely empty. Title to the land was still both theoretically and practically in the hands of 276 separate and partially autonomous feudal barons. These barons had not yet pledged loyalty to the Emperor and held their domains on order from the Shogun.

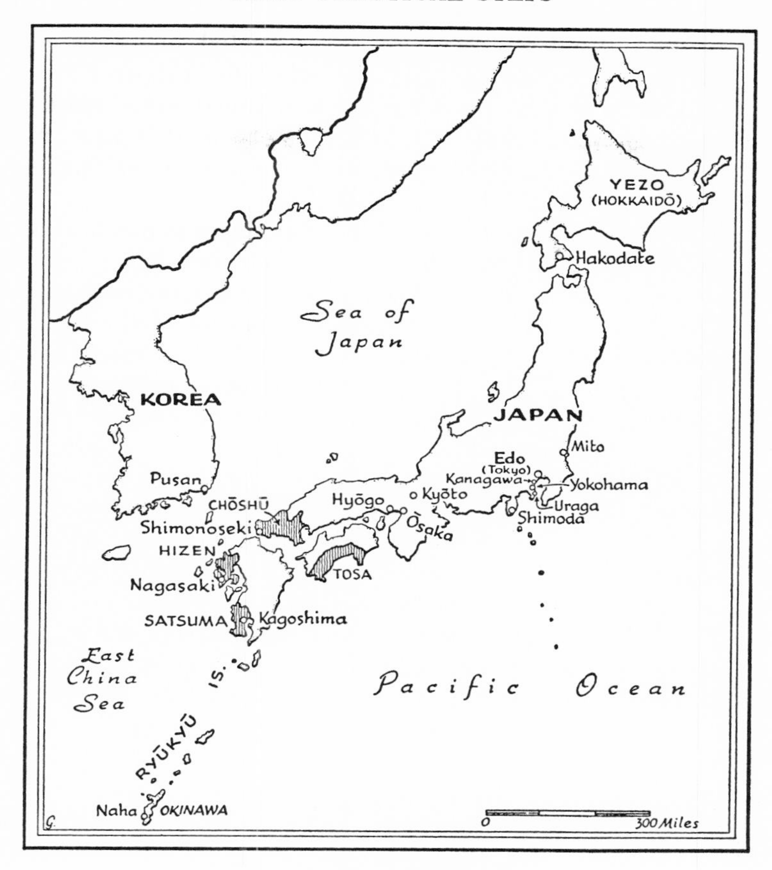

JAPAN IN 1868

There was no standard currency in circulation. There was no agreed pattern for the structure of the new government and no clear concept of the relationship between the Imperial Court and the feudal barons and other classes in society. There were few experienced administrators available to take over the operation of the affairs of state. No foreign power had yet recognized the new government. Militarily, Meiji was defenseless against foreign attack as he had no navy, nor did any of the barons loyal to him have ships of sufficient size or strength to form the core of a new navy.

As Kido Kōin, the sensitive young warrior from Chōshū, described the situation ten months after the Emperor issued his Restoration Proclamation:

If we wish the restoration of a new government to be realized and the prestige of our Emperor to be elevated abroad, we must establish the basis of government by allotting three-fifths of the expenses for military purposes, one-fifth for the government, and one-fifth for relief and for the people.

The new government did not suddenly appear as a fixed pattern. The whole Restoration movement was a continuing process which extended over several years. In fact, the pattern of the new constitutional monarchy was not irrevocably set for roughly twenty years. Under these circumstances, the first few years of the Restoration were full of constant shifts in the form of government. A small group of capable and imaginative men, who had been the leading courtiers and the young warriors in the progressive clans in western Japan, became the key figures in the most important new posts in the government. They constantly shifted from one ministry to another or created new ones as the exigencies of the times demanded. They were completely engrossed with the problem of improving Japan's position through rapid modernization, industrialization, and increased military strength. They were far too occupied with practical matters in the first dozen years of Meiji's reign to have time to work out a master plan for the development of an imperialistic monarchy.

Although there was interest in human rights and liberalism, this interest was in no sense comparable to that which existed in the American or French Revolutions. The Meiji Restoration had not been sparked by Christian idealism, by the principles of equality, brotherhood, and liberty, or even by a class struggle, as the Marxists would wish one to believe. On the contrary, it had been a struggle between rival groups within the warrior class with loyalty to the Emperor as a unifying force among them. Consequently, the first forms of the new government followed a pattern familiar in Japanese history. Two councils of state were formed to be composed of courtiers and the feudal barons from those clans that had supported the Emperor against the Tokugawa Shogun. Seven departments of government were established, one of the most important of which was that of Shintō, the indigenous religion.

In addition to the military action taken against the Tokugawa forces in the early months of 1868, the new leaders made an important decision on the basic policy which should control the new government. This basic policy was formulated by the courtier Iwakura Tomomi (1825–1883), assistant chief of the new State Council, and two of the young clansmen from the west, Fukuoka Kōtei (1835–1919) from Tosa and Kido Kōin from Chōshū. It was proclaimed on April 6, 1868, in the form of an Imperial oath, usually referred to as the Charter Oath. Its famous five articles stated, in familiar terms, the general principles and antifeudal aspirations under which the new monarchy would operate. It read:

1. An assembly widely convoked shall be established, and thus great stress shall be laid upon public discussion.
2. The welfare of the whole nation shall be promoted by the everlasting efforts of both the governing and the governed classes.

3. All subjects, civil and military officers, as well as other people, shall do their best and never grow weary in accomplishing their legitimate purposes.
4. All absurd usages shall be abandoned; justice and righteousness shall regulate all actions.
5. Knowledge shall be sought for all over the world and thus shall be strengthened the foundation of the Imperial polity.[4]

With these broad principles settled, it was possible for Fukuoka and his colleagues to draw up more specific plans for a national government. After they studied Chinese, European, and earlier Japanese systems of government, they presented a plan which recognized the three powers of government, namely, the legislative, executive, and judicial, and delegated them in a rather loose fashion to the Council of State (*Dajōkan*). These powers were to be exercised by a bicameral assembly, the President of the Council, and the various executive departments. This plan, often referred to as the first "Constitution" and called the *Seitaisho,* was formally adopted in June, 1868. Shortly thereafter, the name of the city of Edo was changed to Tokyo (Eastern Capital). The name of Meiji (Enlightened Government) was given to the period. In the spring of 1869 the young sovereign moved his court permanently to the new capital of Tokyo, and the old Edo castle became the Imperial Palace.

As new problems developed, it soon became apparent that the real power in the government rested in the hands of the Councilors (*sanyo*). The Imperial princes, who were the titular heads of the executive departments, became figureheads. The proposed assembly proved to be little more than an advisory body and soon disappeared. On the other hand, with the Emperor's sanction, the Councilors acted either individually or collectively as both the executive and legislative branches of government. They were men largely from the middle-class warriors of the western clans who had had practical experience in local government and had participated in the Restoration. They were comparatively young men when their sovereign ascended the throne; many of them had hardly reached the age of thirty. These were the men of action who were content to wait for a more propitious time before they set up a complicated national administrative structure. These were the people who were to grow as the new state grew and whose power increased with it. Once having tasted the heady effect of power, they could not give it up.[5]

Financial Confusion and Lack of Technical Knowledge

Fortunately for the Imperial Army, there had been a minimum of military resistance by the supporters of the Tokugawa cause. Nonetheless, such battles as were fought in 1868 and 1869 placed a heavy drain on the meager resources of the new government. Of an estimated expenditure of 51.5 million yen for the first two years nearly 9 million yen was spent on the various military campaigns. Furthermore, it was too early for the new government to profit from the confiscation of the vast realm owned by the Tokugawa family. As the chief of the newly established Treasury Office described it, "The expenditures or budget of this office is a fiction. We have only resorted to borrowing and our daily expenses are barely met." Such revenue as existed came largely from the issuance of paper currency, borrowing, and customs duties. For example, during the first year of the Restoration, the government borrowed 29 million yen to defray expenditures of 33 million yen.

The situation was complicated by the fact that no action had been taken to abolish the outward forms of feudalism, and the central authorities still lacked the power to collect a uniform national tax. Furthermore, the currency was in a state of utter confusion. There were different varieties of gold, silver, iron, and copper coins and nearly 1,700 types of gold, silver, and rice certificates with a total value of approximately 146,790,000 yen.

As had been the case a decade earlier, the foreign merchants were quick to profit from this confusion and from the favorable exchange rates between gold and silver in Japan. By exchanging foreign silver for Japanese gold they were able to make a profit of 100 per cent. Consequently, one-half million gold pieces (*ryō*) were exported in the first month of 1869 alone. The new Finance Office resorted to the only means at its disposal. It immediately requested a "loan" of 3 million yen from the rich merchants to meet the emergency and issued 48 million yen in paper currency known as "Council of State Bills" (*Dajōkan satsu*). Of this amount, approximately half was used to meet the expenses of the new government and the remainder was loaned to the leading feudal barons to relieve their financial difficulties. This policy served the double purpose of circulating the new currency and of stimulating industrial production.

Another basic and practical problem which simultaneously confronted the new leaders and demanded adroit handling was the relation of the Imperial government to the Western powers. During the final days of the old Tokugawa government, agreement had been reached to open an additional port for foreign traders, namely Hyōgo (modern Kōbe). In fact, several foreign representatives had come to Ōsaka to observe the opening of the port. In view of the danger of hostilities between the Imperial and Tokugawa armies at the end of 1867, however, the foreigners returned to the new port under the protection of a flotilla of foreign warships anchored in the harbor. At this critical point, every effort was made by the new Imperial government to prevent a deterioration in relations with the Western countries. Their representatives were informed in February, 1868, that the Emperor and his government intended to respect the treaties already signed with the Europeans. Imperial audiences were planned with leading foreign diplomats.

During this first year, at least half of the most influential leaders in the Restoration, especially those who had already been abroad, were appointed as officials in the Office of Foreign Affairs or were in charge of relations with the foreigners in Ōsaka, Yokohama, or Nagasaki, the three places where there were the largest number of Western traders. For example, Inouye Kaoru and Itō Hirobumi, both of whom had already been to England, were successively in Nagasaki, Ōsaka, and the Foreign Office. Kido was an assistant, Ōkuma Shigenobu an Under Secretary, and Gotō Shōjirō an Assistant Secretary of that same office.[6]

A specific example of one of these obligations under the old treaties which was carried on by the new government is that in connection with lighthouses. In 1866, Sir Harry S. Parkes, the British Minister, had negotiated on behalf of England, Holland, France, and the United States, a convention "for various requirements necessary to the safety and well-being of Europeans and Americans." Japan was required thereby to "provide all the ports open to foreign trade with such lights, buoys or beacons as necessary to render secure the navigation of the approaches to said ports."

Through the good offices of Sir Harry Parkes, Richard Henry Brunton (1841–1901) was chosen to supervise the work to be undertaken by the Japanese government. A manuscript which he wrote of his experience in Japan throws pertinent sidelights on conditions in the early years of the Restoration.[7] Brunton arrived in June, 1868, with two assistants and equipment necessary to build lighthouses at eight key points. Surveying of the locations was begun immediately. By the beginning of the next year the light at Kannonzaki, halfway up the bay to Yokohama, was finished, and a temporary light was installed on the tip of Awa at Nojimagasaki, the point first sighted by steamers headed for Yokohama. Furthermore, the British ship "Sunrise" of about 500 tons was purchased as a lightship and anchored off Yokohama to mark the harbor entrance. Construction was also begun on a lightship with the aid of British shipwrights. The ship was finally launched in 1869 for use at Hakodate. By 1876, when Brunton resigned and returned to England, lights had been established at thirty places along the Japanese coast. The official record of the Bureau reads laconically, "He had worked zealously since 1868 so he was given a reward of 2,000 yen." This sum was, of course, in addition to the monthly salary of 600 yen which he had been receiving.

The lack of technical knowledge throughout Japan is poignantly expressed by Brunton at several places in his manuscript. For example, at one point he showed considerable irritation over the refusal of the Governor of Yokohama, Terashima Munenori, to accept his proposal that the city water be conveyed in iron pipes from a reservoir rather than in hollow bamboo and that a filtration plant be built. He also refers with unrestrained disdain to the craze for steamers in Japan. He writes:

> High officers of the government, feudal barons and all who could command sufficient means purchased steamboats. . . . Unfortunately for these first purchasers, steamboats are exceedingly intricate, and, in the hands of the ignorant, dangerous instruments both as regards their guidance across the sea and their internally propelling machinery. Heedless of the fact that their own people were without experience in controlling or working them, the Japanese owners placed unskilled persons in charge of the vessels usually with frequent results of a most disastrous character.

The most common mistake was to fire the boilers without sufficient water in them. He concludes, "Soon learning to estimate justly their own utter incapacity, foreign officers and engineers were appointed to all steamships."

His efforts were not restricted, however, to lighthouses and ships. In 1870 he was asked to construct a bridge without foreign artisans to show the Japanese how bridges were built in Western countries. He designed the bridge, borrowed a punching and shearing machine from an engineering shop, cut the iron plates and made the holes for the rivets. "The whole girders were thus fitted and riveted together by Japanese mechanics who had never in their lives handled similar tools and who were completely ignorant of the exact character of the work in which they were having a part." He concludes with the cryptic remark, "Thus the first iron bridge was erected in Japan without mishap and appeared to be perfectly satisfactory."

Brunton was succeeded by another Britisher, but the Japanese who had been sent abroad to study were soon to replace the foreigners. The role of the Westerners in introducing many of the foreign skills, however, is well illustrated by the large number of foreigners hired in the lighthouse service. For example, forty-seven persons were employed during these early years as engineers, supervisors, metal workers, instructors, lighthouse keepers, and teachers. One of the lightships, the "Meiji Maru," which had been built in England, was manned by British officers until as late as 1884.

Strengthening the Emperor's Base of Power

If it was obvious to Brunton that Japan had made little preparation for the adoption of Western techniques and industrial improvements, the group of reformers were equally convinced that the future prosperity of their country lay in the rapid development of internal economic and military strength. They were painfully aware of the fact that the treaties with the West restricted their autonomy. Foreigners were allowed extraterritorial rights and severe limitations were placed on the import and export duties which Japan could charge. Most of these new leaders had had personal contact with the limited industrial developments in their own clans prior to the Restoration. Hence, they were conscious of the lack of technical knowledge throughout the country. But above all, they realized that the power of the Emperor rested on a flimsy foundation.

When the form of the new Imperial government was announced in June, 1868, the feudal barons were told to govern their fiefs temporarily as in the past and to consider themselves as provincial governors. The promise of the new government that it would assume responsibility for the income and debts of the barons was a substantial incentive to them to remain loyal to the sovereign. The most astute of the young clan leaders realized, however, that if the Emperor was to have any real power both the political and economic autonomy of the feudal barons must be destroyed. In other words, any authority or power which the barons and their retainers derived from the territory inherited by them or assigned to them from the Tokugawa Shoguns must be transferred to the Emperor. Any residual privileges which the warriors retained after the Shogun resigned must first be returned to the throne and then reassigned by the Emperor.

The chief leader in this movement was Kido Kōin of Chōshū. He first persuaded his feudal lord of the advisability of a formal return to the crown of his feudal rights of suzerainty over his fief. He then obtained Ōkubo's reluctant agreement to persuade the lord of Satsuma to do likewise.[8] Consequently, in March, 1869, the four powerful western clans, Satsuma, Chōshū, Tosa, and Hizen (the *Satchō Dohi* clans), petitioned together that the sovereign accept the title to their domains. Their request to "return their registers" (*hanseki hōkan*) was based on the argument that one central body of government and one universal authority was essential for the effective operation of the new Imperial government. Their plea continued, "It is now sought to establish an entirely new form of government. The land in which your servants live is the land of the Emperor and the people whom they govern are his subjects." These clan chieftains then surrendered their "registers" of the persons within their domains and entreated the Emperor to issue decrees as he deemed necessary and to deal as he saw fit with the lands and peoples of the four clans. Other clans vied with each other to follow this example. By 1870, the feudal lords of these fiefs had moved permanently to the new capital of Tokyo and had placed their troops directly under the command of the sovereign.

In August, 1871, an Imperial Decree was issued which formally abolished the clans and converted them into prefectures (*ken*). At that time, all but seventeen of the 276 feudatories had already transferred their fiefs and there was a general feeling of satisfaction over the accomplishments thus far. On that day, Kido Kōin was elated. He was confident of the feasibility of eradicating feudalism and the arbitrary power of the feudal barons. He noted in his diary: "Today my ideal has been realized and Japan's stature has become as lofty as that of the other countries of the world." [9] The outer forms of feudalism were disappearing but the new Imperial government still did not have the power to levy a universal tax in money based on the value, not the crop, of the land.

Much still needed to be accomplished, therefore, before Japan would begin to become a "prosperous country through military and industrial strength," as envisaged by its ambitious young leaders. A free labor supply, technical knowledge, an abundance of capital, an integrated plan for industrialization, and a uniform system of taxation were necessary. The first of these prerequisites came about as the result of the social changes which accompanied the Restoration. The barriers between the provinces no longer existed, people were permitted to travel at will and obtain employment wherever they desired. The social classes were abolished. Even the warriors lost their identity. The jinrikisha had been invented and transportation was rapidly developing. As has already been intimated, technical knowledge was obtained by hiring foreigners and by sending groups of young men abroad to learn new skills.

On the other hand, it was more difficult to solve the problem of lack of capital. Japan's extended seclusion had reduced the possibilities of growth of a strong mercantile class. The owners of such capital as had been accumulated from internal commerce and trade were reluctant to risk investment in enterprises sponsored by a government in which they had little confidence. If capital was to be obtained, it would come about by the untiring efforts of the government leaders. It was not enough to collect a special levy on the wealthy families or to increase the paper money in circulation. Government-sponsored commercial companies (*Tsūshō Kaisha*) were established in the open ports but these failed to compete successfully with the foreign trading companies or to increase confidence in the new government's currency.

Two bold steps were taken in the field of national finance. In the first place, two of the key figures in the Restoration movement were ordered to improve the currency. Ōkuma Shigenobu and Itō Hirobumi were assigned to the Finance Office. They proposed that the yen should be the unit coin, that the decimal system should be used, and that only one metal would be the standard. Shortly thereafter, Ōkuma was promoted to be Vice-Minister of Finance and Itō became his assistant. Itō was sent to America early in 1870 to study foreign currency systems. Since the gold standard was the most prevalent one abroad, he urged its adoption. Contrary to his recommendation, the government first settled on the silver standard. As a result of the continued objections of the European traders who practically monopolized Japan's foreign trade, the gold standard was finally adopted in 1871.

Before Itō went abroad, he and Ōkuma made a second important financial decision. They recognized the absolute necessity for a railway and yet had no funds for constructing one. Horatio Lay, a former Commissioner of the Chinese Maritime Customs, was in Tokyo at that time and persuaded them to appoint him both as the commissioner for a loan for the construction of the new railroad and as the contractor for it. In June, 1870, however, because of his questionable activities, the Japanese government severed its relations with him and authorized the Oriental Bank of London to take responsibility for the loan. Bonds paying 9 per cent interest, redeemable in 1881, were successfully floated, for which Japan received £930,000. Work on the first section of the line from Tokyo to Yokohama had already begun under the supervision of the British civil engineer, Edmund Morell. The line was officially opened two years later. Simultaneously a branch office was established in Ōsaka to supervise construction work of the main line in western Japan. But progress in the mountainous terrain was discouragingly slow. In 1872 only eighteen miles of track were completed and there were only ten locomotives in the country. Nine years later, 128 miles of track were finished so that many of the cities on the Pacific coast of the main island were connected by this latest method of transportation.

This step in Japan's industrialization was also significant for two other reasons. In the first place, the loan floated in London was the first of only two foreign loans sought by Japan during the formative years and was of such a limited amount that Japan was able to remain independent of financial dominance by Great Britain. In the second place, this transaction indicated the predominant position, financially and economically, which Great Britain had over the other Western powers engaged in Far Eastern trade. For example, both the United States and France had hoped that they would be selected to finance a railroad, but they lost out to their commercial rival. As for the United States, it was also vitally interested in railroads at this time. It hoped that it would be able to recover some of the trade lost during the years of the Civil War and of the Reconstruction Period. The same year that the British loan to Japan had been floated in London, the Union Pacific Railroad had completed the final link in the first transcontinental system. It was the dream of its builders that this new route would draw some of the European–Oriental trade through the United States. Such was not to be the case. Neither the recently reunited American Republic nor Imperial Japan had yet learned how to compete successfully in Oriental trade with the more experienced British financiers and traders.

Government-sponsored Industrialization

In addition to railway construction, the Japanese government also took an early interest in strategic industries. These included communications, the old Tokugawa munitions plants, and mining. In the communications field, energies were concentrated on building a telegraph line. Technicians and experts were hired from England and the first line was opened between Tokyo and Yokohama the first year after the Restoration. Due to the lack of technical knowledge of the Japanese and the fear and objections of the peasants to this new invention, there were only sixty-five miles of line by 1871. Some believed the rumors that the wires were to be used for transmitting their blood to quench the thirst of the foreigners. Others objected to the line crossing their property and cut the wires or tore down the poles. Despite these obstacles, the Council of State persisted in its opinion that the telegraph should be extended and that it should be owned by the government for security reasons. When faced with civil war a few years later, public ownership of the telegraph assured effective communication between the capital and the troops in the field and was one of the factors which contributed materially to victory. The Council was vindicated in its decision.

After the Tokugawa dictatorship had capitulated, the new Imperial government immediately confiscated such military industries as had already been started. This move had a twofold effect. In the first place, the government had direct control over the most important strategic industries, a situation that assisted the rapid rise of a strong and effective military machine. In the second place, the normal order of industrial development from light to heavy industries was reversed in Japan. Consequently, consumers' goods industries were to develop far more slowly than heavy industries.

One of the first examples of confiscation undertaken by the Meiji authorities was that of the Nagasaki shipyard and foundry. It had been built by the Hizen clan in 1861 and was placed under the supervision of the Nagasaki city office in 1868. The Yokosuka foundry and shipyards, planned by the feudal government with the assistance of French technicians and the promise of a loan, were formally seized in 1868 and operated as a government naval yard until 1945. The two chief arsenals at Tokyo and Ōsaka were likewise appropriated, foreigners were employed to operate them, and instruction was given in the manufacturing of small weapons. The difficulty in putting these plants in operation is clearly illustrated by the history of the Ōsaka arsenal. Its confiscation was not formally consummated until two full years after the Restoration; it was not ready to operate until after machinery had been shipped from the Nagasaki foundry and was installed and adapted for arsenal use.

Mining also was important both for the growth of strategic industries and for the growth of industry as a whole. The Meiji government took over the mines owned directly by the Tokugawa government and profited from earlier geological surveys made in northern Japan. It proceeded on the theory that while it theoretically owned the natural resources below the surface of the ground, private persons could open new mines with the government's permission and could sell their products to the government. In many cases the government operated the mines directly and invited European miners, geologists, and engineers to Japan to assist in their operation and to train Japanese who would eventually run them completely. In other cases, the government was glad to have the mines developed by private enterprise.

One of the most important mining projects in the latter category was the coal mine at Takashima, an island ten miles offshore from Nagasaki. Before the Meiji Restoration, the exploitation of this mine was planned as a joint enterprise of the local feudal baron and the British firm of Thomas B. Glover & Co. They installed steam-driven hoisting machinery for raising the coal from the pits, a railway for hauling the coal through the mines and a ventilating system. This equipment enabled the mine to produce 200 tons of bituminous coal daily. It continued to be operated after the Restoration by Glover until 1873 when it was purchased by, and put under the direct operation of, the government for ten months. At this point, Gotō Shōjirō of Tosa, who was familiar with Nagasaki and with members of the Glover firm, purchased the mine. Several years later it was bought by the Iwasaki interests.

Confusion and ineptness in the early industrialization were inevitable when so many problems pressed on all sides for immediate solution. Progress was made, however, on the important problem of an organized plan of industrialization by the formation of the Ministry of Industry (*Kōbushō*) in November, 1870. This new department had the double purpose of encouraging industry among the people and enabling the state to profit financially and militarily from this industrialization. It was the center of Japanese mercantilism and the nursery of Japanese capitalism. Specifically, the Ministry was charged with the supervision over all matters relating to the opening of industrial schools, encouragement of industry of all kinds, and the supervision of all mining activities. Furthermore, it was to construct, repair, and maintain railroads, telegraphs, lighthouses, and navigation buoys; construct and repair ships and warships;

carry out the forging and casting of metals, such as copper, iron, and lead; manufacture various types of machines; and survey land and sea areas.[10]

Some of these responsibilities were new ones and required extended planning and development; others had been transferred from the all-powerful Finance Ministry or from the experimental Ministry of People's Affairs (*Mimbushō*, 1869–1871). It is extremely significant that the Ministry of Industry was directed almost exclusively in its earlier years by Itō Hirobumi. He was appointed Vice-Minister in December, 1871. As there was no Minister at that time, he had final and complete charge of its activities. This situation was formalized by his appointment to be Minister in 1873, a post he held for five years. A man like Itō, who was to play such an important role in the formation of the constitutional government, seemed to have had no time in those early years to argue about the form of government most suitable for Japan. He and his colleagues were too absorbed with other more practical matters. They postponed the formation of a constitutional monarchy until Japan was strong enough economically to withstand the various forces at work, at home and abroad, that might have destroyed the new Imperial state.

At this point, two questions present themselves. Was it possible that Kido, Ōkubo, Itō, and their colleagues had decided at an early date that the best government for Japan immediately following the Restoration was a minimum of government? Was it more likely that they had no real choice because of lack of full powers and no time to consider the matter seriously, and were fortunate in the choice that was made by default? Perhaps no definitive answer can ever be made to either of these queries. On the basis of what actually happened, however, one can venture a guess. In view of the innumerable problems which confronted the small group of active members of the government and which demanded immediate attention, the latter explanation is the more likely.

In any event, the net result for Japan's future development was the same. The concentration on practical problems accelerated industrialization and strengthened Japan militarily. This reduced interference from groups outside the clan oligarchy to a minimum during the first few years because the oligarchs alone had the technical knowledge to be leaders in the industrialization movement. Having secured important posts within the government during this transition period, they could easily shift their efforts to constitutional problems when the country was ready for them. (See Chapter 8.) In so doing, they selected and trained their own group of assistants, the lower-ranking bureaucrats; there was no room for members of the opposition. In other words, this concentration on practical problems made possible a simultaneous political unification and the formation of a strong, centralized state.

Feudal Forms Abolished

But an extremely important reform still needed completion: the abolition of feudalism and, in its stead, the establishment of a system of private ownership of property. As noted above, in the summer of 1871 an edict was issued formally abolishing all of the fiefs and turning them into prefectures. A few months thereafter, the new Minister of Finance, Ōkubo, and his assistant, Inouye Kaoru, developed a plan for the private ownership of land. They recommended the sale of land in perpetuity, the issuance of new deeds to specify ownership of land, and the establishment of a value of the land so that annual taxes could be collected in money. But the difficult problem was to set a fair value for the land. Heretofore, farmland, the basic source of revenue for the government and the ruling warrior class, had been graded and evaluated in terms of the amount of rice that each plot produced. If land was to be sold or assessed and taxes on it collected in money, some formula was necessary to establish its monetary value.

Ōkubo and Inouye devised such a formula on the basis of facts available to them. They decided that 6 per cent should be considered to be a fair return on investment in land. Hence they argued that, as the landowner's income was the annual crop or yield from his land, this should equal 6 per cent. By equating these two factors, the crop and the 6 per cent income, the value of the land could be fixed. Since each plot of land represented the capital investment of the landlord, and since the interest on that investment was arbitrarily established at 6 per cent, the total value of the land was 16⅔ times the value of the crop. As the value of the crop of any given field was a matter of record, the value of the field or plot could be determined by multiplying its yield by 16⅔.

Having established the cash value of each plot of land, the Finance Ministry used the generally accepted formula for rent as the basis for the tax rate. Throughout the Tokugawa period taxes varied considerably but half the crop was normal rent. Hence, the new tax was set as equal to half the value of the crop. As the crop had been determined as equal to 6 per cent of the value of the land, half of that amount, or 3 per cent, was the new land tax.

In 1873, the old methods of collecting taxes were abolished as new surveys were begun of all land, new deeds were issued to the owners, and taxes were assessed under the new system. The immediate effect of this move was obvious. As the new tax in money was to be levied universally on the land value and not on the annual crop the tax income of the government would be fixed and would not vary with the crop. Furthermore, since the new tax was equivalent to half the value of the crop, it would be no more severe in its actual effect on the farmer than the old tax collected in rice.

Through this new cadastral survey of both agricultural holdings and their yield, the government also hoped to correct the traditional underestimation of crops and hence insure more revenue to the national treasury. But this objective was difficult to achieve. The main work of the surveys was undertaken by the landowners and the villagers, both of whom had a vested interest in under-reporting the yield. For the former, lower estimates of the crop would result in a low evaluation of his land and hence lower taxes. For the tenant, a low estimate would mean a lower rent. Both underevaluation of the yield and concealment of land continued, therefore, until the detailed and highly supervised surveys of the 1880's were completed.[11]

But the establishment of a land tax in money was not the only unsettled problem connected with the abolition of feudal rights. The new government had assumed the burden of paying the annual rice stipends of the feudal barons and of the warriors. While this arrangement assured the loyalty of many of them to the new regime, it placed a heavy charge on the impoverished treasury. In 1871, of total government expenditure of 42.5 million yen, stipends to the warriors amounted to 15 million yen. Naturally, the government was anxious to be relieved of this obligation as rapidly as possible in view of the fact that the warriors comprised a nonproductive class and most of them were useless to the Emperor even as soldiers. By 1871, when the movement to transfer the fiefs to the throne gained momentum, the government offered to commute those privileges into government bonds. Such a procedure enabled it to transform immediate cash requirements into long-term obligations. In other words, it no longer would have to make heavy annual payments in rice or the cash equivalent, but would only be required to pay interest on the bonds issued.

Even though this scheme, originally devised by Ōkubo and later developed by Ōkuma, relieved the strain on the national treasury, cash was needed immediately to pay 8 per cent interest on the bonds. Furthermore, warriors with less than 500 bushels of rice income could commute half of their pensions into cash and half into bonds. Consequently, funds were sought from every possible source. The Ministry of Finance issued a new series of convertible treasury notes. The name and credit of the Mitsui family, the strongest bankers in Japan, was called upon to bolster the value of these new notes. Credit was again sought and obtained in London for £2,400,000, at an interest rate of 7 per cent, for a period of twenty-four years.

By 1876, the financial position of the government was sufficiently strong to make possible the forced commutation of all of the feudal pensions. In that year, an edict made it compulsory upon all of the former members of the warrior class to transform their incomes, if they had not already done so voluntarily, into government bonds. The interest rate of these bonds and their date of maturity varied according to the former rice income of the warrior.

From the point of view of the warriors, especially those with small income, this transfer of their perpetual feudal claims into cash or government bonds had several disadvantages. By Imperial Decree, their assets had already been reduced to less than half of their original value. Furthermore, traditionally the warriors considered money matters as degrading so that few of them had had any practical business experience. When payments were made to them in negotiable securities, many of them soon lost their assets through poor investment policies; others dissipated their limited resources in extravagant spending. Within a few years, all but 20 per cent of them had lost control of their original holdings.

On the other hand, the old feudal barons with large incomes suffered far less than the average warrior. The former tended to hold on to their government securities. Furthermore, a former feudal baron with an old income of 500,000 bushels of rice ended up in 1876 with an annual income from interest on his government bonds equal to 80,000 yen.[12] In comparison to the landholder during the French or Russian Revolutions whose lands were confiscated, however, the old warrior class had come out handsomely.

Simultaneous with the abolition of the old feudal contracts of the warriors, they lost many of their special social privileges. (See Chapter 10.) For example, after 1871, they could voluntarily give up wearing their swords if they desired. In other words, the sword no longer symbolized social prestige and power. The feudal barons and the courtiers formed the new nobility; the warriors (*samurai*) comprised a new class in society called *shizoku* (gentry); all other persons became commoners. Thus the warriors lost their special exemptions and became a class in name only.

They lost even their distinction as a separate class when a modern army, based on universal conscription, was substituted for the old armies composed of hereditary warriors. The movement for a strong army coincided with Japan's industrialization and social reorganization and was made possible by it. On the other hand, these far-reaching changes did not come about easily. Ōmura Masujirō, who had been influential in modifying the Chōshū army before the Restoration, was convinced that Japan could not become a modern state unless the new national army was composed of all elements in society. In 1869, he was appointed Minister of War and proposed the adoption of universal conscription. This move was strongly resented by many members of the warrior class.

In fact, a band of Chōshū warriors was so indignant that it murdered him for his action. But he had laid the groundwork for universal conscription and his work was largely brought to successful conclusion by Yamagata Aritomo, one of the young Chōshū warriors who had previously served under Ōmura.[13] After assisting in the subjugation of the Tokugawa forces during the early months of the Restoration, Yamagata went to Europe to study the French and Prussian armies. After his return in 1870, he was appointed Second Vice-Minister of War. Since his superior was an Imperial prince with little practical knowledge and there was no Vice-Minister, Yamagata was the actual head of the ministry. In 1873 he became full Minister.

Courtesy of The Bettmann Archive

EARLY CONSCRIPT ARMY

During this short interval, the Imperial Japanese Army was formed. The first conscription law was enacted in 1870. It provided for three years of active service and two years in the reserve. It also permitted exemption from service through payment for a substitute. Many of the farmers objected to this provision and refused to serve. Consequently, national quotas could not be filled until 1873, when a new conscription law was promulgated. Although exemptions still existed which placed the heaviest burden on the lower classes, the new conscripts were chosen by lot. For the next few years, not more than 10,000 men were called to the colors annually. In fact, it was not until after the Satsuma Rebellion of 1877 that Yamagata was able to organize a strong and effective army.

Signs of Unrest and the Iwakura Mission

The military campaigns between the Imperial and Tokugawa forces in the first two years of the Restoration were not extensive operations and affected only a small portion of the people. The great social and economic changes of the Restoration movement were not brought about, however, without creating more extensive disorder than these military campaigns. As more drastic changes were pushed by the authorities, more disturbances developed. These took the form of peasant uprisings similar to those of the Tokugawa days. Universal conscription, the liquidation of the fiefs, and the introduction of a tax in money were the most common causes for the uprisings. Others resulted from the abolition by decree of the four classes, the designation of a single currency as the medium of exchange, the introduction of innovations such as the telegraph, and the forceful separation of Buddhism from Shintoism. The greatest number occurred in 1873, the year in which both the land reforms and effective conscription were started. In most cases, they were local affairs arising from local conditions. In a few cases, as in Kyūshū in 1873, over one-quarter of a million persons were involved. Except for some of the political riots connected with the people's rights movement, they were not of national significance. (See Chapter 6.) Practically none of them was directly connected with the struggle between the Emperor and the Tokugawa forces. They were a symptom of the times, however, which showed that the oligarchs were not yet completely in control.

But an even more significant sign of discontent was the split which was rapidly growing within the ranks of the Emperor's chief ministers and advisers. The split came about over the policy toward Korea. In effect it was the result of a basic rift between those who advocated the further strengthening of Japan internally before expanding overseas, and those who supported expansion before the home base was secure. In 1871, the former group argued that a special mission should be sent abroad to secure as much knowledge as possible concerning Western technological progress. As the treaties with the Western powers provided that revisions could be considered that year, the further question arose as to whether such a mission should also be given powers to negotiate such revisions. If changes in the treaties were possible, the tariffs could be raised increasing the government's income and the warriors could be given a larger compensation for their old feudal rights. It was finally concluded that Japan had not yet made sufficient progress with its internal reforms to be able to negotiate successfully with the Western nations. Consequently, the mission was instructed to seek as much practical knowledge as possible on foreign governments, industries, and public works.[14]

Iwakura Tomomi, Vice-President of the Council and Minister of Foreign Affairs, was selected to head this special mission. He was accompanied by several of the most powerful officials in the government and especially those who were primarily concerned with first strengthening Japan internally. For example, Ōkubo Toshimichi, Minister of Finance, was an important member of the group. He had been largely responsible for the plan just inaugurated which deprived the warriors of their feudal privileges. Itō Hirobumi, newly appointed Vice-Chief of the Ministry of Industry, was another member of the mission. He was young and inexperienced but eager to make his new department the dynamic center of Japan's modernization. His fellow clansman Kido Kōin, who had drafted many of the edicts which actually brought about the Restoration, was also included. There were fifty subordinates and assistants as well as the first Japanese women to be sent abroad to study.

When the Iwakura Mission arrived in Washington, it was received cordially by President Grant and Secretary of State Hays. Furthermore, the United States Congress appropriated a special fund of $50,000 for its entertainment. While the atmosphere for negotiating the unequal treaties seemed propitious, Iwakura finally decided not to do so. The true nature of the Iwakura Mission is evident from Brunton's description of its four months' stay in England. Home on leave from his lighthouse services in Japan, he greeted the group upon its arrival in London. He wrote that Itō and his young assistants showed special interest in twenty-eight London business establishments in September alone. These included factories for candles, skivers, glue, gelatine, bricks, cement, and iron foundries and shipyards. They spent far more time in the factories than in diplomatic talks in the Foreign Office.

The group then crossed over to the continent where they were favorably impressed with Prussia and Bismarck. Iwakura's conversation in

Courtesy of The Bettmann Archive

IWAKURA PRESENTS HIS CREDENTIALS TO PRESIDENT GRANT, 1872

Berlin in March, 1873, with Germany's Under Secretary of Foreign Affairs made him and his Mission realize how many reforms at home were necessary before the Western Powers would consider Japan an equal. At that interview, Iwakura was asked how soon foreigners would be allowed to travel freely in the interior of Japan. He had to admit that permission for this could not be granted until legal administrative reforms were perfected and the national police were trained. The Under Secretary replied that the Japanese government should make a request for opening negotiations to revise the treaties only after such reforms had been perfected.

Iwakura and his colleagues were in a receptive mood, therefore, when they dined with Bismarck. They listened attentively to his advice that if Japan was to become strong like Germany it must rely on its own strength. He told them that nations could not be trusted and that international law was followed only so long as it was in the self-interest of a state to do so. Iwakura and his entourage never forgot this lesson.

In less than a decade, he was advocating a Prussian-type Constitution for Japan. Itō was sent back to Berlin to study Prussian political philosophy in preparation for drafting Japan's Constitution.

Saigō Resigns over Korean Issue

But this quest for practical knowledge by those most directly responsible for the program of industrialization was abruptly terminated by the ascendancy at home of a group advocating expansion. This latter group was composed of talented Councilors who had been excluded from many important conferences at which basic policies had been determined. They were disgruntled because the real power was wielded by others. They were also jealous of having been left out of Iwakura's Mission.

The most dynamic among them was Saigō Takamori, a fellow clansman of Ōkubo's from Satsuma. He had carried much of the brunt of the fighting for the Emperor against the Tokugawa Shogun at the time of the Restoration and had negotiated the settlement in early 1868 for an armistice. (See page 71.) He was, therefore, one of the key figures in the Restoration. Always an idealist and a man of action, he deplored the gradual degradation of the warriors as a class and more particularly the concentration of governmental power in the hands of such men as Ōkubo, Kido, and Itō. In other words, he realized that he was less and less influential in the government.

To assure continuance of their policies during their absence, Iwakura and the key members of his Mission had obtained assurances from Saigō and their other political rivals who remained at home. The latter had promised that no important appointments or policy changes would be made during the absence of the Iwakura Mission. In view of the struggle for power which was developing within the government and of the problems which demanded immediate settlement, it was impossible to expect that such a pledge would be kept. In fact, it was to be honored more in its breach than in its observance.

The problem of Japanese–Korean relations was the central issue which caused an open break between the two opposing factions. In the early months of 1872, Japan had sent official envoys to Korea to negotiate a treaty and to open that country from its seclusion. The envoys had been rebuffed and insulted. Subsequently, several Japanese subjects in Korea were attacked and the Korean problem was placed before the Council of State. Saigō, who had great confidence in the newly established conscript army, recommended an aggressive policy for two reasons. In the first place, Japan's national honor and pride demanded that Korea pay for its insulting conduct. In the second place, a successful military campaign would solve the distress of the dispossessed warrior class by making new territory available to them for exploration. His Foreign Minister Soejima Taneomi, who believed that Japan could subjugate Korea in a hundred days, advocated the immediate seizure of that peninsula and the control by Japan of North China and the Shantung Peninsula.

Saigō, who apparently never doubted the successful outcome of this venture, was fully aware of the possibility that such a military move might result in hostilities with Russia. Nevertheless, he argued that such an eventuality would give Japan a welcome chance to extend its frontiers. "Should Japan's borders be restricted to Hokkaidō?" he queried. Rather, they should be expanded to include the territory south of a line from Possiet Bay to Nikolaevsk. By these arguments and his forceful personality, he was able to win support in the Council for a positive policy against Korea. Other Councilors, such as Etō of Hizen, and Gotō and Itagaki of Tosa, had also been piqued by the monopoly of important government positions held by Satsuma and Chōshū clansmen. They were glad to sponsor a project which would challenge this monopoly. The plan, as adopted by the Council, included Saigō's appointment as envoy to force Korea's capitulation. Confident that his efforts would lead to hostilities and a successful campaign, he was delighted at a chance to die, if necessary, for the glory of his country.

On the other hand, the members of the Iwakura Mission had been sobered by what they had observed abroad and were more convinced than ever that Japan's first task was to strengthen her internal economy and her military power. When reports from home reached them of the danger of the outbreak of war against Korea, they feared not only for their own political power but also for the future of their country. They returned home immediately and finally won support for the reversal of the decision of the Council to send Saigō to Korea and to fight if necessary. In October, 1873, the Emperor ordered the government to concentrate on internal improvements and to forget about a military expedition to Korea. The rancor created over the Korean issue caused serious repercussions for the next few years. Saigō was enraged; he immediately resigned from the government and returned to his home province of Satsuma. Other members of the opposition such as Gotō and Itagaki of Tosa and Etō of Hizen also resigned.

From external appearances, the Imperial government had successfully weathered the storm generated by the rejuvenation of the Emperor's power. The basic principle had been universally accepted that the government should be controlled and operated by a coterie of Imperial advisers and councilors. A uniform currency had been adopted. Studies had been made in important fields of industrialization with the assistance of foreign experts. Railway lines were rapidly expanding. Several industries were sponsored by the government. Feudalism was formally abolished by the liquidation of the fiefs and the commutation of the pensions of the warriors. Only two foreign loans of limited extent, and free from any political commitments, had been necessary to put the government on a comparatively sound financial basis. An official mission to America and Europe had obtained much practical knowledge from its trip. The first major crisis within the government had been solved to the satisfaction of the rulers. There had been few important revolts at home since the Tokugawa forces capitulated. This apparent tranquillity was, however, only the lull before the storm.

Notes

1. See Itō Hirobumi, "Some Reminiscences of the Grant of the New Constitution," in Ōkuma Shigenobu (compiler), *Fifty Years of New Japan,* English version edited by Marcus B. Huish (2 vols.; London: Smith Elders, 1909), I, pp. 121 ff.

2. Fukuzawa Yukichi (1835–1901) was born into a low-class samurai family from northern Kyūshū. His father was in charge of the clan's treasury in Ōsaka. Young Fukuzawa learned at an early age a high sense of duty and loyalty, self-control, contempt for worldly goods, and an aversion to restrictions which feudal society placed on those who lived under it. In 1854 he was sent by his clan to Nagasaki to learn Dutch and Western-style gunnery. This experience increased his disbelief in the value of the old traditions and myths of Japan. After starting a school in Edo for the warriors of his clan, he realized he must learn English if he were to understand the West. Toward this end he secured a position as servant to Katsu Kaishū, the captain of the "Kanrin Maru" which sailed for San Francisco in 1860. Though he never filled a post in the government, he became one of the most effective interpreters to his fellow countrymen of foreign institutions and thinking. He founded Keiō University, one of Japan's outstanding private universities. For an excellent account of Fukuzawa as a *philosophe* and of his most important writings see Carmen Blacker, *The Japanese Enlightenment, a Study of the Writings of Fukuzawa Yukichi* (Cambridge: Cambridge University Press, 1964). See also Eiichi Kiyooka (ed.), *The Autobiography of Fukuzawa Yukichi* (New York: Columbia University Press, 1966), and G. B. Sansom, *The Western World and Japan* (New York: Alfred A. Knopf, Inc., 1950), pp. 427–51.

3. Emperor Meiji (1850–1912). It is practically impossible to obtain detailed and objective biographical information about Emperor Meiji. His early training and outlook were strongly influenced by the court nobles such as Iwakura Tomomi and Sanjō Sanetomi. In 1871, Motoda Eifu (1818–1891), a conservative and a Confucian scholar, was appointed Lecturer in Chinese Studies to the Emperor. Motoda, who considered his chief task to be that of developing the young Meiji's mind, remained his tutor and close associate for nearly twenty years, advising him on various important moral and political problems.

Some of Meiji's biographers describe his chief pastimes as writing poetry, horsemanship, and reviewing troops on maneuvers. As an individual in the Restoration he was less important than his ministers. As a symbol, he was extremely important. His public appearances added much to the budding spirit of nationalism but he was always kept away from normal contacts with the people. In times of crisis, however, his opinion was sought and followed. But the key to obtaining general approval for any policy was for his closest advisers and ministers to obtain Imperial sanction for such a policy. Hence, as will become apparent below, Emperor Meiji is important in history for the manner in which his chief ministers were able to use his name and his position to gain acceptance of their plans.

4. W. W. McLaren, "Japanese Government Documents," *Transactions of the Asiatic Society of Japan,* XLII (1914), p. 8.

5. These key councilors included Ōkubo Toshimichi and Saigō Takamori from Satsuma; Kido Kōin, Itō Hirobumi, and Yamagata Aritomo (1838–1922) from Chōshū; Gotō Shōjirō and Itagaki Taisuke (1837–1919) from Tosa; and Soejima Taneomi (1828–1905) and Ōkuma Shigenobu (1838–1922) from Hizen. For Japanese sources on the background of the government changes see Ishin Shiryō Hensan Kakari (ed.), *Ishin Shi* (6 vols.; Tokyo: Meijishoin, 1939–1941), I. The names of the officials appointed to the various posts are given chronologically in *Meiji Shiyō* (2 vols.; Tokyo: Kinkō-dō shoseki k.k., 1933). For special studies on the period see Nobutake Ike, *The Beginnings of Political Democracy in Japan* (Baltimore: Johns Hopkins University Press, 1950); R. A. Wilson, "Seitaisho," *Far Eastern Quarterly* (May, 1952), pp. 297–304, and Johannes Hirschmeier, *The Origin of Entrepreneurship in Meiji Japan* (Cambridge: Harvard University Press, 1964), p. 91. The social origins of the key leaders of this period are analyzed in Bernard S. Silberman, *Ministers of Modernization: Elite Mobility in the Meiji Restoration* (Tucson: University of Arizona Press, 1964).

6. Inouye Kaoru (1836–1915). Inouye was born of a family which had served the feudal barons of Chōshū for generations. In his youth he studied "English and Dutch Learning," concentrating on Western artillery methods. After 1854 he served as a sort of aide-de-camp for his feudal lord and soon joined other convinced partisans in the clan who worked for an Imperial restoration. He also was in the forefront of the antiforeign movement and was among the group which set fire to the British legation in Edo in 1861.

In the spring of 1863 he and Itō Hirobumi went abroad for study. While in England, he realized that the idea of "expelling the barbarians" was nonsense and henceforth concentrated his attack on the Tokugawa dictatorship. His views were not appreciated by some of his fellow clansmen, one of whom attempted to assassinate him one night while returning home. He hovered between life and death for several days but finally recovered. During the turbulent civil war days, he traveled about in disguise on various missions. After 1868 his most important posts were in the Ministries of Foreign Affairs and Finance.

Ōkuma Shigenobu (1838–1922) was one of the few outstanding leaders of the Restoration who came from the province of Hizen. Born in a warrior's family, he was sent to the various clan schools in Nagasaki where he became proficient in both Dutch and English studies. During this period he came in contact with other future leaders of the Restoration such as Saigō Takamori and Gotō Shōjirō.

In the spring of 1866 he vainly sought permission to obtain an audience with the Shogun to try to persuade him to give up his powers to the Emperor. When the Imperial Restoration was announced in 1868, Ōkuma was Governor of Nagasaki. Since he had been appointed to this position by the Shogun, he left office precipitately, only to be appointed to the same post by his feudal baron. In view of the number of foreigners at that trading center, Ōkuma's chief responsibilities were toward the foreign merchants and representatives. One of the most serious problems which faced him was the appearance of about 5,000 Japanese Christians, who had been in hiding near the city. As the anti-Christian edicts were still in force, Ōkuma began rounding them up. The representatives of the Western powers protested vehemently but before Ōkuma could offer any solution, he was called to Tokyo to serve in the Foreign Office. After holding various posts, he became Under Secretary of Foreign Affairs in 1869. Since at this period the heads of the departments of the government were either courtiers or feudal barons appointed for prestige purposes, Ōkuma in reality controlled the country's foreign affairs. Like many of his colleagues he shifted from one government department to another. He even became Prime Minister but much of his public life was devoted to various problems of foreign relations.

7. Richard Henry Brunton, "Pioneer Engineering in Japan, A Record of Work in Helping to Relay the Foundations of the Japanese Empire 1868–78," Ms in Rutgers University Library, New Brunswick, N. J. I am greatly indebted to the Rutgers Library for permission to use Brunton's manuscript. It is part of their valuable manuscript collection of the "Griffis Papers." The transfer of the Lighthouse Bureau, to which Brunton was appointed, from the jurisdiction of one Ministry to another during the early years of the Restoration was indicative of the unsettled conditions within the government and of its general policy of improvisation. The Lighthouse Office, *Tōdaikyoku,* was first established in 1868 as part of the Yokohama City Office. In the next year it was transferred to the Finance Ministry (*Ōkurashō*), then to the Foregin Office, after which it became a branch of the People's Affairs Ministry (*Mimbushō*). Following the formation of the Ministry of Industry (*Kōbushō*) in 1870, it was one of its important branches until the general reorganization in 1885.

8. Ōkubo's reluctance to approve of this key move for the abolition of feudalism detracts somewhat from Iwata's claim that he was the predominant leader of the new government during its first three years. See Masakaza Iwata, *Ōkubo Toshimichi, the Bismarck of Japan* (Berkeley: University of California Press, 1964), pp. 124–27.

9. Oka Yoshitake, "Seijishi," in Yanaihara Tadao (ed.), *Gendai Nihon Shōshi* (Tokyo: Misuzu-shobo, 1961), II, p. 18.

10. The official history of the Ministry of Industry is entitled "Kōbushō Enkaku Hōkoku," in Ōuchi Hyōe and Tsuchiya Takao (eds.), *Meiji Zenki Zaisei Shiryō* (21 vols.; Tokyo: Kaizō-sha, 1931–1936), XVII. For reference to the questionable maneuvers of Horatio Lay concerning the railway loan and the subsequent successful flotation of it see Grace Fox, *Britain and Japan, 1858–1883* (Oxford: Clarendon Press, 1969), pp. 386–93.

11. For an extremely valuable study of this problem and its relation to the rate of growth of Japanese agricultural production and economic development, see James I. Nakamura, *Agricultural Production and the Economic Development of Japan 1873–1922* (Princeton: Princeton University Press, 1966), pp. 7 ff.

12. This figure is derived as follows: the income of the feudal barons holding land with estimated income of 500,000 bushels of rice or more had been reduced twice by Imperial decree. First the income was cut in half. In 1876 it was reduced to one-fourth the previous amount, bringing the original

500,000 bushels down to 62,500 bushels with an estimated cash value of 80,000 yen. This amount was then capitalized at 1,600,000 yen by the issuance of irredeemable government bonds paying 5 per cent interest.

13. Ōmura Masujirō (1824–1869) first studied military tactics under the Dutch and opened a school in Edo.

Yamagata Aritomo (1838–1922), the power behind the throne from 1909, when Itō died, until his own death in 1922, was also the person most responsible for Japan's modern army. Born in Chōshū on June 14, 1838, his father was able to provide him with a good education. At the age of nineteen he was sent to Kyōto to serve as a clan spy and there met some of the earliest loyalists. Like his fellow clansman, Itō, he was inspired by the loyalist teacher Yoshida Shōin to work for the restoration of the power and prestige of the Emperor. He received his first military experience as an officer in the "people's army" of Chōshū, which proved that spirit and training were superior to tradition and prestige. Yamagata was wounded during the bombardment of the coastal defenses of Chōshū in 1863 by the Western powers. Subsequently, his clique within the clan came to power and its policies resulted in the outbreak of civil war against the Shogun. In February, 1867, Yamagata and Saigō of Satsuma began to work together to form an Imperial force strong enough to defeat the Tokugawa. In the campaign of 1868–1869, he was in command of the loyalist forces which defeated the Aizu clan troops in northern Japan. For an account of the early years of the Japanese army see Yamagata Aritomo, "The Japanese Army," in Ōkuma, *op. cit.*, I, pp. 194–217; Hyman Kublin, "The Modern Army of Early Meiji Japan," *Far Eastern Quarterly,* IX (1949), pp. 20–42; and Ernest L. Presseisen, *Before Aggression; Europeans Prepare the Japanese Army* (Tucson: University of Arizona Press, 1965), p. 27.

14. I am indebted to Prof. Marlene Mayo for this clarification of the purpose of the Iwakura Mission. When the leaders of the Mission met with President Grant and Secretary of State Hays they were greeted with enthusiastic cordiality. As a result, they decided that negotiations for revision of the treaties should be undertaken immediately and so Itō and Ōkubo were sent home to obtain plenipotentiary powers. By the time they returned to Washington, however, Iwakura had again changed his mind and no formal negotiations were begun. See her forthcoming study of the Iwakura Mission entitled: *In Search of Enlightenment: the Iwakura Mission to the West.*

6

The Oligarchs Establish Their Power, 1873–1880

In the previous chapter, the early practical steps taken by the young Imperial advisers and government leaders of the Meiji Restoration and their pragmatic approach to the intricacies of government have been emphasized. Munitions factories made possible a conscript army. A conscript army deprived the warrior class of their monopoly of martial virtue. The abolition of the fiefs and application of a universal tax based on the value of the land, not the crop, enabled the national treasury to be assured of a fixed income and to operate on a budget. Modern railroads and the telegraph, built by the government, helped to tie the country into a single geographic unit which could be readily protected from internal revolts or external attacks. The implementation over several years of these various reforms increased, both directly and indirectly, the strength of the Emperor and the power of the state.

When Iwakura and his group received Imperial sanction for their policy to give up the expedition against Korea and to concentrate instead on internal improvements, the responsibility for running the government became restricted to an even smaller handful of oligarchs. Led by Iwakura, Okubo, Kido, Okuma, Yamagata, and Itō, they entrenched themselves in the key positions in the government. At times, they vied among themselves as individuals for favor and power. On the other hand, when they were challenged by the advocates of "people's rights" and by the champions of a representative, elective assembly, they gave way on unimportant issues only and presented a united front. Whenever they agreed to structural changes which ostensibly gave the people more power, they implemented such agreements as they saw fit and promulgated, in the name of the Emperor, legislation which gave them extensive powers.

They found little difficulty in obtaining approval for their policies from Emperor Meiji. His chief tutor, Motoda Eifu, was ultraconservative.

Concerning his teaching, he wrote in 1874, "I always discussed the essential points of the sovereign's virtues, the importance of duty . . . , reverence for *kokutai* [national polity], purity of the Confucian way, the harm of Christianity and the error of Buddhism . . . , the reason that an Imperial and republican constitution would not be the same." [1]

The period immediately following the decision on the Korean issue, therefore, is characterized by two distinct, yet interrelated, features. There was an intensification of opposition to the oligarchs by various antigovernment groups in the form of a public demand for new, representative institutions. On the other hand, the government leaders husbanded the power they had acquired. As Sir George Sansom has aptly expressed it:

> Almost all the national energy seemed to be devoted to political questions, and the country was divided into two main camps—progressives . . . against conservatives.[2]

The political struggle precipitated by the resignation of the disgruntled Councilors in 1873 must not be thought of simply as a struggle between advocates of progressive and conservative political views. As Sir George is careful to note, the course of events was not governed by adherence to accepted political theories. Even though ideas were given European labels such as "liberal," "progressive," or "conservative," these words cannot be interpreted in their usual Occidental meaning. They have always had their peculiar Japanese connotations.

Thus, if the term "progressive" is defined broadly to mean greater freedom and more rights for the people, it is not fully applicable to the political philosophy of all of the antigovernment leaders. For example, Saigō, who led a formidable revolt in 1877, was far from "progressive" politically. Furthermore, even the most outstanding progressives were unbelievably conservative on some subjects.

Conversely, the conservative oligarchs might be defined as those who believed in the superiority of absolute rule and in the inferiority of democratic institutions. But they, like their opponents, were often motivated by a personal thirst for power. By 1873, their initial loyalty and enthusiasm for the Emperor had begun to wear thin. Each of the young clan bureaucrats had experienced the giddying and exhilarating effects of power in his own hands. They would not and could not give it up easily. The Ministers of State came to consider themselves individually, rather than collectively, responsible to the Emperor. A new political atmosphere developed in which personal jealousies, antagonisms, and ambition often became stronger than clan ties or even a common loyalty to the throne.

Itagaki Taisuke, who was the personification of the "progressive" movement, befriended some strange fellow-travelers in his crusade to obtain a representative assembly. Saigō, the ultraloyalist, became jealous of his fellow clansman Ōkubo and willingly gave his life in open rebellion. Ōkuma, at once a "progressive" and an oligarch, was summarily ejected from power when he challenged his colleagues, the clan bureaucrats. At a later stage, though fellow clansmen imbued with the same conservative beliefs, Yamagata and Itō became political enemies.

Opposition to the Oligarchs

The resignation of Saigō on October 24, 1873, and that of the four other Councilors on the next day, created an immediate crisis; and Iwakura and his group acted quickly to retain control over the reins of government. On October 25, Itō of Chōshū was designated to fill one of the vacancies on the Council. Though only thirty-three years old, he had impressed Iwakura favorably during the trip abroad and thus became one of the inner circle. He was soon preoccupied with the problems of the Ministry of Industry. By the beginning of 1874, though no decision had yet been made on the final form for the new government, this group of bureaucrats from the western clans formed a tightly knit body. They were confident that they were in undisputed control and that their position could not be successfully challenged.

It came as a shock to them, therefore, to discover that those who had resigned over the Korean issue had closed their ranks and were actively engaged in antigovernment activities. In January, 1874, all those who had resigned from the Council, except Saigō, presented a caustic memorial to the throne demanding the formation of an elected assembly. These memorialists were motivated by both a fervent desire to enhance their own political power and an urge to increase the rights of the people. Furthermore, they were from the two clans of Tosa and Hizen and were keenly aware of the inferior position which their clansmen had held in the central government.

Among the chief Ministers and Councilors, Ōkuma, who was appointed Minister of Finance in 1873, was the only representative from either of these two clans left in the government. Itagaki Taisuke and the other memorialists saw in the people's rights movement a possibility of support to overthrow the bureaucrats from the rival Satsuma and Chōshū clans. They also hoped that they might become the new leaders. Their memorial was, therefore, outspoken in its denunciation of the leaders of the government. It accused them of usurping the governing power and of depriving the crown of its prestige. It claimed that the Councilors prevented the people from expressing their grievances. If reforms were not effected, the state would be ruined. It continued:

> We have sought to devise a means to rescue the state from this danger and we find it to consist in developing public discussion in the Empire. The means of developing public discussion is the establishment of a Council Chamber chosen by the people. Then a limit will be placed to the power of the officials and both governors and governed will obtain peace and prosperity.[3]

This indictment was too severe to be ignored. A direct reply to the memorial was made a week later by Katō Hiroyuki (1836–1916), as spokesman for the government. Katō had studied both the Dutch and German languages as a youth. He was in charge of the government school which later became Tokyo Imperial University. He was the author of various books on political science. He began as an advocate of liberal equalitarianism but became conservative as his age and administrative responsibilities increased.[4] He also served as tutor on western subjects to the young Emperor Meiji. His arguments in 1874 against Itagaki's memorial for a deliberative assembly, however, reflected his basically conservative point of view. He noted that even in the civilized and enlightened states of Europe, public opinion is not invariably just and enlightened. As neither Prussia nor Russia had deliberative assemblies, he saw no reason why Japan should have one. In fact, he concluded that only wise leaders were capable of determining what was suitable for the country under the present circumstances.

The antigovernment forces were not to be silenced. In fact, the action of some of them reflected the discontent and unsettled conditions of the times. As already noted, Saigō had returned to Satsuma and rallied a hard core of fanatical loyalists around him. Etō Shimpei lost patience and returned directly to his province of Hizen. He immediately led an open rebellion under the slogan of "War with Korea, the restoration of the feudal barons to their rightful place in the government, and the expulsion of the foreigners." When he was unable to receive active support from Saigō or from other antigovernment groups, he capitulated after fifty-two days of rebellion.

On the other hand, Itagaki and his immediate supporters did not resort to direct action but continued their attack on the government through public written statements. In February, 1874, they elaborated further on their demands for a deliberative assembly in a written rebuttal to Katō's views. This document is important not only because the authors quoted from John Stuart Mill to defend their position, but also because it reveals their own conservative, rather than radical, political philosophy. At the time their reply was written, Itagaki was the most important and most vociferous member of the movement for people's rights. If his reply is a true indication of his basic beliefs, there is little to distinguish him as a champion of equalitarian individualism, liberty, and the basic human rights as these concepts have been understood in France, England, or the United States. He and his colleagues were liberals or progressives, therefore, only in a relative sense.

As was true of most Japanese intellectuals of his day, Itagaki had accepted those concepts which impressed him favorably. He then modified or superimposed them on a basically conservative native belief. For example, he condemns the government as oligarchic and hence in need of rectification. He quotes Mill to prove that men of high caliber do not require despotic power to enable them to exert great influence. Furthermore, he deplores the extreme submissiveness of the people. He argues, with Mill, that the government should take responsibility for the people's advance to the next stage of political development, namely, a deliberative assembly.

At this point, Itagaki injects his own concepts. He recommends that the assembly, or Council Chamber, as he calls it, be given only restricted and limited powers. As he defined it:

> If the Council Chamber is established, we do not propose that the franchise should at once be made universal. We would only give it in the first instance to the samurai and the rich farmers and merchants.

In other words, the Council would be selected by an elite minority. Furthermore, there is no demand that the Council be the most powerful executive organ of the government. In fact, it is doubtful whether even Itagaki conceived of an Assembly to which the Cabinet or Imperial Councilors would be responsible. As Yanaihara Tadao points out, a movement of pure liberalism had not yet arisen from the people. Rather, Itagaki was motivated by what has been termed "national liberalism." [5] He was convinced of the superiority of his own class; he saw little reason to give the majority of the citizenry, the masses in the city, and the tenant farmers a vote.

The Formosan Expedition

Ōkubo Toshimichi, who had been appointed Minister of Home Affairs in November, 1873, was rapidly becoming one of the strongest officials in the government. As his office was responsible for internal peace and order, he had dealt directly with the rebellion in Saga. When he returned to Tokyo in April, 1874, after having successfully accomplished his mission, war with China seemed inevitable. The crisis arose from the refusal of China to take responsibility for the murder, in 1871, of fifty-four shipwrecked Ryūkyū fishermen by Formosan aborigines.

During the absence of the Iwakura mission from Japan, Saigō Takamori and his Foreign Minister had been encouraged by the American Minister in Tokyo, Charles E. DeLong, to launch an expeditionary force against Formosa and to obtain redress from China for the action of the Formosans. DeLong also recommended the appointment of General Charles Le Gendre, former American consul at Amoy, as adviser to the Japanese Foreign Office. He also encouraged Japan to occupy Formosa and assured Japan that China was too weak to resist. Although DeLong was reprimanded by the United States government for his activities and transferred from his post, Japan decided to organize an expedition. Such a decision received Ōkubo's approval and Saigō Tsugumichi, a native of Satsuma and younger brother of Saigō Takamori, was appointed commander-in-chief of the forces. Despite subsequent protests from both Great Britain and the United States, Ōkubo, with strong pressure from the elder Saigō, proceeded with the invasion of Formosa. With discontent at home arising over the earlier cancellation of the Korean campaign, the Formosan venture offered a convenient diversionary action.

Although it required 3,600 soldiers and 289 sailors, and cost 3,600,000 yen, the expedition was eminently successful from the Japanese point of view. Not only did a large band of hotheaded warriors have a chance to practice their newly acquired skills, but business interests also profited from it. The merchant-banker Iwasaki of Tosa made a handsome profit on the expedition. (See page 131.) The government purchased thirteen ships which it leased to him to operate after the expedition was over; it later gave them to him with a subsidy sufficient to develop his own shipping line. Furthermore, through Ōkubo's hard bargaining in Peking, and with the assistance of the British Minister to Peking, Sir Thomas F. Wade, Japan gained a clear diplomatic victory over China. The latter finally recognized its responsibility over Formosa and the right of Japan to send the expedition to protect its own subjects.[6] This agreement of 1874 also gave Japan a strong legal claim for the Ryūkyū Islands which were incorporated into the Japanese Empire in 1879. (See Chapter 9.)

Criticism of the Government Continues

Even though Ōkubo had achieved notable success with his Peking negotiations and had avoided war with China, he and the other Satsuma and Chōshū leaders in the government were in a vulnerable position. Kido had resigned because of his opposition to the Formosan expedition. Itagaki of Tosa refused to return to the government and had concluded that progress in the people's rights movement would be possible only when public interest in governmental affairs was sufficiently aroused. With his fellow clansman, Kataoka Kenkichi (1834–1903), he formed the Society of Independence (*Risshisha*). It started as a purely local group with the avowed purposes of fighting for the rights of the individual, perfecting the people's welfare, and advancing the concept of an elected public assembly. Its membership was restricted to the gentry class.

Furthermore, the writings of Fukuzawa Yukichi were having a marked impact on the people's political philosophy. In a constant stream of publications, he insisted that Japan was making a mistake by continuing to rely on orthodox Confucian principles and teachings which stultified progress. He noted that the peoples of Western nations who enjoyed freedom became imbued with the spirit of enterprise, initiative, and responsibility. In 1872 he wrote, "Heaven made no man higher than another and no man lower than another." As every man possessed equally the right to preserve his life, his property, and his honor, he concluded that all men are equal. Fukuzawa also believed that governments were established to guarantee the rights of the people so that a good government was one which interfered the least with the normal activities of society.

He deplored the reliance the people placed in government which caused them to fear and flatter it and thereby stifled their independence of spirit. Progress would come, he insisted, when both government and the people operated in their respective spheres and carried out their respective responsibilities. While criticizing the government for its irresponsible and harsh treatment of the leaders of the movement for people's rights, he chided the latter for having failed to protect their own rights.[7]

To meet these challenges of the opposition, the oligarchs resorted to an oft repeated device. They held a conference in Ōsaka in 1875 of as many of the dissident leaders as would attend. Significantly, Saigō and his followers refused to come. A valiant attempt was made to patch up the differences among the incumbent Councilors and those who had left the government. Itagaki insisted that some type of deliberative and representative assembly be formed. The final agreement, which was incorporated into an Imperial Proclamation, provided that:

1. A Senate or *Genrō-In* be called to discuss legislative matters.
2. A Supreme Court be organized.
3. A conference of Prefectural Governors be called to consider, along with the Senate, the future form of the national government.
4. The functions of the Councilors and Ministers of State be separated.

The implementation of the agreement reached at Ōsaka is illustrative of another technique which the clan oligarchs used to great effect. The Imperial Proclamation, which they had prepared, provided for these changes in general terms. At the same time, it warned, "Our subjects . . . must not yield too impulsively to a rash desire for reform." While it appeared to be sanctioning democratic institutions, in reality such was not the case. The detailed interpretation and implementation of the new policy was left to conservatively minded Ministers of State and their bureaucratic assistants. War Minister Yamagata, for example, was convinced that persons in the antigovernment movement planned to overthrow the government. He remonstrated, "Every day we wait, the evil poison will spread more and more over the provinces."

Thus the oligarchs, in order to be assured of control over the opposition, enacted strict laws. For example, in 1875 new press and publication laws provided for severe penalties for those who openly wrote against established policy. More than sixty persons were arrested within a year for violating these new laws.

As new "freedoms" were given the people, new power to guide and to suppress them was acquired by the Emperor's responsible Ministers. This same procedure was followed in general in 1887 when strong objections were raised to the lack of progress on the revision of the treaties, in 1889 when the Constitution was promulgated, and in 1924 when universal manhood suffrage was approved. Even in 1931, when elements of the Japanese Army engineered a coup d'état in Manchuria, the same pattern was followed in modified form. In any of these or other crises in Japan's modern history, the Emperor's ministers were convinced of the justice of their cause. They firmly believed, or made themselves believe, that they knew better than anyone else what was best for the country and for the people. Consequently, they sponsored legislation or Imperial decrees which gave them sufficient authority to carry out their beliefs.

Obviously, Itagaki's efforts had resulted in some progress toward the formation of representative institutions; but the new pattern of government continued to be conservative and slow in forming. Administratively, the powers and functions of the Home Ministry were broadened. The Home Minister was responsible directly to the Emperor and had full charge of matters related to public safety, local government, taxes, and public works. With the national police force under his direct supervision, he became one of the most powerful men in the government.

The edict of 1875 which created a Senate and a lower house to be composed of prefectural governors and the designation of the Council of State (*Dajōkan*) as the executive body acting like a Cabinet seemed to augur well for greater rights for the people. On the other hand, membership in the Senate was restricted to nobles and persons of the two highest court grades who had rendered meritorious service to the throne. The meetings of the lower house were mere convocations of the prefectural governors controlled by the Home Minister. The Council of State consisted of members of the oligarchy and was the body through which they exerted their control. Their authority was further strengthened in 1876 when an Imperial edict overruled Itagaki's plea that the members of the Council of State should not perform both executive and administrative functions. Itagaki resigned in protest and the Council members determined policies and also administered them.[8]

Saigō Takamori Challenges the Clan Bureaucrats

No one was more aware of the concentration of power in the hands of a few favored Imperial Councilors than Saigō Takamori. After his resignation in 1873 from the Council and as commander-in-chief of the Imperial guard, he had returned immediately to his home province of Satsuma. He was accompanied by his former feudal baron, the Imperial Advisor Shimazu Hisamitsu. Both men were strong supporters of the right of the Emperor to rule and they believed firmly that he was being ill-advised. They refused to participate in any of the government's activities. They had not been included in the compromise meeting in Ōsaka in early 1875. Consequently, Saigō was both shocked by and apprehensive of the news that a Senate was to be established. The conferences of prefectural governors held shortly thereafter filled him with even greater forebodings. Reportedly, they were discussing an appropriate form of a Constitution for Japan which would mean further limitation of the Imperial prerogatives.

In the meantime, Saigō had established his own private school in the prefectural capital of Kagoshima. Since many of his faculty had formerly served under him in the Imperial guards, infantry and artillery squads were formed. Chinese classics were an important part of the course of study. Saigō's purpose was to train young men adequately for government service. Eventually he hoped to have a hard core of well-disciplined persons who would take over the central government under his leadership. Furthermore, his small group of fanatic followers insisted that the warriors as a class should be supreme above all others and should rule the empire. Among the warriors, they believed none were better equipped to bear that responsibility than themselves.

Satsuma was one of the most isolated provinces in Japan, and its inhabitants had long cherished a feeling of independence from central control. Many of the graduates of Saigō's school were given positions in the Satsuma prefectural government and the governor was in agreement with Saigō's objectives.

Personal rivalries and antagonisms also contributed to the bellicose attitude of Saigō's band of warriors. They were attached to his cause by a strong personal loyalty and had an intense antipathy toward any who opposed him. The Satsuma men were particularly resentful of the power wielded within the central government by their fellow clansman, Ōkubo. Their feelings were intensified by the fact that as Home Minister he was responsible for public safety throughout the country, including Satsuma. When he requested Ōyama, the prefectural governor, to come to Tokyo to explain his insubordination and partisanship toward Saigō, the governor refused to appear. When special police agents were sent from Tokyo in retaliation to spy on the activities of the Saigō clique, its members considered it an insult to their leader. Finally, the Satsuma warriors were dissatisfied with the central government's plan for the forceful commutation of their feudal pensions. The special interest rate of 10 per cent for bonds held by Satsuma warriors, as compared to a rate of 5 to 7 per cent for all other warriors, was not a sufficient incentive to force them to change their minds. They did not desire to be tied, either financially or politically, to the fate of the new government.

The final, unbearable insult, from the point of view of Saigō's henchmen, was an order from Tokyo in January, 1877, to transfer the Army and Navy ammunition stored in the city of Kagoshima to a safer district. The Satsuma men ignored the order and took the initiative by seizing the depots. Saigō then led a force of 15,000 men northward ostensibly to carry on negotiations with the national government in Tokyo. Actually, he had revolted against the Imperial government and his campaign was supported and sanctioned by Governor Ōyama. Although the governor's jurisdiction was limited to Kagoshima Prefecture, in the extreme south of Kyūshū, he ordered all the garrisons in the entire island to give the rebels safe conduct. They were not challenged until they had marched six days and 115 miles to reach Kumamoto.

The Commander of the Imperial Army garrison of that city, who was responsible to the Chief of Staff in Tokyo, refused to permit the rebels to pass without a pitched battle. Saigō's forces, fired by his zeal and leadership, began a siege of the Imperial troops in the castle at Kumamoto. Reinforcements arrived just in time to save the castle. The entire peacetime army of 32,000 men was committed against Saigō. They were supplemented by a reserve of 10,000 men and many of the national police. It took the government nine months and cost 42 million yen to suppress the revolt. In September, 1877, Saigō, his officers, and the last of his men died in their den near Kagoshima.

As a result of the rebels' defeat, the Imperial Government had successfully met its greatest challenge. The new Imperial Army, recruited from all classes of society, proved that it could successfully meet an army composed exclusively of the old warrior class. As none of the other dissident groups, such as that led by Itagaki in Tosa, had joined Saigō's rebellion, it was clear to the central government that a widespread, effective opposition did not exist. Rather, the rebellion was a personal affair of Saigō and was motivated by his frustrations and misplaced loyalties.[9] Consequently, after the suppression of the uprising, the clan bureaucrats were in a position to push forward with the business of the formation of a permanent governmental structure and of economic development and expansion which would contribute directly to Japan's national strength.

Increased Demands for People's Rights

But the oligarchs were not as free to pursue their policies as appeared on the surface. They still had to deal with increasing political opposition. The continuing problem which faced them was how to retain the power and dignity of the throne and their own favored position and at the same time to give the people enough rights and privileges to keep them satisfied. No one had yet developed a satisfactory solution to this problem. In fact, a solution might have been ignored if it had not been forced on the clan bureaucrats by the challenges thrown at them by the advocates of "people's rights."

Fukuzawa Yukichi aided the opposition by the publication in 1876 of a treatise entitled *Bunken Ron* on the division of the judicial, legislative, and executive powers of government as practiced in America and Great Britain. Another important influence had come from France. Although French thought was not accepted as extensively as British political philosophy, it served as the basis for the most radical reformers. By the time of the Satsuma Rebellion in 1877, the works of both Montesquieu and Rousseau had been translated; Rousseau's theory of man's natural rights, as set forth in his *Contrat Social,* had been enthusiastically accepted by a small group of Japanese radicals. The concepts of "liberty and equality" became the basis for their demands that the social and political privileges inherited from feudalism should be abolished.

One of the most prominent of this group was Nakae Chōmin (1847–1901), a Tosa native who studied Dutch and French at Nagasaki before the Restoration, and then became interpreter for the French Minister Leon Roches. At Itagaki's suggestion he was sent to France as a student on a government scholarship. After his return in 1874 he became secretary of the Senate and later devoted his time to journalism. He was always in the forefront of the fight against the oligarchs. Although his views were more radical than those of Itagaki and his immediate followers, he never advocated overt action against the government or revolution.

Perhaps the most important single act, at this time, of Itagaki and the *Risshisha* was the sponsorship of a memorial drafted in the name of Kataoka, its President. These leaders of the opposition had no responsibility for such things as suppressing Saigō's rebellion and were free to devote their energies to political problems. In view of the dangers of arrest under the new press and libel laws, the sponsorship of antigovernment views took considerable courage and personal conviction. They presented their memorial in June, 1877, while the rebellion was still in progress. In it they claimed that the unrest was the direct result of the despotic power exercised by the Emperor's ministers and of their refusal to take heed of the opinion of the nation.

Laws have been enforced, taxes imposed, the collection of the land-tax reformed, wars declared against foreign countries, portions of the empire exchanged; solely at the caprice of several officials, without allowing public opinion to have a voice in the matter. The sacred oath taken by the Emperor on his accession to the throne has been altogether set aside.[10]

The memorial then lists eight evils which prevailed. The first was the arbitrary action of the Cabinet which imposed its own oppressive measures on the people in disregard of the Emperor's will expressed in his decrees of 1868 and of 1875. The memorial decried the fact that the provincial governors had not met again and that the press and libel laws stifled all expression of public opinion. Other evils noted were the random and confused way in which the government was conducted and the concentration of authority and power in Tokyo. Furthermore, it complained that the common people were given no political rights and had no control over their welfare. While the memorial did not oppose the concept of military conscription, it disapproved of such a system so long as it was operated by a despotic government.

On financial matters, the memorial accused the authorities of favoritism in the exploitation of Hokkaidō and other regions and complained that the system of collecting taxes in cash was unfair. The eighth evil cited by the *Risshisha* was referred to as the mismanagement of foreign affairs, a point on which the government was particularly vulnerable because no progress had been made in revising the unequal treaties with the European powers. The memorial was a formidable document in its caustic attack on prevalent evils as well as in its length. It concluded with a plea to the Emperor to "put an end to all despotic and oppressive measures, and to consult public opinion in the conduct of the government. To this end a representative assembly should be established so that the government may become constitutional in form."

The memorial was ignored officially on the grounds that it contained impolite language. Its demand for an elected assembly and charges against the oligarchs for obvious mistakes could not, however, be so easily dismissed. It was public knowledge that the Satsuma and Chōshū clansmen were acting arbitrarily and that their foreign policy belied their claim that Japan was a nation comparable to any in the Western world. Many of the other evils described in the memorial were easily recognizable by the increasing number of persons influenced by Occidental political philosophy. By the issuance of this statement, the *Risshisha* had greatly intensified the struggle for people's rights.

As already noted, steps taken thus far by the Imperial government to increase the rights and privileges of the people were not dictated by a great revolutionary movement. Furthermore, except for the Etō and Saigō Rebellions, the popular revolts or uprisings which had exploded were restricted to the peasantry, were often isolated cases, and rarely had any political motivation. In fact, they were unimportant enough to be ignored by the government in the sense that they did not demand or dictate the agrarian changes that were inaugurated. On the other hand, the movement for people's rights could not be ignored. Unrest and disturbance after 1877, although never comparable to that of Saigō's Rebellion, increased and included influential groups in society such as the landowners and manufacturers of consumers' goods. (See Chapter 7.) Even the farmers and city workers were beginning to become politically conscious and to be influenced by political leaders such as Itagaki.

It is difficult to assay the influence exerted by the *Risshisha* or any of the advocates of greater people's rights at any given time. A prominent constitutional historian, Professor Ōtsu Jun'ichirō, goes so far as to claim that the demands of Kataoka and others expressed the real desire of the people and changed the political complexion of the country. As he expressed it, "The government officials, who had been oppressing public opinion, found that they had lost face and realized for the first time that they could not suppress the will of the people." The facts do not seem to justify giving so much importance to the influence of the "progressives."

The Meiji oligarchs had already begun to form their conservative views on a constitutional monarchy. For example, as early as 1876 the Emperor requested the Senate to study various constitutional systems and to establish a Committee under Prince Arisugawa to prepare a draft constitution. Furthermore, in 1877, there was a general reorganization of the governmental structure which attempted to separate the executive, legislative, and judicial powers of government. The next year, Ōkubo, one of the strongest of the oligarchs, was assassinated. His assailants charged that he had suppressed the rights of the people and monopolized administrative powers, sponsored unnecessary government expenditures, weakened the authority of the patriotic samurai, and handled foreign affairs improperly. Revenge for Saigō's death, for which Ōkubo as Home Minister was responsible, was doubtless another motive for the murder. Consequently other oligarchs became apprehensive for the safety of their own persons and of their positions.

Under the circumstances, the government took additional steps to placate the opposition. The Ōsaka Conference and the subsequent proclamation in 1875 had promised the formation of an assembly of prefectural governors to consider the question of a constitutional system. Such a meeting had been held for a few days under the chairmanship of Kido. Many of the governors regretted that the time for discussion had been limited and no further meetings had been called.

Just prior to his death, Ōkubo called the governors together to approve a plan for local assemblies. Consequently, in July, 1878, it was announced that prefectural assemblies would be established and their members would be elected by a restricted male electorate. The assemblies were to be used to discuss prefectural budgets and other local matters. On the other hand, their power was limited by the fact that the Governor initiated all bills and could veto them. He also had power to dissolve the assembly if it became too cantankerous. Although these assemblies were a far cry from an elective national parliament, the government claimed that it was taking appropriate steps to determine the will of the people.[11]

The Conservative Oligarchs State Their Views

Far more important than any of these reforms, however, was the awakened consciousness of the Emperor's advisers and the oligarchs to the fact that they must crystallize their own views on the question of the permanent governmental structure. Motoda Eifu, the Emperor's chief tutor, was constantly suggesting new ways in which the Emperor could become more familiar with political matters through consulting Ōkubo and others. In 1877, Motoda set forth certain principles of political strategy which the Emperor should follow. These included winning the hearts of his people, becoming acquainted with the prefectural officials, creating public discussions, and stressing the importance of a Cabinet.[12]

At the same time, advice on these problems was sought from former President of the United States Ulysses S. Grant when he visited Tokyo in 1879 on his trip around the world. Some of the same persons who had asked him six years earlier in Washington about treaty revisions now sought his opinion on the knotty problem of how much power to give to the people. General Grant was well aware of the fact that the Japanese people as a whole had had little education or experience in politics. Universal education had theoretically been in operation for a few years (see page 202), but in reality illiteracy was more prevalent than literacy. Furthermore, the average Japanese subject had had little firsthand experience with problems which required political decisions and had not been given responsibility in government. People were content to leave such matters up to the authorities.

In view of these facts, when Grant had a conference with the Emperor Meiji, he advocated adoption of representative institutions but urged the Japanese to consider the matter with great care. He warned them that if rights of suffrage and representative institutions were once given to the people they could not be withdrawn. Hence, they should be given gradually. Under the circumstances, he urged delay in establishing an elected national legislature with full powers.

With Ōkubo's assassination in May, 1878, the last of the triumvirate of Kidō, Saigō, and Ōkubo had disappeared. This meant a marked change in the leadership of the government. Itō, Ōkuma, Matsukata, and Yamagata emerged as the most powerful officials. Itō, who became the new Home Minister, had already shifted his interests from practical problems of reconstruction, which he encountered as Minister of Industry, to those of a political nature and came to play an increasingly important role in the government. When he learned that the draft Constitution proposed by the Senate contained liberal provisions which he believed to be dangerous to the future of the state, he turned to his old mentor, Prince Iwakura, for help. As President of the Council of State, Iwakura was a key figure in any move to get Imperial sanction for a new policy. He was opposed to the submission to the Emperor of the Senate's draft of a Constitution on the grounds that parts of it did not conform properly to his concept of the role and authority of the Emperor. Consequently, in December, 1879, when Iwakura received a letter from Itō suggesting that the Senate be asked to revive its work on a draft constitution, the former readily agreed. Shortly thereafter, obviously on Iwakura's advice, the Emperor issued such an order. At the same time, each of the members of the Council of State was requested to present his views to the throne on the question of a constitution.

By this move, Itō had outmaneuvered both the Senate and those outside the government who clamored for a parliament. In the first place, he knew that the Councilors, with the possible exception of Ōkuma, would support his own general position that extreme caution was necessary in granting additional powers to the people. Any public demands for action could now be silenced by the reply that the Emperor had requested his most esteemed advisers to give him their views. It could logically be argued that until these views were in hand, the government could take no action. Even more important, the people could be kept in ignorance of the contents of the opinions of the Councilors in the event that the

Courtesy of The Bettmann Archive

Itō Hirobumi, 1841–1909

views were not acceptable to Iwakura and Itō. As President of the Councilors, Iwakura would forward the memorials to the throne, and could screen them at will. At one blow Itō had thus assured himself of support for a conservative governmental system and deprived the opposition of a means of criticizing his maneuver.[13]

As was expected, the views of all the Councilors except Ōkuma were conservative and reflected the heritage of Confucianism and the German doctrine of the supremacy of the state expounded by political philosophers such as Blüntschli and Biederman. Yamagata Aritomo, who had been Minister of War until 1878, was the first Councilor to send in his reply. He was also one of the most representative of the advocates of Prussian political philosophy. Although his memorial is rambling in parts and is a combination of generalities and references to modern concepts of government, the type of government he supported is clear.

He pointed to three evils which he believed retarded Japan's governmental progress. The first evil was the rapid development of events which resulted in hasty decisions and a deviation from "the right way." The second evil was a change on the surface of society brought about by new innovations. In reality, he argued, only limited groups had benefited from changes which had already occurred. Finally, Yamagata concluded that the Restoration had caused some of the warriors and other groups to revolt. These examples were proof to Yamagata that the majority of the people had not shown proper respect for the government and refused to obey its orders. To meet these evils, Yamagata proposed that the people cease their search for novelty and follow the example of the Councilors and Ministers. The action of the latter should be based on a constitution established on sound principles. For Yamagata, such sound principles included continuance of the special prerogatives of the Emperor and of the privileges of his court.

Courtesy of The Bettmann Archive

YAMAGATA ARITOMO, 1838–1922

Yamagata's views were equally conservative on the question of division of powers. He wrote:

> As for the division and establishment of the three powers of executive, legislative and judicial, though there are models in existence, these should be completely modified [to suit Japan's unique needs]. The extent of power of these branches of government should be settled. If the legislative and judicial power are not restrained by the executive power and if provision is not specifically made in the constitution for such restraints, it will be impossible to avoid contradictions.[14]

In other words, he disregarded the concept that the three estates should balance each other. Rather, he championed the position that the executive branch of the government should have power to check the legislative and judicial branches.

In view of the controversy over the question of the people's rights which Itagaki and others had aroused, Yamagata's memorial also contained his views on this issue. Like practically all key persons in the government, he opposed the idea of an elective parliament. He advocated, on the other hand, a modification of existing governmental institutions such as the appointive prefectural assemblies. The capable persons from these assemblies should be "pulled out," regardless of the prefecture from which they came, and should be used to form a single assembly. This hand-picked assembly should then discuss the principles for a new constitution. After this type of assembly had functioned for a few years, it could be changed into an elective body. As he argued:

> Put an assembly in practice secretly, learn from experience and at a time when there is no fear of contradiction and trouble, change its name, speak about it openly, and it will not be too late. Make a mixture of direct and indirect election as through an electoral college. Slowly a people's assembly could thus be organized.

In conclusion, he recognized that persons might object to his proposals on the grounds that such an assembly would be merely advisory and would automatically approve governmental policies. He was not impressed, however, by the fact that citizens of European countries participated directly in their governments. Japan could not be compared with the West. As he expressed it:

> As Japan is just beginning a new type of government, you cannot expect the Japanese to have one ten-thousandth of the rights of Europeans.

Yamagata's memorial has been quoted extensively both because of the key position he held in the Restoration government and because most of the other Councilors agreed with his conservative position. For example, Itō Hirobumi, who was to be primarily responsible for drafting Japan's new constitution, held views essentially the same as those of Yamagata.

In his earliest proposals for an elective assembly, which he presented in 1879, Itō recommended that the Senate (*Genrō-In*) should be expanded and that its members should be elected from among the nobility. He believed that the chief function of a Parliament (*kokkai*) should be to protect the Imperial Household and to preserve ancient customs. Its opening should, however, be postponed. Such a plan, he maintained, would have the dual advantage of controlling changes and broadening the base of public discussions. As for an election for members of Parliament, a specific office should be formed to investigate the question before any decision should be made on it.

Finally, the Emperor's chief tutor, Motoda Eifu, strongly supported the oligarchs' views. In 1879, he insisted that a national assembly should be formed before popular demand forced the government to create something less acceptable to it. In creating such an assembly, there should be no compromise with the direct rule of the Emperor and no concessions should be made to the concept of popular sovereignty. Motoda's main principles for a national constitution, drafted in 1880, included the concept of a divine Imperial rule by an Emperor who was sacred and inviolable and who would wield the power of government and educate his people in the basic principles of benevolence, duty, propriety, deference, loyalty, filial piety, and honesty.[15]

Continued Antigovernment Pressure, 1880

As if to underline his proposal that a decision be postponed on the question of an elective parliament, Home Minister Itō sponsored a new law which restricted political activity. This new edict of 1880, entitled "A Law of Public Meetings," made the usual forms of political activity illegal. Henceforth, all political meetings must be approved by the police, including the speakers, their topics, and the membership and governing rules of the body sponsoring such a meeting. The police had additional authority to disband a meeting if the speaker wandered from the approved subject or if the meeting were deemed prejudicial to public tranquillity.

Another move of the oligarchs was aimed directly at reducing participation in politics by those persons who had been the most active supporters of the movement for people's rights. An Imperial decree forbade members of the armed services, and teachers and students in both government and private schools and universities, from attending political meetings. Finally, political associations were prohibited from advertising their meetings, soliciting membership, or combining or communicating with similar societies. In other words, persons who wished to lecture on subjects such as democratic political institutions, or the right of the people to be represented in the government, and any group which wished to discuss these questions were carrying on activities branded as subversive by the government.

Despite these stringent public safety and public assembly laws, political activity advocating people's rights not only survived but increased. Many persons, such as Fukuzawa Yukichi, who had previously questioned the advisability of establishing a national assembly, by 1879 became strong advocates of such a procedure. During the summer he wrote a series of articles which started a wave of enthusiastic support for a national parliament and kept up his barrage against the oligarchs on this issue. In 1881 he wrote Itō and Inouye: "We have decided that whatever kind of political parties arise, the reins of government must go fairly and squarely to the party with a majority of popular votes." [16]

Another reason for the growth of the people's rights movement and its demands for a parliament was the close alliance of the organizers of the first political party and the landowner–entrepreneur group. (See Chapter 7.) Furthermore, Itagaki and his followers decided to formalize their *Risshisha* into a national political party. In December, 1880, they published their projected covenant for the *Jiyūtō* or Liberal party. It promised to work for the extension of civil rights, the advancement and prosperity of the nation, and for constitutional government. It also called for the publication of newspapers to expand the beliefs in liberty and to cultivate public opinion on political issues. Despite the new laws of 1880 which made such activity illegal, it advocated public lectures and a membership drive. After the platform was published, however, no immediate steps were taken to organize the party formally. This move awaited the crisis within the government created by Ōkuma's challenges of the oligarchs in 1881.

From a political point of view, therefore, the oligarchs were still faced in 1880, as they had been faced in 1873, with an irritating and embarrassing, if not formidable, opposition. They had been forced to make some concessions to the advocates of greater rights for the people, but had not capitulated on any of the vital issues. If the conservative recommendations, which the Councilors had already forwarded to the throne, could be incorporated eventually into a new, national, governmental structure, they would have no objections to such a move. On the other hand, they were in no hurry for such a change and were content with conditions as they existed.

There was one flaw in this situation. Ōkuma Shigenobu had not yet expressed his views on the question of a parliament and had shown a tendency to favor the opinion of the progressives such as Itagaki, Kataoka, and Fukuzawa. Ōkuma was an outsider; he was from Hizen rather than from Satsuma and Chōshū. Finally, he was becoming one of the strongest men of the government. A showdown between Ōkuma and the other Councilors seemed inevitable but no one was aware of the acuteness of this major political crisis. The final act in the Meiji Restoration was still to come.

NOTES

1. Donald H. Shivley, "Motoda Eifu, Confucian Tutor to the Meiji Emperor," in David S. Nivison and Arthur F. Wright (eds.), *Confucianism in Action* (Stanford: Stanford University Press, 1959), p. 310.

2. G. B. Sansom, *The Western World and Japan* (New York: Alfred A. Knopf, Inc., 1950), p. 343.

3. Itagaki Taisuke (1837–1919) of Tosa was one of the chief signers of this memorial. He had served creditably in the campaign against the Shogun's forces at the time of the Restoration of Emperor Meiji. He was appointed Councilor in 1869. He supported the general concept of the separation of powers. In 1874 he returned to his native province of Tosa where he established the *Risshisha,* a political club. For the text of the memorial see W. W. McLaren, "Japanese Government Documents," *Transactions of the Asiatic Society of Japan,* XLII, pp. 426 ff.

4. For example, Katō's *Shinsei Taii* (A General Outline of True Government) which appeared in 1870, was a precursor of later works by authors who demanded democratic reforms in the government. In 1875, his *Kokutai Shinron* (A Basic Treatise on National Polity) was critical of the traditional ideas of the Japanese state. He accused the leaders of believing that the Emperor is sublime and that the people are base. He argued that the nationalist scholars did violence to the truth and were despicable because they advocated complete obedience to Imperial commands without question. Shortly thereafter he recanted and withdrew the book from circulation. His later writings were conservative.

5. For Yanaihara's views see Yanaihara Tadao (ed.), *Gendai Nihon Shōshi* (Tokyo: Misuzu-shobo, 1952), I, pp. 14 ff. The text of Itagaki's and his colleague's reply to Katō is in McLaren, *op. cit.,* pp. 440 ff.

6. See Masakazu Iwata, *Ōkubo Toshimichi, The Bismarck of Japan* (Berkeley: University of California Press, 1964), pp. 185–224, for a detailed account of the key role Ōkubo played in the Formosan Expedition and the negotiations in Peking.

7. See Carmen Blacker, *The Japanese Enlightenment, a Study of the Writings of Fukuzawa Yukichi* (Cambridge: Cambridge University Press, 1964), pp. 30 ff. and pp. 101 ff.

8. This general pattern of gradual approach to a national assembly was that advocated by Kido Kōin in his proposals for a constitution. See George M. Beckmann, *The Making of the Meiji Constitution* (Lawrence: Kansas University Press, 1957), pp. 35 ff.

9. Although I have referred to Saigō as a rebel and to his campaign as a rebellion, the reader should not infer that he has been treated in Japanese history as a traitor. On the contrary, because he revolted in the name of the Emperor to protect him from evil influences, he was admired by many of his contemporaries and he has become a great national hero and a favorite subject

for novels, plays, and stories of knightly valor. Even a post-World War II theater audience will weep over a classical play in which he is the hero.

10. For a complete translation of this memorial see McLaren, *op. cit.*, pp. 452–79. It is purported to have been written by Ueki Emori (1854–1892), one of the more radical members of the Tosa group. Called Itagaki's "brain trust" by some, Ueki took a strong position in defense of freedom of speech and thought and insisted that the people be informed of the actions of officials in regard to public affairs. On the other hand, like his contemporaries, his "liberalism" was tempered with conservatism. He favored a constitutional monarchy with the state organized on a hierarchical basis. Members of his own class, the warriors, should be the backbone of the electorate and should constitute the political elite. Kataoka had been selected in 1871 as one of two representatives from Tosa to study abroad. When he returned from Europe, he became an official in the Navy Department. He resigned with Itagaki over the Korean issue in 1873. He was arrested later for his political indiscretions but finally was elected to Parliament.

11. The most significant and numerous changes and developments within the prefectural governments took place between 1868 and 1878. After 1876, the prefectural governments became largely administrative units. Two years later, their structural form, which was to last for the next forty years, had been settled. For an analysis of the rapid structural and functional differentiation which took place within the prefectural governments see Bernard Silberman, "Structural and Functional Differentiation in the Political Modernization of Japan," in Robert E. Ward (ed.), *Political Development in Modern Japan* (Princeton: Princeton University Press, 1968), pp. 337–86.

12. See Shivley, *op. cit.*, pp. 310–24.

13. Contrast this procedure with that of John Jay, James Madison, and Alexander Hamilton who in 1787–1788 pleaded through their papers in the *Federalist* with the people of New York to adopt the American Constitution. The policy in Japan was to keep the people from thinking on basic issues, rather than giving them the facts and then letting them decide.

14. For the complete text of Yamagata's views see Tokutomi Ichirō, *Kōshaku Yamagata Den* (Tokyo: Yamagata Aritomo Kō Kinen Jigyō-kai, 1933), II, pp. 842 ff. For the opinions of Itō, Yamada, Inouye, and other Councilors, see Ōtsu Jun'ichirō, *Dai Nihon Kensei Shi* (10 vols.; Tokyo: Hōbun-kan, 1927–1928), II, pp. 370 ff. For English translations of the memorials of Yamagata and Itō, see Beckmann, *op. cit.*, pp. 126–36.

15. See Shivley, *op. cit.*, p. 326.

16. See Blacker, *op. cit.*, pp. 117–21.

7

The Victory of Conservatism in 1881

In the years immediately following the crisis over Korea in 1873, events such as the Saigō Rebellion of 1877 and the demands of the people's rights movement compelled the oligarchs to concentrate on the solution of political problems. Nevertheless, many of the practical difficulties which had absorbed the time and energy of the chief government officials in the period prior to 1873 (see Chapter 5), had not been resolved. In fact, continued industrialization and increased economic and military power were prerequisites for the creation of conditions under which a constitutional monarchy could be established. In other words, the political power and the economic strength of the Imperial government were interdependent and the oligarchs could not have acted in one field without support from the other. Hence they devoted much time and energy to the further solution of many of these practical problems. They used as their model the only one at their disposal, namely, laissez-faire capitalism in America and Western Europe. On the other hand, in line with their inherent capability of *adapting* foreign models to their own special circumstances and needs, they emphasized the establishment of state-supported enterprises and government encouragement and guidance of private companies.

What, then, were the most significant developments, from the formal abolition of feudalism in 1873 to the challenge of Ōkuma in 1881, which gave the leaders in the government additional strength to combat this serious threat to their authority from within their own ranks? What was the position of the government in relation to the nation's industrialization? What role did private capital play in Japan's modernization? What specific measures did the oligarchs take to facilitate victory for their political and economic policies?

Government Encouragement of Foreign Trade

The economic program during the first few years of the Meiji Restoration might be characterized as one of improvisation. It was an apprenticeship for acquiring technical skills and for creating what the young oligarchs believed to be the minimum politicoeconomic essentials for a modern state: an infant Navy, a conscript Army, the beginnings of a system of transportation and communication, a tax collected universally in money, and a single currency. After 1873, the national government continued to encourage and control industry so that the country could guarantee its military and economic, as well as its political, independence. There developed a new tendency, however, to concentrate on stimulating new industrial and commercial activity, especially in the field of consumers' goods. After his return from Europe in 1873, Minister of Home Affairs Ōkubo Toshimichi expressed the government's position as follows:

> The wealth of the country is dependent on the quantity of goods produced. . . . The people's industries have not had sufficient encouragement from the government as they have just begun to develop. Skill and knowledge must be given to the people and complete regulations established. The government and officials all must exert every effort to encourage industry and to increase production.

To give substance to his words, he proceeded to establish a special division of industrial and agricultural development within his Ministry. One of its first tasks was to try to force foreign trade into the hands of Japanese traders. Ever since Japan was opened to the Occident, foreign traders and foreign commercial houses had monopolized foreign trade in the open ports. As late as 1877, foreigners handled 94 per cent of the export and 97 per cent of the import trade. The Japanese merchant class had been weak for several reasons. In the first place, the largest and most experienced group of merchants were in Ōsaka but they had suffered heavy losses with the abolition of feudalism. Their business and financial structure was based on a feudal economy and the warriors were heavily in debt to them. When feudalism was abolished, the ports were opened to foreigners, and the debts of the feudal barons were nullified, the old merchant families were in no position to carry on the work of economic modernization. They were ignorant of international trading practices and shunned the chance to participate in foreign trade. A new, select group of entrepreneurs was to develop. To circumvent the obstacles created by the lack of merchants with a new outlook, Ōkubo and his colleagues concentrated on developing native skills, raising the quality of goods, and educating foreigners about Japanese products.[1]

Technical education was stressed. For example, the agricultural experimentation station first established in Tokyo was moved in 1874 to

Sapporo, the capital of Hokkaidō. It was placed under the supervision of Horace Capron, United States Commissioner of Agriculture. This institution was the forerunner of the University of Hokkaidō. The Ministry of Finance established a school of banking and finance. The Tokyo Technical School was transformed in 1877 into the Engineering Department of Tokyo Imperial University. Furthermore, great importance was given to international expositions abroad. Elaborate preparations were made for representation at the Vienna Exposition of 1873. Since it was Japan's first participation in that type of activity, two years were spent on the plans. A special office was established with Ōkuma as director for which 600,000 yen was appropriated. The general purpose of the program was to advertise Japanese goods abroad and to transplant to Japan as many European production methods as possible. Seventy government officials were sent to the Exposition to assist in exhibiting Japanese products which might compete in the world markets. They had an additional assignment following the close of the Exposition. Under the general direction of a European adviser, they traveled throughout Europe to study modern methods of manufacturing and marketing.

In order to capitalize on any foreign interest in Japanese products that might have been stimulated, consulates were formed wherever possible with capable persons in charge. For example, the Finance and Home Ministries each sent a representative to England and to America to "distribute samples of Japanese products, investigate conditions of industry in those countries, and to make secret investigations of the advantages and disadvantages of Japanese products in the markets of those countries."[2] Special reports were soon sent home by the new consular officers and trade agents on subjects such as the market for silk-egg sheets in Italy, porcelain in San Francisco, flannel in Shanghai, and black tea in India. The practical results of some of these reports were soon apparent. In 1875 Ōkubo announced that the policy henceforth would be to encourage exports through Japanese hands. A Tea Examination Bureau was established and the first tea was exported to the United States in October, 1875. Tea soon grew to be a large trade item. Matches were sent on consignment to special offices in China.

In fact, attempts were made to enter a field in which foreigners had practically a monopoly, namely, the sale of raw silk. The Occidental traders had been isolated in special compounds in each of the treaty ports where they lived a life apart from the country around them. Because of the extraterritoriality provisions in the treaties, they were beyond the reach of the Japanese law. For many years they had their own police, post offices, and currency, which gave them a feeling of superiority over the "natives." Naturally, their arrogant and superior attitude was carried over into any business dealings which they had with the Japanese. On many occasions the foreign merchants arbitrarily disregarded price agreements previously reached between themselves and Japanese sellers. At other times, the foreigners refused to countenance legitimate Japanese demands for a higher price of raw silk and paid a lower price of their own choice.

Every effort was made by government officials, such as Ōkubo, to develop direct Japanese shipments of silk abroad to circumvent the necessity of dealing with the unprincipled Westerners. These silk shipments began in 1876 and slowly increased in volume. Four years later, the Yokohama silk merchants formed their own association and the government lent one million yen without interest to the Japanese wholesalers to protect their profits and to give them an advantage over the foreigners. In 1880, the Yokohama Specie Bank was organized to have charge of foreign bills of exchange and to assist the Japanese with their foreign trade transactions.

Faced with these drastic developments, the foreign merchants became more tractable and amenable. They began to abide by their agreements lest they be forced out of business prematurely. As a result of the government's conscious effort to increase foreign trade, total trade nearly doubled from 1870 to 1880 to a value of approximately 65 million yen. As a result of these efforts, and thanks to a silkworm disease in Europe in 1868 and 1876 which resulted in heavy exports of silkworms from Japan, some favorable trade balances were realized in the early years. But the situation was adversely affected by the heavy loss of specie.

Shipping and Industrial Growth

Shipping was another branch of Japan's economic activity which illustrates the struggle to break down a foreign monopoly through active assistance from the government to a selected group of entrepreneurs. Special government commercial offices and exchange companies had been established immediately after the Restoration to stimulate trade. They were soon found to be ineffectual against competition from such well-established companies as the American Pacific Steamship Company and the British P. & O. Company. Consequently, the government ordered the wealthy Mitsui family to form a new company. Despite public loans to the amount of 850,000 yen granted at favorable terms this company was eventually dissolved. The eighteen ships which it had operated, together with thirteen ships which the government had purchased in 1874 for the Formosan expedition, were all transferred to the Iwasaki-owned Mitsubishi Steamship Company. Home Minister Ōkubo extended his policy of protectionism still further by promising the new company an annual subsidy of 310,000 yen. The Japanese government further augmented the resources of the Mitsubishi Steamship Company during the Satsuma Rebellion of 1877. Funds totaling 700,000 yen and nine ships were given to it to meet the needs for army transports to suppress the uprising. After the rebels were pacified, the Mitsubishi interests kept the ships.

Obviously private foreign lines could not compete with this type of direct subsidy. Consequently, the American Pacific Steamship Company gave up. It sold to the new Japanese company three of its ships, which it used in the Yokohama-Kōbe-Nagasaki-Shanghai trade, and its warehouses in Kōbe and Shanghai. An additional government grant was given the Mitsubishi Company to enable it to compete successfully with the British P. & O. Company for the trade between Shanghai and Yokohama. As Minister of Finance, Ōkuma had enabled Iwasaki to develop a virtual monopoly in Japanese coastal shipping. When two rival Japanese companies developed, the government offered a new subsidy in 1885 to an amalgamated company which was to be known as the Nippon Yūsen Kaisha (Japan Mail Line). Thanks to the close interrelationship of government and private enterprise and the active support of men like Ōkubo, within sixteen years Japan had absorbed a large part of its ever expanding trade into its own hands. In fact, it had forced its foreign rivals out of business and finally obtained another sovereign right—a monopoly of its intercoastal trade.[3]

In the 1870's, the government tried to encourage investment of private capital in business and industry. Except for an increase of banking capital of 2½ million yen in 1875 to 43 million yen in 1880, of which the former warriors owned three-fourths of the stock, the government had little success persuading private investors to support the new industries. On the other hand, the government was far more successful, at least in the long run, in encouraging Japan's rapid industrialization through the formation of model factories as incentives to private industrialists to form their own companies. From the latter part of 1869 to December, 1873, the government had invested 11 million yen in such enterprises. For the next seven and a half years it invested an average of approximately 3 million yen a year. One of the most significant companies financed by public funds was the Sapporo Machine Shop in Hokkaidō which was developed as a part of the general colonization program of that frontier area. Steam-powered machines were imported from the United States. Forges and steam-driven sawmills and machines for manufacturing water wheels were all part of the project. In fact, Hokkaidō became the center for the manufacture of machinery, implements, sawmills, and wheat mills. (See below, pages 139–41.)

In 1874, the second year Itō was chief, the Ministry of Industry constructed at government expense an equally important factory at Akabane, then a suburb of Tokyo. It was originally built on British models to encourage the production of machines and other iron products. It was particularly proud of its smelting plant and the forty-horsepower steam-driven machinery. Like many of the other machine shops and heavy industries, it was later absorbed by the military, being transferred to the jurisdiction of the Navy Department in 1883. In order to create the foundation for a new Army and Navy, the government had been spending large sums annually on the military. For example, from 1875 to 1880, annual naval expenditures averaged over 3 million yen and army costs were over 7 million yen, which together totaled more than three times the annual investment in government enterprises.[4]

Along with this emphasis of the government on heavy industry and on those features of Japan's economy which would strengthen the country militarily, there was also a conscious attempt made to encourage the manufacture of consumers' goods. In some areas, such as Kagoshima in Satsuma, where limited industrialization had taken place before the Restoration, progress had already been made in cotton spinning. The first modern-type factory in Japan had been established there in 1867, and four years later when Brunton visited the city, he noted a huge cotton factory which was seemingly in perfect order and operating at full capacity. The machinery had been imported from Oldham, England, through Glover & Company.

The successful operation of large spinning mills depended, however, both on the development of a uniform thread and on the training of skilled operators. Consequently, the government established a large silk thread factory at Tomioka in 1872 to improve the quality of thread and encourage the adoption of mechanical reeling by private producers. The factory was built by a French company; its design, materials, machines, and tools all came from France. By 1873 it employed 400 Japanese workers and two years later the foreign advisers were dismissed. Other spinning plants followed the customary pattern of direct government sponsorship and construction with machines imported from England, France, or Italy; operation for a limited period by the government; and final sale to private purchasers at a ridiculously low price. Such a procedure was followed for the spinning plants at Nagoya and Hiroshima and numerous other western cities and for the waste-silk plant in Shimmachi.

Cotton spinning mills also developed under both private and government auspices. Prior to the Meiji Restoration, Satsuma had established two spinning mills. In 1872, a pioneer entrepreneur Kashima Mampei had built in Tokyo a plant whose success was enhanced by its own wholesale store. During the next decade the government built two model plants with 2,000 spindles each and subsidized operation of ten other mills.

They were constructed with the dual purpose of encouraging the production of raw cotton and providing yarn for weaving plants. The first privately financed, large-scale cotton spinning mill, completed in 1883, with 10,500 spindles, was financed by Shibusawa Eiichi. His firm, the Ōsaka Cotton Spinning Company, had former feudal barons and wealthy Ōsaka and Tokyo merchants as its stockholders. As a result of the technical knowledge and skill of Yamabe Takeo, whom Shibusawa had had trained in Lancashire,[5] it was an immediate success.

Financial reforms were also introduced to keep pace with the industrial advance. Ōkuma had been appointed Finance Minister in 1873 and remained in that post until 1880. New convertible notes had been issued in 1873 to help meet the expense of commuting the rice incomes of the warriors. National banks had been organized to fill the needs of the country for currency but the First National Bank would have collapsed but for the efforts of its president, Shibusawa Eiichi. Furthermore, an unusually heavy drain on the gold reserve had reduced the value of the new government notes, which shortly had to be turned into the banks for conversion. During the period of 1875–1876, therefore, the circulation of money practically stopped. New gold and silver coins were stamped and inconvertible notes were issued. In fact, the government was forced to meet the extra expenses arising from the Satsuma Rebellion by borrowing 15 million yen from the National Bank and by issuing 27 million yen in paper currency. This act brought the total paper money in circulation up to a total of about 100 million yen. As a contemporary popular saying had it, "The Meiji Government ruled the Empire by cutting paper."

As paper money increased, prices rose. For example, from 1877 to 1880, wholesale rice prices doubled in the largest cities. The multifarious programs undertaken by the government required additional funds. Nevertheless, for a few years national expenditures were kept within reasonable limits through the ability of an expanding economy to absorb the increases in paper notes. In 1881, when Matsukata Masayoshi (1835–1924) became the new Finance Minister, a retrenchment policy was inaugurated.[6]

Another characteristic of this period was the ambivalent attitude of the government officials toward the foreign experts on whom they relied heavily. This fact is substantiated by the official history of the Ministry of Industry which frankly admitted that foreigners, mostly British, had in reality brought about a revolution in Japanese industry and were largely responsible for increased scientific knowledge. On the other hand, the lighthouse adviser, Brunton, noted on the basis of his own experience that after the Iwakura Mission failed to obtain revisions of the treaties in 1873, his Japanese superiors were less cooperative and his colleagues less willing to take his advice. He observed an increasing desire to be rid of the foreigners as quickly as possible.

On November 15, 1879, the Council of State made an important policy decision on this problem. It specifically requested the Ministry of Industry to reduce its expenses by asking the foreigners to resign as soon as possible. At that date, it employed 130 foreigners whose salaries totaled 342,000 yen, nearly three-fifths of the fixed expenses of the whole Ministry. Whenever possible, the foreign experts were to be replaced by Japanese graduates of the newly formed technical schools.[7] The period of apprenticeship was fast drawing to a close.

Effect of Industrialization on Political Rivalries

The industrial capital structure, built under state auspices, had a direct bearing on the political structure of the country. In the first place, this program of government sponsorship of trade and industry had caused a close alliance between the government and the financial and industrial leaders. With the exception of a few families, such as the Mitsui family, which had acquired its wealth in the seventeenth century, the new capitalists had not been wealthy before the Restoration. They were not, as one might expect, the direct descendents of the largest feudal barons nor of the Ōsaka merchant houses. Rather, the political and ideological forces were more important than class origin in molding the new entrepreneurs. A belief in the new Japan of the future, a willingness to cut one's ties with the past, a decision to migrate to the centers where foreigners were active in trade, and experience and practical knowledge were common characteristics of those who became the new industrial leaders. They profited from a close political and economic alliance with those in power. In fact, many of the richest industrialists of the Meiji period became officials within the government or were appointed to the peerage.[8]

Furthermore, there had not been a wealthy, effective group of merchants, financiers, or industrialists who could afford to be exponents of a European-style liberal state. Such wealth as existed was dependent on the continuance of both the new economic and political structure. The new capitalists and the new government found themselves in a mutually beneficial alliance; neither desired to challenge the other and both profited from this alliance.

At the same time, this government sponsorship of industrialization resulted in two other developments which determined the social composition of the groups that opposed the government and that simultaneously supported greater rights for the people. If this alliance of oligarchs and *nouveaux riches* was to continue to their mutual profit, new industries must be protected. Such protection would normally come about through high tariffs. Because of Japan's treaties with the foreign powers, however, Japan did not have tariff autonomy. Hence, the only remaining way to protect industry was by a discriminatory tax policy.

It was to be expected that the oligarchs would not tax the infant industries which they had created. Land had traditionally been the chief source of revenue for the government and logic dictated that it should continue to be so. Consequently, land taxes continued to comprise the greatest source of income. For example, from 1875 to 1879, taxes from land equaled 80.5 per cent of the total, and from 1880 to 1884 amounted to 65.5 per cent. Furthermore, industrialization led to urbanization, which created greater interest in the cities with a proportionate neglect of rural areas. As spinning mills developed and sugar refineries were built, the farmers found that their home industries in spinning and refining could not compete with the machines. No attempt was made to recompense them nor was any program conceived to rehabilitate them.

On the contrary, in 1881 just prior to the time when Ōkuma presented his first memorial, the new Finance Minister, Matsukata, inaugurated a retrenchment policy. Rice prices fell so that the landowner, the owner–cultivator, the part-tenant, and tenant all suffered. Many of the small landowners were also entrepreneurs who manufactured products such as rice wine, bean paste, and soy sauce. Hence their businesses were likewise adversely affected by the new financial measures. This large group of discontented people naturally blamed the government for their plight. Consequently, they readily supported persons such as Itagaki and his colleagues, and later Ōkuma, who were fighting the oligarchs.

At the same time, the leaders of the "liberal movement" actively sought the support of the discontented landlord–entrepreneurs and occasionally organized them against the government. For example, in 1880 when the government proposed a special yeast tax to defray the cost of a projected naval expansion program, a Council of Rice Wine Brewers was formed to oppose the tax. Ueki Emori, who allegedly had drafted the famous memorial of 1877, was one of the founders and most active members of this council. He was one of two representatives who presented a formal protest to the government against its interference in private enterprise and against the tax. When he was arrested, he called a meeting of the Brewers' Council in Ōsaka only to have it banned by the authorities.

Thus by the beginning of 1881, political and economic policies of the oligarchs had produced three groups with a single common interest. Two of these groups, the advocates of greater rights for the people and the landlord–entrepreneurs were beginning to work together. The third group was composed of past and present members of the government who were not members of the Satchō clique but who came from other clans. All three groups were united through their hatred of the clique of former Satchō warriors who held the key posts in the government.

Ōkuma Shigenobu was the outstanding member of this last group. At this time, even though he had come from the province of Hizen, he was the senior member of the Council of State and one of the strongest figures in the government. Furthermore, he was known to be opposed to the views of all the other Councilors on the question of the early formation of a representative and elected national assembly. There was also a possibility, therefore, that Okuma could rally around him all these anti-government forces and thus become undisputed leader of Japan.

Ōkuma Defies the Conservatives, 1881

Without doubt, in the early months of 1881, the possibility of a united front was in Ōkuma's mind as he planned his strategy against his colleagues on the Council. Since he was the only Councilor to oppose the conservative views of the oligarchs, he was reluctant to state his position in an official memorial. On the other hand, Itō and the other conservatives were anxious to isolate Ōkuma sufficiently to prevent him from causing too much trouble. Since all the other Councilors except Oki and Ōkuma, both from Hizen, had expressed their opinions in writing on the constitutional issue, the Satchō group insisted that Ōkuma state his position. After receiving a promise from Arisugawa, Vice-President of the Council, that his views would be kept confidential, Ōkuma presented a memorial to the Emperor on March 11, 1881.

This document, which was drafted by Yano Fumio, one of his disciples, was a challenge to the views of the Satchō Councilors. He prefaced his memorial with an explanation of the operation of a parliamentary form of government. Next he outlined six steps which he believed to be prerequisites for the creation of such a government. He proposed that, after the question of membership for Parliament was settled, a definite date should be set for its opening and that this date should be publicly announced. To assure conformity of the government's policy with the will of the people, the leader of the majority party in Parliament should become Premier and should resign when he lost the confidence of the legislature. As in the British system, provisions should also be made for separate parliamentary secretaries and civil servants who would not be affected by the rise and fall of cabinets and who would afford a continuity of personnel.

Yet this was the extent of his liberalism. He could not bring himself to the point of trusting the majority. A product of his times, his views were almost as conservative as his colleagues on the question of how to draft the constitution. He believed that it should be framed by Imperial command and should not be forged from heated debate in a constituent assembly or a constitutional convention.

But the point in his memorial which was most embarrassing to the oligarchs concerned the date for the opening of Parliament. Itō and the others had urged postponement of such a move to avoid any threat to their power or to the prerogatives of the Emperor. On the other hand, the public was increasing its demands for the early formation of an elective body. Ōkuma capitalized on this movement and argued that the calling of a national assembly was an urgent matter. In fact, he insisted that the form of the new national government should be decided within the year (1881), that an election should be held in 1882, and that a Parliament should be called the next year.[9]

The impact of Ōkuma's demands, when they became known to Itō and the other Councilors, was tremendous and was the immediate cause for a showdown between the conservative Satchō leaders and Ōkuma and his supporters. It set off a chain reaction which led to Ōkuma publicly challenging the government's proposal in July to sell most of the properties owned and developed by the Hokkaidō Colonization Office. These two moves caused a crystallization of thought among the conservatives and acted as a catalyst for the precipitate steps taken by them against Ōkuma. In the end, this struggle resulted in the concentration of autocratic control in the hands of the Satchō oligarchs under Itō's leadership. It also spelled defeat for the supporters of representative government. This defeat had both an immediate and lasting effect. The immediate result was that the oligarchs allowed the formation of a constitutional monarchy with only limited powers granted to the people. Control was concentrated in the hands of the chief ministers. The lasting effect, as will be evident from subsequent accounts of the futile efforts of the liberal forces to direct Japan's policies prior to World War II, was to stifle the growth of democracy.

Obviously, Ōkuma's views, as expressed in his memorial in March, 1881, were not acceptable to such conservative Councilors as Iwakura and Itō. In fact, Iwakura had told Ōkuma personally that his request for an election the next year was ridiculous since it would be impossible to make the necessary preparations in time. When Itō saw the memorial —whether he was officially given a copy or took one surreptitiously from the files is an open question—he was enraged that Ōkuma should make such sweeping demands.

There had been disagreements before among the chief advisers of the Emperor, but never of such a deep-seated nature. Perhaps Itō foresaw that this rift over policy would evolve rapidly into a struggle for power between the conservatives and the "liberals." In a Council meeting on July 6 he openly challenged Ōkuma, accusing him of having formed an alliance with Fukuzawa and having reversed his previous support for a conservative constitution. Itō and the other Satchō oligarchs were fighting for a form of constitutional government which would protect the interests of their sovereign and themselves. Ōkuma was fighting for continued favor with the Emperor and for a constitutional monarchy which would give the people at least a minimum of rights.

Later that month, Ōkuma challenged the government's economic policy. He charged that his colleagues were aiding, abetting, and profiting from the proposed sale of the Hokkaidō Colonization Office. By his cry of scandal, he made the question of the disposition of government-owned industries a vital issue in the national debate on people's rights and constitutional government. In reality, by this act he forced a showdown on the question of who was the strongest man in the government. His position made the split between himself and the Itō–Iwakura–Yamagata clique irreparable.

The Hokkaidō Scandal

To understand the significance of Ōkuma's move, it is necessary to revert temporarily to the importance of Hokkaidō to the nation as a whole and to the program of liquidation of government-sponsored industries. At the beginning of the Meiji Restoration in 1868, the northern island of Hokkaidō was the one area in Japan which was not heavily populated nor developed. Colonization had been retarded because of its inaccessibility, its high mountains and heavy forests, and its cold climate. Geological surveys had revealed that it was one of the richest regions of natural resources throughout Japan and that it had great potential industrial possibilities. To capitalize on these potentialities, the government formed the Hokkaidō Colonization Office in 1869 and sponsored an energetic colonization and development program. Model factories and mines, breweries, machine shops, and sawmills were built with government funds. In fact, during the first eleven years of its existence, over 14 million yen had been invested by the Colonization Office.

The exploitation of this northern frontier had largely been the result of the energy and vision of Kuroda Kiyotaka, a clansman from Satsuma.[10] After his appointment in 1869 as Vice-Commissioner of Colonization, he visited the United States and solicited the technical assistance of leading American scientists and educators. Some of the most prominent of these included General Horace Capron, United States Commissioner of Agriculture, and Dr. William S. Clark, President of Massachusetts Agricultural College. These men, together with approximately seventy other foreign advisers and experts, developed the pattern which enabled Hokkaidō to become an important asset to the empire, as well as a laboratory for experiments in methods of colonization to be used later in Korea and Formosa.

Kuroda was also keenly aware of Hokkaidō's strategic importance. In this connection, he gave priority to the expansion of heavy industries. Simultaneously, colonists were transported at government expense and were formed into militia. This militia, which was organized as a defensive force against Russia, offered some protection but was not sufficient to prevent an attack from the north. To lessen the increasing tension between Japan and Russia, Kuroda urged abandonment of claims to Sakhalin and concentration on strengthening Hokkaidō. This policy led to the settlement with Russia in 1875 of Japan's northern boundary. The latter gave up all claims to Sakhalin in exchange for full control over all the Kurile Islands. (See Chapter 9.)

As in other parts of the nation, the successful operation and expansion of many of the industries started by the Colonization Office corresponded with the general shift in government policy from direct to indirect control and operation of nonstrategic industries, most of which no longer needed direct government subsidies for technical development, although many were operating at a loss. If the nonstrategic industries could be sold to private industrialists, they would no longer be a burden on the financial and technical resources of the state. Furthermore, the state then became free to devote its efforts toward enlarging the Army and Navy and developing the industries necessary to support them.

Heretofore, no clear-cut policy had been developed for disposing of a particular industrial plant or enterprise. In some cases, particularly among the strategic industries, the government retained control and ownership. In others, the factory or plant was sold to the original promoter at a nominal price. In still others, the industrialist who had built the factory himself was given a subsidy to encourage expansion. In all cases, there was a close relationship between key figures in the government and the new industrialists.

In view of the criticism which was growing against this apparent collusion between industry and government and the losses which the latter was sustaining, a new policy was formulated. In November, 1880, a Law on the Sale of Factories (*Kōjō Haraisage Gaisoku*) was promulgated. The government claimed that since the factories which were established for encouraging industrial development had become prosperous, they should be turned over to private ownership. It looked forward, however, to selling unprofitable enterprises at a low price to encourage the growth of private enterprise. Such a general program released the government of responsibilities that it no longer wished to carry. It also gave undeniable advantages to private enterprise and permitted questionable deals between businessmen and key officials in the Ministry of Industry, the Home Ministry, or other branches of the government responsible for the program.

Since the ten-year, government-sponsored program for Hokkaidō expired in 1881, the future of the Colonization Office had to be settled. A group of merchants including a fellow clansman of Kuroda's from Satsuma and some members of the Hokkaidō Colonization Office saw a rare opportunity to profit from the application of this law to the government projects under the office. In July, 1881, they set up two companies to purchase the real estate, distilleries, factories, mines, ships, shipyards, and other tangible assets of the Colonization Office. Their plan provided for the payment of a total of 387,000 yen for property whose actual value was probably fifty-four times that amount or 21,000,000 yen. It was also proposed that the new companies purchase the property in thirty yearly installments and that no interest be charged on the unpaid balance. Thus the entire investment could be purchased for a down payment of 10,000 yen or 1/2,000 of its estimated cost. This scheme was presented to Kuroda who approved it and forwarded it to the Council of State with a recommendation that it be accepted.

The question of whether to sell the Hokkaidō property immediately became a major political issue both within the Council of State and among the people at large. In July, the Council had rejected outright Ōkuma's proposals for a constitution and for the formation of an elected assembly within a year. Itō and other members of the Council, who had been enraged at Ōkuma for daring to present views which differed from theirs, saw in the move an attempt to oust them from leadership in the government.

At the same time Kuroda had been most reluctant to approve of any policy advocating a national assembly or parliament. He threatened to resign from the Council if it did not approve his Hokkaidō sale proposal. As the Satchō leaders were reluctant to go against Kuroda's wishes they finally approved the plan on July 30.

The Hokkaidō proposal gave Ōkuma an excellent means by which he could embarrass the government. He denounced Kuroda's proposal for what it obviously was—a colossal and brazen attempt by some within and close to the government to make enormous profits at the expense of the taxpayer. The leading newspapers, with encouragement and financial support from Iwasaki and the Mitsubishi interests, denounced it and the Satchō leadership within the government. Fukuzawa Yukichi, who had been encouraged to form a government-sponsored newspaper but now found Itō and the other leaders turned against him, was also vehement in his opposition to the Hokkaidō deal. Mass meetings sprang up at which the clan bureaucrats were severely criticized and Ōkuma's position was eulogized. He also found his position supported by such important figures in the government as the Minister of Finance Sano and Vice-President of the Council Sasaki. Many of the followers of Itagaki and persons who were shortly to organize the Liberal party (*Jiyūtō*) were eager to join the chorus of criticism against Kuroda, his plan, and his fellow clansmen and supporters from Chōshū.

Iwakura's Principles for a Constitution

In view of the power which the conservatives had already wielded in the government, it was unlikely that they would let this threat to their power and authority pass unchallenged. In fact, they were biding their time and knew that time was on their side. For several weeks, the Emperor had planned a tour of inspection to the north and northwest. It was the fifth of such carefully planned trips throughout the Empire and the first to the interior of Hokkaidō. The Imperial party, which included Ōkuma, departed from Tokyo on August 1 and did not return until October 11, 1881. In this interval, the oligarchs who remained behind in Tokyo planned their strategy carefully and well on three vital, interconnected problems. These were (1) the basic principles for the Constitution, (2) the future of the Hokkaidō Colonization Office, and (3) the disposition to be made of Ōkuma. In reference to the all-important question of the Constitution, Ōkuma's challenge for an immediate election had been rejected but no substitute proposal had been offered.

Specific ideas were taking shape, however, in the minds of several of the key officials. Minister of the Right Iwakura, who had always been close to the Emperor, was taken ill early in the summer. Before his departure for a rest cure on July 6, 1881, he presented a memorial to Prince Arisugawa on constitutional government and the methods which should be followed in drafting a constitution. This memorial had been prepared for Iwakura by Inouye Ki (Kowashi) reflecting the strong influence of Hermann Roesler, the German scholar of constitutional law and legal adviser to the government.[11] As these views on the procedure for adopting a constitution and on its basic principles were largely followed in the next few years, the importance of this memorial is obvious. Iwakura advocated:

1. Public announcement of the formation of a constitution-investigation commission.
2. Establishment of a drafting office within the palace under the direction of a Minister, secret preparation of the draft, and its presentation to the Council for discussion.
3. The secret preparation by three or four ministers of the draft constitution and the accompanying Imperial proclamation.

In this same memorandum, he was equally explicit on the basic principles for a constitution. He argued that the Emperor should be the source and authority for all steps connected with drafting a constitution. Furthermore, procedures should be followed which permitted the gradual adoption of constitutional government. Some matters, such as the rules for succession of the Emperor, did not properly belong in the constitution. Any such basic document should permit the Emperor to retain the following powers: supreme command of the Army and Navy; the right to declare war, make peace, and conclude treaties with foreign powers; supervision of the coinage; conferring of honors; granting of an armistice; and authority to close, prorogue, dissolve, or open the Diet. He should also be given the right personally to appoint or dismiss the highest officials in the government.

Iwakura also recommended certain features for the Cabinet and Parliament which were designed to increase the power of the former and reduce the strength of the people's elected representatives in the latter. For example, he suggested that Cabinet members did not necessarily have to be members of Parliament. The various Ministers of State should be individually responsible for their action to the Emperor in contrast to the accepted concept in most constitutional monarchies of collective responsibility of the Cabinet. The Imperial Diet should be bicameral; the Senate, or upper house, was to be composed of Imperial appointees or persons elected by the peerage. The lower house, the People's Elected Assembly (*Minsen In*), should have only restricted power. In the first place its members should be selected by an electorate restricted to those who were property owners. Furthermore, Parliament should not have the right to interfere with the formation of a Cabinet.

His memorial contained three other important suggestions designed to strengthen the position of the Emperor and that of his chosen ministers. Significantly, all three of these proposals were incorporated in the Constitution when it appeared eight years later. Perhaps the most important of these points was that concerning the budget. He recommended that if Parliament rejected or refused to pass the budget as presented by the government, the budget of the previous year should automatically go into effect.[12] As such a constitutional provision would deprive Parliament of its all-important control over finances, its adoption made a non-confidence vote meaningless. Second, Iwakura recommended that limitations should be placed on the other powers of Parliament. Third, similar restraint should control the judiciary.

He concluded his memorial by pointing to what he considered to be the weaknesses in the British parliamentary system. He noted that in England the King's wishes were subject to the majority will of Parliament and that "the Cabinet was at the mercy of the dominant party" in the House of Commons. Iwakura argued that if the British pattern were followed, the Japanese tradition of supreme power of the Imperial throne would be broken. Consequently, he urged adoption of the Prussian pattern in which Parliament was consulted, but in which the sovereign had the real authority and power.[13] Having presented his position, Iwakura left for the west and remained away from the capital for two months.

Ōkuma Is Ousted

In the meantime, opposition among some of the other Councilors was mounting against Ōkuma. In fact, if Itō and some of his colleagues had had their wish, Ōkuma would have been forced to resign rather than be permitted to go with the Emperor on his northern tour. Shortly after Ōkuma left Tokyo, rumors circulated that he was responsible for the foundation of a close alliance with the writer and educator, Fukuzawa Yukichi, and the entrepreneur, Iwasaki Yatarō. Kuroda claimed that the former was Ōkuma's political strategist and the latter his financial supporter and that all three were working to overthrow the Satchō oligarchs and to set up a constitutional government acceptable to them. Much was also made of the failure of Ōkuma's financial policies as Minister of Finance and of the fact that the national reserve was found to be 4 million yen less than he had reported.

These rumors were not as fantastic as they appeared. If Ōkuma had retained Imperial favor and formed a Cabinet, he would, in all probability, have supported a constitution based on a political philosophy similar to that which Fukuzawa advocated. Iwasaki, who came from Tosa, doubtless would have been delighted to see the clansmen from Chōshū and Satsuma ousted. If a new regime were established under the direction of his friends and with his financial support, he would be sure to profit from it. Moreover, there were indications of close financial ties between Ōkuma, Fukuzawa, and Iwasaki. While Ōkuma had been Minister of Finance, he had received a memorandum from Fukuzawa on the advisability of establishing a new bank. Shortly thereafter, Iwasaki helped to finance the government's new bank for foreign transactions, the Yokohama Specie Bank. Furthermore, Fukuzawa had acted as intermediary for Iwasaki when the latter purchased the Takashima Coal Mine. Finally, all three men were openly opposed to the proposed plan to sell the Hokkaidō properties for a mere pittance.

Even though Iwakura, Itō, and the other oligarchs had not yet developed a plan to oust Ōkuma, the Hokkaidō scandal continued to be increasingly embarrassing to the government leaders. In early September, 1881, Sanjō Sanetomi, acting President of the Council, became concerned over the turn of events. He wrote Iwakura, who was still away from the capital on a rest cure, that since Ōkuma had labeled the Hokkaidō sale plan as graft, the Council of State was becoming pressed to the limit and should postpone the sale of the Hokkaidō properties but stand firm on the constitution issue. He pleaded that Iwakura return to the capital. This letter was followed by an urgent telegram three weeks later which brought Iwakura to Tokyo less than one week before the return of the Emperor and Ōkuma. The stage was rapidly set for the final scene of the drama.

Upon Iwakura's return, he agreed with Sanjō that the government had made a mistake in approving the Hokkaidō deal. He realized that postponement of the sale would automatically deprive the opposition of one of its main points of grievance. Hence, he urged that Imperial sanction should be sought for a cancellation of the plan to sell the properties. Second, he recommended that a formal announcement should be made that the Emperor favored the formation of a constitutional government and that a parliament was to be opened by a specific date.

During the next few days, five of the Councilors (Sanjō, Itō, Saigō Tsugumichi, Yamada, and Iwakura) met to clarify these decisions and to put them in writing for the Emperor's approval. They also decided on procedures to be followed to oust Ōkuma. They agreed that the chief ministers should confer with the Emperor immediately upon his return. At that time they would seek his consent to the resignation of Ōkuma and the postponement of the Hokkaidō sales. They would also present him with a draft edict for his signature, which would announce a date for the opening of a parliament and would order changes in the Council of State and the Senate.

On October 11, 1881, the Emperor and his party returned to Tokyo. That night the Councilors, except Ōkuma, who purposely was not invited, met with the Emperor. They obtained his consent to Ōkuma's resignation; they also received his approval of an innocuous announcement about the opening of a national assembly. When Ōkuma went to the Imperial Palace the next day to submit his resignation, he found the situation so radically changed that he was reduced to being treated "as a criminal," was firmly rejected by the guards, and could not even be received in audience. He was then told that he had been dismissed from the government. The edict proclaiming the establishment of a parliament in the future set the date, not two years hence, as urged by Ōkuma, but in nine years or by 1890. It continued with the request that necessary preparations should be made in the meantime for formation of a constitutional government. It added that a subsequent proclamation would deal with matters such as "the limitations upon the Imperial prerogative and the constitution of parliament." Lest the opposition misinterpret what the Emperor had in mind, the edict concluded:

> We perceive the tendency of Our people is to advance too rapidly, and without that thought and consideration which alone can make progress enduring, and We warn Our subjects, high and low, to be mindful of Our will, and those

who may advocate sudden and violent changes, thus disturbing the peace of Our realm, will fall under Our displeasure.[14]

Thus the die was cast on the fateful night of October 11, 1881. The counsels of the conservatives had prevailed and the Japanese were to be granted by 1890 a constitution drafted secretly by the men who had successfully ousted Ōkuma, the main threat to their position. It is quite true that this announcement of a parliamentary government stimulated the activities of the so-called political parties. It is also true that Itō, who was to be in charge of drafting the Constitution, went abroad to study foreign forms of government.

But it is equally true that Iwakura and Itō had finally realized that their concepts of a limited constitutional monarchy were threatened if Ōkuma gained control. Perhaps his criticism of the Hokkaidō proposal presaged a movement to challenge the economic policies and program of the government. It was too great a risk for the oligarchs to run. During his absence with the Emperor on his two and a half months' journey, Itō and Iwakura had worked effectively and well among their colleagues to win support for Ōkuma's ouster. They had also drafted and obtained approval of an edict on the new Constitution which permitted the acceptance of Iwakura's political philosophy. Nine years was more than enough time to win support for a form of constitutional monarchy which gave the sovereign and his ministers wide powers and limited the rights of his subjects. The conservatives had met successfully the first real challenge to the continuance of their favored position.

In conclusion, it is important to remember that many of the accounts of Japan's political history have put greater emphasis on the years *subsequent to,* rather than *prior to,* Ōkuma's ouster. Some stress the Prussian influence on Itō after 1882, others the importance of the suppressive laws of 1885 and 1888 in throttling the opposition when the Constitution was being drafted. Still others emphasize the rise of the political parties and certain "democratic features" of the Constitution.

But none of these interpretations seems to stand up against the facts. Let it be re-emphasized that Ōkuma's challenge had two phases. His first memorial in March, 1881, challenged accepted political concepts; his criticism of the Hokkaidō deal in July, 1881, was directed against basic economic policies. In reality, by his two memorials, he had raised the basic and fundamental issue of whether he or Itō was to be the leader under the new Constitution. Furthermore, the ideas expressed in Iwakura's memo of July 6, 1881; the political maneuvers during the summer and fall of that year; and the reversal of the policy on Hokkaidō all point conclusively to the fact that the key figures in the government had agreed, prior to October 11, 1881, when Ōkuma was ousted, on the type of constitution Japan should have. The important decisions were made and the stage was set for an autocratic type of government *before* rather than *after* Itō received his appointment in 1882 as Minister of Constitutional Matters. The details of content and of the drafting of the Constitution remained to be settled, but nine years was ample time for that.

Notes

1. Tsuchiya Takao, *Zoku Nihon Keizai Shi Gaiyō* (Tokyo: Iwanami, 1941), p. 66. Johannes Hirschmeier, *The Origin of Entrepreneurship in Meiji Japan* (Cambridge: Harvard University Press, 1964), p. 30.

2. Tsuchiya, *op. cit.*, pp. 87 ff.

3. Two of the largest trading and financial firms owned by a single family were the House of Mitsui and the Mitsubishi Company. The House of Mitsui was near collapse at the end of the Tokugawa period but it decided to support the new Meiji regime. By 1874 it held 3.8 million yen interest from money loaned the government. During the Satsuma rebellion of 1877 it supplied two-thirds of the provisions for the campaign. The leader of the firm, Mitsui Hachiroemon, held key positions in fifteen different government-supported enterprises. The success of Mitsui was also due to the organizational ability of Minomura Rizaemon, its head director, who had knit the organization together by the time of his death in 1877. He moved the firm's headquarters to Tokyo in 1873 and was a close friend of Inouye Kaoru.

Iwasaki Yatarō (1834–1885) was the founder of the Mitsubishi Company. As indicated earlier, he developed a trading company in Tosa and through his close friendship with Ōkuma early received favors from the government. See Hirschmeier, *op. cit.*, pp. 213 ff.

4. See Thomas C. Smith, *Political Change and Industrial Development in Japan: Government Enterprise, 1868–1880* (Stanford: Stanford University Press, 1955), p. 64.

5. Shibusawa Eiichi (1840–1931) was the son of a rich farmer. In the early years of his life he vacillated between supporting the movement to overthrow the Tokugawa regime and working for it. Having been raised to warrior rank by the Tokugawa government, he served it loyally until its downfall. In 1867, he accompanied the Shogun's brother to the Paris Exposition. He remained abroad a year during which time he was struck with the importance of businessmen in European countries and vowed he would spend his life on the modernization of Japan's economy. Upon his return home in 1868, he was persuaded by Ōkuma Shigenobu to accept a position in the Ministry of Finance where he worked closely with Inouye Kaoru. He finally left the government in 1872 to devote himself exclusively to private business and finance. He continued to oppose excessive military expenditures such as the expedition to Formosa in 1874. In addition to the spinning and weaving factories which he built, Shibusawa was a pioneer in banking. He helped organize the "First National Bank" (*Daiichi Ginkō*) in November, 1872, and later saved it from ruin. As its president, he not only played a key role in the development of new banks but in the training of their leaders and the development of national banking policies. Through the successful operation of the Ōsaka Spinning Mill, which by 1888 had become one of the largest industrial establishments in Japan, Shibusawa was considered the leader in cotton spinning. In later years, as one of Japan's leading entrepreneurs, he invested heavily in private

railways and shipping and strongly advocated the joint-stock company as the best means to develop Japan's economy. This latter policy led to rivalry between the two largest family companies, the Mitsubishi and Mitsui. Before his retirement in 1909 he had been influential in the establishment of over 240 companies. See Yasuzo Horie, "Modern Entrepreneurship in Meiji Japan," and Johannes Hirschmeier, "Shibusawa Eiichi: Industrial Pioneer," in *The State and Economic Enterprise in Japan,* William W. Lockwood (ed.) (Princeton: Princeton University Press, 1965), pp. 183–247.

6. Total paper currency in circulation in 1881, when Matsukata's policy of retrenchment and conversion was inaugurated, equaled 154 million yen. See Asahi Shimbun (eds.), *Meiji Taishō Shi* (Tokyo: Asahi Shimbun, 1930–1932), III, p. 42.

7. Ōuchi Hyōe and Tsuchiya Takao (eds.), "Kōbushō Enkaku Hōkoku," in *Meiji Zenki Zaisei Keizai Shiryō* (21 vols.; Tokyo: Kaizōsha, 1931–1936), XVII, pp. 265 ff. In 1873, at Itō's request, a six-year school of engineering was established within the Ministry by Henry Dyer. Dr. Dyer, a distinguished graduate of the University of Glasgow, remained in Japan until 1882. For these and other British influences on the development of Japanese science see Grace Fox, *Britain and Japan, 1858–1883* (Oxford: Clarendon Press, 1969), pp. 457 ff.

8. For example, Yasuda Zenjirō (1838–1921), founder of the Yasuda interests, was the son of a poor warrior who came to Edo where he became a daring banker, stressing maximum profits for his enterprises. Ōkura Kihachirō (1837–1928) was a landowner–farmer who sold rifles during the Restoration, went abroad, and returned with an unquenchable desire to improve Japan. The Ōkura Trading Company, founded in 1873, thrived on government contracts and expanded into construction, trading, mining, and maritime insurance. For these and other examples see Hirschmeier, *The Origin of Entrepreneurship . . . , op. cit.,* pp. 226 ff.

9. Ōtsu Jun'ichirō, *Dai Nihon Kensei Shi* (10 vols.; Tokyo: Hobun-kan, 1927–1928), II, pp. 420 ff.; and Andrew Fraser, "The Expulsion of Ōkuma from the Government in 1881," *Journal of Asian Studies* (February, 1967), pp. 217 ff.

10. Kuroda Kiyotaka (1840–1900) was born in Kagoshima and had fought against the British when they attacked the city in 1863. He was influential in cementing the alliance of his clan with that of Chōshū before the Restoration. He later became Prime Minister, Privy Councilor, and finally Elder Statesman.

11. Inouye Ki (Kowashi) (1844–1895) had considerable knowledge of constitutional law. In 1874 he translated the Prussian Constitution. Later he was to become the chairman of the group largely responsible for the drafting of the Constitution and the Imperial House Laws. In 1881 he relied heavily on Roesler for advice and learned from him about the operation of the Prussian Constitution.

Hermann Roesler (1834–1894) was Professor of Law at the University of Rostock from 1862 to 1878. An ardent advocate of "monarchial constitutionalism," he was selected in 1878 by the Japanese representative in Berlin, Aoki Shūzō, as legal adviser to the Foreign Office. For his first three years in Japan he worked on treaty revision problems. In 1881 he became legal adviser to the government as a whole and began to exert a significant influence on problems of constitutional and legal reform. In 1877 he had written a strong criticism of Bismarck and the Prussian Constitution, indicating his belief that a parliamentary form of government was the ideal. His memoranda to Inouye in 1881 strongly supported monarchial constitutionalism as the model for Japan. He envisaged the monarchy as the institution around which law and order could be built. He also condemned the British Parliamentary system as an absorption of political power by the majority through the Cabinet, thus preventing the monarch from governing.

In Johannes Siemes' study, *Hermann Roesler and the Making of the Meiji Constitution* (Tokyo: Sophia University Press, 1966), much new information on Roesler is available. This book corrects some of the "highly inaccurate" information which its author has accused me of passing on in the first edition of this book (see Siemes, *op. cit.*, p. 2). I have corrected the name of the university where he taught and the spelling of his name. Furthermore, Siemes' accusation that such an important figure deserves more than "fragmentary" treatment is partially met by the present footnote and further reference in the text to Roesler's role in connection with the drafting of the Constitution.

Siemes is obviously an ardent advocate of Roesler and his political philosophy and seems to overemphasize his importance. For example, it is clear from the memorials on the future form of government which the oligarchs presented to the throne in 1878 and 1879 that they had already formed their own firm views on the philosophical basis of a parliamentary government in Japan, influenced by their visit to Prussia in 1872. Roesler, like Rudolph von Gneist and Lorenz von Stein, who taught Itō in 1882, seems to have acted more like a catalyst on the oligarchs in solidifying beliefs they had previously acquired, rather than presenting them with a new political philosophy. Roesler's role in connection with the Meiji Constitution was not known publicly until fifty years later. See Siemes, *op. cit.*, pp. 1–12; Suzuki Yasuzo, "Hermann Roesler und die Japanische Verfassung," *Monumenta Nipponica*, IV (1941), pp. 443–53; and Suzuki Yasuzo, *Kempō Seitei to Roesure* (The Making of the Constitution and Roesler) (Tokyo: 1942). See also George Akita, *Foundations of Constitutional Government in Modern Japan, 1868–1900* (Cambridge: Harvard University Press, 1967).

12. This provision of the old budget carrying over was strongly urged by Roesler. The Prussian budget crisis of 1862–1865 had convinced him of the need for such a provision if the Emperor and his advisers were to retain control over Parliament. See Siemes, *op. cit.*, pp. 29–30, 105–8, and 111–12.

13. See Ōtsu, *op. cit.*, II, pp. 411–19, for the text of Iwakura's memorial.

14. W. W. McLaren, "Japanese Government Documents," *Transactions of the Asiatic Society of Japan*, XLII (1914), pp. 86–87.

8

The Adoption of the Meiji Constitution, 1881–1889

Although Itō and his conservative colleagues had won their battle with Ōkuma, their preferential position was not unassailable until their views and their authority had been incorporated into a new constitution. The Emperor had cautioned against precipitate action and had set nine years hence as the target date for the calling of Parliament. If the oligarchs were to capitalize on their victories thus far, they would have to be on constant guard against any significant threat to their position during the period in which the forms of a constitutional monarchy were being worked out.

By their decision to reverse themselves on the Hokkaidō deal as a result of widespread, articulate, and indignant opposition, the oligarchs had lost considerable prestige and popularity. Furthermore, there was always the possibility that an extremist might rally enough support among the general populace to resort to direct action either against the chief ministers individually or against the government as a whole. Ōkubo had been killed only a few years earlier as an aftermath of the Saigō Rebellion. Another fanatical nationalist might attack those who had ousted Ōkuma or any other Councilor for an alleged act of disloyalty. Furthermore, the nation faced a financial crisis which was going to require Finance Minister Matsukata to take severe and unpopular measures.

Thus the history of the seven and a half years, from Ōkuma's dismissal on October 11, 1881, to the promulgation of the Constitution on February 11, 1889, is one in which the government took such action as it considered necessary to maintain control while it prepared a constitution.

New rules and regulations kept the Liberal and Progressive parties within bounds and caused their demise only a few years after they were formed. A short depression and the government failure to obtain the cancellation of "unequal clauses" in the peace treaties were prevented from creating a strong and effective antigovernment movement by strict police surveillance. The secrecy which surrounded the drafting and approval of the new Constitution by a handful of selected Ministers assured the acceptance of a document which preserved the special prerogatives of the throne and granted only a minimum of rights and privileges to the people.

No sooner had Ōkuma been eliminated than a complete reshuffle took place in the government. The first move was to order the creation of a new, semiexecutive, semilegislative body called the "*Sanji-In.*" Its functions were to assist in drafting laws and regulations forwarded from the Council of State. At the same time, it could present drafts of new laws on its own initiative for the Council's approval. The heads of the six sections of the *Sanji-In*—Foreign Affairs, Home Affairs, Military Affairs, Finance, Justice, and Legislative—were to be appointed by the President from among its members. These executive departments continued to operate until the formation of a Cabinet in 1885.

As had been true of all the organs of the central government, however, the most important point was not what the avowed functions of the organs might be, but who were the key figures in these organs. Hence, it was of special significance that Itō Hirobumi was Chairman of the new *Sanji-In* which he had helped to create. Furthermore, Terashima Munenori (1833–1893) from Satsuma was the new President of the Council of State, having replaced a Hizen clansman. In other words, the Satchō oligarchy had consolidated its hold over the key positions of a reorganized government.

Formation of the Liberal and Progressive Parties

These acts of the oligarchs, especially their dismissal of Ōkuma, only stimulated the leaders of the people's rights movement into action. Despite the fact that they were fighting against heavy odds, the antigovernment forces refused to be silenced. Before the end of 1881, the Liberal party (*Jiyūtō*) completed its formal inauguration and Itagaki Taisuke was elected its first president. As intimated above, it supported a form of government which would give the people a voice in public affairs. It opposed government interference in the private affairs of the individual and advocated general education so that there would be an enlightened public opinion. As Ueki Emori, one of the most articulate leaders stated, "To criticize freely the merit of legislation is necessary for the well-being of the state."

The more the leaders of the Meiji government made secret decisions, the more irate the Liberal party leaders became over the fact that they and the people were in ignorance of what transpired. Despite strenuous efforts to increase the party's numerical strength, however, it never had an important national membership. Even its advocacy of lower taxes and other policies favorable to the peasants did not materially increase its size. It was primarily a local group in Tosa and its membership was ridiculously small. Only 101 members are recorded for the early months of its existence; just prior to its dissolution in 1884 there were about 2,100 members. But the influence of its leaders was far greater than that of its actual membership.

The other important antigovernment party, the Progressive party (*Kaishintō*) was founded by Ōkuma. In the previous discussion of him and his role in the struggle for a liberal constitution and for greater people's rights, he has been treated as one of the regular members of the oligarchy. Although he was the chief spokesman within the government who opposed ultraconservatism, it is not correct to classify him as a "liberal" in the same category with Itagaki, a practice followed by many of the writers on the democratic movement. It is true that in October, 1881, Ōkuma was so vitally interested in a constitution which would guarantee the rights of the people that he was willing to be broken politically for these views.

It is equally true, however, that he, like any realistic politician, hoped that his moves, plus the people's exacerbation over the Hokkaidō scandal, would increase his power and enable him to challenge Itō successfully. In other words, whereas he was interested in the movement for popular rights and constitutional government, he was a conservative liberal on the one hand and a politician on the other. Moreover, there are certain other factors which make Ōkuma seem of only secondary importance as a liberal. For example, he did not begin actively to organize a political party until after he was outside the government. Furthermore, his willingness in 1888 to come back into the government during the premiership of Kuroda Kiyotaka, whom he had fought on the Hokkaidō issue, indicates a vacillation and opportunism not evidenced by Itagaki.

As a politician, Ōkuma rallied around himself the urban intelligentsia, industrialists, and some conservatives outside the government. He formed his Progressive party in March, 1882, which adopted the motto of "Slow and Steady." It favored preservation of the dignity of the Imperial Household, extension of internal reforms, strengthening of local government, and the extension of the franchise. Like the Liberal party, it was small numerically but symbolized and represented the views of a much larger group. But these two parties were to go out of existence long before the Constitution was promulgated or a national election was held, so that they should not be thought of as political parties in the strict sense. They were more like political clubs whose members were loyal to the leaders and supported the loosely defined "people's rights movement."

The tragedy of the early liberal movement, from the point of view of the political parties becoming an effective leavening influence in Japan's constitutional development, was that the parties and political leaders fought among each other. Rather than closing ranks when governmental pressure increased and directing their attack at the evils of the oligarchy, the Liberal and Progressive parties allowed the government to drive a wedge between them and to increase their animosity for each other. If they had swallowed their pride and stood together against any move to suppress the people's rights, they would have been far more effective.

Rivalry Within the Party Movement

The outstanding example of this rift within the party movement was the treatment accorded Itagaki and the reaction it created among the followers of Ōkuma and the Progressives. In the first place, an attempt was made on Itagaki's life in April, 1882, after one of his political speeches. He was wounded but not mortally and soon recovered. His convalescence was speeded by receipt of an Imperial gift of money, a gesture which indicated the high esteem in which he was held. At the same time, the government feared his political potentialities. Consequently, several of the chief ministers conceived of a plan whereby his influence could be temporarily diminished and he could be weaned away from his party.

They sought financial assistance from the Mitsui interests for an extended trip abroad for him and his colleague Gotō. He accepted the offer and announced his plans for the trip. Several important party leaders, including the popular writer and novelist, Suehiro Tetchō, violently opposed the project. They claimed that a trip at this critical juncture of Japan's political development was equivalent to abandoning the movement for representative government. Others, particularly members of the rival Progressive party, claimed that the funds for the trip came from a questionable deal made by the government and the Mitsui interests. They maintained that the Japanese Army had renewed its contracts with Mitsui after the latter had promised to finance Itagaki's trip. The Progressive party's newspapers insisted that he had no right to go unless he divulged the source of his support.

No one was quite sure whether Itagaki was aware, when he left, that he was traveling on Mitsui's funds. His supporters ignored the issue and launched a frontal attack on his critics. They called for the destruction of the "Sea Monster," the Mitsubishi interests, which financed the Progressive party. In doing so, they referred to the steamship monopoly which Iwasaki Yatarō, founder of the Mitsubishi, had developed largely through close association with Ōkuma while he was in the government.

Their criticism was an appropriate one as the Mitsui interests had been able to form a rival steamship company only after Ōkuma had left the Finance Ministry and been forced out of the government.

It was a public secret that the two largest financial houses, the Mitsui and Mitsubishi, had found it to their self-interest to be closely associated with a political party. Hence, the incriminations were well-founded and a close Liberal party–Mitsui and Progressive party–Mitsubishi liaison developed. Not only was this close relationship to continue as the old parties evolved into modern parties but business rivalries came to be added to political antagonisms. In the 1880's, this ill feeling created an irreconcilable schism between the parties. The recriminations and equally vehement denials diverted the energies and the venom of the antigovernment forces from the central issue of oligarchical control under an absolute monarchy. When Itagaki returned from his trip, his colleagues were fighting the rival party, not the clan bureaucrats. Furthermore, the scandals and strife between the parties antagonized the public toward the democratic movement.

In the meantime, the conservatives took advantage of this conflict and made it even more difficult for the parties to function. The laws regulating the press and public meetings and associations were strengthened. Proprietors, managers, and editors of newspapers and magazines were made personally responsible for statements critical of established policy. The law restricting political meetings and prohibiting attendance at them by members of the armed forces, by public servants, and by teachers and students was strictly enforced. Political arrests increased, and it became almost impossible for the parties to survive.

Economic conditions also weakened the popular movement. Matsukata had become the new Finance Minister in 1881 and immediately began a deflationary program. He froze government expenditures for four years, retired the notes in circulation, purchased specie abroad, and brought business expansion to a halt. Prices tumbled and land taxes increased. Whereas previously the landowner had had funds to support the party movement, after 1881 he was struggling to keep from being dispossessed from his land.

At the same time, the radical elements in the two parties, particularly those in the *Jiyūtō,* found support among the hard-pressed and discontented tenants and small farmers. Revolts of farmers faced with heavier taxes or foreclosures increased in number and size. The party leaders were justifiably accused of instigating them. Many of the revolts occurred in the silk-growing area northwest of Tokyo as a result of the fall in silk prices. A noteworthy episode was the uprising in May, 1884, in Takasaki in Gumma Prefecture. One of the ringleaders was a member of the prefectural assembly and another was a leader of the Liberal party in the adjoining prefecture. Members of the Tokyo branch of the party came to Takasaki and attended meetings with the local officials and inhabitants. They advocated direct action against the government and began to train their own special military units. Their plot to assassinate several high officials was uncovered in time to frustrate an open attack on the city's army garrison. The central government became alarmed lest the general economic depression lead to a general uprising under the leadership of the parties. Consequently, it passed new laws which made it impossible for the parties to function effectively. With a loss of their main financial support, the parties disappeared in 1884. The *Jiyūtō* dissolved and the *Kaishintō* lost its leadership.

The Clan Bureaucrats Plan a Constitution, 1882–1887

With the party movement for representative government securely under control, the Emperor's chief ministers and advisers were free to proceed with the preparation of a constitution which reflected their political philosophy. In particular, the steps which were taken reveal the skill of Itō Hirobumi as a politician in achieving his objectives. As early as 1876, when Arisugawa, Vice-President of the Council, presented a draft of a constitution which would have placed the revenues of the Imperial Household under legislative control, divided legislative powers between the Emperor and a separate legislative body, and given the Senate the right to impeach the state ministers, Itō's objections eventually killed the draft.

In March, 1882, only five months after the Emperor stated that a constitution would be promulgated by 1890, Itō Hirobumi received an Imperial command to proceed abroad to study foreign constitutions. He later wrote that he had been sent on his mission:

> . . . to make as thorough a study as possible of the actual workings of different systems of constitutional government, of their various provisions, as well as of theories and opinions actually entertained by influential persons.[1]

As President of the newly formed *Sanji-In,* he was the key person in the government concerned with the drafting of the basic laws of the land. The Imperial Councilors had already approved a constitutional monarchy, which preserved the position, authority, and dignity of the throne.

They also clearly realized, from their visit to Prussia ten years earlier, that it offered one of the most fruitful plans for study. This belief was reinforced in the minds of the ruling oligarchy by Hermann Roesler who looked on the current people's rights movement with distrust and apprehension. He was diametrically opposed to the concept of individual freedom and saw the movement as a threat to the sovereignty of the

Emperor. It is not surprising, therefore, that Itō went directly to Berlin where the Japanese Minister, Aoki Shūzō, had arranged for the famous political scientist, Professor Rudolph von Gneist, to give Itō a special series of lectures on constitutional law. In these lectures, which Gneist held thrice weekly for nearly three months, he argued against adopting characteristics of the American or French Constitution. In his opinion, problems of diplomacy, the organization of the military establishments, and property owned by the Imperial family should not be subject to the decisions of the legislative body. In fact the power of Parliament should be limited and that of the ministers of state strengthened. Specifically, there should be a limit on the former's budgetary power and on those eligible to vote.[2]

From Gneist, and later from Lorenz von Stein in Vienna, Itō found ample evidence to use on his return to refute the arguments of those who opposed his political philosophy. In another sense, he found verification of the basic ideas which he and Iwakura had already accepted and which had been expounded by Roesler. Itō could well afford, without jeopardizing his objectives, to stop in England on his return trip to listen to a single lecture on representative government by Herbert Spencer.

Itō and his party returned to Tokyo in 1883. The government, obviously guided by Itō's experience, set about making the necessary administrative changes to assure the formation of a limited constitutional monarchy consistent with his political philosophy. Gneist had argued that it would be unwise to establish a constitutional convention. Itō had been impressed with his reasoning on this point and forthwith recommended a special office for the study of constitutional and administrative reforms. A bureau, known as the Commission to Investigate the Constitution (*Seido Torishirabe Kyoku*), was announced in March, 1884. It was made a branch of the Imperial Household Ministry and Itō was appointed its Chairman. Consequently, work could be carried on in strictest secrecy and in collaboration with the personal wishes of the Emperor. Under these conditions, the public would neither be permitted nor dare to intervene directly.

At the same time, the system of nobility was remodeled so as to strengthen the hands of the conservatives. Finally, at the end of the next year (1885) the old system of Councilors was reorganized and a Cabinet system was set up. Itō became the first Prime Minister while several of the key posts within the Cabinet were assigned to his fellow clansmen.[3]

At the age of forty-four, he had achieved a position in the new government with powers comparable to that of his European idol, Bismarck, the German Chancellor. He was concurrently Prime Minister, Minister of the Imperial Household, and Chairman of the Commission to Investigate the Constitution. Furthermore, the new power given his fellow clansman

Yamagata as Home Minister had already caused the dissolution of the political parties and broken the back of the agrarian movement. The office of Lord Keeper of the Privy Seal was created and a national civil service organized. Finally, the government talked in general terms about representative institutions which would be created by the new Constitution, but no document had yet been drafted and no official recommendations as to its contents had been made public. Consequently, the opposition had nothing tangible to criticize and simply had to wait and hope for the best. Itō and his colleagues must have been well satisfied with the way opposition to their plans had been kept to a minimum.

In the face of these developments, public interest in politics began to decline. People as a whole resigned themselves to what had always been considered as inevitable in the operation of the government; namely, that "the authorities" who were in positions of responsibility would take matters into their own hands and inform the public of their decisions after they had been made. As Fukuzawa expressed it:

> The general mass of the people is indifferent to political power and ignorant of its value. They are satisfied if the government issues an order.

Hence, there was a general apathy toward the whole question of drafting of the Constitution. This attitude was somewhat offset by a general curiosity as to how much power would be granted Parliament and what rights would be assured the Emperor's subjects.[4]

Concentrated work on the Constitution by Itō and his colleagues was not begun until 1886. In passing, it should be noted that after it had been announced in 1881 that a constitution would be prepared, the bureaucrats had taken five years to reach the point of beginning to draft the basic document. By postponing their work, much of the ardor of those who urged greater rights for the people had been cooled by the passage of time. Furthermore, Itō had been preoccupied with other duties. He had been holding conferences with Li Hung-chang on the thorny question of Japanese and Chinese rights in Korea. (See Chapter 9.) Itō also realized that the longer he postponed the completion of the final draft of the new Constitution, the less time his opponents would have to organize and solidify the opposition prior to the deadline of 1890. With important administrative changes well behind him, therefore, Itō assigned specific tasks to his associates. Inouye Ki was primarily responsible for the preparation of the drafts of the Constitution and of the Imperial House Laws. He kept in close touch with Roesler and consulted him constantly but always acted as the leader of the group.[5] Itō Miyoji, who had gone to Europe with Itō Hirobumi in 1882–1883, worked on the laws for Parliament; and Kaneko Kentarō, a former student of Harvard University, compiled the election laws.

All of them operated under certain general principles which had formed in Itō Hirobumi's mind after his return from Europe. In the first place, he believed that since the Imperial system had been the essence of the country, the new Constitution and its supporting laws must preserve the Emperor's dignity and power. He insisted that, in granting rights and limited freedom to the people, special care should be taken not to limit the prestige of the Emperor. He later explained that in European countries religion was made the axis of the state, but that in Japan neither Confucianism nor Shintōism had sufficient power to control the people. Hence, neither of these religions could appropriately become such an axis. He concluded, therefore, that the Emperor alone should be the axis of the Japanese state and that the Constitution should verify and emphasize that principle. Another general principle that Itō had learned from von Stein was that the text of any constitution should be as simple as possible to permit broad latitude in its interpretation. Finally, he insisted that heavy reliance be placed on Prussian political theory.

By the spring of 1887 three drafts were completed; two were compiled by Inouye on the basis of Itō's suggestions and principles, and the third had been written by Roesler. In the summer of that year Inouye, Itō Miyoji, and Kaneko visited Itō Hirobumi at his summer villa. There all four of them, with the three drafts at hand, worked without interruption until they had produced a fourth draft to which only a few changes were made prior to its formal presentation to the Emperor and Privy Council. Except for the fact that a copy of one of the drafts had been stolen, their work was kept secret from the public. In fact, they had not even given any indication to the public of the contents of the proposed draft; nor did the public know how far the drafting had proceeded.

Complications Over Revisions of the Treaties

Just at this juncture, international developments shifted general interest away from the problems of the proposed Constitution. By their position in the Cabinet and by the methods used to prepare an official draft text, Itō and his colleagues had protected themselves from effective criticism. On the problem of the revision of the treaties with Western powers, however, they found themselves in a vulnerable position. They had constantly insisted that all their actions were motivated by a desire to exalt and strengthen their country and their Emperor. On the other hand, the lack of progress on treaty revision seemed to belie this purpose. Several clauses in the treaties with the Western powers clearly infringed on Japan's sovereignty and national dignity. For example, the clauses which permitted extraterritoriality for Europeans and limited Japan's freedom to determine its own import and export duties still remained unchanged. A rising patriotism and national pride had produced violent objections to the extraterritoriality clauses.

Practical considerations created demands for revisions of the tariffs. When Ōkuma became Minister of Finance in 1873 he realized that tariff autonomy was essential if he was to place the country's budget on a firm basis. Whereas in 1888 a country such as the United States derived half of its revenue from tariffs, Japan collected only 5 per cent of its income from import and export duties. It was imperative, therefore, for Japan to obtain tariff autonomy as soon as possible.

But early attempts at revision had failed miserably. After the Iwakura Mission had been rebuffed by the Western powers in 1873, the government leaders had realized that many domestic reforms were necessary before successful negotiations for revisions could be completed. For example, none of the Western powers would approve of revisions until modern Western-style civil and criminal codes and law courts were in operation. No European nation would be willing to have its citizens tried under a feudal code of ethics. So long as the old codes continued, the Western powers insisted on the continuation of extraterritoriality.

Futile negotiations dragged on intermittently for several years while the people clamored for their successful conclusion. After the British Minister reminded the Japanese government in 1884 that revision of the treaties was contingent upon the adoption by Japan of Western legal standards, the work of drafting new codes by foreign legal experts such as Roesler was accelerated. Their efforts had impressed the United States favorably enough for it to be willing to revise the unequal clauses, but other governments still claimed that insufficient progress had been made.

The next step was a joint British–German proposal of 1886 which recommended only partial abolition of extraterritoriality. It provided that the countryside should be opened to foreigners for unrestricted travel. In the meantime, the new civil, criminal, and commercial codes and the law courts should be put in operation. Import duties would be raised, in some instances by as much as 25 per cent, but the export tariff rate would remain at 5 per cent. In spite of these concessions, however, the foreigners insisted that certain aspects of extraterritoriality should remain. For example, consular jurisdiction should be retained for a limited period in the large cities. Finally, foreign judges and procurators would be appointed in cases in which foreigners were involved. When these proposals became known, the public was indignant. The objections were chiefly against the provisions for the continuing use of foreign judges and for permitting foreigners unrestricted residence throughout the nation.

Opposition to the foreigners' proposals was so strong that in September, 1887, Foreign Minister Inouye Kaoru was forced to resign.[6] (See also page 208 below.)

It was precisely at this point that Itō and his colleagues had completed their fourth draft of the Constitution. The success of their efforts in this regard was threatened by the impasse over the revision of the treaties. There was a real possibility that a leader of the opposition might be able to capitalize on this failure of the government to revise the treaties. If anyone could unify the various political elements opposed to Itō and his colleagues, the whole future of the oligarchs was at stake. In fact, all the carefully laid plans to produce a constitution which preserved the special prerogatives of the Emperor and the position of his Ministers might be for nought.

Consequently, the Cabinet took strong measures to prevent further embarrassment both on the treaty negotiations and on the type of constitution to be adopted. In the first place, Itō temporarily assumed the post of Foreign Minister. In late December, 1887, his Home Minister, Yamagata, promulgated strict regulations to preserve law and order. Under the new regulations, persons suspected of causing disturbances or "judged to be scheming something detrimental to public tranquillity" could be banished from Tokyo. Both those who were the Cabinet's political opponents and those who objected to the proposed treaties with the foreigners were either intimidated or banished from the city. Under virtual martial law, nearly 600 persons active in the people's rights movement were forced to leave the political heart of the Empire.

Such was the domestic atmosphere in the spring of 1888 when Itō and his three assistants met again to put the finishing touches on the Constitution and on the texts of the Imperial House Laws. The time had also arrived to settle the question of how the basic laws should be adopted. While there had been some clamor for a constitutional convention, Itō had never favored such a procedure, and the disturbances caused by the treaty-revision fiasco made him even less enthusiastic about it. Some persons claimed that only the Emperor's approval was necessary. A partial compromise of these two extremes was adopted. In April, 1888, a Privy Council was created by Imperial Ordinance. The Emperor gave the following reasons for this move:

> Whereas We deem it expedient to consult personages who have rendered signal service to the State, and to avail Ourselves of their valuable advice on matters of state, We hereby establish Our Privy Council which shall henceforth be an institution of Our Supreme counsel.

In other words, the Emperor and a select group of his most trusted servants would discuss the draft of the Constitution in the new Council and would approve it. It would then be proclaimed as the immutable law of the Empire.

From the shifts which followed in the highest posts in the government, it is obvious that the oligarchs, under Itō's guidance, had engineered this whole scheme. He immediately resigned as Premier and became President of the Privy Council. His three assistants were made secretaries of the Council. Kuroda Kiyotaka of Satsuma, a loyal protégé of Yamagata, was the new Premier. In the second place, the two strongest adversaries of the clan oligarchs, Ōkuma and Itagaki, were asked to join the Council to make it impossible for them to lead the opposition. Ōkuma accepted a position in the Cabinet as Foreign Minister with an assignment to solve the explosive problem of the unequal treaties. It will be noted later how dangerous this undertaking became for him. (See below, page 208.) On the other hand, Itagaki remained outside the government and refused to join the Council. Nevertheless, Yamagata's strong-arm rule made it impossible for anyone opposed to the government to cause any significant trouble.

The Meiji Constitution of 1889

In May, 1888, with Yamagata having squelched or eliminated the subversives, the Privy Council began its deliberation on Itō's draft of the Constitution in the presence of the Emperor. During forty-three subsequent sessions throughout the next nine months, the Emperor and his most trusted advisers debated the text of this basic document. Ōkuma, who was busy with negotiations with the foreigners, was the only important official to keep away from the meetings. Since he had long disagreed with Itō on many points, he was glad to have this excuse for not attending.

As in the case when the first drafts were made by Itō and his colleagues, no records are available as to what exactly transpired in the Council meetings. It seems probable that such changes as were made did not materially affect any of the important provisions of the document. In any event, the draft was approved by the Privy Council. February 11, or Empire Day, the day when the first mythological Emperor presumably ascended the throne, was selected for the promulgation of the new Constitution.

The ceremony held on February 11, 1889, was a simple one. According to Dr. Erwin Baelz, a German professor at Tokyo Imperial University, who observed the ceremony, the entire procedure lasted about ten minutes. He writes:

> On either side of the throne a high dignitary now stepped forward, one of them Duke Sanjo . . . , each of them with a roll of parchment. The one Sanjo

held was the Constitution. The Emperor took the other document, opened it, and read it in a loud voice.[7]

Emperor Meiji, who by that time was thirty-seven years old, proclaimed that he promulgated the present, immutable fundamental law for the sake of his subjects and their descendents. He attributed Japan's successes in the past to the virtues of his ancestors and to the loyalty of his subjects. He concluded that since his subjects descended from his ancestors, he had no doubt that they would be guided by his views, sympathize with his endeavors, and make manifest the glory of his country, both at home and abroad.

After his speech (containing slightly more than two hundred words in the official English translation), he handed the parchment on which the Constitution was written to the Prime Minister and left the room. Thus Japan's first Constitution was given to the people more than twenty years after the Restoration was started. For fifty-eight years, from that day until May 3, 1947, when the post-World War II Constitution came into force, not a single change was made in the document which implemented Itō's desire that the Emperor be the center, the axis of the constitutional monarchy.

Although the importance of the Constitution will become apparent from the interpretation of events subsequent to its adoption, some of its features must be emphasized at this point if those events are to be understood. The late Professor Robert K. Reischauer, an outstanding authority on Japan's government, has succinctly described the fundamentals of Japanese political theory which must be grasped if the history of Japan's constitutional government is to be understood. To him, these concepts are that society is more important than the individual, that all men are by nature unequal, that politics and ethics are synonymous, that government by men is superior to that by law, and that the patriarchal family is the ideal state.[8] To explain the document another way: it is a compromise between the concepts of statism and liberalism, with a strong preference toward statism.

But the Constitution can best be understood by an analysis of its most salient features. (See Appendix II.) While it delineated the three basic powers of government, it strengthened the Emperor's power on all sides. The preamble stressed the immutability of the document and the necessity of eternal allegiance to it in its present form. The power, dignity, and central position of the Emperor were guaranteed. He was sacred and inviolable. As Itō expostulated in his *Commentaries*,[9] not only should no irreverence be shown the sovereign but he should not be made the subject of discussion nor the topic of derogatory comment. The Constitution further provided that the Emperor exercise the rights of sovereignty and of legislative power with the consent of the Diet. It also gave him wide powers to issue ordinances. It recognized his Supreme Command of the Army and Navy and his authority to determine the organization of the armed services. He had the power to make war and peace and to conclude treaties. Finally, as the initiator of amendments to the Constitution, he could control any future attempts to limit his power.

His position was further secured by the Imperial House Law. Its purpose was to assure the continuance of the Imperial line without outside interference. If amendments were necessary, they would be decided by the Emperor with the advice of the Imperial Family Council and of the Privy Council. The Imperial Household Ministry had charge of the personal affairs of the Emperor and his family, as well as restrictive control over the right of his subjects to approach him. As a result, this group of bureaucrats, who originally were conservative but in the 1930's stood up against the ultranationalists, became influential personal advisers to the sovereign and wielded much power behind the scenes.

Despite the new outward form, the Constitution perpetuated the strength of the executive branch of the government. In reality, it gave legal sanction to the wide powers already exercised in the name of the Emperor by a small group of ministers. While it established legislative and judicial branches of the government, it was careful not to give them sufficient power to infringe on the executive. Consequently, the Privy Council, which was the body composed exclusively of Imperial appointees, was continued with authority to deliberate upon important matters of state referred to it by the Emperor. In practice, it came to operate as an ultraconservative force in the government.

The concept of individual responsibility of Ministers of State toward the Emperor, which had existed heretofore, was strengthened. Article 55 read:

> The respective Ministers of State shall give their advice to the Emperor and be responsible for it.
>
> All Laws, Imperial Ordinances and Imperial Rescripts of whatever kind, that relate to the affairs of state, require the countersignature of a Minister of State.

The Constitution did not mention a Cabinet as such nor refer to the concept of collective responsibility. Rather, the compilers consciously omitted this important feature of parliamentary government whereby the legislative has a check on the executive. This lack of provision for collective Cabinet responsibility on the one hand, and the assignment to the Emperor of supreme command over the Army and Navy on the other, led to a policy of dual diplomacy and gave free rein to the military. Since the ministers were appointed by the Emperor, and acted for him, they were nearly as far above reproach as their sovereign. In time of crisis, if they were able to retain the Emperor's personal approval for their action, they could weather the storm of criticism.[10]

Confucian teachings and feudal concepts of loyalty had combined to create a deep reverence for one's elders in Japanese society. Japan's history is replete with examples of those who ruled indirectly from retirement. As the old leaders developed a loyal cadre of trained followers there was a tendency to promote new leaders to positions of authority. For example, Kuroda, the Premier, was from the younger group. At the same time, even with the fundamental pattern of government settled, the old leaders were neither willing nor able to relinquish control. Consequently, the informal conferences of two or more of the older statesmen came to be formalized into a body known as the *Genrō* or Elder Statesmen. The members of this extraconstitutional body were selected by the Emperor from among his most venerable contemporaries. It was used to advise him on the most important decisions and for several years was the strongest body in the governmental structure. In many respects it exercised the executive functions for him.[11]

Weaknesses of the Imperial Diet

This tendency in Japan's political development to rely on the experience and wisdom of the conservative elite elements in society was further increased by the constitutional provisions for Parliament. The Imperial Diet was divided into a House of Peers and a House of Representatives. Membership in the former came from the nobility and a few Imperial appointees. Only the members of the lower chamber were elected. To guarantee, as Itō desired, that the appointive House of Peers serve as a stabilizing and conservative force within the legislative branch, it was given powers practically equal to the House of Representatives. The only exception was the right of the latter House to initiate financial bills, but in practice even this difference did not exist. Hence, the Peers had a virtual veto over legislation forwarded to it by the lower body. The basically conservative Peers could and did control any move by the Representatives to circumscribe the power of the executive and rarely took sides with the Representatives in their battle to strengthen the legislative branch of the government. Furthermore, the Constitution was worded carefully to avoid any indication that the Diet shared any sovereign power with the Emperor.

The powers of the House of Representatives, the only elective body in the national administration, were limited to such an extent that it was difficult for the political parties to operate effectively. Together with the House of Peers, it was subject to prolongation or dissolution at the will of the Prime Minister. As dissolution made an election for members of the lower house compulsory, this device was frequently used effectively by the oligarchs in their fight with the party representatives. Furthermore, when the Diet was actually in session, it met infrequently and for only a few hours each day. There was no real opportunity to discuss adequately important national and international issues. As a Minister was not responsible collectively to the Cabinet, even a vote of nonconfidence did not, as in the case of Premier Tanaka in 1928, cause his resignation.

But the numerous Premiers who ignored the wishes of the Diet were able to act independently also because of the limited budgetary powers given to the people's elected representatives. Iwakura had been impressed with the operation of the Prussian government whereby the budget of the previous year was declared to be operative when both branches of Parliament failed to act on a new budget prior to adjournment. He had recommended, therefore, that this principle be incorporated into the Constitution. Roesler argued for it strongly for he saw this as a device whereby a Cabinet could stay in power regardless of the wishes of the legislators. In the American and British governments, the executive is completely dependent on the legislative branch for finances to operate the government. Since Itō and his colleagues wished to avoid such an eventuality, Article 71 of the Constitution specifically stated that:

> When the Imperial Diet has not voted on the Budget or when the Budget shall not be brought into actual existence, the Government shall carry out the Budget of the preceding year.

Because of this provision the political parties and members of the opposition in the lower chamber knew full well that if they disagreed with the Cabinet, their views would have only a limited effect. Even though a vote of nonconfidence were pushed through Parliament, which was unlikely because of the right of dissolution, the government would automatically have funds to continue operations. This provision, perhaps as much as any other, permitted a degeneracy in politics in the earliest sessions of the Diet.

Privileges of the Military and Restrictions on People

The treatment accorded two other groups by the Constitution must be noted. The first of these groups, the militarists, were given special privileges and advantages which enabled them to become the strongest single force in Japan's history. As indicated in the discussion of the role of the Emperor, his power of Supreme Command and authority to determine the organization of the services enhanced the special position of the military through what was termed "direct access to the throne." In other words, if the military wanted Imperial sanction for an exploit such as the invasion of Manchuria in 1931, they claimed that these provisions in the Constitution gave them the right to go directly to the throne for the Emperor's approval for their plans. The Premier and other members of the Cabinet might not even be aware that such a decision had been made. Faced with a *fait accompli,* the Cabinet would be forced to capitulate.

This predominant position of the military in Japanese politics was also the result of another unique feature of the operation of the Japanese government. Under most parliamentary governments, if a new cabinet is being formed, the Prime Minister has a comparatively free hand in selecting his ministers for the various portfolios, including those of the War and Navy Departments. In Japan, however, those available to serve as Minister of War and Minister of Navy were closely circumscribed by an Imperial Ordinance. The first of these ordinances was issued in May, 1900, while General Yamagata was Premier. It provided that only Generals and Lieutenant Generals on the active list could be appointed to the post of Minister of War. Only Admirals and Vice-Admirals on active duty could be appointed as Minister of Navy.

This ordinance, more than any other single piece of legislation, gave the militarists a life-and-death hold over all subsequent Cabinets. Its operation was very simple. If the military leaders, or any strong clique in either the Imperial Army or the Imperial Navy, opposed the policies of a Prime Minister or his Cabinet, the Minister of War or Navy threatened to resign. If the government failed to heed the warning, the Minister would resign and cause the downfall of the whole Cabinet. The small group of high-ranking officers eligible for these Cabinet posts were then ordered not to serve on any future Cabinet until a Premier acceptable to the military was selected. Consequently, if a Premier wanted to stay in power, he had no choice but to bend to the wishes of the military. In 1913 this ordinance was modified to make reserve officers eligible for appointment. In 1936 it was changed back to its original form.

Finally, there remains to be considered the position of the people under the Constitution. To the extent that persons such as Itagaki and Ōkuma spoke for the people, they had forced the issue of a constitution. However, they had no part in drafting it. The central issue of the movement for a constitution and for people's rights had not been whether all men were created equal and hence should have equal rights. Furthermore, no one had seriously advocated the thesis that sovereignty resided in the people rather than in the Emperor. On the contrary, the question was the extent of the rights to be granted to the people, if any. One of the points vigorously urged by Roesler was that the rights of the people should rest on the principle that they had to be determined by law and expressly stated in the Constitution. In his view, there was nothing inalienable about them. He persuaded Inouye to accept this principle, which was upheld in the Privy Council. Itō Hirobumi condescendingly described the subjects of the Empire as "public treasures." He conceived of them as treasures, however, which should be protected and controlled. This acceptance of the principle of inequality within Japanese society had an obvious result.

In the first place, the Constitution referred to the people as subjects and placed more emphasis on their duties than on their rights. Even the basic right to vote was limited to property owners. At the time of the promulgation of the Constitution, those eligible to vote for members of the House of Representatives equaled less than half a million persons. This meant that only about 1¼ per cent of the population had the right of franchise.

As for basic human rights, they were restricted. Freedom of conscience, of religion, of thought, and of speech were all recognized but were made subject to the limits of the law. Hence, a Parliament composed of representatives from the elite classes passed stringent laws, such as the Peace Preservation Law, which limited the people's freedom. If a subject were arrested, custom, the Constitution, and the Civil and Criminal Codes provided for a far different "due process of law" than the traditional Western European practice. A trial by a jury composed of one's peers, the right to be confronted with the charges against the accused, the right of counsel and a speedy trial for the defendant were all principles and practices foreign to Japanese judicial practice. In fact, a man was considered guilty until he could prove his innocence. In a stratified society, privileges and judicial protection were allotted in proportion to the importance of one's social status. As for the duties of the subjects, the Constitution specified that they were "amenable" to service in the armed forces and to the duty of paying taxes.

Such was the general heritage of the Japanese people under the Meiji Constitution. It was not a heritage which was conducive to the growth of individual freedom or representative institutions. It had in no sense been designed for that purpose. In fact, it was clearly designed to establish the supremacy of the throne and to enable the state to control the people. It had been conceived and nurtured in an atmosphere in which freedom was considered to be less of a virtue than obedience; equality less important than inequality; brotherhood less appealing than suspicion.

The process of modernization from a form of modified feudalism to a limited constitutional monarchy was similar in many respects to that of Germany, from which so much had been borrowed. As Veblen has pointed out, in Japan, as well as in Germany, the concept of the state as an overruling personal—or quasi-personal—entity had prevailed from former times. In both countries, the government rested on the suzerainty of the crown, not on the discretion of a parliamentary body, and was a government of "constitutionally mitigated absolutism" with little or no libertarian tradition to temper this absolutism. In the economic sphere, both of these nations decided to modernize their economies to meet the strategic needs of the state. The technology necessary for industrialization was taken over ready-made from other countries which had previously developed it. Such things as parliamentary tradition, democratic government, or even the needs of the people could be ignored if the state's preparation for war made it necessary.[12]

In 1890 Japan was in a particularly advantageous position. Both German absolutism and technological development were at an advanced stage when the key figures of the Meiji Restoration visited Europe in 1873 and again in 1882. These leaders were perceptive enough to recognize that they could avoid innumerable mistakes and perhaps even disaster if they relied heavily on Germany's experience. The process of modernization in Japan, therefore, so long as its national objectives were the same as those of Germany, could be speeded up by an emphasis on adaptation of those features applicable to Japan. The process of modernization described thus far, therefore, is really that of adaptation. Its success was enhanced by the economic and territorial accruals which had occurred by the time the Constitution was promulgated. Its success was assured by society's acceptance of the philosophy that the highest calling of the subject was to serve the State and to follow its dictates for the glory of the Empire.

Notes

1. Itō Hirobumi was accompanied by three younger men, Itō Miyoji (1857–1934), Hirata Tōsuke (1849–1929), and Saionji Kimmochi (1849–1940). Itō Miyoji, who was no relation to the other Itō as they had different family names, was assigned with the other two to study the Constitution of the Third Republic in France. He was the only one of the assistants to aid in the preparation of the final draft of the Constitution a few years later. For reference to Itō Hirobumi's concept of his mission see Itō Hirobumi, "The Japanese Constitution" in Ōkuma Shigenobu (compiler), *Fifty Years of New Japan*, English version edited by Marcus B. Huish (2 vols.; London: Smith Elders, 1909), I, p. 127.

2. Aoki Shūzō (1844–1914), the Japanese Minister in Berlin, was a strong supporter of Prussian concepts of government. The first Japanese to study in Germany, he absorbed much of the political atmosphere around him in his student days and especially that of Bismarck after the latter became Chancellor in 1875. Aoki had, as mentioned previously, selected Roesler as an adviser to the Foreign Office. The latter, along with von Gneist, were the leaders of a national school of constitutional law which supported self-government. Thus

both Roesler and von Gneist held many of the same views on constitutional law. Father Siemes claims that both von Gneist and von Stein only convinced Itō of the truth of Roesler's views and consequently the latter had the greatest influence of any foreigner on Itō. The point is difficult to prove and becomes largely academic as all three European advisers accepted the same basic concepts of "constitutional monarchies." See Johannes Siemes, *Hermann Roesler and the Making of the Meiji Constitution* (Tokyo: Sophia University Press, 1966), p. 11.

3. Inouye Kaoru was the new Foreign Minister; Yamagata Aritomo was Home Minister; the important portfolios of Finance, Army, and Navy were held respectively by three Satsuma clansmen, Matsukata Masayoshi, Ōyama Iwao, and Saigō Tsugumichi.

4. A similar disinterest of the public toward modern political crises was evidenced in February, 1936, and in March, 1946. On February 26, 1936, a radical group in the army staged an abortive coup d'état but held parts of the heart of Tokyo under their grip for several days. The public felt no personal responsibility for what was happening or for the future course of events. If a complete military dictatorship had resulted, they would have been as complacent as they were under Hirota's Cabinet. (See *infra* page 388.) In March, 1946, when the Japanese were expected to accept SCAP's proposals for a new constitution, their capitulation was rapid and complete, and there was little outside reaction to the decision. (See *infra* page 468).

5. Sessions of the drafting were begun as early as 1884. See Siemes, *op. cit.*, pp. 11–12.

6. Since the issue of the unequal treaties was the only problem of international relations which had aroused the people during this period, it has been discussed at this point. For the other international problems see *infra* page 181.

7. Tobu Baelz (ed.), *Awakening Japan: The Diary of a German Doctor: Erwin Baelz,* translated by Eden and Cedar Paul (New York: Viking Pres, Inc., 1932), p. 81.

8. See R. K. Reischauer, *Japan, Government and Politics* (New York: Thomas Nelson & Sons, 1939), pp. 22–35.

9. Following the deliberations by the Privy Council on the draft of the constitution, Inouye Ki turned over to the government a series of notes and comments he had compiled on its interpretation. This material was then edited and published in April, 1889, as the government's official interpretation of the text under the name of Itō Hirobumi and entitled *Dai Nihon Teikoku Kempō Gikai.* An English translation was made by Itō Miyoji and appeared in August, 1889, as *Commentaries on the Constitution of the Empire of Japan.* More or less simultaneously, from July, 1888, to March 12, 1891, Roesler wrote his own "Commentary" which appears verbatim in Siemes, *op. cit.,* pp. 40–113.

10. Itō states in his *Commentaries* that the Prime Minister had no control over his Cabinet Ministers and they were not responsible to him. Roesler argued that as each Minister was appointed by the Emperor he "is independent in his respective branch of the government and also has full independence of opinion with regard to the common affairs of the Cabinet." In view of the concept of the Imperial Command, the military had even greater independence of action.

11. For a survey of the *Genrō* see Roger F. Hackett, "Political Modernization and the *Genrō*," in Robert E. Ward (ed.), *Political Development in Modern Japan* (Princeton: Princeton University Press, 1968), pp. 65–97.

12. See Thorstein Veblen, *Imperial Germany and the Industrial Revolution* (New York: The Macmillan Co., 1915), pp. 80 ff.; and Thorstein Veblen, "The Opportunity of Japan," Leon Ardzrooni (ed.), *Essays in our Changing Order* (New York: Viking Press, Inc., 1934), pp. 248–66.

9

National Strength in 1890

The power at the disposal of the Emperor and his Ministers at the time of the promulgation of the Constitution was dependent on much more than the provisions of that document. It depended on certain specific factors such as the condition of agriculture, potentialities for self-sufficiency, financial stability, the extent or success of the industrialization program, and the growth of the armed services. At the same time, national strength could be dissipated if dreams of territorial expansion went far beyond ability to absorb territory overseas, or were thwarted by another power or powers. Conversely, if expansionism was commensurate with an integrated national growth, it could cause a net increase in national strength.

All these power potentials, as well as the sovereign rights and authority of the Emperor which were confirmed by the Constitution, were also affected by numerous variable factors and national characteristics. For example, the loyalty of the people toward the Emperor and the throne, their patriotism, their willingness and ability to work, their aptitudes and ambitions, and their subservience to authority were crucial elements in the state's program of amalgamation of the entire national effort to strengthen the Empire. On all these counts, as well as on many more which would augment the national strength, the people were not found wanting. An analysis of Japan's national strength in 1890 will necessitate, therefore, a brief account of Japan's general economic status, of the territorial limits of the Empire, and of the contemporary cultural and social scene.[1]

The Conditions of Agriculture

Particularly after World War I, Japan has been referred to as a "have-not" country. A paucity of natural resources, a small area, extremely limited arable land, and an ever increasing population have added to its economic plight. Good or bad standards of living and conditions within a country are relative, however, and the ordinary Japanese subject compared his plight with that of a few years earlier, not with a comparable person in one of the advanced Occidental countries. In the years immediately following the Meiji Restoration of 1868, the country was far from modernized and standards of living were low in comparison with the Occident. Nevertheless, conditions gradually improved and the main home islands were able to produce enough rice to feed the population without imports of cereals. The population had not yet begun to take a sudden spurt upward and the people's tastes were still relatively simple. Despite isolated uprisings by peasant groups, there was general acceptance of conditions as they existed.

One of the most significant features of the agrarian economy is the fact that though only one-seventh of Japan's land area is arable, the country's population is predominantly agrarian. For example, in 1875, about three-fourths of the gainfully employed were agricultural workers and four years later the proportion was slightly higher; as late as 1920, half of the total workers were engaged in agriculture. From these figures it is obvious that agricultural conditions affected more people than did the conditions of any other industry; if there were weaknesses in the agrarian economy, they would eventually weaken the national economy.

During the first two decades of the Meiji Restoration, both strong and weak characteristics of agriculture appeared. As for the former, the traditional small-scale farms, many of them less than two acres, permitted the continuance of farm operations with a minimum of capital when capital funds were needed for industrialization. Moreover, the competition for good farm land had forced an intensive use of all available space. Improved methods of cultivation and better seeds increased production sufficiently to meet the demands made by a growing population. The farmer's income was also supplemented by the sale of raw silk and the products of home industries. As silk exports doubled, the growing of silkworms became an important phase of farming. So long as the market was firm, silk remained the most profitable cash crop. The agrarian economy was also bolstered by the fact that the farm population was hard working, expected little from life except enough to eat, and was inherently conservative.

On the other hand, there is strong evidence to indicate that agricultural production did not increase at the phenomenal rate which heretofore has been described as a unique characteristic of Japan's modern development. This conclusion, which had been effectively argued by Professor James Nakamura, is based on the assumption that the previously published figures on arable land reported in the earliest surveys were too low. It seems evident that landowners, as a means of evading the new land taxes, understated their holdings. For example, in 1881, after the first series of cadastral surveys was completed, the official figures for the total of arable land was 4,486,000 *chōbu* (1 *chōbu* = 2.45 acres). By 1885, this had increased by less than 1 per cent to 4,514,000 *chōbu*. As it was apparent to officials in the central government that considerable land was still being concealed, a second and more thorough survey was taken from 1886–1889. As a result, by 1890, the total figure for arable land had risen by over 11 per cent to 5 million *chōbu*. As the increase in arable land during the next thirty years totaled only 4.4 per cent, the conclusion seems obvious that the abrupt increase in the quintennial prior to 1890 was largely the result of improved methods of surveying rather than the sudden increase in total arable land. It is generally agreed, therefore, that a downward adjustment is required in the arable land area statistics. Such being the case, the agricultural sector actually did not have the phenomenal rate of growth of production that has been implied by these figures.

At the same time, faced with the unreliability of statistics, especially for the early years, it is unlikely that economists will agree on the rate at which agricultural production actually increased. On the basis of arguments mentioned above, Professor Nakamura believes statistics on crop yields from 1878–1882 to 1913–1917 should be re-estimated to show a growth rate of 1 per cent a year. On the other hand, Professor Ohkawa Kazushi and Henry Rosovsky, who give more credence to the official figures, originally estimated the annual growth rate at 2.4 per cent and more recently have accepted a 1.8 per cent rate. (See Table 2.) In any

TABLE 2

COMPARATIVE FIGURES ON RICE PRODUCTION AND YIELD
(ANNUAL AVERAGES, 1878–1917)

	Long-Term Economic Statistics *		Nakamura's Estimates **	
Years	Rice Production (1,000 *koku*)	Yield per *chōbu*	Rice Production (1,000 *koku*)	Yield per *chōbu*
1878–1882	33,951	12.44	43,060	16.36
1883–1887	36,660	13.45	44,525	16.72
1888–1892	39,273	14.05	46,160	17.09
1893–1897	37,673	13.40	47,449	17.47
1898–1902	42,480	14.96	49,222	17.86
1903–1907	46,286	16.11	51,091	18.26
1908–1912	50,588	17.19	53,322	18.67
1913–1917	55,242	18.39	55,733	19.08

* Ohkawa Kazushi (ed.), *Chōki Keiza Tōkei: Nōrin* (Estimates of Long-Term Economic Statistics of Japan since 1868: Agriculture and Forestry) (Tokyo: Tōyō Keizai Shimpō, 1966), IX, pp. 166–67.

** James Nakamura, *Agricultural Production and the Economic Development of Japan 1873–1922* (Princeton: Princeton University Press, 1966), pp. 43 and 92.

event, the general consensus is that the estimates should be reduced. Consequently, in terms of Japan's overall economic development, the primary sector of the economy apparently made only a modest contribution to the increases in the national product. If such is the case, Japan's development appears to have been much more comparable to that of other countries than has previously been believed.[2]

In contrast to these limited food resources, there were indications that the population of the nation would increase at a rapid rate. During the Tokugawa dictatorship, natural calamities, social practices such as infanticide and abortion, and disease had resulted in a stagnant population. Modernization, including the introduction of sanitation and hygiene and improved living standards, was bound to force a rapid rise in the net increase. Although the population had risen less than 10 per cent in the decade from 1880–1890, any increase, no matter how small, put a strain on the food supply. Furthermore, as the standard of living for all classes of society improved, per-capita consumption of rice increased.

This relentlessly increasing pressure of population on food supply is graphically demonstrated by reference to the statistics on rice exports and imports. In the 1890's there was an abrupt change from a surplus to a deficiency in the national crop. In the quintennial prior to 1892 the average annual exports of rice amounted to 290,000 *koku* (1 *koku* = 4.96 bushels); in the next five-year period, the average annual imports of rice stood at 332,000 *koku*. Thereafter, production at home could not keep up with demand so that rice imports steadily increased. (See Table 3, in Chapter 14.)

The long-range prospects of agriculture were not good. Domestic production of foodstuffs was not going to be sufficient to meet the demands of a rapidly growing population. Hence, Japanese industry would have to manufacture goods for export to provide the foreign exchange to purchase vital food imports. If this balance could not be maintained, the national economy would be in jeopardy. For the period under discussion, however, this issue had not yet become acute but the trends indicated that it soon would be.

Another feature of the agrarian economy during this early period, which came to be permanent, was a marked increase in tenancy. This movement was greatly increased by the effects of the Restoration. After the feudal holdings were transferred into private property, the new Imperial government was obliged to establish a universal land tax. In addition, in order to meet the requirements of a centralized state, the tax was to be paid in money and paid regularly. These common features of a modern national economy became insurmountable obstacles for many of the farmers. The abolition of the fiefs had made the landlord–peasant relationship an impersonal one.

In feudal times, if the peasant were in arrears in the payment of his taxes in rice, the feudal baron knew that dispossession would only reduce the amount of rice produced within his domain. Since the feudatory was interested in as much rice income as possible, he often permitted postponement of tax payments until the farmer had a good harvest. After the certificates of ownership of land were issued, the owner had to either pay his tax in cash or borrow money to do so. Moreover, he must pay the same amount each year, regardless of whether there was a good harvest, and could no longer count on the beneficence of a paternalistic feudal lord. Instead, he was confronted by an impersonal tax collector who insisted on adherence to an impersonal law.

Under these circumstances, the position of the small landowners was extremely vulnerable and many of them were forced to give up their holdings. The figures on tenancy and increased dispossessions attest to this fact. For example, in 1873 the proportion of tenants to proprietors was 1:5, but by 1887 it had doubled to 2:5. For the seven years from 1883 to 1890, about 7 per cent of the total farm households were forced to sell their land. The most tragic aspect of this development was the fact that three-fourths of the dispossessions resulted from nonpayment of taxes while the value of the land confiscated by the government and auctioned for sale was twenty-seven times the value of the total taxes in arrears.

This tendency toward concentration of landownership in the hands of fewer landlords and the decrease in the number of cultivator-owners had additional weaknesses and permitted widespread abuses. The owner, by exaction of a heavy rent from the tenant, could pass on to the cultivator any new taxes which the government might require. On the other hand, the tenant was in a weak bargaining position because he had little freedom of action. There was only a limited demand for unskilled farm labor and a heavy demand for dwellings. Hence, the tenant held on to the job and the house which he had and accepted a heavier burden of rent. On balance, in 1890 the agrarian economy showed more signs of weakness than of strength, but these weaknesses were not yet significant enough to cause any serious embarrassment to the government.[3]

Fiscal Policy

These weaknesses of the agrarian economy were partially mitigated by the increased stability in the nation's finances but aggravated by its fiscal policy. As for the former, when Matsukata Masayoshi became Minister of Finance in 1881, the nation's finances were in a chaotic condition. The experiment in national banking had been unsuccessful. The bank notes had different values in terms of silver yen coins. In 1880, 1.50

yen exchanged for 1.00 yen of silver; by the next year 1.79 yen of paper money was needed to buy 1.00 yen of silver. Prices of commodities also rose. Rice cost 5.15 yen in 1877 but rose to 10.48 yen in 1881. Despite the temporary suffering which sweeping reforms might inflict on some of the population such as the farmers, Matsukata adopted radical steps to place the country on a solid financial base.

His first steps were to freeze the national expenditures and create a sinking fund to redeem the public debt. He had inherited the inconvertible notes issued to pay for the Satsuma Rebellion in 1877 and for other national expenses. When an accumulation of specie permitted it, he recalled these notes, reducing the total money by some 20 per cent. In 1884 the general price level dropped to 75 per cent of the 1881 level. Four years after he took office, the total currency had been decreased by 15 per cent and the value of the paper money rose by one half its face value to a level equal to that of silver. Furthermore, during the decade 1880–1890 the public debt rose only 2 per cent while the service charges paid by the government on its indebtedness were reduced. Interest charges, which had been as high as 19 per cent, declined to 5 per cent; a foreign loan for a new section of the railroad across the central mountains was secured at only 6 per cent.

An analysis of the annual receipts and expenditures for the nation shows the improved condition of the exchequer. In 1869, the first full year after the Restoration, both receipts and expenditures approximated 21 million yen. In 1875–1876, when the new land tax was collected over a large portion of the country, receipts rose to 86 million yen and expenses were only 60 million yen. In 1882, after Matsukata had taken office, receipts and expenditures were equal again to 63 million yen. As a result of his having frozen expenditures at that amount for the next few years, the situation improved so noticeably that in 1890–1891 receipts stood at 106 million yen, 24 million yen above expenditures.[4]

This improvement in national finances was also the result of institutional reforms inaugurated by Matsukata. He abolished the old National Banks because of their inability to meet the financial demands made upon them. In their stead, with the National Bank of Belgium as a model, he organized the Bank of Japan as the central banking institution. He also created special banks to perform specialized functions such as the Yokohama Specie Bank and the Hypothec Bank. The Yokohama Specie Bank acted as the chief foreign exchange bank. The state provided one-third of its capital and the Minister of Finance appointed its president and vice-president. Reserves in the treasury could be called upon for use in foreign bills of exchange. Thus by 1887, when the Specie Bank began to function effectively in foreign exchange, a Japanese financial institution was at hand to deal with foreign trade. Local producers of silk, rice, tea, and other items of export no longer dealt through foreigners in the port cities. Similarly, necessary raw materials or finished products for the growing armament program could be imported directly through Japanese firms. Finally, the Hypothec Bank accepted immovable property as security for long-term loans. Within less than a decade, the country's finances were on a firm basis, economic activity was stimulated, the foreign trade balance shifted from excess imports to excess exports, and a firm basis was established for armament expansion.

Certain aspects of the government's fiscal policy, however, had an adverse effect on the agriculture sector. The extraction of large sums of money in taxes from the farm population was generally detrimental to agriculture, particularly since much of this revenue was used for military purposes. For example, it is estimated that out of the total government revenue of 116.5 million yen for the five-year average (1889–1893), 53.4 million yen came from land taxes. In the year 1890, 66.6 per cent of expenditures went for state services, such as the operation of the legislative-executive branch of the government, fiscal requirements, foreign affairs, military (20.5 per cent), and justice, and only 4.4 per cent was allotted to primary industries (agriculture, forestry, and fisheries).[5] While military expenditures may have given some stimulus to the economy, as Japan was still largely underdeveloped and faced a shortage in the aggregate supply of goods, the demand-generating effect of these expenditures added impetus to inflationary tendencies. This effect might well have stimulated the collapse in business activity after both the Sino-Japanese and Russo-Japanese wars.[6]

Industrial Growth

Although the limited agricultural resources and increased population pressure boded ill for Japan's economic future, the general policy of government sponsorship of industries brought encouraging results. Some of them, such as those in Hokkaidō, became extremely profitable. (See Chapter 7.) In 1882 Ōkuma reported that the following were owned by the Imperial Japanese Government:

3 shipbuilding yards
51 merchant ships
5 munitions works
52 factories
10 mines
75 miles of railway
1 telegraph system

Capital investment by the government in such enterprises up to 1881, exclusive of shipyards, arsenals, and the Tomioka mill, totaled 34.6 million yen.

As some of these factories, mills, plants, and mines were offered for sale by the government at bargain prices, private capitalists were eager to absorb them. This policy of bargain sales was advantageous for both the government and the new owners. It permitted the former to devote its energies to new fields or to concentrate on key strategic industries. It eliminated nepotism, the possibility of discriminatory and unfair subsidies, and the competition between government and private enterprise in several important industries.

As for the private industrialist, it permitted him to start out with a small amount of capital. Other things being equal, he would make a handsome profit from his new adventure. To give a few random examples, the Mitsui interests were delighted to purchase the Shimmachi Spinning Mills. Asano Sōichirō (1848–1930), who became the wealthy cement tycoon, purchased the Fukugawa Cement Company in 1884. All the large combines strengthened their position of monopolistic control of many industries through shrewd purchases.[7] This sale of government-owned industries contributed materially, therefore, to Japan's industrial strength prior to 1890.

Progress and expansion also continued in the textile industry. By 1890, Shibusawa's Ōsaka Spinning Mill had been enlarged sevenfold to a total of 70,000 spindles. The demands of this plant and those of many other new ones boosted raw cotton imports from a mere 12,000 bales in 1868 to a peak of 158,000 in 1888.

As for mining and heavy industries (many of them under government ownership), progress was equally notable, but it started from a low base and therefore is not too significant. In coal mining, for instance, the average annual output increased rapidly. During the period 1877–1884 less than a million tons were mined annually, but in the next decade a yearly average of 2,600,000 tons was produced. As Japan was deficient in iron ore and coking coal, metal production was never sufficient to meet domestic needs and developed more slowly. Even after the Sino-Japanese War of 1894–1895, home output of pig iron was sufficient to meet only 40 per cent of domestic needs.

Shipbuilding, which was to be so important after World War I, was still in its infancy. In fact, only one steamer over 1,000 tons had been built in Japan before 1895. Nevertheless, the importance of a merchant marine had been recognized by the authorities. The largest shipping firm was the Mitsubishi Shokai founded by Iwasaki Yatarō in 1871. It received strong support from the government and developed into the powerful Japan Mail Steamship Company (N.Y.K.). In 1885 it owned

58 ships aggregating 65,000 tons, practically all of them having been built in foreign yards. Moreover, it received a subsidy which guaranteed for fifteen years a return of 8 per cent interest on the capital investment.

This rapid industrial progress was naturally reflected in the sudden shift in foreign trade from an unfavorable balance prior to 1881 to an excess of exports over imports for several years in the next decade. By 1881 the adverse balance had totaled 79 million yen with invisible foreign services having cost Japan 70 million yen in gold exports. From 1881 to 1893, however, some of the years showed a favorable trade balance. The character of foreign trade also reflected the changing economic pattern. Imports of finished manufactured goods increased and the export of foodstuffs and raw materials declined. In other words, Japan's population was absorbing all of the domestic food supply and there was a demand for finished foreign goods. Furthermore, its industries were far enough advanced to use the total production of raw materials, but it relied on foreign factories for complicated machinery. (See Table 10, in Chapter 14.)

Military Strength

If the assumption is correct that the Meiji leaders modernized their country to meet its strategic needs—and the facts thus far strongly substantiate this assumption—it was to be expected that the expansion of the Army and Navy would be commensurate with industrial growth. A review of military expenditures shows this to be true. During the period between the Satsuma Rebellion and the Sino-Japanese War (1877–1894), the Imperial Army spent approximately 200 million yen and the Imperial Navy an additional 130 million yen. Following the difficulties which the government had encountered in suppressing the Satsuma Rebellion of 1877, War Minister Yamagata was able to convince his colleagues that the Army needed to be expanded and modernized. In 1878 he organized the Army, established a General Staff, and laid down a ten-year expansion program. The plan included building the ground forces into an Imperial Body Guard Division and six other divisions.

But the uncertain financial conditions delayed some of this program until Matsukata had stabilized the nation's finances. In the meantime, in 1883, an extremely important first step toward the formation of a new, modern army was taken. An Army Staff College was established. While both French and German instructors were employed during its first few years, the appointment in 1885 of Major K. W. J. Merkel to the College faculty and as adviser to the General Staff meant that Japan's Army would follow the German pattern. Major Merkel was primarily responsible for the complete reorganization of the army in 1887. The old garrisons located at various cities throughout the Empire were changed into Division Headquarters. Divisions were formed with specializations in infantry, artillery, supply, and engineers. The organizational structure called for the Chiefs of Staff to be responsible for military affairs, the Minister of War to be the chief administrative officer, and the Inspector General to be in charge of all aspects of military training. These three positions together formed the top policy-making body of the Army through which "Supreme Command" was carried out. By the time Major Merkel returned to Germany, an effective peacetime army of 73,000 men, with a wartime strength of 274,000, had been hammered out and the foundation for subsequent successful fighting on the continent had been laid. In essence, this structure of the army continued down to the end of World War II.[8]

In view of the insular character of Japan's geography, a navy was as essential as an army for security reasons. Consequently, during the same period an ambitious naval construction and development program was pursued. Naval expenditures were used largely to meet the costs of the naval building program. In 1881 a program was started which included the construction of six warships, twenty-four middle- and small-sized auxiliary craft, and twelve torpedo boats. It called for annual payments of 3.3 million yen. After 1883 the additional expenses of the program were financed largely by special bond issues which totaled 17 million yen. The program was further expanded to permit the construction of 23 ships between 1883 and 1889. But even though the Navy built its own hulls and rig, much of the machinery and armament for the vessels had to be imported. In fact, the war against China in 1894 was fought largely in ships purchased from abroad or built overseas on special order.

A strong military machine was already in the making. Although expenses were far greater toward the end of the period, during 1877–1894 Japan spent an average of 20 million yen yearly on armaments. In terms of the national expenditure, which Matsukata froze at 63 million yen in 1882, these Army and Navy expenses equaled one-third of the total.[9] These expanded military establishments immediately became two of the chief pillars which supported Japan's national strength.

At the same time, as was true of the agrarian problem, there were circumstances which made this strength more apparent than real. This program of modernization enabled Japan to win the Sino-Japanese War in 1895, the Russo-Japanese War in 1905, and to profit materially from World War I. On the other hand, military expenditures placed a heavy burden on the taxpayer and kept living standards down. The scarcity of raw materials, such as coking coal and iron ore, tempted the militarists to undertake the conquest of Manchuria and China to obtain these resources. Since they were not stopped by their own government or people, the Empire had to endure the consequences of eventual expansionism. This in turn led to a clash with the United States and its Allies in World War II and eventual defeat and humiliation. One is tempted to ask, therefore, whether this newly created strength in 1890 was real or illusory. In any event, the modernization movement of the first two decades of the Meiji Period had contributed directly to a limited expansion of the territorial boundaries of the Empire.

The Beginnings of Empire: The Kurile and Bonin Islands

Thus, by 1890 various aspects of Japanese economic life had shown marked virility and potentialities for growth. Some of these aspects, such as the rapidly expanding program of military preparedness, gave indication of bursting their bonds. But the time had not yet arrived for a correlation of political, economic, and military forces which would result in a successful, full-scale war, and the acquisition of important colonial territories. Nothing like a master plan for imperialistic expansion had been developed or accepted.

On the contrary, it was a period of trial and error in questions concerning territorial expansion. Many years earlier, individuals such as Saigō Takamori had dreamt of the conquest of territory on the mainland of Asia, but a basic policy on this question had not been decided. For example, the decision in 1873 not to send a military force to Korea resulted in Saigō's resignation from the government. The next year, however, Ōkubo sanctioned, on an *ad hoc* basis, a naval expedition against Formosa, and Japan might well have occupied Formosa permanently at that time if the Western powers had not reacted so strongly against the whole project. Improvisation, which was such an outstanding characteristic of the economic and political growth of the nation in these formative years, was the only consistent element in Japan's early foreign relations. Nevertheless, two of the territorial questions which arose prior to 1890, the issue of the Ryūkyū Islands and the question of Korean independence, had a direct bearing on the formation of the subsequent policy in relation to the continent. Furthermore, the problems which these issues raised came to be basic causes of both the Sino-Japanese War of 1894 and the Russo-Japanese War of 1904.

Even the less significant question of the final disposition of the Kurile Islands, the chain which extends from Hokkaidō northeasterly in an arc to Kamchatka, was a crucial element in Russian–Japanese relations. In the earliest treaties with Russia, the Kuriles had been divided between the two countries and the status of the Island of Sakhalin (Karafuto) had been left unsettled. In the years after the Restoration, there were

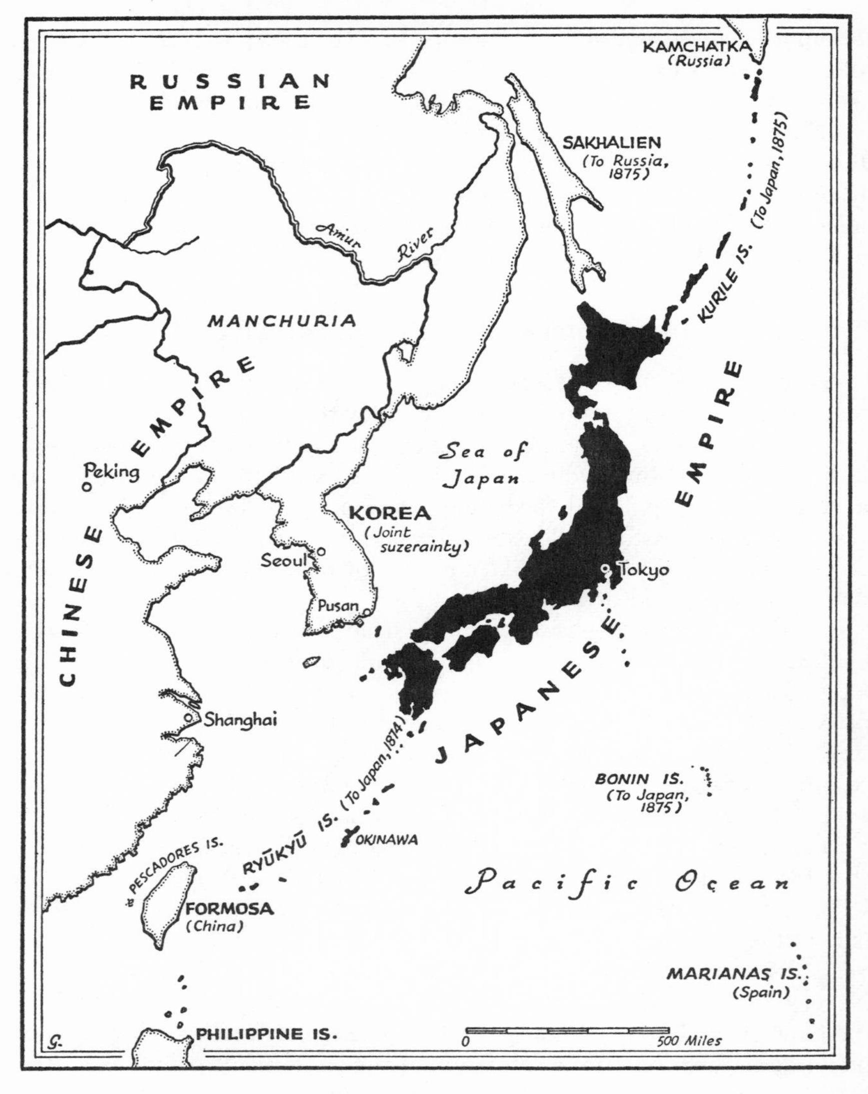

THE JAPANESE EMPIRE, 1890

divergent views within the Japanese government on the disposition which should be made of these territories. One group, stimulated by the visit to Tokyo in 1870 of the former United States Secretary of State, William H. Seward, favored a policy of expansion. This school of thought urged that negotiations be started with Russia for the purchase by Japan of the northern half of Sakhalin. In addition, Russia should be forced to accept Japan's demand for the southern half of the island and all of the Kuriles.[10]

The other group, led by Kuroda Kiyotaka, the chief of the Hokkaidō Colonization Office, supported a policy of conciliation toward Russia. He realized better than anyone else how slim a hold Japan had over Hokkaidō and how a war with Russia at that time would have meant the loss of Hokkaidō for Japan. (See Chapter 7.) Since Kuroda wanted to avoid an open break at all cost, he even advocated Japan's abandonment of any claim for Sakhalin to relieve Russian–Japanese tension.

His views prevailed. Admiral Enomoto Takeaki was sent to St. Petersburg in 1874 with instructions to settle the Russo-Japanese boundary questions as amicably as possible. After lengthy discussions, a treaty was concluded the next year in which both countries made concessions. Japan gave up all claims to Sakhalin; Russia gave up claim to the northern half of the Kuriles and agreed to cede the entire chain of islands to Japan. This settlement remained in force until after the Russo-Japanese War when Japan acquired, by the Treaty of Portsmouth of 1905, the southern half of Sakhalin. Because of their geographic position, the Kuriles were important to Japan strategically and were incorporated into Hokkaidō and administered as an integral part of that prefecture. Because of the abundant fish in their waters, they were valuable economically. After World War II, in accordance with the Yalta Agreement of February, 1945, the Soviet Union occupied all of the Kurile Islands. Unfortunately, President Franklin Roosevelt had not obtained a specific definition from Stalin as to what islands were to be included in the Kuriles. Consequently, the Soviet Union has deprived the Japanese of access not only to the Kurile chain but also to Shikotan and Habomai islands just off the northern shore of Hokkaidō. This problem remains one of the basic issues between Japan and the Soviet Union.

Another group of offshore islands, the sovereignty of which was disputed in the early Meiji Period, is the Bonin Islands (Ogasawara). Historically they had been considered an integral part of the Empire but their chief fame had been as a place of exile for political criminals. Claimed by the British in 1827 and by Perry for the United States in 1853, neither country had pressed its claim, but Japan had undertaken their active colonization. In 1873 United States Secretary of State Hamilton Fish had ruled that they had never been officially recognized as an American possession; two years later the United States persuaded the Western powers to agree to recognize the Bonins as Japanese territory. Despite the fact that they lie 560 miles to the southeast from Tokyo, they were incorporated in 1880 into Greater Tokyo (Tokyo Fu). They remained as part of the capital district until occupied by United States naval forces during World War II. Their poor water and mountainous terrain have made them of little value other than as a protective outpost for Japan as a whole and especially for the metropolitan areas of Yokohama and Tokyo. In 1968, the United States turned them back to Japanese administration and control.

The Ryūkyū (Liuchiu) Islands

One of the most important territorial issues in the early Meiji Period concerned the Ryūkyū Islands.[11] They extend for 570 miles in a southerly direction below Kyūshū and were the most important territory in dispute during this period. In 1875 they sustained an estimated population of 167,572 that had distinctive cultural and linguistic characteristics of its own. In language and customs the Ryūkyūans show similarities to both the Chinese and Japanese, but are more closely related to the latter. From the fourteenth to the seventeenth centuries they were predominantly under Chinese influence. After the seventeenth century, they were conquered by the Japanese feudal baron of Satsuma. He continued to exact tribute rice from them until modern times. This relationship of suzerainty did not prevent the islands from paying tribute simultaneously to China, however, and from carrying on an active trade with both China and Japan. Furthermore, the "King of the Liuchius" considered himself independent enough of both Japan and China to sign treaties on his own behalf with the Western powers. In 1854 Perry signed one of the first of such treaties for the United States.

With the formal abolition in 1872 of the feudal domains in Japan, the disposition of the Ryūkyūs became important. The Japanese gave little credence to any Chinese claims to the territory and took steps to eradicate such claims. The King was forcibly transported to Tokyo and forbidden to leave. The United States Minister to Japan, DeLong, was informed in October, 1872, that the Ryūkyū Islands had been formally incorporated into Japan but was assured that the terms of the American treaty with "the Kingdom of the Liuchius" would be observed.

In 1873 the Japanese Foreign Minister was dispatched to China to obtain redress for the killing of some Ryūkyūan waifs by an aboriginal tribe in southern Formosa. He sought an admission from China that these aborigines were beyond its control. Furthermore, he pressed for Chinese recognition that Ryūkyūans were Japanese subjects and Japan had a right to send an expedition against the Formosan tribesmen. According to Japanese accounts of these official conversations in Peking, members of the Chinese Foreign Ministry agreed orally to these demands. Consequently, the Japanese Foreign Minister and DeLong, the American Minister in Tokyo, concluded that China had thereby renounced its claim to the Ryūkyū Islands.

Japan then proceeded to make plans for a Formosan Expedition. As already noted, Ōkubo as Minister of Home Affairs personally endorsed it and sanctioned the dispatch of the fleet under command of Saigō Tsugumichi. This military move against a defenseless Formosa was not challenged militarily by China and enabled Japan to obtain a written agreement for indemnification of losses sustained by the Ryūkyūans. In October, 1874, the Japanese plenipotentiary and the Chinese Minister of Foreign Affairs signed a convention at Peking which recognized the Ryūkyūans as Japanese subjects. The Convention stated specifically that "certain Japanese subjects" were "wantonly murdered by the unreclaimed savages of Formosa." Japan agreed to withdraw its expeditionary forces from Formosa; China promised not to blame Japan for its action and to drop all further discussion on the matter. Furthermore, China promised to pay an indemnity of 500,000 taels, one-fifth of which was paid immediately for the families of the shipwrecked "Japanese" who were killed.[12]

Two points are of special significance. In the first place, the agreement makes no mention of Ryūkyūans but always refers to them in the text as "people from Japan." Secondly, China signed the agreement and paid the indemnity without any reservations. It never realized that both of these acts constituted recognition on its part of Japanese sovereignty over the Ryūkyū Islands.

Consequently, when China protested in 1879 against the incorporation of the islands into Okinawa Prefecture, it was in an extremely weak position from the point of view of international law. Nevertheless, when ex-President Ulysses S. Grant stopped at Peking on his world tour, China placed the matter before him and asked for his intercession. He proposed the appointment of a High Commissioner to settle the question. After his arrival in Tokyo, he informed China that he believed Japan would be willing to make sacrifices if China would approach the negotiations in the same spirit. This move of General Grant resulted in the renewal of direct negotiations between the Chinese and Japanese. As Grant had predicted, the Japanese proposed a compromise solution, namely, that the southernmost group of the Ryūkyūs, the Sakishima Group, be ceded to China in return for a revision of the Sino-Japanese Treaty of 1871 to include a most-favored-nation clause which would give Japan the same privileges that China had granted the other powers.

Negotiations over this thorny issue continued throughout 1880. At one point, Viceroy Li Hung-chang agreed to limit China's claim to the southern group but refused to consent to revision of the old Sino-Japanese treaty. In October, 1880, the Chinese negotiator promised the Japanese Minister at Peking that he would sign an agreement which included both of Japan's demands. Two months later, the Chinese had not signed and reversed themselves. The Japanese Minister at Peking was informed that an Imperial Decree had ordered that the whole matter be taken out of the hands of the Chinese Foreign Ministry and that it was to be considered by the Northern and Southern Superintendents of Trade. By mid-January, 1881, the Japanese government was fed up with Chinese vacillations. It considered that the failure to keep the promise to sign the treaty was in reality equivalent to forfeiture of Chinese claims to the islands. It notified the Chinese government that it considered the matter closed and that its Minister had been recalled.

Apparently the Chinese government had followed these tactics to prevent signing an agreement which recognized Japanese sovereignty over the Ryūkyū Islands. In March, 1881, Li Hung-chang told the United States Minister to China that his government would never agree to the division of "the Liuchiu Islands" between China and Japan. At the very most, it would sign a treaty whereby both powers guaranteed their absolute independence. But Li was not willing to make their disposition a cause for war and was content to leave the matter in abeyance.

He and his colleagues had underestimated the importance of actual possession of territory in such a dispute. Time was on the side of the Japanese. They continued to administer the islands as an integral part of their Empire and refused to reopen negotiations. Whether from indifference or from misjudgment, the entire archipelago, including the two southernmost islands nearest Formosa, had been lost to China indefinitely.

The issue was revived again during World War II by Generalissimo Chiang Kai-shek. In a revised Chinese edition of *China's Destiny,* he described the Liuchius, along with other border regions, as strategic areas necessary for the protection of China's existence. He assumed that the islands were Chinese territory. He concluded that "their severance from the rest of China takes away the natural defenses of the country." [13] This Chinese claim was never taken seriously, however, by the other Allies in discussions on the postwar disposition of the Ryūkyūs. In the spring of 1945, Okinawa, the largest of the islands, was captured and occupied by American armed forces. After the war it was developed into a large American base and remained under United States military occupation. In November, 1969, President Richard M. Nixon and Prime Minister Eisaku Satō agreed that during 1972 Okinawa should revert to Japanese administration. (See below, page 535.)

Although the dispute over the Ryūkyūs did not lead to open hostilities between China and Japan, it laid the groundwork for the distrust and animosity which were to increase during the next decade. Each country interpreted the results of the negotiations differently. Japan believed that China's oral commitments could not be trusted and that action was preferable to endless negotiations. On the other hand, China was resentful of the arrogance of the Japanese officials and of their insistence on following Western procedures in international law. It was fearful of the military machine which Japan had developed, and was apprehensive that there would be a repetition of the Formosan affair with negotiations backed by military or naval pressure. It considered that all of the outlying territories, such as the Ryūkyūs and Korea, were under Chinese suzerainty and that Japan had no right to claim them. It was not sure, however, that Japan could be stopped or controlled.

Korean Independence and Suzerainty of China and Japan

As in the dispute over the disposition of the Ryūkyū Islands, the issues arising from the question of Korean independence went beyond the limits of that country. In fact, the problem of Korean autonomy has always, whether in the late sixteenth century, the late nineteenth century, or mid-twentieth century, involved two or more other countries. Partly because of its geographic location as the land bridge between Japan and the Asiatic mainland, partly because of its endemic weakness in comparison with its neighbors, Korea has often been one of the most baffling of international problems. In the third quarter of the nineteenth century, Korea was an independent country with its own King and separate government, yet paid tribute to both China and Japan. Each of these countries considered that it had a special interest in Korea to the exclusion of the other. Each regarded with suspicion any moves by the other within the Korean peninsula. In fact, each considered such moves as a direct threat to its national interests. For many centuries, however, Korea had had a closer relation to China than to Japan.

Under these circumstances, when Japan attempted to negotiate a treaty with Korea which would have abolished the latter's seclusion and put Japan's relations with that country on a par with those of China, complications immediately developed. In 1872–1873, when its envoys received rebuffs from the arrogant Koreans, there was violent reaction in Japan. (See Chapter 5.) Japan then sought to clarify the situation by asking China to explain its position on Korea. The answer was the same as that for the Ryūkyūs. China maintained that it possessed the right of suzerainty over the Korean kingdom and that the King was a Minister of the Chinese Emperor.

Not satisfied with this answer, Japan attempted to force the issue by following a policy which Perry had used so successfully in Japan some twenty years earlier. In 1875 Japan sought a treaty with Korea through a show of naval force along the Korean coast and through diplomatic negotiations. The mission failed; so the next year Japanese naval boats surveyed the Korean coast despite gunfire from shore batteries. The Koreans were warned that the survey was in preparation for a military force which would support the next Japanese diplomatic move.

It was a bluff but it worked. China, which had only recently agreed to concessions in the Ryūkyūs as a result of the Japanese military expedition against Formosa, was afraid of future Japanese moves. Hence Viceroy Li Hung-chang told the Koreans to receive the proposed Japanese diplomatic mission. Direct negotiations between the Japanese and the Koreans resulted in the Treaty of Kanghwa of 1876. By this first modern treaty, Korea opened two ports to Japan and granted partial extraterritorial rights to Japanese subjects. In return, Japan recognized Korea as an independent state enjoying the same sovereign rights as Japan.

But Korean and Chinese reactions to this treaty were as important for the future as were its contents. One of the objectives of the Japanese negotiators had been to obtain an agreement which clearly established Korea as a country independent of Chinese or any other foreign influence. If this fact could be established, there was some chance of Japan being able to compete successfully for the control of Korea on an equal footing with China. Either on their own initiative or on the advice of Li Hung-chang, however, the Korean negotiators had questioned the powers of the Japanese envoy and so raised questions on the validity of the Kanghwa Treaty. Furthermore, they had kept the Chinese informed of all stages of the negotiations and had not acted as free agents. As for China, it refused to take seriously the clause in the treaty about Korean independence. In fact, the whole affair made no difference in China's attitude. Regardless of the Kanghwa Treaty, China continued to assume that it had a right to expect Korea to follow its lead on foreign affairs and to be partially subject to it.

This policy is illustrated by subsequent negotiations of the United States with Korea. The American envoy, Admiral Robert W. Shufeldt, first approached the Japanese in the hope of getting them to mediate for the United States. This move aroused Li Hung-chang into action. Since he was anxious to keep Japan from obtaining a favored position, he offered to act as mediator himself. Shufeldt assumed that this offer meant that China was agreeable to recognizing Korean independence. He soon discovered, however, that such was not the case. In fact, he was asked to include a statement in the treaty which recognized Korea as a dependent state of China. Such a clause would have been a diplomatic victory for China over Japan in its relations with Korea. When Shufeldt refused to comply with this wish, the Koreans indicated that they might not be willing to sign any treaty with the United States.

The question was finally settled in a manner which protected the desires of both the United States and China. The Shufeldt Treaty, the first Korean treaty with a Western power, was signed in 1882. It provided for perpetual peace and friendship between Korea and the United States. At the same time, a letter from the Korean King accompanied the Treaty which described his country's status as inferior to China's. This letter stated specifically that Korea was a dependency of China but that the intercourse between Korea and the United States should be carried on in every respect on terms of equality. It concluded:

> In the matter of Corea being a dependency of China in any question that may arise between them in consequence of such dependency, the United States shall in no way interfere.[14]

Hence both Japan and the United States had presumably negotiated treaties with Korea as a free and equal nation. China had permitted such negotiations, however, on the assumption that there were no inconsistencies between these treaties and the concept that Korea continued in reality to be a Chinese dependency. In other words, the issue of Korea's status relative to China and Japan was as unsettled as ever.

At the same time, the effects of implementing the Kanghwa Treaty and domestic intrigues within Korea complicated Japanese–Korean–Chinese relations. During preceding decades, the autocratic and corrupt court of the Korean King at Seoul had broken into several factions, each of which supported a contender for the throne. The lines of loyalty were further confused by the support which China and Japan gave to the contending factions. One of the two most important groups was led by the father and Regent of the young King, the Taewŏnkun. In general, the Taewŏnkun and his adherents were conservative, reactionary, and antiforeign, and were supported by China.

After 1873, when the King came of age, the Taewŏnkun was in retirement and watched the policies of his rival faction, which the Queen and the Min family, who now controlled the King, put into effect. The Queen's position was relatively progressive, proforeign, and pro-Japanese. After the Treaty of Kanghwa was signed with Japan in 1876, the King and his court were relatively circumspect toward the new Japanese Minister. In July, 1882, however, an anti-Japanese riot in Seoul, instigated by the Taewŏnkun, exacerbated the situation. Both the King and Queen escaped assassination; the Japanese Minister, Hanabusa, and his guard fled in a small boat and were returned to Japan on a British survey ship. The Japanese immediately sent reinforcements to guard their legation and China countered with a similar move. At the same time, the latter captured the Taewŏnkun and whisked him away to Tientsin on the grounds that he had revolted against the Chinese Emperor. In reality, he was in safe keeping until such time as China might want to use him for political purposes. In the end, the King retained temporary control. He apologized to Japan for the revolt started by the Taewŏnkun, granted an indemnity to Japan for the losses sustained, and permitted an increase in the Japanese Legation Guard. Two years later, the Japanese canceled the remaining indemnity payments.

The Li–Ito Convention of 1885

During the next few years, the history of Korea's foreign relations is one of intrigue and coercion, especially by both China and Japan in their endeavor to obtain control over Korea's destiny. Russia's interests in Korea only complicated the picture. As foreign pressures increased, the Korean King was placed in an untenable position. For example, China was clearly unwilling to accept the concept of Korea as an "independent and sovereign state" and proceeded to act toward it as a dependency. In 1883, when China issued new trade regulations, it declared them to be "commissions on the part of China to her tributary state [of Korea] and are not within the scope of the 'Favored Nation Rule' existing between the several Treaty Powers and China." [15] In early December of the next year, Pak Young-hyo, a brother-in-law of the King, Kim Ok-kiun, and other leaders of the Independence Party who had close connections with liberals in Japan, especially Fukuzawa Yukichi, staged a coup d'état. The Japanese Minister and his staff were clearly implicated in the plot. He dispatched troops from the Japanese Legation to protect the King after the leaders of the coup had entered the palace and killed several of the King's ministers. The plot was conceived ostensibly because Min Yong-Ik, a nephew of the Queen, had begun to cooperate with the Chinese thus further endangering Korean independence. Following attacks by Koreans against Japanese and their property and attempts to capture the Japanese Legation, the Japanese Minister and civilians, under the protection of Japanese troops, escaped to Inchon and the safety of a Japanese ship. Kim and Pak, the Korean revolutionary leaders, fled with them to Japan. In the meantime, the Korean King had taken refuge in the Chinese camp. Foreign Minister Inouye Kaoru then negotiated with the Koreans alone for an indemnity and an apology, refusing to release Kim and Pak. In 1885, Yüan Shih-kai, whom China appointed as its chief resident in Korea, openly befriended the Korean King and aided and abetted those Koreans opposed to Japan. The situation had deteriorated to such an extent that the differences between China and Japan had to be settled either by negotiations or by war.[16]

As neither side was yet ready for war, both agreed to negotiate. Despite strong popular opposition in Japan to diplomatic negotiations, in March, 1885, Itō Hirobumi went to China to work out a solution with Viceroy Li Hung-chang. The two leaders met in Tientsin, and after brief negotiations, they signed the Li–Itō Convention whereby both countries agreed to withdraw their troops from the Korean peninsula within four months. Furthermore, if disturbances within Korea required either of the signatories to dispatch troops, written notice of such intention would be sent to the other. Finally, they agreed that neither Chinese nor Japanese were to be employed in the organization or training of a Korean army. This agreement settled the crisis temporarily. The Japanese government then undertook measures to see that terms of the agreement were carried out. The Japanese troops were withdrawn within the allotted period; Korean extremists in Japan were apprehended to prevent further political assassinations. While there were several difficult problems which arose over Korea during the next few years, Japanese–Chinese relations did not reach a crisis until 1893.[17]

In the meantime, Russia's moves began to make it clear that it was the European power most concerned over Korea's future. So long as China and Japan vied for control over Korean affairs without the issue being settled in favor of one or the other, Russia was content to await a more propitious moment to exert its influence. Even before the Li–Itō Convention forbade the use of Chinese or Japanese advisers in the Korean Army, Russia was in an enviable position. When Von Mollendorf, a German in the employ of the Chinese Maritime Custom, went to Korea as a foreign adviser, he advocated the use of Russian officers to modernize the Korean Army. In return, Russia was to receive exclusive permission to use Port Lazaroff, the warm-water port of Wonsan. Both China and Japan protested against this move, so that Russian influence was temporarily kept out of the crucial area. For the moment the Li–Itō Convention had prevented the crisis over Korea from deteriorating but had not settled the question of whether China or Japan would dominate the peninsula. Peace in the Far East was contingent on the willingness of both of these countries to postpone a final showdown.

When the Japanese Constitution was promulgated in 1889, therefore, the various components of the nation's strength indicated growth and expansion, both economically and territorially. Agriculture, the country's basic industry, had produced enough staple food to meet domestic needs with a surplus for export. The difficulties of increased production, a limited acreage of untilled arable land, greater per-capita consumption, and a steady rise in the birth rate were to combine, in the near future, to create a deficit in the rice supply. The deficiencies were met, however, by imports paid out of exports of raw silk and a limited amount of finished goods. Moreover, a more serious agrarian crisis was to be averted by the outbreak of war.

Financially, the nation was stronger in 1890 than at any other time in its recent history. The policy of retrenchment and fixed annual expenditures sponsored by Finance Minister Matsukata had effectively reduced the public debt, regained confidence in the currency, and increased annual revenues by more than half so that they were well in excess of expenditures. Industrial growth continued in both consumers' goods and heavy industries. Foreign trade showed an excess of exports over imports. With these auspicious developments, Japan absorbed an annual military budget of 20 million yen, about one-third of the total expenses, without showing any outward signs of strain. Could it be that fate had destined Japan to become the new leader of Asia?

A survey of Japan's territorial problems prior to 1890 tends to substantiate a positive answer to this question. There were few signs which indicated that Japan could easily be held in check if it decided to expand. Thus far it seemed to have succeeded in obtaining most of what it sought. The Russian boundary question had been settled; Hokkaidō was rapidly becoming more and more secure. The Ryūkyū Islands had been incorporated into the Empire. China's demands concerning them had been ignored. Only a war could wrest them from Japan.

As for Korea, Japan had not yet recognized it officially as a key to the control of the continent. So far, efforts had been partially successful in neutralizing Chinese influence in Korea. The best that could be hoped for at the moment was recognition by China, in word and in deed, that Korea was an independent country. As the realization grew that China intended to persist in its overlordship of Korea, Japan became obsessed with the desire to control the peninsula. It was an easy step in reasoning, therefore, to conclude that this control was necessary for national survival.

Japan had gone a long way in less than forty years. When Perry arrived it feared for its very existence. Now it dared to consider the use of force to obtain acceptance of its desires in territories such as Korea, which had not traditionally been considered a real or potential part of Imperial Japan. The thirst for empire was just beginning, as the thirst for power had already held the oligarchs in its grip.

Only one basic international question still remained unsettled. This was the revision of the unequal treaties with the Western powers. But even in the face of these difficulties, the oligarchs had retained complete control over the opposition. In the immediate future, however, this question of treaty revision and the problem of Japan's relations toward Korea were to absorb much of their thought and energy. For the next three decades, they were to be primarily concerned with carving out and consolidating an Empire which made Japan the dominant force in East Asia.

Notes

1. As in Chapters 5 and 7, references in this chapter to the various sectors of Japan's economy are restricted to trends and the most significant developments to indicate the extent of national strength up to 1890. A more detailed analysis of Japan's economic base in 1915 is presented in Chapter 14. This treatment seems appropriate for two reasons. First, the economists Ohkawa and Rosovsky have divided Japan's century of economic growth from 1868 into three phases. The first phase, that of a transition, extends to about 1885; the second phase, that of initial modern economic growth, covers the next twenty years. Second, economic statistics are less reliable for the first than for the second phase.

Several significant recent economic studies have added notably to our understanding of Japan's modern development. On the other hand, the disagreement among economists on such basic problems as the rate of economic growth complicates the analysis of this growth. For a summary of these and other aspects of Japan's economy see William W. Lockwood (ed.), *The State and Economic Enterprise in Japan* (Princeton: Princeton University Press, 1965), especially Kazushi Ohkawa and Henry Rosovsky, "A Century of Japanese Economic Growth," pp. 47–77; James I. Nakamura, "Growth of Japanese Agriculture 1875–1920," pp. 249–325; Harry T. Oshima, "Meiji Fiscal Policy and Economic Progress," pp. 353–91. See also James I. Nakamura, *Agricultural Production and the Economic Development of Japan 1873–1922* (Princeton: Princeton University Press, 1966).

2. See Nakamura, *Agricultural Production . . . , op. cit.*, pp. 22 ff.; Ohkawa and Rosovsky, *op. cit.*, p. 69; and Ohkawa Kazushi (ed.), *Chōki Keizai Tōkei: Nōrin* (Tokyo: Tōyō Keizaishi Shimpōsha, 1966), IX, pp. 166–69.

3. It will be recalled that even the distress among the landowners, entrepreneurs, and farmers, on which the *Jiyūtō* attempted to capitalize, had largely subsided by 1889. (See *supra* page 155.)

4. Matsukata Masayoshi, "Japan Finance," in Ōkuma Shigenobu (compiler), *Fifty Years of New Japan*, English version edited by Marcus B. Huish (2 vols.; London: Smith Elders, 1909), I, pp. 364–65.

5. Oshima, *op. cit.*, pp. 359–71.

6. The role of military expenditures in the economy is difficult to predict. It has been claimed that if these expenses had been used for nonmilitary purposes, the nation would have profited. The difficulty with this premise is that there was no assurance an equivalent amount of money would have been spent if there had not been the threat to Japan's security.

7. The following figures indicate the large differential between the cost to the government and the sale price to the purchaser for some of these industries.

	Date Sold	Government Investment (Yen)	Sale Price (Yen)	Purchaser
Fukugawa Cement	1884	169,631	61,700	Asano Sōichirō
Nagasaki Shipyard	1884	628,767	459,000	Iwasaki Yatarō
Kosaka Mine	1884	547,476	273,000	Kuhara Shōzaburō
Annai Mine (copper)	1885	1,606,271	337,000	Furukawa Ichibe
Shinagawa Glass	1885	189,631	80,000	Nishimura Katsuzō

See Thomas C. Smith, *Political Change and Industrial Development in Japan: Government Enterprise, 1868–1880* (Stanford: Stanford University Press, 1955), pp. 90–91; and Johannes Hirschmeier, *The Origin of Entrepreneurship in Meiji Japan* (Cambridge: Harvard University Press, 1964), p. 242.

8. That the army was rapidly growing up is illustrated by Yamagata's willingness to shift from Minister of War in 1878 to other posts and to Home Minister in 1885. For an excellent detailed account of the problem facing the new Army and the role played by foreign advisers in its formation, especially Major Merkel, see Ernest L. Presseisen, *Before Aggression; Europeans Prepare the Japanese Army* (Tucson: University of Arizona Press, 1965), pp. 95 ff.

9. Edwin A. Falk, *Togo and the Rise of Japanese Sea Power* (New York: Longmans, Green and Co., Inc., 1936), p. 125.

10. Seward made these suggestions on the basis of his own experiences with Russia. He had purchased Alaska for the United States in 1867. For a detailed account of Japan's shifting policies toward Sakhalin and the final settlement, see George A. Lensen, *The Russian Push toward Japan: Russo-Japanese Relations 1697–1875* (Princeton: Princeton University Press, 1959), pp. 442 ff.

11. The changing status of the Ryūkyū Islands over the years poses a real problem as to what name to use for them. The Chinese reading of the characters used for the islands as a whole is Liu-ch'iu; the Japanese reading of the same characters is Ryūkyū. After World War II, Okinawa, the name of the biggest of the islands, came to be used both for that island and for all of them. I have decided to use the term Ryūkyū Islands when referring to them as a whole for the period before 1945. Thereafter I have used Okinawa.

12. As the clauses in this treaty have an important bearing on the Chinese claim, the last clause reads as follows in the original:

日本國從前被害難民之家

See United States Government, *Chinese Treaties 1908*, II. For details of the Sino-Japanese negotiations see *United States Department of State Archives 56*, "China," James B. Angell, November 16, 1880–February, 1881; Dispatch No. 103, January 25, 1881. See also T. F. Tsiang, "Sino-Japanese Diplomatic Relations, 1870–1894," *Chinese Social and Political Science Review* (1933), pp. 45 ff.; George Kerr, *Okinawa* (Tokyo: Charles E. Tuttle Co., 1959); and Grace Fox, *Britain and Japan, 1858–1883* (Oxford: Clarendon Press, 1969), pp. 286 ff.

13. For the Chinese edition of Chiang's work see Chiang Kai-shek, *Chung Kuo Chih Ming Yun* (Chunking: December 15, 1945), pp. 6–7.

14. United States Department of State, *United States Foreign Relations 1888*, Part II, pp. 255–56.

15. See Hilary Conroy, *The Japanese Seizure of Korea: 1868–1910* (Philadelphia: University of Pennsylvania Press, 1960), p. 115.

16. *Ibid.*, pp. 124–68.

17. I am indebted to Professor Hilary Conroy for having raised serious doubts concerning the inference reached in the first edition of this book (page 167) that by 1885 Japan had clearly defined designs on Korea and planned to conduct its foreign relations in such a way as to be able to take Korea after fighting a successful war against China. Professor Conroy discovered the quotation I used from Frederick Nelson, *Korea and the Old Order in Eastern Asia* (Baton Rouge: University of Louisiana Press, 1946), to be

incorrect. He points out that in the years immediately following the Li–Itō Convention of 1885, Japan was primarily interested in Korea's reform and independence and in inducing it away from Chinese control. As examples of this policy he cites Japan's attempts to break the Chinese telegraph monopoly by constructing one of its own and to change the monopoly of Chinese advisers at the Korean court and to increase Japanese–Korean trade. See Hilary Conroy, *op. cit.*, pp. 169–201. For an analysis of the Conroy thesis that there is little evidence to support the existence of a Japanese plot to annex Korea, see George Totten, *et al.*, "Japanese Imperialism and Aggression: Reconsiderations. I," *Journal of Asian Studies,* XXII (1963), pp. 469–73.

10

The Social and Cultural Scene

Something of the conglomerate character of Japanese society in 1890 can be imagined from the preceding material, but the contributions of this society to the aggregate strength of the growing Empire have yet to be analyzed. The problem at hand is more than an elaboration of national characteristics and habits and a description of the social scene in the chief urban centers and in the remote villages. Rather, it is essential to determine the extent and effectiveness of the efforts of the Imperial government to mold the masses of society to become obedient, loyal, and industrious subjects of the Emperor. It is also important, if the true nature of the Japanese people in modern times is to be understood, to indicate the influences and acceptability of other forces on both those who led and those who followed. The subsequent description of the social scene will enumerate, therefore, some of the specific reforms deemed necessary to complete the process of national modernization. It will give illustrations of the effects, in many cases incongruous and unpredictable, of the conflict between an innate conservatism and nascent nationalism on the one hand, and an insatiable appetite for Western knowledge on the other. It will note the growth of a state-controlled educational system and a new legal system both of which attempted to preserve old concepts and to make all subjects amenable to the duties imposed upon them by virtue of the fact that they were Japanese.

As has been pointed out previously on numerous occasions, a highly developed ability to *adapt* foreign cultural attributes, an extensive eclecticism, has been a significant national characteristic of Japan. At no time in its history was this more clearly illustrated than in the first twenty years of the Meiji Period; in no aspect of life was this more apparent than in the effort toward modernization. In fact, thanks to this ability to select rather than to a blind desire to imitate, much of the friction which would normally be expected from the clash of Occidentalism with traditional

Oriental customs and thought was avoided. In its place, the new government and many of the most brilliant young men of the country were able to combine a strong belief in the national heritage with technical knowledge of Western civilization.

The Two Currents of Nationalism and Occidentalism

In 1884, when Itō had returned from Germany and began to think specifically about drafting a constitution, a young man, twenty years his junior, had just been sent to the United States as a student. This young man, Nitobe Inazō, was to personify in his life this eclecticism in a unique manner. In the year that his country promulgated the Constitution, he was expounding on the two currents of Western civilization and of Japanese culture. Later he wrote eloquently of the conflict between the former, with its scientific, practical, and democratic approach, and the latter, with its literary, artistic, and aristocratic base. Learning in Japan meant a knowledge of religion, belles lettres, and Chinese ethics; education in the West covered all branches of knowledge. He concluded:

> Japan is experimenting with Western arts and sciences to see how far she can make them her own. . . . She will not repeat the folly . . . of introducing an exotic civilization wholesale; she could not do it now as she has too much at stake.[1]

To Nitobe, as well as to his contemporaries, the new Japan was not an accretion produced by foreign cultures, but the result of the application of an innate eclecticism to new circumstances and new stimuli.

In the first years of the Meiji Period, this sophistication was not as apparent as was the blind eagerness to learn the English language, a naïve belief that all foreigners had a superior knowledge of any subject, whether the foreigner was a drunken sailor, a profligate, a merchant, or a pious missionary of the Gospel. But by 1890 modernization had come to mean to people of all ranks, whether urban resident or lowly peasant, the prohibition of many of the customs and practices which had been accepted for centuries. The famous Charter Oath of 1868 set forth some of the basic objectives for the new society. All classes were to have a chance to fulfill their proper functions, absurd usages were to be abandoned, and knowledge was to be sought throughout the world. (See page 82 above.)

All general policies of this nature required time and effort to implement. Since an agrarian society such as that of Japan is inherently averse to change, and since the government's leaders had more important issues to solve than social changes, many of the old customs disappeared slowly. Social mobility was sanctioned and encouraged and people were free to travel and seek employment at will. Nevertheless, nearly everyone

Chūō Suraido Company

TOKYO'S GINZA IN 1882

remained conscious of rank and class; few ventured away from familiar haunts in exchange for the insecurity of a strange place or the uncertainty of a new position.

Fukuzawa Yukichi, who zealously awaited all decrees which abolished many of the outward signs of feudalism, relates a personal experience which illustrates this aversion to social change. Feudal custom and the common law had required that if a farmer or merchant were on horseback and met a warrior, he must immediately dismount and prostrate himself at the side of the road while the warrior passed by. Beginning in 1871, many new privileges had been given to the "commoners" to elevate their status. They could use a family name, ride horseback, marry into a warrior family, and even refuse to dismount when passing a warrior.

Sometime after the issuance of the edict canceling the custom of dismounting before warriors, Fukuzawa, who by his attire gave away the fact that he was a member of the warrior class, met a farmer on horseback. The latter immediately jumped from his horse. Fukuzawa then ordered him to remount or he would beat him. Both the farmer and Fukuzawa showed that they were victims of the society in which they had been raised. The peasant, fearful lest he be beaten for observing the new custom, observed the old. On the other hand, though Fukuzawa intellectually accepted the new custom, he reacted in the old tradition as a warrior toward a peasant by threatening to force him to accept the new custom by a flogging.

Certain attributes of a modern state, however, dictated certain changes in custom. For example, the topknot, a kimono with long flowing sleeves, and a full skirt might have been little hindrance to a knight in battle who relied on old weapons and who dueled with a sword. For a modern army, however, requiring concerted action, mobility, and the use of modern firearms, all of these customs were a hindrance. The modern soldier wore a hat and had no time after reveille to fix an elaborate "hair-do." He had to be ready to move easily and freely and to march with a group. He could not be encumbered by broad kimono sleeves which were drafty in winter and easily snared at all times. Hence the Army was the moving spirit behind the abolition of many old social customs. To cut one's hair in the Western style, or to wear Western-style hats, coats, shirts, and trousers on official government duty first became voluntary and then compulsory. To give incentive to the reform movement, the adverse reactions of the foreigners to old customs were often emphasized.

But the process of acculturation often produced a hodgepodge. A young blade might consider himself well-dressed with a derby, waistcoat, kimono, and wooden clogs. A Tokyo barber, with a beautifully styled headdress, and flowing kimono sleeves kept out of the way by a Western-style apron, would see little incongruity in the fact that he was giving his client a Western-style haircut. The government official, on the other hand, was not considered appropriately dressed unless he wore a morning coat, striped pants, and a high silk hat to his office. When he returned home, he would change into his native dress.

The new national telegraph bureau was more disturbed than pleased over the farmer's misunderstanding of this new device. To the simple peasant, if men's thoughts could be transmitted over wires, it seemed logical that men's possessions likewise could be sent by the new invisible force. Consequently, they would constantly hang packages on the wires in the naïve belief that they would be mysteriously spirited away to their destination. Such practices, plus the farmer's fear of the purpose of the telegraph, became so prevalent that riders had to patrol the line constantly to keep it clear.[2] The peasant also had little use for the new law which forbade him to appear naked in public. His habit of not wearing clothes was dictated by utility. It was cooler in summer without them and it was far simpler to clean himself than his clothes after a day in the muck of the rice fields.

Mixed Reaction to Westernization

Many of these new restrictions on old customs, however, were full of political overtones. The peasant who was on the lookout for a way to ameliorate his economic plight used the enforcement of such decrees as conscription into the army as the immediate cause for local uprisings. The warrior who had been taught from childhood that it was more honorable to part with his life than with his sword, and who still considered himself superior to all other groups, received a blow to his pride and social status when forbidden after March 22, 1876, to wear his swords in public. He had been well prepared for this eventuality, however, by a decree issued as early as 1871 which made sword-wearing optional. Consequently, there was no public demonstration when the edict went into force. As observed above, by this time almost everyone (except Saigō and his men in Kyūshū) had accepted the inevitable changes which accompanied the elimination of the outward forms of feudalism.

Since these specific "reforms" were believed to be requisites on the road toward "modernization," they covered a wide range. For example, the government encouraged eating of beef for health reasons. When much publicity was given to the fact that the Emperor had eaten a dinner with roast beef, meat eating became a fad. Men believed that they understood modern civilization if they wore watches and jewelry, lit their houses with gas lamps, and rode in trains.

On some occasions, the nation was shocked by the official sponsorship of exhibitions of some of the less commendable manifestations of "Western civilization." One of the most notorious examples of this type of activity was the construction in 1883 by the government of a Western-style pavilion, the *Rokumeikan,* for social engagements. Here meetings were held on foreign cooking and dressmaking, Western music, the renovation of art, novel writing, and the theater. Regular dances and social gatherings with the foreign community were officially sponsored by Foreign Minister Inouye. A fancy dress ball, held on April 20, 1887, brought severe criticism on Prime Minister Itō and his Cabinet, most of whom had attended the affair.[3] The public was shocked at the spectacle of a leading statesman cavorting in public over a dance floor in the arms of a foreign woman and dressed in a ridiculous costume. Their excuse for these activities was that they would bring a *rapprochement* between the Japanese and the foreigners and the revision of the unequal treaties that much closer. The argument soon lost weight, however, since negotiations for treaty revision were broken off only a few weeks later.

But all of this private and public interest in westernization made little difference to some of the basic, ingrained social practices and concepts. Far more progress was made in changing superficial practices than in creating new social concepts. A feminist movement, including sponsorship of foreign education for a select group of young women, the first of whom were chaperoned as far as the United States by the Iwakura Mission in 1871, had little effect on the inferior position of women in Japanese society. The Constitution and the new codes verified this unequal status. The attempted liberation in 1871 of the professional entertainers (*geisha*) and of the prostitutes, who were indentured to their masters, was a useless gesture and had no effect on the universal acceptance of a double standard of morality for men and women.

The abolition of the pariah class (*eta*), who had performed the "unclean" tasks of scavengers, executioners, slaughterers, and tanners, was ordered in 1871, but their absorption into the general ranks of the common people was more theoretical than real. This group of three-quarters of a million persons continued to live in separate villages, married out of their group with difficulty, and were limited in the occupations open to them. In fact, their disparity was recognized by the opprobrium attached to "new commoner" which was given to them.

Former social classes were abolished but a strong consciousness of class distinction continued. A new class, the nobles (*kazoku*), took the place of the former ruling warrior class in the minds of the common people. The Confucian concept of superior and inferior continued and was underscored by the constitutional provision for a House of Peers to "be composed of members of the Imperial Family, of Nobles, and of Deputies who have been appointed by the Emperor." Likewise, the family pattern continued largely unchanged on the basis of a vertical relationship. Marriages were arranged through a "go-between"; the daughter-in-law, who lived with her husband's parents, was subservient to their wishes; the head of the household was supreme and considered that the family existed for him and was subservient to his demands.

Temporary Educational Reforms

Despite the tenacious hold which tradition had on society, old concepts and institutions gave way to new ones. As in the case of economic and political institutions already described, there were tremendous renovations in education but they came about slowly and their general purposes and patterns did not take final shape until shortly after the Constitution was promulgated. Traditionally, education had theoretically been limited to the warrior class, had been based on Confucian learning, and had been the responsibility of the feudal clans. The word of the teacher was not open to question and the greatest of deference was due him. Did not the pupil walk seven feet behind his instructor to avoid indiscreetly treading on his shadow? Many of the townsmen had been sufficiently educated to read popular literature. Time and patience were required before the concept was accepted that teaching was a science and that education was something to be organized into a system.

The leaders of the new government under Emperor Meiji had early recognized, however, the importance of education and the need for technical information on the subject. This need had been expressed in the Charter Oath of 1868 by the provision which specified that knowledge should be sought for "all over the world." (See page 83.) In the first years of the Restoration, foreign knowledge on education was largely limited, however, to that of the French system. Hence the Education Law of 1872, which established compulsory elementary education, was based on a French model. Education was described as being essential for success in all lines of pursuit, whether farming, manual arts, or business.

The system, as it was laid down on paper, was magnificent. It provided that boys and girls of all classes should receive primary education and that the more gifted should be given advanced training. The country was divided into university, middle school, and primary school districts with interlocking supervision. Many of the old urban schools and their teaching staffs were brought within the system, thereby giving it continuity with the old educational concepts and methods. But in reality, much had to be done to implement this new code. It could not be put into practice overnight or even within a few years. Buildings had to be constructed, teachers trained, curricula established, textbooks written and published, and the people educated to accept and cooperate with this new concept of compulsory education. Actually, as late as 1890 only half of those eligible for a primary education were taken care of.

Some of these obstacles were partly overcome by a firsthand survey of conditions abroad, by the employ of foreign advisers in key spots, and by improvisation. For example, the Iwakura Mission had a special educational section which spent several weeks in the United States surveying the American educational system. It was greatly assisted by the Japanese Minister in Washington, Mori Arinori,[4] and by the United States Commissioner of Education. During this visit, members of the Mission made other important personal contacts with leading American educators and decided to employ some of them as advisers to their government.

For example, Professor David Murray (1830–1905) of Rutgers University was appointed adviser to the Ministry of Education in 1873. After his arrival in Japan, he spent nearly a year traveling and observing the newly created educational system at work and investigating the nation's needs before he wrote his first report in which he made several significant recommendations. In the first place, he urged instruction in Japanese rather than in foreign languages. The dearth of teachers and the immediate need for adequately trained instructors had necessitated the employment of a large proportion of foreigners. In the seven most important government schools, for example, there were fifty-one Japanese teachers and forty-six foreigners. He concluded:

> No system of universal education can be successfully carried out which shall not employ as its vehicle the common language of the people. . . . It must, therefore, be fully understood that the efforts to carry forward the national education in the languages of Europe are only temporary expedients.[5]

In the second place, Murray outlined the general lines to be followed in training future teachers. A select group of persons should first be trained in the principles of the projected primary school system. They should then become the staff of a normal school to introduce to others the new methods of teaching. Simultaneously, textbooks should be prepared and the requisite number of normal schools should be established to supply the needs of the country. For the next few years, his general recommendations were followed.

Another American, Marion M. Scott, trained the first teachers; American primary school textbooks were translated *in toto* for use in the Japanese schools. Foreign experts, estimated at 5,000 persons at the peak of the program, were used to instruct Japanese students especially in the sciences and technology. For example, British instructors in the various naval schools were largely responsible for the growth of the modern Imperial Navy. As soon as a core of Japanese were trained in the new techniques, the foreigners were replaced by their Japanese understudies.

Education To Serve the State

But this initial emphasis of education on the needs of the individual, rather than those of the state, was gradually but effectively replaced by an educational system whose purpose was to train the individual to serve the state. This shift in policy followed the general political trend toward oligarchical control. By about 1880 the government leaders had developed a philosophy based largely on Prussian concepts. This new Prussian influence was soon reflected in the general reorganization of the national government and in the functions and authority delegated to the Ministry of Education. The new regulations of December, 1880, were directed against an attempt made the year before by Vice-Minister Tanaka Fujimaro to decentralize the system by the formation of local school boards.[6]

The new law bluntly decreed that the educational affairs of the whole country would be administered by the Department of Education. Furthermore, any important act of the Minister of Education had to be approved by the Privy Council. A new educational proclamation, or law, the selection of members of an educational mission or of students to go abroad, the framing of rules for government-sponsored schools, or any deviation from existing rules, all had to receive the sanction of the Councilors. Since these same Councilors also determined the political policies of the government, it was obvious that the final shape of the educational system was going to be such as to strengthen the state.

During the decade from 1880, when the concept of a strongly centralized school system was accepted, to the issuance of a conservative, reactionary Edict on Education in 1890, most vestiges of liberalism in education disappeared. The mania for Western knowledge was replaced by a conscious effort to teach the old concepts of morality based on Confucian doctrines and national patriotism. After 1882, university courses in which the instructor lectured in a foreign language were dropped. Three years later, Mori Arinori, who had become converted to Bismarck's political philosophy, was appointed Minister of Education. He was convinced that the primary purpose of education was to serve the state. The primary object of the schools (whose curricula now emphasized Oriental morality, the Chinese classics, and Japanese language and history) was to train the pupil in complete obedience to the wishes of the state.[7] Privately established schools, such as Keio University in Tokyo, founded by Fukuzawa, or the special school of Ōkuma, which developed into Waseda University, were not allowed to issue the same type of degree as that of the leading Imperial Universities, so that their graduates were unable to obtain government employment. The private institutions did serve a useful purpose, however, in training the core of leaders in the fields of industry, finance, and private education.

The final act in the transformation of the new educational system into an arm of the state was yet to be enacted. Motoda Eifu, the Emperor's tutor, had been pressing for several years for the acceptance of Confucian concepts and moral principles as the bases of education and public morality. On the other hand, Minister of Education Mori wished to emphasize Western philosophy. In 1888, however, Motoda and some of the other Councilors in the Imperial Palace recommended that responsibility for determining national morals and ethics should rest with the Imperial Household Ministry. Mori was enraged at this suggestion, insisting that the Department of Education should have charge of such matters.

With the assassination of Mori in February, 1889, however, the initiative for issuance of a formal statement by the Emperor remained with the Imperial Councilors. The new Premier, Yamagata Aritomo, and his Minister of Education supported this proposal. It was inevitable, therefore, that Motoda contributed much of the material that went into the statement which is known as the Imperial Rescript on Education. It was promulgated on October 30, 1890, and read as follows:

Know Ye, Our Subjects:

Our Imperial Ancestors have founded Our Empire on a basis broad and everlasting and have deeply and firmly implanted virtue; Our subjects ever united in loyalty and filial piety have from generation to generation illustrated the beauty thereof. This is the glory of the fundamental character of Our Empire and herein also lies the source of Our Education. Ye, Our Subjects, be filial to your parents, affectionate to your brothers and sisters; as husbands and wives be harmonious; as friends be true; bear yourselves in modesty and moderation; extend your benevolence to all; pursue learning and cultivate arts, and thereby develop intellectual faculties and perfect moral powers; furthermore, advance public good and promote common interests; always respect the Constitution and observe the laws; should emergency arise, offer yourselves courageously to the State; and thus guard and maintain the prosperity of Our Imperial Throne coeval with heaven and earth. So shall ye not only be Our good and faithful subjects, but render illustrious the best traditions of your forefathers.

The Way here set forth is indeed the teaching bequeathed by Our Imperial Ancestors to be observed alike by the Descendants and the subjects, infallible for all ages and true in all places. It is Our wish to lay it to heart in all reverence in common with you, Our subjects, that we may all attain to the same virtue.

This pronouncement says much more about patriotism, loyalty, and moral principles than it does about education. In a sense it was a reversal of the fifth paragraph of the Charter Oath of 1868 which advocated seeking universal knowledge throughout the world. It was a clear-cut victory for the conservative oligarchs over the advocates of Western liberalism and representative institutions. It was a boon to Itō Hirobumi's philosophy that the Emperor and loyalty to him should be the axis around which the state and its subjects should revolve. It became the ultimate expression of the nation's philosophic basis for an autocratic government.[8] In terms of modern methods of propaganda, it was a powerful weapon of thought control. *In fine,* it was a conscious and effective way of steering the people away from the exotic Western stream of civilization toward an amplified, intensified, national stream of culture which was to sweep all before it for the next half century.

A New Legal System

The problem of the creation of a legal system which would serve the needs of the new constitutional monarchy was extremely complicated. It involved both the conflict between Western and traditional concepts, a difficulty which was common to most of the reforms, and a diplomatic struggle between the Western powers and Japan over the question of revision of the treaties. It was necessary to reconcile such diametrically opposed ideas as the old feudal belief of complete subservience to authority and the modern concept of individual rights. Right of ownership of property was more essential than the right to receive an annual rice stipend. The state's power to collect a tax on personal holdings and recognition of individual indebtedness were a far cry from the old practices whereby the feudal baron possessed economic and financial autonomy within his own fief and the head of the household was held responsible for the debts of any of its members.

As for the conflict over the revision of the unequal treaties, various aspects of this problem have already been discussed (see Chapter 8), but its relation to the formulation of a new legal system has only been implied. In 1858, when the Western powers insisted that their nationals be tried in their own consular courts rather than in the local courts, the Japanese legal system left much to be desired. Such laws as existed discriminated in favor of the warrior. The townsman, craftsman, or peasant was intimidated by the overbearing warriors, lived in constant fear for his life, and was kept in ignorance of the law. Whenever anyone was arrested, he was expected to confess the crime of which he was accused. If no confession was forthcoming, it was exacted from him by ingenious and effective torture. Since the foreigners refused to be placed under the jurisdiction of this type of legal system, they had insisted on their own consular courts and other special privileges.

On the other hand, the nationalist-minded reformers were eager to eliminate these inequalities as rapidly as possible while the political opponents of the oligarchs kept relentless pressure on the government to revise the treaties. Many of the responsible ministers realized, however, that drastic reforms in the legal system would have to be inaugurated before any real progress could be made in treaty revision. Like many of the other features of the Restoration, it was not until after the Iwakura Mission returned in 1873 that the Council of State realized how formidable the problem was. Iwakura had hoped to revise the treaties while abroad but had met with rebuffs in Washington, London, Paris, and Berlin. When he and his colleagues saw the differences of Western legal practices with those of Japan, they were forced to admit that their laws were inadequate.

The first written penal code, which was largely a codification of seventeenth-century Chinese legal concepts, had not been promulgated until 1870. Japanese jurists began to study Western legal institutions, particularly those of France, and a special law section of the Department of Justice translated French codes and gave instruction in French law. Foreign legal specialists were appointed to assist in the modernization program; Gustave Boissonade de Fontarabie, a Frenchman, began drafting a new criminal code. With the *Code Napoleon* as a model, it was completed in 1882 and remained in force until a decade after the Constitution was promulgated.

Since there had been even less progress in the codification of the civil law than of the criminal law, the government emphasized the importance of local usage in civil cases. In 1875, in an attempt to regularize civil procedure, orders were issued which provided that civil cases, in the event that there was no written statute, were to be decided according to custom. In default of common procedure, they were to be settled by reason and justice. In reality, the judge decided cases on the basis of whatever legal system he might have studied. Simultaneously, work continued on various drafts of a civil code which was finally placed under Boissonade's supervision.

By 1885, when Itō became Premier and was prepared to begin the serious preparation of the new Constitution, the legal system was in complete confusion. A Criminal Code, similar to that of the *Code Napoleon,* was in force; the draft of the new Civil Code was unsatisfactory; a Commercial Code had yet to be accepted. The Western powers were in no mood, therefore, to concede that the Japanese legal system had been revised sufficiently to permit them to abandon extraterritoriality.

In 1886 the negotiations were again begun with the foreign powers to conclude a new series of treaties. (See page 159.) At the same time, a

Bureau to Study the Legal Codes was formed. It produced a revised Civil Code as well as new drafts for the treaties. When it was published in 1888 the public became indignant at its recommendations, which permitted use of foreign judges in cases that involved foreigners, and which opened the hinterland to them. The Japanese people objected strenuously to having the foreigners roam over their country at will. They also saw no further need for any form of extraterritorial rights. Despite this widespread opposition, a series of Imperial Conferences was held in 1889 to consider these recommended revisions for the treaties. At this point, public indignation produced dramatic consequences. Ōkuma had been appointed Foreign Minister to solve the knotty treaty problem. (See page 161.) He was considered responsible, therefore, for these unpopular proposals and criticism was aimed at him. As he returned home from one of the Conferences a bomb was thrown at him which resulted in the loss of his leg. It also postponed the settlement of the issue of unequal clauses in the treaties for another few years.

By 1890, however, when Parliament first met, a strict Criminal Code was in effect, a new Civil Code had been drafted, and the German jurist, Hermann Roesler, had codified the Commercial Code on the basis of the German model. As the new parliamentary government began to function and as the foreigners insisted on further legal reforms before they would agree to revision of the treaties, innumerable changes were made in the Codes before they were acceptable. At the same time, these changes in the legal system strengthened the state's control over the individual. France's influence in the Civil Code had been replaced by that of Germany.[9]

Some of the unique features of Japanese society were preserved under the new laws. For example, they recognized that all persons in a household were under the control of the head of the house. Nevertheless, new rights were given individual members of the house, such as the right to own property. Furthermore, since property was inherited by members of the house rather than by the group as a whole, the head of the household was no longer liable for the debts of all its members. Society's assumption that women had an inferior status was recognized in the marriage, divorce, and inheritance laws. From the point of view of the government, the legal system was an effective partner of the educational system in making the subject a servant of the state to be used by the state to make it strong.

Religion and Thought

In the early years of the Meiji Restoration, the national government had taken a direct interest in the control of religion. This interest was reflected in the first reorganization of the government, which placed the Bureau of Shintō Religion above all of the other departments of the Council of State. This temporary elevation of Shintōism, an indigenous polytheistic animism and ancestor worship, to become the state religion created a violent anti-Buddhist movement (*Shimbutsu bunri*). For a few months immediately following the abolition of the Shogunate in 1868, all Shintō shrines were forced to rid themselves of Buddhist influence or risk destruction at the hands of fanatical exponents of the new national faith. But the movement petered out as rapidly as it had arisen and Shintōism was temporarily forgotten.

The active interest of the government in religious problems was next aroused by the activities of the Christians. The traditional anti-Christian attitude of the country and its people has already been emphasized. (See Chapter 2.) Despite bans proscribing it as a religion and the imposition of the death penalty for all believers, a number of households in southwestern Japan had secretly maintained their faith in Catholicism. Even before the Restoration, both Catholic and Protestant missionaries appeared in Japan but were restricted in their evangelical activities because of the continuance of the anti-Christian edicts and of the laws forbidding foreigners to leave the port cities. As late as 1870, the government received complaints from the Buddhist priests that the ban on Christianity was being flouted. Consequently notices were again posted which proclaimed that "the evil religion of Christianity was strictly prohibited as heretofore," and nearly 4,000 Catholic communicants were removed from the Nagasaki area.

This move had a calamitous effect on both Protestants and Catholics as many of the native Christians gave up working for the missionaries. But the picture abruptly changed in 1873 when the edict against Christianity was removed. As Dr. Daniel Crosby Greene, a missionary of the Congregational Church in Kōbe, recorded:

> Soon there followed the dawn of a better day. The edicts against Christianity were taken down from the notice board; Roman Catholic Christians were restored to their homes and it was a privilege to minister to some of them as they passed through the streets of Kobe. Gradually the consciousness of freedom spread among the people and our little chapel was thronged with curious listeners.[10]

Evangelical activities were now openly undertaken by the small band of Protestant missionaries, and a committee began to translate the Bible into Japanese. New converts were made but progress was slow. The Japanese had difficulty in comprehending some of the basic Christian concepts, and other aspects of Western civilization seemed more appealing and more utilitarian than the new religion. English Bible classes were often attended more for the practice which they afforded in the language than for the theology which was taught. By 1881, there were roughly 4,500 Protestants and 25,000 Roman Catholic converts; by 1889 the numbers had risen to 32,000 and 26,000 respectively, together with 16,000 Greek Orthodox adherents.

But the strength of this new movement can better be measured in terms of official and unofficial reaction to it rather than by citing the number of converts. Aside from the relaxation of the restrictions on Christians, the government took little interest in the movement until it decided in 1890 to issue the Imperial Rescript on Education, a general statement on the moral principles which should guide the Empire. By that time, thanks to the tireless efforts of several outstanding Christians and a small band of their ardent followers and believers, Christianity began to make an impression, especially on the Japanese intellectual world. Some of the most successful, such as Dr. William S. Clark at Sapporo Agricultural College, used education as a means for Christian evangelism. He was brought from Massachusetts Agricultural College to train leaders for the exploitation of untapped resources of Hokkaidō. At the same time, he was strongly motivated by his Christian New England background. He refused to teach a class in ethics unless he was permitted to teach the Bible. As he had a strong sense of piety and knew how to respond to the intellectual curiosity and needs of his students, he had an influence far out of proportion to his comparatively brief sojourn in Japan. After teaching from July, 1876, to April, 1877, his parting words to his students, "Boys, be ambitious," became a slogan for Japanese youth.

Two outstanding Japanese Christians, Niishima Jo (1843–1890) (Reverend Joseph Hardy Niishima) and Uchimura Kanzō (1861–1930) had a particularly strong impact on Japanese Christianity and also exemplified by their lives the basic conflicts which arose in the Japanese Christian movement. Niishima, after graduation from Amherst College, was ordained as a Congregational minister and returned home to establish a Japanese center of Christian training which later became Dōshisha University in Kyōto and which still maintains a close connection with Amherst College. He believed that a clear distinction should be made between a mission school, established primarily for evangelistic purposes, and a Christian college and that Dōshisha should be primarily the latter. In 1884, he toured the United States for funds to build Dōshisha into a first-class Christian university. His return coincided with the increasingly intense conflict between Christianity and the new nationalism. This retarded Dōshisha's expansion at a time when the state-supported universities were receiving greater support. Dōshisha also suffered from the conflict between the Japanese Christians, who were developing their own leadership and ideas as to how they could serve Japan and not oppose its national aims, and the missionaries, who were primarily interested in increasing the number of converts.

Uchimura and Nationalism

The growing conflict between Christianity and Japanese nationalism, as well as the impact of foreign Christians, such as Dr. Clark, is best illustrated by the life of Uchimura Kanzō. Born into a warrior's family, he entered Sapporo Agricultural College in 1877 after studying English in Tokyo. Although the college was a government-supported institution, it had a strong Christian flavor. For example, when Uchimura arrived he learned that the entire freshman class had been baptized by the Methodist missionary, M. C. Harris. He was later converted to Christianity through Dr. Clark's influence.[11]

After graduation, Uchimura worked in the Ministry of Agriculture but interrupted his bureaucratic career to go to the United States to see a Christian country in action. He hoped that such a trip would teach him how to serve his own country better. He was at first disillusioned by what he found but was later inspired by those who befriended him. He, like Niishima, graduated from Amherst College, studied theology, and returned home in May, 1888. Unlike Niishima, however, he refused to cooperate with the foreign missionaries and declined to teach at Dōshisha because of the foreign support it received.

This emphasis on a native Christian Church, independent of foreign support, which later grew into the strong *Mukyōkai*, brought Uchimura into personal conflict with the new nationalism and with the authorities. After his return to Japan, he became an English teacher and spiritual adviser to 600 dormitory students in the First Higher School, one of the chief preparatory schools for Tokyo Imperial University. Subsequent to the promulgation of the Rescript on Education, the Principal of the First Higher School announced a meeting of the faculty and students of the school to acknowledge formally the receipt of this document. Each member of the faculty was ordered to go singly to the platform and to bow to the Imperial signature affixed to the Rescript.

Uchimura considered this performance similar to the obeisance required at Buddhist and Shintōist ceremonies. His basic philosophy was that one should be a man first and then a patriot. He concluded:

> I took a safer course for my Christian conscience and in the august presence of sixty professors . . . and over one thousand students, I took my stand and did not bow.[12]

The effect of his adamant stand was electrifying. The national press and public opinion branded him as a traitor. Despite a subsequent compromise with his conscience and promise to bow before the Rescript, pressure was so strong and opinion was so united in the view that he had committed lese majesty that he was forced to resign from the school.

This incident, while it did not prevent Uchimura from becoming one of the most effective advocates of Christianity, sharpened the schism between those who believed their greatest loyalty was to God and those who considered their paramount patriotism and loyalty was to the throne. It was used by Christianity's arch enemies as an illustration of the incompatibility of Christianity with the ideals set forth in the Rescript. The most eloquent advocate of this position was the outstanding philosopher, Professor Inouye Tetsujirō. In a famous article published in 1893, which expressed the views of most of the Imperial University scholars, Inouye argued that Christianity was contrary to the concept of national polity (*kokutai*), that monotheism and undivided loyalty to God were subversive to the principles of obedience, loyalty, and nationalism as expounded in the Rescript. Inouye's blast was only the first round of an extended polemic whose results were inconclusive.

The Constitution provided that ". . . subjects shall within limits not prejudicial to peace and order, and not antagonistic to their duties as subjects, enjoy freedom of religious beliefs." (Article 28.) The matter boiled down, therefore, to the question of whether the beliefs of the Japanese Christians or missionaries forced them, as had been true of Uchimura, to run counter to existing laws and whether these laws were strictly enforced. In reality, Christianity and a strong nationalism coexisted and tolerated each other. The government was confident, however, that the universal dissemination of morals and ethics based on traditional nationalism would more than counteract any subversive effect of Christianity.

Control of Newspapers

Even before the Restoration, no aspect of life was free from the influences of the Western stream of culture which had been trickling past the curtain of isolation. Since this stream brought with it new knowledge, new concepts, and new techniques, the curtain became perforated and ever more numerous aspects of Occidental culture appealed to the imagination of the Japanese. But the mysteries of this new culture could not be solved unless its languages could be understood. Prior to Perry's arrival no one had considered it important to learn any foreign language other than Chinese or Dutch.

After the country was formally opened to the West and foreign consulates were established, however, there was a shift away from the study of Dutch toward English and French. Increased contacts with the foreigners required a much larger body of competent interpreters than heretofore. Official communications between the representatives of the foreign powers and the central government, business transactions between foreigners and Japanese merchants, trips abroad of individuals and official missions, all required a minimum language competence at least by a corps of interpreters. Consequently, by 1868, the first year of the Meiji Restoration, more than a decade had elapsed to permit comparatively widespread competence in European languages by many of the leaders of the country. Under the new Imperial regime, this movement gained momentum.

At the same time, not only these persons but any Japanese who had direct or indirect contact with the foreigners became exposed to new media for the dissemination of ideas and new forms of writing. One of the most significant of these innovations of the foreigners was the newspapers. The first of these was the *Japan Herald,* published in 1861 under the editorship of John R. Black until 1867, when he started his own paper in Yokohama, the *Japan Gazette.* Black was outspoken in his support of the Tokugawa government. The *Herald*'s rival, the *Japan Times,* which first appeared in 1865, supported the restoration of power to the Emperor. One of its regular contributors was Ernest Satow, the young interpreter of the British legation. While it criticized the British Minister, Sir Harry Parkes, for the corruption in the Consular courts, it was quick to praise him for his early recognition of the new Meiji government.

During the next few years, stimulated by the innovations inaugurated by the new Imperial government, a host of papers, many of them small and published irregularly, appeared in the Japanese language. Toward the end of 1870, the *Yokohama Mainichi,* a single sheet published daily on foreign paper by movable lead type, became the first regular Japanese daily. It was followed shortly by papers published by foreigners or sponsored by individuals who used them to gain support for their point of view. But their influence was restricted because their distribution was limited to the metropolitan areas, particularly Yokohama, Ōsaka, and Tokyo, and only a small number of copies were printed. The largest paper, the *Nisshin Shinjishi,* printed by John R. Black, after 1872, had a daily circulation of only 1,500 copies.[13]

In 1874, when the leaders of the movement for people's rights, such as Itagaki Taisuke, used their own papers to criticize the policies of the oligarchs, the central government moved in. It could not afford to let such issues as the national financial crisis, the Korean expedition, or the form and content of a constitution be discussed indiscriminately by the budding journalists. It might be disastrous to the privileged position of the oligarchs, particularly in view of the adoption of universal education and the rapid increase in literacy, if these papers were allowed freedom of expression and if this concept were accepted by their readers as a fundamental right of the people. Consequently, restricting legislation was adopted in this field just as it had been imposed in others.

In 1875, while the debate raged between the "liberals" and the government on the question of liberty and rights for the people (see Chapter 6), the Meiji government issued a Press Law which gave it extensive powers of control. There followed a struggle, which was to continue until the 1930's with varying degrees of intensity, between the government which tried to enforce the laws and the papers which sought ways and means of evading them. The latter, as they received public support, became bolder and more open in their criticism which stimulated the issuance of even more restricting laws. Specifically, the Press Law of 1875 provided for a fine and imprisonment of editors whose papers criticized government policy. The papers evaded the laws by hiring dummy editors, who were popularly known as "prison editors," who paid the fine and served the jail sentence for the paper while it continued to appear. The government remedied this weakness in the law the next year by an amendment which called for suspension of publication as well as the penalties of fines and imprisonment.

Humorous as this contest may seem in retrospect, the authorities zealously kept control over public opinion and never allowed it to get out of hand. When the issues of the Constitution and the revision of the treaties with the foreigners were still unsettled, the laws were again strengthened in 1883 and 1885. Under the new laws, each paper had to deposit 1,000 yen which was forfeited any time the Home Ministry decided an article was inimical to the public welfare.

As a result of these limitations, as well as the need of extensive capital dictated by modern plant facilities, the number of newspapers was radically reduced and there was a shift away from polemics to the reporting of facts. The outstanding leader in this new trend was the *Asahi* papers published by Murayama Ryūhei in Ōsaka and Tokyo. He founded the papers in 1879 and immediately introduced innovations. He developed his own wire and news services to enable his papers to base their stories on facts rather than on hearsay reports. These innovations had a leavening effect on the standards of the entire newspaper world.

In 1882, Fukuzawa Yukichi vainly waited for a government offer to be editor of a new, officially sponsored newspaper. He then began publication of his own paper, the *Jiji Shimpō.* By this time he had abandoned his earlier belief that utopia could be achieved by the operation of natural moral laws. He now saw only natural laws devoid of ethical content as valid. He argued that this logic, which was inherent in science, was essential for Japan to grasp and follow if it were to survive in a highly competitive world. Hence, he declared the basic aims of his newspaper to be the dissemination and encouragement of the principles of independence in learning, commerce, law, and religion. He concluded, "We have made the independence of our country our lifelong objective, and all who share these aspirations with us are our friends, all who do not are our enemies."[14] With the opening of Parliament in 1890, the best papers had their permanent correspondents in Tokyo and other important cities, subscribed to foreign telegraph services through Reuters, speeded publication through the use of the revolving press, and relegated police stories to the third page.

Early Translations and Novels

A unique contribution which the newspapers made to the nation's cultural development was through the publication in serial form of many of the early novels and translations of Western books. While it is true that some published separate books, many of the literati supported themselves by writing novels in serials for the newspapers. Although the novel had long been a popular type of literature in Japan,[15] it had differed in form from the Western-style novel, had lacked the concept of a sustaining plot, and, in later years, had fallen under the influence of Chinese literary tradition. With the influx of the numerous practical aspects of Western civilization and a popular desire to learn about Europe, the newspapers sponsored the translations of Occidental novels. These translations, which at one time comprised nearly 90 per cent of the books published, were accepted with great enthusiasm by their readers.

During the period from 1877 to 1890, these translations of foreign novels awakened the Japanese writers and the public to new possibilities of literature. Such works as Bulwer Lytton's *Ernest Maltravers,* which was translated in 1878, or Disraeli's *Coningsby,* which received the translated title of "Spring Warblings" in 1884, caused a sensation. They appeared just when political problems absorbed men's minds and motivated their actions. Some of the most popular Japanese authors, both out of political conviction and because of the profits involved, began to turn to political problems. The result was the emergence of a new, virile novel which recorded the disappointments, the hopes, and aspirations of its author. It centered about the history of Japan and hinted at dissatisfaction with existing political conditions.

One of the most representative and popular authors of the political novel was Suehiro Tetchō (1848–1896). He was educated in his fief's school, became one of its teachers, and went to Tokyo in 1870 to continue his studies. He was an active member of Itagaki's "liberal movement" and first expressed his views in the newspapers for which he worked.

When he criticized the Press Law of 1875, he was fined and restricted to his home for three months. His first important political novel, *Setchū Bai* (1886), dealt with contemporary politics and indirectly advocated, by its descriptions of governments in other countries, the adoption of a popular representative government in Japan. This was followed the next year by another novel (*Kakan-ō*) which ends with the Liberal party (*Jiyūtō*) triumphant in the national political struggle. After the new Constitution was promulgated in 1889, however, his political writings, as well as those of his contemporary political novelists, lost their popularity.

Two other important influences on the development of the modern novel must be noted. Tsubouchi Shōyō (1859–1935) had a profound influence on the form and substance of the novel. At the age of fourteen, he began the study of English at the Foreign Language School in Nagoya. Shortly thereafter, he was sent to Tokyo where he continued his studies of English and began translations of Shakespeare and Scott. By 1885, after he had been greatly influenced by the English literature which he had read, translated, and taught, he wrote *The Essence of Fiction* (*Shōsetsu Shinzui*). This work was the first to explain the meaning and purpose of a European-style novel. He emphasized the necessity to free the novel from the deadening effects of traditions of the Tokugawa Period, to emphasize realism, and to depict life accurately. He also advocated a psychological penetration which was new to Japanese authors and readers. This work was so important that some literary historians consider its appearance as the beginning of the modern novel in Japan.

The final stage in the development of modern Japanese literature was reached with the publication of Futabatei Shimei's (1864–1909) famous novel *Drifting Cloud* (*Ukigumo*) in a semicolloquial style. Its first installment appeared in 1888. Futabatei, unlike both Suehiro and Tsubouchi, who had largely been influenced by British thought, was a follower of Russian writers such as Tolstoy and Gorky, whose works he also translated. The characters in his books were taken from the crowds and, like those around him, were tormented and uncertain. His style was simple and his works were the inspiration for future young writers of the naturalist school and made the novel understandable to the average graduate of the new educational system.[16]

By the opening of the first session of Parliament in 1890, when the new Constitution began to operate, the cultural and social phases of society reflected the same tendencies as those in the political and economic spheres. While certain practical manifestations of Western civilization had been incorporated into new social customs, into the national educational system, in the law courts and legal codes, in journalism and modern literature, there was not blind acceptance of both the form and substance of these foreign practices. Rather, a highly developed eclecticism permitted the adaptation of elements compatible with traditional customs and beliefs and amenable to regulation and control by the state. In the first few years of the Meiji Period, both the government and people were confused by the complexity and number of the problems which had to be solved. The impact of Christianity and of British and American advisers in various branches of the Imperial government, notably in education, bode well for the universal acceptance of democratic principles and concepts of government by and for the people. The widespread influence of France in the early organization of the Army and in the legal codes gave added strength to the movement.

But as the power of the central government increased, a small group of oligarchs defeated the supporters of a modified form of the political philosophy of Mill and of Rousseau and kept these advocates under close surveillance. The clan bureaucrats sought, by every means at their disposal, to make their country strong and to perpetuate and to enhance the privileges and prerogatives of the Emperor and of themselves. Consequently, the oligarchs turned to the supervision of the cultural traits of society to make them consistent with accepted political philosophy. By the time that Itō and his colleagues had agreed that a modified form of Prussian-style constitutional monarchy was applicable to Japan, that the state was supreme, and that the subject existed to serve the state, changes were ordered in the educational and legal systems.

By 1890, when the new Constitution was in operation, the earlier democratic influences of England, the United States, or France had been eradicated from the national system of education, from the law codes, and from the press. As an extra precaution against the re-emergence of these influences or against an untoward increase in the effectiveness of Christianity, the conservatively minded statesmen obtained Imperial sanction for the issuance of a new set of moral principles to which all loyal subjects must prescribe on pain of social ostracism, economic purge, or even death. Hence men's thoughts, as well as the form of government and the economic system under which they lived, were to be cast into an increasingly rigid, nationalistic mold. The first half century of Japan's modern history had seen a phenomenal modernization, but it had also witnessed a centralization of control, a subordination of the individual to serve the purposes of the state, and a pronouncement of acceptable and prescribed beliefs and practice. Those who conformed to the will of the state, whether neighboring nations or Japanese subjects, would receive the benevolent blessings of the Emperor. Those who dared to challenge that will would have to be forced to accept it or perish.

Notes

1. Nitobe Inazō (1862–1933) was born into a warrior family of Morioka fief. While a student at Sapporo Agricultural College, he came under the influence of Dr. W. S. Clark and was a close personal friend of the outstanding Christian, Uchimura Kanzō. Nitobe studied at Johns Hopkins University, married a Philadelphia Quaker, and returned to Japan in 1891 to be a professor at his alma mater. After holding various teaching posts he was Under Secretary-General of the League of Nations (1920–1926). Long an advocate of internationalism, he was an arch opponent of the Army's policies toward Manchuria and North China in the 1930's but died on a visit to America when it appeared as though he had given up his opposition to them. The quotation is from his *Western Influences in Modern Japan* (Chicago: University of Chicago Press, 1931), p. 22.

2. For illustrations of the strange mixture of the exotic strains of the East and the West see *Gahō Kindai Hyakunenshi,* No. 3–6 (Tokyo: Kokusai Bunka Jōhōsha, 1951). One picture is of special interest, a photograph of the Iwakura Mission taken at San Francisco in January, 1872, showing Ōkubo, Kido, Itō, and Yamaguchi in formal Western attire, and Iwakura in a Japanese costume and topknot. *Ibid.*, No. 3, p. 203.

3. *Ibid.*, No. 5, pp. 394–95, for description, cartoons, and pictures of what it refers to as the Rokumeikan Period.

4. Mori Arinori (1847–1889) was from Satsuma. He realized at an early age the need for information on foreign affairs and hence devoted himself to "Western studies." After his clan's bombardment by the British in 1863, promising young men were sent to England to study. Mori was one of them and arrived in London in June, 1865. There he studied mathematics, chemistry, physics, and Russian naval techniques. He returned home in 1868, to be sent to Washington as Japanese Minister in 1870, where he immediately started a survey of the American educational system. Fifteen years later, when he was to become Minister of Education, he had abandoned American concepts of education for those of Germany. He was murdered in 1889, purportedly for not having shown proper respect to the Emperor.

5. United States Bureau of Education, *Circular of Information,* No. 2, 1875, p. 20.

6. Tanaka Fujimaro (1846–1909) was, like several of the members of the Iwakura Mission, a student of the American missionary, Guido F. Verbeck. The latter had been in Japan since 1859. Despite his connection with Christianity, Verbeck was president of a school which was the forerunner of Tokyo Imperial University. Tanaka became Vice-Minister of Education in 1876. With the preference for German pedagogical methods after 1880, his influence rapidly declined. Dr. David Murray, who supported Tanaka's views, had left Japan in 1879.

7. This Herbartian pedagogical philosophy was expounded after 1887 at Tokyo Imperial University by the German philosopher and educator, Emil Hausknecht. His conservative philosophy became prevalent not only because it appeared to be applicable to Japan but because it was consistent with the whole philosophy of the state developed by the oligarchs. Obviously, if they had not approved of his point of view, they would not have approved his ap-

pointment. For an interesting discussion of Hausknecht's influence, see Nitobe, *op. cit.*, pp. 43 ff.

8. See Donald H. Shivley, "Motoda Eifu, Confucian Tutor to the Meiji Emperor," in David S. Nivison and Arthur F. Wright (eds.), *Confucianism in Action* (Stanford: Stanford University Press, 1959), pp. 330–31.

9. The chronology of the drafting and promulgation of the Civil Code indicates the confusion which existed. The part of the Code dealing with property was published in 1890. In 1893 the effective date of the entire code was postponed to permit further changes. Three books, those on General Provisions, Real Rights, and Obligations were promulgated in 1896. The entire code was revised and published just prior to the effective date of the new treaties in 1898. For a careful and significant study of the changes in the legal system see Dan Fenno Henderson, "Law and Political Modernization in Japan," in Robert E. Ward (ed.), *Political Development in Modern Japan* (Princeton: Princeton University Press, 1968), pp. 387–456.

10. The timing of this edict was doubtless the result of two important factors. Sir Harry Parkes, the British representative in Japan, had constantly been pressing the Japanese government to change its anti-Christian policy. At the same time, the Iwakura Mission had just returned from Europe where it found constant criticism of Japan's anti-Christian policy. See Evarts B. Greene, *A New Englander in Japan* (Boston: Houghton Mifflin Co., 1927), p. 113; and Grace Fox, *Britain and Japan, 1858–1883* (Oxford: Clarendon Press, 1969), pp. 482–501. Figures on Christian converts vary widely. Those quoted are accepted by Masaharu Anesaki, *History of Japanese Religion* (London: Kegan Paul, Trench, Trubner and Co., Ltd., 1930); and Otis Cary, *A History of Christianity in Japan* (2 vols.; New York: Fleming H. Revell Co., 1902).

11. In a recent study on Japanese Christians and American missionaries, Uchimura and Clark are among the five most important in their respective categories. See John F. Howes, "Japanese Christians and American Missionaries," in Marius B. Jansen (ed.), *Changing Japanese Attitudes Towards Modernization* (Princeton: Princeton University Press, 1965), pp. 337–68.

12. It was the universal practice for all schools to have copies of the Rescript on Education. The Rescript and the portrait of the Emperor were considered to be the most valuable possessions of the school. Yearly ceremonies were held at which the Rescript was read to the entire school, during which everyone bowed reverentially. The quotation from Uchimura is from a letter, dated March 6, 1891, to David C. Bell, a Minneapolis banker, ardent Christian and lifelong inspiration to Uchimura. It is contained in Uchimura's *Collected Works* (Tokyo: Iwanami Shoten, 1932–1933). The most thorough study of Uchimura in English to date is that of John Howes, *Uchimura Kanzō (1861–1930)*, Master of Arts Thesis, Columbia University, New York, 1953.

13. Black was fearless in his criticism of the Formosan Expedition and published a new paper to challenge the severe Press Law of 1875. He was forced to cease publication when Minister Parkes declared it illegal. For much new valuable material on British influence prior to 1881 on the British press, the Japanese press, and Japanese science and medicine, see Fox, *op. cit.*, pp. 451–83.

14. Both the *Jiji Shimpō* and the *Asahi* continue to be published today, but the latter remains the more powerful paper. See Carmen Blacker, *The*

Japanese Enlightenment, a Study of the Writings of Fukuzawa Yukichi (Cambridge: Cambridge University Press, 1964), p. 17; and Albert M. Craig, "Fukuzawa Yukichi: the Philosophical Foundations of Meiji Nationalism," in Ward, *op. cit.*, pp. 99–148.

15. The reader is doubtless familiar with *The Tale of Genji* (London: George Allen & Unwin, Ltd., 1935) through the admirable translation by Arthur Waley of the eleventh-century novel *Genji Monogatari* by Murasaki Shikibu. This novel has always been popular with Japanese readers. In the eighteenth century there was a rash of "realistic" novels, many of them centering around life in the licensed quarters in the cities.

16. See *Japan's First Modern Novel: Ukigumo of Futabatei Shimei*, translation and commentary by Marleigh Ryan (New York: Columbia University Press, 1967).

PART III

ESTABLISHMENT OF THE JAPANESE EMPIRE 1890-1915

There is a Law of Nations, it is true,
But when the moment comes, remember,
The Strong eat up the Weak.

From a Song of Diplomacy *by Komuro, translated by G. B. Sansom, in* The Western World and Japan

Chronology

1890–1915

1890	November	First Diet opened
1892	February	Violence in elections
		Itō becomes Premier
1894		Treaty with Great Britain abolishing extraterritoriality
	July 25	Outbreak of Sino-Japanese War
1895	April 17	Treaty of Shimonoseki
		The Triple Intervention, forcing the return of Liaotung
1898		Acquisition of Liaotung by Russia
		Rosen–Nishi Agreement
1899		The Open Door Policy
1900		Boxer Uprising
		Yamagata–Itō rivalry; Itō forms Seiyukai
1901		Katura's first cabinet
		Saionji–Katsura compromise
1902		Anglo-Japanese Alliance
1904	February 8	Outbreak of Russo-Japanese War
1905	July	Taft–Katsura Agreement
		Anglo-Japanese Alliance renewed and strengthened
	September 5	Treaty of Portsmouth
	November	Itō becomes Resident General of Korea
1907	July 25	Protectorate over Korea
1908		Katsura Cabinet
1909	October	Itō assassinated at Harbin
1910	August 22	Korea annexed by Japan
1912	July 30	Death of Emperor Meiji
	December	Taishō political crisis
1914	April	Ōkuma becomes Premier
	August 23	Japan declares war on Germany
	November	Japan completes capture of German-leased territory in Shantung
1915	January 15	Twenty-One Demands presented to China
	May 25	China reluctantly agrees to demands

11

The Oligarchs in Power Under the Constitution 1890–1895

In a little more than a generation, from Perry's arrival in Japan in 1853 to the promulgation of the Constitution on February 11, 1889, Japan had undergone dramatic changes. Some of this transformation was, however, more superficial than real. Most of it had been inspired and directed by a small group of oligarchs. Many of the reforms which they had inaugurated, such as the promulgation of a new Constitution, had yet to be tried by experience. Nevertheless, the basic prerequisites for a modern state were at hand: an effective central government, a conscript army, a system of universal education, an abundant labor supply, a potentially important industrial and commercial society, and an agrarian production sufficient to meet immediate demands. Obviously Japan had met the challenge of Western civilization by *adapting* the basic elements of Westernization.

The significant question to be answered in 1890 was not whether Japan was to become a modern state. It was rather, "What type of state and how important a country was it to become?" Would the oligarchs continue to retain control through the manipulation of the constitutional government which they had created? Would the civil or military group among the oligarchs finally gain the ascendancy? What influence would modernization have upon the country? Could the economic and political aspirations of a virile people be met within the territorial confines of the empire as of 1890? If not, what effect would international forces have on the course of the Japanese Empire? How significant would that empire become? Could it possibly become strong enough to play a leading part in world politics? What would be the net effect of the interaction of these forces on Japan and on the world during the next generation?

In view of the fact that the next quarter century covered by this study saw the creation of a strong Japanese Empire with significant colonies, international problems dominate the scene. As the empire grew, Japan became increasingly involved in world politics. By May, 1915, this involvement had reached its climax. Japan took advantage of the preoccupation of the Allies in the war in Europe to consolidate its position in China. It demanded and received preferential treatment and special privileges on the Asiatic continent and became the undisputed leader of East Asia.

While achieving this prominent position as a world power, the oligarchs had successfully met every challenge to their supremacy from the people and from the political parties. Such struggles as took place between Parliament and the Cabinet, or between the party members in the House of Representatives and the oligarchs were over domestic issues and for control of the reins of government. On the all-important issue of establishment of a strong empire, all groups supported an aggressive foreign policy. Such differences as existed on questions of diplomacy were on matters of method rather than on questions of policy.

Oligarchs' Advantages over Political Parties

Before describing Japan's successes in the war against China in 1894, it is necessary to turn to the bitter domestic struggle between the political parties and the oligarchs after the new Constitution went into effect. The conclusion of the short ceremonies on February 11, 1889, which promulgated the Meiji Constitution, was the signal for the renewal of the political battle silenced two years earlier by the harsh measures enforced by Home Minister Yamagata. The oligarchs were confident that the new Constitution protected the special prerogatives of the Emperor and their own position as advisers to him and that Parliament's power could be kept to a minimum.

On the other hand, although they were resentful of the conservatives' notion of the Constitution, the party leaders placed great hopes in the power they would be able to exert through Parliament. Despite the constitutional limitations on the powers of the House of Representatives, they fully expected that the new national government would be operated on the principle that the Premier would be selected from the largest party in the House. With elections for members of the House of Representatives in the offing, the political parties (*mintō*) had a new *raison d'être*.[1] At last, they had a legitimate opportunity to prove both their strength and their worth by the election of their members to Parliament. The party leaders anticipated that if a majority of the members of the House of Representatives belonged to the parties, the political parties and those who supported "popular rights" would be in a strong position to counteract the influence of their opponents, the clan oligarchs. In fact, the parties might even be able to control the executive as well as the legislative branch of the government. As the strength of the parties lay in the general unpopularity of the oligarchs among the people, every effort was made to capitalize on this situation. For example, the party candidates criticized the slow progress of the negotiations for the revision of the unequal treaties with the Western powers. They also challenged the right of the oligarchs to continue to monopolize the key positions in the government and to refuse to inaugurate democratic practices.

For their part, the clan bureaucrats had no intention of allowing the Constitution to deprive them of their authority. They had moved adroitly and cautiously toward a constitutional monarchy. Whenever they made concessions toward popular representation in government, they contrived safeguards to protect the prerogatives of the throne and to assure the predominance of the executive over the legislative. They had conceived and drafted the Constitution in such a way as to provide a minimum of representative institutions and a maximum of Imperial absolutism.

Certain ingrained social concepts and patterns of action gave the oligarchs a distinct advantage over the political parties in the fight to retain control. In the first place, the Constitution had been granted by the Emperor to the people. This act was a natural consequence of the feudal concept of subordination of the inferior to the authority of the superior. Furthermore, the basic social concept of group responsibility greatly assisted the leaders of the government. Anyone familiar with contemporary Japan is aware of the importance of group consideration (*sōdan*) of a problem before a decision is made. This traditional procedure of passing judgment on any issue—whether a family or national problem—had not been affected by the Meiji Restoration. On the contrary, examples already cited clearly indicate that group decisions determined basic policies throughout the Restoration Period. Such a procedure exonerated any single individual from blame if the policy proved unsuccessful. In society in general, individual opinions and private initiative had to give way to compromise and group harmony. Diversity of views and individual responsibility were sacrificed for the good of the whole. Hence these traditional practices tended to strengthen support for the oligarchs and to handicap the popular movement.

But perhaps the greatest advantage for the oligarchs in their struggle with the parties was the fact that the former had held the reins of government for the past twenty-three years. When the Constitution was promulgated, all of the key posts in the government were filled by oligarchs.[2] There was no indication that they would abdicate their favored position just because a Parliament was to be formed. On the contrary, it was clear from what they had already done and said that they intended to continue to rule and to fight the concept of popular government. It was inevitable, therefore, that the first period of parliamentary government should be one of conflict between the party representatives on the one hand and the oligarchs on the other.

Oligarchs' Victories over Parties

During the first five years of constitutional government, the constant changes in Cabinets, the frequent dissolution of the Lower House, and the violence during the general elections all indicate the extent and intensity of the struggle for control of Parliament. In this half decade there were four separate Cabinets and three general elections. The demise of the first Cabinet, even before the elections were held, illustrates the instability of the political scene.

Foreign Minister Ōkuma had been having great difficulty with the Western powers, with his political opponents, and with the public on the question of revision of the unequal clauses in the treaties. Because of his willingness to compromise, an attempt had been made on his life on October 18, 1889. (See above, page 208.) The shock of this terroristic act had been too great for Prime Minister Kuroda to withstand. His Cabinet resigned *en bloc* within ten days. The oligarchs had been challenged in this first instance not by those who clamored for greater people's rights but by ultranationalists. As was to be the case so often in the future, the terrorists were to achieve their aims by illegal direct action to the detriment of the plans and policies of the moderates.

The selection of the new Prime Minister was of the utmost importance to the oligarchs. They realized that the first national election scheduled for July 1, 1890, and the opening of the first session of the Diet would put a great strain on their position. To assure continuance of their control, they needed a strong, steady hand to guide the Cabinet. Consequently, General Yamagata was chosen as the new Prime Minister. Aoki, the Minister in Berlin when Itō was studying the Prussian Constitution and who looked and behaved more like a German than a Japanese, was selected as Foreign Minister. Yamagata and Aoki were known for their opposition to representative institutions. All of the important Cabinet positions were filled by men from Satsuma and Chōshū. Thus the oligarchs hoped to keep Parliament from interfering with the operation of national affairs. They talked about the "transcendental" character of the Cabinet. Leaders such as Itō argued that since the administrative rights of the government were part of the Emperor's prerogatives, Cabinet ministers were responsible for their actions to the Emperor and to no one else. They were above the political parties and beyond the reach or the reproach of Parliament.

As a result of this attitude, considerable opposition to the Cabinet developed prior to the election. The party leaders made full use of this discontent and of the popular demand for immediate revision of the treaties. Consequently, at the first national election, the Liberal party (*Jiyūtō*) and the Progressive party (*Kaishintō*) together were able to obtain 170 seats out of a total of 296 in the Lower House.[3] A large number of the remaining members of the Lower House were independents. Prime Minister Yamagata controlled only 84 votes. When he met the First Diet in November, 1890, the lines were clearly drawn between the oligarchs and the party members of the House of Representatives. In his opening speech, which was arrogant and contemptuous, he represented the extreme attitude of the bureaucrats. He assumed that his colleagues, with their twenty-five years' experience in statecraft, knew what was best for the country. His omission of any reference to his legislative program indicated his intention to ignore Parliament.

On the other hand, the people's parties had a clear majority of votes in the House of Representatives. Although they were not united behind a single leader, they were united on several issues. They were enraged that no progress had been made on revising the treaties. They were anxious to challenge the Satchō (Satsuma Chōshū) clans' monopoly in government and to exercise fully the powers given them under the Constitution. When the national budget was presented to the Diet, the Lower House immediately slashed 10 per cent off the appropriations. These reductions were primarily concentrated on the salaries of the civil and military officials who had actually been operating the government for the past two decades. The newly elected members of Parliament were disdainful of the civil service which was replete with conservative bureaucrats who were as uncompromisingly opposed to the political parties as were the oligarchs.

In the face of this possible reduction in available funds, Yamagata adopted two separate tactics; one was parliamentary but the other was of questionable propriety. He contended that the Lower House was exceeding its power in demanding reductions in the budget and prorogued the Lower House for a week. He justified this action on the basis of Article 67 of the Constitution, which prohibited the reduction of fixed expenditures without the concurrence of the Cabinet. The questionable tactics which he espoused included hiring thugs to intimidate the members of Parliament who were opposed to the government and to prevent them from entering the Diet Building. At the same time, bribes and special favors were used to induce other members to abandon their party allegiance. In the end, the budget was passed but Yamagata had weakened his position.

He was criticized by his colleagues for the tactics which he used. Itō, the leader of the civil group among the oligarchs, questioned the applicability of Article 67 to the Diet's decision to reduce the budget.[4] These were the first signs that cracks were appearing in the armor of the oligarchs. Divisive tendencies, created by jealousies and the rivalry between civil and military leaders were increasing. This criticism of the Prime Minister led to his resignation in May, 1891. Nevertheless, during his tenure of office, the Diet had been unable to exert its influence effectively in the operation of state affairs. In fact, the independence of the executive from the legislative branch of the government had only increased.

Two important precedents, which had been established in selecting the last two Prime Ministers, were again followed in 1891. In the first place, the oligarchs decided among themselves by informal conferences who should be selected from among their group to head the Cabinet. Their choice was in complete disregard for the strength of the parties in Parliament. Thus, the hope and dream of the advocates of people's rights that the leader of the largest party in Parliament would be the Prime Minister remained only a dream. There was apparently no effective way that the parties could break up the oligarchs' monopoly.

The second precedent which the oligarchs followed was to choose the new Premier alternately from Satsuma and Chōshū. Thus, Matsukata Masayoshi from Satsuma, who had been such a successful Finance Minister a decade earlier, was selected to head the government. Like his predecessors, he had little patience with the political parties or respect for their representatives in the Diet. He soon antagonized the legislators, who retaliated by obstructing any new legislation by a filibuster. Faced with these tactics, Matsukata answered in kind. He received Imperial consent to dissolve the Diet in December, 1891, making a new election compulsory.

Politicians in Diet Outmaneuvered

The election of February 15, 1892, was a sordid example of the ruthless attitude of the oligarchs toward the people and their parties. The politicians maintained that Matsukata's dissolution of Parliament was a retaliatory act and was contrary to the public will. Consequently, the parties' candidates were bitterly opposed to the oligarchs and all they stood for. On the other hand, the government took an equally uncompromising attitude. It hoped to smash the direct connection of the popular parties with the people and to strengthen its own representation in Parliament at the expense of the parties. Men like Itō, who now recognized that the Diet could not be ignored completely, were beginning to advocate a government party. They realized that they must have a legislative program and win the support of the legislators for such a program.

As the first move in a campaign of the Cabinet to win greater support in Parliament, Shinagawa Yajirō, a ruthless and ultraconservative bureaucrat from Chōshū and henchman of Yamagata, was appointed Home Minister. He ordered all of the prefectural governors and the police, who were directly responsible to him, to support the government's candidates in each district. The result of these instructions was the bloodiest election in Japan's history. Twenty-five persons were killed and nearly 400 wounded. Police and troops had been sent to the home villages of Itagaki and Ōkuma. Ballot boxes were seized by the authorities while they were being transported to a central location for official counting. Bribes began to be offered to the electorate. Yet despite these ruthless and strong-arm methods, only 95 government candidates were elected in contrast to 163 representatives from the "people's parties."

After such violence and in view of the comparatively poor showing of the government's candidates in the election, the struggle between the oligarchs and the parties increased in intensity. A resolution to impeach the Cabinet lost in the Lower House by only three votes. The Third Diet, which met in May, 1892, refused to pass the annual budget. But in effect, like so much of Parliament's obstructionism, it made little difference. The Constitution provided that if a budget was not approved, the one for the previous year automatically went into effect.

Despite this rebuff, therefore, Matsukata continued as Premier until challenged by the military. The furor created by the election scandal had been partially placated by the removal of Shinagawa as Home Minister. His successor tried to restore public confidence by the transfer or dismissal of the prefectural governors who had been responsible for the outrages. Since Shinagawa was a representative of the military faction of the oligarchs, such action was a direct affront to the military. Consequently, both the Ministers of War and of the Navy showed their disapproval of the policies of the bureaucrats in the Cabinet by resigning. This action, like many other precedents set in these early years, was to become a common practice in later years and assured control of the cabinets by the military.

When Matsukata was forced to resign in mid-summer of 1892, the party leaders were elated. They believed that their uncompromising attitude and the refusal of their representatives in the Diet to cooperate with the oligarchs had shown conclusively that the concept of a transcendental Cabinet was both impractical and inoperative. They assumed that the constant turnover in Cabinets and the resignation of three Premiers since

October, 1889, was attributable to their maneuvers. They saw the resignation of Matsukata as Premier as a sign of a breach among the oligarchs. The parties anticipated that the oligarchs would soon offer concessions in the hope of obtaining cooperation from the Diet. If such an eventuality came about, the importance of the House of Representatives would be established and the parties would become the dominant power in Japanese politics.

It is impossible to determine how much of this reasoning, accepted largely both by Itagaki and Ōkuma, was wishful thinking and how much of it reflected the actual position of power of the parties. In historical retrospect, however, several facts become patently clear. The party leaders had underestimated the solidarity of the oligarchs whenever their power was challenged. Furthermore, the proponents of people's rights had not yet realized that the Constitution had created a political paradox —a parliamentary form of government, yet one in which the Emperor and his advisers retained autocratic power. Finally, severe divisiveness among the party leaders and members increased their ineffectiveness.

Political developments during the next Cabinet demonstrated both of these facts. The elder statesmen immediately closed ranks and selected the most venerable civil oligarch as Prime Minister, namely, Itō Hirobumi. He proceeded to use the politicians to discredit themselves. For example, in November, 1892, when the antioligarch members of the Lower House presented a memorial to the throne censuring the Cabinet, Itō refused to show any signs of weakness. He arranged for the Emperor to call together the Cabinet ministers and leaders of both houses of Parliament, to admonish them and to order them to compose their differences. After the Emperor offered to contribute one-tenth of his income for defense expenditures, he asked the members of Parliament and other officials to allocate a similar proportion of their own salaries for the same purpose. It would have been impossible for them to have refused and still retained their jobs. This use of the prestige of the throne to placate the opposition had the desired effect. The party members became dispirited and even agreed to approve the national budget with only minor changes. Itō had clearly won his first round.

During the next year and a half prior to the outbreak of the Sino-Japanese War in August, 1894, Itō and the oligarchs were at loggerheads with the House of Representatives. Parliament was dissolved twice and Itō carried out his policies despite a hostile legislature. When the parties began to fight each other, the Prime Minister encouraged their disunity. In December, 1893, they united again over the issue of revision of the unequal clauses in the treaties and sent a resolution to the Emperor which requested the dismissal of the Premier. On the other hand, Itō feared that discussions of the revisions of the treaty would endanger negotiations with the Western powers.

At this point, the prestige of the Privy Council was brought to bear on the obstreperousness of the Representatives. Answering for the Emperor the Privy Council made the terse statement, "As for the resignation of my Chief Minister, I will not permit outside interference."

In a crisis, the oligarchs, not only in the Cabinet but also in the Privy Council, had stood firm against the people's representatives in Parliament. Finally, Parliament was dissolved and the use of strong tactics against the opposition was renewed. These took the familiar form of suppression of the opposition's newspapers, prohibition of political meetings, and the liquidation of the most "radical" organizations.

In the elections in March, 1894, voting at most of the polls was without incident but resulted in a House of Representatives hostile to Itō. As previously, it passed a nonconfidence resolution, but this time by an overwhelming majority of 253 to 17. Both Itō and the Emperor refused to accept the resolution and did not even give the Representatives the satisfaction of a written reply. In effect, the parties had again brought the legislative branch of the government to a standstill. They seemed determined that if they could not control the government, they would obstruct its operation whenever possible. In retaliation for their lack of support and because he did not wish to have the treaty revision negotiations discussed in the Diet, Itō dissolved it again on June 2, 1894. Actually, his action had been precipitated by the crisis in Korea. Before Parliament met again, Japan was at war with China and domestic political differences were forgotten.

Revision of Unequal Treaties

Nothing more effectively quieted the futile efforts of the political parties to control the reins of government than the international crisis. In fact, international problems dominated Japan's development during the years to come and were of far greater import than domestic political struggles. Heretofore, the two most crucial international questions following the Restoration had been the revision of the unequal treaties and the struggle for the dominance over Korea. (See Chapters 8 and 9.) Both of these questions became acute, however, during the premiership of Itō.

The question of treaty revision was always a politically explosive issue. Many a Foreign Minister had been forced to resign and several Cabinets had faced a crisis over their inability to persuade the foreigners to relinquish their extraterritorial rights. Even when war clouds thickened over Korea, Parliament was more critical of Itō's inability to solve the question of treaty revision than of his policy toward China. Treaty revision was the central issue of the debates on foreign affairs in 1893 and 1894. Prime Minister Itō had used Parliament's attitude on the treaties as the excuse for dissolution.

Just prior to the outbreak of the Sino-Japanese War in 1894, however, the thorny issue was largely resolved. Aoki Shūzō, who had been Foreign Minister under Yamagata, was sent to London on special assignment to negotiate with Great Britain for the abolition of consular courts (extraterritoriality) and for tariff autonomy for Japan. As a result of Aoki's successful mission, the first treaty with Japan abolishing the unequal clauses was signed in London on July 16, 1894, to be effective in 1899. Similar treaties with other powers soon followed. The end of the fight for equality with the West was in sight.

War With China 1894–1895

The controversy with China over Korea was incomparably more significant for Japan than the revision of the treaties with the Western powers. If China gained undisputed control of Korea, Japan's chances for expansion on the Asiatic continent were lost. In 1885 the possibility of a Sino-Japanese war had been averted by the successful conclusion of the Li–Itō Convention. (See above, page 190.) At that time, both China and Japan had temporarily forsaken their claim for exclusive control of Korea. They also promised to notify each other if either power intended to send troops into the Korean peninsula. Nevertheless, China continued to contend that it had jurisdiction over Korean foreign affairs. For example, it had asked that the United States Chargé d'Affaires Foulke be recalled from Seoul because of his activities on behalf of Korean independence. Furthermore, Yüan Shih-kai had continued as the Chinese Resident and was unusually successful in obtaining Korean compliance with China's wishes. At the same time he aroused Japanese antagonism by advocating an export ban on Korean goods which were vital to the continuance of Japanese trade with Korea.

On the other hand, Japan tenaciously refused to accept China's special position. The conservative clique in Tokyo had restrained the ultranationalists from going to war over Korea in 1873 because their country was not politically and economically solidified. Twenty years later such arguments were no longer convincing or pertinent. Furthermore, Itō and his Cabinet colleagues had not forgotten what they considered to be China's procrastination and pusillanimous attitude over the question of the disposition of the Ryūkyū Islands. They had not given Korea up but were waiting for a more propitious moment to settle permanently the question of whether Japan or China was to control Korean affairs. Foreign Minister Mutsu took the position that it was imperative to conclude the revision of the unequal treaties with the Western powers prior to undertaking the solution of the Korean problem.

But certain events in the first half of 1894 forced the issue. The assassination in the International Settlement in Shanghai of the Korean reform leader Kim Ok-kiun, who had been strongly pro-Japanese, aroused the liberals in Japan against their government's Korean policy. When a band of anti-Japanese nationalists, known as the Tonghaks, revolted in South Korea, a crisis rapidly developed. The Tonghaks were a reactionary group of Korean patriots inspired by a desire to preserve "Eastern Learning" and to expel all vestiges of Western civilization as well as Japanese influence from their court. They considered the Japanese as Oriental renegades and as degenerate as Occidentals. Politically the Tonghaks were the enemies of the Min or Queen's family and were supported by the former Regent, the Taewŏnkun. After the Tonghaks revolted, the Japanese Minister in Seoul telegraphed his government that they probably were not strong enough to overthrow the King but that their revolt might endanger the lives of Japanese nationals.

Since the Korean King's troops were defeated in their first skirmish with the rebels, he decided on May 31, 1894, to ask Yüan Shih-kai for Chinese military assistance. Yüan was reported as boasting that he intended to settle the riot immediately to avoid a chance for the overthrow of the Korean government. Two days later the Japanese Cabinet had decided, under strong pressure from the Deputy Chief of Staff, Kawakami Soroku, that Japan should counter any Chinese troop movements with its own and that a General Headquarters should be set up in Korea.[5] Shortly thereafter the Emperor approved this plan. Even though the Koreans claimed they had the Tonghaks under control, Japan dispatched a mixed brigade to Korea. By June 7, in accordance with the provisions of the Li–Itō Convention, each side informed the other that troops were being sent to suppress the rebellion. In doing so, China referred to restoring order in its "tributary state" while Japan refused to recognize China's special status there.[6]

From this point, events developed rapidly. By June 10, 1894, Chinese troops were south of the Korean capital of Seoul. Despite the fact that the rebel Tonghaks were under control, both Japan and China refused to withdraw their troops. When Great Britain and other powers inquired about the intentions of the two countries, Japan gave evasive answers. At home, it completed preparations for the mobilization of both its land and naval forces. Hostilities seemed inevitable. When Itō's offer to send a joint Sino-Japanese Commission to Korea to guarantee reform of the corrupt Korean government was rejected by China, Japan concluded it would have to act independently. It presented extensive demands to the Korean King. These included treatment of Japanese officials and private subjects as equal to those from China and the establishment of a competent judicial system, a modern army, a new police force, a new currency, and a means of supervising government expenditures. When the King ignored these requests and British attempts at mediation between China and Japan failed, the Japanese Cabinet agreed on July 11 that it would go to war if necessary to force China out of Korea. China was warned that the dispatch of more troops to Korea would be considered as a hostile act. On July 23, 1894, the King's palace was entered by Japanese troops. As a captive, the King signed an agreement for the expulsion of the Chinese. Two days later a Chinese troopship of British registry, the "Kowshing," was sunk by the Imperial Japanese Navy.[7]

In Japan, opposition to Itō and his Cabinet vanished instantaneously with the outbreak of war. During the special Diet session in the fall of 1894 and the regular session in 1895 the opposition parties acted as though they had forgotten their previous animosities. In February, a war budget passed easily. Fukuzawa Yukichi wrote that the war supported Japan's cultural advancement and progressive plans for the future.

The entire nation realized that the stakes in Korea were too high to be lost by internal bickering. Moreover, the party members in the House of Representatives had opposed the oligarchs not because of the latter's aggressive China policy. On the contrary, the various factions, regardless of their differences on matters of internal politics, had never disagreed on the advisability of greater Japanese control on the Asiatic mainland. Such differences as had appeared had been more over the method and the timing of such control rather than over the wisdom of control. In 1891, for example, the *Jiyūtō* had demanded a more, rather than a less, aggressive policy. Since Itō had taken the nation into a war which might give Japan control over Korea, everyone willingly bent to the task of winning that war as rapidly as possible.

Because of this sudden disappearance, with the outbreak of war, of the struggle between the oligarchs and the politicians, it has been claimed that Itō started hostilities to extricate himself from a difficult position politically. Such an argument is, however, an oversimplification of a very complex problem. In fact, many factors indicate its fallaciousness. Naturally, it made his political life much simpler to have Parliament's support for his war effort. But he was far more fearful of the extension of Chinese hegemony over Korea than of the continuous bickerings of the politicians. He had drafted a Constitution which assured the pre-eminence of the executive and the Emperor's advisers. During the previous five years, the parties had not seriously threatened that pre-eminence, so that Itō could continue, if necessary, to ignore Parliament. If Japan's international status was not to be impaired, however, he could not ignore Chinese troop movements in Korea. Whether war meant the political solidification of the home front was of only secondary importance. Of supreme importance was whether China could be forced to give up its suzerainty over Korea.

First Fruits of Victory

The Declaration of War by Japan on August 1, 1894, six days after the Chinese troopship had been sunk, was an anticlimax. So, too, was the government's decision in mid-August that Japan recognize Korean independence as its basic policy and be willing to defend it indefinitely. On August 26, 1894, through the influence of the Taewŏnkun, whom the Japanese had persuaded to operate the Korean government, an agreement was signed which formalized Japan's position of maintaining Korean independence and expelling the Chinese troops. From the beginning of hostilities, there was no question as to the outcome of the struggle. China was weak and disorganized. The Imperial Court was still living in a blissful isolation. Its army was practically as outmoded as that of Japan thirty years earlier. Although two of the Chinese battleships outclassed those from Japan, the training and equipment of the Chinese Navy were inferior. By mid-September, Japan controlled the Gulf of Chihli which meant that it could effectively prevent the shipment of Chinese reinforcements to Manchuria and Korea. Port Arthur fell on November 21. Three months later, Japan was in possession of all of Korea and of the rich Liaotung Peninsula, the entrance to South Manchuria.

Having completed these valuable conquests within little more than six months, Japan was willing to negotiate for peace. Its demands as a price for an armistice indicated, however, that it hoped to profit directly from its military victories. The armistice conditions specified that Viceroy Li Hung-chang be sent as the chief Chinese envoy and that three important northern Chinese cities be ceded to Japan. These cities were Shanhaikwan, gateway through the Great Wall to the north; the industrial city of Tientsin; and its port of entry, Tangku. As possession of these three centers by Japan would be a constant threat to the capital city of Peking, Li refused to accept the demands. Nevertheless, he came to Shimonoseki to see if he could negotiate a settlement.

The deadlock in the preliminary negotiations was broken and Japan's attitude toward China was abruptly changed by an unexpected attack on Li's life. Although he was not seriously wounded, this terroristic act caused immediate repercussions in Japan and abroad. Throughout the war, Japan had gone to considerable pains to demonstrate to the world that it was "modern" enough to be able to follow the practices prescribed by international law. Its failure to declare war after hostilities had started had not been considered too serious an infraction. The unwarranted shooting of an official peace envoy, however, was an entirely different matter.

The Japanese government suddenly realized that unless amends were made speedily and magnanimously, this one irresponsible act might jeopardize all of the prizes of the war. Consequently, Itō, the Japanese Premier and chief peace delegate, visited Li and apologized to him officially. The Emperor sent his personal physician to care for the wounded envoy and issued a decree deploring the incivility of the act. The conditions for an armistice were withdrawn and Japan made concessions in its peace demands. The proposed war indemnity was reduced by one-third and the demands that Japanese subjects be given exceptional privileges in the interior of China were dropped. The right of occupy Mukden in South Manchuria as a guarantee that the terms of the treaty would be carried out was also waived.[8]

As a result of this attack on Li, the final settlement was far more moderate than originally intended by Japan. By the Treaty of Shimonoseki, which Li and Itō signed on April 17, 1895, China "recognized definitely the full and complete independence and autonomy of Korea." It also agreed to cede to Japan in perpetuity and full sovereignty the island of Formosa and the adjacent Pescadores Islands and the Liaotung Peninsula in South Manchuria. It promised to pay an indemnity of 200 million taels of silver (350 million yen) to defray the cost of the war. Four additional Chinese cities were opened for commercial and industrial purposes. Finally, the treaty specified that the port of Weihaiwei, on the northern shore of the Shantung Peninsula, would continue to be occupied by Japanese forces until the indemnity was paid and a treaty of commerce was negotiated between the two nations.

The Sino-Japanese War had been eminently successful for the victor. Japan had conclusively defeated one of the strongest nations in the Orient. The indemnity was more than sufficient to repay Japan for its war effort. New, rich colonial territories had been acquired both in the south and on the continent of Asia. Formosa, which was contiguous to the Ryūkyū Islands, formed a natural bridge to further expansion southward. In Japanese hands, the Liaotung Peninsula was a protection from future encroachments by China or by Russia on Korea. Finally, Chinese hegemony over, and special privileges in, Korea had been eliminated and the political vacuum created thereby was rapidly filled by Japan.

The American Minister in Seoul claimed that there was evidence everywhere that Japan was running Korea. The Korean Army was drilled and officered by Japanese. The post office, the telegraph system, and the railway from Seoul to Pusan were taken over and operated by them. Taxes were assessed according to Japanese laws. China had more than given up suzerainty over Korea. The peninsula kingdom was at the mercy of a rapidly expanding Japanese Empire which had become the predominant force in East Asia.

The Bitter Price of Victory—The Triple Intervention

Such appeared on the surface to be the rewards of victory. One of the leading dailies, the *Kokumin Shimbun,* had boasted:

> As a result of the war, Japan's position in the world has been changed by the revelation of three basic Japanese characteristics. First, the Japanese people excel throughout the world in their patriotic love of country. Secondly, they have a unique ability to digest, utilize, and apply modern civilization. Thirdly, they have a solid and strong nature or temper.[9]

But no historical event is isolated or detached from other contemporary developments and the peace negotiations at Shimonoseki were no exception to this rule. The Western powers had begun to look upon Japan's activities with considerable misgivings. They were particularly apprehensive lest Japan win special privileges in China. Some of them were determined to prevent such an eventuality from coming to pass. When the Japanese Minister in London had asked in 1893 about Britain's attitude in the event of a war between Japan and China, he had been told that while Great Britain would welcome an amelioration of the internal chaos in Korea it would not tolerate the transfer of Korea to Japan.

The Russian Minister in Tokyo had likewise stated that his government would not countenance the violation of Korean independence. The newspaper *Novoye Vremya* had warned Japan not to go too far lest a joint Chinese–Russian protectorate be necessary for Korea. Vice-Foreign Minister Hayashi had been told by some of the European diplomats that a demand for territory on the Chinese mainland might result in intervention by the powers. Despite these warnings, Foreign Minister Mutsu recorded in his journal his hope that Japan could acquire both the Liaotung and Shantung peninsulas. At the end of the war, the Japanese Chiefs of Staff had insisted that they receive territorial concessions and an indemnity as the reward for military victory. Consequently, the clauses which ceded Liaotung to Japan had been included in the Treaty of Shimonoseki.

Prime Minister Itō was fully aware, however, that it was unlikely that the Western powers would allow Japan to retain this territory. He also knew that the powers had been kept informed of the progress of the negotiations. Viceroy Li, who was conscious of the value of international support for his position, had kept the foreign diplomats abreast of the developments. For example, on April 1, 1895, nearly three weeks before the Treaty was signed, they learned of Japan's request for the Liaotung Peninsula.

Itō and his colleagues did not know until later, however, the extent of the impact which this news had had on the Western powers. It was particularly startling to Russia. That country had long desired a warm-water port either in Korea or in the Liaotung Peninsula. Such a port would be a natural eastern terminus for the Trans-Siberian Railway which had been under construction for three years. The Sino-Japanese War had decreased the chances of Russia obtaining a port in Korea. From the Russian point of view, therefore, the Liaotung Peninsula remained as an alternate potential Russian sphere of influence so long as it did not fall into Japanese hands.

After learning of Japan's request for Liaotung, the Russian Minister of Finance, Count Serge Witte, who was one of the chief architects of Russian Far Eastern policy, acted quickly to forestall Japan. He proposed to Great Britain, France, and Germany that intervention was in order to discourage Japan from asking for Liaotung. Great Britain, fearful of Russian advances on the Asiatic continent and contemptuous of China, preferred to see Japan rather than Russia in a favorable position in Korea and South Manchuria. Hence it showed little interest in Witte's proposal. On the other hand, France and Germany were quick to agree that if Port Arthur and the Liaotung Peninsula were in Japanese hands, they would be a menace to the peace of the Far East.

As soon as the contents of the Treaty of Shimonoseki were announced on April 17, 1895, Russia formally approached the powers concerning intervention. Thus Japan's destiny became entwined in the intricacies of European diplomacy. It had asked for something which conflicted with the self-interests of one of the European powers. From the point of view of this self-interest, such interference could not be tolerated, especially by an upstart nation which might be impertinent enough to defy the "advice" of a single power. A week later, the first formal step of the tripartite intervention took place. Vice-Foreign Minister Hayashi was jointly "advised" by the French, German, and Russian Ministers in Tokyo that Japan should renounce its claims to the Liaotung Peninsula.

Two days later, a formal note from Russia stated:

> The Government of His Majesty the Emperor of all the Russians, in examining the conditions of peace which Japan has imposed on China, finds that the possession of the Peninsula of Liaotung, claimed by Japan, would be a menace to the Capital of China, would at the same time render illusory the independence of Korea and would henceforth be a perpetual obstacle to the peace of the Far East.

It concluded, in diplomatic language, by "advising" Japan to renounce its claim.

Despite the fact that Itō and some of his Cabinet had expected this *démarche*, they found it difficult to accept the inevitable. It was clear that Russia had taken the initiative and had challenged Japan to a show-down. The Japanese Minister at St. Petersburg reported that Russia was adamant and was making military preparations for any eventuality. It was common knowledge that the Russian Pacific fleet was concentrated at Vladivostok ready for action at a moment's notice. Faced with these unpleasant facts, an Imperial Conference was hastily called at which it was tentatively decided that the "advice" would have to be accepted. Foreign Minister Mutsu, who could not attend because of illness, argued for postponement of a decision. He hoped, by diplomatic means, to find those who would oppose Russia's move but his efforts came to naught. At one point, Japan made a compromise proposal that it would retain only the southern tip of the Liaotung Peninsula but Russia rejected this suggestion.[10]

As for the public at large, they had been kept in ignorance of the latest developments. News of the Russian demands had leaked out and caused an immediate wave of antigovernment criticism. The government immediately closed all of those newspapers which had referred to the matter in an unfavorable light. The only news available on this vital issue came from the foreign press, *The Japan Times and Mail.* The Foreign Minister was unable, therefore, to capitalize on public support for his position.

The original Russian demand that Liaotung be given up was finally accepted by Japan with the proviso that Japan receive additional indemnity, which was later settled at 30 million taels. The Emperor tried to soften the blow for his subjects and to minimize the humiliation by stating in an Imperial Rescript that Japan had accomplished its aims in the war. He concluded that the retrocession in no way reflected on Japan's honor and hence the people should accept the decision passively. In November, 1895, the Treaty of Shimonoseki was revised accordingly by a special protocol.

The Triple Intervention Stimulates Nationalism

But even the prestige of the Emperor was not sufficient to make the Japanese public willing to accept this forceful intervention in their affairs by Russia and its allies. In fact, the official and formal acquiescence to the demands of the European *triplice* had both immediate and far-reaching results. The immediate effect was seen in the outburst of violent public indignation directed against the contents of the treaty and the Itō Ministry. All shades of political opinion criticized the government's action. For example, Gotō Shōjirō, one of the leaders of the *Jiyūtō* and former Agriculture Minister in the Itō Cabinet, advocated an expansionist program in a memorial which he forwarded to the Cabinet. He proposed the acquisition of the Three Eastern Provinces in Manchuria and of Korea. He recommended that these territories be linked by the construction of a Japanese-owned railway. He also urged necessary political alliances to protect China from European encroachments.[11]

This international capitulation also acted as a stimulant to ultranationalists who found a receptive public ear for their proposals for an aggressive foreign policy. Heretofore, leaders of nationalist thought had taken a negative attitude. They had hoped to preserve certain basic national characteristics and to protect them from the deleterious effects of European civilization. Henceforth, a new national self-consciousness concentrated on how to improve Japan's international position in the world at large. As one of the new intellectual leaders, Takayama Chogyū, expressed it:

> The Constitution, which was promulgated in 1889, clarified Japan's unique national polity, destroyed the empty principles of democracy and thereby unified national political thought. Likewise, the Imperial Edict on Education of 1890 is a model for national morality and in its turn unified national moral thought. Thus for the first time the spirit of Nipponism was able to control the public spirit of society. . . . It became the principle which was to represent the clearly awakened consciousness of Japanese nationalism.

A new type of patriotism, to be known as Nipponism (*Nihon Shugi*) had arisen during the war. It was a virulent nationalism which throve on self-sacrifice and adversity. The war period had raised the people's loyalty to a high pitch. As a contemporary writer expressed it, "The special features and most glorious points of Japan's constitutional government were made manifest at home and abroad."

The far-reaching results of the aftermath of the Sino-Japanese War of 1894–1895 are difficult to assay in view of the congeries of forces which molded Japan's modern development. But one development is clear. Slowly but steadily the Japanese people and nation came to be convinced that their chance for an important place in the sun was in direct proportion to their material and spiritual strength. They adopted a slogan of "Perseverance and Determination" and willingly accepted budget increases for greater military expenditures. The Army grew from seven to thirteen divisions in eight years and during the same period the Navy nearly tripled its tonnage. This dogged determination of the entire nation was further strengthened by the intervention of the Three Powers. The bitterness of the humiliating experience was intensified in

1898 when Russia acquired for itself the same territory it had forced Japan to renounce.

One can make a strong case, therefore, for the contention that the tripartite intervention was the most important single event in recent times which diverted Japan toward a policy of nationalistic aggression. The nation had been struggling peacefully for over twenty years to revise the unequal clauses in the treaties with the Western powers. At last, real progress had been made toward that end. The recent victory against China had been won at the cost of a concerted, national effort. Furthermore, in asking for territory from its former enemy, Japan was following what it believed to be accepted international procedure. Spain, Portugal, the Netherlands, and Great Britain had long since carved out empires in Asia as a result of military conquest. Germany, Russia, and France showed clear signs of following a policy whereby "might makes right."

In the face of victory, more and more Japanese, both statesmen and humble subjects, were convinced that these three powers had taken advantage of Japan's weakness to prevent it from acquiring territory which they believed was essential for them to hold to prevent Russia's encroachments in Asia and threats to Japan's security. Henceforth, anyone within Japan who opposed a strong, aggressive policy toward China, toward Russia, or toward the West found scanty historical evidence to support the position that cooperation and concessions would win more respect than aggression and an adamant position. It was argued with cogent consistency that the only true steps to national survival and salvation were by perseverance and determination through military strength and aggressive nationalism. Consequently, it will constantly be noted that the emphasis for the next half century was on military preparedness, expansion, and making the most out of the weaknesses of China or of the Western powers. Russia, Germany, and France had sown the wind; a half century later, the United Nations were to reap the whirlwind.

Notes

1. A word of caution is in order concerning terms such as "political parties" (*mintō*) and "popular rights" (*minken*). These terms are used loosely by Japanese political scientists to refer to the various groups who favored greater rather than fewer rights for the people and who supported candidates not sponsored by the government for the House of Representatives. A more exact meaning of these terms will become clear as the controversy between the oligarchs and the parties is explained.

2. On February 11, 1889, Itō Hirobumi was President of the Privy Council, Kuroda Kiyotaka was Prime Minister, Matsukata Masayoshi was Home Minister and concurrently Finance Minister. Ōkuma Shigenobu, who had opposed Itō and his colleagues so bitterly seven years earlier, was Minister of Foreign

Affairs. Other Cabinet members were Oyama Iwao, Minister of War, Saigō Tsugumichi, Minister of Navy, Yamada Akiyoshi, Justice, Mori Arinori, Education, Enomoto Takeaki, concurrently Minister of Agriculture and Commerce and Communications. Inouye Kaoru was Secretary of the Privy Council and Director of the Cabinet's Legal Office. Yamagata Aritomo had resigned as Home Minister two months earlier and became Prime Minister in December.

3. During the first decade of the operation of the Constitution, Itō and the other oligarchs were amazed at the opposition and resistance they encountered in the Diet, especially in the House of Representatives, and were distressed with their own inability to control the Diet to the extent they desired. For this whole problem as well as Itō's "mastery of the art of the possible," see the perceptive study by George Akita, *Foundations of Constitutional Government in Modern Japan, 1868–1900* (Cambridge: Harvard University Press, 1967).

The qualifications for voting which limited the franchise to males over 25 years of age and paying an annual real estate tax of ¥15 meant that only 1¼ per cent of the population voted. See Oka Yoshitake, "Seijishi," in Yanaihara Tadao (ed.), *Gendai Nihon Shōshi* (Tokyo: Misuzu-shobo, 1961), II, p. 42. A comprehensive study of this election has been made by R. H. P. Mason, *Japan's First General Election, 1890* (Cambridge: Cambridge University Press, 1969).

4. When Article 67 was drafted, Itō apparently had in mind such expenditures as the ordinary expenses of the Army and the Navy, of diplomatic missions, of the Diet, and of the obligations on the national debt. See Itō Hirobumi, *Commentaries on the Constitution of the Empire of Japan*, tr. by Itō Miyoji (Tokyo: Chūō Daigaku, 1931), pp. 128–31.

5. One of the first of the Japanese nationalist societies, the *Genyōsha*, and one of its leaders, Tōyama Mitsuru, had sent intelligence agents to the Asiatic mainland. Some of these, supported by the War Ministry's secret service funds, had made intimate contact with the Tonghaks and were able to send the Japanese General Staff reports on their activities. See Richard Storry, *The Double Patriots* (Boston: Houghton Mifflin Co., 1957), pp. 9–12; and Marius B. Jansen, *The Japanese and Sun Yat-sen* (Cambridge: Harvard University Press, 1954), pp. 45 ff.

6. Hilary Conroy, *The Japanese Seizure of Korea, 1868–1910* (Philadelphia: University of Pennsylvania Press, 1960), pp. 221 ff.

7. F. Nelson, *Korea and the Old Order in Eastern Asia* (Baton Rouge: University of Louisiana Press, 1946), p. 206.

8. H. B. Morse and Harley F. McNair, *Far Eastern International Relations* (Boston: Houghton Mifflin Co., 1931), p. 402.

9. Ōtsu Jun'ichirō, *Dai Nihon Kensei Shi* (10 vols.; Tokyo: Hobun-kan, 1927–1928), IV, pp. 216–21.

10. *Ibid.*, p. 476.

11. *Ibid.*, pp. 451–56.

12

International Pressures and the Growth of Empire, 1895–1904

It has just been shown how the rivalry between Japan and China for the control of Korea was the central issue leading directly to the Sino-Japanese War. This issue was presumably settled by the Treaty of Shimonoseki of 1895 by which both countries recognized Korea's complete independence. The intervention of the three Western powers in 1895 had forced Japan to give up its hopes of acquiring the Liaotung Peninsula. But during the next decade, the same struggle for control over Korea persisted, with Russia replacing China as one of the challengers. Furthermore, this was the period in which the leading European countries carved out concessions and spheres of influence for themselves in China. This movement was an outcome of their drive to maintain a balance of power in Europe and led to Japan's involvement in an alliance with Great Britain against Russia.

Even the United States, which had been largely absorbed with its own internal problems, suddenly became a colonial power with important possessions in the central and western Pacific Ocean. Likewise it became implicated in the future of China through the advocacy of the Open Door Policy and the outbreak of the Boxer Uprising in North China. The decade closed with the conclusive defeat of Russia by Japan in the Russo-Japanese War of 1904–1905. Obviously it was a period in which international forces were predominant among those which directed Japan's course of history. The question to be answered, therefore, is: What was the effect of these international events on the growth of the Japanese Empire?

The Political Background

Before this question is answered, we should turn briefly to the political background within Japan against which these international events took place. With the conclusion of the war with China in 1895, political instability continued. But the decade following the war saw the beginning of accommodations between the different Cabinets headed by the oligarchs on the one hand and one or more of the larger parties in the House of Representatives on the other. When such arrangements broke down, the House of Representatives opposed the program of the Cabinet and the latter dissolved Parliament or used more devious means to resolve the deadlock. The situation was further complicated by the fact that no party had a majority in the House until 1900 when the newly formed Seiyūkai Party claimed 155 seats out of the total of 300.

For example, Itō Hirobumi, who continued as Prime Minister until 1896, received the cooperation of Itagaki and his Liberals in return for his appointment to the Cabinet. On the other hand, when Itō insisted that Ōkuma, Itagaki's long-time political rival, should also receive a Cabinet post, the Liberals withdrew their support and the Itō Cabinet fell. According to custom, it was now Satsuma's turn to provide the new Prime Minister so the Elder Statesmen selected Matsukata Masayoshi. He in turn relied on Ōkuma, who was made Foreign Minister, for support from the Progressive Party. Matsukata's Cabinet lasted for less than a year and a half.

In January, 1898, Itō was again called upon to form a Cabinet but this time he excluded party members from it. In the elections in the spring both the Liberals and Progressives increased their seats in the Lower House so together they held a clear majority. At the special session of the Diet, in June, the parties combined to defeat Itō's bill to increase taxes so he dissolved it. At the same time, he became convinced that he should form his own party and sought financial support for it. When he reported his plan to the Elder Statesmen he received an immediate and violent reaction from Yamagata who insisted that the only purpose of the political parties was to oppose the government and their existence only increased political instability. Itō retorted that parties were advisable for the operation of the national government. He had little interest in the principle of mass participation in the governmental process but realized from a practical point of view that a Cabinet needed party support to be successful.

Heretofore, except for Ōkuma's dismissal from the Council of State in 1881, there had been no significant disunity among the oligarchs, especially when they were challenged by the political parties. By 1898, however, Itō and Yamagata had become political rivals, if not enemies. Although they were fellow clansmen from Chōshū, personal jealousies and antagonisms between the civilian group, led by Itō, and the military faction, under Yamagata's tutelage, caused an open break between these two men. This antagonism is clearly apparent from Itō's action in 1898. In late June, Ōkuma and Itagaki had decided to forget their differences and to combine their two parties into a new one. They subsequently formed the Kenseitō whose basic aims were the formation of party cabinets, cabinets responsible to the Diet, and greater self-government. As the Kenseitō controlled the Lower House, Itō saw no alternative but to resign.[1] Furthermore, as no Elder Statesman appeared available for selection as Prime Minister, Itō went to the Imperial Palace and recommended that Ōkuma and Itagaki, as representatives of the majority in the Lower House, be asked to form a Cabinet jointly. In making this recommendation, Itō had indirectly insulted Yamagata and also given himself time to develop his own party. Itō's recommendation was accepted; Ōkuma became the new Prime Minister and Itagaki held the second strongest position in the Cabinet, that of Home Minister. With this recognition having been given to the concept that the Prime Minister should be selected from the leaders of the largest party in the Lower House, the leaders and rank and file of the Kenseitō believed that the time had finally arrived when future Cabinets would be led by party men rather than the oligarchy.

But events were soon to show that these were vain hopes. From the very start, the military faction opposed Ōkuma's Cabinet. Both the Army and Navy refused to nominate candidates for their respective ministries but this impasse was resolved when the Emperor ordered them to appoint someone. The Ōkuma Cabinet fell in four months and in November, 1898, Yamagata became Prime Minister for a second time. He was able to survive through a shaky understanding with the Kenseitō. He also greatly strengthened the future position of the military by issuance of Imperial Ordinances in 1900 which decreed that only officers on active service in the two highest ranks of the Army and Navy were eligible for appointment as Ministers of War and Navy respectively. These ordinances restricted the eligible list to a mere handful, which meant a small clique could control and divert the policy of a Cabinet by a threat from one or another of the service ministers to resign or to refuse to serve. He also gave added impetus to increasing military expenditures for an enlarged Army and Navy. Yamagata's Cabinet fell, however, because of his rivalry with Itō.

In the summer of 1900, the Kenseitō showed signs of breaking up and of becoming dissatisfied with Yamagata and his policies. At the same time, Itō's plans to form a new party were progressing. In September,

1900, he announced the formation of the Rikken Seiyūkai. Its primary purpose was to expand constitutional government, as Itō interpreted it, and to give him and his protégés support in any future transcendental cabinets they would control. It would also serve as a bulwark against Yamagata and his military faction. Itō welcomed into his new party members of the Kenseitō but insisted the latter be dissolved before its members entered his party. He also made it clear that party members must follow his instructions explicitly. Furthermore, as he believed the appointments of Ministers of State to be the prerogative of the Emperor, party members could not interfere in any manner with a Minister in the discharge of his official duty.

When Itō announced the formation of the Seiyūkai, Yamagata resigned immediately as Prime Minister in the hope that Itō would fail in his plan to rally widespread support for his new party. At this point both men were only partially successful in achieving their objectives. Itō became Prime Minister and appointed only two Seiyūkai men to his Cabinet. His party was not yet fully organized and he soon ran into opposition among Yamagata's supporters in the House of Peers, the Privy Council, and the bureaucracy. By June, 1901, he recognized that he faced insurmountable obstacles and resigned.

The fall of the Itō Cabinet was a significant turning point in Japanese politics. It marked the beginning of Cabinets led by a new generation. The oligarchs, who had participated in the Meiji Restoration over thirty years earlier, henceforth exerted their influence behind the scenes. During the next twelve years, the office of Prime Minister was exchanged between General Katsura Tarō (1848–1913), a protégé of Yamagata, and Saionji Kimmochi, a follower of Itō. At the same time, the Seiyūkai, through the astute leadership of Hara Kei, became the largest party in the Lower House and strong enough to force Yamagata's followers to make political compromises with it.

Thus when General Katsura became Prime Minister in 1901, he had to rely on the Seiyūkai for support to obtain approval of his budgets and other vital legislation in the Diet.[2] When he resigned in 1906, he had already agreed with Hara that Saionji, the President of the Seiyūkai, would be the next Premier. But the rivalry and antagonism of the two most powerful individuals of this period, Yamagata and Itō, and of their military and civilian factions, continued though they operated largely in the background through their protégés, Katsura and Saionji.[3]

Failure of Japanese Coup in Korea

To revert to international developments after peace was concluded with China in 1895, Korea remained the central issue. The war had eliminated the menace of Chinese control over Korea but the designs of the Russian Empire represented an even greater menace to Japan. After the threat of military action by Russia and its intervention with the support of France and Germany to force Japan to relinquish the Liaotung Peninsula, both the government and the people of Japan had resigned themselves to "suffering privations for the sake of revenge."

At the same time, it was hoped that Korea could be kept independent of foreign control and amenable to Japan's wishes. Toward this end, on June 3, 1895, Prime Minister Itō's Cabinet had decided that future policy toward Korea "will have the objective of leaving off interference insofar as possible and causing Korea to stand by herself . . . and to take up passive objectives."[4] The Japanese Resident Minister Inouye had been largely unsuccessful in reorganizing the political and financial structure of the Korean government but hoped for financial support for railway construction. In September, 1895, he was recalled to Tokyo.

The new Japanese Minister in Seoul was Miura Gorō (1846–1926). Before leaving for his post he had told the Cabinet that Japan could follow one of three alternative policies in Korea: (1) to protect and reform Korea by Japan's power, (2) to protect Korea in concert with impartial Western Powers, or (3) to divide Korea into Russian and Japanese spheres. Minister Miura did not obtain specific instructions to follow any one of these alternatives. Upon his arrival in Korea, he soon took matters into his own hands to make the first alternative a reality.

Shortly after Inouye's departure in September, the Korean Court began destroying such reforms as he had been able to inaugurate, including the dismissal of the commander of the Japanese-trained Korean troops. To counteract these moves and in an attempt to strengthen Japan's position and control over Korean affairs, Miura and members of his staff plotted with the Taewŏnkun to run Korea in accordance with what he conceived to be Japan's wishes. The plot called for a military coup d'état under the direction of Japanese officers, the capture of the Korean King, and the appointment of the Taewŏnkun as his chief adviser. During the early hours of October 8, 1895, a military party under Japanese leadership, forced its way into the palace, placed the King in protective custody, and murdered the Queen, the leader of the strongly anti-Taewŏnkun family of Min, and many of her followers. When the news broke, the foreign diplomats in Seoul were shocked, and the Korean people were enraged. Since Miura's implication in the plot was publicly known, the Koreans held Japan accountable for what had happened and that country immediately lost influence and prestige both in Korea and among the Western powers.

The incident is also significant as an early example of two recurring and dangerous themes in Japan's recent history: dual diplomacy and the refusal of the Japanese courts to convict political assassins. As for the first of these themes, when the American Minister in Tokyo inquired about the incident, he was assured by the Foreign Minister in the most positive fashion "that the recent revolution at Seoul was a complete surprise to the Japanese Government and that the Japanese Government had nothing whatever to do with it." Prime Minister Itō insisted that the usurpation of power by the Taewŏnkun must be immediately repudiated by Japan.

After the Foreign Office received a report a few days later on what had transpired, the American Minister was told that Miura and his staff were being recalled. The Japanese Government now knew that their Minister had been in direct communication with the Taewŏnkun concerning the plot. It also knew that Miura had acted independently of instructions from the Foreign Office and that it could repudiate his acts only with difficulty. The harm had been done and Japan had to face the consequences.[5]

As for the reluctance of the courts to act against political assassins or their accomplices, Miura's treatment was surprisingly lenient. He, members of his staff, and several military officers stationed at Seoul were arrested upon their return to Japan. They were tried at a court martial held early in 1896. The tribunal found that prior to the murder of the Queen, Miura did "enter into conspiracy with the Taewŏnkun to overthrow the existing government and murder the Queen." The court concluded, however, that despite their findings there was not sufficient evidence to prove that any of the accused actually committed the crimes which they had originally planned. Consequently, six military officers, General Miura, and forty-seven civilian members of his staff were all acquitted. On January 29, 1896, the *Official Gazette* announced that Miura's ranks and honors, of which he had temporarily been deprived, had been restored. As far as both he and his government were concerned, the matter was closed.

Miura and his henchmen had hoped to improve both their own position and that of their country in Korea by their participation in the plot to murder the Queen. On the contrary, however, they had aroused widespread resentment. It became increasingly difficult for Japan to gain support within Korea for its policies. On the other hand, Russia was quick to take advantage of this situation and to fill the breach caused by China's withdrawal and by Japan's self-incrimination.

Ascendancy of Russian Influence

For the next few months following the murder of the Queen in October, the King continued to be under the control of Japanese-trained

Korean troops. By February, 1896, counterrevolutionary forces were of sufficient strength for the Russians to land reinforcements to protect the King. On February 11, he and the Crown Prince sought refuge in the Russian Legation. Their escape and liberation from the Japanese automatically destroyed any *de facto* or *de jure* basis for Miura's projected puppet regime. Under this new protection and in view of the sudden appearance of a strong anti-Japanese feeling, the Korean King was quick to brand the pro-Japanese members of his Cabinet as traitors. A new Cabinet was created and annulled the "reform laws" which had been imposed on Korea by Japan. For the next year, during which time the King continued to reside in the Russian Legation, Russia's influence in Korea was predominant. At the same time, the King had considerable freedom and by May, 1896, willingly sent his brother-in-law to Moscow to ask for Russian protection over Korea.

In order to strengthen its position in Eastern Siberia and East Asia, after Japan's victory over China in 1895, Russia became increasingly involved in Chinese and Korean affairs. It came to realize that its strategic position in East Asia and the proposed Trans-Siberian Railway would be secure only if it were able to acquire a concession from China to construct a shortcut for the Trans-Siberian Railway across Northern Manchuria to Vladivostok. Toward this end, in April, 1896, Russia had sponsored a Franco-Russian loan to China of 400 million francs. On June 3, China and Russia had, in the Li–Lobanov Treaty, agreed on a fifteen-year Defense Alliance in which each party promised to come to the assistance of the other if Japan attacked Korea or the territory of either power. At the same time, Russia obtained permission to construct the Chinese Eastern Railway from the Trans-Siberian Railway across Northern Manchuria to Vladivostok. Construction and exploitation would be carried out by the Russo-China Bank, the railroad would be tax-free, autonomous, and responsible for its own security, and would revert to China after 80 years. Russia then began negotiations for a commission for another railway from the Chinese Eastern to a seaport on the Yellow Sea but this request was rejected by the Chinese government. China's attempts to exploit Manchuria and construct a railway of its own were nullified by the action of the powers in 1897–1898.[6]

Yet both Russia and Japan found themselves in vulnerable positions. Neither of them was strong enough to force the other to capitulate. It was impossible for Russia to compete with Japan in the Far East so long as the Trans-Siberian Railway connecting Vladivostok and the Far East with European Russia was not expected to be completed until 1902. Japan's position was equally weak. Russia had suffered a severe setback in Korea by Miura's indiscretions. Thus far it had made only limited economic investments in Korea. Most of its proposed expansion of the

Army and Navy was still in the planning stage. It would take several years to build them up to the projected strength.

Though Japanese–Russian rivalries for Korea's control were intense, both sides were forced to make concessions for the next few years. For example, when General Yamagata was sent to Russia in 1896 to represent Japan at the coronation of the Russian Czar, Nicholas II, he suggested that Korea might be divided into two spheres of interest with the thirty-eighth degree parallel as the dividing line. By this arrangement Russian encroachments could be kept within bounds and Japan would have time to build up southern Korea and to solidify its position.

Russian Foreign Minister Lobanov rejected this suggestion but by the Lobanov–Yamagata Convention of 1896, both countries reached a general understanding which in effect placed them on an equal footing in Korea. They agreed to render friendly advice and mutual financial assistance to Korea and to assist the King in modernizing the police and armed forces. The agreement also provided that each of the signatories could send an equal number of guards for protection of the telegraph lines and of their respective settlements. If they found it necessary to dispatch troops to Korea they would consult each other prior to such action. While Russia was primarily interested in Manchuria and Japan considered Korea of special importance for its security, both sides were avoiding antagonizing the other.

Such an unstable balance could not be maintained for long. Although the Korean King was given personal freedom, he governed with Russia behind the throne. Even after he moved into his new palace in the early months of 1897, he discovered that he was a victim of Russian machinations. The new Russian chargé d'affaires in Seoul, De Speyer, both advocated and implemented an aggressive policy. He increased pressure on the Korean government to bend to his will and to that of the Czar. He threatened to force out of office those Korean officials who opposed him. He obtained an acknowledgment that Kir Alexeev was to be chief Financial Adviser and Superintendent of Customs with power to control and supervise all matters relating to Korea's finances. Further concessions concerned Russia's long-standing request for a coaling station in southern Korea. Deer Island in Pusan Harbor was agreed upon as the site. Alexeev arrived in October and by mid-February, 1898, the Russo-Korean Bank opened for business with authority to handle all of the government's revenue. Russia's predominant position appeared assured and De Speyer's policies seemed to have been accepted.[7]

But an abrupt change in Russian policy in Korea, as well as limited moves which Japan was able to take in both Korea and China, can be understood only within the context of events in East Asia as a whole. Most of these events emerged from the whole complex of European rivalries and balance of power. They involved the struggle for foreign concessions in a China too weak to defend itself, the emergence of the United States as a world power with colonial possessions in the Pacific, and the recognition by Great Britain and Japan of their common interest in preventing Russia's encroachments in East Asia.

Spheres of Influence of the European Powers in China

The participation of Germany and France, on Russia's initiative, in the demand on Japan in 1895 that the Liaotung Peninsula be returned to China was representative of their growing interest in Asia. Although both Great Britain and the United States had maintained a strict neutrality on this issue, these countries also were by no means disinterested observers in the fate of China or in the growth of the Japanese Empire. In fact, all of these Western powers were on the point of consolidating their spheres of influence in Asia either on the continent or in the Pacific.

These acts of imperialism had a dual result. They not only dismembered China but also had a controlling effect on Japan's foreign relations and hence are an essential element in this narrative. For example, Germany's constant search for an effective means to reduce the strength of France turned the attention of William II to China. He recognized that if he could obtain Russia's support for his plans in the Far East, he might reduce the effectiveness of the new Franco-Russian Alliance. Hence he had been glad to join Russia in 1895 in a common move to check Japan.

Furthermore, he was in immediate need of a commercial and naval base in Pacific waters to protect his farflung empire. Specifically, he sought a coaling station for German naval and commercial vessels as a counterbalance against British-held Hong Kong. Surveys were made in the Philippines, the Pacific Islands, and along the China coast to discover a suitable location for such a base. Kiaochow Bay, on the south-central coast of Shantung Peninsula, was finally agreed upon as the most desirable site. The only question which remained was how to secure this territory with a minimum of resistance from China and without causing hostilities with another European Power. Consequently, William II, while visiting in Russia, personally sought the blessing of Nicholas II for the German moves in China. The Czar vacillated but finally said he could not approve or disapprove of the German squadron going to Kiaochow Bay.

In November, 1897, two German missionaries in Shantung were killed by Chinese robbers. This incident gave Emperor William the excuse for which he had been waiting. Despite effective Chinese action against the robbers, Germany acted. Tsingtao, the important port at the mouth of Kiaochow Bay, was successfully occupied by a small German military

JAPANESE EMPIRE AND EUROPEAN CONCESSIONS IN CHINA, 1900

contingent. Germany then demanded complete compensation for the murder of its subjects, the granting of railway and mining concessions on the Shantung Peninsula, and a naval base at Kiaochow Bay.

When China balked at some of these demands, William II jumped at the chance to become the self-appointed protector of the Holy Church. He claimed that it was his duty to defend Christendom from the peril of the infidels and the barbaric hordes of the "Yellow Race." He organized a squadron to be sent to China to enforce his demands and to save Europe from the "yellow peril." By the time his brother, who headed the naval force, arrived, China was ready to capitulate.

Germany's action in Shantung gave Russia a pretext for making its move for an ice-free port in the Pacific. On December 11, 1897, Czar Nicholas II overruled his ministers and decided that the Russian fleet should be ordered immediately to enter Port Arthur "temporarily." No troops were landed for two months but in the end China agreed to Russia's demands for a twenty-five-year lease to Port Arthur and Dairen in the Liaotung Peninsula. Russia also received the right to construct a railway from Mukden to both of these ports. Port Arthur was to be a Russian naval base and Dairen was to be an open port.[8]

In view of Britain's extensive commercial and strategic interests in the Far East, with Hong Kong as the pivot, the reaction of Great Britain against both the German and Russian moves was predictable. Great Britain saw Germany's actions as a threat to her special interests in the Yangtze River Valley. Consequently, in March it extracted a promise from China not to alienate any of the territory along the Yangtze to any other powers. At the same time Britain gave China a loan of £16 million which enabled China to make its final indemnity payment to Japan as part of the peace settlement of 1895. In order to strengthen its position against Russia's naval base at Port Arthur, Great Britain found it expedient to turn to Japan for help in solving its problem.

As part of the peace settlement with China in 1895, it had been specified that Japan was to occupy the strategic harbor of Weihaiwei on the northern coast of Shantung until such time as China completed its indemnity payments. With China having just obtained the necessary funds from Britain for this final payment, Japan prepared to withdraw its forces from Weihaiwei. Great Britain then suggested that Japan should continue to occupy the harbor but Prime Minister Itō insisted that withdrawal take place as planned. When the British Cabinet decided that China should grant Great Britain a lease there and that British forces should replace the Japanese as a strategic reply to Russia's action, Japan was eager to cooperate in making the transfer.[9]

Relieved of this responsibility, Japan then turned toward solving the problem of Korea and obtaining privileges of its own on mainland China. Within the Japanese government there had been considerable support for a policy of exchanging its rights in Manchuria for Russian recognition of Japan's special rights in Korea (*Mankan kōkan*). On April 2, 1898, Prime Minister Itō, who consistently looked for ways to come to terms with Russia, persuaded his Cabinet to agree to this policy. Simultaneously, Russia, considering it imperative to avoid a showdown with Japan over its action in the Liaotung Peninsula, was willing to reverse its policies in Korea. De Speyer and other Russians were ordered home, the Russo-Korean Bank was closed, and negotiations were started with the Japanese. At the end of April, the Rosen–Nishi Agreement was signed outlining the procedures which Russia and Japan would follow in the immediate future in Korea. The signatories recognized Korea's independence and promised to refrain from direct interference in Korean internal affairs. They would nominate, at Korea's request, only those military instructors and financial advisers approved by both Russia and Japan. Russia recognized Japan's economic and commercial position in Korea and promised not to interfere in these activities and developments. But the Agreement did not implement the policy of recognizing special interests of Japan in Korea in exchange for those of Russia in Manchuria. Japan hoped, however, that this agreement would mean that the Russian dominance in Korea was over.

At the same time, Japan was able to wrest a concession from China, namely, the recognition of Japan's special interests in Fukien Province, opposite its colony of Formosa. To Japan these gains seemed scant recompense in comparison with what other powers were obtaining throughout Asia. In fact, this disparity of position in Asia between Japan and the leading European powers made a deep and lasting impression on the Japanese. A little over a generation later, when Japan followed similar tactics in Manchuria, European action in 1895 was taken as a precedent. The argument ran as follows: Japan happened to modernize in 1930 not in 1895. If it had been strong at the earlier date, it could have kept Liaotung. If it had insisted upon doing so, it might have obtained a lease in China when the powers carved out their spheres. It might even have acquired possession of Korea at the same time. Why should it be condemned for similar action a few years later when it had much greater provocation for its action?

The United States Becomes a Pacific Power

Simultaneously with these manifestations of imperialism by the European powers, the United States likewise became a victim of the expansionist fever. The disunity and weaknesses caused by the struggle over slavery, the stultifying effect of the tragedies of the Reconstruction in the South, and the challenge of vast undeveloped areas had kept the United States occupied primarily with national issues. Since 1856–1862, when Townsend Harris was the first American Consul, it had played only a limited role in Japan's historical development. Most of the technical foreign assistants, with the exception of those selected by Kuroda for Hokkaidō, had come from Europe. The preference for American ideas and materials for the educational system was of short duration. American political institutions, which were based on a philosophy incongruous with the basic concepts of the oligarchs, had never been accepted. Japan's trade with America was only a fraction of that with other foreign countries.

By 1895, therefore, there were only a limited number of basic interests which the United States and Japan had in common. On the other hand, a rapid industrialization, the growth of transcontinental transportation, and the desire for overseas markets were underlying forces which contributed to a new American nationalism. This expansionism, which was advocated by the Republicans, collided with Japan's ambitions in the Pacific and with Europe's designs in China.

The collision with Japan was the result of both American and Japanese desires to possess the Hawaiian Islands. By a treaty with Hawaii in 1887, the United States had obtained a naval base and the use of port facilities in the Islands. In the previous year, Hawaii had made an agreement with Japan concerning the immigration of Japanese laborers. Japan, on the basis of an earlier commercial treaty, insisted that its subjects receive treatment equal to that of native Hawaiians. On the other hand, it had disregarded the quota for immigrants as set by the treaty. To stop this limitless flow of foreign laborers, the Hawaiian government permitted only those with valid permits to land. Japan countered this move by the dispatch of a warship to Honolulu and by demanding unrestricted entry privileges for Japanese subjects.

American reaction to these Japanese maneuvers varied with the party in power in Washington. The Democrats, who headed the government when the treaty was concluded in 1887, were against formal annexation of the Islands. In 1896, William McKinley, a Republican, won the election by a considerable majority and the annexation movement was revived. The *Honolulu Star*, in commenting on Japan's request for unlimited immigration, wrote, "It is the white race against the yellow. . . . Nothing but annexation can save the islands."

This plea fell on sympathetic ears. By the middle of 1897, McKinley had resubmitted the treaty for the annexation of Hawaii. This action brought a fiery protest from the Japanese Minister in Washington, Hoshi Toru. In an official communication to the American government, he claimed that the maintenance of the status quo in the Hawaiian Islands was "essential to a good understanding of the powers which have interests in the Pacific." He feared that annexation would postpone the settlement of Japanese claims in the islands. Finally, he argued that the residential, commercial, and industrial rights of Japanese subjects would be endangered by annexation.

Despite these protests, the United States pushed ahead with its plans for annexation. The American Minister at Honolulu was prepared for any eventuality. His instructions read that if the Japanese resorted to forceful occupation, he was to consult with the local authorities and the American naval commanders, "land a suitable force and announce provisional assumption of a protectorate by the United States over Hawaii pending consummation of the annexation treaty." [10]

In the Congressional debates on the treaty, the chief argument for annexation was the danger to the United States of Japanese infiltration of the Islands. Other senators noted the need for a coaling station for American ships in the mid-Pacific. Finally, it was claimed that annexation was the only way to assume protection of American property which amounted to over three-fourths of the area of the Islands. The Senate Foreign Relations Committee reported in a prophetic vein:

> The present Hawaiian–Japanese controversy is the preliminary skirmish in the great coming struggle between the civilization and the awakening forces of the East and civilization of the West.[11]

After the United States entered the war against Spain in 1898, which John Hay had characterized as both necessary and righteous, the fate of Hawaii was sealed. The defeat of the Spanish fleet in Manila Bay stimulated Congress to pass a Joint Resolution for annexation. The Hawaiian Islands were formally annexed on August 12, 1898, and the United States immediately became a power with colonial territory in the Pacific. Two days later, the Japanese Minister was assured that the Japanese on the Hawaiian Islands would receive just and equitable treatment. Faced with a *fait accompli,* as in the case of Russia in Liaotung, the Japanese government was powerless to push its objections further, and remained skeptical as to future developments.

The American acquisition of the Philippine Islands, though a much richer and larger prize than Hawaii, had only an indirect bearing at this juncture on Japanese–American relations. No mention was made of the need to place the islands under American sovereignty to keep Japan from acquiring them. On the contrary, after Manila's occupation by American forces, Japan formally expressed its acquiescence to the extension of United States sovereignty over the Islands. It added that such a solution of the question would be entirely satisfactory to Japan.[12]

This solution was likewise satisfactory to the American people. They were proud of their colonial empire and gloried in it. They were too naïve to realize that empire building carried heavy responsibilities. They had little suspicion that the protection of these possessions forty years later would involve them in a war against Japan. In 1898, the American sphere of influence, though not on the Asiatic mainland, was even more real, more comprehensive, and more exclusive than that of the European powers in China, or of Russia in Manchuria or Japan in Korea.

The Open Door Policy

At the same time, the United States was apprehensive lest the European powers exclude it from trade in their respective spheres of influence in China. If the expansion of these spheres continued, American commercial interests would suffer. When John Hay circulated his famous Open Door Note in 1899, Western imperialism had reached its peak in Eastern Asia. The United States had taken possession of the Philippines and of the Hawaiian Islands. Germany had acquired concessions in Shantung and the Micronesia Islands north of the equator. Russia was ensconced in Manchuria and was threatening Korea. France was negotiating for territory in South China.

Although Great Britain was a free-trade country and would have welcomed imports from America in its sphere in China, its actions appeared to follow the same pattern as the other European countries. It had received recognition from China of its special sphere of influence in the rich Yangtze River Valley. It had acquired a leasehold on the northern shores of Shantung at Weihaiwei. In June, 1898, it had doubled the size of its crown colony of Hong Kong by obtaining the New Territory of Kowloon. Its ships hauled two-thirds of the tonnage of the goods in the China trade and it was determined to retain this commercial advantage.

The Open Door Policy, which was designed to preserve and enhance American commercial interests in China, became one of the basic elements in American foreign policy. Like many such policy pronouncements, however, it underwent elaboration and expanded interpretations. By the time of the abortive negotiations with Japan in November, 1941, the United States referred to the Open Door Policy in terms such as the inviolability of territorial integrity, the noninterference in the internal affairs of other countries, and the equality of commercial opportunity. At its inception at the end of the ninteenth century, however, the Open Door Policy had a very limited connotation. It was not an attempt to get the powers to give up their recently acquired concessions in China but rather a plea for the maintenance there of the commercial status quo.

In view of Britain's large commercial interests in the Far East and its desire to protect this trade, especially from Germany and Russia, immediately following the German seizure of Tsingtao in 1897 the British proposed to the United States that the two countries work together to insure equal economic opportunity in China. The United States was, however, completely absorbed with the question of war with Spain and turned down Britain's suggestion. By September, 1898, the fighting with Spain was over and America was suddenly conscious of the Far East as a new area in which to exert its influence. John Hay was appointed Secretary of State and selected as one of his advisers, W. W. Rockhill, an old China hand.

At the same time, many persons in the United States had developed a new consciousness of East Asia. They argued that America should take positive steps to assert its own rights and interests in China. By his Open Door Note, Secretary Hay hoped to restrain those who urged a vigorous, positive American policy in Asia and to notify the European powers that he expected American interests to be respected in their spheres of influence. He asked Rockhill to prepare a memorandum on American policy for China. Rockhill, in turn, consulted a life-long friend and fellow-resident in China, Alfred E. Hippisley, a British subject who had been Commissioner of the Chinese Maritime Customs. His experience in that position had made him keenly conscious of the dangers to China of the predatory commercial and territorial policy advocated by the foreign powers. From a practical viewpoint, he believed that monopolistic trends could best be checked by a new policy which gave equal opportunity to everyone.

The recommendations which he sent to Rockhill, therefore, concentrated on the question of how equal economic opportunity could be achieved within the framework of conditions as they actually obtained in China in 1899. He advocated acceptance of the existence of the various spheres of influence, arguing that it would be impossible for citizens of any country to obtain treatment within a sphere equal to that of the nationals of the state controlling that sphere. Specifically, United States citizens could not expect preferential treatment. Nevertheless, the United States could and should insist that its citizens be given treatment in these spheres equal to that afforded other nations.

This memorandum of Hippisley's to Rockhill became the basis for Hay's Open Door Note of September 6, 1899. The Note was concerned primarily with customs problems and nondiscriminatory commercial treatment within the spheres of influence. It asked the powers with concessions in China to agree that they would not interfere with any foreign investments within the spheres or leased territory which they had in China, and it requested that Chinese tariffs be applied to goods shipped to these ports. Finally, it proposed that equal harbor dues and railroad fares be levied on the goods of all countries.[13]

Secretary Hay's note was circulated to England, France, Germany, Japan, Italy, and Russia. As was to be expected, Great Britain readily accepted this move which would protect its commercial interests in the spheres of other powers. Germany also sent a favorable answer. Russia, which assumed it had exclusive rights in territories it controlled, was not interested. Japan's reply was evasive and equivocal, but it agreed to accede to Hay's proposal if the other powers did likewise. Secretary Hay seized upon this indecisive attitude of Japan to make the first expansion of the Open Door Policy. He informed the Japanese Foreign Minister that the other governments intended, so long as the other powers acted in the same manner,

> . . . to maintain liberty of trade and equality of treatment for all the world within the territory in China over which they can exercise control or influence.

There was one important flaw in the American proposal. It came from a country which had no leasehold and no sphere of influence in China. When Hay claimed that the principle of commercial equality had been accepted by states with interests in China, he assumed that these powers would deny special privileges for their own subjects within their spheres. At the same time, the United States adopted a closed door policy in its own Asiatic possessions. It is not surprising, therefore, that the various powers to whom the Open Door Note had been sent saw little reason to take their commitments seriously. To Japan, the whole proceedings seemed naïve and useless.

The Boxer Uprising

The internal events in China were to endanger its territorial integrity even more than the avarice of the Western powers. Ever since China's defeat in 1895, political and economic conditions had deteriorated and an antiforeign feeling had increased. In 1898, a few enlightened Chinese leaders, such as the reformers K'ang Yu-wei and Liang Ch'i-ch'ao, had persuaded the young Emperor to adopt far-reaching reforms to prepare China to modernize and to meet the challenges of the Western powers. Unfortunately, the reformers lacked a broad base of support and the young Emperor was no match for the reactionary leaders of the Imperial Court and the shrewdness of the Empress Dowager. The Hundred Days Reform came to an end when the Emperor was seized, the reform edicts were rescinded, and K'ang and Liang fled to Japan. At the same time the Empress Dowager decided to adopt a strong policy against the foreign powers. She ordered the Army reorganized and in November, 1899, issued an Imperial Decree to the viceroys and provincial governors ordering that they should resist forcibly any future unacceptable demands made by the aggressive powers.

Such was the atmosphere in China when a widespread, anti-Christian, antiforeign revolutionary movement, abetted by famine, floods, and banditry, sprang up in Shantung and Chihli Provinces. The so-called Boxer Uprising rapidly spread to the chief cities with foreign settlements in North China. The vacillation of the Imperial Court and the ambiguous decrees issued to the provincial governors only encouraged the movement. Joint declarations by the foreign representatives in Peking demanded that the Chinese government suppress the rebellion, but to no avail. By early June, 1900, stations on the Tientsin–Peking railroad had been destroyed and foreign troops had skirmished with bands of Boxers.

By June 10 the Boxers had entered Peking in force and the foreign representatives in Tientsin had decided to send an international force to keep the rail connection open between Peking and the coast. This force was intercepted and the Powers had to wait nearly two months before they were strong enough to proceed inland. The Imperial Court ordered its generals in the north to resist further foreign landings and the Empress Dowager was prepared in the event of war to use the Boxers against the foreigners. On June 19, a foreign flotilla attacked and silenced the forts at Taku at the entrance of the Peiho River leading to Tientsin. Two days later China declared war. The siege of the Legations in Peking began on June 20; Tientsin fell before the Boxers. In the meantime, Russia had dispatched troops from Port Arthur, and Japan supplied a force of 22,000 troops, about half of the total Allied Army. By July 14, Tientsin had been recaptured by the Allied Powers. During the next month, the Legations were under constant attack in Peking, the Allies were victorious on their march to the capital, and the Imperial Court fled to the west. Allied troops relieved the siege of the Legations on August 14 and shortly thereafter Li Hung-chang was ordered to come to Peking to negotiate with the powers.

The United States, which was aware of the tepid reaction of the powers to the Open Door Policy, was fearful that the Boxer Uprising would be used by them as an excuse to demand even greater concessions from China. To forestall such a move, Secretary Hay issued a new policy statement on China a month before the Allied forces were ready to advance from Tientsin to relieve the Peking legations. This statement of July, 1900, required no reply from the other powers. It left no question in their minds, however, as to America's attitude. It stated:

> The policy of the United States is to seek a solution which may bring about permanent safety and peace to China, preserve Chinese territorial integrity and administrative entity, protect all rights guaranteed to friendly powers by treaty and international law and safeguard trade with all parts of China.

In less than a year after the Open Door Note had been circulated, therefore, the United States had added another important element to its China policy. Henceforth, it was committed to the principle of preserving what was left of Chinese territorial integrity.

The final settlement of the Boxer Uprising required the payment by China of an indemnity to the powers of 450 million taels ($334,000,000). The special privileges, which the powers required as guarantees for the safety of their diplomatic representatives and their nationals, were far more important than the cash settlement. They were made at the expense of Chinese sovereignty and to the military advantage of the powers. China was prohibited from importing arms and materials for their manufacture. Furthermore, each power acquired:

> The right of maintaining a permanent guard for its Legation, and of placing the Legation Quarter in a condition of defense. Chinese not to have the right of residing in the Quarter.

The forts at Taku were to be razed and points between Taku and Tientsin were to be occupied by the Allies to assure access of foreigners from the sea. China's internal disintegration and inability to suppress rebellious elements within its borders had left it at the mercy of the foreign powers.[14]

Increased Russian Threats

Although the emergency created by the Boxer Uprising and the subsequent threat to all foreigners in China had forced them to act jointly to save their nationals in North China, each of the powers watched any move of the others to improve their special privileges. In fact these mutual suspicions and national jealousies were far more effective than the Open Door Policy in saving China from worse dismemberment. This suspicious attitude was particularly true of Great Britain and Japan toward Russia's designs and actions in Manchuria. With its leasehold in the Liaotung Peninsula, including the naval base at Port Arthur, and a contiguous border with China along the Amur River, Russia was in a strong position to wrest concessions from the Chinese Imperial Court. In the summer of 1900, the Boxers had spread to Manchuria where they endangered the construction of the Russian-owned Chinese Eastern Railway. On July 6, 1900, an Imperial edict ordered the regular Chinese troops to attack the Russians in Manchuria. Finance Minister Witte countered this Chinese move by having Russian troops dispatched from Siberia to crush Chinese resistance. By October, the Russians had completed the conquest of Manchuria where they deployed over 170,000 troops; Russia then turned its attention to securing a separate agreement with China on the future of Manchuria. In November, 1900, the Tseng–Alexeev Agreement was signed at Port Arthur, permitting Russian troops to remain to protect the Chinese Eastern and South Manchurian Railways, and calling for the disbandment of Chinese troops and a Russian

Resident to reside in Mukden to supervise communications and negotiations between the "Tartar Generals" and the Russian government in Liaotung. The Chinese representative signed the agreement pending authorization from his government.[15]

Contrary to fears of the European nations which participated in the defeat of the Boxers, Japan took a conciliatory attitude toward China. Its troops acted in an exemplary fashion. Half of its forces were withdrawn soon after the relief of the Legations. On the other hand, while the Boxer Uprising was in progress in the north, Kodama Gentarō, Governor-General of Korea, and the Navy Minister developed a plan for Japan's occupation of Amoy, in Fukien. Yamagata was also in favor of strengthening Japan's position in the south. But the proposal came to naught when Itō, as Prime Minister, forced its cancellation.

So long as Russian troops remained in Manchuria, they were always a threat to Korea. Even though Prime Minister Itō personally favored a *rapprochement* with Russia, he could not countenance the latter obtaining such privileges as those provided in the Tseng-Alexeev Agreement. He was forced to concur with Yamagata and the Privy Council that Japan should speed up its military preparations because of the danger of war with Russia. On March 25, 1901, his Foreign Minister, Katō Kōmei, sent Russia a stiff note taking exception to the proposed Russo-Chinese agreement as a violation of Chinese sovereignty.

Russia refused to accept the Japanese note and thereby created a diplomatic crisis which had widespread repercussions. It united the proponents within Japan of an Anglo-Japanese Alliance. It led Russia to re-examine its Manchurian policy in view of the likelihood of future hostilities against Japan. Russian Foreign Minister Lansdorf became convinced that Japan would go to war unless Russia promised not to sign a separate agreement with China. When Peking objected to ratifying the agreement, Russia dropped the matter. While Lansdorf had overestimated Japan's preparedness for war at that time, he was correct in assuming Japan would brook no interference with areas which it considered essential to its self-interest, such as Korea.

With the downfall of the Itō Cabinet in June, 1901, and the selection of Katsura Tarō as Prime Minister, Japan's policy toward Russia and Great Britain changed markedly. General Katsura, a protégé of Yamagata, was strongly anti-Russian. He and his colleagues in the Cabinet were determined to keep the Russians out of Korea. They interpreted the Russian occupation of Manchuria as a direct threat to Korea and at the appropriate time were prepared to go to war to erase that threat. They estimated that victory would be assured if the war was fought before Russia completed the Trans-Siberian Railway and if France was kept out of the struggle.

The Anglo-Japanese Alliance

With a view to attaining these goals, it was decided to explore further the possibility of an Anglo-Japanese alliance. Ambassador Hayashi Tadasu was recalled from St. Petersburg and assigned to London with instructions to renew negotiations which had been broken off by Katō three years earlier. The successful conclusion of this proposed alliance was hindered by several factors. In the first place, there was Germany's desire to check Russia and the question of what role, if any, it should play in an alliance. In the second place, despite Britain's apprehensions as regards Russian moves in Asia, there was considerable question in London as to how much advantage it would be to Britain to make a defensive alliance with Japan. Finally, acceptance of the alliance in Japan was complicated by the lack of agreement among the Japanese leaders.

The idea of including Germany in the alliance was soon dropped by both Britain and Japan. The doubts within the British government concerning an alliance with Japan were allayed for several reasons. Foreign Minister Lansdowne and Francis Bertie, Chief of the Asiatic Department of the Foreign Office, were apprehensive lest Japan receive financial aid from France and be susceptible to Russian advances for a *rapprochement.* In a memorandum on this subject, Bertie wrote as follows:

> Unless we attach Japan to us by something more substantial than general expressions of goodwill, we shall run the risk of her making some arrangements which might be injurious to our interests.[16]

Another positive factor in persuading Great Britain was the economic and strategic advantages it saw to the alliance. If Japan could be induced to make its naval forces available for the protection of British interests in the Yangtze Valley, such an arrangement would be equivalent to an increased British fleet in the Far East.

On the matter of differences over the alliance within Japan, as noted earlier, Itō believed that Japan's interests in Korea could best be preserved by an alliance with Russia rather than with England. Nevertheless, on July 31, 1901, Hayashi in London was instructed to begin official conversations with Lansdowne and discussions between the two governments continued throughout the next few months. On November 6, Hayashi was presented with a draft approved by the British Cabinet.

At this point, the negotiations were complicated by Itō's maneuvers. He had been invited to Yale University to receive an honorary degree at its bicentennial celebration in October, 1901. Itō had accepted the invitation and was determined to extend his trip to Europe and especially to Russia. Apparently he hoped to negotiate an agreement with Russia which would assure Japan's hegemony over Korea, prevent a war with

Russia, and forestall the necessity of an alliance with England. He was too powerful a figure to be ignored and so was allowed to take his trip.

Premier Katsura authorized him to "carry out an informal exchange of views" in Russia. Hayashi was ordered to meet Itō in Paris and to bring him up to date on the negotiations. The latter cabled Prime Minister Katsura that he had no objections in principle to the agreement but believed it sound policy to delay a final decision until views were exchanged with Russia. On November 28, three days after Itō arrived in St. Petersburg, the Japanese Cabinet approved the draft of the Alliance but the Emperor withheld his sanction of it pending Itō's reply. On December 8, Itō reported that he thought it unwise not to include Germany in the alliance and that final approval should await a reply from Russia to his conversations there. Itō's views did not change the opinion of the Cabinet and the *Genrō*. Prime Minister Katsura and Foreign Minister Komura persuaded the Emperor to approve the final draft. Hayashi was sent instructions to proceed with the final discussions.

The Anglo-Japanese Alliance was signed on January 30, 1902. It recognized the special interests of Great Britain in China and of Japan in Korea. It provided that either of them could take necessary measures to safeguard those interests if threatened by the aggressive action of another power or by disturbances within China or Korea. Both countries promised to remain neutral if either of them should become involved in a war to protect those interests. They also pledged themselves to come to the assistance of the other if a third power should join in any such hostilities. The agreement was to remain in force for five years. The naval agreement, which was kept secret, was contained in an exchange of diplomatic notes. It made the docking and other facilities of each power available to the other. It also provided that each of the signatories maintain, so far as possible, a naval force superior in strength to that of any other power in Far Eastern waters.[17]

The effect of this alliance was immediate. While the victory over China in 1895 had increased Japan's prestige abroad, the alliance with Great Britain was far more significant. Japan was elated over the fact that it was an ally of one of the most powerful European states. Moreover, it had achieved by diplomacy one of its objectives, namely, the prevention of another power entering a war with Russia as the latter's ally. In view of Britain's pledge, it was certain that France would not come to Russia's aid in the event of a Russo-Japanese War. Furthermore, Great Britain had recognized Japan's special interests in Korea.

On the international scene, the first concrete result of the new alliance was the promise of Russia to withdraw its troops from Manchuria. These troops had been in occupation since the Boxer Uprising and previous efforts to force their removal had been fruitless. In April, 1902, a Russo-

Chinese agreement was signed which specified that evacuation of troops would begin forthwith and would be completed within eighteen months. China also successfully resisted a Russian plea for special privileges in connection with the railways in Manchuria.

From the British point of view, the alliance was accomplishing its purpose. Plans for a Japanese–Russian alliance had been frustrated. Furthermore, Russia had not only been checked in China, it was apparently being forced to withdraw. On the other hand, the alliance produced results of questionable value. Russia's suspicions of England's designs and ambitions were increased to such an extent that Great Britain went to some lengths to explain that the alliance in no way threatened the present position or the legitimate interests of any other power. Russia was not impressed by these explanations. Its ally, France, announced that the Dual Alliance would henceforth be applicable to the Far East as well as to Europe. But this move did little to change the new balance of power in East Asia. The Anglo-Japanese Alliance had established Japan, rather than Russia, as the strongest force in that area.

Such were the apparent, tangible effects of the alliance with England. In retrospect, however, it appears as a symbol of one of the most remarkable national transformations in modern times. It signified not only that Japan had come of age as a modern nation but that its manhood, its vitality, and its potentialities of power and of growth had been recognized and condoned by one of the strongest nations of the world. When viewed in its proper historical perspective, it is nothing less than amazing that Japan had reached a point where Great Britain, at a time when Britannia undisputedly ruled the waves, should have turned to Japan to make an agreement on terms of equality.

Collapse of Japanese–Russian Negotiations

The first signs of this nascent feeling of invincibility began to emerge in the hardening of the attitude toward Russia. With Great Britain as an ally, the Japanese leaders quickly moved to a solution of other basic outstanding issues. They were not interested in a solution unless it was favorable to Japan. They had previously discovered that the endemic political crises had little effect on the international policies which they formulated. The ineffective struggle of the politicians in the Diet against the oligarchs continued but Katsura met the challenge to his domestic policies in the usual manner. He dissolved Parliament and operated on the budget of the previous year. On matters of foreign policy, he simply ignored the wishes of Parliament.

Foremost among the unanswered questions involving Russia, from Japan's point of view, was whether Russia would recognize and respect

Japan's special position in Korea. For the past few years, Japanese subjects had slowly acquired increasingly important concessions and property in Korea. Permission had been obtained to build the Pusan–Seoul and Chemulpo–Seoul Railways. Important strategically located real estate had been purchased around the most important harbors. The Bank of Japan had acquired special whaling, fishing, and mining rights. As the Anglo-Japanese Alliance had stated, Japan was "interested in a peculiar degree, politically, industrially and commercially in Korea." It intended to increase these interests and to improve its strategic position in the peninsula. It would brook no interference. It took a dim view of Russia's plans for exploitation of timber in the Yalu River Valley in northwest Korea. In April, 1903, Japan had reason to fear Russia's future moves. Rather than carry out the second phase of the scheduled withdrawal of its troops from Manchuria, Russia presented China with seven demands as prerequisites to such withdrawal. If China had not rejected these demands, Manchuria would have become a Russian protectorate. While Japan was willing to recognize that Russia had special rights and interests in Manchuria, it was apprehensive about Russia's real designs.

Japan was faced, therefore, with the alternatives of trying to negotiate its differences with Russia or settling them by force. Katsura and his Foreign Minister, Komura Jutarō, believed that war with Russia was inevitable. At an Imperial Conference on June 23, 1903, the latter argued that Russia was determined to control Manchuria; this would lead to its conquest of Korea which would then be pointed like a dagger at the heart of Japan. Komura was willing for negotiations to be undertaken, providing Japan's rights and interests in Korea were not compromised. It was agreed that the basis for the diplomatic discussions with Russia would be the old formula of acknowledging Russian rights in Manchuria in exchange for Russian recognition of Japan's special interests in Korea, including the right to send troops and advisers to Korea.[18]

This decision in Japan coincided with the development of a new Russian Far Eastern policy and with the struggle for power between contending groups among the Czar's ministers and advisers whose disagreements made Russia's moves unpredictable and complicated the negotiations. Finance Minister Witte had devoted his vast resources and energies toward building Russian strength in the Far East through the construction of the Trans-Siberian and Chinese Eastern Railroads. He now pressed hard for the withdrawal of Russian troops in Manchuria, had little interest in Korea, but was rapidly losing favor with Nicholas II. His position as close adviser to the Czar was being taken by the aggressive entrepreneur Alexander Bezobrazov. The latter urged that Russian timber concessions on both the Manchurian and Korean banks of the Yalu River be exploited by the use of Russian Army reservists. In

June, lumbering operations were begun in North Korea. Even though they were abandoned in October, from Japan's point of view, its future interest in Korea was being directly threatened by Russia.

Furthermore, on August 12, 1903, the day official negotiations were begun with Japan, the Czar established a Viceroyalty of the Far East with powers to unify all Russian military, economic, and diplomatic activities in regions east of Lake Baikal. Admiral E. I. Alexeev, Commander of the Far Eastern Fleet and of the Kwantung garrison at Port Arthur was the new Viceroy. Japan had no way of knowing that the Czar believed a conflict with Japan could be avoided if he yielded on Korea and so had decided "to allow the Japanese complete possession of Korea, maybe to the boundary of the Tumen and Yalu Concessions." [19]

Japan was encouraged, however, to discover that Russia was agreeable to entering into negotiations. The first Japanese note of August 12 proposed that both nations recognize mutual respect for the independence of China and Korea and the maintenance therein of equal commercial opportunity. Furthermore, Russia and Japan should recognize the special interests of the other in their respective spheres of interest, namely, Manchuria and Korea. Japanese exploitation of Korea, including construction of a railway in north Korea, was not to be impeded. Finally, Japan was to have the exclusive right to advise the Korean government on administrative reforms and on military assistance.

The Russian counterproposals of October 3, 1903, were only partially satisfactory to Japan. Russia was willing to agree to Japan's request to advise Korea on reforms providing such advice and assistance improved the "civil administration" of the Korean Empire and did not infringe upon its independence. No Korean ports were to be used for strategic purposes and no coastal defenses were to be built along the Korean Straits. Korea north of the thirty-ninth parallel—a line just south of the cities of Wonsan and Py'onyang—should be a neutral zone. Russia also insisted that Manchuria and all of its littoral be completely outside of the Japanese sphere of influence. In other words, Russia intended to keep Manchuria as its exclusive sphere and wanted an unimpeded line of communication by sea from Dairen and Port Arthur to Vladivostok.

Negotiations continued for the next three months. Japan's counterproposals, presented on October 30, substituted a fifty-kilometer buffer zone on each side of the north Korean border for the one north of the thirty-ninth parallel. Nothing was said about using Korea for strategic purposes. In December, when Russia refused to budge from its original position, Japan insisted that an understanding concerning Manchuria must be included in any final settlement. On January 6, 1904, Russia again insisted that Japan should pledge not to use Korea for strategic purposes.[20]

The choice left to Japan was clear. It could go to war with the hope that it would drive Russia from Manchuria and emerge as the chief power in northeast Asia. In general, public opinion supported this position. Most people believed that a war with Russia was inevitable and the sooner it was over the better. Premier Katsura and his military colleagues were convinced that they could defeat Russia. The Japanese Navy was equally confident though less vociferous. The other alternative was to settle for a restricted Japanese hegemony over Korea, exclusion from Manchuria, and the continued menace of Russian naval bases on both flanks of Korea at Port Arthur on the west and Vladivostok on the northeast.

To the military-minded leaders in Japan who had easily won a war only a decade earlier, the first alternative seemed both sensible and reasonable. At an Imperial Conference of January 12, 1904, of the Cabinet, the *Genrō,* leading financial and military authorities, and the Emperor, as Chairman, Japan's minimum terms were decided on. These included recognition of Manchuria as outside Japan's sphere providing Russia respected the territorial integrity of Manchuria and China and permitted legitimate activities of Japan and other powers in Manchuria. In return, Russia would pledge not to interfere with Japan's activities in Korea. If no satisfactory reply was received to these minimum demands, the issues would be settled by war. The nation as a whole was solidly behind its leaders. As the American Minister in Tokyo reported:

> The Japanese nation is now worked up to a high pitch of excitement, and it is no exaggeration to say that if there is no war it will be a severe disappointment to the Japanese individual of every walk of life. . . . The Japanese nation is in the position of having finally made up its mind to fight, and its costly preparations have been made.[21]

Notes

1. Details of the political developments from the downfall of the third Itō Cabinet on September 18, 1896, were as follows: the Matsukata Cabinet lasted from September 18, 1896, to January 12, 1898. As an incentive for cooperation from the Progressives, Matsukata not only appointed Ōkuma as Foreign Minister but also promised administrative and financial reforms and support for the principle of collective responsibility of Cabinets. When Matsukata then proceeded to ignore these promises, Ōkuma resigned in disgust and the Kenseitō opposed the government's proposals during the Diet session early in 1898. Matsukata then dissolved the Diet, which made a general election mandatory, and resigned as Prime Minister. The Premiership shifted back to Chōshū control under Itō. As a result of the elections in March, 1898, the nongovernment parties received an overwhelming majority. Itō was unsuccessful in overthrowing the opposition in the Lower House. His bill for increased taxes was defeated and he was roundly criticized for a weak policy toward China and for allowing Germany and Russia to obtain Chinese

concessions. He dissolved Parliament, the fifth dissolution in eight years, and resigned as Prime Minister half a year after his appointment. See Robert A. Scalapino, *Democracy and the Party Movement in Prewar Japan* (Berkeley: University of California Press, 1953), pp. 167–82; George Akita, *Foundations of Constitutional Government in Modern Japan 1868–1900* (Cambridge: Harvard University Press, 1967), pp. 121 ff.; and Mitani Taiichirō, *Nihon Seitō Seiji Keisei* (Tokyo: Tokyo University Press, 1967), pp. 231 ff.

2. In 1901, when Katsura became Prime Minister, the Seiyūkai had 158 of a total of 300 seats in the Lower House. When Itō went abroad, dissident members of the party tried to reverse Itō's pledge to Katsura that the party would support him. On Itō's personal instructions to the dissidents, party unity was restored and Katsura survived the Diet session. In the regular election of 1902, the Seiyūkai increased its seats to 191. Katsura then ran into trouble with the passage of a new tax bill to pay for increased armaments. He dissolved Parliament, elections were again held, and the Seiyūkai still maintained a comfortable majority. Even though Seiyūkai members publicly opposed the government's program, when the votes were taken, Itō's demand that the party support Katsura was carried out. But Yamagata was jealous and fearful of Itō's political power and Katsura was fed up with the opposition of Itō and the Seiyūkai. Consequently, to show his indignation, on July 1, 1903, Katsura threatened to resign as Premier. Yamagata then persuaded the Emperor to isolate Itō from politics by appointing him President of the Privy Council. This move had the results Yamagata anticipated. It persuaded Katsura to continue as premier; it forced Itō to resign as President of Seiyūkai. He remained President of the Privy Council until 1905 when he was sent to Korea as Resident General. With the outbreak of war with Russia in 1904, Katsura had widespread support and remained in power until 1906.

3. Katsura Tarō (1848–1913) was born in Chōshū. Before the Meiji Restoration in 1867, he became a member of that clan's specially trained Army. In 1870 he went to Germany for three years to study military organization and tactics and returned again from 1875–1878. He became a follower of Yamagata and helped introduce the German military system into the Imperial Army. He was Military Attaché in Berlin, Vice-Minister of War, and then Governor of Formosa from 1896–1897. The next year he was appointed Minister of War, the post he held until six months before he became Prime Minister.

Hara Kei (1856–1921) was born into a warrior family in Morioka in northeastern Japan. In 1872 he entered a French Catholic school in Tokyo, later studied law at the Ministry of Justice's school but was expelled in 1879 for protesting against the school's policy. He then became a newspaper reporter, was befriended by Inouye Kaoru, and in 1883 married the latter's stepdaughter and entered the Foreign Ministry the same year. After 1890 he attached himself to Mutsu Munemitsu who did much to advance the career of the young bureaucrat. In 1900, after three years as a special political editor of the *Ōsaka Mainichi*, Hara gladly helped organize the Seiyūkai. He served as Minister of Communications during the last six months of the Itō Cabinet. In 1902 he was elected to the House of Representatives from his home district. His role in the party was greatly strengthened by the fact that, in 1903, he was its Secretary-General and controlled its funds. Itō had become President of the Privy Council and Saionji, who was not interested in politics, became the new President of the party. As Home Minister in both the Saionji and Yamamoto Cabinets, Hara greatly strengthened the base of the Seiyūkai in rural areas. In 1914, he was elected president of the party and became Prime Minister in 1918. He was killed by an assassin on November 4, 1921. His diary, *Hara Kei Nikki* (13 vols.; Tokyo: Kangen Sha, 1950–1951), contains invaluable material on his thoughts and activities. For his shrewdness as a politician see Tetsuo Najita, *Hara Kei in the Politics of Compromise 1905–1915* (Cambridge: Harvard University Press, 1967).

4. See Hilary Conroy, *The Japanese Seizure of Korea, 1868–1910* (Philadelphia: University of Pennsylvania Press, 1960), p. 298.

5. For a detailed account of the Queen's murder and subsequent events see *ibid.*, pp. 306 ff.

6. The Defense Alliance, as well as future agreements, was facilitated by large Russian bribes. In this case Li Hung-chang was apparently paid 3 million rubles. Andrew Malozenoff, *Russian Far Eastern Policy 1881–1904* (Berkeley: University of California Press, 1958), pp. 77 ff.

7. For an account of these rivalries see Malozenoff, *op. cit.*, pp. 69–93; and C. I. Eugene Kim and Han-kyo Kim, *Korea and the Politics of Imperialism, 1876–1910* (Berkeley: University of California Press, 1967).

8. See Hosea Ballou Morse, *The International Relations of the Chinese Empire* (3 vols.; London: Longmans, Green and Co., Inc., 1918), III, pp. 101 ff.; and Malozenoff, *op. cit.*, pp. 93 ff.

9. On April 2, 1898, the Japanese Cabinet decided to make no commitments to Great Britain other than to concur with the latter's occupation of Weihaiwei when Japan withdrew on May 23, 1898. See Ian Nish, *The Anglo-Japanese Alliance: The Diplomacy of Two Island Empires 1894–1907* (London: University of London Athlone Press, 1966), pp. 53 ff.

10. O. Clinard, *Japan's Influence on American Naval Power, 1897–1917* (Berkeley: University of California Press, 1947), p. 10.

11. *Ibid.*, p. 12; and Payson J. Treat, *Diplomatic Relations Between the United States and Japan, 1895–1905* (Stanford: Stanford University Press, 1938), pp. 30 ff.

12. This note was dated September 8, 1898. On September 16, President McKinley instructed the Peace Commission not to seek advantages in the Orient which were not common to all. He was ready to accord open door treatment to all. Only the island of Luzon was to be retained. A month later, however, public opinion in the Midwest convinced him to change his instructions to the Commissioners to acquire all of the islands. When Spain balked, the United States offered to buy them for $20,000,000. The Treaty of Paris, which assigned the islands to the United States, was signed December 10, 1898. Guam was also included. Wake Island was claimed in 1900.

13. For a new approach to the Open Door Policy see Akira Iriye, *Across the Pacific: An Inner History of American–East Asian Relations* (New York: Harcourt, Brace and World, Inc., 1967), pp. 79–82.

On the matter of British influence on the development of the Open Door Policy, Professor Nish states that Hippisley "probably had an influence on the drafting" but that this "does not implicate the British government" and that the distribution of the Note at this time owed nothing to British Foreign Office personnel. While the latter point may be true, there is no doubt about the importance of Hippisley's influence as seen from the Hippisley–Rockhill correspondence. See Nish, *op. cit.*, pp. 75–76, and A. Whitney Griswold, *The Far Eastern Policy of the United States* (New York: Harcourt, Brace and Co., 1938), pp. 65 ff. and 475 ff.

14. A preliminary note containing the basis of the settlement with the Allies was signed in Peking on January 10, 1901. The final Protocol, which included punishment by death of those Chinese officials who had aided the Boxers, was signed September 7, 1901. See Chester C. Tan, *The Boxer Catastrophe* (New York: Columbia University Press, 1955), for a detailed and thorough study of the rebellion.

15. For the text of the Tseng–Alexeev Agreement, see *ibid.*, p. 165.

16. This memorandum, as well as much other valuable material, is to be found in the excellent and exhaustive study of the Anglo-Japanese Alliance by Nish, *op. cit.*, p. 154. For an important analysis of the alliance, especially from the point of view of the balance of power in Europe, see William Langer, *The Diplomacy of Imperialism 1890–1902* (2 vols.; New York: Alfred A. Knopf, Inc., 1951), II, pp. 725 ff.

17. For a complete text of the alliance and the diplomatic notes on the naval clauses, see Nish, *op. cit.*, pp. 216–18.

18. At this point, both Itō and Yamagata were opposed to precipitous action and believed that Katsura and Komura intended to undertake protracted negotiations. For an extremely careful analysis of the process of foreign-policy decision making at this time see Shumpei Okamoto, *The Japanese Oligarchy and the Russo-Japanese War* (New York: Columbia University Press, 1970).

19. Alexander Bezobrazov had at one time received the Czar's approval for a semiprivate corporation to exploit timber and other resources in Korea and Manchuria but his recommendations had been rejected by Witte and the company was abandoned. After Bezobrazov returned from the Far East on a mission expressly ordered by the Czar, in June, 1903, at a special conference with his Ministers, the Czar approved the formation of the Russian Timber Company of the Far East. It was active cutting timber until October, when Bezobrazov again fell into disfavor because his views were contrary to the Czar's desire to avoid war with Japan. The Czar's view that Japan might be allowed "complete possession of Korea" was sent to Bezobrazov in July while en route to the Far East. It was meant to be passed on to Admiral Alexeev and the Russian Minister in Tokyo but Bezobrazov decided against doing so. See Malozenoff, *op. cit.*, pp. 208 ff. and 220.

20. The Czar continued to be hopeful that if Russia gave up Korea to Japan, war might be avoided. He cabled Admiral Alexeev on January 6, 1904, that he should not consider Japan's occupation of Korea up to the thirty-ninth parallel as an act of war. For details of the negotiations see Malozenoff, *ibid.*, pp. 237–49.

21. Treat, *op. cit.*, p. 194.

13

The Consolidation of the Japanese Empire 1904–1915

It is no mere coincidence that two significant periods in Japan's recent history encompass approximately a decade. There was a marked change in Japan and its world position in the period from the end of the Sino-Japanese war in 1895 to the breakdown of negotiations with Russia in 1904. In 1895 Japan was largely an unknown quantity. Despite its victory over China, it was still considered by the Western powers as a backward, semifeudal, inferior country. Just prior to the outbreak of the war with Russia, Japan had consolidated its position. It was an ally of Great Britain. It had important and special interests in Korea and had obtained British and Russian recognition of those interests. It was beginning to be recognized as an important world power, and was confident enough in its own strength and ability to be willing to defy Russian threats.

Similarly, the decade from the Russo-Japanese War (1904–1905), to the reluctant acceptance by China of the Twenty-One Demands in May, 1915, forms another distinct period in Japan's recent history. In that short time, Japan not only increased but consolidated its empire. In February, 1904, Japan had decided to win control of Korea at all costs and to throw down the gauntlet at Russia's feet. Although it was recognized as a significant force in East Asiatic politics, there was no proof that it was strong enough to challenge a European power successfully. There was even less evidence that it could or would become a successful colonial power, that it would be able to support an efficient modern army and navy, or that it would become a permanent threat to European and American interests in China.

At the end of this second decade, in May, 1915, there was no question as to Japan's capabilities, intentions, or potentialities. It had been transformed into a world power which dominated the entire Far East. It seemed to have been catapulted onto the world stage by an uncontrollable and compelling urge to become strong, to force its will on any who challenged its position, and to be the leader of Asia. Both external and internal developments during this decade must be analyzed, therefore, to determine whether the success in this growth of empire was the result of caprice, of the clever implementation of a master plan, of wise decisions made at times of crises, or of a combination of all of these factors.[1]

The Russo-Japanese War, 1904–1905

This analysis logically begins with the outbreak of the war between Russia and Japan. Having received no reply to what Japan considered to be its final note of January 12, it was decided at an Imperial Conference on February 4, 1904, that the time for waiting had passed and direct action should be taken. Admiral Tōgō Heihachirō was ordered to begin naval operations and two days later Japanese troops sailed for Chemulpo. The Japanese Minister in Russia was ordered to break off diplomatic relations and Russian troops crossed the Yalu River into Korea. On the night of February 8–9, without warning, Japanese naval forces torpedoed the Russian naval fleet in its base at Port Arthur and inflicted heavy damage. On February 10, Japan declared war on Russia. Thus Nicholas II's attempts to prevent war through compromise and negotiation had failed. Japan's special position in both Korea and Manchuria was to be resolved on the Manchurian plains and in the Tsushima Straits.[2]

Within three months after the outbreak of war, the Russian land forces had been driven out of Korea and the naval forces at Port Arthur were crippled. In the Motherland, it was apparent that the heart of the Russian people was not behind the war. Liberal intellectuals and businessmen welcomed military reverses hoping they would force the autocratic Czarist regime to make political concessions while the radicals turned to revolutionary agitation. Russian activities in Korea and Manchuria were associated with the private machinations of the Czar and irresponsible adventurers close to the throne.[3] On the other hand, the entire Japanese nation was solidly behind its military endeavor which it considered imperative for its future survival.

These contrasting characteristics of a divided Russia and a strongly united Japan had their effect on the outcome of the war. General Nogi, the Japanese Army Commander, captured Port Arthur on January 2, 1905, after a five months' siege. He then prepared to engage the enemy in what became the largest battle to be fought in modern times up to that date. For two weeks, 400,000 Japanese fought tenaciously against

350,000 Russians before the city of Mukden fell in March, 1905. As noted below, moves to bring about peace had already been started, but the defeat of the powerful Russian Army was not enough to settle the issue. The Russian Baltic fleet under Admiral Rodjestvensky had been sent around the world to engage the Imperial Japanese Navy. Admiral Tōgō, the Japanese fleet commander, was prepared for the attack, had taken a calculated risk, and had estimated that the Russian fleet would take the most direct route to Vladivostok through the Korean Straits.[4] The main Japanese fleet was at hand when the Russian ships appeared near Tsushima Island on May 27. Within two days, Japanese naval superiority and skill practically annihilated the Russian fleet. Russia's military power in the Far East had been shattered. It was only a matter of time until peace negotiations began and hostilities ceased.

Diplomatic Victories, 1904–1905

Both during and immediately following the successes on the battlefields of South Manchuria and in the Tsushima Straits, Japan achieved equally important victories on the diplomatic front. All of these moves were interrelated and directed toward the consolidation of a favored position in Korea and in northeastern Asia. The first of these steps, which took place within a fortnight after the Russo-Japanese War broke out, was the easiest to accomplish. On February 23, 1904, Japan forced the young Korean King to sign a protocol which established a modified Japanese protectorate over Korea. Japan guaranteed to protect the safety of the Korean royal family and the integrity and independence of its country. In return, Korea became a Japanese ally and promised to act on administrative matters only on the advice of Japan. The immediate effect of the protocol was to permit the occupation by Japanese military forces of all important strategic points on the peninsula. In a matter of days all of Korea was secure. On May 30, 1904, Japan decided that it should obtain full military and political protective rights in Korea and plan for its economic development. Furthermore, it should secure control of Korean defense, foreign affairs, finances, and communications. In effect, the first irrevocable steps had been taken to make Korea an integral part of the Japanese Empire. Japanese merchants and carpetbaggers followed in the wake of their army of occupation and considered themselves above the law. A new and significant sphere of influence had been created on the Asiatic continent.

Economic uncertainty and financial chaos were, however, hampering the exploitation of this newly acquired sphere of influence. Consequently, within six months, Japan moved again. A new protocol was signed in August, 1904, whereby the Korean government agreed to engage Japanese financial and diplomatic advisers. Megata, who became the first financial adviser, immediately inaugurated far-reaching reforms. He established a uniform system of coinage, prepared a budget for the Korean government, and eliminated bureaucratic inefficiency and bribery. Necessary authority was at hand to confiscate land, and to obtain preferred fishing rights and cabotage privileges for Japanese subjects for inland and coastal waters. The communications system was taken over for purposes of security. Martial law prevented sabotage or other acts inimical to Japan's rapid exploitation of the hard-pressed country. All these moves had been made with the full knowledge that they had the tacit approval of both Britain and the United States.

From the beginning of hostilities, President Theodore Roosevelt had shown a strong personal interest in the war and its outcome. While he was careful to do nothing which prejudiced his position of strict neutrality, he had made it clear to the Japanese that if they were victorious he expected they would wish to establish special controls over Korea. By February, 1905, he told Japan that it should succeed to Russia's rights in and around Port Arthur but hoped Manchuria would be restored to China. At the same time, he urged Russia to seek peace before the Japanese pushed on to Mukden so that the latter would be confined to the south. Thus, he saw no immediate danger to the United States in Japan's limited continental expansion and hoped that the peace treaty would establish a situation whereby Russia and Japan would offset each other.[5]

Even several weeks before the arrival of the Russian fleet in the Tsushima Straits in May, 1905, Japan had seriously considered an armistice. After the defeat of the Russian Army in Manchuria, the Japanese Chief of Staff had reported that 250,000 more men and an expenditure of 1.5 billion yen would be needed for complete victory. This news dampened the ardor of those who pressed for an annihilation of the Russian Army and made a negotiated peace seem to be the logical solution. But Russia showed no signs of wanting to negotiate. In the meantime, Japan complicated matters by letting it be known that it expected an indemnity and new territory after the war.

After Japan's naval victory near Tsushima, Foreign Minister Komura requested President Roosevelt "directly and on his own initiative" to invite Russia and Japan to negotiate for peace. By mid-June, 1905, both belligerents had accepted the President's good offices. On August 10, 1905, the Peace Conference began at Portsmouth, New Hampshire.

Japan's position at the Portsmouth Peace Conference was augmented by two diplomatic developments. In the first place, President Roosevelt had warned Germany and France that if they made any move against Japan, as they had done in 1895, he would support Japan.

At the same time he feared that Japan's new position of dominance in the Pacific might endanger American interests in the Philippines. He instructed his Secretary of War, William Howard Taft, who was en route to the Philippines, to reach an understanding with the Japanese Prime Minister. Taft informed Katsura that the United States would not interfere if Japanese troops established "suzerainty over Korea to the extent of requiring that Korea enter into no foreign treaties without the consent of Japan." In return, he sought Katsura's assurances that Japan did not have any aggressive designs upon the Philippines.[6] These assurances were incorporated into the Taft–Katsura Agreement of July, 1905. Indirectly, at least, the Agreement showed Japan that it would have America's sympathy at the peace conference.

A second diplomatic victory for Japan was the successful extension and broadening of the Anglo-Japanese Alliance. Because of the increased rivalry between Germany and England in 1904, France and Great Britain had developed a strong community of interest. The latter continued to fear Russian pressure and rivalry in Asia. Consequently, Japan's initial suggestion in February, 1905, that the alliance be strengthened, was favorably received in London and negotiations for a stronger alliance continued for five months. Only a few days after the Portsmouth Conference began, therefore, a second Anglo-Japanese Alliance was signed. The new alliance, which was directed against both Russia and Germany, was expanded to include the regions of East Asia and India. Furthermore, a new proviso required that one of the signatories automatically would come to the assistance of the other when war resulted from an attack on these territories by a third power. In return, Great Britain recognized Japan's paramount political, military, and economic interests in Korea and its right to take "measures of guidance, control and protection" in Korea to safeguard those interests. The alliance was to remain in force for ten years. Unlike the first alliance, it contained no secret clauses nor secret notes modifying any of its provisions.[7]

The Treaty of Portsmouth

When the Portsmouth Peace Conference opened in August, 1905, Japan's international position had been rapidly improving. It took a strong position and demanded that Korea be recognized as entirely within its sphere of influence. Secondly, the Russian Army should be withdrawn from Manchuria. Thirdly, Russian leases in the Liaotung Peninsula and of the railroad from Harbin to Port Arthur should be transferred to Japan. Additional demands, which the Japanese government considered desirable but not essential, included the surrender of Russian vessels in neutral ports, granting of fishing rights off the maritime provinces, the cession in full sovereignty of the entire island of Sakhalin, and the payment by Russia of an indemnity to cover the costs of the war.

As the negotiations progressed, the Japanese delegates were in no mood to make concessions. Nevertheless, Japan was not in a position to make unlimited demands. The war had created a financial and economic crisis at home. If negotiations broke down and hostilities were resumed, there was a lack of manpower to assure a quick victory. Russia, on the other hand, found world public opinion swinging to its side as the conference continued. Furthermore, the Czar was adamantly against Russia ceding any territory or paying an indemnity.

By August 18, the conference had reached an impasse and President Roosevelt intervened directly by urging the Czar to transfer all of Sakhalin with Russia paying for Japan's cost of occupying it in lieu of an indemnity. The substance of Roosevelt's compromise was far less important than the fact that it came at a time when the chief Russian delegate, Witte, had been instructed to break off negotiations if Japan did not drop its demands for an indemnity and all of Sakhalin. As Roosevelt had received no reply from his appeal to the Czar, Witte refused to break off negotiations. By August 23, American Minister Meyer in St. Petersburg persuaded the Czar to agree to cede the southern half of Sakhalin. Roosevelt then prevailed upon Japan to drop the indemnity request and settle for southern Sakhalin. Consequently, the Treaty of Portsmouth, which was signed on September 5, 1905, provided for:

1. The recognition of Korean independence and of the paramount political, military, and economic interests of Japan therein
2. The transfer to Japan of Russia's leases and rights in Liaotung and of the South Manchurian Railway
3. The withdrawal of foreign troops from Manchuria except Japanese railway guards
4. The acquisition of the southern half of Sakhalin in full sovereignty by Japan and of special fishing rights in adjacent waters
5. The noninterference by the signatories in measures which China might take in Manchuria for the commercial and industrial development of that area

As with the Treaty of Shimonoseki a decade earlier, the Japanese people expected much more from the war. Their hopes had been raised by earlier announcements by the Katsura government that Japan would receive an indemnity. The people reacted emotionally and violently against the terms of peace. They demanded Katsura's resignation. They insisted that he should have pressed for an indemnity 50 per cent greater than the cost of the war, for the northern half of Sakhalin, and even for some of the Maritime Provinces in Siberia. Some of the most influential newspapers recommended rejection of the treaty. The comparatively sedate *Asahi* editorialized that the terms of peace had lifted the crown of victory from the nation's head. Other papers suggested the assassination of Cabinet members and the Elder Statesmen. Riots broke out in Tokyo with resultant heavy casualties. Martial law was immediately established. But this time no group of powers forced Japan to give up what it had been granted by the Treaty. Its sphere of influence now encompassed both Korea and Manchuria, and Japan was well along the road toward acquiring a controlling influence over all of Eastern Asia.[8]

A Limited Protectorate Over Korea

When the populace demanded the resignation of Premier Katsura because of his failure to win greater spoils at the Portsmouth Peace Conference, he would have gladly resigned. He was not, however, a free agent. He owed his position and his tenure of office to the Elder Statesmen and the Privy Councilors. They, in turn, realized that there was still important unfinished business to be settled. Japan's new status with Korea had to be regularized. Furthermore, China had not yet recognized the legality of Japan's claim to the former Russian leases in the Liaotung Peninsula. Hence, the Elder Statesmen insisted that Katsura remain at the head of the government until negotiations were completed with both Korea and China.

As for Korea, the two agreements of February and August, 1904, had given Japan a modified protectorate over that country, including the right to appoint financial and diplomatic advisers. These concessions had been obtained during wartime, however, and Japan was insistent on obtaining a more comprehensive and permanent arrangement. Although by the Portsmouth Treaty, Russia recognized the paramount political, economic, and military interests of Japan in Korea, it was another matter to get Korea to verify and to guarantee these interests. Itō Hirobumi, the most venerable statesman, was called upon to negotiate a convention at Seoul with the helpless and hapless peninsular kingdom.

The Korean King requested help from the United States but to no avail. Willard Straight, the American Minister at Seoul, told him that he had had ten years in which to improve Korea's situation but had failed to do so and lost his chance for help. President Roosevelt had already declared that Korea was incapable of governing itself. When Japanese gendarmes surrounded the royal palace, the Korean King capitulated. On November 17, 1905, an agreement was signed which provided for the extension of rights obtained in the earlier conventions and the appointment of a Japanese Resident General to reside in Seoul with authority to direct diplomatic affairs and to have private and personal audiences with the King. Itō, who was the first Resident General, explained that propinquity and Japan's own safety had made this action necessary.

Secret requests of the Korean King for help from the United States were of no avail. President Roosevelt declared he saw no practical action open to him in view of the earlier agreements between Japan and Korea. In November, 1905, the United States Minister was ordered to close the American Legation in Seoul. For all practical purposes, Roosevelt considered Korea as a Japanese protectorate and had no objection to such an arrangement.

There was another piece of unfinished diplomatic business before the Katsura Cabinet. China had not yet completed the transfer to Japan of Russia's former rights in the Liaotung Peninsula. By the Portsmouth Treaty, Russia was bound to relinquish its rights in favor of Japan. But Russia had received its rights from China. Since China was not a party to the Portsmouth Treaty, a separate agreement between China and Japan was necessary to make this transfer legal. Consequently, a special mission under Foreign Minister Komura went to Peking to settle the issue. In December, 1905, an agreement was signed which transferred the former Russian leasehold in Liaotung to Japan, granted Japan timber rights and permission to build and operate the railroad from Antung to Mukden, and opened several cities in Manchuria to foreign trade. By a secret protocol, China pledged not to construct a railroad line parallel to the Japanese-owned lines in Manchuria (the South Manchurian Railway). With the successful conclusion of these negotiations, in January, 1906, Katsura gladly resigned.

The Saionji Ministry and Itō as Resident General

Katsura's resignation as well as political events in Japan during the next seven years were largely unconnected with the political realities. In fact, this period witnessed the operation of some of the most blatantly nondemocratic aspects of a constitutional monarchy. In the first place, the premiership shifted back and forth between two men, Katsura and Saionji. These shifts were made with complete disregard for their party affiliations and the strength of the parties in the House of Representatives. At the same time, it was a period in which the strength of the Seiyūkai, under Hara's leadership, was such that there developed a "mutual understanding" (*jōi tōgō*) between the parties and the cabinets.

As noted earlier, Hara and Katsura had agreed that when the latter resigned as Prime Minister, Saionji, the President of the Seiyūkai, should succeed him. As Katsura had previously secured Yamagata's approval for this arrangement, Saionji was selected to head the new government. Although his new Cabinet was not in any sense a party cabinet, two important posts were filled by Seiyūkai members. Hara Kei was appointed Home Minister from which point he secured increased support for the party through his power to disburse funds for local construction projects and to appoint governors and other important local officials. Matsuda Masahisa, the additional Seiyūkai member of the Cabinet, was appointed Minister of Justice. The other positions were filled by former bureaucrats and oligarchs. Despite the new Cabinet, there was no basic shift in policy. A balanced budget, the increased nationalization and expansion of railways, and larger appropriations for the Army and Navy were sponsored and approved. Hara's attempt to abolish the system of counties (*gun*) as a means to weaken Yamagata's political power was, however, defeated.[9]

The two most important events of the first Saionji Ministry (1906–1908) were the extension of Japanese control over Korea and the resolution of the "war crisis" with the United States in 1907. As for the former, while the agreements already signed with Korea had given Japan direction over Korean foreign affairs, the arrangement proved to be far from satisfactory. As Resident General, Prince Itō proposed a comprehensive program of internal "reforms." His plan included the improvement of agriculture and transportation facilities, industrial development, and the reorganization of the courts and the police system.

Since his powers and those of his subordinates appointed to the executive branches of the Korean government were only advisory and since Koreans resented and opposed these infringements on their independence, little progress was made. The King refused to listen to Itō's pleadings that he should approve a protectorate to prevent appointment of a Japanese military governor and outright annexation. When the Japanese Foreign Minister arrived to discuss a new treaty in 1907, the King abdicated rather than be forced to compromise his country's independence.

A new convention was immediately negotiated with his son, the new sovereign. This convention of July 25, 1907, made Korea a protectorate and placed it at the mercy of the Resident General. He could instruct and guide the Korean government on all matters relating to the reform of the Korean administration. His preliminary approval was required for all laws and ordinances and for appointments and removals of high Korean officials. Finally, the Korean government was bound to accept the appointment of any Japanese subject he recommended. To avoid any possible international complications from this action and to protect the Japanese flank, Japan and Russia signed a special agreement on July 30, 1907. By its secret clauses the latter recognized the validity of the Japanese protectorate over Korea and Japan acknowledged Russia's special status in Outer Mongolia. Furthermore, it established North Manchuria as a Russian sphere and South Manchuria as a Japanese one.

Even under the protectorate, the reforms advocated by Itō did not progress as rapidly as Japan desired. When one considers the basic attitude of Itō and his colleagues toward the Koreans, it is not surprising that such should be the case. On the one hand, the Japanese had operated under the delusion that the Koreans would willingly accept any "advice" offered them. Such an approach was consistent with Itō's public career. Throughout his long and distinguished service, he had always assumed a paternalistic attitude toward the common man in Japan. He and his contemporaries had displayed a strong self-confidence in the righteousness of their cause and in the wisdom of their decisions.

Naturally, he took this same attitude with him to Korea as Resident General and imbued his subordinates with it. It was strongly tinged with a feeling of superiority over all Koreans. He took immediate steps to implement the new powers granted Japan under the protectorate. Japanese vice-ministers, lesser officials, and clerks and secretaries were attached to the executive departments of the central Korean government. A Japanese secretary and an Inspector of Police with clerical assistants were assigned to each provincial office. Chief justices and procurators were appointed to the principal courts. The Oriental Colonization Company was organized to exploit Korean resources and expand Japanese industry.

On the other hand, Itō found that he had grossly underestimated Korea's love for independence. He had failed to realize that a hard core of Korean nationalism still existed. The more he tried to submerge it, the more buoyant it became. The King and his officials refused to be intimidated. They acted as independently as possible of the Resident General. On all levels of the Korean administration, a conscious policy of obstructionism was followed. Itō believed annexation would be avoided, Japan's security from outside attack assured, and Korean reform accomplished through the combined efforts of the Resident General, the Korean Court, and a Korean Reform Ministry. By the time he resigned from office in June, 1909, he recognized that his policies in Korea had failed.[10]

The second most important event of Saionji's ministry was the crisis which arose over the anti-Japanese movement in California. This movement flared up after the San Francisco earthquake of 1906. It was exacerbated by the action of the San Francisco Board of Education in October, 1906, when it excluded Orientals from all but Oriental schools. President Roosevelt, in his message to Congress in December, scored this move as a "wicked absurdity" and asked for special legislation which would give him power to regulate aliens entering the country, such as Japanese immigrants from Hawaii. California and other western states were inflamed by his speech and were finally placated only after agreement was reached in February, 1907, for the restriction of Japanese immigration. Animosity against the United States was stimulated once more during the summer. In an official Army and Navy policy statement, Russia was depicted as the "theoretical" enemy for the Army and the United States for the Navy. To quiet war rumors which persisted in Europe and on both sides of the Pacific, on July 4, 1907, President Roosevelt announced that the United States fleet was starting on a world cruise and would call at Japan. When the fleet arrived in 1909, it received a rousing welcome, an indication of improved Japanese-American relations.

The Second Katsura Cabinet and Korea's Annexation, 1910

The growing dissatisfaction within Japan with the Saionji Cabinet also brought Korea's annexation closer. Paradoxically, this dissatisfaction had not been reflected in the regular elections of May, 1908. Despite the unpopularity of Saionji's financial policies, his party (the Seiyūkai) had won eight new seats in the House of Representatives, which gave it a majority for the first time in five years. But Yamagata, the most powerful Elder Statesman, had never let the wishes of the electorate stand in his way. He and his clique had agreed that it was time for a change. Itō was considered a failure in Korea and Saionji was unpopular at home.

The latter feigned illness and resigned as Prime Minister in July, 1908. His capitulation to the desires of the Elder Statesmen in the face of increased support from the voters was taken as a matter of course. His recommendation that Katsura succeed him was accepted. Hara and the Seiyūkai, despite the party's majority in the House of Representatives, had no alternative but to accept the change of premiership.

Katsura was little perturbed over the thought that he would be faced with a hostile Parliament. He had always been disdainful of the parties and their elected representatives. In fact, he was confident that he could force his policies through the Diet despite the opposition. In the final analysis, if he faced a political crisis, he could always turn the premiership back again to Saionji.

Katsura's second Cabinet, composed largely of his own henchmen and representatives from the militarist clique, remained in power for three years (July, 1908–August, 1911). Its domestic policy emphasized austerity and a balanced budget. The naval building program and increases in military expenditures were correlated with a long-term expansion program. To win support for his program, he resorted to bribery and intimidation. The scandals which came to light after the bankruptcy in 1909 of the Japan Sugar Refining Company further weakened the prestige of the politicians. Twenty Diet members were arrested because of bribes which they had received. Furthermore, the legislators evinced a lack of interest in democratic processes. The House of Peers defeated a proposal for universal manhood suffrage. In his speech in opposition to the law, one of the Peers noted: "Nowhere in our Constitution is it stated that the chief object in the creation of the Diet was to give expression to the will of the people."

In the meantime, events were rapidly unfolding toward a climax in Korea. On the international front there were few indications of opposition to its annexation by Japan. On November 30, 1908, Secretary of State Elihu Root and Japanese Ambassador Takahira signed an agreement whereby their countries promised to press for territorial integrity and the principle of equal commercial opportunity in China. By inference, Japan could assume that it had a free hand in Korea as it was not mentioned in the joint declaration. In addition, when Japan rejected Root's proposal the next year to internationalize the Japanese-owned South Manchurian Railway, the United States dropped the matter.

On the domestic scene, Katsura and his Cabinet continued preparations for formal annexation of Korea. Even Itō raised no objections to the specific plans previously approved by Katsura and Yamagata that Japan should annex Korea at an appropriate time. In June, 1909, Itō resigned as Resident General and returned to his old post of President of the Privy Council. In October, he was sent on an inspection trip to Manchuria during which he conferred with the Russian Finance Minister in Harbin. While leaving the meeting, Itō was assassinated by a fanatical Korean representing a group of Korean émigrés at Vladivostok. In Japan, his death was taken as an adequate pretext to annex Korea as soon as possible. Popular opinion clamored for such action; those who had previously opposed it remained silent.

The Katsura Cabinet then acted to incorporate Korea into the Japanese Empire. In the process, the Premier followed the usual policy of not disclosing his plans to Parliament. To do so might jeopardize his scheme. After the Diet adjourned in March, 1910, the Cabinet appointed a military man as the new Resident General, as Itō had predicted. General Terauchi Masatake (1852–1919), who had been War Minister continuously from 1902, was assigned to the post. In mid-June, 1910, a detachment of Japanese marines was dispatched to Korea to enforce law and order. A special Cabinet Bureau of Colonial Affairs was established with authority over Korean problems. It was made directly responsible to the Premier.

In July, General Terauchi arrived in Seoul under heavy guard. The entire country had already been under the equivalent of martial law. He suspended or suppressed all organs of public opinion. The Korean King and people were at his mercy. Within a month, after a series of conferences with the King and other officials, Terauchi telegraphed to Tokyo that "the government of Japan and Korea were in complete accord" and sought Imperial sanction for "Korea's request for annexation." On August 22, 1910, Terauchi and the Korean King signed the Treaty of Annexation proposed by Japan.

The Treaty of Annexation was the culmination of a long-standing and deep-seated desire of some Japanese to conquer Korea. In 1873, nearly forty years earlier, there had been many who favored an attack on Korea, but the plan was abandoned as impracticable. In the intervening years, Japan had fought successfully in two wars to prevent Korea from falling into the hands of China or Russia. It was now in a position to force its will on the youthful King and proceeded to do so.

By the Treaty, Japan acquired complete sovereignty over Korea and assumed responsibility for its entire government and administration. Korea ceased to exist as a country. Henceforth, Koreans were to be subject to Japanese rulers and to Japanese law. Unfortunately for both the Koreans and the Japanese, this rule was administered by the military who ruthlessly suppressed any signs of opposition. Every effort was made to eradicate Korean nationalism. This stern attitude toward the people of Korea and disregard for their sensibilities and political aspirations intensified their hatred for their masters. Despite their thirty-five years under Japanese rule, Koreans never lost their thirst for independence.

Having completed the annexation of Korea, Japan moved to consolidate its position by other international agreements. In the same year, a protocol was signed with Russia whereby the contracting parties recognized each other's right to take necessary action to safeguard their interests in Manchuria and Korea. In 1911 Japan pushed for another renewal of the Anglo-Japanese Alliance. The disquietude created over Japan's competition for the China market had caused a certain degree of British opposition to the continuance of the alliance. Nevertheless, fear of German imperialism was more of a formative force in British foreign policy than fear of Japan. As a result, the alliance was renewed for ten years and some of the provisions were strengthened.

Second Saionji Cabinet Opposes Increased Armaments

Having secured a prominent position on the continent of Asia, the military leaders were convinced that this position could be maintained or improved only through the expansion of the Imperial Army and Navy. Thus, the main attention of the leaders of the government shifted, at least temporarily, from the international to the domestic scene. In January, 1911, Katsura had been able to obtain acceptance of his budget with the help of the Seiyūkai after he promised Hara that funds for the construction of new railroads would not be cut off. In the spring and summer, the Army and Navy pressed for additional funds for military expansion. Rather than face these demands, Katsura resigned and turned the problem over to Saionji.

The second Saionji Cabinet lasted from August 30, 1911, to December 21, 1912. The most difficult problem it faced was how to survive in the face of strong pressure for new funds for expansion from the Army leaders, backed by Yamagata and the Chōshū faction, and from the Navy, supported by Satsuma. The former argued that the acquisition of Korea and the revolution in China in October, 1911, dictated the formation of two new Army divisions. Yamagata insisted that national defense should take precedence over financial considerations. The Navy argued that Japan's new position in the western Pacific could be maintained only by comparable increases in the Imperial Navy.

The military had already perfected their procedures whereby they could keep either an obstreperous Cabinet or Parliament in line. For example, in the elections in 1912, the Seiyūkai party increased its majority in the Lower House placing Saionji in a position of having full support for his policies. Retrenchment had been a popular election campaign slogan so Saionji, with Seiyūkai backing, refused to approve the budget increases necessary for two new Army divisions. At the same time, his approval of the Navy appropriations stimulated the military leaders to resort to a device which was to be "standard operational procedure" throughout the turbulent years after the invasion of Manchuria in 1931. The War Minister, on orders from his superiors, sent in his resignation directly to the Emperor in protest to the Cabinet decision. This action automatically caused the downfall of the Saionji Cabinet because no successor could be found to fill his post.

In 1900, an Imperial Ordinance was issued under pressure from Prime Minister Yamagata, whose leadership was being challenged by Itō, which said that only Generals and Lieutenant-Generals and Admirals and Vice-Admirals on the active list could serve as Ministers of War and of Navy respectively. This ruling restricted to a mere handful the persons eligible for these two Cabinet portfolios. When the Minister of War resigned in 1912, therefore, all of his colleagues eligible for the post had also been ordered not to accept appointment under Saionji. Saionji knew that he had lost the confidence of the military and had no alternative. He must resign.[11]

The Death of Emperor Meiji

Before we proceed further with the discussion of the political history of the prewar years, the death of Emperor Meiji on July 30, 1912, at the age of sixty, must be noted. Since the operations of the constitutional monarchy had become more complicated, the Emperor had participated less and less as an individual in governmental affairs. Imperial Conferences, over which he presided, were called less frequently than in the earlier years of his reign. Now they were held only when the most vital issues, such as those of war and peace, were at stake and their purpose was to secure Imperial consent for decisions already reached by the chief ministers. It was not until the waning days of World War II that they were used to settle differences between contending factions in the government. (See page 441.) On practically all other matters, the Emperor's prerogatives were delegated to his various ministers. On routine matters, his approval was given through the Imperial Household Ministry and the Lord Keeper of the Privy Seal. On formal functions, such as the opening of Parliament, his speech was prepared for him and the whole ceremony was carefully prearranged according to precedent. Meiji as a person had reigned but had not governed. He was protected from public affairs and kept from personal contacts with the people. Divine characteristics were beginning to be attributed to him. The Emperor as a symbol became more important than the Emperor as a person. His death made little difference to the policies of the government.

Meiji's son, whose reign was known as Taishō, died in 1926. He was of even less importance in politics than his father. His inexperience, his isolation from the realities of life, and his mental ill-health in the latter part of his life made him a figurehead rather than a leader. As a new national consciousness emerged as a result of the victories against China and Russia, the institution of the Emperor increased in importance. It became a symbol of patriotism and was to serve as an important and useful instrument of ultranationalism and aggression in the near future.

The Taishō Political Crisis

Shortly after the death of Emperor Meiji, clear signs developed that the oligarchs would have to change their tactics of shifting the premiership from Saionji to Katsura. No progress was being made in Parliament with the armament program. As noted above, the resignation of the War Minister forced Saionji out of office on December 21, 1912. The political crisis which developed immediately thereafter, when practically all of the political groups in the Lower House were united solidly against the oligarchs, has come to be known as the Taishō Political Crisis.

The immediate cause of the crisis was Saionji's refusal to approve of the Army's request and his subsequent resignation. When Katsura returned from Europe in the summer of 1912, he had lost much of his political support. His mentor, Yamagata, had turned against him and arranged for his "retirement" from politics by his appointment as Grand Chamberlain to the Emperor. Consequently, when Saionji threatened to resign as Premier in December, the *Genrō* tried unsuccessfully to persuade someone other than Katsura to become Prime Minister. After holding ten sessions, they reluctantly turned again to Katsura.[12]

The announcement of his reappointment was the signal for the smoldering opposition of the parties to the whole political system to burst into flame. It took the form of a Movement for Protection of the Constitutional Government which resolved that "the arbitrariness of the military clique had reached such a pass that constitutional government was endangered and we are firmly against government by the oligarchs and are resolved to protect the constitution." Consequently, after taking office on December 21, 1912, until his forced resignation two months later, Katsura met with rigid opposition and obstructionism in the Diet. In fact he postponed its reopening for two weeks in the hope that he could force the opposition to break up. On the contrary, when the Diet finally opened on February 5, 1913, one of the most outstanding and consistent of Japan's liberals, Ozaki Yukio, was brutally frank in his denunciation of the Cabinet. In a speech in Parliament on February 5, 1913, he claimed that the oligarchs:

> . . . always mouth "loyalty" and "patriotism" and advertise themselves as the sole repositories of these qualities but what they are actually doing is to hide themselves behind the throne and shoot at their political enemies from their secure ambush.[13]

A nonconfidence resolution against the government was passed by the Lower House so Katsura prorogued the Diet to February 10. Angry mobs in Tokyo battled with the police in protest against the arbitrary rule of the oligarchs. There were simultaneous riots in other cities. Katsura had no choice but to resign. Before the year ended he had died of cancer. The oligarchs realized that if they were to continue to control future cabinets, they would have to appoint as premiers those who could secure at least partial support from the strongest political parties. They were not yet prepared to recommend the formation of party cabinets.[14]

The conciliatory attitude of the next Premier, Admiral Yamamoto Gombei (1852–1933), made such an arrangement possible. He appointed Hara as Home Minister and two other Seiyūkai members to his cabinet: Matsuda Masahisa as Minister of Justice and Motoda Hajime as Minister of Communications. In April, 1914, the *Genrō* selected Ōkuma Shigenobu as the next Premier. As leader of the former Progressive party, he had shown some interest in party government and still commanded respect within the Diet. As a Cabinet Minister on several earlier occasions, he had proved to be tractable to policies dictated by the oligarchs. He appeared to be well qualified to control the political scene. He also was amenable to a deal with the military in return for the offer of the office of Prime Minister. The Army apparently secured his approval and support for the two new divisions which they had planned for several years. In any event, after Ōkuma took office on April 16, 1914, his Cabinet members became little more than puppets manipulated by the Elder Statesmen and by the leaders of Yamagata's military clique.

This capitulation of Ōkuma to the desires of the military became clear from his dealings with the Diet. When it rejected his bill which provided for the enlarged Army, he immediately dissolved it. The elections in March, 1915, under the close surveillance of Home Minister Ōura, gave the Cabinet a majority and assured the approval of the Army's plans.[15] It is ironical that Ōkuma, one of the party leaders, should have been the instrument through which the military achieved their aims. It was inevitable, however, from the fact that when he accepted the premiership he had not insisted on Cabinet responsibility to Parliament or other manifestations of representative government. Rather, he capitulated to the wishes of the oligarchs and became their willing tool. Perhaps it was too much to ask of a party leader to press for such reforms in view of the history of the constitutional monarchy up to this point. In any case, it is clearly evident that when he took office, the elements for a truly representative and responsible government simply did not exist.

Japan Enters World War I

The outbreak of war in Europe in August, 1914, and its global repercussions swiftly shifted interest from the national to the international stage. Here, too, Ōkuma was to follow an aggressive policy. Despite his interest in earlier life in parliamentary government and the rights of the people, he did not apply his modified concepts of the rights of man to questions of international relations. Indeed, the policies he advocated toward China were a sad commentary on his "liberalism." As Premier in 1915, he sponsored a policy which forced China to become subservient both politically and economically to Japan. To Ōkuma and his colleagues, such liberalism as they advocated could not be allowed to interfere with Japan's destiny to secure a predominant and ruling position in East Asia.

Japan's leading statesmen were constantly on the alert for any opportunity that would permit them to achieve this objective. They had been apprehensive of the effect on Japan of the Chinese Revolution and of the downfall of the Manchu dynasty on February 12, 1912. Although the Japanese public in general supported the revolutionaries, the government announced that it would remain neutral. While the clan bureaucrats were casting covetous eyes on Manchuria and north China and were hopeful that they would be able to extend Japan's influence on the continent, World War I gave them the chance they were seeking.[16]

A new China policy developed rapidly under the leadership of Foreign Minister Katō Kōmei. While Ambassador to London, he had already received assurances from British Foreign Minister Viscount Grey that England would not object to Japan's taking up with China, at an appropriate time, the question of the extension of the leases in Kwantung (Liaotung) and South Manchuria. Upon his return to Tokyo to become Foreign Minister in the third Katsura Cabinet, Katō continued his efforts to support a strong Japanese policy toward China. When the Ōkuma Cabinet was formed in April, 1914, Katō was again appointed Foreign Minister. It was not surprising, therefore, that with the outbreak of World War I in August, 1914, he advocated an aggressive foreign policy. He had concluded that the preoccupation of European countries with the war against Germany and the Entente would leave Japan free to act as it desired in China.[17]

Before we consider Japan's demands on China, however, brief mention should be made of the early effects of World War I on Japan. From the outbreak of hostilities, the Japanese government realized that under the terms of the Anglo-Japanese Alliance it might be called upon to enter the war. On August 7, when Great Britain formally requested Japan's assistance in the destruction of German men-of-war in Chinese waters, Foreign Minister Katō had already decided on his answer. He immediately championed his country's entry into the war on the side of the Allies. He rejected suggestions advanced by Great Britain that the scope of operations of the Imperial Navy be restricted. He clearly saw an opportunity simultaneously to destroy German prestige in Asia and to increase Japanese power. Two days later he had persuaded his colleagues and the *Genrō* to accept the same point of view.

On August 15, 1914, an ultimatum, which set forth Japan's position, was sent to Germany. It demanded that all German men-of-war be withdrawn from Chinese waters or be disarmed. Within a month, the German Leased Territory of Kiaochow in Shantung was to be delivered to Japan with a view to its eventual restoration to China. Finally, an unconditional reply must be received within a week. This decisive action under Katō's leadership had a dual effect. It forestalled any move by Great Britain to limit Japan's zone of operations, and it gave ample cause for entering the war and seizing Germany's possessions in China. On August 23, 1914, no reply having been received within the time specified, Japan declared war. A special session of Parliament was called immediately which gave Prime Minister Ōkuma unanimous support for his war budget. Foreign Minister Katō's address on foreign relations was a mere formality and gave no explanation of the reasons for entering the war.

Actually, Japan's entry into World War I placed far less strain upon the nation than had either of the two previous wars. The naval and military operations were on a much smaller scale than those against China or Russia. Unlike France, Great Britain, or even the United States, Japan had no fear of the power and might of Germany. It was not, in any sense, fighting for its self-preservation or existence. Rather, it was acting in those areas where it was to its direct advantage to do so. Hence, Japanese military and naval operations were confined to the Shantung Peninsula, to the Pacific Ocean and to Siberia. In Shantung immediate action was taken to assure the capitulation of the German forces in Kiaochow Bay. On September 3, 1914, Japanese marines landed at Lungkow on the northern shore of Shantung Peninsula. This move, though it was in violation of Chinese neutrality, permitted a rapid encirclement of the German forces. By November 7, the German contingents and warships had capitulated and the former German-leased territory was in Japanese hands. Furthermore, Japanese troops spread out westward along the Tsinan–Tsingtao Railway disregarding a new war zone delimited by the Chinese Government.

An interesting sidelight on Japan's attitude toward its partner in the Anglo-Japanese Alliance is revealed by the treatment accorded the British during the Shantung campaign. In view of the alliance, it was decided for political reasons to permit a British contingent to participate in the campaign against Kiaochow. To avoid any complications in the future, the British forces were kept in complete ignorance of the Japanese plan of attack. The British attachés from the Embassy in Tokyo, who were assigned to the expedition as observers, were not allowed to "observe" any of the actual operations. Upon their return to Tokyo after Kiaochow's fall, they reported that they had been treated to lavish hospitality, had enjoyed a vacation, but had nothing further to report. To Japanese in all walks of life, the war was equally unreal.

The operations in the Pacific Ocean were even more routine. Naval patrols were set up to search for German ships or submarines but few were encountered. The German-owned Marianas, Caroline, and Marshall Islands surrendered without any real resistance. By the beginning of 1915, therefore, Japan considered that its military and naval operations in the war were largely over. It had no military problems comparable in any sense to those created by the entrenchment of the German Army on the Aisne after the Battle of the Marne, by the struggle to win the channel ports, or by the attack being launched on the Eastern Front which was to defeat the Russians in May, 1915. On the contrary, Japan refused a request of the Allies to send troops to Europe. It settled back to profit

THE JAPANESE EMPIRE, 1915

economically from the manufacture of munitions and other war goods and from the logistic support its merchant marine gave to the Allies. It also was in the enviable position of being able to carry on a diplomatic offensive of its own when the other Allies were concentrating their every effort on survival.

THE TWENTY-ONE DEMANDS OF 1915

Consequently, Foreign Minister Katō sought ways and means of capitalizing on the preoccupation of the European powers. In September, 1914, while the campaign against Kiaochow was under way, he had already decided, and so informed his Minister in Peking, that Kiaochow should be under Japanese control, Japanese power should be extended into the interior by taking over the railroads in Shantung Province, and these matters should be negotiated directly with China. Other crucial issues were obtaining an extension of the leases in the Liaotung Peninsula and Manchuria and greater rights in Inner Mongolia. Katō's thinking on outstanding issues and the maximum desiderata of his country were sharpened and stimulated by the memorandum sent from Peking by Major General Machida Keiu and by ideas proposed by Koike Chōzō, Chief of the Political Affairs Bureau of the Foreign Office. These men, together with Vice-Admiral Moriyama Keisaburō, hammered out proposals for an overall settlement with China. Their recommendations became the basis for the Twenty-One Demands.

Plans for presenting these demands to China were worked out as carefully as their content. In the first place, inspired articles in the press appeared after Kiaochow's surrender which advocated immediate transfer of the German rights to Japan and the extension of Japanese interests on the continent. Japanese Minister Hioki was recalled from Peking and told to present the Twenty-One Demands to the Chinese Government on a suitable occasion. By the time Parliament had convened at the end of December, 1914, Hioki was back in Peking waiting for a propitious moment to make his *démarche*.

He did not have long to wait. In connection with the capture of Kiaochow, Japanese troops had occupied the Tsinan Railway line well outside of the war zone established by China. China was, quite naturally, apprehensive of the results of the continuance of such a situation. Consequently, on a suitable occasion, it announced the abolition of the military zone in Shantung and requested that all foreign troops be withdrawn from Chinese territory. Hioki promptly retorted that this act of revocation was improper and arbitrary and betrayed a lack of confidence in his country's good faith. On January 18, 1915, he delivered the Twenty-One Demands directly to the Chinese President, Yüan Shih-kai.

Negotiations concerning these famous Demands began on February 2 and continued through April 17. On Hioki's insistence, no minutes were taken of the discussions. The negotiations were broken off by Japan whenever China showed signs of intransigence. Although Foreign Minister Katō refused to support an expeditionary force against China, he readily agreed in mid-February to the dispatch of Japanese troops to Shantung and Manchuria, "to relieve the garrison." The Chinese government was informed that these additional troops would not be withdrawn "until the negotiations could be brought to a satisfactory conclusion." Through the tried expedient of conscious leaks, the Chinese negotiators circumvented the secrecy of the conference and kept the United States and Great Britain *au courant* with developments. The moral support which China received from these countries helped to offset the military pressure from Japan. In the final analysis, however, China knew that it was powerless to resist Japan unless it had positive help from outside.[18]

In the course of the negotiations, China raised two fundamental questions. The first question concerned the relative importance of the various demands. They had been divided into five groups, the last one being most obnoxious to China. The first four groups, which contained fourteen articles, concerned such items as the transfer to Japan of the former German rights in Shantung, the right of Japanese capitalists to build the Chefoo–Weihsien railroad, the opening of additional localities for trade and residence and the nonalienation of any territory in the province to another power. The second group concerned Manchuria and Inner Mongolia. It extended the Port Arthur and Dairen leases and the South Manchuria and Antung railway agreements for ninety-nine years. Japanese were allowed extensive business rights in the area and permission to exploit mines. In separate notes, China agreed to use Japanese capital for railway construction in Manchuria if foreign financial assistance was needed, and financial, military, and police advisers when necessary. Other demands guaranteed Japanese rights in the operation of the iron deposits near Hankow. The fifth group provided for extensive Japanese rights within China and the appointment of advisers to the government. If this last group had been accepted, the result would have been a practical Japanese protectorate over China. In the early part of the negotiations Japan insisted that all five groups be accepted. China gradually conceded on most of the demands in the first four groups but adamantly refused to accept Group V. It received strong indirect support from Great Britain and the United States in maintaining this position.

The second basic point which China pressed concerned the manner in which the demands were presented. It insisted that it was being forced to accept them under duress. When it took a firm stand in mid-April, Foreign Minister Katō urged his government to issue an ultimatum to China demanding acceptance of the Demands. When Katō ran into strong opposition from the *Genrō*, he agreed to the withdrawal of all of Group V. On May 7, he sent China an ultimatum in which it was given two days to make a favorable answer to all of the demands except Group V or accept the consequences. The simultaneous preparations for the mobilization of the Japanese armed forces left no doubt as to what these consequences would be. China capitulated and the main features of Groups I–IV were incorporated in two treaties signed on May 25, 1915. At the Paris Peace Conference China constantly stressed the fact that it had signed the agreements unwillingly and only under duress.

In the decade from the Treaty of Portsmouth of 1905 to the new treaties with China in 1915, the consolidation of the Japanese Empire had been effected. In fact, the main boundaries of that Empire had already been determined. Korea had been made into a colony. Broad concessions had been obtained in Shantung. The Marianas, Caroline, and Marshall Islands were securely under military occupation. There seemed every likelihood that these new acquisitions would be confirmed by the peace conference after World War I. If possession or territorial propinquity had any bearing on the final outcome, Japan's claims would be accepted and confirmed. If such were the case, the unchallenged leadership of Japan in East Asia would be assured. No Japanese official took seriously the note which Secretary of State Robert Lansing sent in protest to the Twenty-One Demands. It said that the United States government could not recognize any agreement which impaired the rights of the United States and its citizens in China, the political and territorial integrity of the Republic of China, or even the Open Door. Surely, they argued, his protest was only for the record and any future conflict of American and Japanese interests in China could be resolved. The world was to wait thirty years to discover, however, that Japan had taken another irrevocable step in 1915 on the road to eventual defeat.

Notes

1. It may be argued that Japan's entry into World War I in August, 1914, is a more logical date to use as a terminal one for this period. I would point out, however, that there was never any real doubt as to which side Japan would join either before or after the outbreak of hostilities. The Anglo-Japanese Alliance was only an outward manifestation of a general feeling that it was decidedly to Japan's interest to side with Great Britain in any struggle against Germany. The important decision, therefore, in relation to the consolidation of the Empire, was not to declare war and capture the German possessions in Shantung. Rather, the significant decisions were those made late in 1914 and early in 1915 to force China to accept the Twenty-One Demands which would assure Japanese hegemony over China and over all of East Asia.

2. It was ironical that Russia's last proposals, which had been transmitted on February 2, did not reach Baron Rosen, the Russian Minister in Tokyo, until February 7, three days after Japan's final decision to go to war. Furthermore, these proposals included Russia's willingness to give up the idea of a neutral zone in northern Korea. Of even more significance, however, was the fact that Witte, who might have extricated Russia from its diplomatic tangle, was in disfavor with Nicholas II. His favorites, such as Admiral Abaza, actually misrepresented to the Japanese Minister in St. Petersburg the Emperor's decision to drop the demand for a neutral zone in Korea. See Raymond A. Esthus, *Theodore Roosevelt and Japan* (Seattle: University of Washington Press, 1966), p. 22; and Andrew Malozenoff, *Russian Far Eastern Policy 1881–1904* (Berkeley: University of California Press, 1958), pp. 247 ff.

3. See George A. Lensen, *Russian Eastward Expansion* (Englewood Cliffs, N. J.: Prentice-Hall, Inc., 1964), p. 124.

4. As the Russian fleet was off the Indochina coast during the winter, this conclusion was a natural one to make. Admiral Tōgō Heihachirō (1848–

1934) was the commander responsible for this victory. Upon his return home, he was idolized by boisterous crowds in Yokohama and Tokyo. Upon his death, an Imperial rescript declared: "Your sincerity put you in communion with the ancestral gods and your foresight decided victory or defeat." The hero of the capture of Port Arthur, General Nogi, became even more of a deified figure as he followed the Emperor Meiji in death in 1912.

5. The Japanese had made a wise move at the beginning of the war. They had sent Kaneko Kentarō to the United States as a special public relations officer to assist Minister Takahira. Kaneko had been a personal friend of Roosevelt since they were at Harvard together. As the war progressed Kaneko obtained from Americans an increasingly friendly attitude for Japan's cause. For a recent study of Roosevelt and the war, shedding much new information on his peacemaking role, see Esthus, *op. cit.*, pp. 3–97. For the war in the broader context of Japanese–American relations, see Akira Iriye, *Across the Pacific: An Inner History of American–East Asian Relations* (New York: Harcourt, Brace and World, Inc., 1967), p. 68.

6. Tyler Dennet, *Roosevelt and the Russo-Japanese War* (New York: Doubleday and Co., Inc., 1925), pp. 112–13.

7. Ian Nish, *The Anglo-Japanese Alliance, The Diplomacy of Two Island Empires 1894–1907* (London: University of London Athlone Press, 1966), pp. 301–33.

8. For details of the negotiations see Esthus, *op. cit.*, pp. 80–93. For an informative account of public reaction to the terms of the Portsmouth Treaty and the resultant riots see Shumpei Okamoto, *The Japanese Oligarchy and the Russo-Japanese War* (New York: Columbia University Press, 1970).

9. The growth of Seiyūkai power through Hara's activities is ably set forth in Tetsuo Najita, *Hara Kei in the Politics of Compromise 1905–1915* (Cambridge: Harvard University Press, 1967), especially pp. 32 ff.

10. It seems clear that Itō believed the rival militaristic, expansionist faction at home could be kept from getting the upper hand in Korea so long as a civilian was assigned Resident General. He seems to have changed his mind in favor of annexation after his resignation in the summer of 1909. For his failure to achieve his objectives in Korea see Hilary Conroy, *The Japanese Seizure of Korea, 1868–1910* (Philadelphia: University of Pennsylvania Press, 1960), pp. 325–80. For an account of the close relationship of the presence of Japanese military forces in Korea and Itō's methods of obtaining its reluctant acceptance of the Protectorate Treaty, as well as the powers and functions of the Resident General, see C. I. Eugene Kim and Han-Kyo Kim, *Korea and the Politics of Imperialism, 1876–1910* (Berkeley: University of California Press, 1967), pp. 128 ff.

11. The War Minister was within his legal rights in presenting his resignation to the Emperor. Article XI of the Constitution designates the Emperor as the Supreme Commander of the Army and Navy. Article XII gives him responsibility for its organization. Consequently, the military leaders claimed that they had a constitutional right of "direct access" to the throne on military matters. As we shall see, this concept of "direct access" was the basis for the dual diplomacy which evolved from World War I. (See *infra,* page 375.)

12. For the background of the Taishō crisis, which many historians describe as an important turning point in Japanese history, see Najita, *op. cit.*, pp. 87 ff.; and Ōkubo Toshiaki, *Kindai Shi III, Nihon Zenshi* (Tokyo: Tokyo Daigaku Shuppan Kai, 1964), X, pp. 37 ff.

13. Quoted in Robert A. Scalapino, *Democracy and the Party Movement in Prewar Japan* (Berkeley: University of California Press, 1953), p. 194.

14. See Najita, *op. cit.*, pp. 122 ff., and Ōkubo, *op. cit.*, pp. 54 ff.

15. The fifteen-year expansion plan for the Imperial Army, approved in 1907, called for a gradual expansion to twenty-five divisions. After Ōkuma's bill was approved, the total divisions authorized totaled twenty-one. The Navy's building program received setbacks under Katsura and Ōkuma.

16. From the first visit of Sun Yat-sen to Japan in 1895, ultranationalists had befriended him in the hopes of strengthening Japan's position in China. When the revolution came, Japan had no clear-cut policy toward it and support for Sun vacillated. Various Chinese factions were backed, as no one knew which one would win. See Marius B. Jansen, *The Japanese and Sun Yat-sen* (Cambridge: Harvard University Press, 1954).

17. Katō Kōmei (Takaaki) (1860–1926) was born in Aichi Prefecture in 1860. He sought his fortune in Tokyo where, it turned out, he literally found it. After graduation from Law School of Tokyo Imperial University in 1881, he entered the Mitsubishi firm, attracted the attention of its President, Iwasaki Yatarō, was sent to England for study, and returned to marry Iwasaki's eldest daughter. In 1886 he began his career in the Foreign Office, later serving as Ōkuma's private secretary. In 1895 he was Minister to England and became Foreign Minister under both Itō and Saionji. In 1911, he formed a *rapprochement* with Katsura which led to his election as president of the *Dōshikai,* the political party which Katsura founded in 1913, and eventually became Prime Minister. As noted below, his arrogance and aloofness were exemplified by his refusal to keep the *Genrō* informed of contents of the ultimatum he issued to China in 1915. This action antagonized Yamagata and resulted in Katō's resignation as Foreign Minister in August, 1915, but he had advocated policies toward China which coincided with the younger, active military leaders. At the time of his death in 1926 he was Prime Minister of a "party Cabinet."

18. For details of the development of the Demands and their presentation to China see Ōkubo, *op. cit.*, pp. 87 ff.; James W. Morley, *The Japanese Thrust into Siberia, 1918* (New York: Columbia University Press, 1957), pp. 12–13; and Arthur S. Link, *Wilson: The Struggle for Neutrality, 1914–1915* (Princeton: Princeton University Press, 1960).

14

The Economic Basis of the New Empire, 1890–1915

The economic metamorphosis within Japan during the quarter century before World War I was almost as phenomenal as the outward expansion of the boundaries of the Empire. By 1890, at the inception of the constitutional monarchy, the nation's finances had finally been placed on a sound basis for the first time. National receipts had actually surpassed expenditures. Agricultural resources had been able to keep pace with the increases in population. In fact, there had been a surplus of rice since the quinquennium 1878–1882 which permitted an average annual export of 272,000 *koku*.

Although some progress had been made in the country's industrialization, particularly in the textile and silk industries, there were still many significant gaps. Heavy industries were notably underdeveloped and there was practically no steamship building. Foreign trade, which was carried on almost exclusively in foreign ships, had only just begun to show a favorable balance from 1885 to 1889. Increases in annual expenditures by the central government, which amounted to more than one-third the total, were diverted toward building a modern Army and Navy.

By May, 1915, when Japan confronted China with an ultimatum demanding compliance with four of the five groups of the Twenty-One Demands, the general economic picture had changed radically. Japan had passed through its initial phase of economic growth and had entered a period of accelerated increase in the individual worker's productivity, in capital investment, in industrial specialization and concentration.[1]

The wars against both China and Russia and the newly created and enlarged military establishments had placed a heavy drain on the nation's finances. With the increase in population, annual rice imports rose to five per cent of the national crop. Little new land was available for reclamation and there were few other prospects for increasing rice production. The needs of the national economy for raw materials were reflected by a shift in the international trade balance from an excess of exports to an excess of imports. Added to this fact was an even greater loss in international payments in gold and interest payments. In 1913, the total foreign indebtedness equaled about 1,100 million yen.

Between 1890 and 1914, Japan's economic growth had increased at a remarkable rate but also showed clear signs of strain. Just when a crisis seemed inevitable, the acute demands of the Allied Powers for munitions, shipping, and supplies during World War I enabled Japan to solve, at least temporarily, its major economic and financial problems. So long as the foreign market for Japanese goods and services held, the country's economic future could be left to take care of itself. The present chapter is devoted, therefore, to an analysis of these developments and of their effect on Japan's future.

The displeasure of the Japanese nation with the results of the victory over China in 1895 had been aroused by the intervention of the *triplice* which had forced Japan to retrocede the Liaotung Peninsula to China. This intervention dramatically convinced all classes of society of the validity of the philosophy which had motivated the Meiji leaders in the formulation of political and economic reforms. They had maintained that the country must strengthen itself industrially and militarily if it were to achieve its objectives. This condemnation of the action of the three European powers, this emotional and psychological reaction to foreign meddling, had tended to divert men's minds from the actual and potential results of the war.

In the first place, the war had acted as a proving ground for the general operations, tactics, and use of equipment of the Imperial Army and Navy. This first full-scale test of the newly created military and naval forces had been a severe one but had not been prolonged enough to place too heavy a drain on resources and on personnel. Nevertheless, the war had been extensive enough to reveal a lack of scientific and up-to-date armaments and a weakness in ability to give logistic support and to coordinate the movements of Army and Navy units. It had taught the Chiefs of Staff, in a realistic fashion, what improvements and expansion were necessary before Japan could dare to face successfully a powerful Western nation such as Russia.

Furthermore, the territorial settlement of the war provided new areas for economic development and exploitation. The colony of Formosa, with its estimated population of 2.6 million in 1898, offered new and tempting markets for the products of Japanese industry. Its area was equal to almost one-tenth of Japan proper; its climate was tropical with abundant rainfall. With a minimum of investment and with the establishment of internal security, the island soon became a valuable source of important raw materials and agricultural products. Camphor, lumber, rice, and sugar were shipped to Japan, and were to become important elements in the Empire's economy.

By the peace treaty of 1895 China had recognized the independence of Korea. From an economic point of view, this meant that so long as political stability could be maintained in Korea and discriminatory tariffs against foreign goods could be enforced, Japanese merchants and investors were free to exploit Korean markets and resources. In fact, such exploitation would increase in direct proportion to Japan's control over Korea. On the other hand, Korea's strategic importance would have the greatest impact on Japan's economic development. As it was argued that control of Korea was essential for the nation's security, the creation of a military machine of sufficient strength to achieve this goal was a matter of the highest priority. Specifically, this meant that an enlarged and modernized Army and Navy were requisites for preventing Russian encroachments in Korea. These requirements accelerated the growth of existing government-owned and private industries and forced the creation of new ones. Simultaneous demands for more consumer goods and services generated enlarged government spending for state-owned enterprises such as railways, public works, telegraph, and telephone.[2]

Consequently, the future, viable, economic development of the nation would be dependent on a delicate balance of several basic factors: the demands of a rapidly increasing population on limited domestic food supplies; current financial resources to meet increased government expenditures, particularly for military expenses; capital needs for raw materials and industrial expansion; the growth toward greater self-sufficiency in heavy industries; and the ability to find expanding foreign markets for the products of this new industrialized complex. Therefore, after the problem of population pressure on agrarian production has been analyzed, Japan's financial condition, industrial development, and foreign trade will be presented in order to obtain an estimate of its economic strength in 1915.

Population Pressure and Agrarian Production

In the first quarter century of Japan's modernization, there had been no serious population problem in the sense that the demand for rice, the staple food, could not be met from domestic production. In fact, in these early years rice had been one of the export items and had not been imported until after 1890. During the next quarter century, from 1890 to 1915, there was a complete reversal of this trend and the beginnings of new problems created by continued increases in the population and a higher standard of living. Net rice imports began in the years just before

TABLE 3

RICE PRODUCTION AND CONSUMPTION: ANNUAL AVERAGE SUPPLY AND DEMAND; ESTIMATED YIELD PER *Chō*, PER-CAPITA PRODUCTION, AND CONSUMPTION IN *Koku* (1878–1967) [3]

Year	Rice Production in 1,000 *Koku* (1)	Yield per *Chō* (2)	Net Import of Rice in 1,000 *Koku* (3)	Rice Consumption in 1,000 *Koku* (4)	Population (000) (5)	Per-Capita Rice Production (6)	Per-Capita Rice Consumption (7)
1878–1882	33,951	12.44	— 219	33,732	36,649	.926	.924
1883–1887	36,660	13.45	— 308	36,352	38,313	.983	.978
1888–1892	39,273	14.05	— 290	38,983	39,902	.984	.977
1893–1897	37,673	13.40	332	38,005	41,557	.907	.915
1898–1902	42,480	14.96	373	43,853	43,847	.978	1.00
1903–1907	46,286	16.11	474	50,760	46,620	.993	1.09
1908–1912	50,588	17.19	2,263	52,851	49,184	1.03	1.07
1913–1917	55,242	18.39	2,695	57,937	52,752	1.05	1.09
1918–1922	58,920	19.23	5,876	64,796	55,391	1.06	1.17
1923–1927	58,023	18.51	8,956	66,979	59,179	.985	1.13
1928–1932	60,468	18.88	9,418	69,886	63,872	.947	1.09
1933–1937	62,757	19.06	18,019	80,776	68,662	.914	1.18
1938–1942	63,514	19.82	12,612	76,126	71,400	.888	1.07
1943–1947	60,291	21.51	3,197	63,488	72,200	.835	.879
1948–1952	64,752	21.43	3,242	67,994	83,200	.778	.817
1953–1957	69,466	21.85	6,488	75,914	89,276	.778	.840
1958–1962	83,707	24.60	1,680	85,387	93,419	.896	.914
1963–1967	85,403	27.04	3,901	89,304	98,182	.870	.910

the war with China and rapidly mounted. By 1915 they averaged 2.7 million *koku* or about 4.7 per cent of the total rice consumed. The pressure on foreign exchange to purchase these imports was relieved considerably by the fact that about half of the rice imported at this time came from the new colonies of Formosa and Korea. (See Table 3.)

The vital facts to be noted in the relationship of these figures on the supply and demand of rice and on the increase in population are that they point to major difficulties ahead. As for the years 1913–1917, the average annual demand for rice imports of as much as 2.7 million *koku* underlines the fact that Japan was no longer able to produce for its own food needs. For the future, the steady increase in population meant only one thing: a greater demand for rice. There was no assurance, however, that these demands would continue to be met by improved production techniques or by imports paid for from excess exports.[4]

The population and food problems could only be solved, therefore, by their close correlation with the overall economic program. Contemporary writers and government officials, however, failed to recognize the dangers inherent in the nation's demographic trend. They were fully cognizant of the fact that there was little hope of material increases in the production of staple foods, yet did little to discourage or to prevent rapid population increases.

On the contrary, they considered a large population a boon rather than a hindrance to the growth of the nation. It was argued, for example, that a large population made possible a large army and hence augmented the national strength. The Chief of the Colonial Bureau suggested that the ills from any surplus population could be remedied by industrialization and by the fullest possible use of the new colonial territories such as Korea, Formosa, and Southern Sakhalin (Karafuto). It was not, therefore, until after World War I that Japanese economists and demographers regarded the increases in population as an essentially antagonistic factor in their country's economic welfare. But by that time, their prognostications had little effect on national policy. A militant nationalism had become the accepted policy and foreign nations were told that population pressure made it inevitable and necessary for Japan to expand on the Asiatic mainland.[5]

The amalgamation of the old, feudal, agrarian economy with the new capitalist state had also had other important effects on agriculture and on the nation as a whole. In 1915 the nation was still predominantly rural, so that any impact on the agrarian population was immediately felt throughout the entire empire. The farmer, who traditionally had had difficulty eking out a living, was hard pressed by increases in the size of his family. He supplemented his income from rice by growing silkworms and reeling the silk thread at home. Silk became a profitable cash crop so long as the foreign markets were steady. Furthermore, he found that his daughters formed an abundant, cheap labor supply for industry, particularly for the textile plants.

On the other hand, he was forced to pay a large share of the nation's taxes. The national policy of encouragement of heavy industries, including public ownership and management of the most important strategic industries, carried with it an obligation to protect these industries whenever possible. Consequently, the state imposed only light taxes on industry despite the need for greater revenue, and the farmer carried a disproportionately heavier tax burden than industry. This helped to cause a decrease in the number of farmers who owned their land, an increase in tenancy and rural indebtedness, and a greater concentration of the population in urban areas. The farmer's difficulties were increased by the importation of cheap rice from the colonies. This policy forced down the price of rice grown in Japan and decreased the farmer's income. As a result, many persons on the farms were underemployed and thus willing to accept employment in industry for extremely low wages. Insuperable problems, therefore, would appear in the agrarian economy unless drastic reforms in land ownership and in taxation policies were inaugurated. It was far easier for the national government to ignore the growing crisis in agriculture or to hope that it would be solved by Japanese domination of China or by some other diversionary tactics than to sponsor unpopular reforms.

The nation's finances were also far from stable. Annual budgetary increases had put a strain on limited resources. The war against China had cost an estimated 232.6 million yen, a sum over two times the normal national expenditure in the fiscal year prior to the war. These costs had been partially paid by the issuance of special bonds. At the peace settlement Japan was awarded an indemnity of 360 million yen, payable in sterling, but this amount was not sufficient to meet the needs of the expansionist program resulting from that war. On the other hand, Japan had won considerable prestige abroad by its quick victory in 1895. In 1897, it strengthened its financial position further by adoption of the gold standard and sought assistance overseas. During the next six years it marketed abroad domestic bonds totaling 93 million yen and floated a 10-million-pound loan in London. When war broke out with Russia in 1904, foreign borrowing rapidly increased. Between 1904 and 1913, sterling and franc loans from Britain and France aggregated 145 million pounds and 650 million francs. The net inflow of capital in the form of loans, indemnities, and investments from 1896 to 1913 equaled more than 1.6 billion yen, which was used largely to cover deficits caused by heavy military expenditures. As is shown in Table 4, the net deficit balance of international payments in the decade 1904–1913 equaled 1.08 billion yen.[6]

TABLE 4

BALANCE OF CURRENT INTERNATIONAL PAYMENTS OF THE JAPANESE EMPIRE, 1873–1936
(MILLIONS OF YEN)

	1873–1895	1896–1903	1904–1913	1914–1919	1920–1929	1930–1936
Net balance of current transactions and gold			*–1,083*	*2,431*	*–2,272*	*1,302*
Merchandise trade	*30*	*–355*	*– 707*	*1,198*	*–4,216*	*– 538*
Invisibles			*– 436*	*1,838*	*1,897*	*1,032*
Interest and dividends	–25	– 41	– 637	– 314	– 603	– 665
Income on undertakings and services abroad			274	441	1,094	1,049
Freight receipts			252	1,357	1,424	968
Government payments abroad			– 330	166	– 344	– 660
Other			4	187	326	340
Gold	*72*	*– 62*	*60*	*– 604*	*– 452*	*808*

These strains on the nation's finances were reflected in the instability of its financial institutions. For example, in 1899 an imminent financial panic was avoided by the outbreak of the Boxer Uprising in China. When the Japanese financial world learned of the siege of the foreign legations at Peking, it rallied to this challenge to the nation's prestige abroad. After 1900, however, financial conditions worsened as a result of a cumulative unfavorable trade balance which caused a heavy loss in gold specie. Furthermore, the limitless issuance of convertible loans also weakened the financial market. Annual military appropriations had continued to rise by about 10 per cent until they were equivalent to the cost of the war with China (230 million yen.) The breaking point had been reached so that a run on the Ōsaka Bank on April 16, 1901, culminated in numerous bank failures and was followed by general economic inactivity for the next two years.

But financial conditions were not serious enough to cause despair. Despite the increased threat of war with Russia, further financial crises were avoided. Practically the entire nation was convinced that such a war was inevitable and a part of Japan's destiny; so it willingly bore the burden of war preparation. Increases in government expenses were partially met by greater revenue. In 1899 a new tax law was promulgated which increased tax returns. Furthermore, under the terms of the new treaties with the Western powers, which went into effect the same year, Japan had acquired tariff autonomy which increased the income from the new tariffs. Additional funds were available from the increase in total currency. This stood at approximately 201 million yen in 1890, rose 30 per cent during the next five years, had risen to 317 million in 1900, and climbed another 48 per cent to a total of 469 million by 1906.[7]

The costs of the Russo-Japanese war, which were estimated at about two billion yen, placed an even heavier strain on the nation's finances. Furthermore, the decline in war orders and the expenditures of huge sums on nonproductive enterprises produced an unsound stock market. Stocks began to decline; new bubble companies went bankrupt; more banks closed in 1907 and 1908. The unfavorable trade balance continued at a yearly average of over 50 million yen. In contrast to the financial situation in 1894, the outlook in the summer of 1914 was precarious.

Industrial Development

The growth and consolidation of the Empire during the quarter century after the promulgation of the Constitution could not have been achieved without a phenomenal growth in industry. In the period prior to 1890, industrial expansion had resulted from two causes. In the first place, the government had initiated the construction of model factories and the exploitation of resources in the homeland. Many of these plants had then been sold to private capitalists at unusually low prices in order to encourage private capital to form companies. In the second place, private investment had sought new sources of profit. But industrial expansion in old fields and the mushrooming of new enterprises from 1890 to 1915 was not so much the result of direct government participation in industry as the expansion of the private sector resulting from increased government spending.[8]

An analysis of Table 5 will illustrate both the extent and the characteristics of national growth during the period under discussion. From 1888–1892, near the middle of the period described as Japan's initial modern economic growth, to 1913–1917, a decade after the beginning of its differential structure, the average annual production index for textiles rose more than sixfold, from 3.6 to 22.3. In comparably new industries the growth was even more phenomenal: metals 1.3 to 20.1; machinery 2.7 to 20.8. All manufacturing tripled.

After Japan defeated Russia in 1905, several factors produced a slightly different type of industrial growth. In the first place, foreign capital was readily available which permitted the growth of new industries. Secondly, some industries had progressed to the point where their products could compete successfully with foreign manufactures. These interests sought to preserve the domestic market for their own goods through tariff protection. Furthermore, the needs of the new

TABLE 5

PRODUCTION INDEXES FOR MANUFACTURING INDUSTRIES: ANNUAL AVERAGES (1935 = 100)[9]
(1888–1940)

	Foods	Textiles	Forest Products	Chemicals	Stone, Clay, and Glass	Metals	Machinery	Miscellaneous	All Manufacturing
1888–1892	28.78	3.62	26.48	5.07	4.45	1.32	2.72	11.15	8.67
1893–1897	32.31	7.28	32.69	7.17	6.00	2.78	4.41	13.65	11.66
1898–1902	36.85	10.41	43.42	8.89	6.74	4.27	4.22	17.99	14.31
1903–1907	37.08	11.75	46.25	11.30	9.55	5.09	6.64	27.35	16.13
1908–1912	41.33	14.51	48.41	11.95	15.48	10.17	12.87	32.69	19.47
1913–1917	49.46	22.34	54.91	19.94	20.52	20.16	20.78	40.66	27.84
1918–1922	67.96	33.83	62.28	29.32	32.53	24.63	46.32	42.45	40.26
1923–1927	82.56	45.84	64.72	38.23	50.09	32.54	33.50	55.17	48.22
1928–1932	88.02	64.32	71.80	54.63	61.03	46.90	45.91	73.11	62.71
1933–1937	95.73	97.25	115.47	101.78	96.98	86.79	94.93	98.16	96.13
1938–1940	115.98	96.22	127.21	157.34	147.51	145.52	272.68	122.17	141.30

colonial territories of Formosa and Southern Sakhalin created new challenges to industry. Finally, the successful elimination of the threat of both Chinese and Russian economic and political control over Korea opened vast opportunities for venture capital in that area. No other power was in a position to challenge Japan economically in the exploitation of this market of some 15 million persons. Little Korean capital was available to profit from the use of the rich resources in that peninsular kingdom, which was over half the size of Japan.

There were new indications that Japan had reached a new level of self-sufficiency. Japanese textiles were beginning to compete favorably in the Chinese market with British, American, and Indian goods. Battleships, steamships, and steam locomotives were no longer purchased abroad but made at home. As one authority expressed it:

> The Russo-Japanese war was a turning point in the history of Japanese industry. After the war, the newly started or developed industries were extended more than ever owing to the post-bellum restoration. The governmnt encouraged the use of domestic products which resulted in the establishment of Japanese industry on an equal footing with their foreign rivals.[10]

But progress toward a self-sufficient economy, particularly in view of expanded military appropriations, was retarded by deficiencies in natural resources such as iron and coking coal. This situation, in turn, had resulted in a late start in iron and steel production. Nevertheless, political necessity, such as the Russian threat in Korea, had forced the government to build its own iron and steel plants. For example, in 1901 the

Yawata Iron Works was built in northern Kyūshū at a cost of 43 million yen. For many years it was the main steel-producing plant in the entire Empire and its completion had a pronounced effect on the total production of iron and finished steel. In 1896, 26,000 tons of pig iron were produced annually. By 1906, after the Yawata works were operating, the figure had risen to 145,000 tons; by 1913 it had increased to 243,000 tons. Since the general demands of industry for iron increased with over-all expansion, however, the domestic smelting plants were able to meet only 48 per cent of requirements.

The steel industry had a similar history. When the war ended with China, this industry had hardly been born. By 1896 only 1,000 tons were produced, which equaled only 0.5 per cent of domestic needs. By the end of the war with Russia, however, the Yawata steel mills had been going full blast and total annual steel production was 69,000 tons. By 1913 this figure had risen to 255,000 tons. But this amount was sufficient to take care of only one-third of the nation's demand for steel.

In the important supplementary coal mining industry, the coal mines near Nagasaki had been developed in the 1860's. Thus by 1894, over 2.5 million tons of coal were mined yearly and ten years later the total had climbed to 8 million tons. In another ten years, by 1913, the total production of 22.3 million tons was sufficient to permit the export of 3 million tons.[11] The production of other minerals also increased rapidly, the total in 1913 equaling four and a half times that of 1897. Thus, by 1915, although Japan had only limited iron ore deposits and poor coking coal, important advances had been made toward supplying finished iron and steel needs.

As for the other heavy industries, it has been indicated previously that attempts were made to encourage the rapid growth of shipbuilding, as well as that of shipping companies, through direct government subsidies. Government yards at Nagasaki and Kōbe were transferred to private ownership and subsidies were paid on all goods shipped in vessels which were over 700 tons and which had been built in Japanese shipyards. Since this policy did little to increase the shipbuilding industry, a double subsidy of 40 yen per ton of cargo was offered to owners of ships built in local yards. The cumulative effect of this direct support from the government was a rapid increase in the tonnage of ships launched and of the percentage of the foreign trade carried in Japanese bottoms. Whereas in 1898 there was an annual average launching of a total of 10,000 tons of ships over 100 tons displacement, by 1909 the launchings totaled 50,000 tons yearly. This tonnage amounted to half of the current domestic output of durable goods. Moreover, as will be observed from Table 6, there was a marked shift in the proportion of the total exports and imports carried in Japanese ships. In 1893, only 7 per cent of ex-

TABLE 6

TRENDS TOWARD SELF-SUFFICIENCY IN SHIPPING AND SHIPBUILDING [12]

Year	Average Annual Tonnage Launched Ships Over 100 Tons	Percentage of Exports Carried in Japanese Ships	Percentage of Imports Carried in Japanese Ships	Percentage Japanese Tonnage Entering Ports	Percentage Foreign Masters, Engineers, and Navigators on Japan Mail Line
1893	10,000	7	9	14	40
1903		40	34	38	
1909	50,000				
1913		52	47	51	25

ports and 9 per cent of imports were carried in national ships. By 1913, the proportion had risen to nearly half of all foreign trade. In only two decades, therefore, Japan had reached the halfway mark in having met its shipping needs even in the face of an ever larger total in foreign trade.

The significance of the increasing importance of durable equipment and its changing composition is apparent also from the statistics available for domestic capital formation in this field and for the composition of output of this type of equipment. In the first place, in the decade of 1892–1901, private investment averaged 71 million yen of which only 10 million yen was for durable goods. In the 1912–1921 decade, these figures had risen to 615 and 253 respectively. Total government investment for the same decades equaled 91 and 546 million yen. Of these latter amounts, durable goods amounted to 41 and 290 million yen. In other words, private investments had increased nine times while the durable goods proportion had multiplied twenty-five times. The increase in government investment had been sixfold and durable goods accounted for half of the total.[13]

An analysis of the composition of the output of durable goods during this period is also revealing. As indicated in Table 7, as late as 1909, well over half of the total output (61.8 per cent) was in transportation, of which shipbuilding accounted for 92 per cent. Engines and turbines and industrial machinery each comprised 12 per cent of the total and electrical equipment and optical and scientific equipment divided the remainder about evenly. By 1919, transportation had risen to nearly 69 per cent with shipbuilding taking a notably less proportion of that amount. Engines and turbines fell off to 7 per cent and industrial machinery rose to 14. Electrical equipment remained constant and optics and scientific equipment fell to 2 per cent.

TABLE 7

COMPOSITION OF DOMESTIC OUTPUT OF DURABLE EQUIPMENT INCLUDING MILITARY *

Year	Engines and Turbines	Industrial Machinery and Equipment	Textile Machinery as a Percentage of Column 2	Metal Process Machinery as a Percentage of Column 2	Electrical Equipment	Transportation	Ship Building as a Percentage of Column 6	Optical and Scientific Equipment
	(1)	(2)	(3)	(4)	(5)	(6)	(7)	(8)
1909	12.2	12.8	26.3	2.6	7.1	61.8	91.8	6.1
1919	7.3	14.5	27.9	8.1	7.1	68.7	83.7	2.3
1929	8.3	22.3	28.1	5.2	20.5	42.4	26.0	6.5
1939	10.0	39.6	4.4	33.8	21.2	23.8	28.9	5.5

* Reprinted with permission of the Macmillan Company from *Capital Formation in Japan 1868–1940* by Henry Rosovsky (New York: The Free Press of Glencoe, Inc., 1961), Table 51 on Composition of Domestic Output of Durable Equipment.

As the Meiji Period progressed, the textile industry became particularly important in the nation's economy and in foreign trade. Both spinning and weaving had been significant industries at an early date, but it was not until after the defeat of China in 1895 that Japanese cloth captured the markets in Korea and China. The large population of otherwise underemployed women was easily absorbed into the industry which retained many characteristics of a feudal society. The mill owners took a proprietary and paternalistic attitude toward their employees. The girls were often under contract for a year or more. They were housed in company dormitories, ate in company restaurants, and had their entire lives regulated by the plant according to a rigid schedule. Bells sounded not only at the close of work but at reveille and at taps.

While this type of labor was cheap and docile, the lack of raw materials increased production costs. For example, raw cotton had to be imported from China, India, or the United States. Nevertheless, the finished product competed with those from Lancashire or southern Europe. In fact, Japan had the highest rate of growth of cotton fabrics exports in the world. By 1918, Japan exported more cotton fabrics than the United States and in the 1930's surpassed those of Great Britain. In the formative years of the textile industry in Japan, the decrease in the number of spinning companies was in no sense a sign of weakness; it merely indicated a concentration of ownership in the hands of comparatively few companies, each of which increased in size. From 1893 to 1913, the total spindles grew from 382,000 to 2,415,000 and the yearly cotton yarn production rose from 88 million pounds to 607 million pounds. Similar trends appeared in the silk industry, as silk thread exports became one of the largest items in overseas trade. (See Table 8.) Finally, light

TABLE 8

JAPANESE TEXTILE DEVELOPMENT [14]
(1893–1913)

Year	Cotton Spindles (in thousands)	Cotton Yarn (in million lbs.)	Spinning Companies	Power Looms	Silk Thread (in thousand *kan*)	Silk Exports (in thousand *kan*)
1893	382	88	40	900	1,110	662
1903	1,381	317	51	5,000	1,924	1,110
1907	1,504	393	42	9,000		
1913	2,415	607	44	24,000	3,375	2,563

industries, and especially textiles, were a special characteristic of Japan's industrial growth. For example, in 1895, light industries accounted for over 80 per cent of industries' contribution to the national income. By 1930, the proportion was nearly 60 per cent. Of these amounts, textile production accounted for one-fourth in 1895 and one-fifth in 1930.

Providing constant access to important sources of raw materials, such as oil, iron, coking coal, commercial salt, and raw cotton, could be assured, the base was rapidly being laid in heavy industries, in utilities, and in consumers' goods industries for an economy capable of continual growth. So long as these resources were not within the limits of the Japanese Empire, they could be secured in one of two ways. Profits from exports of raw silk or finished goods could be used to purchase necessary imports of food and of raw materials for processing. Alternatively, territories in which essential natural resources existed in abundance, such as Korea, Manchuria, or North China, could be placed under direct or indirect Japanese control by diplomacy or by force of arms. In reality, both of these alternatives were used. As political unrest threatened accessibility to raw materials in East and Southeast Asia, heavier reliance was placed on territorial expansion than on other methods.

FOREIGN TRADE

The last basic factor which had a determining influence on the strength of the economic base of the new Empire was the character of foreign trade. With the increased need for greater imports of raw materials to supply the new industrial complex, new and expanding markets for finished goods had to be found if an adverse effect on international payments was to be avoided and if the nation's finances were to be kept intact. As can be seen in Table 9, except for the period from 1885–1894 prior to the outbreak of World War I, the steady increase in exports failed to keep up with imports essential for the modernization process. As one would expect, the resultant unfavorable balance

TABLE 9

GROWTH OF TRADE OF JAPAN PROPER WITH FOREIGN COUNTRIES, KOREA AND FORMOSA:[15] ANNUAL AVERAGES
(Unit values: 1868–1955 in million yen; 1956–1968 in hundred million yen)

Annual Averages	Exports	Imports	Balance
1868–1869	14	16	— 2
1870–1874	18	27	— 9
1875–1879	25	35	— 10
1880–1884	33	31	— 2
1885–1889	55	47	8
1890–1894	86	84	2
1895–1899	163	206	— 43
1900–1904	274	308	— 34
1905–1909	413	468	— 55
1910–1914	606	650	— 44
1915–1919	1,663	1,423	240
1920–1924	1,875	2,440	— 575
1925–1929	2,494	2,849	— 355
1930–1934	2,058	2,212	— 154
1935–1939	4,029	3,927	102
1940–1944 *	4,091	3,646	445
1945–1949 *	58,318	92,269	— 33,951
1950–1954	458,104	709,409	—251,305
1955–1959	9,866	11,962	— 2,096
1960–1964	18,239	22,043	— 3,804
1965	30,426	29,408	1,018
1966 (fiscal year)	36,190	35,407	783
1967 (fiscal year)	38,793	43,409	— 4,616
1968 (fiscal year)	49,320	47,880	1,440

* No figures available for 1944 and 1945.

in foreign trade was particularly pronounced in quinquennials which included the wars against China and against Russia. Not until the first full year of World War I (1915) was this trend dramatically reversed. As we shall see later, this fact was a strong force in saving Japan from financial collapse.

An analysis of the changing structure of this foreign trade reflects the extent to which Japan was shifting from its first phase of modern economic growth to a differential structure. (See Table 10.) For example, in the period 1868–1872, the value of goods from the primary sector—food, drink, and raw materials—totaled nearly as much as the value of all

TABLE 10

STRUCTURE OF FOREIGN TRADE [16]
(Percentage of Total Value)

	Food and Drink		Raw Materials		Semimanufactured Goods		Finished Goods		Other	
Years	Import	Export	Import	Export	Import	Export	Import	Export	Import	Export
1868–1872	29.0	25.4	4.1	23.1	20.2	40.0	44.5	1.9	2.2	8.8
1878–1882	14.8	37.1	3.5	11.6	29.9	40.4	48.6	7.2	3.2	3.7
1893–1897	20.8	16.8	22.7	10.3	19.1	43.3	35.1	26.2	2.3	3.4
1903–1907	23.5	11.9	33.0	9.1	16.7	45.3	25.5	31.1	1.3	2.6
1908–1912	12.0	11.1	44.3	9.2	18.9	48.1	24.1	30.5	.7	1.1

other exports. Conversely, there was a heavy demand for finished goods (44.5 per cent) and semimanufactured products from abroad to meet the needs of the new military machine and of an expanding industrial structure. After the Sino-Japanese War, the value of exports of manufactured goods was equal to the value of food, drink, and raw materials shipped overseas; semimanufactured goods equaled 43 per cent of total exports. Finished goods purchased abroad still led the list of items imported.

From 1908 to 1912, the period before World War I, the value of imports of finished goods had dropped to 24 per cent and raw materials were by far the largest import item (44 per cent). As for exports, one-third of their value was in finished goods and nearly a half was in semifinished products.

In other words, the mills and factories which had already been built were now in need of raw materials such as iron ore, coking coal, and cotton to keep the machinery and mills operating. To a large extent the domestic demands for consumers' goods were met by the products from these mills, and their surplus was shipped abroad. But despite this increase in exports, the national economy had two weaknesses: exports had not been able to keep up with imports, and a large proportion of these exports was in a single item, raw silk. By 1913, silk thread amounted to 30 per cent of exports. If the bottom should drop out of the price of raw silk, Japan's economic plight would immediately become precarious.

Finally, the distribution of Japanese overseas trade was showing new tendencies which reflected political as well as economic developments. In the year prior to the Sino-Japanese War, exports were almost evenly divided among the United States, Europe, and Asia, with China, including Manchuria and Hong Kong, acounting for 25 per cent of the total. Imports for the same year came largely from Europe and Asia, especially the United Kingdom (about one-third the total). China and India were the next largest sources while the United States supplied a scant 7 per cent. Ten years later, however, China took an unquestioned lead in exports, climbing from 25 to 30 per cent; the United States moved into second place with 26 per cent; and the United Kingdom fell to less than 5 per cent. As for imports, in 1913 Asia became the main source, supplying over half of the total. India accounted for the largest amount for any single country (about 21 per cent), followed by the United Kingdom and the United States with almost exactly 15 per cent each. In other words, Japan was rapidly developing a primary dependence on Asia for imports, though China had not yet become as important in this respect as either the United Kingdom or the United States. Furthermore, since over half the markets for all exports were to be found in Asia, its political stability became of paramount concern to Japan.[17]

In 1914, the overall economic picture was far gloomier than a quarter of a century earlier. For example, the population was beginning to show an accelerated rate of increase but production of rice in the main islands had slowed almost to a halt. The disproportionate share of taxes borne by the farmer drove him either to greater indebtedness or to tenancy. The country had survived the rigors of the wars against both China and Russia, and added important outposts to the Empire, but at a heavy financial burden. This fact, together with the cumulative effects of an excess of imports over exports appeared in the rise of commodity prices, in a larger amount of currency in circulation, and in the net deficit balance of international payments which had reached 1.1 billion yen. The spate of new companies and factories which had sprouted between the two wars had helped Japan become more self-sufficient. Complete economic independence was impossible, however, in view of scarcities in iron, coking coal, oil, commercial salt, and staple food. Many of the new industries contributed to a healthier foreign trade structure, but Japan seemed unable by its own efforts to eliminate the annual unfavorable balance of foreign trade. An economic basis of empire had been built, but it rested on a shaky foundation.

The outbreak of World War I in the summer of 1914 immediately changed Japan's economic status. Japan's limited military operations throughout the war put no special strain on the nation's economy. Furthermore, the immediate purchases by the Allies of Japanese goods and services in the last four months of 1914 were almost sufficient to bring that year's total exports even with imports. The unfavorable trade balance had been cut to a mere 5 million yen. In 1915, the favorable trade balance of 176 million yen was greater than the combined deficit in foreign trade for the previous four and a half years. Just as Japan had benefited politically in China in May, 1915, from the preoccupation of the European powers in the war (see Chapter 13), so it gained financially and economically from the continuation of hostilities. Any misgivings which the industrialists or politicians might have had as to Japan's future were dispelled by the profits derived from both military and economic participation in the war on the side of the Allies.

In its own war against China in 1894–1895 and against Russia in 1904–1905, Japan had acquired new colonial territory and had gained prestige. New profits again appeared from war in 1915. Within two decades Japan had successfully increased and consolidated the Empire as a result of three wars in which it had participated. By 1915, the last one was not yet over but it was fast becoming more profitable and less costly to Japan than any of the others. Consequently, it became increasingly difficult to dissuade even the most "liberal" Japanese that war did not pay.

If in the future, the leading world powers agreed to disarm, history had taught Japan that it should be willing to follow their lead providing it did not weaken itself in relation to the other powers. On the other hand, if international conditions created a changed atmosphere and any important nation resorted to aggression to achieve its objectives, past experience had taught Japan the value of acting in its own self-interest. In any event, the establishment of its hegemony over Eastern Asia had been accepted by practically all groups within the nation as a steadfast principle of foreign policy. If any foreign power, particularly a Western power, failed to recognize Japan's special prerogatives on the Asiatic mainland, it would have to be forced to do so. In the quarter century after 1915, therefore, nothing was to be permitted to interfere with the emergence of Japan as the leader in Greater East Asia.

Notes

1. This process, which economists describe as "the creation of the differential structure," is characterized by the development of a gap between the traditional sector and the modern sector of the economy. The rate of the former declines while that of the latter increases. In their study of Japan's economic growth during the past century, Professors Ohkawa and Rosovsky have divided the period as follows:

A. 1868–1905: First Phase of Modern Economic Growth
   1) Transition 1868–1885
   2) Initial Modern Economic Growth 1885–1905
B. 1906–1952: Second Phase of Modern Economic Growth
   3) Differential Structure: Creation 1906–1930
   Differential Structure: Economic and Political Consequences 1931–1952

Studies are still progressing (as of 1970) on Japan's gross national product and rate of growth. Professor Rosovsky's most recent estimates indicate a

3.4 per cent growth from 1889 to 1905 and 3.7 per cent from 1905–1919. Those readers wishing to pursue further the problem of the growth rate of Japan are referred to Kazushi Ohkawa and Henry Rosovsky, "A Century of Japanese Economic Growth," in William W. Lockwood (ed.), *The State and Economic Enterprise in Japan* (Princeton: Princeton University Press, 1965), pp. 47–92, and their forthcoming book *A Century of Economic Growth;* James Nakamura, *Agricultural Production and the Economic Development of Japan 1873–1922* (Princeton: Princeton University Press, 1966); William W. Lockwood, *The Economic Development of Japan: Growth and Structural Change 1868–1938* (Princeton: Princeton University Press, 1968), and Lawrence Klein and Kazushi Ohkawa (eds.), *Economic Growth: The Japanese Experience Since the Meiji Era* (Homewood, Ill.: The Dorsey Press, 1968).

2. For a concise analysis of fiscal policy in this period and the proportion of expenditures for both the functional operations of government and for services, see Harry T. Oshima, "Meiji Fiscal Policy and Economic Progress," in Lockwood (ed.), *op. cit.*, pp. 353–89. For estimates of Japanese national wealth in terms of both private and government capital investment, see Henry Rosovsky, *Capital Formation in Japan, 1868–1940* (New York: The Free Press of Glencoe, Inc., 1961).

3. Sources for statistics in Table 3 are as follows: Column 1, Ohkawa Kazushi (ed.), *Chōki Keizai Tōkei: Nōrin* (Tokyo: Tōyō Keizaishi Shimposha, 1966), IX, pp. 166–68. For the years 1963–1967 from Bureau of Statistics, *Nihon Tōkei Nenkan, 1968* (Japan Statistical Yearbook; Tokyo: Prime Minister's Office, 1969), p. 112.

Column 2, estimated by dividing the average annual rice production in each quinquennial by the average annual paddy field area for the same periods. For years prior to 1943 from Ohkawa Kazushi (ed.), *op. cit.*, pp. 166–69 and 217; for 1943–1967 see Bureau of Statistics, *Nihon Tōkei Nenkan, 1953* (Tokyo: 1952), p. 96; *ibid., 1963* (Tokyo: 1964), p. 90; and *ibid., 1968* (Tokyo: 1969), p. 112.

Column 3, annual averages to 1948 from Bureau of Statistics, *Nōrin Shō Ruinen Tōkeihyō 1868–1953* (Department of Agriculture and Forestry, Yearly Statistics; Tokyo: Department of Agriculture, 1955), pp. 160–61. For years from 1948–1967, *Nihon Tōkei Nenkan, 1963, op. cit.*, pp. 260–61; and *Nihon Tōkei Nenkan, 1968, op. cit.*, p. 308. As rice exports are not listed after 1948, net imports of rice will be slightly under the figures given for the most recent years.

Column 4: derived from columns 1 and 3.

Column 5, annual averages to 1962 from Statistics Bureau, Bank of Japan, *Meiji Iko Hōmpō Shūyō Keizai Tōkei* (Tokyo: Bank of Japan, 1966), pp. 12–13; for 1963–1967, *Nihon Tōkei Nenkan, 1968, op. cit.*, p. 11.

Column 6: Column 1 divided by column 5.

Column 7: Column 4 divided by column 5.

As all statistics after 1953, except those in *Chōki Keizai Tōkei,* which includes data up to 1962, are given in the metric system, the following formula was used to transform the figures into *koku* and *chō:*

6.67 *koku* equal 1 metric ton of brown rice (*gemmai*)
1.0083 *chō* equals 1 hectare

For comparative purposes and illustrative of the differences in estimates in the early years of yield and production growth between those of *Chōki Keizai, op. cit.*, and of Professor Nakamura, see Table 2, above.

4. Professor Lockwood points out that a slower population growth would have allowed more of the natural resources and man-made assets to have been devoted to the requirements of technical progress and an overall higher living standard. While such a development might have taken place, it would not necessarily have occurred. Lockwood, *Economic Development . . . , op. cit.*, p. 139.

5. Ryoichi Ishii, *Population Pressure and Economic Life in Japan* (London: P. S. King and Sons, 1937), pp. 39 ff.

6. Lockwood, *Economic Development . . . , op. cit.*, pp. 254 ff. Copyright 1954 by Princeton University Press. Table 4 is taken from p. 257 with the permission of the publisher.

7. Bank of Japan, *Keizai Tōkei, op. cit.*, p. 166.

8. Professor Lockwood emphasizes the importance of private capital even in the early period in investments in new enterprises. He states, "After 1882, the state receded into the background as an entrepreneur. Thereafter it confined its own industrial undertakings within Japan to a few strategic industries, notably iron and steel." See Lockwood, *Economic Development . . . , op. cit.*, pp. 234 ff.

9. Adapted from Yuishi's "Pattern of Industrial Output" in Klein and Ohkawa, *op. cit.* pp. 102–03, with permission of the publisher.

10. Uchisaburo Kobayashi, *The Basic Industries and Social History of Japan* (New Haven: Yale University Press, 1930), p. 170.

11. Japan continued to be largely self-sufficient in low-grade bituminous coal. High-grade coking coal had to be shipped from overseas.

12. George C. Allen, *A Short Economic History of Modern Japan, 1867–1937* (with a supplementary chapter on economic recovery and expansion, 1945–1960) (New York: Frederick A. Praeger, Inc., 2nd revised edition, 1963), pp. 76–77 and 86.

13. Rosovsky, *op. cit.*, p. 2.

14. Allen, *op. cit.*, p. 65.

15. Lockwood, *Economic Development . . . , op. cit.*, p. 313; and Bank of Japan, *Keizai Tōkei, op. cit.*, pp. 278–79. Figures for 1966–1968 are calculated from statistics in *Nihon Keizai Shimbun,* May 27, 1969.

16. Allen, *op. cit.*, p. 181.

17. Lockwood, *Economic Development . . . , op. cit.*, p. 395.

PART IV

LEADERSHIP IN GREATER EAST ASIA 1915-1941

Our best policy of action is to make skillful use of the War to erect a lasting national policy for the Empire.

From a report of the
Japanese Army Chief of Staff
October, 1917

CHRONOLOGY

1915–1941

1915		Resignation of Foreign Minister Katō
1916	October	General Terauchi becomes Premier
1917		Secret Treaty with Allies, reference Shantung and Pacific Islands
1918		Siberian Expedition
	September	First party cabinet under Hara
	November	Armistice in Europe
1919		Paris Peace Conference
	June	Versailles Treaty
1921		Washington Disarmament Conference
	November	Assassination of Premier Hara
1924		Japanese Exclusion Act
1925		Universal Suffrage for men
		Peace Preservation Law
		Shidehara's conciliatory policy toward Russia
1927		General Tanaka is Premier
1928		Murder of Chang Tso-lin in Manchuria
1930		London Naval Treaty
	November	Shooting of Hamaguchi
1931	September 18	Manchurian Incident
1932	February	Formation of State of Manchukuo
		Assassinations of Inouye, Dan, and Inukai
1933		Occupation of Inner Mongolia by the Japanese
		Tangku Truce
1934		Rise of Nationalist philosophy under Araki
1936	February 26	Coup by young officers in Army
		Anti-Comintern Pact
1937	June	First Konoye Cabinet
	July 7	Incident at Marco Polo Bridge
		Widespread war in China
	December	Rape of Nanking
1938		Enactment of National Mobilization Law
		New Order in East Asia
1940		Tripartite Treaty of Alliance
1941	April	United States–Japanese negotiations begin
	July	Japan decides to move southward
		United States freezes Japanese assets
	September 6	Imperial Conferences support war plan
	October	General Tōjō becomes Premier
	November 3	Final decision for war
	December 7	Japanese attack on Pearl Harbor

15

The Fruits of Victory in World War I

From the previous discussion of the manner in which the Japanese Empire was extended and consolidated, it is clear that one of the primary concerns of all groups within the nation was to establish their country as the undisputed leader of Eastern Asia. During the first year of World War I, Japan had moved quickly to replace Germany in China and the Pacific Ocean. It had reinforced its new privileged position on the Asiatic mainland by forcing China to sign the Twenty-One Demands. (See page 293 above.) Its chief interest in the war and in the peace settlement continued to be to improve its economic and political position on the Asiatic continent and its strategic advantage in the Pacific. The secret negotiations with Russia and the Allies, the *rapprochement* with the United States, the special Nishihara loans arranged with Chinese leaders, the agreements extracted from China in 1918, and the Siberian Expedition were all undertaken with these objectives in view. The demands which Japan presented at the Paris Peace Conference were also dictated by this basic policy of expansion.

Domestic Political Scene

A brief description of the domestic political scene is necessary, however, before considering the negotiations of the secret treaties with Russia and the other Allies. As noted above, when the Twenty-One Demands were served on China, in 1915, Ōkuma Shigenobu, one of the earliest supporters of the concept of party government, was Prime Minister and his protégé, Katō Kōmei, was Foreign Minister. On the matter of Japan strengthening its position toward China, the views of both of these men coincided with those of the military leaders who sought support for expanded military appropriations. Ōkuma and Katō were severely criticized, however, for their political tactics. In the election in March, 1915, which was marked by extensive bribery and interference by the Home

Minister, Ōkuma's supporters in the Lower House increased at the expense of the Seiyūkai membership. Nevertheless, the election scandals embittered the Seiyūkai against the Cabinet and seriously damaged Ōkuma's prestige.

Furthermore, the Elder Statesmen, and especially Yamagata, were always alert for an opportunity to embarrass and discredit the politicians. Consequently, Yamagata was the leading critic of the Cabinet, especially of the methods it used in implementing its policies. Specifically, he became angry at Foreign Minister Katō for having ignored a memorandum on policy toward China which he had sent the Foreign Minister, and for the latter's refusal to inform the *Genrō* of his plan to issue an ultimatum to China on May 7, 1915. As a result, he was forced to resign in August to draw some of the criticism away from his friend and protector, Prime Minister Ōkuma.[1]

But the causes of the struggle between the oligarchs and the leaders of the "political parties" were so deep-seated that the former were not satiated by Katō's resignation. Yamagata had always been inexorably opposed to parliamentary government and still believed that it was against the spirit of the Constitution and the best interests of the country to select the leader of the majority party as Premier. Consequently, when Ōkuma talked of turning the Cabinet over to the leadership of his former Foreign Minister, Katō, the issue was clearly drawn. Yamagata immediately accepted this recommendation as a challenge to the power and prestige of the oligarchs and especially to himself. He seized the initiative and won support for his own candidate, General Terauchi Masatake, the Governor-General of Korea. Through his friends, Yamagata had the Governor recalled. In early October, 1916, while Ōkuma's resignation was pending, Terauchi was ordered to form a new Cabinet. This simple maneuver forestalled the appointment of Katō and signaled once more the victory of the conservative oligarchs over the party leaders.

General Terauchi Masatake formed a "transcendental Cabinet" with many of its members coming from the House of Peers. He failed to win the confidence of the politicians and within a year was faced with the danger of a vote of nonconfidence. Consequently, he was forced to rely on the support of Hara and the Seiyūkai members of the Lower House to survive. Terauchi continued in this precarious position until he was toppled from office by the extensive Rice Riots in the summer of 1918.[2]

Although the nation had profited to an unprecedented extent from the demands of the Allies for its goods and services during World War I, this new prosperity had not reached down to the farmer and urban worker. Further, real wages had been decreasing with the increase in prices of commodities, especially rice. Government efforts to control the situation failed. From July, 1914, to August, 1918, when the riots started, the Tokyo price index had doubled. The riots, which had begun in the provinces, swiftly spread to the cities. On August 15, they had reached such proportions in Tokyo that troops were called out to quell them. Before they started to subside several days later, an estimated 700,000 persons had rioted in 36 cities and 130 towns throughout the nation.

As a direct result of this defiance of central authority, the selection of a new Prime Minister was a crucial matter.[3] It was further complicated by the changes which the passage of time had made among the *Genrō* and in the availability of persons of sufficient stature and capability to become Prime Minister. As for the *Genrō,* since Inouye's death in 1915, they were reduced to three members, Yamagata, Matsukata, and Saionji. Besides these three men, Ōkuma and Yamamoto were the only previous Prime Ministers still alive. From the recent showing of their Cabinets, neither of these last two men seemed capable of guiding the government under existing pressures. Neither Yamagata nor Matsukata desired to take a direct or active leadership again so they once more turned to Saionji. When he refused to consider the appointment, Hara Kei, the leader of the Seiyūkai which had more seats in Parliament than any other party, was the logical choice. Yamagata had been impressed with his astuteness and finally accepted the inevitability of the most powerful party directing the affairs of state under Hara's guidance. Thus the three Elder Statesmen recommended that he be appointed.[4]

The three most significant facts about his selection were that he was from the north of Japan, was a commoner, and was the leader of the strongest political party. As noted earlier, Hara had worked his way to the top as a loyal member of the Seiyūkai party. He had consistently been an advocate of party cabinets and made numerous compromises during the past years to achieve that end. He immediately appointed Seiyūkai members to all of the posts of his Cabinet, except the Ministers of War and Navy, who were selected, as before, by their colleagues.

Although his Cabinet came closer than any previous one to being a party cabinet, as noted later, its operation left much to be desired compared to those in other parliamentary governments. During its first year, his Cabinet was able to create considerable internal stability and his basic foreign policy was largely the same as his predecessor's.

Consolidation of Gains Through Secret Treaties, 1916–1917

From the outbreak of the war to the Versailles Treaty of 1919, the basic theme of Japan's wartime foreign policy remained constant. It was to consolidate and enhance the gains already achieved in the war. Having successfully concluded its negotiations with China, Japan now turned to the West to obtain a closer understanding with the leading Allied and

Associated Powers and with the United States. Negotiations were first started with Russia which resulted in a secret treaty being concluded in July, 1916, whereby the signatories formed a defensive alliance to protect their "vital interests" in China. They agreed to protect China from domination by a third power hostile to them. Thus Japan had assurances of Russia's assistance in preventing third-power interference with the special rights secured through the Twenty-One Demands.

Even before the Bolshevik Revolution in Russia was to annul the benefits which might have been derived from this treaty, negotiations were begun with Great Britain for support for Japan's war claims. On January 27, 1917, the two governments exchanged views on a secret treaty in which each hoped to gain concessions from the other. The British sought support for their claims to the former German islands in the Pacific, south of the equator. Since Germany announced its resumption of unrestricted submarine warfare a few days after the negotiations began, the Allies were anxious to receive both logistical and naval escort support from Japan for the Atlantic and Mediterranean convoys. Furthermore, the Allies were hopeful that Japan would be able to persuade China to break off diplomatic relations with Germany.

In return for these services, Great Britain was willing to support Japan's demands for the former German rights in Shantung and to the Pacific Islands north of the equator. Despite Japan's refusal to comply with all of the Allies' requests, the British Government agreed on February 16, 1917, to:

> . . . support Japan's claims in regards to the disposal of Germany's rights in Shantung and possessions in islands north of the Equator at the Peace Conference, it being understood that the Japanese Government will treat in the same spirit Great Britain's claims to German islands south of the Equator.[5]

Similar assurances were received in secret by Japan from Russia, France, and Italy in exchange for little more than a promise that efforts would be taken to get China to sever relations with the common enemy. Thus the necessary diplomatic agreements had been made with the Allies to assure transfer to Japan at the Peace Conference of those territories which had been acquired by military conquest.

But in the early months of 1917, there was still one important flaw in Japan's diplomatic offensive. No understanding had been reached with the United States. In fact, on the basis of proposals of the American Minister in Peking, the Japanese feared the United States was moving toward active support of China against Japan. So long as this situation obtained, Japan could not be certain that its gains would be verified by the peace treaty. On the other hand, if a successful *rapprochement* could be concluded with the United States, and if no new crises arose in the Far East, Japan could sit back and await Germany's defeat by the other Allies.

There were some real difficulties, however, which prevented Japan and the United States from reaching an understanding. Although the two countries were Allies, financial and economic rivalries in China were full of potential dangers. For example, during the war years, Japan had replaced the Allies as creditors for China and hoped to retain its preferential position. As indicated by the Twenty-One Demands, it considered Shantung, South Manchuria, and Eastern Inner Mongolia to be special spheres in which it had exclusive investment and other rights. When Ishii Kikujirō was dispatched to Washington as head of a special mission to negotiate a settlement, he discovered that President Woodrow Wilson stood firmly behind the concept of the Open Door and equality of economic opportunity in China. The President insisted that Japan's encroachments in China had already violated the high moral principle of China's territorial integrity.

After two months of negotiations in which both sides stood firm, Secretary of State Robert Lansing proposed a general statement of principles which was finally acceptable to both parties. On November 2, 1917, the Lansing–Ishii Agreement was signed. It stated that neither country would infringe on the independence or territorial integrity of China, that they both would adhere to the Open Door and equal opportunity for commerce and industry in China, and that they would not take advantage of its current condition to obtain special rights or privileges which would abridge those of citizens of other states. Furthermore, the United States recognized that "territorial propinquity creates special relations between countries" and hence Japan had special interests in China, especially in areas contiguous to Japanese possessions.[6]

Secretary Lansing had hoped for a much broader agreement but President Wilson would not countenance it. The agreement served as a harmless temporization with each of the signatories interpreting the generalities to suit its own interests. To avoid giving the impression that the United States was abandoning its traditional Open Door Policy for China, the United States announced its intention to join the other powers in a financial consortium in China. Before a final understanding was reached on this subject, however, other more significant events arose in the Far East which required American attention if Japanese expansion was to be prevented from getting out of hand.

The Nishihara Loans

From the diplomatic point of view, the Secret Treaties with the Western powers and the Lansing–Ishii Agreement had secured Japan's flank from attack at the Peace Conference. Presumably, there would be no question about the Allies confirming and supporting Japan's demands after victory. On the other hand, there was the constant danger that unpredictable events, which often had unforeseen consequences, such as the constant shifts within the Chinese government and the Bolshevik Revolution in Russia, might jeopardize the chances of reaping the fruits of victory. Thus, whenever it became apparent to the planners within the government that events might be turned to Japan's advantage, direct action followed. Two of the most important results of such actions, both of which were closely interrelated and had an important bearing on the Paris Peace Conference, were the conclusion of a new series of Sino-Japanese agreements and the formation of an Allied Siberian Expedition in which Japan played the decisive role.

As for the former, during the negotiations of the Secret Treaties, Japan had promised to use its good offices to persuade China to enter the war against Germany. As early as June, 1916, Prime Minister Terauchi had dispatched one of his trusted advisers, Nishihara Kamezō, to China to urge it to sever diplomatic relations with Germany. Nishihara, who was to be a key figure in Sino-Japanese diplomatic and financial negotiations for the next year, secretly established close relations with the Chinese Premier Tuan Ch'i-jui and the pro-Japanese members of his Cabinet. He offered loans to them in exchange for China's entry into World War I. Consequently China declared war against the Central Powers on August 14, 1917. Subsequently, the Japanese government publicly declared that its policy was one of nonintervention in the internal affairs of China, but Nishihara quietly followed an opposite policy.[7]

He constantly sought to bind the two countries together through the use of Japanese capital and technicians in the exploitation of China's natural resources. Between the early part of 1917 and September, 1918, he is reported to have negotiated seven separate loans totaling 145 million yen for the development of the telegraph system, mines, lumbering, and railroads. They were often accompanied by agreements giving Japan special concessions. This personal influence in China of Nishihara, as well as the effects of the large funds at his disposal, must be kept in mind as a specific policy developed toward Siberia and as new political and military agreements were simultaneously made with China.

The Siberian Expedition

The rapid successes of the Russian Revolution and crumbling of the Eastern Front in Europe had led to British speculation on the advisability of asking Japan to intervene in Siberia. The French had proposed that both Japan and the United States should take possession of the Trans-

Siberian Railway at Vladivostok and Harbin, and lead an expedition to Moscow. In the fall of 1917, the General Staff of the Japanese Imperial Army had already made a careful estimate of the problems involved. It had concluded that logistic difficulties made it unwise to undertake a major effort on the Eastern Front. Consequently, Japan agreed with the United States that force should not be used to intervene in Russia against the Bolsheviks. The Imperial Army urged, just as Nishihara recommended, that efforts be concentrated on securing political and economic supremacy in China through the exploitation of natural resources.[8]

But it was one thing for the Army to decline to participate in a campaign in European Russia and quite another to refrain from taking advantage of the Bolshevik Revolution to improve Japan's position in Eastern Siberia or Northern Manchuria. Furthermore, nearly three-quarters of a million tons of Allied war material had accumulated at Vladivostok and would be a valuable prize for the Russian revolutionaries or for the Austrian or German prisoners of war in Siberia. In the hands of an army unfriendly to China or to Japan, these supplies might be a decisive factor in the future peace of East Asia. Consequently, after Japan had rejected outright a British suggestion that the United States be asked to protect this property, the British War Cabinet decided to send a cruiser from Hong Kong to Vladivostok to protect the Allied munitions. When Japan learned of this move, it immediately dispatched two warships to Vladivostok for the avowed purpose of maintaining peace and order and protecting the foreign consular corps. One of the ships arrived on January 12, 1918, to be joined two days later by the British cruiser from Hong Kong. In April, after a robbery of Japanese property and shooting of three Japanese, their marines were landed.[9]

This might have remained only a local incident if events in Siberia had not given the chief Army policy makers the opportunity for which they had been waiting. In February, 1918, an important shift had been made in the planning personnel of the Chief of Staff. General Tanaka Giichi, one of the Army's leading specialists on Russian affairs and currently Vice-Chief of Staff, was appointed chairman of a newly created Siberian War Planning Committee whose purpose was to complete all preparations required for an expedition to Siberia. Tanaka and his Committee recommended that the plight of the foreign residents in Siberia be used as the pretext for sending two divisions into the Maritime Provinces and three into the Trans-Baikal to crush the Bolsheviks. They also recommended the use of anti-Bolshevik forces for this purpose and the conclusion of a military agreement with China. One of the motivations for these recommendations was a deep-seated fear within the General Staff that the United States was becoming increasingly interested in economic resources in the Amur River. The General Staff was anxious, therefore, that Japan move into the region as soon as possible to forestall the United States from doing so. The Foreign Minister approved the recommendation of the Tanaka Committee but the Advisory Council on Foreign Relations insisted that the expedition be undertaken only in self-defense.

In the meantime, Tanaka had pressed forward to obtain an agreement with China for joint Sino-Japanese participation in a Japanese expedition in Siberia. A military agreement of May, 1918, permitted joint planning and tactics, joint use of the transportation system, and the attachment of expert Japanese military advisers to Chinese units. Although the Japanese Army was to operate mainly in North Manchuria, Eastern Mongolia, and Eastern Siberia, this agreement formed a legal basis for its movements within Chinese territory. The first obstacle to a successful Siberian Expedition, mainly, an insecure rear, had been overcome.[10]

At the same time, the United States was apprehensive, on the basis of the moves already made, that Japan would use the unstable conditions in Siberia to assert its hegemony over Siberia and Manchuria. On the other hand, President Wilson was reluctant to become militarily involved in the area. A new element emerged, however, which made President Wilson reverse the negative stand he had been taking against the Allied proposal that intervention in Siberia was advisable. Part of the Czecho-Slovak Army, which was fighting for the independence of its country from Austria-Hungary, had been permitted to leave Russia to return to the Western Front via Siberia and the Pacific. While en route along the Trans-Siberian Railway, this Army had refused to be disarmed, had revolted, and rapidly took over sections of the railway. It soon became the strongest force in Siberia. In June, 1918, it captured Vladivostok and the Czechs immediately received sympathy from the Allies.

Wilson now saw the plight of the Czecho-Slovak Army as a reasonable excuse for the United States to commit a limited number of troops to Siberia. In July, Secretary Lansing suggested to the Japanese Ambassador that the United States and Japan each send 7,000 troops to Vladivostok to protect the Allied supplies there and to assist the Czech Army. In a subsequent formal answer to the Supreme War Council's request for intervention, Wilson gave an ambiguous reply but granted that military action in Russia was admissible to help the Czecho-Slovaks consolidate their forces and to guard military supplies which subsequently might be needed by Russian forces.

Although the American proposal fell short of the wishes of the Supreme War Council and of the recommendations of General Tanaka's Committee, it was accepted by Great Britain and was too intriguing to Japan to be ignored. After bitter debate between the General Staff and members of the Cabinet, on August 1, 1918, it was finally agreed that, in harmony with the Allies, suitable forces would be dispatched to support the Czecho-Slovak forces. To permit as much freedom of movement as possible for its troops, Japan informed the United States that it would be necessary for Japanese troops to advance beyond Vladivostok and to increase these forces in response to circumstances as they developed. It also announced that a total of only 12,000 troops would be sent to Vladivostok and that the Allies would be notified if they were moved westward.[11]

The General Staff was enraged, however, by this apparent independent decision of the Cabinet. It considered itself deprived of a chance to carry on "a great war in Siberia to decide the fate of the nation." Once the expedition was launched in early August, troops flowed into the Chinese Eastern Railway zone and the Amur Valley. By the time of the Armistice, they had concentrated in the Maritime Provinces and Northern Manchuria and totaled 70,000. They had completely outnumbered all of the other Allied Forces and put Japan in *de facto* control of the area.

The Siberian Expedition is a fascinating case study of how the General Staff achieved its objectives in the face of strong national and international opposition. It is equally important as an illustration of power politics at work. While there were small contingents of Allied forces in Vladivostok and the Trans-Siberian Railway was jointly operated, nevertheless, control of the hinterland was in Japanese hands. This situation continued throughout the months of discussion on the peace settlement at Paris. When the issues of racial equality, of Japanese rights in Shantung, and of the Twenty-One Demands were all under discussion, the Japanese Army was well entrenched from Vladivostok to Harbin to Chita to Baikal.[12] The constant realization that the Japanese might remain permanently in that huge area of Siberia acted as a strong incentive to persuade the Allies to accept Japan's demands at Paris. As is so often true in international negotiations, the choice before the Allies was not between a good or bad solution, but rather that of the least objectionable of several unpleasant alternatives. The narrative now shifts away from eastern Siberia to Paris where Japan fought to obtain by negotiations the fruits of victory which it had been promised in the Secret Treaties.

Expectations from the Paris Peace Conference

On November 11, 1918, when the Armistice was signed in Europe, Japan viewed the cessation of hostilities with a far more detached attitude than any of the other belligerents. The battlefields of Europe had seemed a long way off and no Japanese soldiers had been involved in the main theater of war. Moreover, in September, 1918, the rice riots had absorbed the immediate interests of both the people and government. But in the realm of foreign affairs, the course of the Empire was firmly set. Even the appointment of the head of the Seiyūkai party, Hara Kei, as Prime Minister had not caused any deviation in this policy. Internationally, Japan was in a strong position to press at the Peace Conference for acceptance of its demands. The Army was rapidly spreading westward in Siberia to Lake Baikal and northward into the Amur Valley; the international character of the Siberian Expedition had little retarding effect on this advance. No international agreement had yet been reached on the control of international investments in China, so Japan still operated there with a free hand.

It was taken for granted in Tokyo, therefore, that the Paris Peace Conference would legalize the promises of the Allies set forth in the Secret Treaties. They had promised that the German possessions in Shantung and the Pacific Islands north of the equator would be ceded to Japan. It was also assumed by Japan that it would be free to negotiate bilaterally with China on all outstanding issues and that the latter would play only a minor part in the peace negotiations.

Finally, the Japanese government and people had caught something of the contagious feeling instilled by President Wilson's proposals for a League of Nations which presaged the dawn of a new day for international relations. They accepted the concepts of the League and anticipated that the negotiations concerning it would afford an excellent opportunity for the Asiatic countries to seek recognition of both the principle and practice of racial equality. United States Ambassador Roland Morris telegraphed from Tokyo on November 15, 1918:

> It is hoped by the Japanese that the organization of a League of Nations will offer an opportunity to assert the equality of the yellow race, a question which underlies all discussion on the subject.

On January 15, 1919, three days after the Paris Peace Conference was formally opened, Tokyo's leading daily newspaper, the *Asahi,* editorialized that racial inequality was the real obstacle in the way of the brotherhood of nations and that Japan should represent the colored races of the world in seeking equality.

Rejection of Racial Equality

The issue of racial equality was important to the Japanese people and their delegates at Paris because of the discriminatory treatment which Oriental immigrants had received in the United States and Australia. (See page 345.) Since Japan sought world recognition of its status as a leading world power, it could not tolerate the continuance of what the Foreign Minister described as "discriminatory treatment based upon racial prejudice." But the real significance of the debate on racial equality at the Peace Conference was the effect it had on Japan's attitude toward its other demands. Consequently, an account of Japan's role at Paris necessarily begins with its endeavors to obtain a solution to this explosive problem.

All of the leading delegations, including the Japanese, were cognizant of the fact that the whole question of racial equality was an extremely delicate one. After the representatives of the principal powers had been warned that the issue was to arise, President Wilson assigned Colonel Edward M. House to obtain preliminary agreement on a statement which recognized the general principle of racial equality. This statement would then be inserted in the Covenant of the League of Nations. In conversation with Lord Balfour of England, House insisted that the policy of discrimination toward the Japanese could not continue. Balfour was noncommittal but Prime Minister Hughes of Australia refused to budge from his position of opposition to any proposal for racial equality.

The issue first came up formally in the middle of February, 1919, at a meeting of the Commission to draft the Covenant of the League of Nations. Makino Nobuaki, the Japanese member of the Commission, proposed that a clause be added to the draft text of the Covenant which provided for equal treatment for all nationals of all states members of the League, regardless of their race or nationality. In making this proposal, Makino consciously avoided the issue of immigration by referring only to general principles. In defense of his amendment, he argued that the new demands of the League, such as participation by member states in joint actions against aggressors, made it natural that all nationals wanted to be placed on an equal footing with the people they defended with their lives. As was expected from the resistance which Colonel House had encountered, the Japanese proposal was particularly embarrassing to the British. They did not want to offend the Japanese in view of the fact that the Anglo-Japanese Alliance was still in force. They were poignantly aware, however, of the adamant opposition of Hughes of Australia to any proposal which recognized racial equality.[13]

To extricate themselves from this uncomfortable dilemma, the members of the Commission finally decided to delete from the Covenant the entire article which Makino proposed to amend. The delegates from both the United States and Japan had consented to this deletion, however, on condition that they had the right to bring the question of racial equality up again. Thus a final decision was sidetracked for the next two months. But official and nonofficial Japanese statements made it patently clear that they were disappointed and doubted Wilson's sincerity when he spoke of the League as a means to obtain justice and equality.

At this point, the Japanese Ambassador in Washington, Ishii, in the hopes of allaying the fears of the critics of racial equality, inadvertently weakened the chances of success of his government's proposals. In March, 1919, he presented a memorandum to President Wilson in which Ishii stressed the importance which his government placed on the non-discriminatory treatment of races. He concluded his note with the prediction that if this principle were not accepted at the Paris Conference, it would be impossible to eliminate "perpetual friction and discontent among nations and races."

Ten days later, in a public address, he attempted to separate the question of the acceptance of the principle of racial equality, which was before the Peace Conference, from the question of immigration, which was a domestic issue for each nation to decide. Consequently, the ambassador insisted that his government had no thought of trying to force a decision on the immigration issue. But he had not calculated on an emotional, rather than a rational, reaction to his speech. The anti-Japanese pressure groups in the United States irrationally concluded that the Japanese government was pressing for acceptance of the concept of racial equality in order to force the United States to revise its immigration laws. (See page 347.) Senator J. D. Phelan of California, one of the most outspoken advocates of Oriental exclusion, dispatched a telegram to the American delegation in Paris. He claimed that Californians were alarmed at Japan's demands for free immigration and aroused at the prospect of illegal purchases of land by Japanese. He concluded with the categorical statement that the drafters of the Covenant should "under no circumstances concede to the Japanese demands."

Before the principle of racial equality was officially presented again at the Paris Conference, the Japanese delegation learned that Hughes of Australia would not agree to any reference in the League's Covenant to the principle of racial equality. From the Japanese point of view, however, the matter had now become one of national honor. If they were to participate in the League, they wished to do so on terms of equality with other members. They had not yet received assurances that they would succeed to Germany's former rights in China or in the Pacific Ocean. They saw no reason why they should be intimidated by alarmists in the United States or by Australia's threats. At a subsequent meeting of the Commission to draft the Covenant, the Japanese delegation proposed that the text of the preamble to the Covenant include a clause which recognized the principle of the equality of nations and of the just treatment of their nationals. In making this proposal, it was intimated that the failure to accept such a clause might result in Japan's refusal to join the League of Nations. But for Great Britain, since the alternative was between the solidarity of the British Empire or the friendship of Japan, there was no question as to which course should be taken. Hughes remained adamant; Lord Robert Cecil bowed to his wishes rather than those of the Japanese. He refused to approve the proposed clause on the grounds that it would encroach on the sovereignty of member states.

President Wilson, who was Chairman of the meeting on April 11, 1919, hoped that the Japanese would withdraw their proposal. When they insisted on a vote, in which only eleven out of seventeen delegates favored inserting the clause, Wilson ruled that the lack of unanimity had defeated the motion. In an attempt to alleviate any hard feelings which his ruling might engender, he emphasized that the League was obviously based on the principle of the equality of nations and hence such a clause would be superfluous. But it was obvious to everyone, including the Japanese members of the Commission, that the views of the British Dominions had prevailed in London. Even though Makino insisted that he would raise the matter again in the Plenary Session of the Conference, for all practical purposes the question was already settled.

Japan Wins Germany's Rights in Shantung

Bitterly disappointed by the fact that the powers would not even recognize racial equality in principle and convinced that discrimination would continue, Japan was determined that it would not change its position on the Shantung question. Before the Peace Conference had convened, it had assumed that the Secret Treaties of 1917 with the various European Powers assured support for its claims and made negotiations on them unnecessary. After the Conference got under way, however, Japan realized that some of the powers, notably the United States, questioned Japan's claims and even intended to befriend China and its cause. In the face of this opposition, Japan took the position that the issues outstanding between China and Japan concerned those two countries alone. Consequently China should not be permitted to participate in any of these discussions at the conference. Thus, when the question of the disposition of Germany's rights in Shantung first came up at a meeting of the Council of Ten, on January 27, 1919, Baron Makino insisted that the Chinese representative should not be present. His proposal was overruled and the Chinese attended the meetings.

Makino then presented the views of his government, concentrating on its legal aspects. He argued that his country's contribution to the victory of the Allies rendered it only just and proper that Germany's rights in Shantung should be ceded to Japan. He reminded the delegates that Japan had captured Kiaochow from Germany in the early months of the war and had continued to occupy the province of Shantung. He also maintained that by the Sino-Japanese Agreements of 1915 (the Twenty-

One Demands), China had acquiesced in the direct transfer of German rights to Japan. Furthermore, on September 24, 1918, China had signed another set of agreements which were a further recognition of the validity of Japan's position. These later agreements provided for the withdrawal of the Japanese civil administration (military government) from Shantung, for the joint Sino-Japanese management of the railroad from Tsingtao to Tsinan, and for loans from Japan for funds for two new lines.[14]

This position was vehemently and effectively attacked by Dr. Wellington Koo, the chief Chinese delegate. He noted that the Province of Shantung, with its thirty-six million inhabitants, was the cradle of Chinese civilization and the birthplace of the two great sages and philosophers, Confucius and Mencius. Since Shantung was endowed with valuable natural resources, the encroachments of Japan in that region could only be for the purpose of exploitation and Japanese permanent occupation of Kiaochow would also be a constant threat to the capital of Peking.

He then raised the question of the legal basis of Japan's claims in China, maintaining that the Agreements of 1915 had been signed only under duress and had never been considered as permanently binding by his government. Finally, when China had declared war on Germany, it had abrogated "all treaties and conventions theretofore concluded between China and Germany." Consequently, he concluded that there was no legal basis for Japan's claims and that one of the conditions of a just peace required that Shantung should be restored completely and without encumbrances to China.

Dr. Koo immediately won support for his position from practically all the members of the Council of Ten. Popular opinion in the United States and elsewhere recognized China's strong moral position. Consequently, the Japanese delegates became alarmed and emphasized that their country was intent on seeing that it received only what it considered to be its just rewards. Although the Peace Conference concentrated on other matters during the next seven weeks, both China and Japan kept the issue alive by the distribution of memoranda to the other delegations and of pamphlets to the general public in which they set forth the arguments for their respective positions. In this battle of words, the Chinese delegation was the more effective of the two. One of its memoranda, which harped on the moral issue, concluded with a plea that the restoration to China of all rights and territories in Shantung would redress a wrong and be to the best interest of all nations in the Far East.[15]

By the middle of April, circumstances tended to make both sides begin to show some interest in a compromise solution. On the one hand, Japan had run into strong opposition to its proposal for racial equality. Its position on the Shantung issue was becoming increasingly unpopular. If it were to gain anything at Paris, it might have to make concessions. On the other hand, China realized that its legal position was weak because it had voluntarily acquiesced in the agreements of September, 1918. The promises which the powers had made to Japan in their Secret Treaties might prove to have more force than Chinese eloquence. When the issue was raised at a meeting of the Council of Four on April 15, 1919, four days after the defeat on the issue of racial equality, Makino emphasized that Japan had agreed to the eventual return to China of the leased territory in Shantung. President Wilson vainly sought to solve the problem by suggesting a joint trusteeship for the area. When the Council of Four considered the question a week later, the representatives were confronted with new complications. The Japanese delegation stated that it had received instruction not to sign the peace treaty in the event that the Shantung issue was not settled in its favor. It added that its government would be willing to restore the former German territory in Shantung to China on two conditions. First, Kiaochow should be a free port with a Japanese concession in the city. Second, the railroad in Shantung should be a joint Sino-Japanese enterprise with a Japanese police force to maintain law and order. China continued to press for complete expulsion of Japan from Chinese territory.

President Wilson was torn between two conflicting desires. He was determined to do all in his power to obtain approval for the League of Nations. He considered its formation essential to create an atmosphere in which its members would think primarily of their duties toward each other, rather than of their self-interests, and act accordingly. He also wanted to rectify any injustice that Japan might have done against China. Lloyd George announced that Britain considered the secret treaties binding and hence would support Japan's position in Shantung. This development made it impossible for Wilson to continue to oppose Japan's claims and still keep Britain's support for the League. The whole future of the League had been threatened only the day before by the action of the Italian delegation. It had walked out of the Conference because of dissatisfaction with the proposal to assign Fiume and the Dalmatian Coast to Yugoslavia. Wilson was convinced that if Japan did not receive satisfaction in Shantung, its delegates would follow the example of the Italians. If such an eventuality arose, the League would be lost. Lloyd George and Clemenceau had already made their decision in Japan's favor. Wilson desperately sought for a solution to his dilemma. The Japanese delegation was adamant. It opposed the idea of a mandate but finally declared that on receiving Germany's former rights it would be its policy "to hand back the Shantung Peninsula in full sovereignty to China retaining only the economic privileges granted to Germany and the right to establish a settlement . . . at Tsingtao" and that special railway police would be used only to insure security for traffic.[16]

Despite strong opposition from Secretary of State Lansing and from other members of the American delegation, President Wilson agreed to Japan's wishes. On April 30, the Council of Three (Wilson, George, Clemenceau) approved the transfer of Germany's rights in Shantung to Japan. When the Chinese were told of this decision, they raised strenuous objections. As a last resort, they demanded that they be allowed to sign the Treaty of Versailles with reservations on the articles referring to Shantung. When their request was rejected, they refused to sign the Treaty. Thus by the Versailles Treaty the Allied Powers had recognized Japan's new rights in Shantung. China had not done so and Japan's armed forces continued in occupation of the Shantung peninsula. Its diplomats insisted that the decision at Paris implied recognition of the validity of the Agreements of 1915 and of 1918 and began to implement many of their provisions. They ignored China's cries of exploitation and infringement of the Open Door. The problem remained unsolved until the Washington Disarmament Conference of 1922.

In the meantime, there was a tragic sequel to the Paris decision. President Wilson had traded his acquiescence to Japan's demands concerning Shantung for Allied support for his dream of a League of Nations. He had neglected to judge accurately the effect which this compromise would have on the American people and Congress. Popular opinion in the United States insisted that a wrong had been done a weak and helpless China to win favor from a militarily powerful Japan. This opinion, combined with a renascent postwar isolationism, resulted in the rejection of the Versailles Treaty by the United States Senate in March, 1920. Japan was securely entrenched in Shantung. The United States was outside the League. Wilson was a broken man physically and spiritually. New means would have to be found to rectify any injustices perpetrated against China.

Japan's Mandated Islands

Another Japanese objective at Paris was to acquire the former German Islands in the Pacific north of the equator. The Secret Treaties of 1917 had specified that the signatories would support Japan's claims to these islands. Makino and other delegates had referred to this fact on several occasions but it was not until near the end of the conference that a final decision was reached. The Council of Four, with President Wilson's consent, agreed to assign the Caroline, Marshall, and Marianas Islands to Japan as a Class C Mandate under the League of Nations. Although it would have preferred to receive them in complete sovereignty, Japan consented to this arrangement.

When the Versailles Treaty was signed on June 28, 1919, therefore, Japan had attained most of its objectives at the Paris Peace Conference. It had been defeated on the issue of racial equality. On the vital issue of new rights in Shantung, however, it had received almost exactly what it had demanded. It had replaced Germany in China. It had bound China to agree to its plans by liberal loans and by promises to transfer, at an indefinite date in the future, any sovereign rights which it held. Although the Pacific Islands were granted Japan under the new system of mandates, as a Class C Mandate the islands could be treated as an integral part of the Empire. The only drawback, from a Japanese point of view, to such an arrangement was that no fortifications were allowed in Class C Mandates. But this limitation was unimportant when the general tendency in the world seemed to be toward less, rather than more, armaments.

In any event, Prime Minister Hara encountered only mild opposition in Parliament to the Versailles Treaty. When asked why the legislature had not been kept informed of the progress of the negotiations, he replied that his government was always ready to supply information consistent with the public interest. He then reminded Parliament that traditionally it had never interfered with the treaty-making prerogatives of the Emperor. He asked for acceptance of the treaty. In view of the general agreement that World War I had strengthened Japan's leadership throughout East Asia and that much had been won at only very limited cost, opposition in Parliament very soon disappeared.

Notes

1. For details of these political developments see Ōkubo Toshiaki, *Kindai Shi III, Nihon Zenshi* (Tokyo: Tokyo Daigaku Shuppan Kai, 1964), X, pp. 128 ff.; Robert A. Scalapino, *Democracy and the Party Movement in Prewar Japan* (Berkeley: University of California Press, 1953), pp. 293 ff.; Peter Duus, *Party Rivalry and Political Change in Taishō Japan* (Cambridge: Harvard University Press, 1968), pp. 86–106.

2. Terauchi Masatake (1852–1919) was basically a soldier. Born in Chōshū in a warrior family, he lost an arm fighting against Saigō in the Satsuma Rebellion of 1877 but remained in the Army. In the Sino-Japanese War he distinguished himself as a brigade commander. He was promoted to Vice-Chief of the Army General Staff and was Minister of War 1902 to 1910 when he became the first Governor-General of Korea. Yamagata's maneuvers had included receiving assurances from Hara, head of the Seiyūkai party, with 104 seats in the Lower House, that he would support Terauchi.

On the other hand, Katō was piqued by the fact that he had not been selected as Premier. The Dōshikai party, of which he was the leader, had won 150 seats in the election of March, 1915, at the expense of the Seiyūkai, which had dropped from 184 to 104. He formed a new party, the Kenseikai, the day after Terauchi became Premier. Katō publicly denounced the arbitrary action of Yamagata and the Elder Statesmen and promised to fight Terauchi from Parliament. The Kenseikai, an amalgamation of three groups, controlled 197 seats in the House of Representatives. Just when Katō hoped to pass a vote of nonconfidence against Premier Terauchi, Parliament was dissolved. In the elections of April, 1917, the Seiyūkai party, which supported the Cabinet, increased its strength to 160 at the expense of the Kenseikai, which dropped to 119. Hence, Terauchi had vastly improved his political strength. Criticism of foreign policy was kept to a minimum by the Advisory Council on Foreign Relations composed of leaders of the various parties. Katō Kōmei doggedly boycotted the Council.

3. Professor Ōkubo attributes the riots to the sudden increase in the price of rice due to higher wartime prices, hardships of the lower classes, popular reaction against wartime profiteers, demands for rice for the Siberian Expedition, and general repressive measures of the government on the masses. See Ōkubo, *op. cit.*, pp. 170 ff.

4. Hara's selection as Prime Minister was a final tribute to the carefulness with which he had cultivated the *Genrō*, especially Yamagata. In view of the shock he had received from the rice riots, Yamagata was not prepared for a confrontation with Hara in the event he had not been selected. For Yamagata's "capitulation" see Duus, *op. cit.*, pp. 102 ff.

5. Ray Stannard Baker, *Woodrow Wilson and the World Settlement* (New York: Doubleday, Page & Co., 1922), I, p. 61. For a detailed account of the Secret Treaties see A. Whitney Griswold, *The Far Eastern Policy of the United States* (New York: Harcourt, Brace and Co., 1938), pp. 205 ff.

6. Burton F. Beers, *Vain Endeavor: Robert Lansing's Attempt to End American–Japanese Rivalry* (Durham, N. C.: Duke University Press, 1962), pp. 92–109.

7. Nishihara Kamezō was well qualified to carry out Terauchi's wishes. He was in Korea in 1908 as head of a group promoting trade between Japan and Korea and Manchuria. When Terauchi became Governor of Korea he was favorably impressed with Nishihara's zeal and interest in expanding Japanese hegemony over the continent. In May, 1915, Nishihara was dispatched to Manchuria to report on the reaction to the Twenty-One Demands. He became a sort of secret emissary of Terauchi and liaison person with both Chinese leaders and Japanese military officials in China. His activities obviously helped Japan in obtaining further concessions from China. See James W. Morley, *The Japanese Thrust into Siberia, 1918* (New York: Columbia University Press, 1957), pp. 14 ff.

8. For Britain's first approach to Japan and the subsequent position of France, see *ibid.*, pp. 29 ff.

9. For a description of the preliminary plan of the Japanese Army and the race of the Japanese and British navies to reach Vladivostok, see *ibid.*, pp. 50 ff., and Richard R. Ullman, *Anglo-Soviet Relations 1917–1921: Intervention and the War* (Princeton: Princeton University Press, 1961), pp. 90 ff.

10. General Tanaka Giichi (1863–1929) was born in Chōshū and graduated from the Military Staff College and served in the Sino-Japanese War. He then studied in Russia from 1898–1902, returning to rise rapidly as a Russian specialist in various administrative and staff positions. He was a strong advocate of army expansion and in 1910 founded the Imperial Reserve Association. He was Vice-Chief of Staff from October, 1915 to October, 1918. Later he

became Minister of War in two Cabinets, president of the Seiyūkai party, and finally Prime Minister (1927–1929). See Morley, *op. cit.*, p. 102; also pp. 161 ff., for details of the agreements with China.

11. Morley gives a fascinating and detailed account of the rise and fall of persons such as Semenov and Hovarth and of the Japanese and Allied attitude toward them. He also describes how the General Staff eventually ignored the Cabinet and its opposition to Tanaka's original plan.

One of the most ironical aspects of the whole expedition was the fact that Hara, the leader of the Seiyūkai and strongest party in Parliament, opposed the expedition, except in self-defense, and was particularly against a Japanese move into the Amur River Valley. By the time he became Prime Minister in September 29, 1918, Khabarovsk on the Amur had fallen to Japanese troops and others were on their way westward to Irkutsk. See Morley, *ibid.*, pp. 260 ff., and Ullman, *op. cit.*, pp. 191–229. The most penetrative study in Japanese is Hosoya Chihirō, *Shiberia Shuppei no Shiteki Kenkyū* (Tokyo: Yuhi Kaku, 1955).

12. The Japanese forces in Siberia were not withdrawn until 1922, over two years after the forces of the other Allies had left. Japan had also occupied Northern Sakhalin in 1920 and its forces remained there until 1926.

13. House had worked closely with the Japanese in an attempt to obtain a formula which would be acceptable to Hughes but the latter rejected every proposal. Charles Seymour (ed.), *The Intimate Papers of Colonel House* (4 vols.; Boston: Houghton Mifflin Co., 1928), IV, pp. 313 ff.

Makino Nobuaki (1861–1949) was a disciple of Ōkubo's. At the age of eleven, he had gone to the United States to study and entered the Foreign Office upon his return in 1879. He served as Minister in Italy and Austria and was Minister of Education in 1906 in the Saionji Cabinet and Foreign Minister in the Yamamoto Cabinet in 1913. He was Minister of the Imperial Household during the Army revolt of February 26, 1936, and narrowly escaped with his life.

Former Premier Saionji was chief delegate at Paris. Despite his familiarity with France during his student days, he was less active in the conference discussions than Makino. For a text of Makino's proposal, which was to be added to Article 21 of the Covenant, see David Hunter Miller, *My Diary at the Conference of Paris* (New York: Appeal Printing Co., 1925), V, Document 355.

14. For the text of the agreements see Miller, *ibid.*, VI, pp. 204 ff. For a careful and detailed account, based on American diplomatic archives, of Japan's demands at the Paris Peace Conference, with emphasis on the Shantung Question, see Russell H. Fifield, *Woodrow Wilson and the Far East: The Diplomacy of the Shantung Question* (New York: Thomas Y. Crowell Co., 1952).

15. Miller, *op. cit.*, VI, p. 130.

16. Fifield, *op. cit.*, p. 279. There has been considerable controversy over whether President Wilson and Secretary Lansing were as ignorant as they claimed to have been about the contents of the Secret Treaties prior to April 24, 1919, when Wilson opposed Japan's claims. Lord Balfour maintained that he had told them both about the treaties when he visited Washington in May, 1917. More conclusive still is evidence presented at a hearing of the Munitions Investigation Committee. This evidence is a paper prepared for the Committee by the Department of State from which the Chairman of the Committee, Senator Nye, reached the following conclusions: "For the sake of the

record it ought to be noted here that by reason of that paper the committee is informed by the highest possible sources that Secretary Lansing and President Wilson were fully apprised by Balfour of the secret treaties to which Great Britain had been committed; and . . . that both the President and Secretary falsified concerning this matter." As the Department of State had requested that the specific contents of their paper be kept secret, Senator Nye did not quote directly from the paper. Griswold, *op. cit.*, p. 219.

16

The Precarious Position of Parliamentary Government, 1920–1931

The relatively peaceful years between the signing of the Versailles Peace Treaty in 1919 and the outbreak of war in Manchuria in September, 1931, were crowded with contradictions. In reality these events reflected the conflict of diametrically opposed forces which was so typical of modern Japan. They also stand out clearly in retrospect as portents of an unquenchable aggressive nationalism which was to sweep everything before it. For example, the assassination of the two most "progressive" Prime Ministers, Hara and Hamaguchi; the reoccupation of Shantung by Japanese troops; and the independent, overt acts of representatives of the Imperial Army in Manchuria were preliminaries to the military occupation of that entire area following the carefully planned explosion near Mukden on September 18, 1931.

On the other hand, the formation of party cabinets, the singularly powerful position attained by Premiers Hara and Hamaguchi, active participation in world disarmament, and the conciliatory China policy of Foreign Minister Shidehara Kijurō, all attest to the existence of strong groups in favor of following parliamentary processes at home and cooperation abroad. Finally, the inconsistencies of America's policy toward Japan added to the confusion. After taking the lead in checking Japan's international power through naval disarmament and the other Washington agreements of 1922, the United States increased international suspicion and ill will by the passage of an immigration law which excluded Orientals from its shores. The history of the postwar decade is, therefore, that of the interaction of these and many other forces which made the ascendency of internationally minded civilian leaders over the military only an illusion.

Hara's Party Cabinet

As already noted, Prime Minister Hara's inflexible position on the Shantung issue at the Paris Peace Conference had supported the position of the military. At home he had worked for the acceptance of the principle of party Cabinets. On the other hand, he and his Cabinet seemed to lack either an interest in or an understanding of some of the basic elements of responsible parliamentary government. For example, he favored increases in the number of Imperial universities to make higher education available to a larger number of students and modified the rules of colonial administration to permit civilians to be governors of Korea and Formosa. At the same time his Home Minister aroused the ultrapatriotism of the youth of the country through the eulogization of the Crown Prince and the sponsorship of a militant, nationalistic Young Men's Association. Hara was more interested in a new law to gerrymander the election districts, which would favor his party, than in support of a universal suffrage law. In fact, when the opposition parties presented a bill for universal manhood suffrage to win the favor of labor organizations, he dissolved Parliament to forestall a showdown on the suffrage issue. He believed it was premature to extend the franchise in this manner. He was content to have his support come from the bourgeois landholders. While the election returns of May, 1920, gave his Seiyūkai a three-fifths majority in the House of Representatives, Hara had qualms about the political stability of the nation. He lamented the increased prevalence of radicalism and the beginnings of a vocal labor movement.[1]

Unlike the American Federation of Labor, which refused to champion radicalism and concentrated on improvement in the economic status of the skilled workers, the Japanese labor movement had its origins in socialism. As early as 1912, Suzuki Bunji, a socialist, went to the United States and became inspired by the activities of Samuel Gompers and the American Federation of Labor. Upon his return to Japan, Suzuki formed the Friendly Society (*Yuaikai*) which became the nucleus for organizing the first trade unions. But it was not until after World War I that either the number of strikes or their participants became significant or the proletarian movement became strong enough for legitimate concern. For example, in 1914, there were only 50 labor disputes with slightly less than 8,000 participants. In 1919, the number of disputes had risen to 497 with 63,000 participants. Workers demanded the right to organize and to strike, the abolition of child labor, a minimum wage, and restricted working hours. Few of the early strikes were successful, but in 1921 that of the Kawasaki Dockyard workers in Kobe was an exception. This strike, which was conducted comparatively peacefully, resulted in the workers being granted an eight-hour day.

Following the traditional pattern of the oligarchs toward nonconformity, Hara's government was ruthless in its suppression of strikes and of any other signs of the beginnings of a labor or proletarian movement. Thus the growth of organized labor, which was painfully slow, was retarded by its close connection with the radical movement. The police made numerous arrests, and thugs hired by ultranationalists manhandled and otherwise intimidated persons considered as radicals. But Marxism had become popular among many professors and intellectual leaders who advocated the immediate establishment of a communist state in Japan. Students eagerly responded to their pleas to participate actively in strikes and demonstrations. In 1921, there was a severe clash between the police and the marchers in the May Day parade. A general wave of unrest and a desire for direct action swept over the workers in the cities.

Hara's policy of suppression of these activities only increased the bitterness of labor, not only toward management but also toward the Cabinet and the Seiyūkai. To the worker, there seemed little to recommend a party government as compared to a transcendent cabinet. To some, Premier Hara seemed the personification of all that troubled the nation. On November 4, 1921, he was assassinated by a government railway employee. The reins of government were taken over by Finance Minister Takahashi Korekiyo, but the Seiyūkai had lost its real leader. Despite his genius as a financier Takahashi was not effective as a politician. He soon lost the confidence of the various factions of the party, some of whom challenged his leadership. Desertions made the Seiyūkai a minority party in the House, so Takahashi resigned in June, 1922. For the next two years the government reverted again to nonparty cabinets.[2]

Convening the Washington Disarmament Conference

Even though a party cabinet had been in power since 1918, Japan had shown only a few indications of a willingness to change its foreign policy. One such change was in the field of international finance. As early as June, 1918, the United States government had worked toward the formation of a four-power Consortium to make loans to China on the basis of nondiscriminatory, equal economic opportunity. The Consortium, composed of France, Great Britain, Japan, and the United States, was organized to prevent the continuance of the highly political and exclusive loans negotiated with China by Nishihara and other Japanese agents. After it was conceded that the Consortium would not be applicable to the South Manchurian Railway zone and other areas in which Japan already had special concessions, final agreement for the plan was reached in October, 1920. On paper, at least, a check had been placed on unlimited Japanese investments in China, especially those for political purposes.[3]

Furthermore, from the waning months of World War I to the summer of 1921, the United States entertained deep misgivings concerning the effects of Japan's gains from the war and the Versailles Treaty on the future peace and security of Eastern Asia and of the world. While Premier Hara had agreed to reduce the size of the Japanese armed forces in Siberia, multilateral participation in the Expedition had not achieved America's hopes that Japan would be restrained from occupying northeastern Asia. By the summer of 1921, Japan had not carried out its promises made in Paris to return Shantung to China.

A most significant postwar American proposal to check Japan's military expansion, therefore, was the calling of the Washington Conference. By the summer of 1921, several events had contributed to the willingness of the American government to take such a step. In the first place, prior to their victory in the election of November, 1920, the Republicans had advocated general disarmament. Furthermore, many Americans were searching for ways other than the use of the League of Nations whereby future wars could be prevented. The United States placed great hopes on disarmament. It became convinced that a Pacific disarmament conference could bring about a significant reduction of both naval and military armaments, could make a renewal of the Anglo-Japanese Alliance unnecessary, and could hamper and obstruct Japanese imperialism in China and Siberia. If these objectives could be achieved, the possibilities of war would be greatly lessened.

Consequently, formal notes were transmitted to Japan, Italy, France, and Great Britain requesting their views on the advisability of holding such a conference. All of the powers accepted, but Japan raised certain questions. It requested a more concise definition of the scope of the problems proposed for discussion; it clearly indicated that questions concerning Sino-Japanese relations, such as the Twenty-One Demands and Shantung, should be scrupulously avoided. But Secretary of State Hughes, like Hay in 1899 when announcing the answers to his Open Door Notes, ignored these objections and declared that all four of the countries approved of such a conference.

In August, 1921, formal invitations were extended to these four powers and to China, the Netherlands, Belgium, and Portugal to convene in Washington. The scope of the conference was expanded to include all of the important outstanding issues in the Pacific area. These were naval disarmament, the Open Door, Japan's position in Shantung, the integrity of China and Russia, the renewal of the Anglo-Japanese Alliance, the status of the German possessions, the Pacific cable, and narcotics. Despite Japan's earlier objections to placing some of these items on the conference's agenda, Premier Hara was deeply interested in the possibilities of such a conference enhancing world peace. Furthermore, a general curtailment of armament expenditures would be to everyone's advantage. If China was to be discussed at the conference, he did not want to give the Western powers a chance to agree among themselves on a policy designed to limit Japan's freedom of action in China and East Asia. Hara eagerly accepted the invitation and personally told his chief delegate, Admiral Katō Tomosaburō, that the peace of Japan and America and of the world depended on the success of the conference. Hara's assassination, a week before the conference opened, had no effect on Japan's attendance.

Treaties on Pacific Islands, Naval Disarmament, and China

Representatives of these nine powers with possessions in the Pacific Ocean met in Washington from November, 1921, to February, 1922. Seven treaties and twelve resolutions resulted from the deliberations. These agreements were both interdependent and separate; some of them were signed by only two members, others by all the nations attending the conference. The treaties and agreements generally covered three subjects: nonaggression, naval disarmament, and China. The Four Power Treaty on Insular Possessions laid down certain general principles of nonaggression. In this pact, France, Great Britain, Japan, and the United States pledged to respect each other's insular possessions in the Pacific Ocean. They also agreed to consult jointly whenever a potentially dangerous controversy arose over their rights in the Pacific area.

The two most significant decisions concerning the limitation of naval armaments were the Five Power Naval Disarmament Treaty and the agreement between Great Britain and Japan to terminate their alliance. Secretary of State Hughes proposed early in the conference that the most effective method to control naval armaments was by a limitation on the number of capital ships (battleships) to be retained by each of the naval powers. He recommended, therefore, that all capital shipbuilding programs be abandoned, that old capital ships be scrapped, and that the number of battleships owned by each of the five leading naval powers (France, Great Britain, Italy, Japan, and the United States) be reduced in proportion to the existing strength of their respective navies. For Japan, this proposal meant that it would be allowed to retain capital ships at a ratio of three to five in comparison with Great Britain or the United States.

An island empire such as Japan, however, had to rely heavily on its navy for protection and could consider favorably proposals such as a reduction of capital ships or the abandonment of the Anglo-Japanese Alliance providing the potential striking force of the British and American navies was eliminated. In view of the necessity in those days for a task force to have a base from which to operate, Japan would remain safe from attack if American and British naval bases were restricted. Consequently, Admiral Katō, the chief Japanese delegate, proposed that the status quo be maintained with respect to fortifications and naval bases in the Pacific. The United States and Great Britain agreed to this counterproposal so long as it did not apply to their respective naval centers in the Hawaiian Islands and Singapore. These limitations on building new fortifications were incorporated into the Five Power Disarmament Treaty. Having obtained these specific provisions which would protect Japan from attack, it agreed to the capital ship ratios as follows: Great Britain (5), United States (5), Japan (3), France (1.75) and Italy (1.75). Neither Japan nor Britain pressed further for the renewal of the Anglo-Japanese Alliance.[4]

As for the treaties dealing with the problems centering around China's integrity, they were also interrelated. By the Versailles Treaty, Japan had obtained special rights in Shantung, but it had not withdrawn its troops or returned the province to Chinese control. Hence, the United States had insisted that both this specific issue and the broad question of the overall relations of the Powers toward China should be considered by the Washington Conference. Secretary Hughes proposed that the Open Door Policy be defined in terms of equal economic opportunity for everyone in China. Furthermore, he recommended that a Board of Reference be created to study how this policy could be most effectively carried out and to report and investigate on any infringements of this policy. Since Japan considered that such a Board would be used by the Western powers to keep a constant vigil over its activities on the Asiatic continent, it vigorously opposed the plan. All mention of a Board of Reference was dropped from the Nine Power Treaty, but a new definition was given to the Open Door concept. The treaty required the signatories to respect China's territorial integrity, to refrain from interference in the growth of a stable government, and to take no action which would hamper equal economic opportunities for all.[5]

Progress was also made on the thorny Shantung issue despite the diametrically opposite positions taken by China and Japan. China insisted that there was no real legal basis for any of Japan's claims in Shantung. Japan pointed to the Versailles Treaty and adamantly refused to permit the conference to reopen the question of the legality of the Twenty-One Demands. Nevertheless, under pressure from Great Britain and the United States, both China and Japan agreed to negotiate the Shantung problem under the eyes of "observers." In January, 1922, Japan's delegate, Foreign Minister Shidehara, made a conciliatory move. He announced that his country had no designs on either Chinese or Russian territory and would begin immediate withdrawal of its troops from

Shantung. Under these circumstances, China had little choice but to agree to the Sino-Japanese Treaty of February 4, 1922, in which Japan promised to restore Shantung to China in full sovereignty and to give it a loan to enable it to buy the Tsinan-Tsingtao Railway.

By the various treaties which resulted from the Washington Conference, therefore, many of the most serious problems in the Pacific had been at least temporarily "frozen" and the international atmosphere had been eased. As one authority has expressed it:

> The treaties went as far as pen and ink could go to preserve a peace founded on such antithetical elements as those inherent in the *status quo* in the Far East.[6]

Japan's withdrawal of its military forces from Shantung, shortly after the conference, and from Siberia in October, 1922, added to a new feeling of amity. The disarmament program also relieved the national expenditures of the five leading naval powers. There was general confidence that the treaty prohibiting new fortifications would be observed and that militarily the status quo would be maintained.

But conditions on the continent continued to be less reassuring. Propinquity, availability of venture capital, and readiness to make the most of China's endemic political instability were too great temptations for Japan's nationalists to withstand. Before they moved to secure extension of their rights in China, however, they received unexpected support for their policies because of America's new exclusion law. Whatever success the Washington Conference may have achieved in easing international tensions in the Pacific was soon to be dissipated by the effects of this exclusion law.

White Man's America and the Exclusion Law

Discrimination against colored races in the United States was as old as the Republic. Slavery, which was an extreme form of discrimination, was abolished only after a civil war had devastated the South. In the far West, where the Oriental immigrants were concentrated, prejudice against them arose at an early date for both economic and emotional reasons. In the 1860's, the Central Pacific Railroad Company imported thousands of Chinese workers to provide cheap labor to construct the transcontinental line across California. By 1880, the economic competition created by the piteously low wages paid to Chinese laborers created the basis for an anti-Oriental movement. Two years later, both skilled and unskilled Chinese laborers were excluded from the United States in order to protect the American labor market.

As for Japanese laborers, they were first brought to the sugar cane and pineapple plantations of Hawaii on a contract basis and later came directly to the continental United States. By 1900, there were about 61,000 Japanese in the Hawaiian Islands, where they comprised the largest element in the population, and 24,000 on the continent. Most of the latter were on the West Coast but equaled only 1 per cent of the California population.

Despite this comparatively small number of Japanese immigrants in California, a strong anti-Japanese movement emerged under the prodding of Mayor James D. Phelan of San Francisco. Mass meetings were held which demanded outright exclusion. The Japanese government moved, however, to check such an eventuality by discontinuing the issuance of passports for laborers to the United States. But the corrupt political situation in San Francisco and California only aggravated the anti-Japanese movement; the politicians used the anti-Oriental movement as a diversionary tactic to squelch criticism of their unscrupulous administration.

Popular opinion against the Japanese had been sufficiently aroused to result in numerous unpleasant incidents. Following the San Francisco earthquake in April, 1906, several Japanese were molested and their property attacked by the excited populace. The movement reached its peak in October, 1906, when the San Francisco Board of Education passed a resolution excluding Orientals from the city's schools. Since there were only ninety-three persons affected by this order, it had obviously been motivated by racial prejudice against the Japanese. President Roosevelt considered the action an unnecessary and unworthy affront against a sensitive people and "wicked stupidity." He threatened to sue the San Francisco Board. He also recognized that the basic cause for this antagonism against the Japanese was an immigration problem. Consequently, he made a bargain with the California leaders of the anti-Japanese movement that if the Board would rescind its order, he would stop immigration by executive order. The Board finally accepted this compromise.

To fulfill his promise, Roosevelt had to prevent immigration from two sources, namely, directly from Japan and indirectly from Hawaii and Canada. He achieved the first objective through diplomacy. Early in 1907, Japan agreed not to grant passports to either skilled or unskilled Japanese laborers to the mainland of the United States except to settled agriculturists. This action was formalized the next year by what came to be known as the Gentlemen's Agreement. Henceforth, immigration directly from Japan ceased. Roosevelt was equally successful in stopping immigrant Japanese from coming into the mainland of the United States from Hawaii and Canada. He persuaded Congress to adopt an amendment to the Immigration Law of 1907 making such entry illegal.

In the meantime, the jingoistic press on both sides of the Pacific wrote of the imminent danger of war between Japan and the United States. The war scare psychology did not infect the leaders of either country but Roosevelt took the precaution of announcing that the American Fleet would visit the West Coast and make a world cruise for training and goodwill purposes.[7]

To return to the issue of the exclusion of Japanese from the United States, when the Democrats came to power in 1912 under the leadership of Woodrow Wilson, the tension over Japanese exclusion increased between the federal government and California. Phelan was again at the head of the exclusionist vanguard. He sponsored and secured passage of a state law whose purpose and intent was to keep Japanese subjects from owning land. The fact that the law classified them as aliens ineligible for citizenship did not deceive anyone, least of all the Japanese.

The question of exclusion of Oriental immigrants became acute again when the United States Congress began debate on a general immigration law. Mr. Phelan, who was by this time a U.S. Senator, had whipped up extensive support for an exclusion bill. On the other hand, there was a strong group in Congress opposed to any type of discriminatory immigration law. In February, 1924, Secretary of State Hughes wrote to Congressman Albert Johnson in an attempt to restrain Congress from taking precipitous action. Hughes pointed out that the passage of the exclusion bill which was before the House of Representatives was ill-advised and would undo much of the good will created by the Washington Conference.

When the House, ignoring these warnings, was on the point of acting on this bill, the Japanese Ambassador protested against its discriminatory character. At this point, Hughes misjudged the mood of Congress. He thought that the antiexclusionist cause would be helped by sending the Ambassador's note to the Congress. The House reacted in exactly the opposite way. On April 12, 1924, it approved the bill with an exclusion clause attached to it. In the debate in the Senate, Henry Cabot Lodge twisted the Ambassador's note so that it appeared that he had maligned the United States. The Ambassador had said that while he did not question the right of any country to regulate immigration, he found it

> difficult to believe that it can be the intention of the people of your great country . . . to resort . . . to a measure which would not only seriously offend the just pride of a friendly nation . . . but would also seem to involve the question of good faith and therefore of the honor of their government. . . . I realize, as I believe you do, the grave consequences which the enactment of the measure retaining that particular clause would bring upon the otherwise happy and mutually advantageous relations between our two countries.[8]

Senator Lodge claimed that the term "grave consequences" implied a threat to the United States. The exclusionist movement spread like wildfire in the Senate, which favored retention of the exclusion clause by a vote of 76–2.

The result was the exclusion of Japanese from entry into America. The reaction of the Japanese press was bitter, but on the whole, restrained. Some Tokyo papers correctly called the bill inequitable and unjust; others described it as a deliberate slap in the face. Officially, the case was closed after the Japanese government sent a formal protest taking exception to the discriminatory aspects of the new law. Although some of them were too polite to say so, the Japanese people understood the action for just what it was—an act of discrimination provoked by an irrational, narrow-minded, militant group with a distorted sense of patriotism and by an emotional reaction in Congress to the explosive problem of race prejudice.

It was all the more difficult for the Japanese to accept this discriminatory treatment with equanimity because only a few months earlier the American people had generously contributed to the relief of those devastated on September 1, 1923, by the earthquake and fire in the Tokyo area. In that holocaust, two-thirds of Tokyo had been wiped out, and Yokohama was a complete shambles. An estimated 157,000 persons had lost their lives. Wild rumors created panic among the survivors. Martial law was declared to protect innumerable Koreans against attacks and to restore order. American gifts and subscriptions to special earthquake bonds materially helped the capital city area return to normal.

As relations between Japan and the United States deteriorated during the next few years, the Exclusion Law of 1924 was used to arouse suspicion and hatred of America among ordinary citizens and especially among new recruits in the Japanese Army and Navy. At the very least, it was used as sufficient proof of the American attitude of disdain and superiority toward Japan. Pronouncements to the contrary by the State Department or by the American Ambassador, notwithstanding, the Japanese people were convinced that Americans wanted to discriminate against them. To the extent that this immigration law was used by the militarists to arouse anti-American hatred in the prewar years, it did contribute to "grave consequences."

Katō's Party Cabinet, Universal Suffrage and the Peace Preservation Law

With the passage in 1924 of the law which excluded Japanese from entry into the United States, the center of the stage shifts abruptly from Washington to Tokyo. The crucial issue during the next few years, the outcome of which was to determine the peace of the world, was whether the advocates of military expansionism or of international cooperation were to win control over the government. In terms of domestic politics, it was a question of whether the supporters of party cabinets and constitutional government could control effectively the proponents of Army control and direct action.

In the summer of 1924, conditions were more favorable to the former group than at any previous time. All of the older generation of Elder Statesmen had died and Saionji remained as the only regular member of the *Genrō*. He preferred a party system of government rather than a continuation of oligarchical control. Furthermore, the experiments during the previous three years with nonparty cabinets had been most unsatisfactory. For example, during his premiership of January–June, 1924, Viscount Kiyoura had failed completely to win the confidence of the people. Party members of the House of Representatives had refused flatly to cooperate with the Cabinet. They also united to combat the danger of the continuation of cabinets controlled by the oligarchs. Under the leadership of Katō Kōmei, President of the Kenseikai, the three leading parties in the House of Representatives took an unusually strong stand. They proclaimed:

1. The establishment of a system of party cabinets
2. The suspension of the arbitrary and monopolistic power and special privilege of the oligarchs
3. Joint action to achieve these purposes
4. Repudiation of the Kiyoura government [9]

This impressive demonstration of unity among the parties and the popular support which they received from the press forced the dissolution of Parliament at the end of January, 1924.

In the elections which followed, the political parties won 284 seats while the oligarchs mustered only 180. Among the former group, the Kenseikai's total of 153 was by far the largest number of any of the political parties. On the basis of the joint declaration by the leading parties, it was clear Katō could count on a majority of votes for his program. Finally, since Hara's assassination, he was the strongest political figure in Japan. On June 11, 1924, Katō finally achieved his long-sought dream. He was designated Prime Minister and began to put into practice the principle of party cabinets which he had so long advocated. He remained in office until his death in January, 1926. His first Cabinet began an eight-year period during which the leaders of the strongest political parties alternated as Prime Minister.[10]

A brief analysis of the most significant event of Katō's premiership gives some inkling as to why the party cabinets were to disappear so quickly. In the first place, just when a labor and social democratic movement was beginning to organize and might have become a strong social and political force against ultranationalism and militarism, the conservative elements in the government, including the leading political parties such as the Seiyūkai and Kenseikai, revealed their bias toward conservatism and took harsh measures to suppress this movement. On the other hand, this social democratic movement showed its propensity for theoretical controversy, fragmentation, political ineptness, and aloofness from the masses. These characteristics of both elements in society are readily seen in the movement for universal manhood suffrage. During the Hara Cabinet, Katō, largely to gain popular support, had supported universal suffrage. As indicated above, Hara had opposed it as too radical a move. At this point the labor movement, such as it was, had become disillusioned with all politicians and dropped universal suffrage as one of its basic objectives. The radical leaders of the labor movement had advocated an activist, anarcho-syndicalist approach to the labor movement rather than the use of political means to achieve their ends. In 1923, the year before Katō became Prime Minister, there had been a severe clash on May Day between the police and radicals. Over 200 persons were arrested but the police made little effort to determine whether those arrested were real subversives who advocated overthrow of the government, members of labor groups seeking normal rights, or persons merely expressing their criticism of the Cabinet.[11]

Fear and mistrust of the masses and of radicalism were greatly increased the next month when the authorities discovered the existence of a secret communist party. Its leaders were immediately arrested and the police tightened their surveillance of all radical groups. In the midst of the fear and unrest which followed the Tokyo earthquake in September, the police had arrested, "as a security measure," socialists, anarchists, and communists. Nine communist leaders were shot. An overzealous captain of the gendarmes killed Ōsugi Sakae, the leading anarchist, his wife, and child. These acts increased the bitterness of those who considered themselves unfairly suppressed. Many of the strikes, demonstrations, and overt acts were manifestations of a new ferment in society and a desire of the people for greater political rights.

Consequently, to meet this dissatisfaction, the Katō ministry sponsored a universal manhood suffrage law. Some party members of the House of Representatives, such as the liberal Ozaki Yukio (1860–1954), had been fighting unsuccessfully for several years to abolish the restrictions on the right to vote. Prime Minister Katō, who had likewise been eager to extend the franchise, capitalized on the majority which his coalition government commanded in the House of Representatives to obtain passage of a new suffrage law. This new law, which was promulgated on May 5, 1925, gave all male citizens above twenty-five years of age the right to vote, thus increasing the electorate from three million to fourteen million. As the first election under the new law was not held until 1928, the political effect of this new legislation was postponed.

This step toward broader participation by the people in the governmental process had been accompanied by strong opposition from the most conservative elements in both the House of Peers and the Privy Council. In fact, the Universal Manhood Suffrage Law, which had been considerably modified by the Peers, would not have been acceptable to them if both houses of the Diet had not previously approved a measure which permitted the continuance of ruthless control over almost any form of activity in opposition to the government and throne. The Katō Cabinet had inherited earlier attempts to have a Peace Preservation Law (*Chian Iji Hō*) passed by the Diet. Recent activities of the radicals had made him and his colleagues apprehensive lest the strong executive power of the central government be threatened. He was, therefore, a willing supporter of this new law to counteract any ill effects to the Establishment which might result from the extension of the franchise to the adult male population. It had, in fact, been approved by the House of Peers a week prior to passage of the suffrage law. Furthermore, it was to become effective almost immediately, giving the police full powers to cope with the radicals, the advocates of "dangerous thought," and subversives.

The Peace Preservation Law provided ten years of penal servitude for those convicted of knowingly joining societies or parties advocating alteration of the Constitution, of the existing form of government, or of the system of private ownership of property. Thus the Katō Cabinet, despite its emphasis on the principle of party cabinets and cabinet responsibility, followed the same pattern as Itō and the earlier oligarchs. If rights were granted the people, such as universal suffrage, new power was given the executive branch of the government to control the people.[12]

Militarists Criticize Shidehara's Conciliatory China Policy

Another important social change which took place during the Katō Ministry was the reorganization of the Imperial Japanese Army. In line with the general trend toward retrenchment in armament expenditures launched by the Washington Naval Conference, general military expenditures decreased from 42 per cent of the national budget in 1922 to 27 per cent during Katō's Cabinet. This curtailment in expenditures for the armed services resulted in the abandonment of four divisions and the reduction of the standing army to seventeen divisions. Officers who were members of the disbanded divisions were not retired from active service. On the contrary, they were assigned to the middle and higher schools and to the universities to be in charge of the new compulsory military training in the schools.

These moves, rather than decreasing the militaristic character of the country, increased it. The reduced number of divisions was adequate for the defensive needs of the country. The money which was saved thereby was invested into new equipment which had been developed during and after World War I. The inauguration of nationwide military training within the schools and colleges, and assignment of regular Army officers to them, exposed a far larger number of persons to militarism that heretofore had been the case. It afforded an excellent opportunity to inculcate into the youths' minds the philosophy of ultranationalism and of the invincibility of the Japanese armed forces.

Finally, these years saw a shift in the social composition of the personnel of the armed services. The predominant influence of leaders of the old warrior class, such as Yamagata, Kuroda, and Terauchi, from Chōshū, was waning. The new cadres of officers were composed increasingly of members from families of the mercantile or small land-owning class. They were not inhibited by personal loyalty to the oligarchs and became more and more dissatisfied with the corruption of the members of Parliament and with the collusion of the Cabinet with big business. They also opposed what they described as an unnecessarily soft policy toward China and toward the Soviet Union.

This criticism by the militarists of Katō's foreign policy was directed against Foreign Minister Shidehara. In general, he supported a conciliatory attitude toward both the Soviet Union and China. As for Japanese–Soviet relations, they had continued to be strained by the lack of a commercial treaty between the two countries, by Japanese demands for restitution for the massacre in 1920 of Japanese residents at Nikolaevsk, and by the presence of Japanese troops in the Soviet portion of Sakhalin. By January, 1925, Foreign Minister Shidehara had reached agreement with the Soviet Union on the most important outstanding issues. He announced that diplomatic relations between the two countries were to be resumed and that earlier fisheries agreements would be revised. In return for a Soviet promise to recognize the provisions of the Treaty of Portsmouth of 1905 (see page 276), Japan promised to withdraw its troops from Northern Sakhalin. By the end of the year, new contracts had been signed for Japanese to exploit petroleum, coal, and timber in the Maritime Provinces in Siberia and in Northern Sakhalin. Relations with the Soviet Union were better than at any time since the Revolution; diplomats appeared to be more successful than militarists in easing Soviet–Japanese tension. Yet the young officers feared that Japan had conceded too much and had revealed its weakness.

But Shidehara was criticized even more severely for his policy toward China. When he had promised at the Washington Conference that Japan would withdraw its troops from Shantung, he had aroused the enmity of his military colleagues who had dreams of the role Japan was destined to play on the continent. In 1925, when he refused to interfere in the civil war in Manchuria, the General Staff considered him an obstructionist. In that year, General Chang Tso-lin, who had exercised independent control over the three Manchurian provinces since 1922, was faced with a civil war. The Japanese commander of the Kwantung Army, who had jurisdiction over the Japanese-owned South Manchurian Railway, declared that the railroad zone was neutral. Since this order had prevented Chang's enemy from moving his troops on the railway, it contributed to Chang's victory.

The Japanese militarists then pressed Shidehara to obtain special concessions from Chang in return for the favor shown him. But Shidehara insisted that Japan should concentrate on the promotion of foreign trade and economic solidarity and should avoid unjust infringement on the interests of any nation. He refused to be a party to deals with Chinese warlords even though such a position would prevent Japan from obtaining special privileges in Manchuria. If these views were to prevail, any expansionist dreams of the Kwantung Army or of any other branch of the Japanese Imperial Army were in jeopardy.

Tanaka's Cabinet Oppresses Opposition

After Katō's death at the end of January, 1926, the shaky coalition of contending political groups began to fall apart. Wakatsuki, former Minister of Home Affairs, assumed the Chairmanship of the Kenseikai and was selected Premier. Furthermore, General Tanaka Giichi had been elected the new president of the Seiyūkai and began to attract some of the smaller parties into his fold. A temporary compromise, formed by the parties to avert rising public criticism against apparent bribes and scandals, was shattered when the Privy Council refused to approve the Cabinet's financial schemes to support the Bank of Taiwan. Premier Wakatsuki was forced to resign. Prince Saionji, the only surviving *Genrō*, was persuaded to continue with party cabinets. On April 20, 1927, he selected General Tanaka, leader of the largest opposition party, to be Prime Minister.[13]

Before proceeding with an account of the results of the new aggressive foreign policy of General Tanaka, two internal events cannot be overlooked. The first of these was the death of the Taishō Emperor on December 25, 1926, and the succession to the throne of his son, Hirohito.

Born in 1901, the new Emperor had been carefully trained and prepared for his new responsibilities. His grandfather, the Emperor Meiji, had personally selected General Nogi as principal of the Peers school where the young Prince would study and had set forth the principles which should guide his education. These were: health should receive first consideration; no hesitation should be shown in rectifying any misconduct; no leniency or favoritism should influence those grading the work of the Prince; there should be strict adherence to drill and practice; simplicity should be followed constantly; in reference to military obligations, the Prince should, at all times, pay strict attention to his teachers.

Obviously, during his years of training, Hirohito was closely guarded and protected from the real world around him. On the other hand, he had spent half a year on a European trip just prior to his becoming Regent in 1921 because of his father's illness. When he became Emperor at the age of twenty-five, Hirohito continued to be exposed to the outside world through private instruction from experienced Foreign Ministry officials. While his chief interest was in marine biology, in times of crisis he became personally involved in making national policy. At the close of World War II he played a courageous and significant role in bringing about its end. Ironically, the new name given to his reign was Enlightened Peace (*Shōwa*).[14]

When General Tanaka became Premier in 1927, Japan faced a severe bank crisis. Twenty banks were closed including the government owned Bank of Formosa. Under the astute leadership of the new Finance Minister, Takahashi Korekiyo, the Diet approved bills to compensate depositors for losses they had incurred by bank failures and to authorize the Bank of Japan, the central financial institution of the country, to loan money to the Bank of Formosa to permit it to open. Several banks failed but others amalgamated with larger institutions so confidence returned. For his Home Minister, Tanaka selected Suzuki Seisaburō, a former Chief Prosecutor known for his vehement opposition to liberals and radicals alike. It was to be expected, therefore, that the Tanaka government became notorious for its severe oppressive measures against all opposition.

In January, 1928, the Seiyūkai party, despite its having absorbed some of the smaller parties, was only the second largest in the Lower House and needed some 40 more seats to command a majority. When threatened with a nonconfidence vote, Tanaka adjourned Parliament, thus forcing an election in February. Despite Home Minister Suzuki's strenuous efforts to obtain a clear victory for the Seiyūkai, including intimidation and even the arrest of some opposition candidates, it was still unable to win a majority of seats. Furthermore, Suzuki was both worried and enraged over the fact that, in this first election under universal manhood suffrage, the proletariat parties had succeeded in electing eight persons to the Diet. In retaliation, on March 15, 1928, mass arrests of 1,600 persons suspected of harboring "dangerous thought" were carried out under the authority of the Peace Preservation Law. Among those arrested were the leaders of the Japanese Communist Party. As a result of these activities, the House of Representatives voted to impeach Suzuki and almost approved a bill of nonconfidence in the Cabinet. Suzuki resigned to save the Cabinet.[15]

Tanaka's Aggressive Foreign Policy

Tanaka had shown a similar disdain for public opinion in his foreign policy. When he became Premier, he lost no time in reversing the conciliatory policy of the former Cabinet. He retained the portfolio of Foreign Minister for himself. He was convinced that the threatened unification of China under Chiang Kai-shek and the Kuomintang and recent events in Manchuria were a direct challenge to Japan. He deplored the steady increase in the Chinese population in the Manchurian provinces and a gradual development of a Chinese-owned railway system which could compete with the Japanese-owned South Manchurian Railway. Despite the autonomous control which Chang Tso-lin exerted over Manchuria, these manifestations of Chinese nationalism threatened Japan's special position.

By 1927, when Shanghai fell before the northward advancing troops of the new nationalist leader, Chiang Kai-shek, left-wing elements were in control of the Kuomintang. There had been violent antiforeign outbreaks in central China, in Wuhan and Nanking. Shortly thereafter, Chiang had decided to make an open break with the communists. In April, with the previous knowledge of the foreign powers, he carried out a successful coup d'état in Shanghai, arresting several thousand Communist Party members. The arrests were extended to Kwangtung and he then announced the establishment of an anticommunist government at Nanking. He rapidly expanded his control over the Wuhan area and Changsha. The first period of a United Front in China had ended.

When Chiang crossed the Yangtze River in a continuation of his northern expedition in his unification campaign, Tanaka's military and civilian advisers urged the necessity of positive action by Japan before Chiang and his Kuomintang were victorious. One of Tanaka's most influential advisers was Mori Kaku, Assistant Chief of the Political Affairs bureau of the Foreign Office and a resident in China for many years. During a trip to China early in 1927, he became convinced that Japan should counteract the strong communist influence in China by aggressive action. He was a major influence on Tanaka in carrying out such a policy. Consequently, one month after he became Prime Minister, Tanaka dispatched 2,000 Japanese troops from Manchuria to Tsingtao in Shantung Province to interrupt Chiang Kai-shek's advance. A direct clash between the Chinese and Japanese troops was avoided at the time and Chiang Kai-shek temporarily withdrew from public life. In the interim he went to Japan and visited Prime Minister Tanaka with Mori Kaku in attendance. Chiang proposed that China recognize Japan's rights and interests in Manchuria in exchange for Japan's recognition of a united China under his leadership of an anticommunist Kuomintang. Although there is evidence that Tanaka was intrigued with this proposal, he refused to make a deal.

Chiang's subsequent success in launching a second northern expedition and threatening Tsinan, the capital of Shantung, made Tanaka decide to dispatch more troops to China in April, 1928. Minor clashes occurred between the Chinese and Japanese armies in early May. Faced with superior Japanese forces, Chiang Kai-shek withdrew his troops and headed northward. When the Chinese commander in Shantung refused to surrender, the reinforced Japanese troops bombarded Tsinan killing an estimated 3,600 Chinese. These actions, which were condoned by the Cabinet, created the opposite results from those Tanaka had expected. The bombardment of Tsinan brought world condemnation for the atrocity. It increased the effectiveness of a Chinese boycott of Japanese goods. It convinced Chiang Kai-shek that Japan was his enemy, and he continued his march toward Peking. Having failed in their mission to keep Chiang from proceeding to Peking, Tanaka reluctantly ordered the Japanese troops to leave Shantung.

Although Tanaka temporarily avoided resignation by the adjournment of Parliament, he soon found himself a victim of circumstances. As champion of an expansionist policy, he had anticipated that if Chiang Kai-shek could be checked from advancing northward, then the Manchurian war lord, Chang Tso-lin, could be weaned away from the nationalists and could be won over to a policy of friendship to Japan. In other words, if Chang Tso-lin were willing to become a Japanese puppet, Chiang Kai-shek's new unification drive might come to nought. In any event, Japan would still have a comparatively free hand in Manchuria.

But Tanaka's plans for Manchuria became a partial victim of his action in Shantung. Furthermore, as several of his successors were to learn all too well, he had overestimated his ability to control the hot-headed young officers in Japan's Kwantung Army in Manchuria. On its own initiative, the Kwantung Army had dispatched troops to the border of China proper and wanted to establish a puppet governor in Manchuria completely friendly to Japan, presumably not under Chang Tso-lin. In the meantime, Colonel Komoto Daisaku had plotted to assassinate Chang Tso-lin, hoping this would precipitate general disorder throughout Manchuria, which would offer an excuse for the Kwantung Army to take it over. On June 4, 1928, as Chang was returning to Mukden from Peking, at the spot where his train crossed the tracks of the South Manchurian Railway, his special coach was bombed. Since one of the chief responsibilities of the Kwantung Army was the protection of the South Manchurian Railway zone, even though Tanaka and Japanese military leaders publicly disclaimed any responsibility for the incident, the implication was clear. Chang must have been murdered on orders from someone within the Kwantung headquarters.

Prime Minister Tanaka was blamed for this lawless act. To avoid embarrassment, he gave no publicity to the circumstances surrounding Chang's murder. Actually, despite the fact that Tanaka was a general and favored an aggressive policy toward China, he had lost control of the extremists in the Imperial Army. When he insisted that the culprits be punished, his plea was vetoed by the Army Chief of Staff and others. They argued that disciplinary action against those responsible for Chang's murder would weaken the entire discipline of the Army.

What they were actually saying, however, was that there were independent elements in the Japanese Imperial Army, such as the officers of the Kwantung Headquarters, which were out of control and which must be given their own way. But Tanaka's critics would not be silenced and he was forced to resign in early July, 1929. On the basis of information available at the time of his resignation, it appeared as though the anti-aggressive and moderate forces had won a victory. But time soon proved that the situation was otherwise.[16]

Hamaguchi's Retrenchment Policy Doomed by World Depression

The fate which befell Tanaka, a military man, was a mild preview of what was to confront the last of the party cabinets and the entire Japanese nation from 1929 to 1931. The murder of Chang Tso-lin by the Kwantung Army was nothing compared to its carefully executed plans to conquer Manchuria and North China by force of arms. Tanaka's political defeat was insignificant compared to the murder of the next Prime Minister, Hamaguchi Ōsachi, and the subsequent disintegration of the political parties, which left the operation of the central government in the hands of the military. Even though a combination of forces was eventually to eliminate the party cabinets and to extinguish the party movement, for a limited period the Hamaguchi Cabinet was able to challenge successfully both the oligarchs and the militarists.

When General Tanaka resigned, the principle was continued of selecting the leader of the main opposition party to become the next Prime Minister. Thus Hamaguchi Ōsachi, President of the Minseitō party, was asked to form a Cabinet.[17] He immediately selected persons for his Cabinet who were leaders in his party. In both domestic problems and foreign relations, the Hamaguchi government, formed on July 2, 1929, adopted policies diametrically opposed to its predecessor. For example, the new Cabinet advocated retrenchment in national expenditures, a balanced budget, a return to the gold standard, and governmental reforms leading toward efficiency and broader powers for the legislative branch of the government. In international affairs, with the appointment of Shidehara as Foreign Minister, there was a return to a conciliatory policy toward China.

Turning first to economic and financial problems, in the decade of 1920–1930 there had been marked changes in the economy. Some of these were to the nation's advantage while others, when considered in conjunction with the world depression, placed Japan in a precarious position. In the first place, there was a general concentration of capital into the hands of a few powerful financial concerns or combines, the *zaibatsu*. When Hamaguchi came to power, they had reached the zenith of their strength and influence and, to an increasing extent, were able to impose their wishes on the government. Their wide range of interests included mining, metals, mechanical engineering, electrical apparatus and machinery, textiles, chemicals, shipbuilding, foreign and domestic trade, banking and insurance. Their resources for investment in industrial expansion were an important factor in Japan's increased industrial activity. As can be seen in Table 5 (page 305), from the period 1918–1922 to that of 1928–1932, the annual average production index of manufacturing in textiles and chemicals nearly doubled, and in metals it rose 50 per cent.

Despite this upsurge in overall economic activity, Premier Hamaguchi faced a precarious financial situation. His predecessor had placed a heavy strain on the national finances by his increased military expenditures as a concomitant to his aggressive China policy. To combat these effects and to help balance the budget, Hamaguchi advocated retrenchment in national expenditures, wherever possible. Salaries of government employees were reduced by 10 per cent. Savings were advocated in military expenses.

One of the basic policies of the Hamaguchi Cabinet in achieving a stabilization of the national economy was a return to the gold standard. The gold embargo was lifted in January, 1930. Unfortunately for the future of party governments and of democratic forces, this policy could not have come at a worse time. Three months earlier the prosperity boom in the United States had collapsed, sparking the world's greatest depression, and world prices dropped. For a country like Japan, which was so dependent on foreign trade, it spelled disaster. The repercussions of the depression reached Japan about the same time that it was beginning to feel the effects of the return to the gold standard. The reduced demands in America for raw silk, the largest single export item, depressed prices rapidly. Domestic purchasing power was not sufficiently strong to take up the slack. The unfavorable balance in foreign trade continued. The balance in international merchandise trade for 1914–1919 of 1,198 million yen had changed to an unfavorable balance for 1920–1929 of 4,216 million yen. The net balance of current international payments for these same periods had changed from a net balance of 2,431 million yen to a net deficit of 2,272 million yen. (See Table 4, page 303.) In other words, the Hamaguchi government could not have chosen a worse time to advocate retrenchment and the return to the gold standard.[18]

In addition to the havoc caused by the world depression, a rapidly increasing population had already overtaxed the country's food supply. From an examination of the domestic supply and demand of rice (Table 3, page 300), it will be observed that after 1918–1922 the steadily increasing population and the limited availability of new lands for cultivation caused a decline in the per-capita production of rice and a drastic increase in rice imports. During the quinquennium 1928–1932, when the world depression and the Hamaguchi policies were paralyzing the Empire's economy, the average annual increase in population amounted to 939,000, and rice imports equaled 9.4 million *koku* or 13 per cent of the total amount consumed. Fortunately for Japan, most of the rice imported came from Korea and Formosa, so that a minimum of foreign exchange was needed. But even these areas could not be expected to keep up with the new demands made by an increase in the population of a million persons yearly.

Another economic and social aspect of the population problem was the inability of the national economy to absorb each year approximately 450,000 new workers looking for employment. This increase in the labor force posed an almost insurmountable problem in normal times; it caused a national crisis in years of depression. Finally, although the government had reduced its expenses, it had not lowered the tax burden. The farmer found himself caught, therefore, in a squeeze between the pressure from constant taxes and a reduction in his income. Domestic silk prices had fallen 50 per cent and rice prices had declined almost the same amount. The rural debt rose rapidly, taxes were in arrears, more farmers sold their daughters in prostitution, and tenants sought redress from high rents by resorting to organized tenancy disputes.

Hamaguchi Challenges Supreme Command

Before these ill effects of the depression made an appreciable impact on the nation, Hamaguchi had strengthened his political position in a national election in February, 1930. His Minseitō party obtained an overwhelming victory, increasing its representation in the Lower House from 217 to 273 seats, giving him an absolute majority. On the other hand, during the next eight months he was to face bitter opposition from the Naval General Staff, the Seiyūkai, the nationalists, and the public at large.

This situation resulted from the revised instructions which his Cabinet had approved for the Japanese delegation to the London Naval Conference to save it from collapse and also from his courage in challenging the right of supreme command of the armed forces while obtaining approval of the London Naval Treaty. Consistent with his fundamental interest in reduced expenditures, Hamaguchi had agreed that Japan would attend the Conference aimed at controlling naval construction but under certain specific conditions. These were established in mid-October by the Cabinet with the tacit approval of leaders of the Seiyūkai and the Privy Council. He announced that Japan would seek a 10:7 ratio with the United States in heavy cruisers as this ratio was believed by the naval authorities to be indispensable in the defense of the Empire. He concluded, "We offer no menace to any nation, we submit to menace from none."

As the Conference progressed, it became apparent that the United States was equally adamant on two points: parity with Great Britain, and the application to heavy cruisers of a 10:6 ratio. To prevent the breakdown of a tripartite agreement, Hamaguchi decided, despite strong objections from the Naval General Staff, to accept a compromise formula. This formula permitted the United States to build 21 heavy cruisers but to postpone construction of the last three until after 1933. This meant that, in principle, America's demands for maintenance of a 10:6 ratio would continue to be in effect. In reality, because of the existing strength of the Japanese Navy in 1930, it would have a *de facto* 10:7 ratio. The formula was approved and the treaty, which was to run until 1936, was signed on April 10, 1930. But the most embarrassing aspect of this compromise for Hamaguchi was the fact that he had been forced to accede to a formula which admittedly in theory gave the United States more of an advantage than was necessary for purely defensive reasons. In other words, he had, to that extent, compromised Japan's security.

But Hamaguchi's troubles over the London Naval Treaty had only just begun. In the first place, he was faced with a hostile press which supported the Naval Chief of Staff, Admiral Katō Kanji, who was opposed to changing the ratio from 10:7. Admiral Katō had unsuccessfully memorialized the Emperor in an attempt to get the Cabinet's new decision reversed. He had accused Hamaguchi of having usurped the right of Supreme Command of the Armed Forces as provided in Article XI of the Constitution.

For his part, Hamaguchi had support for his policy and action from the Minister of the Navy and chief delegate to the London Naval Conference, Admiral Takarabe Takeshi. He frustrated his Seiyūkai opponents in the Lower House by refusing to concede that the Diet had any legal grounds to challenge his actions. He obtained approval from the Supreme War Council for reporting to the Privy Council, which legally was required to ratify the Naval Treaty, that the revised instructions which Hamaguchi had sent to London approving the compromise had *not* conflicted with the professional advice of the Navy. Finally, he foiled last-minute attempts by the nationalist-minded Hiranuma Kiichirō, Vice-President of the Privy Council, to challenge the legality of the Prime Minister's action. The treaty was finally ratified by the Privy Council on October 1, 1930.

Hamaguchi's temporary victory over the Naval General Staff and his indirect challenge to the military's right of supreme command for the sake of friendly cooperation with Great Britain and the United States only acted as an incentive to the nascent nationalist forces. Even before the ratification process was completed the Supreme War Council notified the Emperor that the London Treaty created deficiencies in the Imperial Navy and that in the future the defense policies established in 1922 should be followed. It concluded that the Empire should renew its efforts upon the expiration of the London Treaty in 1936 "for the completion of its national defense through whatever policy it considers to be best." [19]

The Lion, Hamaguchi, had won a victory by a *tour de force* but it was to be of short duration. The Seiyūkai party did its best to embarrass the Cabinet for having neglected to follow the advice of the military experts. The retrenchment in government expenditures, the abolition of the gold embargo, and the world depression were causing widespread unemployment and economic stagnation. Society was rapidly becoming polarized. The few, exorbitantly rich *zaibatsu* families controlled an even larger segment of the national economy. Farmers, workers, and small businessmen were mere cogs in a system in which they had little influence. They were skeptical of the collusion of big business interests and the political parties. A strong, independent, liberal-minded middle class was largely nonexistent. The expansionists and ultranationalists in the innumerable secret societies and in key positions in the Imperial Army were convinced that a continuation of Hamaguchi's conciliation toward China and disregard for the opinions of the Chiefs of Staff challenged the foundation of their power. A large proportion of the members of Parliament, the press, and the public at large believed that Japan should continue to have a privileged position in China. They were skeptical of the value of a policy of conciliation.

As was so often the case in Japan's modern century, a single, lawless act dramatized a widespread dissatisfaction with the new policies and caused an immediate reaction against them. In mid-November, 1930, while waiting in the Tokyo station, Hamaguchi was shot by a fanatical patriot and member of a nationalist society. Although he survived for nearly a year, this attack shattered his leadership and destroyed at a single blow the principle of supremacy of the civilian branch of the government over the military and over the oligarchs. His immediate successors were unable to hold the Minseitō party together. Of even greater significance was the inability of the party leaders to stop the drive of the Japanese military in China set off by their coup in Mukden on September 18, 1931. A. Morgan Young, one of the most fearless and objective contemporary foreign observers, expressed it:

> Hamaguchi died on August 26th, and a month later all that he had striven for was flung to the winds, and all that he had saved was squandered.[20]

Notes

1. In the election in May, 1920, Hara's Seiyūkai increased its seats in the Lower House by 120, jumping from 162 to 282. The Kenseikai decreased from 118 to 108. For more extensive accounts of Hara's domestic policies see Peter Duus, *Party Rivalry and Political Change in Taishō Japan* (Cambridge: Harvard University Press, 1968), pp. 86–106; Shinobu Seisaburō, *Taishō Seiji Shi* (4 vols.; Tokyo: Kawade Shobō, 1951), IV, pp. 1044 ff.; and Ōkubo Toshiaki, *Kindai Shi III, Nihon Zenshi* (Tokyo: Tokyo Daigaku Shuppan Kai, 1964), X, pp. 226 ff.

2. There were three nonparty Cabinets from June, 1922, to June, 1924. The first of these (June 12, 1922–September 2, 1923) was that of Admiral Katō Tomosaburō, Naval Minister in the four previous Cabinets and head of the Japanese Delegation to the Washington Conference. With his death from natural causes in August, 1923, his Cabinet resigned. It was followed by that of Admiral Yamamoto Gombei (September 2, 1923–January 7, 1924), which had to struggle with the problems created by the Tokyo earthquake and fire of September 1, 1923, and which resigned after an attempt was made on the life of the Prince Regent. Viscount Kiyoura, President of the Privy Council, was next appointed Prime Minister and survived until June 11, 1924, when he gave way to Katō Kōmei's party Cabinet, and Japan had another short period of party governments.

3. The conditions laid down by the United States included the pooling of preferences and options of any member banks, the exclusive support of the member governments for the banks in the Consortium, and the maintenance of the administrative integrity and independence of China by all members.

See A. Whitney Griswold, *The Far Eastern Policy of the United States* (New York: Harcourt, Brace and Co., 1938), pp. 223 ff.

4. For older, standard accounts of the Washington Conference see R. L. Buell, *The Washington Conference* (New York: D. Appleton & Co., 1922), and Griswold, *op. cit.*, pp. 305–32. In terms of its effect on the U. S. Navy see Gerald E. Wheeler, *Prelude to Pearl Harbor: The United States Navy and the Far East 1921–1931* (Columbia: University of Missouri Press, 1962). With the British Foreign Office files for that period having been made available, new works on the subject will appear by Earnest R. May and Asada Sadao. Official documents and texts of the treaties, from which subsequent quotations are taken, appear in United States Senate, 67th Congress, 2nd Session, Senate Report No. 126, *Conference on the Limitations of Armaments* (Washington: Government Printing Office, 1922).

5. Because of the frequency with which parts of this treaty were quoted in the various official exchanges during the next two decades with Japan, some of the clauses of the treaty follow:

Article I.

The Contracting Powers, other than China, agree:

(1) To respect the sovereignty, the independence, and the territorial and administrative integrity of China;

(2) To provide the fullest and most unembarrassed opportunity to China to develop and maintain for herself an effective and stable government;

(3) To use their influence for the purpose of effectually establishing and maintaining the principle of equal opportunity for the commerce and industry of all nations throughout the territory of China;

(4) To refrain from taking advantage of conditions in China in order to seek special rights and privileges which would abridge the rights of subjects or citizens of friendly States, and from countenancing actions inimical to the security of such States.

. . . .

Article III.

With a view to applying more effectually the principles of the Open Door or equality of opportunity in China for the trade and industry of all nations, the Contracting Powers, other than China, agree that they will not seek, nor support their respective nationals in seeking—

(a) any arrangement which might purport to establish in favor of their interests any general superiority of rights with respect to commercial or economic development in any designated region of China;

(b) any such monopoly or preference as would deprive the nationals of any other Power of the right of undertaking any legitimate trade or industry in China, or of participating with the Chinese government . . . in any category of public enterprise, or which . . . is calculated to frustrate the practical application of the principle of equal opportunity.

6. Griswold, *op. cit.*, p. 331.

7. A most inspiring book on the problem of Japanese in America is Bradford Smith, *Americans from Japan* (Philadelphia: J. B. Lippincott Co., 1949). Two more recent studies are Raymond A. Esthus, *Theodore Roosevelt and Japan* (Seattle: University of Washington Press, 1966); and Charles E. Neu,

An Uncertain Friendship: Theodore Roosevelt and Japan 1906–1909 (Cambridge: Harvard University Press, 1967).

The Gentlemen's Agreement of 1908 was incorporated into the United States–Japanese Commercial Treaty of 1911. In the latter, the Japanese Government agreed "to maintain with equal effectiveness the limitations and control which they have for the past three years exercised in regulation of the emigration of laborers to the United States." The actual net increase of immigrants for a fifteen-year period had been 8,681, all of whom were women. After 1920, even the admittance of women, so-called "picture brides," was forbidden.

8. United States House of Representatives, 68th Congress, House Report No. 350.

9. Itō Masanori, *Katō Takaaki* (Tokyo: Katō Haku Denki Hensan Iinkai, 1928), II, p. 460; and Shinobu, *op. cit.*, p. 1138.

10. Katō's first Cabinet had representatives from the other parties which had joined in the declaration. Seiyūkai members were Takahashi Korekiyo, Minister of Agriculture and Commerce, and Yokota Sennosuke, Minister of Justice. Inukai Tsuyoshi of the Kakushin Club was Minister of Communications. On August 2, 1925, Katō formed his second Cabinet, composed exclusively of Kenseikai members except for the Ministers of War and Navy. When Katō died on January 28, 1926, he was succeeded by his Home Minister, Wakatsuki Reijirō. The latter was forced to resign on April 20, 1927, over disagreement with the Privy Council on financial matters.

11. Other examples concerned outstanding professors. In 1920, Professor Morito Tatsuo of Tokyo Imperial University wrote an article on the social ideas of Kropotkin. He emphasized the advisability of achieving individual freedom but the authorities claimed that he had presented communism and anarchism in a favorable light. The court ruled that his writings disturbed the public peace and order. He was dismissed from the university, fined, and imprisoned. The publisher of the article, Ōuchi Hyoe, was accused as an accomplice. Four years later, Professor Yoshino Sakuzō also considered it expedient to resign from the same university because of his writings. Several years earlier, he had criticized the influence of the military in governmental affairs and claimed that neither the House of Peers nor the Privy Council spoke for the people. He was branded as a radical. The argument still continues as to whether that was a fair accusation. For example, in 1952, at the annual meeting of the Political Science Association of Japan, Shinobu Seisaburō, an outspoken leftist, claimed that Yoshino was nothing more than a liberal. His opponent, Kaji Ryūmei, argued that Yoshino was at least a Socialist.

The study of the origin and growth of the leftist movement in Japan has received an inordinate amount of attention by Japanese political scientists and historians since World War II. For example, Professor Shinobu (*op. cit.*) devotes considerable space to it, giving it a Marxist slant. The reader wishing to pursue the subject in Japanese will find extensive bibliographical references in the thorough and competent monographs by Western scholars such as: George M. Beckmann and Ōkubo Genji, *The Japanese Communist Party, 1922–1945* (Stanford: Stanford University Press, 1969); Robert A. Scalapino, *The Japanese Communist Movement 1920–1966* (Berkeley: University of California Press, 1967); and George O. Totten III, *The Social Democratic Movement in Prewar Japan* (New Haven: Yale University Press, 1966).

12. For translation of the first three articles of the law see Harold S. Quigley, *Japanese Government and Politics: An Introductory Study* (New York: Century, 1932), pp. 57–58. An extensive detailed account of both the Suffrage and Peace Preservation Laws is in Shinobu, *op. cit.*, pp. 1179 ff.

13. In the last Diet before Tanaka's appointment, the Seiyūkai had 158 seats in contrast to the Kenseikai's 166 seats, out of a total of 466, so neither controlled an absolute majority. Because of his military background, he was an acceptable choice to most of the military men. On the other hand, because of the scandals in which he was involved as Minister of War (1918–1921) and had not satisfactorily cleared himself, he was less acceptable to the public at large. He had been charged with using three million yen of the Ministry's funds to bribe parliamentary and party leaders. In the February, 1928, election, the first under universal manhood suffrage, the Seiyūkai won 221 seats; the successor to the Kenseikai, the Minseitō, won 214 seats; and the group of proletariat parties won eight seats. Duus, *op. cit.*, pp. 214–32. Figures for party representation in the Diet are taken from Tōyama Shigeki and Adachi Shizuko, *Kindai Hikkei* (Tokyo: Iwanami Shoten, 1967), p. 123.

14. If previous practice is followed, after his death he will be known by the name of his reign, Emperor Shōwa. Though prejudiced in favor of the Imperial system, an interesting account of Hirohito will be found in Nezu Masashi, *Dai Nihon Teikoku no Hōgai. Tennō Shōwa Ki* (2 vols.; Tokyo: Shiseidō, 1961).

15. Ōuchi Tsutomi, *Fuashizumu no Michi, Nihon no Rekishi* (Tokyo: Chūo Koron, 1967), XXIV, pp. 96 ff.

16. The Japanese public had no way of knowing at the time of Tanaka's resignation that his downfall was due to insubordination within the Army. Having been a general, he was identified with expansionism and militarism. He made no effort to gain popular favor by accusing his colleagues of disobedience. Perhaps it would have been futile to do so, since his willingness to agree to the Pact of Paris had only increased his woes. Some of his enemies accused him of usurping the Imperial prerogatives. Faced with unpopularity on all sides, he was content to retire from public life and died shortly thereafter in the arms of his mistress. Suicide was rumored but actually he died of a heart attack.

Because of the unusual reading of his name, Colonel Komoto has been mistakenly transcribed by some western authors as Kawamoto. See Richard Storry, *The Double Patriots* (Boston: Houghton Mifflin Co., 1957), p. 44. For details of these events see Ōuchi, *op. cit.*, pp. 88 ff. On the drive of Chiang Kai-shek to unify China see O. E. Clubb, *20th Century China* (New York: Columbia University Press, 1964).

17. Hamaguchi Ōsachi (Yuko) (1870–1931) was born in Kōchi Prefecture in southwestern Japan. After graduating from Tokyo University, he entered the Ministry of Finance where he became Chief of the Monopoly Bureau, Vice-Minister of Communications, and later Vice-Minister of Finance. He was elected to the Lower House in 1915 and joined the Kenseikai. He served as Minister of Finance in the Katō Ministry in 1924 and Minister of Home Affairs under Wakatsuki. When the Minseitō was formed in 1927 as the successor of the Kenseikai, Hamaguchi was elected President. He was Premier from July 2, 1929, to November 15, 1930, and from March 9 to April 14, 1931. He died on August 26, 1931. Shidehara acted as interim Premier following the attack on Hamaguchi's life on November 15, 1930. Wakatsuki

became the new President and Premier on April 14, 1931. The Minseitō received financial support from the Mitsubishi interests. Inouye Junnosuke, Minister of Finance, and Shidehara, Foreign Minister, were sons-in-law of the head of Mitsubishi. The Seiyūkai received support from the rival Mitsui firm.

18. The export price of silk in 1929 equaled 1,420 yen per 100 *kin*. By October, 1930, it had dropped to 530 yen and in June, 1932, hit a low of 390 yen. Total exports during 1930 dropped 32 per cent and the value of silk exports fell 50 per cent. See G. C. Allen, *A Short Economic History of Modern Japan, 1867–1937* (with a supplementary chapter on economic recovery and expansion, 1945–1960) (2nd ed.; New York: Frederick A. Praeger, Inc., 1963), p. 111. For summaries of these events see Rōyama Masamichi, *Seiji Shi, Gendai Nihon Bummei Shi* (Tokyo: Tōyō Keizai Shimpōsha, 1950), II, pp. 449 ff.; Ōuchi Hyōe, "Keizai," in Yanaihara Tadao (ed.), *Gendai Nihon Shōshi* (Tokyo: Misuzu-shobō, 1952), I, pp. 157–88, and Ōuchi Tsutomi, *op. cit.*, pp. 181 ff.

19. For an excellent account of the London Naval Conference, especially in terms of the manner in which Hamaguchi outmaneuvered the opposition to the Treaty, see James B. Crowley, *Japan's Quest for Autonomy: National Security and Foreign Policy 1930–1938* (Princeton: Princeton University Press, 1966), pp. 35–82 and a forthcoming study by Arthur Tiedemann.

20. Young, an Englishman, was owner and editor of the *Japan Chronicle*. He continued his attacks on antidemocratic aspects of Japan long after the Manchurian Incident of September, 1931, and after all other foreign or Japanese editorial criticism of militarism within Japan had been silenced. See A. Morgan Young, *Imperial Japan, 1926–1938* (New York: William Morrow & Co., Inc., 1938), p. 61.

17

Militarism and Aggression in China, 1931–1937

The successful coup d'état of the Japanese military in Manchuria in September, 1931, was caused by events of even more importance than the death of Premier Hamaguchi. While he was indispensable for the continued supremacy of his party, his successors might have been able to control the military if other forces had not been stacked against them. Whether considered from the economic, social, or political point of view, Japan was psychologically ready for momentous events and for an imaginative leadership. For the unemployed, for the debt-ridden farmer, for the low-salaried worker, and for the student who saw little chance of employment after graduation, Marxism and communism had their appeal. For the officers in the lower echelons in the Imperial Army and Navy and for the recruits in the ranks, revitalized concepts of a divine mission in Asia and of state control of society seemed to be the salvation for Japan. As economic conditions worsened, ultranationalists found a receptive audience for their grandiose plans of conquest which promised prestige, wealth, and power for the Empire. Furthermore, this active Japanese expansionism emerged concurrently with a new movement for the unification of China under the leadership of Generalissimo Chiang Kai-shek. When he seriously threatened to incorporate Manchuria into China as an integral part of the Republic, he aroused the Japanese militarists.

The imaginative leaders of the Kwantung Army in South Manchuria interpreted these developments as a threat to the special privileges of themselves and of their nation. Inasmuch as they were convinced that their own government leaders were more likely to hinder than to help them, they acted on their own initiative. When the Japanese people realized that the military alone had a plan to solve the economic and international crisis which faced the nation, they followed this leadership. As the military successes on the Asiatic continent were ascribed to the divine attributes of the nation and of its sovereign, the Emperor's subjects willingly acquiesced in whatever demands were made of them. The history of the years between the coup in Manchuria in September, 1931, and the outbreak of war in North China in July, 1937, therefore, is that of these demands. It is also an account of how the nation accepted the philosophy of the ambitious and aggressive military and civilian leaders and of how it willingly followed them into war.

Confrontation of Chinese Unification and Japanese Expansionism

It is obvious from previous references to Chinese–Japanese relations that one of the constant aims of Japan's foreign policy had been to obtain and then to solidify special privileges on the Asiatic mainland. This objective had been comparatively easy to achieve, despite foreign intervention, so long as China continued to be politically unstable and disunited. But conditions were rapidly changing under the leadership of Chiang Kai-shek. By 1928, he had largely pacified northern China and had moved his capital to Nanking. Even the young Manchurian war lord, Chang Hsueh-liang, whom the Japanese military had expected to be able to control after they had killed his father (see page 357), had sworn allegiance to the Nationalist government and thereby defied Japan in Manchuria. In 1930, Chiang had launched his first Extermination Campaign against the communists. The political unification of China seemed closer than it had in many generations. In the spring of the next year, the annual convention of the Kuomintang had proclaimed that Port Arthur, Dairen, the Kwantung Leased Territory, and the South Manchurian Railway all should be returned to China. China had also won some notable diplomatic victories under the impetus of a nationalist resurgence. Great Britain had relinquished its concessions in five Chinese cities; the United States had been only the first of several Western powers to grant China tariff autonomy. By the summer of 1931, plans were afoot for the abolition of extraterritoriality. A certain number of limited agreements had been reached between China and Japan. The latter had recognized China's right to full tariff autonomy. Negotiations were continuing on the issue of extraterritoriality. Foreign Minister Shidehara had indicated that the Manchurian issue might be resolved if China would effect constructive reforms and recognize that the two countries complemented one another. In a word, China appeared to be on the threshold of a new era in which it would begin to guide its own destinies.

In this task it had the blessing and protection of the Nine Power Treaty signed at the Washington Conference nearly a decade earlier. But this independence from foreign domination could not be complete until

Japan's special position in Manchuria had been eliminated. Consequently, a concerted effort was made by the Chinese Nationalist Party (Kuomintang) to integrate Manchuria into the rest of China. Both political and economic means were taken to achieve this objective. In the first place, despite an agreement of 1905 to the contrary, a Chinese railway system was gradually constructed to compete with the Japanese-owned South Manchurian Railway. A special system of preferential tariff agreements was applied to the various Chinese railways which tended to siphon the freight through these lines to the seaboard. With the passing of each month, the Japanese-owned South Manchurian Railway increasingly felt the adverse effects of this plan. In the second place, the Kuomintang was sending its organizers to propagandize the schools and to cement the bonds between Nanking and Mukden. As in the case of the competition of the two railway systems, time was on the side of China rather than Japan. The Chinese population in Manchuria had been rapidly increasing and the Japanese had difficulty in buying land. Finally, Chang Hsueh-liang refused to negotiate with the Japanese on any Manchurian issues. He insisted that all matters should be referred to the Nationalist government at Nanking.[1]

Ultranationalism and Expansionism

Just as the concept of nationalism was taking hold in China, an ultranationalism was firing the imagination of the new civilian and military leaders in Japan. This new ultranationalism, which was redefined as time passed and as new emergencies arose, won acceptability in direct proportion to the growth of Chinese unification and of the anti-Japanese movement. Japanese nationalism also evolved from the reaction against the strengthening of the political parties, against the Cabinet's acceptance of disarmament, and against the increased popularity of the radicals. Since all of these trends were accelerated in the summer of 1931, an explosion at some point seemed more than likely. In fact, in view of the variety and number of the ultranationalist groups, it was surprising that the situation did not get out of hand sooner.

Advocacy of military expansion was not new in Japan. The earliest of the nationalist societies, working in conjunction with the military, had aided and abetted Japanese control over Korea and Manchuria. The philosophy of chauvinism was championed and implemented by the officers in charge of planning in the General Staff, the Intelligence Division, and the Kwantung Headquarters of the Imperial Army. When their plans received tacit support, if not encouragement, from several of the leading, senior Army officers, direct action by the military became the most dominant force in both domestic and foreign affairs.[2]

One of the most important ultranationalists was Kita Ikki (1884–1937). Impetuous and egocentric, Kita advocated a type of state socialism. In his *General Outline for the Reconstruction of Japan,* he set forth his program for a social revolution in which the nation was to be reconstructed by a military coup d'état after which the Emperor would be forced to declare martial law for three years, dissolve the Diet, and abolish the Privy Council and the nobility. A military junta would be elected to run the government. Japan's economic ills would be solved by the state's expropriation of all private property above a fixed amount and by the transfer of all of the Emperor's holdings to the state. British and Russian colonial territories in Asia would be conquered by Japan. Areas such as Manchuria and Siberia would be taken and their resources used to augment Japan's paucity of raw materials. Kita's ideas had a direct influence on various activists, notably the leaders of the attempted coup in February, 1936.[3]

Another leading nationalist was Ōkawa Shūmei, an advocate of a close working relationship with young military officers. He disagreed with Kita on several issues such as the nationalization of large enterprises. He was passionately committed to direct action and became personally involved in various plots.[4]

The strength of this new ultranationalism is illustrated by the plot of March, 1931, in which Ōkawa was to play an important part. In the summer of the previous year, Colonel Hashimoto Kingorō (1890–1957), in charge of Russian affairs in the Army General Staff, and several like-minded officers in the Intelligence Division formed the *Sakurakai* (Cherry Society). They believed that "the poisoned sword of the politicians, who have become exhausted and used up, is pointed at the Army. . . . We will not be defeated as was the Navy at the London Naval Conference." They were determined to save their country by carrying out a coup d'état. Working through Lieutenant General Tatekawa Yoshitsugu, Chief of the Intelligence Bureau of the General Staff, they were able to get support for their secret plans to overthrow the Hamaguchi government and to place it in the firm hands of the generals. The plan called for an attack on the headquarters of the political parties and a march on the Diet building by a crowd of 10,000 persons under the leadership of Ōkawa. General Tatekawa and other Army leaders were then to confront Premier Hamaguchi and demand his resignation and the installation of War Minister Ugaki Kazushige as the new Premier. Sensing the enormity of the plot, General Ugaki balked and ordered General Tatekawa and his colleagues not to go through with the plans. The plot dissolved but Colonel Hashimoto and his fellow members of the *Sakurakai* bided their time.[5]

With such a psychological attitude prevalent among the young army officers, especially those assigned to the General Staff and to the Kwantung Army in Manchuria, it was not difficult for them to find what they believed to be a *casus belli* in almost any act by the Chinese. Traditional Japanese interests in Manchuria were bound to clash with the Chinese Nationalists' attempts to integrate South Manchuria with the Nanking regime. These basic antagonisms began to explode into incidents which occurred at ever increasing frequency.

The Mukden Incident, September 18, 1931

In July, 1931, the Chinese residents of southeastern Manchuria revolted against the encroachments of Korean landowners. The Chinese resented the fact that the Koreans, as Japanese subjects, enjoyed extraterritorial rights and protection by Japan and hence were receiving preferential treatment. When the irate Chinese farmers attacked the Koreans as they constructed irrigation ditches for their community, the Koreans were protected by Japanese guards. This incident led to anti-Chinese riots in Korea and to a retaliatory anti-Japanese boycott in China. Negotiations to settle this incident had barely begun when reports trickled in from Inner Mongolia that a Japanese intelligence officer, a Captain Nakamura, had been killed in June by Chinese troops as a spy. Nakamura's colleagues, who were imbued with the ultranationalism of Ōkawa, argued that the incident revealed Chinese duplicity and hence the need to settle the Manchurian issue by force. They inflamed Japanese public opinion by maintaining that Nakamura was a civilian making a scholarly study and they challenged their own Foreign Office to force a favorable reply out of the Chinese government.

Simultaneously, various groups within the Imperial Army were crystallizing their own views on the future role of Japan in Manchuria and Mongolia. To tell how they gained the support of their superior officers for their plans, and how they acted without authority when their objectives were threatened, is to describe the Mukden Incident and the beginning of the Pacific War.[6]

At the beginning of summer, General Araki Sadao, who headed the Operations Division of the General Staff, had become convinced that Japan must take some type of military action in Manchuria to avoid becoming vulnerable to attack from the Soviet Union. His colleagues in the Intelligence Division of the General Staff had concluded that China should be expelled from Manchuria as a prelude to the creation of an "independent" Manchuria and Mongolia (but under Japanese control). At the same time, Colonel Nagata Tetsuzan, who had previously developed the scheme for the modernization of the Army, had been ordered to prepare a plan to settle the Manchurian problem. This document, which was approved by the Minister of War, the Chief of Staff, and General

Tatekawa Yoshitsugu, concluded that the anti-Japanese campaign in Manchuria was so serious that if these activities could not be controlled by diplomacy, then military action would be necessary. Consequently, the Minister of War, General Minami Jirō, and representatives from the General Staff were to keep in close touch with the Foreign Office and also prepare for ways and means of obtaining public support for such military action as might be necessary. Finally, the General Staff was to make plans concerning the armed forces required for such action. Thus the Minister of War, Chief of Staff, and others were prepared, if diplomacy failed, to initiate military action in Manchuria.[7]

At the same time, the members of the Special Affairs section of the Kwantung Army had worked out details for the military occupation of Manchuria, with the recommendation that the plan be put into effect if Japanese life and property there were threatened. One of them, Major Hanaya, made a secret trip to Tokyo urging the most influential authorities in the Imperial Army to approve of their proposals. Colonels Itagaki Seishirō and Ishihara Kanji, chief authors of the plan, received encouragement from their commander-in-chief and by the end of August had completed their preparations for action.[8]

There were also clear signs of increased friction between the military and the civilian members of the Cabinet. In early August, Minister of War Minami addressed the new district commanders, emphasizing the need for greater military expenditures, and chided the Wakatsuki government for not recognizing this fact. Furthermore, Foreign Minister Shidehara was dissatisfied with the negotiations which General Doihara Kenji was conducting with the Manchurian warlord Chang Hsueh-liang over Captain Nakamura's death. Doihara had insisted that General Chang should take personal responsibility for Nakamura's "murder," should apologize and guarantee that such an incident would not occur again. Chang refused. General Doihara was ordered home and told by the Prime Minister and Shidehara that Chang should not be held responsible for Nakamura's death and that the issue should be settled on that basis. This decision was transmitted to Kwantung headquarters where it was passed on to Colonels Ishihara and Itagaki.

Enraged at this interference of the civilian Cabinet members with military matters, they tried to persuade their commander-in-chief, Honjō Shigeru, to approve of their taking direct action. He was dissuaded by his deputy who, on September 14, 1931, cabled Tokyo that the situation in Manchuria was so critical that General Tatekawa, who had just been appointed Chief of Operations in the General Staff, should be sent to Manchuria immediately to prevent overt action by younger officers. The next day the Foreign Minister received a report from the Consul General in Mukden that a coup was imminent. Shidehara immediately reprimanded War Minister Minami for allowing such a situation to develop. Previously the Prime Minister had also expressed to the War Minister his concern over the trend of events; but the civilian arm of the government found itself helpless.

As a result of these ominous reports, Chief of Staff Kanaya and War Minister Minami ordered General Tatekawa to proceed to Manchuria to caution General Honjō, Commander of the Kwantung Army, to control his subordinates. But this was a vain gesture. The conspirators in Manchuria had too many accomplices in key positions. They had already received tacit, if not explicit, approval for their scheme from General Tatekawa. One of their confreres in the General Staff informed them of the purpose of General Tatekawa's visit and said that he would not meet their commander-in-chief for forty-eight hours. This information gave Ishihara and Itagaki ample time to manufacture an incident. This they obviously decided to do. Colonel Itagaki saw to it that he was on hand to meet General Tatekawa when he arrived in Mukden on the evening of September 18. He was taken to a *geisha* house where he was entertained and stayed throughout the night. At about 11 P.M., a bomb exploded mysteriously on or near the South Manchurian Railway tracks in the section of Mukden where the best Chinese troops were located and where Itagaki was the commander of the Japanese troops. On his own initiative, he ordered his troops to attack the north barracks of the Chinese troops. A few hours later, Commander-in-Chief Honjō, under pressure from Ishihara, ordered the mobilization of all Japanese troops in Manchuria. By the time General Tatekawa met General Honjō, Mukden was under occupation and the first phase of the conquest of China had begun.

The Kwantung Army Defies the Cabinet and the League of Nations

The Tokyo morning newspapers reported that "at 10:30 P.M., a group of lawless Chinese bandits northwest of the northern barracks bombed the South Manchurian Railway. Since they attacked our guards, a battalion lost no time to fight back." On the assumption that Japanese lives and property were in jeopardy, the Kwantung Army and the General Staff in Tokyo urged the complete implementation of the plans already approved for the takeover of Manchuria. But War Minister Minami soon discovered that the Cabinet, which met immediately, disagreed and ordered the incident settled forthwith.

The civilian and military branches of the government continued to disagree and to act at cross purposes. The Premier reported to the Emperor that his Cabinet was seeking a peaceful solution to the Mukden

Incident, as it came to be called. At the same time, General Honjō was informed by the General Staff that, under the Army's right of supreme command, the Cabinet's decision was not necessarily binding. Furthermore, a subsequent directive notified the Kwantung Army that, under the discretionary power of the field commander, it could advance several miles beyond Mukden and "undertake limited operations without waiting for direct orders." [9]

The Wakatsuki Cabinet was further restricted in its freedom of action by developments in Korea. Mindful of an earlier offer of the Commander of the Japanese Army in Korea, General Hayashi Senjirō, to send reinforcements when needed, the Kwantung Army asked for his help. By midmorning of September 19, troops had begun to concentrate in northern Korea. Two days later, without receiving orders from his superiors, General Hayashi commanded his troops to cross the border. By sending his troops into an area not under his command, he had compromised the Emperor's right of Supreme Command. Nevertheless, the Chief of Staff supported his action. Hayashi's troops had already reached Mukden when the Cabinet gave *ex post facto* approval to this "unauthorized crossing of the border." Similarly, the Emperor sanctioned it after the fact and reportedly told his Chief of Staff that the Army should be more discreet in the future. In Geneva, the Council of the League of Nations was informed by the Japanese delegate that his government was taking all measures possible to prevent a local incident from spreading. On September 21, China appealed to the League to prevent further deterioration of the situation and to demand a re-establishment of the *status quo ante*.

Although it had been suspected in Geneva, London, and Washington, and even in some circles in Tokyo, that the Japanese Army was out of hand, many of the world's leading diplomats believed this to be only a temporary situation. Most foreign observers, blinded partly by wishful thinking and partly by ignorance, held to the opinion that, if the Cabinet and Foreign Minister Shidehara were not embarrassed by precipitate foreign action, then they would be able to regain control. Few persons realized that the only possibility of stopping the irresponsible acts of the military would have been for the Prime Minister, the political parties, the League of Nations, and the United States to have opposed these acts in unequivocal terms.

But the realities of the times made any moves along these lines impossible. In fact, a general timorousness and aptitude for procrastination by opposition groups within Japan and by the powers only stimulated aggressive groups throughout the world. The young officers, who had successfully staged the plot near Mukden, realized that they could do it elsewhere in China with little opposition. They or their colleagues might even be able to overthrow the Cabinet and establish a military dictatorship. A Mussolini or a Hitler could argue that, since Japan's aggression was not checked in Manchuria, it was unlikely that anyone would dare to stop a Fascist or a Nazi drive in Europe or Africa.

But to return to the Manchurian Incident, as it came to be called, two basic questions remain to be answered. They are: (1) What were the effects of the action of the Japanese military in Manchuria? (2) What were the reasons for these developments? The explosion in Manchuria on September 18, 1931, set off a chain reaction with results, though not immediate, that were to make inevitable a conflict between the Axis Powers and the Allies. Space will not permit a detailed account of all of the phases of this reaction. Suffice it to refer to a few significant aspects of the events which followed. In the first place, the world and the League of Nations were confronted with all of the dangers and irritations emanating from the operation of dual diplomacy in Japan. While the Japanese representative in Geneva was assuring the Council of the League that his government was taking steps to confine the movement of Japanese troops in Manchuria, the military were executing a plan previously approved by the Chiefs of Staff.

At Geneva, on September 30, Japan agreed to abide by a resolution of the Council of the League. This resolution clearly committed Japan to a speedy withdrawal of its troops to within the South Manchurian Railway zone and to a promise not to aggravate the situation further. Both the League and Secretary of State Stimson assumed that Japan would comply. They had confidence in Foreign Minister Shidehara's ability to negotiate a settlement between China and Japan. But none of the Western powers realized that they were expecting him to accomplish the impossible. In the first place, the Imperial Army took a position contrary to that of Shidehara, the League, and China. The Army insisted that China agree to recognize Japan's special interests and position in Manchuria before its troops withdrew. Secondly, the Imperial Army would give no assurance that it would not advance into North Manchuria or Jehol before a comprehensive settlement had been reached with China. China insisted, with support from the United States, that Japan had acted illegally in Manchuria and its troops must be withdrawn to their former position before serious negotiations could begin.

In the midst of this impasse, in defiance of the League's resolution and the promise of Shidehara to the Council that Japan would not carry out any further aggressive action, on October 18 the Kwantung Army bombed Chinchow, the provisional capital of Manchurian warlord Chang Hsueh-liang.[10] Furthermore, Japan insisted that outstanding differences with China should be settled by direct negotiations between the two countries and that they did not concern the League. In reality, the military were determining policy and also deciding when and how it should be executed. They left to the Foreign Office and its diplomats

Military Aggression on the Asiatic Mainland, 1931–1937

the task of extricating Japan from any international complications which resulted from these aggressive acts. This involvement of the military in policy and in politics, therefore, was another important result of the Manchurian explosion.

Militants Endanger Party Politics

Not only were the Foreign Office and the Cabinet forced to follow the Army's lead in Manchuria, but they found themselves forced into subservience to its desires at home. This situation was the result of both overt and covert actions by elements in the Army. After the outbreak of hostilities in Manchuria, Premier Wakatsuki and his colleagues appear to have leaned over backward to avoid any direct criticism of the War Minister. They seemed to sense that any insistence on their part upon a reversal of policy or upon a demand that insubordinate officers be reprimanded would have caused the War Minister to resign. Such a move would have overthrown the Cabinet and might have meant the end of party governments.

Colonel Hashimoto and other members of the *Sakurakai* became increasingly displeased with the Cabinet and impatient over the lack of success of Shidehara's diplomacy. In early October, with the help of Ōkawa Shūmei, they plotted to exterminate the Cabinet by aerial bombardment and to replace it with a group of extreme nationalists. The plot came to nought when General Araki learned of their plans, reported the matter to his colleagues, and had them arrested. Vice-Minister of War Sugiyama Gen transferred the leaders out of their staff positions and ordered the *Sakurakai* dissolved. To protect the Army's reputation, information about the plot was kept secret. From the actions of the ranking military officers, they were not yet ready to accept the establishment of a fascist-type government.[11]

As the pressure, slight though it may have been, continued to be exerted on Japan by the League's Council and as Prime Minister Wakatsuki became increasingly less able and willing to control the War Minister, the Cabinet became less stable. The Premier wanted to resign but had no appropriate successor to recommend. The Army's direct action in Manchuria was receiving widespread support. Home Minister Adachi was seeking an alliance with the right wing of the opposition party, the Seiyūkai, under the leadership of Mori Kaku. The Privy Council, with prodding from Baron Hiranuma, an avowed ultranationalist, supported an aggressive policy.

After Japan had failed to carry out the League's resolution requiring the withdrawal of troops, the Council met in mid-November, 1931, to consider the next appropriate step it should take. At this juncture, Foreign Minister Shidehara agreed to the appointment of a Commission of Enquiry to be dispatched to Manchuria, so long as it did not interfere with Sino-Japanese negotiations for settling the issue. He had also persuaded the Imperial Army not to advance on the city of Chinchow with the understanding that Chinese troops would be withdrawn southward to the Great Wall. Thus, nearly three months after the explosion at Mukden, the Council unanimously approved the dispatch of a Commission to make a study at first hand and to report to the Council any circumstances which threatened to disturb the peace.[12]

In the meantime, the precarious structure Shidehara had built to prevent further hostilities collapsed abruptly. The Chinese government refused to withdraw its troops from the Chinchow–Great Wall area.

Simultaneously, the Kwantung Army pressed for the expulsion of the Chinese from North Manchuria. Finally, in December, the leadership of the Imperial Army decided to (1) reinforce the Kwantung Army so that it could gain control over North Manchuria; (2) cultivate the formation of an independent Manchuria; (3) invade Jehol Province and thus command the pass through the Great Wall at Shanhaikwan; and (4) select General Araki Sadao as the new Minister of War. There was no alternative for the Wakatsuki Cabinet but to capitulate.

When Wakatsuki resigned as Prime Minister on December 13, 1931, the Elder Statesman, Saionji, decided he would continue the previous policy of selecting the new Premier from the opposition party. On the other hand, he was unwilling to recommend the appointment of Suzuki Kisaburō, President of the Seiyūkai, because of his nationalist tendencies and those of his strongest supporter, Baron Hiranuma. He turned, therefore, to Inukai Ki, who was critical of the unsuccessful foreign policy of Shidehara but was not willing to support the Army's contention that it could act as it wished in Manchuria. When Inukai was informed of his appointment as Prime Minister, he received the following message from the Emperor:

> Meddling of the Army in domestic and foreign affairs is something which for the welfare of the nation must be viewed with apprehension. Be mindful of my anxiety.[13]

Inukai, who was the last Party Premier in prewar Japan, devoted the next, and last, five months of his life to trying to keep the Army in check.

But the trend toward military fascism gained momentum despite Inukai's good intentions and the apprehension of the Emperor. The young officers responsible for starting the occupation of Manchuria had been eulogized by certain elements in the Imperial Army and had not been disciplined; nothing had happened to the civilian colleagues of Colonel Hashimoto, such as Ōkawa Shūmei, who had planned the October coup. General Araki, the leader of the Imperial Way Faction (*Kōdō ha*) of the Army became War Minister. Prince General Kanin was the new Chief of Staff but most of the decisions were made by Vice-Chief of Staff Mazaki Junzaburō, a close associate of General Araki. The people at large were far from satisfied with the government's policy toward China or with their economic plight. Unemployment and social unrest, arising from the world depression, provided fertile ground for nationalistic propaganda. The time was ripe for an appeal to people's innate patriotism to make them champion a policy of expansionism rather than the less spectacular task of improving their plight by retrenchment and austerity. The spiritual yearning of the people was easily satisfied by a plea to return to the way of their ancestral gods. Once launched on a program of aggression, there was no turning back; foreign remonstrances and warnings merely served to arouse national feelings.

Manchuria Conquered and End of Party Cabinets—1932

The strongest of these remonstrances came from Secretary of State Stimson. With great faith in Shidehara's ability to restrain the extremists, he had followed a cautious policy so as not to excite the latter. He was relieved to receive Shidehara's assurances that the Army did not contemplate the capture of Chinchow but was apprehensive when Shidehara was forced out of office. Stimson's worst forebodings became a harsh reality on January 2, 1932, when the Kwantung Army occupied that city, the last vestige of Chinese authority in South Manchuria. Believing implicitly in the value of moral principles, he decided that it was imperative to warn Japan that "the United States does not intend to recognize any situation, treaty or agreement which may be brought about by means contrary to the Pact of Paris." He was more than disappointed when Great Britain refused to join him in this demarche and when Japan was not deterred by his famous "non-recognition formula." [14]

By February, 1932, Japan was already well along the fascist road. The Army had completed its military campaign in Manchuria and had instigated an "independence movement." In February, 1932, the new "state" of Manchukuo declared its independence. The next month, Pu Yi, former youthful ruler on the Manchu throne, who had been taken to Dairen under the protective custody of the Kwantung Army, was inaugurated as Provisional President.

In the meantime, hostilities had flared up in Shanghai after Japanese troops had landed allegedly to protect their fellow countrymen's lives and property from violent anti-Japanese demonstrations. The Chinese 19th Army put up stiff resistance, deprived Japan of a quick victory, and forced it to send extensive reinforcements. The Shanghai attack further alienated the Western powers and solidified American opinion against Japan. Secretary Stimson's hint that such action might result in America reappraising the value of the Washington Naval Treaties only aggravated the situation. Japanese naval leaders used it as evidence that they could no longer rely on the treaties for their nation's security but must strengthen their naval forces and insist on parity at the next naval conferences.

Japanese extremists were taking matters into their own hands. For example, in February, 1932, Inouye Junnosuke, former Finance Minister and campaign manager of the Minseitō party, was shot and killed by a peasant lad. Within less than a month, Dan Takuma, Managing Director of the Mitsui combines, was also murdered. Both of these assassinations were perpetrated in the name of patriotism against men described by their assailants as typical representatives of the politicians and capitalists who were responsible for the ruinous state of the country. Both the civilian and military ultranationalists were also encouraged by the elections for the House of Representatives. Candidates who advocated conservatism at home and an aggressive policy abroad were invariably elected. Prime Minister Inukai's party, the Seiyūkai, which was known for its support of a strong attitude toward China, received an overwhelming majority. There was little likelihood, therefore, that Parliament would place obstacles in the way of the Kwantung Army in its consolidation of Japan's position on the continent.

But the leading politicians of both of the main parties, members of the Privy Council, and heads of the industrial and banking combines, the *zaibatsu,* were anathema to several of the ultranationalists. The latter believed that all of these groups were evil and were obstacles to the blossoming of Japan's pure, imperishable, unique national principle. They insisted that an ideal familial state under the divine Emperor could be renovated only after these leaders were destroyed. Hence, on May 15, 1932, a small group of zealous farmers and naval officers tried to overthrow the government. They assassinated Premier Inukai, attacked other officials, and bombed the Bank of Japan and other key spots in Tokyo. Naïve and ill-conceived though this plot may have been, it rang down the curtain on party cabinets and set the stage for the predominance of the Army in the Japanese government. But resistance from several of the Emperor's key advisers, a struggle for control among factions within the Army, and concern of business and financial leaders for the future of the nation's economy combined to retard, but not prevent, the spread of totalitarianism.[15]

With the sudden demise of Inukai, Saionji was again faced with the question of whether to continue to select a party leader as Prime Minister or a national figure capable of uniting the nation and, hopefully, of controlling the military. As for the former alternative, however, his choice was limited. The clear defeat of the Minseitō at the elections in February made it undesirable to turn to it for leadership. As for the Seiyūkai, five months earlier he had rejected Suzuki Kisaburō as too nationalistic. Consequently, Saionji compromised by choosing the more moderate former Governor-General of Korea, Admiral Saitō Makoto, who formed a nationalist, nonparty cabinet.

Broad Support for Military

In reality, a new era was inaugurated with this new government. Prewar party cabinets ceased to exist. General Araki Sadao, as Minister of War, leader of the Imperial Way Faction (*Kōdō ha*) of the Army and idol of the young officers, was the most influential person in the government. Political leaders, as such, were denied access to the Cabinet. The various Ministers of State became spokesmen for their own ministries, thus enhancing the importance of the bureaucracy. Saionji, who as the only surviving Elder Statesman, had selected the Prime Ministers, was replaced by a group composed of former premiers, known as *Jūshin* (Senior Statesmen). Basic policies came to be decided by Five Ministers Conferences (Prime Minister, Foreign, War, Navy, and Finance Ministers).

One of the most significant aspects of Admiral Saitō's government was the struggle between War Minister Araki Sadao and Finance Minister Takahashi Korekiyo. The former espoused the expansionist aims of the Imperial Army and justified its action in Manchuria, Inner Mongolia, and North China. Takahashi, although basically a conservative, fearlessly opposed the continuous demands of the military for greater military expenditures.

But Takahashi was faced with insurmountable obstacles. Each new move of the Army on the continent required even greater expenditures. After the pacification of Manchuria and the organization of Manchukuo, Japanese forces advanced on Jehol Province in Inner Mongolia and by March, 1933, occupied its key points. In Geneva, the Japanese delegate, Matsuoka Yōsuke, who was a notorious nationalist and pro-Army man, walked out of the League of Nations in protest over its criticism of Japan's actions. In further defiance of world opinion, hostilities were extended to North China. They ceased temporarily, at least, only after the Chinese and Japanese commanders signed a truce at the end of May, 1933, at Tangku. By the Tangku Truce, an area of about 5,000 square miles between Peking and the Manchurian border was demilitarized. The Chinese Army was to withdraw from the area. The Kwantung Army had the right to verify this withdrawal and promised to retire northward to the Great Wall. On the other hand, peace and order were to be maintained by a police force friendly to Japan. Consequently, the Kwantung Army was now committed to protect all of Manchuria and China north of Peking.

Faced with these *faits accomplis,* Finance Minister Takahashi was placed in an untenable position. Military expenditures increased from roughly 500 million yen in 1930 to 873 million yen in 1933, and to 941.8 million yen, or 43.3 per cent of the entire budget, in 1934. When queried in Parliament as to why the armed services needed this amount, Takahashi could only give evasive answers. War Minister Araki insisted that expenditures would continue to increase in the future and that the reasons were none of Parliament's business. If he could persuade the people to have implicit faith in the Army's leaders and in the invincibility of the Army and Navy, then the dictatorship of the military would be complete. He then set about instilling this attitude among both the Armed Services and the people at large. A man of unselfish motives and simple personal habits, he was at heart a soldier. He was also devoted to strengthening Japan through the dissemination of the Imperial Way (*Kōdō*).

Araki's nationalist philosophy, as well as that of many of his colleagues in the Army, was disseminated through a series of Army pamphlets. First published in 1934, these pamphlets emphasized the need of adequate defense to counteract what was described as the menace created by the air forces of the Soviet Union and the United States. The pamphlets argued that the unstable balance of power in the world and the threat of communism dictated a broad economic and social mobilization of the entire nation. The Japanese were destined through the working of the Imperial Way to bring peace and order to the Asiatic continent. War, the father of creation, should be encouraged; a new regime of social justice should be promoted.

Another pamphlet, which concentrated on the international crisis created by the Manchurian invasion, maintained that Japan had been insulted. It added:

> Not only in order to work out our protective measures with respect to Manchuria and Mongolia, but also to show the world our brilliant essence, it is necessary . . . that the entire nation be awakened to the convictions and ideals of the Imperial Army. . . .[16]

As the crisis in Asia increased, persons from all classes in society—the political parties, businessmen, laborers, and farmers—found in the pamphlets philosophical and religious justification for the nation's expansionist program. Those "liberals" who were outspoken in their criticism of the military lived in constant danger of assassination. Political assassins, so long as they pleaded that they had been motivated by patriotism, received ridiculously light sentences from the courts.

As time passed, even the Foreign Office, in addition to sponsoring withdrawal from the League, showed clear signs of supporting a strong antiforeign policy and expansionism in China. This was particularly true after September, 1933, with the appointment of Hirota Kōki as Foreign Minister. For the next five years he was probably the most influential civilian in the Japanese government. He was a staunch advocate of cooperation and harmony between Japan and other nations if the latter agreed to Japan's hegemony over Manchuria and North China. He was determined that Japan accomplish its mission of supremacy in East Asia regardless of whether other nations approved or accepted it. This policy was more specifically enunciated in a statement issued by the Foreign

Office spokesman in April, 1934. Known as the Amau Statement, it declared that China should not avail itself of the assistance of any country other than Japan. Furthermore, the statement warned that if any other country supplied China with military instructors, advisers, or war planes, or provided funds in the name of technical and financial assistance, Japan would oppose such moves as threats to peace and order in East Asia. In other words, any individual or concerted action by the Western powers to bolster the faltering resistance of China would not be countenanced by Japan. If China was to be a united nation, it would be so at the sufferance of Japan and under its tutelage.[17]

There were other indications that Foreign Minister Hirota acquiesced in the general policy of strengthening the Empire's position in Asia. For example, negotiations had begun in 1933 with the Soviet Union for the purchase of the Chinese Eastern Railway, for the settlement of boundary claims, and for the extension of oil and fishing rights. Since the formation of Manchukuo, the Soviet Union realized that the Chinese Eastern Railway had lost much of its strategic and economic importance and hence should be sold. Furthermore, the 2,000 miles of contiguous Soviet–Manchukuo frontier had caused innumerable border clashes and disputes. Although both Japan and the Soviet Union had much to gain by successfully negotiating these issues, it took two years before they could agree to mutually acceptable terms. In the spring of 1935, a sale price was agreed upon for the Chinese Eastern Railway, with Japan guaranteeing the payment in money and goods. The year following, both countries agreed in principle to the formation of a commission to adjudicate disputes and to settle the Soviet–Manchukuo boundary.

Demise of Opposition

Additional evidence continued to accumulate, leading to the conclusion that Japan was preparing for any eventuality. Although the War Minister, General Araki, had been replaced in January, 1934, by the more moderate General Hayashi Senjūrō, members of the Control Faction of the Army were appointed to key posts. General Nagata Tetsuzan, the advocate of total preparedness, was the new head of the Military Affairs Bureau of the War Ministry. General Sugiyama Gen was Vice-Chief of Staff. The Japanese delegates to the preparatory Naval Conference in London were instructed not to negotiate for a new Naval Treaty unless it provided for parity of the Japanese fleet with those of Great Britain and the United States. In December, 1934, Japan gave formal notice of renunciation of the Washington Treaties, thus opening the doors for an unlimited naval construction and fortification program after 1936. At the same time, the American Ambassador, Joseph C. Grew, cabled from Tokyo that: "The armed forces of the country are perfectly capable of overriding the restraining control of the government and committing what might well amount to national 'harakiri' in a mistaken conception of patriotism."

With the northern flank thus secured by agreements with the Soviet Union, Japan turned toward a more permanent solution of the China problem. Basically, the points at issue between China and Japan were clear. China claimed in 1935, just as it had maintained at the Paris Peace Conference, that Japan had no legal basis for the special privileges it demanded on the continent. The Nationalist government maintained that the Mukden Incident of September 18, 1931, the Japanese occupation of Manchuria, their "autonomous independence movement" which created Manchukuo, and their penetration into Inner Mongolia and North China all stemmed from the aggressive and inexcusable action of the Japanese militarists. The Kuomintang insisted that the local military agreement between Chinese and Japanese commanders were designed to secure Japan's dominance over the Asiatic continent. The members of the League of Nations, the Soviet Union, and the United States generally supported China's position. On the other hand, both militarily and politically Japan was entrenched in Manchuria, Inner Mongolia, and North China. None of the Western powers was willing to risk a war by openly challenging Japan's position.

At home, political parties were discredited and party cabinets had given way to coalition governments. Ultranationalists threatened to overthrow the cabinet if it showed any sign of sanctioning liberal thought. This fact is clearly illustrated by the controversy that arose over Professor Minobe Tatsukichi's famous Organ Theory. Professor Minobe (1873–1948), an authority on Japanese constitutional law, had maintained in his scholarly treatises on the Japanese Constitution that the Emperor exercised governmental power not solely in his own right but as an organ of the State. Such a position was anathema to those who stressed the sacred and inviolable attributes of the sovereign, to whom the military, through their right of supreme command, could turn for sanction of their actions. Consequently, as ultranationalism became more aggressive, Minobe was attacked in both houses of the Diet and charged with lese majesty. The Okada Cabinet took an equivocable position on the issue. In September, 1935, the leaders of the Imperial Way faction of the Army forced the resignation of War Minister Hayashi. His successor, General Kawashima Kazuo, with the aid of the conservative members of Parliament, insisted that the government take a firm position on the Minobe case. Consequently, the Cabinet announced that Minobe would be stripped of his honors and his faculty appointment. It proclaimed that the Emperor was the absolute repository of sovereignty and was not an organ of the State.[18]

The last vestiges of a liberal interpretation of the Constitution having been discredited, the Japanese government and people argued, with near unanimity, that old standards of international law were not applicable to the unsolved problems between Japan and China. In other words, the Empire's defense requirements, including its economic needs for natural resources and undeveloped land areas, all necessitated the creation of puppet states on the continent. In this manner, Japan could be assured of the friendliness of the puppet governments and simultaneously be able to control and exploit the resources in those areas which would contribute toward a self-sufficient armament industry. The Japanese argument continued that, if the local or national Chinese authorities could not protect Japanese life and property, then the Japanese Army would take over that responsibility in self-defense. Finally, while Japan recognized that it was natural for China to want to become unified, it should be permitted to do so only if it did not interfere in any way with Japan's plans for expansion on the continent.

Preliminaries to Full-scale War in China

If the events which led to a full-scale war in China and to a united front in the Japanese homeland are to be understood, it is not enough to dismiss Japan's position as illegal and groundless or to claim that the arguments are illogical. On the contrary, it must be recognized that many Japanese were firmly convinced of the validity of these claims. Furthermore, they were coming to believe that their country had to defend its action in Manchuria and Asia if it were to survive as a nation. Though the military might not have accurately estimated the cost of their China policy, they were not going to be sidetracked. Keeping these general arguments in mind, the main events in Sino-Japanese relations in the last half of 1935 take on added significance. They have a twofold importance: first, because of the increased tension which led toward open hostilities and, second, because the rebuff which Japan received in China stimulated direct action at home.

As relations with the Soviet Union had become at least temporarily stabilized, more attention was given to a solution of some of the basic Sino-Japanese problems. From Japan's point of view, it was necessary to eliminate from the areas which it had conquered those persons and organizations unfriendly to the puppet rulers. Consequently, in June, 1935, the Japanese commander, General Umezu Yoshijirō, presented to General Ho Ying-chin, China's War Minister and head of the Peiping Military Council, a series of demands designed to achieve this objective. After a month's delay, General Ho reluctantly accepted the proposals which required withdrawal of Chinese government troops from Hopei and the employment by the Chinese commander in the Peking–Tientsin area of Japanese advisers. General Ho refused to acquiesce in a subsequent Japanese order, however, which specified that only Chinese friendly to Japan should be appointed to local and provincial positions and that Japan should retain powers of supervision and examination over these local entities.

From the point of view of the Imperial Army, which was beginning to think of direct penetration into China proper, Japan's position in North China was only partially secure. Consequently, in September, 1935, General Doihara Kenji was dispatched to the Peking area to form an autonomous government in the north which would sever the five northern provinces from financial and political connections with the Chinese nationalists in Nanking and which would be answerable to Japan's demands. General Diohara was partially successful. An East Hopei Council was formed, subject to the control of the Japanese Army commander. This new move to dismember China was met by new waves of anti-Japanese sentiment. China's challenge of assassinations and student strikes was partially answered by the creation of the Hopei–Chahar Political Council, but Japan was not ready to force the issue further.

Coup of February 26, 1936

For one thing, dissension between the leaders of the Imperial Way Faction and those of the Control Faction deepened. General Araki's replacement as Minister of War in 1934 had been a clear sign of a weakening of the supremacy of the Imperial Way Faction. An even more significant move, and one which triggered a series of events leading to the famous uprising of young officers on February 26, 1936, was the ousting of General Mazaki from the powerful post of Inspector General of Military Education. This move had been skillfully manipulated by the Chief of Staff and the Minister of War with the encouragement of leaders of the Control Faction, especially General Nagata Tetsuzan, Director of the Military Affairs Bureau of the War Ministry. As a result, General Mazaki carried on a personal vendetta against General Nagata.

Shortly after General Mazaki's removal, Lieutenant Colonel Aizawa Saburō, an ardent admirer of General Mazaki, assumed that General Nagata had been responsible for Mazaki's dismissal. Taking matters in his own hands, Colonel Aizawa confronted General Nagata and told him he should resign his post to atone for his action. General Nagata countered by ordering Colonel Aizawa to be transferred to Formosa at the time of the annual August assignments. Enraged by this action, Aizawa made a pilgrimage to the Ise National Shrine where he purified himself, returned to Tokyo, entered General Nagata's office in the War Department, and cut him down with his sword. He was immediately arrested and held for court martial. In the meantime, General Mazaki rallied the support of the Imperial Way Faction on Aizawa's behalf. As already noted, his colleagues had demanded that Minister of War Hayashi resign and be replaced by a general unaffiliated with either faction. They insisted that Aizawa be given a fair and public trial. They also decided that the occasion should be used to criticize the Cabinet for its temerity on the Minobe issue and to advocate a radical reform of the government. When Aizawa's trial began on January 8, 1936, he and his defense attorney, a staunch supporter of the Imperial Way Faction, used the occasion to discredit the Control Faction by revealing the relation of its members with the attempted coup d'état in March, 1931. The effect of this prolonged trial was to make the murdered General Nagata appear as a villain and Colonel Aizawa as a patriot who acted to save his country.[19]

The general disquiet and turmoil within Japan was further aggravated by the political instability of the Cabinet. The Seiyūkai, which had a majority of the seats in the House of Representatives, had forced a dissolution of Parliament in January, 1936. Aizawa had hoped that his harangues against the evils of the government leaders would have a direct effect on the elections scheduled for February 20. On the contrary, the election results were a censure of the extremists by the people. The Seiyūkai, which had been friendly with the Army's China policy, dropped sixty-eight seats, and the more moderate Minseitō party gained seventy-eight seats and became the largest party.

But the greatest challenge thus far to parliamentary government and also to the power exercised by the Control Faction was in the offing. A group of young officers from the First Division, stationed in Tokyo, inspired by the ultranationalist teachings of Kita Ikki and Nishida and frustrated and resentful over the treatment afforded their mentor, General Mazaki, secretly planned for an extensive coup d'état to force their will on all concerned. When the First Division received orders to go to Manchuria in February, the leaders of the revolt were forced to accelerate their planning. In the process, some of the young officers met with senior members of the Imperial Way Faction, and reported on their plans for revolt. Their superiors, notably General Mazaki, gave them, at the very least, their tacit support. Two apparently unrelated events occurred on February 25, 1936, but later proved to be forewarnings of portentous things to come. General Mazaki appeared as a witness at Aizawa's trial but refused to answer several pointed questions. Secondly, a notice was placed in the "Personal Column" of the morning edition of the Tokyo *Asahi,* as a signal for a revolt to take place. It read:

Current Issues Stabilized: There has been a crystallization of the correct judgment of you who are wise and can see into the meaning of things. Let us make every effort—all of us unitedly—to strengthen our national power and to make progress for the Empire by leaps and bounds.

Leader of the Orient
Marunouchi Art Club
Half-Piercing Solid Star

Before dawn the next morning, about 1,500 soldiers in full battle gear, members of the first and third regiments of the First Division, were called out of their Tokyo barracks by their immediate commanding officers. Divided into several units, they set out in deep snow on their mission to murder seven of the Emperor's highest officials and advisers. Three of these, the Lord Keeper of the Privy Seal, Admiral Saitō, Finance Minister Takahashi, and the new Inspector General of Military Education, General Watanabe, were killed. The other four intended victims miraculously escaped. At the same time, the rebels took over the War Office, the Premier's Official Residence, and the newly erected Diet Building, and surrounded the Metropolitan Police Headquarters. When the Tokyo populace went to work that morning, they saw a cordon of soldiers around the area in the center of the city which enclosed most of the government buildings. It was obvious that a coup d'état was under way. But the radio was silent and there was no official announcement of what had happened. Rumors were rampant until that evening when the War Department reported the assassination of the three top ministers and the severe wounding of two others in an army uprising led by young officers.

The next day, martial law was proclaimed and troops of unimpeachable loyalty were brought from outside the city to quash the rebellion. The Navy, which never faltered in its loyalty to the Throne, immediately landed marines to guard the Navy Ministry across the street from the area controlled by the rebels and assembled the First Fleet in Tokyo Bay. When night fell, the fleet made its presence known with searchlights. After three days, in which the Emperor insisted that the soldiers had rebelled against him and should return to their units immediately or be forced to capitulate, the Army planned an attack to suppress the rebellion. By the early afternoon of February 29, all of the officers and men capitulated except one of the ring leaders who committed suicide. The officers were arrested to await trial and the soldiers returned to their barracks.

While these momentous events were taking place, the people showed an amazing attitude toward the whole affair. During the first day of the attempted coup many white collar workers in Tokyo spent their lunch hour walking between the columns of soldiers facing each other on opposite sides of the busy downtown streets. The strollers tried to find out from the soldiers what group they represented, but had little success. The entire Tokyo populace was completely docile and amenable to any inconvenience caused them by the coup. They carried on their routine activities and left the struggle up to the Army, as they left it up to the ruling cliques to settle their future.

Unchallenged Army Control

Technically, the coup had failed. The Emperor had not been molested and had taken a leading role in making plans to cope with the emergency. The young officers had failed to win back control of the Army and of the government for the leaders of the Imperial Way Faction. These young ultranationalists had miscalculated the support they might expect from General Mazaki and others, especially if they failed to carry out all their plans. On the contrary, the power and influence of the Control Faction was enhanced. It was only a matter of time before the government became united behind an aggressive foreign policy, especially toward China.[20]

This new power of the Army expressed itself immediately in the selection of a new Cabinet. Hirota Kōki, though known to be nationalistically minded, was finally chosen as the new Premier. The Army selected a new Minister of War, Terauchi Hisaichi, who threatened to refuse to serve whenever the Premier suggested appointments to the Cabinet of persons not acceptable to him and his colleagues. When a colorless national Cabinet was finally selected, the Army rested temporarily on its laurels and endeavored to leave the impression that it alone had saved the country from revolt (even by its own members) and that it had no further intention of centralizing power under its control. This impression was strengthened by extensive personnel shifts within the Army. Military officials who had had connections with the February revolt were either transferred to inactive reserve or barred from future assignments in the Army's central headquarters. Furthermore, Generals Araki and Mazaki of the Supreme War Council and former War Minister Kawashima were among those placed on the inactive list. When the Emperor opened Parliament in May, he took the unprecedented step of adding the following to what is always a set, formal statement: "As for the recent affair which arose in Tokyo, I am grieved over it." The trials of the leading conspirators were held in secret, and thirteen of the young officers involved were executed in July, 1936. Kita Ikki was condemned to death the next year.

By the end of 1936, however, both internal and external conditions had deteriorated and the trend toward totalitarianism was inevitable. The Minister of Finance, Baba Eiichi, had encountered little opposition to a national budget with heavily increased expenditures to develop Manchuria and to strengthen national defenses. For example, total expenditures had increased from 1.5 billion yen in 1932 to 2.3 billion yen in 1936 with an annual average deficit of 638 million yen. During the same period, the amount of the budget devoted to the armed services had increased from 28 to 46 per cent. Baba introduced new taxes on sugar and tobacco and raised postal charges. A sharp rise in wholesale prices developed and retail prices climbed at an average of 2¼ per cent monthly. Increased military demands on heavy industries stimulated their growth at the expense of light industries. The special economic privileges shown some of the new industrialists antagonized the old established families such as Mitsui and Iwasaki.

On the international scene, Japan was less successful in achieving its objectives. In the summer of 1936, these objectives had been set forth in a Cabinet declaration of fundamental principles of national policy. This statement called for the strengthening of Japan's defenses against the Russian menace in the north. This objective was to be achieved through the development of a closely knit economic and military program for Manchuria, Japan, and North China, and the resolution of basic differences with the Chinese Nationalist government. The policy also advocated the gradual and peaceful penetration into Southeast Asia to guarantee the availability of natural resources necessary for a strong self-sufficient Japanese economy and the growth of a strong navy in the Western Pacific as a counterbalance to the American Navy. In carrying out these policies, steps were to be taken to avoid antagonizing the Western powers, especially Russia, Great Britain, and the United States. All national policies were to be unified, with the military assisting the diplomats and refraining from overt acts whenever possible.[21]

But it was problematical how much longer the military would refrain from some new overt act in China. Incidents of killings of Japanese were occurring with increasing frequency in cities such as Hankow and Shanghai. Kawagoe Shigeru, who had been advanced to the post of Japanese Ambassador at Nanking, made new demands on the Nationalist government. He insisted that China and Japan jointly attack communism, that the Chinese press be controlled, that Japan have the right to inspect the schools to ferret out anti-Japanese cells, and that the Nanking government assist in the formation of an autonomous government over the five provinces in the north. He was rebuffed by General Chiang Kai-shek who countered that Japan should respect China's sovereignty, that the special agreements concerning North China were invalid, and that Japan should cease trading secretly in East Hopei. In October, 1936, when Chinese Nationalist forces won a decisive victory in Inner Mongolia against a Japanese trained and equipped "puppet army," the Sino-Japanese negotiations were broken off.

Finally, the kidnapping of General Chiang Kai-shek in Sian, in December, 1936, by the former Manchurian warlord, Chang Hsueh-liang, exacerbated further the relations of the two countries. From all appearances, in exchange for his release, Generalissimo Chiang consented to call off his sixth extermination campaign against the Chinese communists and to form a united front to combat Japanese aggression.

The political crisis in Japan from January to June, 1937, only enhanced the Army's control over the government. In fact it was induced by the Army leaders who became dissatisfied with the slowness with which the Cabinet and Diet were moving toward adopting basic political, financial, and economic reforms necessary for full-scale national military preparedness. In reality, only those persons acceptable to the leaders of the Army were chosen for Premier and the various Cabinet posts. Although the Minseitō and Seiyūkai parties, which made common cause against militarism and fascism in government in the elections in April, 1937, won three-fourths of the seats in Parliament, they were not officially represented in the Cabinet of Prime Minister Konoye Fumimaro, which was formed in June.[22] In fact, they no longer were important in the formation of policy or in its execution. That task was assigned to a newly created Cabinet Planning Board. It had the power to make recommendations on important national policies and on their coordination, to decide on the importance of proposals presented by the various branches of the government, and to integrate them with overall policies. By July, 1937, when full-scale hostilities broke out in China, the machinery was at hand to mobilize the material and spiritual resources of the nation for war. No group, economic or political, challenged the basic policy of expansion on the continent of Asia. In the immediate years that followed, totalitarianism slowly and steadily spread throughout the Empire.

NOTES

1. See C. Walter Young, *Japan's Jurisdiction and International Legal Position in Manchuria* (3 vols.; Baltimore: Johns Hopkins University Press, 1931).
2. Among the earliest secret societies, the two most famous were the *Genyōsha* under the leadership of Tōyama Mitsuru and the *Kokuryū Kai* (Black Dragon Society) of Uchida Ryōhei. The former was active in fomenting plots in Korea and the latter concentrated on increasing Japanese influence in Manchuria. The growth of the various factions within the Army and the influence of specific groups are extremely complicated. The accounts which follow emphasize only the most important persons involved. Both Richard Storry, *The Double Patriots* (Boston: Houghton Mifflin Co., 1957), and James B. Crowley, *Japan's Quest for Autonomy: National Security and Foreign Policy 1930–1938* (Princeton: Princeton University Press, 1966), contain detailed accounts of them. Crowley's work is particularly valuable for his analysis of the effect of the professional training of the officer corps on the different cliques to which they belonged.

3. Kita Ikki was influenced in his early life by both socialism and the concept of *kokutai* (national polity). He went to China in 1911 on funds from the *Kokuryū Kai* to participate in the Chinese Revolution. When he returned to Japan in 1913, he became interested in Buddhism, returning again to China in 1916. In 1921, he published a history of the Chinese Revolution. His *General Outline* (*Nihon Kaizō Hōan Taikō*) appeared in 1923. He hoped to rally to his banner large numbers of young officers. Although not privy to the plot, he was arrested in 1936 because of the interest which the leaders of the February coup had in his views. He was convicted and sentenced to death in 1937. See Storry, *op. cit.*, pp. 37 ff.; Robert A. Scalapino, *Democracy and the Party Movement in Prewar Japan* (Berkeley: University of California Press, 1953), pp. 334 ff.; and for a monograph on Kita Ikki, George M. Wilson, *Radical Nationalist in Japan* (Cambridge: Harvard University Press, 1969). A partial translation of the *General Outline* is in Ryusaku Tsunoda *et al.* (compilers), *Sources of the Japanese Tradition* (New York: Columbia University Press, 1958), pp. 775 ff.

4. Ōkawa Shūmei (1886–1957) studied philosophy at Tokyo University. He formed the nationalist *Yuzonsha* in 1919 but it dissolved in 1923 after Kita Ikki had joined it at Ōkawa's request. Their ideological differences could not be reconciled and continued throughout their lives. Later, as a member of the East Asia Institute of the South Manchurian Railway, he became a friend of Colonel Komoto of the Kwantung Army, who planned the murder of General Chang Tso-lin. Ōkawa was deeply involved in the planning for the March and October, 1931, coups. He was implicated in the murder of Prime Minister Inukai on May 15, 1932, arrested, and sentenced to prison for nine years. He was granted an amnesty in 1935. After World War II he was named as a Class A War Criminal but received no sentence on the grounds of insanity.

5. There is some doubt as to whether General Ugaki knew the details of the original plot. Two drafts, one of which was a ruse, were prepared and he may have seen only the former. General Tatekawa and Major General Koiso Kuniaki, Chief of the Military Affairs Bureau of the Ministry of War, were clearly involved.

Hashimoto Kingorō (1890–1957) graduated from the War College in 1920. He was Military Attaché in Istanbul when Kemal Pasha reformed Turkey and was impressed with his effectiveness. When he was assigned to the Russian section of the General Staff in 1929, his superior was General Tatekawa. Hashimoto helped to plan the abortive coups in March and October, 1931. After the uprising of February 26, 1936, he was cashiered from the Army and became head of the Young Men's Association. In July, 1937, his commission was reactivated. In December, he was directly involved in the sinking of the British gunboat "Lady Bird" in China. He was convicted by the International Military Tribunal as a Class A War Criminal and sentenced to life imprisonment. Basic objectives of the *Sakurakai* and details of his plans are in Ōuchi Tsutomi, *Fuashizumu no Michi Nihon no Rekishi* (Tokyo: Chūo Koron, 1967), XXIV, pp. 276 ff.

Ugaki Kazushige (1868–1956) was a graduate of the War College. He was Minister of War from 1924–1927, when he antagonized the traditionalists by encouraging plans for the mechanization of the Army, and again under Hamaguchi. He resigned in April, 1931, after he was unable to persuade Hamaguchi to increases in the budget for modernizing the Army. He was then appointed Governor-General of Korea. In 1938 he became Foreign Minister in the Konoye Cabinet for a few months and retired from politics until 1953 when he was elected to the House of Councilors.

A word of caution is in order concerning the various plots against the Cabinet. Whenever a plot of this sort was discovered either by the military police (*Kempei tai*) or by the civilian police, great pains were taken not to reveal it to anyone not already aware of its existence. It cannot be concluded, therefore, that the knowledge of the failure of such a coup necessarily had an immediate effect on the Premier and his Cabinet. In some cases, the most that they might learn after several months was that there had been some sort of plot. For example, Harada Kumao, Secretary to the last Elder Statesman, Saionji, states that August 3 was the first time he heard of the March plot. By this time it was too late to do anything about it. The details of this particular plot did not come out until 1947 at the War Crimes Trial of the International Military Tribunal for the Far East.

For details of the March coup, see Storry, *op. cit.*, pp. 56 ff., and Crowley, *op. cit.*, pp. 94 ff.

6. The background of the Mukden Incident is extremely complicated and some of the evidence presented at the International Military Tribunal of the Far East is vague or contradictory. Nevertheless, certain key figures, both among the field-grade officers and the top echelons, can be identified. The reference material is abundant. The most detailed accounts in English are: Sadako N. Ogata, *Defiance in Manchuria: The Making of Japanese Foreign Policy 1931–1932* (New Haven: Yale University Press, 1963); Crowley, *op. cit.*, pp. 83 ff.; and Storry, *op. cit.*, pp. 54 ff. The most detailed Japanese source is Tsunoda Jun (ed.), *Taiheiyō Sensō e no Michi* (8 vols.; Tokyo: Nihon Kokusai Seiji Gakkai, 1963), I and II. For a review of the latter see Akira Iriye, "Japanese Imperialism and Aggression," *Journal of Asian Studies,* XXIII (1963), pp. 103 ff.

7. Araki Sadao (1877–1966) was a graduate of the War College and was Military Attaché in Russia. He was on the General Staff of the Siberian Expedition. From 1929 to 1931 he headed the Operations Division of the General Staff. An idol of the young officers, he was one of the leaders of the Imperial Way Faction in the Army. In 1931, he was Inspector General of Military Education for a few months and then entered the Inukai Cabinet as War Minister, which post he held until January, 1934. He was Minister of Education from 1938–1939. In 1948, he was convicted as a War Criminal and given a sentence of life imprisonment.

General Nagata Tetsuzan received training in Germany and saw the effects of World War I on a nation's entire structure. In 1927 War Minister Ugaki appointed him head of the new Bureau of Mobilization. During Araki's tenure as War Minister, Nagata was removed from staff work and given a field command. In March, 1934, he returned to become chief of the War Ministry's Military Affairs Division under War Minister General Hayashi. A strong member of the Control Faction of the Army, he was murdered in August, 1935, by an enraged Lt. Colonel Aizawa Saburō, a follower of the rival Imperial Way Faction.

8. There is a slight difference in the account of the activities of the Kwantung officers as presented by Mrs. Ogata and Professor Crowley. The former emphasizes a secret visit of Major Hanaya and a subsequent visit to Tokyo of the Kwantung Commander-in-Chief and Chief of Staff. Professor

Crowley refers to Colonel Ishihara's visit to Tokyo for the usual briefing of senior staff officers at which time "neither Tatekawa nor his staff expressed any serious disapproval" of the plans for Manchuria. In either case, General Tatekawa was aware of the views of the authors of the plan. As he had been moved in September from chief of the Intelligence Section to the Operations Section of the General Staff, he was in an even more crucial position to restrict or encourage the activities of the Kwantung Army. See Ogata, *op. cit.*, p. 54, and Crowley, *op. cit.*, p. 117.

Itagaki Seishirō had such an influence over his Chief of Staff that he was allowed to do things largely as he wished. He was an ardent believer in an independent Manchuria under Japanese control. He became a Major General in 1932 and was sent to General Headquarters the next year. After war broke out in China in 1937, he was a field commander. In June, 1938, he became Minister of War under Premier Konoye and shortly thereafter argued with the Emperor for strong reinforcements to be sent against the Soviet forces on the Korean border at Changkufeng. The Emperor strongly disapproved and told Itagaki he was not to move a single soldier without his consent. He resigned as War Minister in August, 1939. He was condemned to death as a war criminal.

9. Crowley, *op. cit.*, p. 124.

10. The Kwantung Army Headquarters claimed that the bombing, the first of a series of many, was justified by provocative anti-Japanese demonstrations and the threat to the security of their forces from the alleged concentration of Chang's troops for an attack on the Japanese army in Manchuria. These claims fooled no one. See S. R. Smith, *The Manchurian Crisis, 1931–32* (New York: Columbia University Press, 1948), p. 82.

11. The Cabinet which Hashimoto and his colleagues proposed had a strong nationalist cast: Prime Minister and Minister of War, General Araki Sadao; Navy Minister, Admiral Kobayashi; Foreign Minister, General Tatekawa; Finance Minister, Ōkawa Shūmei; Home Minister, Hashimoto Kingorō, and Chief of Military Police, Colonel Nemoto. Tatekawa apparently had not objected to serving when he had been approached about the matter. The coup was set for October 24, 1931.

12. Part of the delay in forming the Commission had been the lack of enthusiasm of the United States and Great Britain for such an inquiry. The United States, after the bombing of Chinchow, had invoked the Kellogg Pact and had agreed to send an observer to the Council meetings. It also agreed to have an observer serve on the League's Commission. In the meantime, the Japanese Army continued its advance.

13. Harada Kumao, *Saionji Ko To Seikyoku* (Saionji–Harada Memoirs) (9 vols.; Tokyo: Iwanami Shoten, 1950–1952 and 1956), December 24, 1931.

14. For the most comprehensive and best account of America's position and relations with Japan during this period see Dorothy Borg, *The United States and the Far Eastern Crisis of 1933–1938* (Cambridge: Harvard University Press, 1964).

15. An analysis of the forces which resulted in the abortive coup d'état of May 15, 1932, and in the selection of Admiral Saitō Makoto as the next Premier illustrates, at once, the vital role of the ultranationalist societies and also the complicated nature of the political scene in this period. It also reveals that there were several interrelated yet independent groups involved, thus reducing the possibility of finding a single conspiratorial group guiding

each move of Japan toward fascism. Different individuals and groups, inspired by different leaders, enter the limelight. For example, those responsible for the assassinations in February and for the abortive coup in May were not inspired by members of Hashimoto's *Sakurakai*. They were from the *Aikyō Juku* (Land Loving Society), a rural organization led by a priest named Inoue Nisshō, and the *Ketsumeidan* (Blood Brotherhood League). They advocated wiping out the political parties, the *zaibatsu*, and traitors, with the assistance of the farmers and laborers. When the status quo was destroyed, a new Japan could be built. Hiranuma, who was advocated in May, 1932, as Premier, had founded the Society for the Foundation of the State (*Kokuhonsha*) in 1924. Members in his society included Generals Ugaki, Araki, Mazaki, and Koiso; President of the Seiyūkai, Suzuki Kisaburō; Managing Director of Mitsui, Ikeda Seihin; and Premier-designate Admiral Saitō.

Within the Army, the struggle was between the Imperial Way Faction (*Kōdō ha*) and the Control Faction (Tōsei ha). The former was led by Generals Araki Sadao and Mazaki Jinzaburō who stressed the need for preparation for a crisis with the Soviet Union by 1936 and the spiritual mobilization of the nation. The Imperial Way Faction was particularly influential from 1931–1934. The Control Faction was made up of officers with General Staff experience, many of whom were convinced that national mobilization of all resources was the only salvation for Japan's future security. Its leaders included General Nagata Tetsuzan, whose ideas had resulted in the formation of a Mobilization Bureau, and General Tōjō Hideki, Japan's wartime Premier. The Control Faction became increasingly dominant after 1935. On the all-important question of nationalism and the extension of Japanese hegemony over Asia, the two groups agreed in principle but differed in the timing and method of implementing policy. *In fine,* all nationalist groups capitalized on the effects of direct action by any of them. For the growth of fascism during this period see Tanaka Sogorō, *Nihon Fuashizumu no Genryū* (Tokyo: 1949) and Ōuchi, *op. cit.* Sources in English include Storry, *op. cit.*, pp. 96–152; Crowley, *op. cit.*; Scalapino, *op. cit.*, pp. 346–92; and Hugh Borton, *Japan Since 1931—Its Political and Social Development* (New York: American Institute of Pacific Relations, Inc., 1940), pp. 36–53.

16. Borton, *ibid.*, pp. 41–45.

17. For America's reaction to the Amau Statement, to Foreign Minister Hirota's foreign policy, and to Saitō's inability to persuade Secretary of State Hull to agree to the issuance of a joint statement of understanding, see Borg, *op. cit.*, pp. 55–96.

Hirota Kōki (1878–1948) was born in Fukuoka. He had relations early in life with the nationalistic *Genyōsha*. A graduate of Tokyo University, he entered the Foreign Office and became Minister to Holland and Ambassador to the Soviet Union. He entered Saitō's Cabinet as Foreign Minister in August, 1933, and continued in that office until he formed his own Cabinet in March, 1936, during which time he served concurrently as Foreign Minister until February, 1937. In May, 1938, he was Foreign Minister in the first Konoye Cabinet and remained a leading statesman up to World War II. He negotiated unsuccessfully with Yakov Malik to conclude the war. He was the only civilian official to receive the death penalty as a Class A War Criminal by the International Military Tribunal of the Far East.

18. Professor Minobe's best known works, which were banned by 1935, were *Nihon Kempō* (Constitution of Japan) written in 1921, *Kempō Setsuyo* (Essentials of the Constitution), and *Kempō Seigi* (Commentary on the Constitution). He had been vehemently opposed by Professors Hozumi and Uesugi but both these men had died by the time Minobe was attacked publicly.

Minobe had argued that the state was a corporate entity which possessed a legal personality with the capacity for rights and duties. In the case of a monarchy, the monarch as well as the subjects were contained within the state; so the Emperor was not synonymous with the state. In fact, the direct personal rule of the Emperor was limited by the Constitution, making him one of the elements of the state. Thus he was an organ of it and he exercised his prerogatives and governmental powers only on the advice of his ministers.

See Frank O. Miller, *Minobe Tatsukichi, Interpreter of Constitutionalism in Japan* (Berkeley: University of California Press, 1965).

19. While Professor Crowley is correct in warning that too much emphasis should not be placed on the Control–Imperial Way Faction rivalry, especially as there were other groups involved in the power struggle, it is important to recognize the strong impact which certain military leaders had on the events of this period and the intense personal antagonisms that developed among them. For additional detailed background material see: Crowley, *op. cit.*, pp. 244–73; Storry, *op. cit.*, pp. 126–80; and Ōuchi, *op. cit.*, pp. 351–88.

20. Among those listed for murder in the coup were Prince Saionji, the *Genrō*, and former Lord Keeper of the Privy Seal, Makino Nobuaki, who both were at their homes outside of Tokyo and escaped harm. Finance Minister Takahashi, though first reported as only seriously wounded, General Watanabe, and the incumbent Privy Seal, Saitō, were killed. Grand Chamberlain Admiral Suzuki Kantarō escaped with only severe wounds, thanks largely to the courage of his wife. In the last days of World War II, he was called on by the Emperor to be Premier. Premier Okada's escape afforded a bit of grim comedy to the melodrama. Okada's brother-in-law, who was in the Premier's residence when the attack came, was a victim of mistaken identity and was killed while Okada remained hidden. The latter escaped next day in the disguise of a pallbearer for the coffin which presumably contained his own remains. His safe conduct through the lines of the insurgents guarding his residence was then announced to the amusement of all in Tokyo.

Another aspect of the uprising which should be noted was its complete lack of any antiforeign feeling. The author walked along the lines of insurgent soldiers on three different occasions without the slightest adverse effects.

For more detailed accounts of the uprising see: Storry, *op. cit.*, pp. 180–92; and Ōuchi, *op. cit.*, pp. 388–422.

21. See International Military Tribunal for the Far East, Defense Exhibit No. 979, Document No. 1634 K, "Fundamental Principle of our National Policy," signed by the Prime Minister and Ministers of War, Navy, Foreign Affairs, and Finance, dated August 11, 1936.

22. The Hirota Cabinet fell on January 23, 1937, after the War Minister resigned in protest to criticisms made against him in Parliament. General Ugaki Kazushige, former Governor of Korea, was unacceptable to the military, so he gave up his efforts to form a Cabinet. Finally, General Hayashi Senjūrō was selected. Without warning, Hayashi dissolved Parliament in

April and won only fifty seats in the subsequent elections. He finally resigned at the end of May. Prince Konoye's first Cabinet (June 4, 1937–January 5, 1939) was composed largely of pro-Army men and new bureaucrats who were under military influence. Hirota Kōki was Foreign Minister and President of the Planning Board. For a detailed account of these developments see Borton, *op. cit.*, pp. 45 ff.

18

Preparation for Total War 1937–1941

In the early summer of 1937, Japan faced an unprecedented series of crises both at home and abroad. To many persons, the nation's China policy had thus far proved to be only partially successful. The leaders of the Kwantung clique and the advocates of state planning for the puppet regime of Manchukuo had prophesied that their program would bring benefits to all. They had also predicted close cooperation from China in their endeavors. But such had not proved to be the case. Japan's prodigious and unscrupulous efforts to improve Sino-Japanese relations through the promotion of autonomous, indigenous, regional "governments" throughout North China and Inner Mongolia had only strengthened China's movement toward national unification. Since December, 1936, when Generalissimo Chiang Kai-shek was kidnapped at Sian and then released through the intervention of the Chinese communists, the possibilities of a united China had increased still further.

The Japanese Army, especially the Kwantung clique, looked upon this situation as a threat to the traditional policy of divide and rule. The Foreign Office saw little possibility of Chiang accepting or implementing its minimum requirements for an overall settlement. It had demanded that China suppress all anti-Japanese activities, recognize the independence of Manchukuo, and cooperate with Japan in the extermination of communism on the Asiatic mainland. Furthermore, China's unification appeared to Japan to be aided and abetted by the Western powers whose special privileges conflicted with its own. In fact, it was claimed that Japan's very existence was being threatened by the encroachments of the United States, Great Britain, and the Soviet Union.

As for the Soviet Union, it had challenged the Kwantung Army's plans for control of all of Mongolia by signing a mutual assistance pact with the Mongolian People's Republic. In fact, General Tōjō Hideki,[1] Chief of Staff of the Kwantung Army, had warned the Army General Staff of the possibility of a coalition of a unified China with the Soviet Union. He advised striking a blow against Chiang at Nanking to prevent such an alliance. To offset this encirclement, Japan had become a partner with Germany in the Anti-Comintern Pact of November 25, 1936. The published clauses of the Pact provided for collaboration in preventing the spread of communism within the borders of the two states and among third powers. The secret clauses were directed against the Soviet Union. They provided that if it launched an unprovoked attack against either of the signatories, the other would not assist the Soviet Union. Furthermore, both parties promised to refrain from making political treaties with the Soviet Union except by mutual consent. Although this single pact was slim protection against a Soviet attack on Manchuria and Korea, it gave Japan moral support in its drive to gain undisputed control of China.

The chief differences of opinion within Japan among the politicians, the financiers, Imperial advisers, and the generals and admirals were on the question of how far Japan should go on the Asiatic mainland. There was no disagreement on who was destined to become the leader of East Asia and possibly of the world. As in previous crises, the differences were over methods rather than over basic aims. The Army extremists were convinced that direct action, regardless of the consequences in Asia, Europe, or America, was the only method. Their opponents, who came from almost all groups including the Imperial Navy and from some cliques within the Imperial Army, are perhaps best described as "moderates." The moderates hoped that Japan's aims in Eastern Asia could be achieved without an open break with the United States, Great Britain, or the Soviet Union. Even after the outbreak of hostilities in China in July, 1937, the moderates naïvely assumed that if the war in China could be terminated successfully in Japan's favor, then the Western Powers would acquiesce in this new "realistic approach" toward Asia.

The various shifts in government, therefore, from the formation of the first Konoye Cabinet on June 4, 1937, to the selection of General Tōjō as Premier on October 18, 1941, were indicative of the struggle for control between the "extremists" and the "moderates." This internal struggle first took the form of an attempt by the latter to prevent the Army from gaining complete political control. As the war in China progressed, however, and as Japan's aims became more closely identified with the Axis powers, the moderates increasingly acquiesced in the plans of the military. They finally capitulated to the admonitions of Tōjō that Japan's national existence could be assured only by waging a successful war against the United States. The present chapter will be devoted, therefore, to an analysis of what steps were taken to centralize political, economic, and social controls, to augment the national strength by alliances with the Axis, and to prevent the moderates from interfering with the war plans.

Outbreak of War in China in July, 1937

In view of the domestic and international crisis which faced Japan in the summer of 1937, the selection of the proper person to fill the post of Premier was of the utmost importance. Those directly responsible for selecting the Prime Minister and influential persons inside and outside of the government agreed that Konoye Fumimaro was the logical choice. A descendent of one of the oldest families of nobility in Japan, Prince Konoye was enthusiastically proclaimed the man of the hour by the militarists, the bureaucrats, the financiers, and the leaders of the political parties. Because of the close contacts he had had in recent years with key figures in the Army, he was acceptable to both the extremists and the moderates.[2] The extremists were confident that, when necessary, they could persuade him to follow their policies. The moderates recognized that the only hope for the acceptance of their views lay in controlling the extremists in the Army. Konoye was the one person who might be able to throttle them. From the beginning, however, it was evident that Konoye tended to accept much of the expansionist philosophy of the militarists and was not willing or able to check them. He adopted the broad policies of the Army which were described as clarification of national policy, the strengthening of the defenses, the renovation of the administration of the central government, and the stabilization of the people's livelihood.

The first step toward clarification of a new policy and renovation of the government was the appointment of persons amenable to Army leadership to key posts in the first Konoye Cabinet of June, 1937. In the second place the Cabinet Planning Board, which had been commissioned just prior to the demise of the last Cabinet, became the most important coordinating agency within the government. Charged with making "recommendations . . . both in regard to important national policies and to their coordination and adjustment," it was directly under the Prime Minister and transcended all departments and agencies. Hirota Kōki was appointed Foreign Minister and Chairman of the Board. Through this Board, the new leaders of Japan planned the expansion and mobilization of the nation's strength for any eventuality. As necessity arose, its functions were broadened. For example, after the outbreak of war in China in July, 1937, its Chairman was given rank comparable to that of a Cabinet Minister. The synchronization of its policies with plans for Manchuria was assured by the fact that the Board's Vice-Chairman was also Vice-Chairman of the Cabinet's Manchurian Affairs Board.

But the Cabinet Planning Board and other new organs of control became important in direct proportion to the enlargement of hostilities in

China. Since the Ho–Umezu agreement of 1935, Japanese troops had been stationed at strategic points in North China. (See page 385.) At the same time, Chinese Nationalist troops were in the same region so the situation was fraught with danger. Fully aware of this fact the Japanese General Staff had persuaded the Cabinet to reconfirm the existing policy, namely, that local military commanders should take all precautions to avoid serious incidents on the Chinese mainland. In the summer of 1937, Japanese officers in the field were again sent instructions to this effect. Nevertheless, during the maneuvers of Japanese troops in the strategically important triangle bounded by the Peking–Hankow and Peking–Tientsin line near Marco Polo Bridge (Lukouchiao), a skirmish took place during the night of July 7–8, 1937. The original disposition of both the Chinese and Japanese armies showed that neither side apparently planned the attack. In fact, despite some continued fighting, on July 11, 1937, a cease-fire agreement was signed between the Chinese and Japanese commanders in North China.[3]

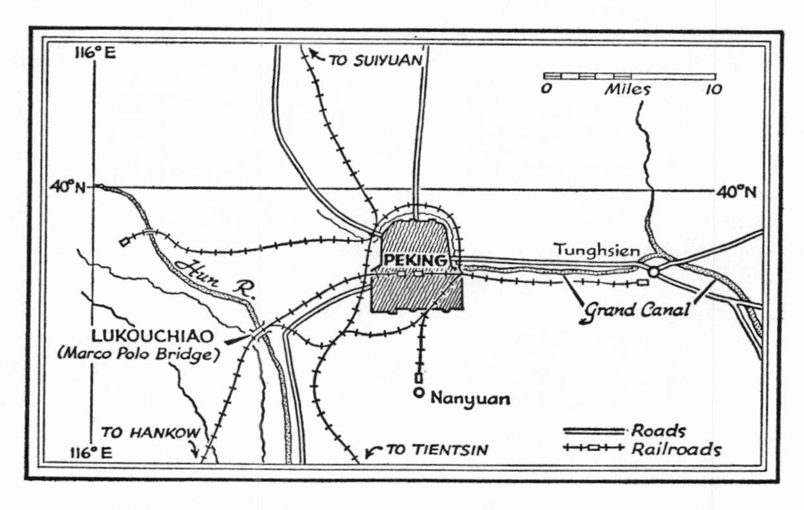

Peking and Marco Polo Bridge, July, 1937

But certain long-standing fundamental differences between Japan and the Nationalist government of Chiang Kai-shek were responsible for this incident flaring into a full-fledged conflict. These differences, as already noted, were that Japan saw the strengthening of Manchukuo and the formation of a buffer zone or autonomous area in North China and Inner Mongolia as essential to its security against the Soviet Union and communism. On the other hand, Chiang Kai-shek had no intention of accepting Japan's demands for greater autonomy in North China, even at the risk of war. Thus the official positions taken in Tokyo and Nanking toward the Marco Polo Bridge skirmish reflected these basic antagonisms and the incident soon developed into full-scale war. For example, on July 11, though the local commanders had worked out a truce, Prime Minister Konoye announced publicly:

> There is no room for doubt that the recent incident is entirely the result of China's anti-Japanese military action. . . . Since the security of North China is a matter of urgent importance for the peace in East Asia . . . the government of Japan has decided on the important steps which should be taken in reference to the dispatch of troops.

On July 18 the Chinese government told Japan that it must continue its military preparations because of the Japanese decision to mobilize and to reinforce its army in North China. In a speech at Kuling, Generalissimo Chiang declared Peking must not fall. Conditions for a peaceful solution were: no infringement of Chinese sovereignty; no unlawful alteration of the Hopei–Chahar Council; no removal of any official appointed by the Nanking government; and no restrictions on the stationing of the Twenty-ninth Army in North China. The Konoye Cabinet refused to take Chiang seriously and believed it could obtain a "fundamental solution" to the China problem by a show of force. Events were soon to show the gravity of this miscalculation. By July 27, 1937, widespread hostilities had broken out and reinforcements were sent from both sides. In a few days, the Japanese became masters of the Peking–Tientsin area. Thus the second Sino-Japanese War, or more accurately, the early stages of the Pacific phase of World War II had begun. In mid-August, as his answer to Japan's terms for further negotiations, Chiang Kai-shek attacked Japanese naval installations at Shanghai. Japan retaliated with force and fully expected a quick victory and Chiang Kai-shek's surrender within a matter of months. But the issues underlying the Marco Polo Bridge skirmish were resolved only by World War II.[4]

Western Protests Ignored—Fall of Nanking

As in previous cases of Japanese aggression on the Asiatic mainland, the Western powers were divided on the best policy to follow. The United States contented itself with an official pronouncement of general principles. In mid-July, 1937, Secretary of State Cordell Hull issued a statement which deprecated the use of force to settle international differences and advocated peaceful negotiation and the faithful observance of international agreements. He wished to avoid any action which could be used by the military in Japan to strengthen their position. Thus he declined an invitation of Great Britain and France for a joint *démarche* and for mediation.

Japan's answer to the American statement revealed, even at this early date, the wide divergence of its policies from those of the United States. The Japanese note maintained that Hull's principles could not be applied to the situation in the Far East unless the Western powers fully recognized the special conditions which existed in that region. In effect, the Japanese government was saying that it would be willing to adhere to these principles only after it had forced the Chinese Nationalist government of Chiang Kai-shek to recognize its position of superiority in China. Throughout the next four years of war and military occupation of China, any protests against Japan's unilateral, aggressive moves were rejected on the grounds that Chiang's government refused to adopt a friendly policy toward it. Hence, it claimed that it had been forced to take matters into its own hands in self-defense. Despite the conquest of ever larger areas, Japan insisted that it had no territorial designs on China.

During the first few months of the war, Chiang Kai-shek was not intimidated by the Japanese claims that they were fighting "to impress Nanking with the necessity of a reconstruction of its attitude toward Japan." On the other hand, Japan had extricated itself from a difficult position in Shanghai, spreading out along the main railway arteries in North and Central China more or less at will. In the meantime, having failed to get the expected support from the Western powers at Shanghai, Chiang appealed to the League of Nations for help. But neither the League nor the powers with special interest in China did much to limit the spread of the war. When the latter met in Brussels in November, they saw no way in which they could bring the conflict to a peaceful conclusion.

Both the people and the governments of Great Britain and the United States were becoming increasingly antagonistic toward Japan. They considered the whole war as the direct result of the aggressive attitude of the Japanese military. They deplored the increasingly frequent bombings of Chinese cities.

The events of December greatly added to this antagonism. Japan increased its preparations to attack Nanking and fully expected that its capture would result in Chiang Kai-shek's surrender. While American and British gunboats on the Yangtze River were evacuating their nationals from the besieged city, on December 12, Colonel Hashimoto led an unauthorized and wanton air attack on the U.S.S. "Panay" and H.M.S. "Ladybird." An immediate apology by Japan and payment of an indemnity settled the issue officially. When Nanking fell later that month, the triumphant Japanese army went berserk. Its troops massacred, looted, and raped at will. This "Rape of Nanking" shocked the world. It could not be eradicated from the minds of either the Chinese or the Western powers. They were nauseated by Premier Konoye attributing the fall of Nanking to "the Emperor's virtue and the loyalty and courage of the Japanese soldiers."

While Japan celebrated the capture of the Chinese capital with lantern parades in Tokyo and anticipated Chiang's early collapse, he moved his capital farther inland and extricated most of his army from destruction. Shortly thereafter, a power struggle within the Japanese government took place between those who advocated the chastisement of China for its refusal to capitulate and those who favored seeking an accommodation with Chiang's government. Contrary to the usual pattern, the General Staff urged a settlement through negotiation while the Cabinet, led by Premier Konoye, Foreign Minister Hirota, and the new Home Minister, Admiral Suetsugu, wanted to continue the attack. On January 16, 1938, Premier Konoye announced the decisions of an Imperial Conference which settled the issue. Henceforth Japan would reorganize its relations with China working through a new regime. It would promote the economic welfare of China, Manchukuo, and Japan, create a new political organization in North China, and establish an autonomous government in Inner Mongolia. But the General Staff was not at all sanguine that Chiang Kai-shek could be destroyed and feared a long and costly war.[5]

National General Mobilization

Reluctantly, both the military and civilian leaders in Japan realized that the war in China could be won and the nation's defense structure strengthened only by the efforts of the entire nation. Konoye bolstered his country's morale by expressing the hope that the Western powers would eventually become cognizant of Japan's stabilizing influence in the Orient. He insisted that, in the meantime, Japan's mission could be accomplished only by complete mobilization. Militarily, the nation had already been mobilized. The General Staff had begun to execute a previously approved plan for the conquest of key positions on the China mainland. By early November, 1937, an Imperial Headquarters was created to coordinate and to centralize all Japanese military efforts in China. Since the Emperor was Commander in Chief of the Armed Forces, the military leaders could, if necessary, take matters up directly with him. Thus the Cabinet's wishes could be ignored and circumvented.

On the other hand, efforts were made to reconcile differences within the nation by the formation of a Cabinet Advisory Council. This Council was composed of representatives from the most important parties. Although largely advisory, it was organized "to participate in the Cabinet's discussion and planning of important state affairs concerning the China Incident." At its semiweekly meetings, the Council made recommendations on basic national policies. The Cabinet Ministers were thus able to concentrate on administrative matters.

In the meantime, the Cabinet Planning Board speeded up its work on the drafting of a National General Mobilization Bill. This bill was largely an enabling act whose provisions became operative upon the issuance of ordinances. It permitted the government to make full use of the nation's strength for defense purposes in time of war or during "incidents," such as that in China. It permitted the mobilization of the entire personnel and material resources of the nation. It provided for control of prices, goods, services, and finances. It allowed the press and media of information to be placed under strict censorship. The government was given powers to employ or discharge workers, to regulate their wages and working conditions, and to prevent strikes. It could control industrial production and place vital industries under its direct operation. A national registration, wartime taxes, and compulsory savings were all provided for in the law.

In September, 1937, when the Konoye Cabinet presented the Mobilization Bill to Parliament, it was opposed by a large number of Representatives. They maintained that its enactment would mean the complete loss of individual liberty and would make the Diet ineffective, and that conditions did not warrant such action. Opposition to the bill dwindled, however, after Konoye promised that its various measures would not be applicable to the war in China. Furthermore, ordinances under the law would be enacted only with the approval of a committee on which Diet members held a majority. Consequently, the Diet passed the new law in March, 1938. In a little over a year, however, ordinances had been approved for compulsory registration of all males between 16 and 50, authorization to the Ministry of Finance to control profits in industry and to appropriate property for war purposes, and compulsory mediation in all labor disputes.[6]

Konoye's New Order in East Asia

Shortly after the passage of the Mobilization Law, Konoye streamlined his Cabinet. He relied heavily on the Five Ministers Conference (Premier, War, Navy, Foreign Affairs, and Finance). All vital and urgent issues were left to this small group to decide. In May, 1938, Ikeda Seihin was appointed concurrently Minister of Finance and of Commerce and Industry. The military played an increasingly dominant role in all vital issues. It directed the war in China through the Imperial Headquarters. It sponsored administrative shifts in the government which deprived the Foreign Office of much of its powers. For example, the new War Minister, Itagaki Seishirō, who had returned from command of the North China forces after the capture of Hsüchow, urged that the China Affairs Board be placed under the direct supervision of the Cabinet and hence of the Army. Insisting that he must retain control of this Board, Foreign Minister Hirota resigned in protest. More Army men appeared in the Cabinet. General Ugaki was the new Foreign Minister; General Araki, former War Minister and advocate of spiritual mobilization through a belief in the Imperial Way, was made Minister of Education. The whole nation was rapidly being cast into a single, submissive unit, subject to the will of the ruling faction.

Premier Konoye also helped to strengthen the position of the military by an expanded interpretation of the purposes of the war against China. By the end of October, 1938, Hankow had been occupied and Canton had fallen. Large-scale territorial conquests had come to an end. On the other hand, Japan's hope of inflicting a decisive defeat on Chiang's main army had come to nought largely due to heavy Japanese casualties during the march of its Second Army up the Yangtze River Valley. Furthermore, Chiang, his government, and a large part of his army had retired to Chungking in mountainous Szechwan Province and gave no signs of a willingness to surrender. It was obvious that Japan now faced what it had hoped to avoid, an extended war on the mainland. Consequently, a new policy was essential to fit the new circumstances. Some formula must be found which gave a rationale to link the recently conquered territories of Manchukuo, Inner Mongolia, North, Central, and South China with Japan, and for continuing the struggle against the Chinese Nationalist government.

To meet this need, on November 3, 1938, Premier Konoye announced the establishment of "A New Order in East Asia." The purpose of this "New Order" was to assure permanent peace in East Asia. This was to be achieved by a tripartite relationship of mutual aid and coordination, under Japanese leadership, in the political, economic, and cultural fields among Japan, Manchukuo, and China. Konoye concluded his announcement by declaring that as Chiang Kai-shek held power in only a small portion of China, a new cooperative effort should be made by Japan and a "reformed China" for their mutual benefit. He expected these three states to retain their respective individuality but to stand united in safeguarding Asia against any and all encroachments.

As a first step toward the formation of an effective economic bloc, it was necessary to coordinate the national economy with that of Manchukuo and China. This integration had been accomplished in Manchuria through the government-owned South Manchurian Railway Company and later by the Manchurian Industrial Development Corporation of Aikawa Gisuke. (See page 415.) Aikawa, through close connections with leaders of the Kwantung Army, had been given special privileges and his enterprises had made a significant contribution to the industrial growth of Manchuria. After the formation of Manchukuo, control of that "state" by Japan was assured through a General Affairs Board. This Board,

PREPARATION FOR TOTAL WAR, 1937–1941

whose Chairman was a Japanese appointed by the Kwantung Army, developed plans and programs for the new state. These plans were coordinated with those in Japan through the Cabinet's Manchurian Affairs Board. After the industrial control provisions of the National Mobilization Law went into effect, the authority was at hand to integrate the economies of Japan and Manchukuo.[7]

In China, political integration was to come through new autonomous regional governments friendly to Japan and economic integration was to be achieved through the Japanese government-owned development corporations which were primarily concerned with the exploitation of the recently conquered areas. The North China Development Corporation made capital and technical assistance available for the mining of coking coal and iron ore in North China in accordance with a plan prepared by the China Affairs Board. Integration and coordination of the activities in all these areas were achieved in Tokyo through the Prime Minister, who was Chairman of the Cabinet Planning Board, the Manchurian Affairs Board, and the China Affairs Board. Although experience and new crises required innumerable administrative changes between the passage of the Mobilization Law in 1938 and Japan's decision to attack the United States toward the end of 1941, the basic machinery for complete national mobilization and for coordination with the conquered regions of China had been established.

Japan Challenges the Western Powers

While Prime Minister Konoye had been consolidating the position of the central government and making preparations for national mobilization, his government had also been confronted with some delicate international problems. Although the war in China had strained Japan's relations with the United Kingdom and the United States, the nearest potential Western enemy was the Soviet Union. With Vladivostok and other Soviet air bases only a few hours' flying time from the industrial and demographic heart of Japan, the fear of Soviet attack always remained in the background. The borders of the Soviet Union were contiguous with those of the Japanese puppet states of Inner Mongolia and Manchukuo, and of Korea. The Japanese General Staff was painfully aware that prolonged hostilities in China weakened Japan's strategic position. They also knew that a deterioration of Soviet–Japanese relations might threaten Japan's whole position on the Asiatic continent.

In mid-July, 1938, Soviet–Japanese relations came to a crisis with the outbreak of hostilities along the ill-defined Soviet–Korean border, in the area near Changkufeng Hill in a bend of the Tumen River. Fighting continued intensely for approximately two weeks. But when Minister of War Itagaki reported to the Throne on the matter, the Emperor made it clear he was strongly opposed to any further expansion of the conflict and urged immediate diplomatic negotiations to settle the dispute. As both sides wanted to avoid war, an armistice agreement was signed in Moscow in August. Despite subsequent temporary disagreements over terms of a new fishing agreement, friendly relations with the Soviet Union were not threatened again until the summer of 1939. Thus Japan was secure on the northern flank and was free to expand southward to Canton and Hankow. It was also in a position to put pressure on the European powers.[8]

When the Japanese Army began the conquest of China in 1937, one of its objectives was the liquidation of non-Japanese, foreign business and commercial interests on the Asiatic continent. As their forces spread farther southward, the Japanese commanders, under the guise of military necessity, constantly placed obstacles in the way of foreign firms. For example, travel on the Yangtze River was restricted to Japanese boats. The Japanese-sponsored currency in North China was the only one recognized officially as legal tender within occupied China. There was constant interference with the shipping facilities of the Western powers.

Despite these challenges and insults, the Western powers, who were in a comparatively weak position, could do little more than endure them. In view of the growing crisis in Europe, one of the basic objectives of British policy was to avoid a frontal attack in either Europe or Asia to gain time for greater military preparedness. Thus it was unwilling to oppose Japan single-handedly. Since isolationist policy was still strong in the United States, it was unlikely to do more than protest each new Japanese move by an official announcement or note. When Konoye announced his policy of a New Order in East Asia, the United States merely protested against the interference with the rights and interests of its nationals by Japan and continued to insist that it would not abrogate any of its rights. On the other hand, it was not yet ready to make a positive move to protect those rights.

By the early part of 1939, therefore, the Japanese Army leaders were convinced that Chiang Kai-shek's refusal to surrender and the prolongation of the war in China were results of the aid he was receiving from the Western powers. In particular, the Japanese Army believed that unless decisive action was taken against France and Great Britain, the China War could not be brought to a successful conclusion. With the northern flank temporarily secured from Soviet attack, Japan defied France, and in February, 1939, occupied Hainan Island off the south coast of China. It also claimed sovereignty over the nearby Spratly Islands. France was too weak to take any countermeasures. Japan had successfully called the bluff of one of the colonial powers. It had, thereby, measurably improved its strategic position.

An even greater psychological victory was wrested from Great Britain in Tientsin. In June, 1939, the Japanese charged that the British and French were harboring in their concessions in Tientsin the suspected murderers of a native collaborator. Consequently, the local Japanese commander blockaded these concessions. The real issue was who was to control the silver bullion held by the British as collateral for the Chinese currency. Japan wanted to obtain the bullion and drive the Chinese currency out of circulation. Foreigners entering or leaving the concessions were searched by Japanese solders; women were made to strip in public on the pretext of smuggling. This policy of degrading Westerners before Asiatics had a tremendous psychological impact both on the perpetrators and on the bystanders. It was a crude but graphic way of deflating the prestige of subjects of the colonial powers. It also tended to elevate the Japanese in the eyes of the Chinese as the self-appointed deliverers of Asiatics from European oppression.

But Japan had to pay dearly for its callous attitude and disrespect for the treaty rights of other states in China. Great Britain adamantly refused to surrender the silver bullion. The United States decided that words would have to be replaced by action. Consequently, at the end of July, 1939, it announced its intention to terminate its Treaty of Commerce with Japan after the specified period of six months. This was another way of notifying Japan that unless it ceased its expansionism and other lawless acts, after the expiration date of the treaty, the United States legally could, and might, impose an embargo on the island empire.

At the same time, another border dispute had broken out with the Soviet Union. This time it was near Nomonhan on the Outer Mongolia–Manchukuo border. The first skirmish began in May. On August 20, the Soviets counterattacked in force supported by tanks, artillery, and planes. By the end of the month two divisions of Soviet troops with superior mechanized equipment had severely beaten the Japanese forces and inflicted 18,000 casualties on them. Once more the local Japanese military commanders had escalated the fighting contrary to orders from the General Staff, which wished to avoid a full-scale war with the Soviet Union. In so doing, these commanders had also jeopardized Japan's position in China.

As these disquieting reports reached Tokyo, word came from Berlin that Germany and the Soviet Union had signed a nonaggression pact. Japan was in danger of isolation from the Axis. It undertook feverish diplomatic activity directed toward improving its international status. A new Cabinet was formed which promised to follow the "immutable policy of Japan in China," to act independently in dealing with the foreign powers, and to oppose anyone who obstructed Japan's mission.[9] With Hitler's invasion of Poland on September 1, 1939, and the outbreak of World War II in Europe, Japan declared that it would not become involved in the war but would concentrate on the settlement of the war in China. At the same time, negotiations were begun in Moscow which settled the Nomonhan affair. For the second time within a year, therefore, a war with Russia was averted.

Japan Joins the Axis

But the war in China, the "China Affair," as Japan insisted on calling it, still remained unsettled. In an effort to prevent a closer alliance between the European Axis and Japan, Great Britain had sought to negotiate the Sino-Japanese War. Furthermore, it withdrew its gunboats from the Yangtze River; its troops were recalled from Peking and Tientsin. But these moves were of no avail. During the next few months Japan concentrated on the formation of a strong, pro-Japanese regime for all of China. To this end, the Japanese-sponsored government of Wang Ching-wei was formally inaugurated at Nanking in March, 1940. But even this act had no influence on Chiang and his Nationalist government. He continued to fight Japan as best he could from his temporary capital of Chungking.

The more stubbornly Chiang refused to give up, the more Japan blamed the foreigners for making this resistance possible. Hence, it sought ways and means of preventing the Western powers from continuing to send him aid. Events in Europe soon afforded the opportunity for which Japan was waiting. After the fall of France in the middle of June, 1940, Japan could intimidate Great Britain without fear of reprisals, for the latter was struggling for its very survival. Consequently, Japan demanded that no more military supplies be sent to the Chinese Nationalists over the Burma Road. Great Britain agreed to close the Road for three months. In return, it had avoided war with Japan and gained valuable time during which it won the Battle of Britain.

In the meantime, sharp divisions of opinion existed within Japan on whether it should join the Axis. In the spring of 1939, the Japanese Ambassadors to Germany and Italy, with strong support from members of the General Staff, had been pressing hard for Japan's alignment with the Axis. On the other hand, the Emperor and his advisers and the Navy were known to be against such a move. By the summer of 1939, although it was willing to give a commitment to fight against the Soviet Union, Japan did not want to commit itself to fight both Great Britain and the United States. Moreover, after Germany signed a nonaggression pact with the Soviet Union and invaded Poland, Japan was all the more insistent that it be free to play an independent role.

The military power which the Nazis had demonstrated in Europe from 1939 to mid-summer of 1940 had greatly strengthened the position of those Japanese advocating an Axis Alliance. The German invasion of Norway, the Netherlands, and France, the flight of the British Army from Dunkirk in May, 1940, and the collapse of France made the Nazis seem invincible. On the other hand, when the Minister of War presented Prime Minister Yonai Mitsumasa with a memorandum from the Chiefs of Staff recommending that Japan join the Axis, Yonai rejected it. From the Army's point of view, therefore, it was time for a change of Cabinet so the War Minister resigned, causing the Cabinet's downfall.

The continued inability to force a favorable settlement in China, the internal economic and political pressures, and the world crisis called for a strong Cabinet. The Senior Statesmen (*Jūshin*) promptly informed Lord Keeper of the Privy Seal Kido that Prince Konoye was their preferred candidate. The leaders of the Army, Navy, political parties, and business agreed that he was the man of the hour. Before completing his second Cabinet, he sought agreement on general policies from the three most important members of his Cabinet: General Tōjō Hideki, Minister of War, Admiral Yoshida Zengo, Minister of Navy, and Matsuoka Yōsuke, Foreign Minister.[10] This inner group concurred with a four-point program: (1) an alliance with the Axis Powers; (2) a planned national economy; (3) a strong economic bloc composed of Japan, Manchukuo, and China; and (4) an impenetrable defense based on a new, revived nationalism.

Matsuoka, who was a staunch advocate of an Axis Alliance, readily accepted the task of negotiating for it. He believed it would strengthen Japan's strategic position and thus prevent war with either the United States or Great Britain. Premier Konoye argued that the pact would enable his government to negotiate a peaceful settlement with China and prevent a war with the Soviet Union. After approval of the alliance by the Privy Council and the Imperial Conference, the Tripartite Treaty was signed in Berlin on September 27, 1940. The Axis Alliance recognized the leadership of Germany and Italy in Europe and that of Japan in greater East Asia through the establishment of a New Order. The signatories promised to come to each other's assistance when attacked by an outside power. Thus the first objective of the Cabinet's policy had been achieved. At the same time, any hopes which the Allies might have had of isolating Japan from the Axis powers in Europe were shattered.

Difficulties with Economic Controls

Despite the passage of the National Mobilization Law in 1938 and the gradual implementation of some of its provisions, the Empire's economy was not operating as a cohesive unit when Konoye formed his second Cabinet in July, 1940. The military leaders, such as his new War Minister Tōjō, insisted that government controls be increased and intensified and that they be based on an overall economic plan. On the other hand, the industrialists, especially the members of the old family combines (the *zaibatsu*) which comprised the backbone of the nation's economy, insisted that they be permitted to unify and organize industry into cartels which they would control independently of the government. This basic conflict between the militarists and the industrialists, and the bureaucratic jealousies between the old ministries and the new control bodies, had produced a national economy which was partly controlled and partly free. For example, wages were frozen but price controls were more nominal than real. Raw materials presumably were allocated to essential industries but an influential businessman could obtain what he needed if he were willing to pay for it. Profit controls had been strengthened and tax reforms had been introduced as a result of pressure from the Army. Its dissatisfaction with economic conditions had been one reason for the overthrow of the previous Cabinet.

It was natural, therefore, that War Minister Tōjō and Foreign Minister Matsuoka were joined in the second Konoye Cabinet by Hoshino Naoki as president of the Cabinet Planning Board. These appointments were clear proof that the aggressive Kwantung clique was going to exert the dominant influence in national economic planning as well as in military strategy and foreign affairs. Since 1932, when he was appointed Vice-Minister of Finance in Manchukuo, Hoshino had been a key figure in the formation of its industrial structure which was controlled by the Kwantung Army. He rapidly rose to become the most important figure in the Manchukuo government, namely, chairman of the General Affairs Board, the body which planned all important operations of that government. He was a logical choice, therefore, to carry out the Army's plan of creating a similar structure within Japan proper, which called for a shift from a semiwartime economy to complete control under direction of the military. But Hoshino soon found that it was far more difficult to obtain approval for his plan in Japan, where the industrialists were relatively strong, than in Manchukuo, where his friends in the Kwantung Army called the tune.

Although tremendous advances in industrial production had been made during the decade 1930–1940, there were certain obvious weaknesses in the national economy. This production had been directed toward the creation of a strong war machine which had put a heavy strain on the national budget. For example, the value of total industrial output had increased from 6 billion yen at the beginning of the period to 30 billion yen by 1941. The main emphasis had been on heavy industry, however, which showed a tenfold increase from 1930 to 1942. Military expenditures, which reflected this trend, and the demands of the war in China were largely responsible for a rapid rise in the total national expenditures. Whereas in 1931, military expenses comprised less than half a billion yen and 30 per cent of the budget, in the first year of the China War (1937–1938) they totaled about 4 billion yen and over 71 per cent of the budget. By the time Hoshino became President of the Planning Board in 1940 they had increased to 7.3 billion yen. Consequently, the cumulated budget deficit had reached nearly one-fourth of the total national income.[11]

The longer the war in China continued, the more imperative it became for Japan to develop effective planning if the nation was to survive. Despite the efforts of the Cabinet Planning Board, such planning and control as existed prior to 1940 had been haphazard. It had been evolved largely on a basis of trial and error. For instance, effective control over foreign trade was not undertaken until 1937 when high prices at home had caused a slump in exports and a dangerously large adverse balance of trade. In the fall of that year, the first list of prohibited imports was published and strict limitations were enforced. Within a year, by 1938, the former adverse balance had been converted into an export surplus.

But the attempts to control general production and distribution through coordinated plans issued by the Planning Board were far less successful than those for trade. The Planning Board, through a materials mobilization plan, attempted to control such important elements of the economy as oil, iron and steel, power, machine tools, light metals, ships, and minerals. Special policy companies were formed for each of these important industries. But competition for limited raw materials and unwillingness to abide by the regulations resulted in confusion. Even in the strategically important iron and steel industry, there was no fixed pattern of control until November, 1941.

The task of creating an effective economic mobilization was also bedeviled by the plan to create a Greater East Asia Co-prosperity Sphere. As the Japanese Army extended its tentacles over the Asiatic mainland, new raw materials and markets were available for exploitation. The nation was faced, therefore, with a triple task: the exploitation of resources and expansion of industry in the colonies, the industrialization of the newly acquired territories, and the coordination of both of these developments with the new planned economy at home.

A New Economic Structure

During the 1930–1940 decade, there was a decided difference in the method of exploitation of the colonies of Korea and Formosa on the one hand, and of Manchukuo and China on the other. As for the two colonies, industrial growth was the result of investment of both private Japanese capitalists and of the Imperial government. In Korea, for example, the sevenfold increase of industrial production in this period was the result of the investment of both the Oriental Development Company and of private companies. The former, which was half-owned by the Japanese government, possessed a large part of the best agricultural land in Korea. It also provided a large share of venture capital. In 1941, it floated 70 per cent of the loans in the colony. On the other hand, the privately owned Japan Nitrogenous Fertilizer Manufacturing Company developed most of the electric power and chemical industry in the Korean peninsula. It reportedly made a profit of 31 per cent. One of its subsidiaries, the

Suiho Power Company, built the large hydroelectric plant on the Yalu River, with a yearly output of 3.8 billion kilowatt-hours. With such favorable conditions for high profits and maximum security, the three leading *zaibatsu* firms readily invested in new light metal plants, railways, mines, cement, and chemical industries. They also profited from special government subsidies awarded to strategically important plants such as those of synthetic petroleum.

But the economic development of Manchuria had been a different matter. When the Kwantung Army took over that rich, undeveloped, predominantly agricultural area in 1931, it hoped to build its own empire. It proceeded forthwith to make this dream a reality through the creation of the puppet state of Manchukuo. It soon discovered, however, that the economic exploitation and industrialization of a country was a difficult and complicated matter which required large amounts of capital and a specialized knowledge. Suspicious of the old-line financial combines, the Kwantung Army sought assistance from one of the most imaginative of the *nouveaux riches,* Aikawa Gisuke. In 1936, he became a special economic adviser to the Kwantung Army and soon worked out a plan to transform his financial interests in Japan (*Nissan*) into the Manchurian Industrial Development Corporation (*Mangyō*).

On March 1, 1938, this new corporation began operation under the most favorable conditions for Aikawa, its president. Half of the 400 million yen capital had been supplied by the Manchukuo government which also guaranteed a 6 per cent interest on the investment and underwrote the capital which came from Japan. Manchurian Industrial then began to absorb many of the existing companies. It concentrated its investments in new concerns, such as iron foundries, steel plants, and automobile and aircraft factories. By the end of 1941, its loans had risen to nearly 1.5 billion yen and earnings had equaled 13.6 per cent. While this huge corporation was a profitable enterprise, it was not always looked upon with favor by financial circles in Tokyo. For example, when a new Five Year Plan of expansion for Manchukuo was established in 1937 under its direction, Tokyo bankers were worried over the predominance of Manchurian loans floated on the domestic market. In some cases, they refused to approve new issues of loans for Manchurian enterprises.

New conquests were started in North China by the Kwantung Army just when it had become difficult to obtain large amounts of new risk capital for investment in Manchuria. These conquests after July, 1937, secured a new supply of resources and opened up new investment possibilities. Exploitation of China was undertaken in various ways. The North China and Central China Development Companies, under Japanese ownership, began an active expansion of transportation, communications, harbor facilities, and natural resources. Private Japanese companies were encouraged to operate industries already developed by Chinese capital. Manchurian companies also participated in the operation of factories and mines. The net result of all this activity was the strengthening of the economic ties among Japan, Manchukuo, and China and the formation of a significant yen-bloc area. For example, in 1940, North China produced 18 million tons of coal and Manchuria mined 21 million tons. By 1941, both areas met all of Japan's salt requirements. In the crucial iron and steel industries, while the continental area manufactured only a small fraction of the ingot and finished steel for the Empire, it produced 30 per cent of Japan's needs for pig iron in 1937 and also in 1941.[12]

Such, in very general terms, was the economic situation within Japan and the occupied areas of China in July, 1940, when Hoshino, as newly appointed President of the Cabinet Planning Board, tried to impose the same sort of controls on Japan proper that he carried out in Manchukuo. He advocated the reorganization and strengthening of the various cartels and the appointment by the Cabinet of their directors. These directors were to be given virtual dictatorial powers to carry out policies formulated by a Supreme Economic Council. But the great family combines were not yet willing to succumb to Army control and refused to relinquish their autonomy. The international crisis was not yet acute enough to convince them that if they did not support the Army they would lose everything. Consequently, the Army had to wait until September, 1941, when a compromise solution was worked out, before it had the power to force industry to comply with state controls. The Second Konoye Cabinet had been less successful, therefore, in the creation of a new economic structure acceptable to the Manchurian clique than it had been in the negotiations for a Tripartite Pact.

In the creation of an impenetrable defense based on a revival of nationalism, the last of the objectives of the Konoye Cabinet, it made notable gains. Although the political parties had not been opposed to Japan's expansion on the Asiatic continent, they had not, on the other hand, been staunch supporters of the program of centralized control at home and indefinite expansion abroad. Even prior to Konoye becoming Prime Minister in July, 1940, he had been active in the formation of a single national party. Under his leadership, several patriotic organizations were merged into a single organization. Later, the old political parties were subjected to "voluntary" dissolution.

The stage was thus prepared for a transcendent nationalist party to assist in the successful conclusion of "the holy war in China" and the renovation of the entire political structure. It came to be known as the Imperial Rule Assistance Association (IRAA). Its preparatory committee was composed of members of the Cabinet, the Diet, political parties, business interests, and national societies. It was formally inaugurated in October, 1940, with the Premier as president. Konoye and many of his close associates and intellectuals saw it as developing into a new force to control the Army extremists. Actually, it failed to do so and in the course of a year became the vehicle through which outright military party control was exercised. Under its inspiration the nation was prepared to begin its historic march to create a new order in the world, to place, as Konoye had expressed it, the universe under a single roof, namely, the benevolent leadership of the Japanese Emperor.

Importance of Southward Expansion

Underlying all of these ultranationalist developments was a special urge on the part of the Imperial Navy to expand to the south. One of the greatest weaknesses in Japan's economy was a lack of oil, the life blood of the Imperial Navy and the Air Force. While large stores of oil were being accumulated, they were not sufficient to sustain a continued, all-out war effort. Synthetic fuels had not been satisfactorily developed. Ample supplies of oil, bauxite, tin, and rubber existed in the Netherlands East Indies and British colonies. Thus the Imperial Navy had constantly stressed the paramount importance of access to these resources to the south. In 1936, the Navy had advocated the enlargement of the fleet to secure command of the Western Pacific. To achieve access to the natural resources in the South Sea, discreet steps were recommended to assure gradual and peaceful progress. As hostilities on the continent expanded, the Navy sought confirmation for a policy of southward expansion.

By 1940, it had become apparent to Japan that if the Netherlands would not guarantee Japan free access to oil supplies in the Netherlands East Indies, then these oil fields would have to be seized by force. At the Liaison Conference in July, the importance of oil was recognized by the adoption of a policy to obtain it by diplomatic means if possible, but by force if necessary. At the same time, in view of the need to expedite a settlement of the war in China, the French would be asked to halt supplies going to Chiang Kai-shek through Indochina but every effort was to be made not to antagonize the United States, Great Britain, or the Netherlands.

This important shift in emphasis on the importance of the south, in contrast to the previous stress on the danger from the Soviet Union in the north, explains the pressure being put on the Governor-General of Indochina to approve the dispatch of Japanese troops to Hanoi and other ports in north Indochina to enforce the interdiction of supplies to Chiang Kai-shek. In September, the French Governor-General gave Japan the right to establish garrisoned air bases in North Indochina and to use that area as a corridor for troops and supplies. These moves created advance bases for any later southern moves by Japan. Great Britain was also forced to close the Burma Road, the other supply route to the beleaguered Nationalist government in Chungking.

Despite the strategic advantages which these moves gave to Japan over the Western powers, there was ample evidence available to show that the latter would not, regardless of circumstances, agree to recognize Japan's new rights in Asia. For example, in September, 1940, the Netherlands East Indies had rebuffed a special Japanese economic mission which sought to obtain special concessions for Indonesian oil. While Britain might have been forced to make temporary concessions concerning the closing of the Burma Road, it had no intention of doing so permanently. Secretary of State Cordell Hull told the Senate Foreign Relations Committee in mid-January, 1941, that the United States had repeatedly tried to persuade Japan that its best interests lay in the development of friendly relations with the United States. The United States had not, and would not, sanction the formation of a New Order in the western Pacific under Japanese political and economic domination.

Foreign Minister Matsuoka's Negotiations

But Foreign Minister Matsuoka exemplified the group of nationalists in Japan who held the diametrically opposite view and who ran the government. They were convinced that since the Empire was invincible, it could obtain what it wanted by force. Furthermore, they believed that it was in a strong enough world position to make even the United States and the Soviet Union bow to its wishes. Matsuoka saw the world dividing into great blocs with Japan the leader in East Asia. Consequently, he outlined an impossible program. He proposed strengthening the ties with the Axis, protecting his country's northern flank by a treaty of nonaggression with the Soviet Union, and working out a general settlement with the United States which would recognize Japan's New Order in Asia. Unfortunately for his own future and that of his country, his arrogance and conceit blinded him to reality. He failed to understand Hitler's motives. He was unable to bring Stalin and Molotov to his point of view. Finally, Matsuoka completely misjudged the seriousness of the basic differences between his own government and that of the United States.

In March, 1941, he started on his incongruous mission, leaving for Moscow and Berlin the day after the United States Congress had passed the Lend-Lease Act and thus squarely placed itself by Britain's side against the Axis. On his first visit to Moscow, he found no interest on Russia's part in a nonaggression pact. In Berlin, Hitler strongly opposed a Japanese–Soviet accord and urged Japan to attack Singapore. As Matsuoka was more concerned with keeping on the best terms with both Hitler and Stalin than with their relations toward each other he did not catch the significance of Hitler's hint that Germany was contemplating attacking the Soviet Union. The Foreign Minister then returned to Moscow and had to be content with a Neutrality Pact. He believed he had protected Japan's northern flank, and turned his attention toward a *rapprochement* with the United States.[13]

Even before the Foreign Minister had gone to Berlin a new Japanese Ambassador, Admiral Nomura Kichisaburō, had arrived in Washington with the promise from his Foreign Office that he would receive support in negotiations for a basic United States–Japanese understanding. On April 16, 1941, Secretary of State Cordell Hull gave the Japanese Ambassador the first of many notes which were to be exchanged between the two countries during the next eight months of negotiations. During this period, neither country budged from its basic position. Thus Hull's first note contained the four basic principles on which he insisted that agreement must be reached before any final settlement was possible between the two nations. These principles were: (1) the respect for territorial integrity and sovereignty of all nations; (2) the noninterference in the internal affairs of other states; (3) the support of the principle of equality, including equality of commercial opportunity; and (4) the nondisturbance of the status quo except by peaceful means.

The basic Japanese position was expressed in a reply of May 12, 1941. It justified Japan's alliance with Germany and Italy on the grounds that it was defensive in nature with a view to preventing neutral countries from entering the European War. In what was considered as an answer to Hull's first two principles, the note requested the United States to persuade Chiang Kai-shek to agree to negotiate a peace treaty with Japan on the bases of friendship, recognition of the independence of Manchukuo, cooperation against communism, and economic cooperation. In reference to the principle of equal commercial opportunity, Japan proposed normal trade relations between Japan and the United States and that each state should supply the other with needed commodities. The last principle was dismissed by defining Japan's expansion as "peaceful." In fact, it asked the United States to cooperate in the production and procurement for Japan of natural resources such as oil, rubber, tin, and nickel in the southwestern Pacific. Despite the basic divergence of his government's reply from the American position, Premier Konoye hoped that the European War could be confined to Europe and that the United States would agree to force Chiang to sue for peace. If these objectives could be achieved, he was confident that other differences could be resolved.

But international developments and a growing support for an aggressive move to the south to assure Japan's access to basic raw materials and to resolve the war in China quickly obliterated any real chance of a successful conclusion of any American–Japanese negotiations. In the first place, in the early part of June, 1941, the Netherlands had again refused to comply with Japan's demands for oil, rubber, and tin from the Netherlands East Indies. A note from the United States, received shortly thereafter, indicated that it would not assist Japan in obtaining these strategic materials. Consequently, if these valuable supplies were to be obtained, so Japan's nationalists argued, they would have to be obtained by force.

Decision To Move South at Risk of War—July, 1941

When Hitler invaded the Soviet Union on June 22, 1941, and failed to advise his Axis partner in the Pacific of his plans, a crisis immediately arose within the Konoye Cabinet. Matsuoka, who had negotiated the Neutrality Pact with the Soviet Union and simultaneously urged closer ties with the Axis, was in an untenable position. To extricate himself, he argued that Japan should attack the Soviet Union on the basis of the Axis Alliance and temporarily postpone the proposed southern push into the Netherlands East Indies. While Hitler's armies poured eastward, continuous meetings were held in Tokyo by the Liaison Conference, the body which coordinated the views of the Cabinet and the Chiefs of Staff. It finally agreed on "An Outline of National Policies in View of the Changing Situation." On July 2, 1941, at an Imperial Conference, the Emperor gave his sanction to the new policies.[14]

The importance of these decisive conferences cannot be overemphasized. In the first place, Japan decided to settle the war in China as quickly as possible by increasing pressure on Chiang and seizing the foreign settlements. Secondly, the plan to advance southward on Indochina and Siam was to be implemented *even at the risk of war with Great Britain and the United States.* Thirdly, the Neutrality Pact with the Soviet Union should be continued. Fourthly, when Germany was on the point of defeating Russia, Japan would intervene in the European war. Thus Japan would have a chance to strengthen its position in Eastern Asia at Russia's expense. The decisions of the Conference were kept secret from the people, who were told simply that: "A fundamental national policy to be adopted in meeting the prevailing situation has been decided." A general mobilization was ordered. All Japanese merchant ships were called home from the Atlantic Ocean. Time for reaching a settlement was fast running out.

As a first step toward implementing the new policy, Prime Minister Konoye resigned in mid-July, 1941. By so doing, he was able to rid his Cabinet of persons opposed to this basic policy, especially Foreign Minister Matsuoka. The third Konoye Cabinet, which was formed almost immediately (July 18, 1941, to October 18, 1941), promised to put these policies into practice with speed and fortitude. Pressure was exerted on France and the Vichy government. They were forced to consent to new Japanese bases in Indochina or suffer invasion. On July 29, 1941, 50,000 Japanese troops poured into South Indochina. As a reprisal, two days later the United States froze all Japanese assets abroad and the negotiations for a general settlement were broken off. In reality, an economic embargo had been imposed on Japan and trade with the United States virtually ceased.

This new development made it all the more advisable, from Japan's point of view, to reach an agreement with the United States, providing such agreement could be achieved on Japan's terms. Premier Konoye proposed, therefore, that he meet with President Roosevelt somewhere in the Pacific to discuss a basic, overall settlement. In reply, the President told Japanese Ambassador Nomura in August, 1941, that unless Japan stopped its military advances, such as those in Indochina, the United States would have to act to protect its interests and national security. As for meeting personally with Konoye, the President insisted that Japan should furnish a clearer statement of its position and intentions before any such meeting could take place.

In the meantime, the position and intentions which were being evolved in Tokyo were making an agreement with the United States impossible. Lack of progress in the United States–Japan diplomatic negotiation, the apparent swift successes of Hitler's army both in Western and Eastern Europe, the realization that in a few months America's increased war potential would far surpass Japan's, and the inaccessibility of oil and other strategic materials had convinced the General Staff and Prime Minister Konoye that they should take advantage of the moment and resort to direct action. Consequently, a basic plan entitled "Essentials for Carrying out the Empire's Policies" was reviewed and approved by the Liaison Conference. On September 6, 1941, it was presented to another Imperial Conference.

The Emperor, however, was unhappy over the turn of events. He was reported to have previously chided the Army Chief of Staff for making an overly optimistic prediction that a war with the United States would last only three months. At the Imperial Conference he expressed his regret that the Supreme Command had not given a satisfactory answer to the question as to why the proposed plan placed far greater emphasis on military preparations than on diplomacy. Nevertheless, the conference agreed to the proposed essential plan and thereby took an irrevocable step toward war with the United States. The Conference reaffirmed the July decision that Japan should not be deterred by the likelihood of war with the United Kingdom and the United States. War preparations should proceed at an accelerated rate and should be completed by the end of October. At the same time increased diplomatic efforts should be made to reach an accord with the United States. The policy concluded, "In the event that Japan's demands were not accepted by the end of October, a decision should be made to open hostilities with the United States."[15]

But the interchange of notes between Japan and the United States which took place during September did little to iron out their differences. On October 2, Hull informed Nomura that Japan's latest proposals formed no real basis for a settlement. He added that the meeting of Konoye and Roosevelt should be put off until there was agreement between the two countries on how the four American principles, originally proposed by him on April 16, should be applied to problems in East Asia.

Final Steps Toward War

Thus, early October had arrived without Japanese diplomacy having succeeded in persuading the United States to change its viewpoint. The Japanese High Command demanded that in accordance with the Imperial Conference decision of September 6, a definite position should be taken on when to go to war. The military leaders resented the latest American note, which insisted that any basic settlement would entail the withdrawal of Japanese troops from the Chinese mainland. General Tōjō haughtily declared that Japan should fight rather than let the United States interfere with its destiny. Although the Navy Minister was not ready to take responsibility for the consequences of a decision for war, Tōjō's views reflected those of both the Army and Navy Chiefs of Staff. Premier Konoye and his Foreign Minister were still hopeful that the negotiations with America might be successful. At a crucial Cabinet meeting in mid-October, General Tōjō insisted that the time for action had arrived, forcing Konoye to choose between two alternatives: resignation or acceptance of the War Minister's position. He chose the former, hoping Imperial Prince Higashikuni would be his successor. But Lord Keeper of the Privy Seal Kido argued that under existing circumstances the new Prime Minister must be familiar with the recent developments within the government and also be able to control the armed services, especially the Army. Consequently, General Tōjō was selected. His new Cabinet, in which he was not only Premier but also concurrently Min-

Tōjō Hideki (1885–1948)

ister of War and Minister of Home Affairs, was formed on October 18, 1941. The war party was securely in control.[16]

When Tōjō was appointed Prime Minister, the Emperor made a last attempt to postpone or avoid open hostilities against the United States. He requested that a thorough re-examination be made of the September decision to go to war if diplomacy failed. Numerous studies were made of Japan's economic and strategic potentialities and estimates of victory. In early November these were discussed at length, often with anger, in Liaison Conferences. Although Foreign Minister Tōgō Shigenori and Finance Minister Kaya Okinori raised doubts as to the wisdom of going to war, everyone became obsessed with its inevitability. The Chiefs of Staff argued that, under the existing embargo, Japan was rapidly exhausting its supplies of such essential strategic materials as oil and the populace was already facing hardships. If Japan did not go to war the nation faced strangulation. While the Chiefs of Staff could not guarantee

Japan's eventual victory, they insisted that simple logic forced the conclusion that the longer hostilities were postponed the less chance there was for victory. Consequently, the basic issue in the discussions at this stage was whether the diplomatic negotiations should be continued. A partial compromise was reached. On November 5, 1941, it was agreed at an Imperial Conference that preparations for war were to be intensified but negotiations with the United States were to continue. If successful results were not achieved by November 30, a decision to go to war would be made at that time. Japan's minimum demands for these negotiations were divided into two alternatives. The first alternative required American recognition of Japan's conquests in China and abandonment of support for Chiang Kai-shek and his Nationalist government. The second alternative was a *modus vivendi* in which the China problem was left for Japan and China to solve; the United States would assure Japan's continued access to oil in Southeast Asia in return for Japanese troop withdrawals from southern Indochina.

As a result of these latest decisions, which required a complete reversal of the American position if they were to be acceptable, negotiations in Washington continued. By November 17, when special envoy Kurusu arrived, the United States had already rejected the first alternative plan. Secretary of State Hull insisted that no settlement was possible until Japan withdrew its troops from China, adopted a policy of equal economic opportunity for all of the mainland, and gave up its alliance with the Axis Powers. As for the *modus vivendi,* Ambassadors Nomura and Kurusu tried to convince President Roosevelt and Secretary Hull of the necessity of a positive response if war were to be avoided, but the United States also rejected this proposal.[17]

In the meantime, Premier Tōjō had activated the war plan and Japan's submarines were on their way to rendezvous at Pearl Harbor on December 7. On November 26, 1941, the United States presented its last note, which reviewed its position and included the basic points which had been presented at the beginning of the negotiations. It stated that permanent peace could be established only when these principles were adopted. Hull indicated that he was not interested in a *modus vivendi* and that the United States would not modify its position. Unless Japan accepted the American proposals, the economic embargo would continue.

The Liaison Conference in Tokyo agreed unanimously to reject the American note and to fight. Tōjō then secured the Emperor's approval for an Imperial Conference which confirmed this decision. Japan's declaration of war was delayed in reaching the United States. It was still in the process of being deciphered in the Japanese Embassy in Washington when Japan struck at Pearl Harbor on December 7, 1941. The war in the Pacific had begun.

NOTES

1. General Tōjō Hideki (1884–1948) had been one of the staff officers associated with General Nagata and other members of the Control Faction of the Army. He had been removed from the General Staff while Araki was Minister of War. After serving as Chief of Military Police of the Kwantung Army, he advanced to become its Chief of Staff. In May, 1938, he returned to Tokyo as Vice-Minister of War under General Itagaki over whom he had a strong and controlling influence. In December he was in charge of the newly created Inspector General of Military Aviation. Under Prime Minister Konoye, he held the key post of War Minister from July, 1940, to October, 1941, when he became Premier and served concurrently as Minister of War. He was forced to resign in the summer of 1944 after the fall of Saipan. He was condemned to death as a war criminal. For an excellent study of his role in leading Japan to war, see Robert C. Butow, *Tojo and the Coming of the War* (Princeton: Princeton University Press, 1961).

2. Konoye Fumimaro (1891–1945) had remained aloof from politics in the sense that he had never held a Cabinet post. He had long been a member of the House of Peers, however, and was its President from 1933 to 1937, and was also President of the Privy Council from January, 1939, to June, 1940. He appeared to be a weak person, vacillating between a moderate and an extremist viewpoint. At the final showdown, however, he did not hesitate. When he learned that he was to be arrested for trial as a war criminal, he committed suicide. There were three Konoye Cabinets as follows: first Konoye Cabinet, June 4, 1937–January 5, 1939; second Konoye Cabinet, July 22, 1940–July 18, 1941; third Konoye Cabinet, July 18–October 18, 1941. The popular spelling of his name is used here.

Konoye's first Cabinet had General Sugiyama Hajime as Minister of War. He had served in that capacity in the previous Cabinet and was one of the strong men in the Army. Admiral Yonai was held over as Navy Minister. Hirota Kōki, leader of the bureaucrats but amenable to Army dictates, was Foreign Minister. Kaya Okinori and Yoshino Shinji, both under the influence of the military, were appointed respectively Minister of Finance and of Commerce and Industry. Baba Eiichi, former Governor of the Hypothec Bank and selected by the Army to be Finance Minister in 1936, was appointed Home Minister. The heads of the two political parties, Nagai and Nakajima, served as individuals on the Cabinet and not as representatives of their parties.

3. On the basis of available sources, it is difficult to establish which side was responsible for the immediate outbreak of hostilities at Marco Polo Bridge. Conditions were such that any incident could have sparked a bigger conflict. Professor Crowley believes this was not a conspiracy by the local military commanders. In fact, if the General Staff had had its way, it would have accepted a local settlement. See Richard Storry, *The Double Patriots* (Boston: Houghton Mifflin Co., 1957), pp. 204 ff.; James B. Crowley, *Japan's Quest for Autonomy: National Security and Foreign Policy 1930–1938* (Princeton: Princeton University Press, 1966), pp. 300 ff.; and Hayashi Shigeru, *Taiheiyō Sensō* (Tokyo: Chuokoron, 1967), pp. 40 ff.

4. Hayashi, *ibid.*, p. 49; and Dorothy Borg, *The United States and the Far Eastern Crisis of 1933–1938* (Cambridge: Harvard University Press, 1964), pp. 277 ff.

5. For the details of this struggle, the half-hearted negotiations with China through the German Ambassador, and the skillful maneuvers of Konoye to obtain acceptance of his philosophy for chastisement of Generalissimo Chiang, see Crowley, *op. cit.*, pp. 835–78.

6. For a more detailed analysis of the law, see Hugh Borton, *Japan Since 1931, Its Political and Social Development* (New York: American Institute of Pacific Relations, Inc., 1940), pp. 60–65 and 129–30; and *Tokyo Gazette,* No. 11 (May, 1938).

7. The Kwantung Army exercised its control over Manchukuo through the General Affairs Board and the Fourth Section of the Army. While all Ministers of State within the Manchukuo government were Chinese, the real power was in the hands of the Vice-Ministers, who were Japanese. All policies, laws, ordinances, and rescripts were first considered by the General Affairs Board under a Japanese Chairman. The Vice-Ministers and Chief of the Fourth Section of the Kwantung Army were the other members of the Board. Thus no action could be taken by Manchukuo without the approval of the Kwantung Army. Aside from the fact that the latter was nominally responsible to the Chief of Staff in Tokyo, the Japanese government was represented at the Manchukuo capital by the Chief of the Kwantung Army.

8. See Storry, *op. cit.,* pp. 233 ff.

9. The shifts in Cabinets which occurred from the resignation of Konoye on January 5, 1939, to the formation of his second Cabinet on July 22, 1940, had little effect in the long run on national policy although there were various efforts made to halt the trend toward war. With the various factions and interests among the military and civilian leaders seeking to gain power or to prevent others from doing so, policies were finally determined by a small group who usually reached an agreed compromise. Hiranuma Kiichirō, President of the Privy Council after 1936, ardent nationalist and leader of the *Kokuhonsha,* was Premier from January 5 to August 30, 1939. When the Emperor ordered his successor, General Abe Nobuyuki, to form a Cabinet he insisted that every effort should be made to develop a foreign policy based on an understanding with Great Britain and the United States. Abe was followed by Admiral Yonai from January 16, 1940, until his resignation on July 22, 1940. Yonai was followed by the second and third Konoye Cabinets.

10. Matsuoka Yōsuke (1880–1949). As a young man, in 1893, he had gone to Oregon where he finished high school. In 1900 he received his law degree from Oregon Law School and he returned home in 1902. These years, which coincided with America's becoming a colonial power in the Pacific, shaped his personality and character. He developed a strong sense of nationalism and later justified Japanese imperialism in terms of the American expansionists at the turn of the century. He saw the frontiers of Manchuria as a challenge to Japan just as the West had been a challenge to America. He had led the Japanese Delegation out of the League of Nations. Before he became Foreign Minister, he had been President of the South Manchurian Railway and a staunch advocate of an aggressive policy.

11. Heavy industries accounted for only 38 per cent of the total production in 1930; they had been responsible for 73 per cent in 1942. Other notable changes during approximately the same period were increases of motor vehicle units from 500 annually to 48,000, airplanes from practically none to 5,000, aluminum ingots from 19 tons to 72,000 tons, ingot steel from 1.8 million tons to 6.8 million, and naval ships from 15,000 tons in 1931 to

232,000 tons in 1937. In view of the excellent study by Professor Jerome B. Cohen on Japan's wartime economy, a detailed economic analysis of Japan after 1940 has been omitted. Figures will be used only where it is necessary to clarify the general narrative.

In seeking a rationale for expansionism, much was made of the pressure from population. While the argument might have some weight in view of export quotas and the need for foreign markets, it does not seem pertinent in reference to food needs. For example, while the population increased from 64,450,000 in 1930 to 73,114,000 in 1940, rice imports from outside Korea and Formosa declined from 5 per cent of total rice imports in the period 1931–1935 to 2 per cent of imports in 1936–1938, with total amounts of imports actually less in 1941 than in 1938. Cohen, *op. cit.*, pp. 288 and 369. These figures, as well as those used in the remainder of this section, are taken from Jerome B. Cohen, *Japan's Economy in War and Reconstruction* (Minneapolis: University of Minnesota Press, 1949), pp. 288 and 369.

12. Cohen, *ibid.*, pp. 45, 128, and 163.

13. In view of the numerous detailed studies of the intricate foreign relations and negotiations of Japan both with the Axis and with the Allies, it seems unnecessary to do little more than sketch in broadest outline the most significant aspects of these negotiations. For those who wish to consult documentary material, the Proceedings, Records and Exhibits of the International Military Tribunal of the Far East should be consulted. Also the Report and Hearings of the U.S. Congress Joint Committee in the Investigation of Pearl Harbor, U.S. State Department, *Foreign Relations 1931–41, Japan* (2 vols.), U.S. State Department, *Nazi–Soviet Relations,* and Nobutake Ike (ed. and trans.), *Japan's Decision for War, Records of the 1941 Policy Conference* (Stanford: Stanford University Press, 1967). Two competent and thorough studies dealing especially with United States–Japanese negotiations, which contain extensive bibliographical material, deserve special mention. They are Herbert Feis, *The Road to Pearl Harbor* (Princeton: Princeton University Press, 1950); and F. C. Jones, *Japan's New Order in East Asia, Its Rise and Fall, 1937–45* (New York: Oxford University Press, 1954).

14. During this period the Liaison Conference was the key policy-forming body. It was composed of the Premier as Chairman, the Ministers of War, Navy, Foreign Affairs, Finance, and Home Affairs, the Chiefs of Army and Navy General Staff, their immediate subordinates, the Chairman of the Cabinet Planning Board, and the Chairman of the Privy Council, who usually spoke for the Emperor. Technically the Cabinet was required to give formal approval to decisions of the Liaison Conference but in reality the latter made the policies. Only the most basic policy decisions of the Liaison Conference were, as in this case, referred to the Imperial Conference, which was composed largely of the same persons plus the Emperor.

15. For a full text of the "Essential Policies" and the records of the Imperial Conference see Ike, *op. cit.*, pp. 133–63. See also Hayashi, *op. cit.*, pp. 234–38.

16. Tōjō's first appointment to his Cabinet was Hoshino Naoki, former author of state control in Manchukuo and President of the Cabinet Planning Board as new Chief Cabinet Secretary. Kishi Nobusuke, another civilian leader in Manchuria, was Minister of Commerce and Industry. Apparently, Tōjō did not actively seek the premiership. In fact, both he and Konoye had agreed that the Emperor should be persuaded to appoint Prince

Higashikuni, but this was strongly opposed by Kido. See Butow, *op. cit.*, pp. 271–302.

Despite the Navy Minister's earlier reluctance to agree to go to war, Navy Chief of Staff Admiral Yamamoto Isoroku was prepared for any eventuality. On October 9, 1941, he called together the Combined Fleet Commanders in Hiroshima Bay and reported that the international situation was such that "Japan may be forced to take up arms against the United States, Great Britain and the Netherlands rather than succumb to strangulation through blockade." He added that Japan faced the greatest crisis in its history but believed it possible to defend the nation and defeat the enemy "if everyone exerts his utmost efforts." See Hara Taneuchi, *Japanese Destroyer Captain* (New York: Ballantine Books, 1967), pp. 43–44.

17. The United States government was aware of the contents of the instructions sent the Japanese negotiators. It had broken the Japanese codes and was deciphering the messages. This information, while helpful, referred to a deadline after which things would automatically happen but gave no inkling of the Supreme Command's battle plans. They were a closely guarded secret kept even from Cabinet ministers. No one in Washington knew when or where war would break out. For the best accounts in English of the discussions on the decision for war, see Ike, *op. cit.*, and Butow, *op. cit.*, pp. 319 ff.

PART V

JAPAN REBOUNDS FROM WAR AND DEFEAT 1941-1970

Unite your total strength to be devoted to the construction for the future. Cultivate the ways of rectitude; foster nobility of spirit; and work with resolution so as ye may enhance the innate glory of the Imperial State and keep pace with the progress of the world.

Imperial Rescript of Emperor Hirohito
August 14, 1945

CHRONOLOGY

1941–1970

1941	December 7	Pearl Harbor attacked by Japan
	December 8	United States declares war on Japan
1942	May–June	Battles of Coral Sea and Midway
1943	February	Recapture of Guadalcanal
	November	Creation of Munitions Ministry
1944	July	Fall of Saipan
		Premier Tōjō replaced by Koiso
	October	General MacArthur returns to Philippines
1945	March	Saturation bombing of Tokyo
	April 1	Okinawa captured
	July 26	Potsdam Declaration of Allied surrender terms
	August 14	Japan agrees to surrender
		General MacArthur appointed Supreme Commander
	September 2	Japan surrenders
1946	November	New Constitution promulgated
1947		Land reform program begun
1948		United States encourages Japanese industrial revival
1949		Chinese communists victorious on mainland
1950	June 25	Invasion of South Korea starts Korean War
		Dulles negotiates nonpunitive peace terms for Japan
1951	April 10	General MacArthur relieved of his commands
	September 8	Treaty of Peace signed at San Francisco
1952	April 28	Peace Treaty in effect, occupation ends
		May Day riot; economy reaches prewar levels
1954		Self-Defense Forces formed
1955		Conservatives continue to rule through Liberal Democratic Party
1960		Extensive demonstrations against U.S.–Japan Security Treaty
	June 18	Security Treaty ratified
1964		Satō Eisaku appointed Prime Minister
1967		Ultraradical student riots increase in intensity
1968		Riots close Tokyo University
		Okinawa reversion becomes a vital issue
		Japan becomes third largest industrial power
1969	January	Riot police oust students from Tokyo University
	July	Tokyo University reopens
	August	Diet approves University Normalization Law
	November	Satō–Nixon Agreement on Okinawa Reversion
	December	Liberal Democratic Party wins at general election

19

World War II: Pearl Harbor to Surrender, 1941–1945

Pearl Harbor and Other Early Battles

At dawn on December 7, 1941, a two-hour Japanese surprise attack hit the naval and air base at Pearl Harbor with devastating suddenness. Eight battleships and ten other ships were either sunk or severely damaged. At one stroke, 90 per cent of the American naval and air strength in the Hawaiian Islands was immobilized. Simultaneously, the Japanese Imperial Navy, Army, and Air Force began attacks against the Philippines, Malaya, Guam, Wake, and Midway Islands, and the British strategic outposts at Hong Kong and Singapore. The United States declared war on Japan the next day and on the other Axis powers shortly thereafter; England, France, China, and the other Allies soon followed suit.

On December 9, the pride of the British Far Eastern Fleet, the "Prince of Wales" and the "Repulse" were discovered in hiding near Singapore and destroyed by air attack. From the Japanese point of view, these bold and carefully planned attacks had been eminently successful. The Japanese forces were free from the start to capture their next objectives without hindrance from the American or British Navy or Air Force. At home, the people and government were elated at the news and such misgivings as some may have had as to the wisdom of fighting both Great Britain and the United States were supplanted by a belief in the invincibility of the Imperial Army, Navy, and Air Force.

During the next six months, the Allies were helpless to stop the surge of Japan. Such isolated outposts as Guam and the Gilbert Islands fell almost immediately. Within the first month, there had been landings on the Philippines, Hong Kong had surrendered, and Manila had capitulated. The pressure increased in such widely separated regions as the Netherlands East Indies in southeast Asia and the Bismarck Islands and New Guinea in the south-central Pacific. In mid-February, 1942, after a spectacular jungle campaign by specially trained troops, the Japanese surrounded the great British naval base of Singapore and forced it to surrender. Despite heroic stands such as that of the Filipino and American Forces at Bataan in the Philippines, the tide rolled on until it reached its outer perimeter in mid-summer. By that time, Japan was in control of a tremendous quadrangle encompassing the entire western Pacific. The four corners of this vast area were the Aleutians in the northeast, the Gilbert Islands in the southeast, Sumatra and Burma in the southwest corner, and Sakhalin in the northwest.[1] (See map, pages 438–39.)

When the Tōjō government went to war, some basic war objectives had already been approved. Others became clarified and refined as the war progressed. These chief objectives might be summarized as follows: (1) the establishment of peace and stability in East Asia through expulsion of the Western colonial powers; (2) the creation of an impenetrable defensive perimeter by the amalgamation of strategic bases such as Manila, Hong Kong, and Singapore with the Empire's defense outposts; (3) the creation of a self-sufficient economy through a Greater East Asia Co-prosperity Sphere; (4) the temporary military administration of former colonial areas to be superseded by "independent governments" friendly to Japan; (5) the successful termination of the war in China; and (6) the enforced acceptance by the United States and Great Britain of peace terms recognizing these accomplishments. These war objectives were based on certain assumptions: (1) the Soviet Union would not enter the war against Japan until the objectives were largely achieved; (2) essential raw materials, especially oil from the Netherlands East Indies, would become readily available after the colonial territories were conquered; (3) the pressure from the Axis Powers in Europe and the impenetrability of Japan's defense perimeter would compel England and the United States to accept terms favorable to Japan; and (4) the war would be of short duration.

In July, 1942, Premier Tōjō claimed that Great Britain, the Netherlands, and the United States had been humiliated and defeated and the first war objective had been achieved. The nation was proud of its Armed Forces and immensely satisfied. The Chiefs of Staff were elated over the fact that their victories had been achieved more rapidly than they had anticipated. On the other hand, they were shocked to discover that, despite the losses they had inflicted at Pearl Harbor, the United States naval and air strength was sufficient to impair seriously two Japanese campaigns. In the naval Battle of the Coral Sea (May 4–8, 1942), the Japanese outward push toward Australia was thwarted. In the Battle of Midway (June 3–5, 1942), heavy losses, including four carriers, were inflicted on a strong Japanese naval force, from which the Imperial Navy never recovered, and the western flank of the Hawaiian Islands was secured. Furthermore, the Japanese Chiefs of Staff were forced to modify their schedule for the capture of the Solomon Islands and Port Moresby.[2]

Wartime Controls at Home and Autonomous Movements in Southeast Asia, 1942–1944

During the first few months of the war, the entire nation had concentrated its energies on purely military affairs. As the pace of conquest was curbed, then halted, and finally reversed, Tōjō and his Cabinet had to cope with two immediate problems. If these conquests were to be solidified and if progress were to be made toward self-sufficiency, he must integrate the various organs of the national government into an effective totalitarian state. In the second place, he must create new administrative machinery to govern the newly conquered overseas territories and to exploit those resources needed by the defense industries and by the armed services. To assist him in building a totalitarian state, the Imperial Rule Assistance Association was transformed into a vehicle to encourage outright military-party control. For example, in April, 1942, it secured the election to the House of Representatives of an overwhelmingly large majority of candidates who had been officially sponsored by Tōjō's government. He was thus assured of political support for whatever he proposed. All of the mass media were strictly controlled; nonconformists were forced to leave their posts in the most influential newspapers and journals. Imperial Headquarters issued only favorable news, distorting the facts to enhance the morale of the people at home. The Battle of Midway was described as a great victory in the Eastern Pacific.

But he found the business world less amenable to his leadership. Despite the wide powers which he wielded, the *zaibatsu* had not yet capitulated to complete governmental control over management, production, and finance. By the summer of 1942, at the height of Japan's military expansion, a compromise system had been evolved whereby industrialists still controlled at least part of their destiny. This cooperation in the government's controls over their affairs was assured by appointment of the cartel heads of the large combines to the highest posts in the Control Associations. The Cabinet Planning Board, in accordance with a general plan which it originated for Japan and overseas territories, transmitted schedules of production to the Control Associations for execution. Since membership in a Control Association was compulsory for all concerns, presumably a national production quota could be attained. But the heavy demands for increased production soon produced competition among the Control Associations for raw materials and supplies. Furthermore, competition among companies within a single Control Association added to the confusion. As the pace of conquest slackened and was reversed, far more complete and drastic reforms in the governmental structure were necessary.

Furthermore, the swift advances of the Japanese forces in the South Pacific created farflung and complicated administrative problems. To cope with the situation, an ordinance was drafted for the creation of a Ministry of Greater East Asia. Its purpose was to supervise and administer all matters connected with overseas territories except in Korea, Formosa, and Karafuto. It was to absorb the functions of the powerful Cabinet boards which had been in charge of affairs in Manchuria, China, and the Pacific Mandated Islands. In effect, Premier Tōjō conceived of the new Ministry as a means whereby the newly conquered areas would be integrated into the Empire. Finally, it relegated to the Foreign Office only formal diplomatic functions and thus prevented it from challenging the activities of the Imperial Army in occupied territories. Consequently, when the Foreign Minister resigned in protest, Tōjō was delighted and temporarily assumed the post himself.

With the creation of the Greater East Asia Ministry, on November 1, 1942, the protection of Japanese overseas interests and the exploitation of resources in the newly conquered territories were irrevocably placed in the hands of the military. Aoki Kazuo, one of the leading civilian members of the Manchurian clique, was made the first Minister of Greater East Asia.[3] He immediately began to coordinate, as far as it was possible to do so, the political and economic exploitation of the newly conquered overseas territories.

Every effort was made to encourage local independence movements in these areas and to strengthen the ties between them and Japan. The Japanese did their best to appear as liberators. They tried to create conditions which would reduce resistance to their occupation. They also hoped to make it difficult for the Western powers, even though they won the war, to retrieve their colonies and their dominant position throughout Asia. This policy was successful in some areas. In Burma, for example, Ba Maw was supported as chief executive. The autonomous movement flourished under his leadership and Japanese tutelage. By August, 1943, the new state was ready to declare its independence and to make a formal alliance with Japan. In the Philippines the reaction was different. Collaborators were at hand who administered the government under Japanese control; when General MacArthur began the reconquest of the islands in October, 1944, however, he was welcomed as the real liberator.

In the British territory of Malaya, and the Dutch colonies in the East Indies, the emphasis was on economic exploitation. In the former, Singapore was developed as a strong Japanese naval outpost and the western anchor of Greater East Asia. Rubber and tin were requisitioned for military purposes but the economy of the Malay States was never successfully integrated into the Co-prosperity Sphere. The Netherlands East Indies were placed under direct military administration with headquarters in Jakarta (old Batavia). Lip service was paid to the aspiration for independence of nationalist leaders such as Soekarno and Hatta, but the Indies were considered important primarily because of their rich resources. Japanese technicians were poured into the islands in an attempt to extract oil and other raw materials in sufficient quantity to bolster the Empire's self-sufficiency. But shipping was insufficient to meet all the pressing needs and time ran out before this was accomplished.

The other important colonial area in southeast Asia, Indochina, was left under French control because it was to Japan's advantage to do so. The Vichy government was in no position to oppose any demands which Japan might wish to impose and it administered the territory until shortly before the war's end.

Lack of Cooperation Among Axis Powers

By the end of the first year of the war, Japan had achieved, at least partially, some of the war objectives proclaimed by Premier Tōjō. But the war in the Pacific had been planned by Tōjō and his colleagues independently of their Axis partners. It seemed to be almost detached from the war in Europe, Africa, and the Near East. No meetings of Hitler, Mussolini, and Tōjō were held. They told each other about their plans after they had started to execute them. They viewed each other with awe and with suspicion. For his part, Tōjō thought almost entirely in terms of Japan's future leadership in Asia and of the fundamental need of forcing the colonial powers out of East Asia. His strategists could not think of the war in global terms. They were content to push to their planned perimeter, to stand firm on their conquests, and to await an inevitable counterattack.

This lack of cooperation was the result of various factors. In the first place, Germany and Japan distrusted each other's motives. Furthermore, the Nordic concept of racial superiority was in direct conflict with the Shintō-inspired Japanese belief in their own racial superiority. Finally, the two countries were in disagreement over policy toward the Soviet Union. Germany was eager to have Japan engage the Soviet Union in the Far East and thus relieve the pressure on the Eastern European front. On the other hand, Japan was determined to avoid war with Russia at all costs. It hoped to be able to persuade Germany to make a compromise peace with the Soviet Union. After Rommel's defeat in North Africa and the decisive German defeat at Stalingrad early in 1943, no Axis arguments could persuade Japan to weaken its own position by going to war against the Soviet Union.[4]

In contrast to the relationship of the Axis powers, the Allied leaders worked together. President Franklin D. Roosevelt and Prime Minister Winston Churchill were particularly close. They met on numerous occasions before and during the war; they had conferences with other leaders of the Allies, notably, with Generalissimos Stalin and Chiang Kai-shek. The exigencies of the war in which they were engaged forced them to think in global terms. They synchronized their campaigns; their objectives included the unconditional surrender of all of the Axis Powers, not just one of them. After Italy and Germany had been defeated, they intended to concentrate all of their war effort on Japan. Before a campaign could be mounted in the Pacific, the immediate demands of the European and African theaters had to be met. Throughout the entire war, despite occasional disagreements on strategy, the United States and Great Britain cooperated closely on both war plans and postwar policies.

Although it falls within the realm of speculation, one is tempted to ask what might have happened if the Japanese leaders had changed their war plans in the summer of 1942. If the three Axis Powers had developed a coordinated, global attack, would they have been able to turn the tide? For example, if Germany had been able to persuade Japan to substitute the conquest of Ceylon for the attack on Midway, would the two ends of the Axis have been joined? Would the Axis Powers have been able to consolidate their position in the eastern Mediterranean and would Japan have had time enough to prepare for a successful attack on Midway to flank the Hawaiian Islands? The answer is probably that even though they had conceived of a coordinated, unified plan, the final results of the war would not have been different.

United States Offensive Against Japan's Outer Perimeter

Since the Axis Powers were acting largely independently of each other, their only hope of success was through complete control of the state. For Japan, the strengthening of control in the home front was increasingly necessary because of significant military and naval reverses in the southwest corner of its outer defense perimeter. By February, 1943, after half a year of some of the most heroic fighting in World War II, the U.S. Marines, Army reinforcements, and emerging American air and naval supremacy had forced Japan to abandon Guadalcanal in the Solomon Islands. Its earlier attempts to capture Port Moresby on the southern coast of New Guinea had resulted in severe losses. These defeats both exposed Japan's flank in this entire quadrant and caused the cancellation of its new attack in southwest China aimed at forcing Chiang Kai-shek to capitulate.

In the face of these crises, Premier Tōjō moved to place greater control directly in his own hands. He appointed one of his former associates in Manchuria as Chief of the Tokyo Metropolitan Police Board, who intimidated or arrested critics of the government. Critics within the Army were either sent to the front or disciplined. Drastic reforms were inaugurated in local governments to increase the production of war materials and to create new, economically self-sufficient, local entities. Thus in July, 1943, Japan proper, including the Ryūkyū Islands in the southwest, and the Kurile Islands and Karafuto in the north, were divided into nine Regional Administrative Districts. These districts were administered by separate councils whose president was the governor of the most important prefecture in each district. Through periodic meetings among the councilors, representatives from the national ministries, and the prefectural governments, conflicts in the enforcement of national policies were eliminated. Furthermore, production quotas were assigned by districts and competitive demands on scarce raw materials were avoided. Finally, in anticipation of damages from air raids, the regions were given discretionary powers over public works to facilitate emergency repairs.

The most significant administrative change within the government, however, was the creation in November, 1943, of the Munitions Ministry. It was set up as the main organ to administer the complete mobilization of Japanese production. The Cabinet Planning Board and the Control Associations proved inadequate to meet the demands for armaments. Thus the new Munitions Ministry had wide powers over any company which engaged in the manufacture of arms, aircraft, warships, and other war materials. As the central control agency for national mobilization, it allotted raw materials, established production schedules, and distributed finished products. It had authority also to regulate capital, labor, and wages. In other words, the family combines, as well as the small companies, were subject to expansion, contraction, or dissolution. After changes were made in the various departments of the government to coordinate their functions with those of the Munitions Ministry, state control over the nation's economy was complete. Prime Minister Tōjō and the Liaison Conference had dictatorial powers in name, if not in fact.[5]

But Tōjō, like all other Prime Ministers in modern Japan, was a victim of his environment. Decisions had always been made, even in the time of war, by the group rather than by a single person. He had been as responsible as anyone else for taking Japan to war but he had obtained the consent of all important groups and individuals for this policy. On the other hand, as the effects of the earliest victories wore off and as Allied pressure caused a break in Japan's outer perimeter in the central and southwest Pacific, Tōjō was in an untenable position. Allied air and naval attacks had drastically reduced Japanese shipping. Technical defi-

Japan in World War II and After

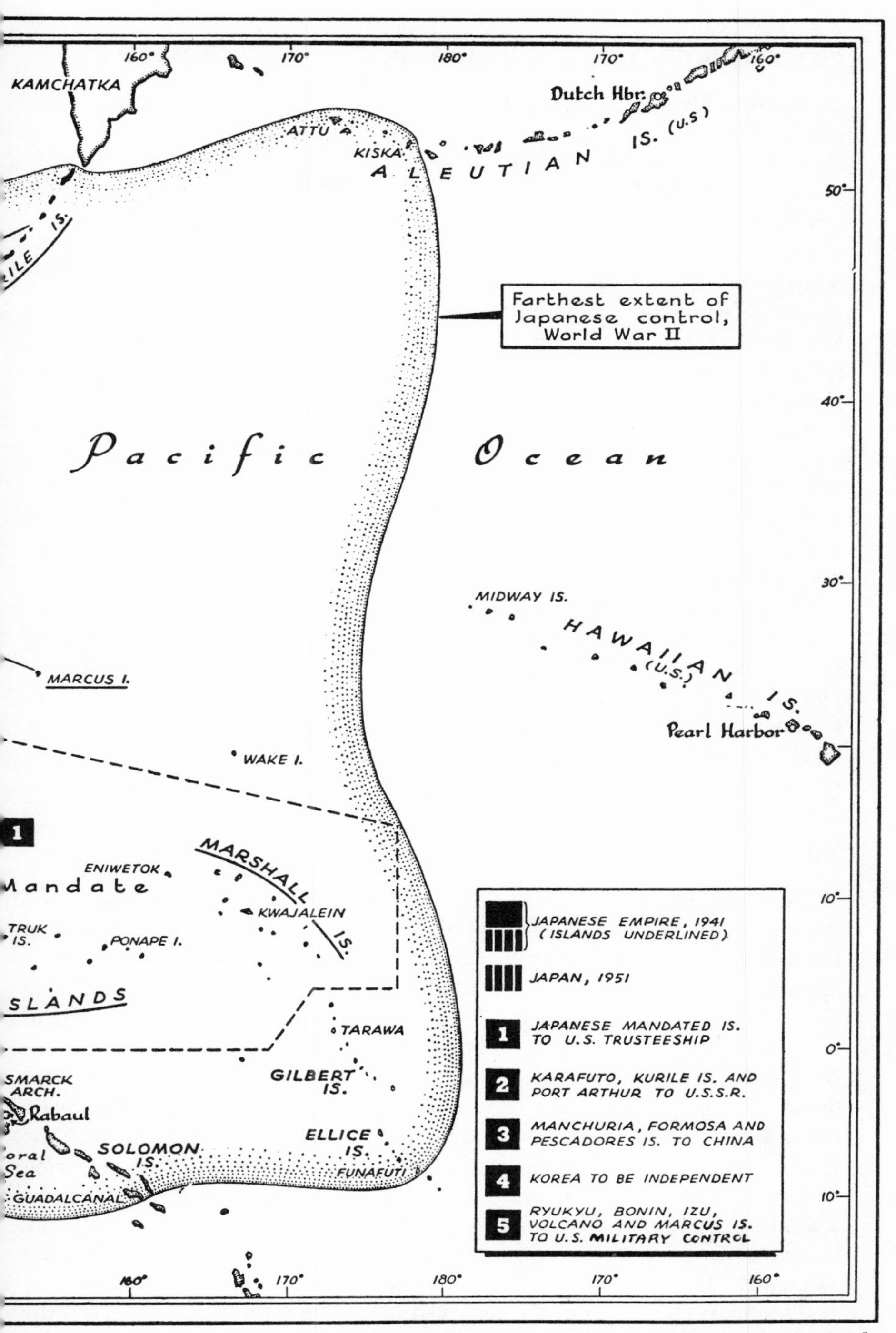

After a map in M.I.T. Series Strategic Area Maps. Copyright by Massachusetts Institute of Technology.

ciency in labor, dwindling stocks of strategic materials, and inefficiency in distribution and production had resulted in a marked decline in war production. Naval and shipping losses and increased demands for supporting airplanes and munitions exacerbated the rivalry between the two armed services. In February, 1944, the Cabinet and the Supreme Command disagreed over strategy for the continuation of the war. Tōjō attempted to solve this dilemma by concentrating greater power in his own hands. He received Imperial sanction for his appointment to still another key position, namely, Army Chief of Staff while retaining the War portfolio. He also had his Minister of the Navy appointed concurrently as Navy Chief of Staff.

But even these maneuvers could not stem the tide of war against Japan nor the wave of discontent against his dictatorial powers. In early July, 1944, the fall of Saipan was the most dramatic and strategically important evidence of the success of the American advance into the central Pacific. The "impenetrable" defense line of Japan had been broken and American bombers were within easy range of its cities.

The Senior Statesmen (*Jūshin*), the former Premiers who acted as special advisers to the Emperor at the time of a Cabinet change, together with Lord Keeper of the Privy Seal Kido Kōichi, decided Tōjō was expendable. When he refused to resign and sought to make changes in his Cabinet, the Emperor agreed with the Senior Statesmen. Thus on July 18, 1944, despite his apparent strength, Tōjō was forced to give way to the will of the group.[6]

The Beginning of the End After July, 1944

The selection of the new Prime Minister, General Koiso Kuniaki, and the members of his Cabinet was the result of a compromise. Some of the Senior Statesmen, though they could not advocate such a policy openly, hoped that the war could be brought to an early conclusion through a compromise peace. They realized that if they even hinted at accepting the territorial settlement proposed by the Allies at Cairo (see page 445), the Army might revolt, liquidate those who opposed it, and dispense with parliamentary government. On the other hand, they were not willing for the Army to retain complete control. They knew that the leaders in the Army advocated an increased national effort to bring victory to Japan. The appointment of General Koiso, a member of the Kwantung clique, as Premier, placated his colleagues. On the other hand, his extremism was balanced by the selection of Admiral Yonai Mitsumasa as Deputy Premier and as Minister of the Navy.[7]

The main objectives of the new Cabinet were twofold: to carry on the war with renewed energy; to be on the alert for a possibility to obtain a compromise peace. Premier Koiso soon discovered that if the war was to progress smoothly closer cooperation between the Cabinet and the High Command must be achieved. The Liaison Conference had been designed to meet this need, but there continued to be a lack of coordination between the government and the armed services. Consequently, in August, 1944, a Supreme Council for the Direction of War was created. It was composed of the Emperor as Chairman; the Prime Minister; the Ministers of War, Navy, and Foreign Affairs; and the Army and Navy Chiefs of Staff. Its function was "to formulate a fundamental policy for directing the war and to adjust the harmonization of combined strategy for politics and war." It differed from the Liaison Conference in one crucial respect. Since the Emperor was Chairman, he could attend whenever he considered it necessary to break a deadlock in the Council or veto any policy decisions which he did not approve. While in effect the Council usually met without him, he cast the decisive vote for peace in August, 1945.

Koiso had inherited an impossible assignment in the face of Japan's mounting reverses and losses in the Pacific. The Supreme Council could do little more than reiterate the necessity for Japan to avoid war with Russia and propose concessions in the hopes of improving Japanese–Russian relations. But nothing came of these or later attempts.

On the military side, four months after Koiso took office, Japan was subjected to constant and heavy air raids from bombers based on Saipan. These raids, which the Imperial Army had insisted would never occur, were made at will over any part of the country. On March 10, 1945, the first saturation bombing of Tokyo took place. These were grim reminders to the Japanese populace that their leaders had grossly miscalculated their country's ability to defend itself from attack. When the people were told that Saipan had fallen, they feared the worst. Despite official pronouncements of plans for a "decisive victory," the populace became convinced that Japan could not hope to win the war, and continued doggedly with the hopeless task of supporting the war effort and trying to survive. In the meantime, the Philippines were recaptured. On April 1, 1945, even Japan's inner line of defense was pierced by the Allied landings on Okinawa, the largest of the Ryūkyū Islands. Within four days, the Koiso Cabinet fell. It was a victim of the unrelenting pressure from the Allied offensive which no Premier could stop.

The war situation had become so critical that an unprecedented procedure was followed in selecting the next Premier. Lord Keeper of the Privy Seal Kido, who technically overstepped his authority, was the chief organizer of an Imperial Conference to decide on the next Prime Minister. On April 5, 1945, the Senior Statesmen met in the Emperor's audience chamber in an atmosphere of tension.

The diehards were represented by former Premier Tōjō, who was appearing for the first time as a Senior Statesman. The news had just been received that the Soviet Union had refused to extend the Neutrality Pact beyond its termination a year hence. In Europe, the Allied Armies had already crossed the Rhine from the west. The Soviet forces were rapidly approaching from the east. The junction of the two forces was expected momentarily. The European end of the Axis was on the point of collapse.

Under these circumstances, the conference immediately turned into a discussion of the question of whether to continue the war or to seek peace. General Tōjō insisted on the former alternative and the selection of a Prime Minister who would agree to fight to the finish. He claimed that he spoke for the Army, which would wreck any Cabinet which followed a contrary policy. He received strong support for his position from ex-Premier Hiranuma.

On the other hand, for several months other Senior Statesmen had been secretly considering ways and means of bringing the war to an end. Together with Kido, they had endeavored to keep themselves informed of the actual military and economic strength of the nation. They had also passed this information on to the Emperor in a series of individual Imperial audiences. They had endeavored to place a representative of the "antiwar group" on the Tōjō Cabinet. They had greatly strengthened their cause when Yonai Mitsumasa was made Deputy Premier and Minister of the Navy under Koiso. Admiral Yonai had learned that one of his colleagues on the Naval Chiefs of Staff, Admiral Takagi Sōkichi, had completed a study on Japan's war potential. On the basis of his survey, Admiral Takagi had become convinced that Japan could not possibly win the war and hence should work toward a compromise peace. When Yonai was appointed Navy Minister, he instructed Admiral Takagi to make a new, documented study of Japan's actual war potential. The report was to contain recommendations on how Japan could extricate itself from a war which appeared already lost.[8]

Even though this report had not been completed when the Senior Statesmen met with the Emperor in April, 1945, a large group of them favored the selection of a person as Premier who would bring the war to an early close. This same group believed that the Emperor would support such a candidate. Specifically, they had reached a previous understanding that Admiral Suzuki Kantarō was the logical man of the hour. He was held in high esteem by all groups within the country. He had escaped assassination on February 26, 1936, only because of the bravery of his wife. For the past months he had served as President of the Privy Council. The Conference finally agreed to his appointment.

When Kido pressed Admiral Suzuki to become Prime Minister, he was fully aware that the Emperor and several of the Senior Statesmen hoped that the war could be terminated in the near future. On the other hand, when he approached General Anami Korechika about serving as War Minister, it was apparent that the Army and the Chiefs of Staff were inexorably opposed to unconditional surrender. General Anami stated he would serve only under the following stipulations: (1) Japan would carry on the war to the end of its ability to resist, (2) the Army and Navy would act in harmony; and (3) the Army's plan to protect the homeland at all costs would be carried out without hesitation. Admiral Suzuki agreed to become Prime Minister and General Anami became his War Minister. The Suzuki Cabinet was committed to continue the war. Those who were known to oppose it were arrested. On the other hand, Tōgō Shigenori, the new Foreign Minister, favored an early end to the war. The movement for an early peace continued to gain support and Foreign Minister Tōgō became actively involved in this movement.[9]

Internal Pressures for Ending the War

In a little over a month after Admiral Suzuki became Premier the Supreme Council met to consider whether Japan was capable of continued, effective resistance. The immediate issue before the Council was a proposal by the Foreign Minister concerning Japan's future relations with the Soviet Union. Japan had been most circumspect in the past in its observance of the Neutrality Pact. It wished, at all costs, to prevent the outbreak of hostilities between the two countries. Germany's capitulation, and Moscow's announced policy that it would not continue the Neutrality Pact, boded no good for the future of these relations. Thus the Foreign Minister was of the opinion that new overtures should be made to Moscow to prevent the situation from deteriorating. Consequently, his plan contained three proposals: (1) the Soviet Union should be prevented from entering the war in the Pacific, (2) the Soviet Union should be enticed into adopting a friendly policy toward Japan, and (3) the Soviet Union should be requested to use its good offices to mediate the war in the Pacific on terms favorable to Japan.

The Supreme Council, though divided on the last point, agreed that negotiations should be begun to improve Soviet-Japanese relations. Ex-Premier Hirota was appointed to approach the Soviet Ambassador in Tokyo, Yakov Malik. At first, Hirota talked only of an improvement of friendly relations between the two countries; later he proposed a non-aggression pact. In both instances, he received a cool reception. In fact, while these conversations were under way, the Soviet Union was beginning to shift its armies from the European front to Siberia in anticipation of a declaration of war on Japan in accordance with the agreement reached at Yalta. (See page 446.)

During the next few weeks events moved rapidly to a climax. With Okinawa as a base constant air attacks on Japan proper had begun. The overseas territories were completely isolated from the home islands. The Japanese civilians and occupation forces in these areas had been all but abandoned. A report prepared by the Cabinet indicated clearly that the warmaking power of the nation had been broken. Shipping losses to submarine and air attack were staggering. The total tonnage of vessels had been reduced from 5.5 million to 1.25 million. It was assumed that the loss of Okinawa would preclude surface communication between Japan and the Asiatic continent. Railway transportation had fallen to one-half that of the previous year. In reference to material resources, the picture was equally grim. Fuel resources had been exhausted; coal production was insufficient to keep industries operating. Steel output had dropped to one-tenth that of the previous year. Despite priorities given to it, aircraft production had fallen rapidly. Destruction of planes and of the Imperial Navy had been so horrendous that Japan could no longer defend itself. The time of decision appeared to be at hand.[10]

This report made a deep impression on Premier Suzuki who agreed with its gloomy estimate. It was forwarded to the Emperor for his information. Despite this estimate, War Minister Anami and the Chiefs of Staff insisted more vigorous steps be taken to prosecute the war. At a Supreme Council meeting on June 6, 1945, it was agreed that the use of suicide squads, a *levée en masse*, and the invincible spirit of Japan would result in a decisive battle for the homeland which would protect "the sacred Imperial soil" and preserve the Japanese polity (*kokutai*). At the very least, the enemy's losses would be so great that he would abandon his demands for unconditional surrender. An Imperial Conference reconfirmed this decision two days later.

During the next two weeks, Kido and others persuaded the Emperor to reverse this decision. Consequently, on June 22, 1945, the Emperor called a meeting of the Supreme Council and took the initiative in asking it to approve of peace negotiations to be carried on through the Soviet Union. After a brief discussion, the Council concurred with the Emperor's request. Conversations were again begun between Hirota and Malik. But the Emperor soon became impatient with the lack of progress. He ordered Premier Suzuki to act immediately and suggested dispatching a special envoy to Moscow with his personal message.

On July 10, 1945, the Supreme Council approved of ex-Premier Konoye as the special peace envoy. In the meantime, the Japanese Ambassador in Moscow was instructed to request the Soviet government to intercede with the Allies on Japan's behalf. The Ambassador was to report that the Emperor expressly wished to end the war promptly. Nevertheless, the Allies should be told that so long as they insisted on unconditional surrender, Japan had no alternative but to continue to fight for its honor and survival. Finally, the Soviet Union was to be asked to act before the Allied leaders met at Potsdam. But these diplomatic efforts of Japan came to nought.[11] The Allies were in the process of deciding what their next move would be.

Allied Postwar Policy Formation

Although the Supreme Council was not aware of the fact, the question of Japan's surrender was one of the items on the agenda of the Potsdam meeting of Truman, Churchill, and Stalin. The United States government was prepared to seek Allied approval of a joint statement which would give Japan an opportunity to surrender or face destruction. In view of the anticipated successful completion of the first explosion of an atomic bomb, a declaration was called for which clearly defined the objectives of the Allies. By mid-summer of 1945, the objectives of the Allies in the Far East had been ill defined. Pronouncements such as the United Nations Declaration of January 1, 1942, had reaffirmed in general terms the principles which Roosevelt and Churchill had proclaimed in the Atlantic Charter. The Allies declared, among other things, that they sought no territorial aggrandizement for themselves and that sovereign rights and self-government would be restored to those who had been deprived of them. Each of the United Nations also pledged not to make a separate peace with their common enemies. At the Casablanca Conference held a year later, Roosevelt and Churchill agreed that the war would end only with "the unconditional surrender of the Axis states." But no further attempt had been made to explain what this would mean.

It was not until December, 1943, that any public clarification was made by the Allies concerning the future of the Japanese Empire. In the Cairo Declaration issued by Chiang Kai-shek, Churchill, and Roosevelt, they declared:

> Japan shall be stripped of all the islands in the Pacific which she has seized or occupied since the beginning of the first World War in 1914, and all the territories Japan has stolen from the Chinese, such as Manchuria, Formosa, and the Pescadores, shall be restored to the Republic of China. Japan will also be expelled from all other territories which she has taken by violence and greed. The aforesaid three great powers, mindful of the enslavement of the people of Korea, are determined that in due course Korea shall become free and independent.

They concluded with a promise to persevere with the other United Nations at war with Japan, "to procure the unconditional surrender of Japan."

But even a declaration as specific as the Cairo Declaration left many basic questions unsettled. As early as 1942, a postwar planning section of the Department of State had attempted to anticipate some of these problems. After February, 1944, this work took on added significance. The War and Navy Departments, for purposes of their own future planning for the military occupation of Japan, requested answers to more than twenty fundamental postwar policy questions. These included: What was the meaning, in practical and specific terms, of unconditional surrender? Did it mean, for example, the nonexistence of a Japanese government? What was to be the extent, duration, and type of the military occupation of Japan? Would it be an Allied or entirely American occupation? If the former, would there be one or more zones? What about the future position of the Emperor? What were the basic objectives of the United States in reference to postwar Japan?

In the preparation within the Department of State of definitive policies on these and other post-surrender problems, it soon became apparent that their military and political aspects were closely interrelated. Consequently, a State–War–Navy Coordinating Committee (referred to as SWNCC) was created with responsibility for coordinating and formulating general policies of the United States government. By early January, 1945, when SWNCC appointed a special Subcommittee on the Far East, agreement had already been reached within the State Department on answers to most of the post-surrender questions. Consequently, when President Roosevelt left for the Yalta Conference later that month, a nearly complete file on studies and recommendations on various Far Eastern problems accompanied him. Although President Roosevelt was too ill to study these documents, those on Japan were used as the basis for both American and Allied postwar policy.[12]

Although the Yalta Agreement of February, 1945, signed by Churchill, Roosevelt, and Stalin, was concerned primarily with China, it had a direct bearing on Japan. It specified, among other things, that the Soviet Union would enter the war against Japan on the side of the Allies not later than three months after the capitulation of Germany. In return, the Soviet Union was to receive special concessions in China and was to reacquire territories lost to Japan, namely, the southern half of Sakhalin (Karafuto) and the Kurile Islands. For obvious reasons, including the fact that the Soviet Union was at peace with Japan, the Yalta Agreement was kept a closely guarded secret. Even James F. Byrnes, who had been to the conference, did not learn of its existence until after he became Secretary of State in July, 1945.

In the first part of 1945, when military events foreshadowed the defeat of Japan, one of the most important problems confronting the United States government was to decide on its postwar Japanese policy. At that time, there was considerable support in Washington for a strict interpretation of "unconditional surrender" which envisaged an occupation of

Japan under which the Allied Commander and his forces would control and govern the country directly and there would be no Japanese government as such. This policy, which reflected the view of Secretary of the Treasury Henry J. Morgenthau, became the accepted policy for Germany. On the other hand, this view was vehemently challenged and finally rejected by the Department of State's planners of postwar policy for Japan. They recommended that the Japanese government, as such, must not be abolished but should be used by the Allied Commander. This position was incorporated into a policy statement which was subsequently approved by SWNCC and the President and was the basis on which General MacArthur's occupation operated.

At the same time, an equally important question was how to develop a workable definition for "unconditional surrender," which the Allies expected of both Germany and Japan. In considering this problem, the Subcommittee on the Far East of SWNCC reasoned that, while unconditional surrender would mean Japan's military capitulation, it would not necessarily mean the annihilation of the Japanese as a people or the complete destruction of their country. It was further argued that if unconditional surrender were defined in specific terms and if this definition were announced to Japan, it might capitulate before an assault would have to be launched against the home islands. If this came about, the Allies would be spared heavy casualties. A document incorporating these ideas was prepared in the State Department and approved by SWNCC, at the beginning of July, 1945. Thus a policy statement, which was to be slightly modified later to become the Potsdam Declaration, was available for Cabinet approval well before President Truman left for the Potsdam Conference.[13]

The Potsdam Declaration

In July, 1945, when the Supreme Council in Tokyo had decided to ask the Soviet Union to mediate for peace, the United States had already decided to issue a declaration calling on Japan to surrender or to take the consequences. Prior to his departure for a conference with Churchill and Stalin at Potsdam, President Truman and his Cabinet also agreed that if the test of the atomic bomb, scheduled for July 16, proved successful, the bomb would not be used against Japan until after the Allies had issued their declaration.

The news of the success of the atomic bomb reached Potsdam as Truman, Churchill, and Stalin were beginning their deliberations. President Truman then sought and obtained the approval of the United Kingdom and of China for the issuance of the Potsdam Declaration on July 26, 1945. (See Appendix I.)

It was an exposition of Allied postwar aims and objectives, an appeal to Japan to surrender, and a warning that the alternative would be complete and utter destruction. It demanded that the authority and influence of militarists and nationalists must be eliminated for all time and that a new order of peace, security, and justice should be established. It continued that Japan's warmaking power would be destroyed and warned that stern justice would be meted out to war criminals. Furthermore, Japanese sovereignty was to be limited to the four main home islands and their adjacent minor islands.

On the positive side, the Allies promised in their Declaration that the Japanese armed forces abroad would be returned home, fundamental human rights would be established, nonmilitary industries would be permitted, and eventual participation would be allowed in world trade. It required the removal by the Japanese government of all obstacles to the revival and strengthening of democratic tendencies among the people. It warned that the occupation of Japan would continue until the Allied objectives had been achieved and the Japanese people had established by their own free will "a peacefully inclined and responsible government." It concluded by calling upon the Japanese government to proclaim unconditional surrender or face utter destruction.

The Decision To End the War

For the next ten days, the Allies waited in vain for a reply from the Japanese government. The only hint as to how their Declaration had been received was to be found in the Japanese newspapers. On July 28, they quoted the Premier as saying that he considered the Declaration of no great value and that he intended to ignore it.[14] When the Japanese government gave no further signs of accepting the Allied terms, the previous agreement to use the atomic bomb automatically went into effect. On August 6, 1945, the first atomic bomb used in warfare was dropped on Hiroshima.

As reported the next day to the Japanese Army General Staff, "the whole city of Hiroshima was destroyed instantly by a single bomb." Although some of the military chiefs were skeptical of the destructiveness of the new bomb, a special commission sent to investigate the results soon confirmed the terrible news. The threat which the Allies had made at Potsdam that "prompt and utter destruction" awaited Japan if it did not surrender suddenly became a reality. Foreign Minister Tōgō conferred immediately with the Emperor and urged him to accept the Potsdam Declaration.

Before a decision could be reached on this vital question, however, the Soviet Union entered the war against Japan. On August 8, 1945,

Soviet Foreign Minister Molotov presented the Japanese Ambassador in Moscow with a declaration of war to be effective the next day. The news that the Soviet Union had entered the war came as a staggering blow. Premier Suzuki and the military leaders knew that they had no effective plan to stop the Soviet troops in Manchuria and Korea. The pride of the Kwantung Army had long since been withdrawn to protect the homeland. The basic question was no longer whether Japan should continue to fight. It was whether the Potsdam Declaration should be accepted with or without reservations.

Thus, August 9 became one of the most fateful days in Japan's history. Premier Suzuki had an early conference with the Emperor. They decided that the Potsdam Declaration should be accepted immediately. A meeting of the six-man Supreme Council was called by midmorning but it immediately became deadlocked. Half of the members (Premier Suzuki, Foreign Minister Tōgō, and Navy Minister Yonai) favored acceptance of the Potsdam Declaration with the understanding that it did not alter the legal position of the Emperor. The other members of the Council (War Minister Anami, Army Chief of Staff Umezu, and Navy Chief of Staff Toyoda) insisted that the Allies' Declaration should be accepted only on four conditions. These conditions were: (1) no Allied occupation of the homeland, (2) demobilization of the Army and Navy to be under Japanese supervision, (3) war criminals to be prosecuted by the Japanese government, and (4) the status of the Emperor to remain unchanged.

The deadlock in the Supreme Council was not broken by receipt of the news at midday of the destruction of Nagasaki by the second atomic bomb. On the contrary, the matter was referred to the Cabinet. In particular, War Minister Anami and the two Chiefs of Staff, General Umezu and Admiral Toyoda, prevented the Cabinet from reaching an agreement on the matter. In desperation, Prime Minister Suzuki and Foreign Minister Tōgō had already decided what course they should follow in such a contingency. They had agreed that the Emperor should be asked to resolve the issue at an Imperial Conference with the Supreme War Council in attendance.[15] Late that night, the Emperor presided over such a meeting in the Imperial air raid shelter. Privy Council Chairman Hiranuma and chief Cabinet Secretary Sakomizu were also present. The two opposing views were again presented. Those favoring acceptance of the Potsdam Declaration suggested a modification which they believed would assure continuation of the special position of the Emperor. They urged acceptance with the understanding that the "prerogatives of His Majesty as a sovereign ruler" would not be affected by unconditional surrender. At approximately 3:00 A.M. on August 10, Premier Suzuki emphasized the urgent need for an immediate decision and made the unprecedented request that the Emperor break the deadlock by expressing his view.

The Emperor then stated that it was unbearable to him to think of the war continuing and that he agreed with the view that Japan should surrender with the understanding that it would not prejudice the prerogatives of the Emperor as a sovereign ruler. His wish was equivalent to a command which was accepted by the Council. The Cabinet immediately gave its *pro forma* approval. The end of the war was in sight.

The decision of Japan to accept the Potsdam Declaration with the reservation concerning the Emperor's status was transmitted immediately to the Allied Powers. When this note was received, the United States government, with the consent of the three other Allied Powers who sponsored the Potsdam Declaration, decided to ignore this Japanese qualified acceptance which attempted to protect the Emperor's special position. The Allied reply made it patently clear that after surrender both the Emperor and the Japanese government would be subject to an Allied Commander who would be empowered to take whatever steps were necessary to effectuate the surrender terms.[16]

Thus four days later, on August 14, Japan again faced the question of complete capitulation. Acceptance would mean peace; rejection would mean destruction. As before, the Emperor was called upon to resolve the opposing views within the Supreme War Council and the Cabinet. That morning he told his chief Generals, Admirals, and Ministers that an immediate and peaceful end to the war was preferable to Japan's annihilation. He concluded the Imperial Conference by ordering the Cabinet to prepare an Imperial Rescript in which he would publicly announce Japan's capitulation. The Emperor's decision brought tears to the eyes of all in attendance. They knew Japan's defeat was complete. As his top ministers and responsible officers of the Armed Services they had failed him and their country. The least they could do was to obey his will.

The next twenty-four hours were "Japan's longest day." While those who had attended the Imperial Conference intended to obey the command of their Emperor, the government found it difficult to put his wishes into effect. For hours, the Cabinet struggled painfully to agree on the actual text of the Rescript announcing surrender. Finally, at 9:00 P.M. it was ready for the signatures of the various Ministers of State which would make it a legal document. It was not finally recorded by the Emperor until two hours later. As rumors spread throughout Tokyo that the Americans were poised for an invasion, that the Emperor personally had decided on capitulation, and that some of the armed forces were in rebellion, War Minister Anami did his best to keep the Army under control. He tried to convince his rebellious subordinates that their highest duty was to obey the Emperor and accept defeat.

Nonetheless, Major Hatanaka Kenji of the War Ministry's Military Affairs Section believed that the Cabinet Ministers had betrayed their sovereign and should be isolated from the palace, and that the war should be continued. He and his colleagues quickly plotted a coup d'état in which the Imperial guards would be used to isolate the Emperor and the Imperial Palace. To accomplish this, they murdered the commander of the guards and forged his signature, placing the guards under their command. They held the Imperial Palace under siege during the early morning hours while they searched in vain for the Grand Chamberlain and Lord Keeper of the Privy Seal who were in hiding. They also could not find the recording of the Emperor's broadcast. When the commander of the Eastern District Army learned of these events he entered the palace grounds and forced the insurgents to capitulate. In the meantime, War Minister Anami took personal responsibility for Japan's defeat, returned to his home, and sought Imperial forgiveness through suicide. By noon on August 15, when the Emperor's bewildered and hushed subjects heard his voice reading the rescript, "most were ready to welcome an end to death and destruction, the hunger and despair of the past months, so long as their country and their Emperor could be preserved." [17] Meanwhile, Japan's reply was immediately accepted by President Truman. World War II was over. The Potsdam Declaration had defined unconditional surrender for Japan and had saved both Japan and the Allies from the horrible cost of invasion.

Preparation for Formal Capitulation

After the Japanese government had sent its conditional willingness to surrender, President Truman proposed to Prime Minister Attlee, Generalissimo Stalin, and Generalissimo Chiang that General Douglas MacArthur be selected as the Allied Commander and that he be designated the Supreme Commander for the Allied Powers. This proposal was approved and General MacArthur's appointment became effective August 14. His immediate task was to make all necessary arrangements for Japan's surrender. His basic assignment was to supervise the occupation of Japan and the execution of Allied postwar policies.

Before the actual surrender ceremonies could take place, however, certain detailed arrangements had to be made. Representatives of the Japanese Chiefs of Staff had to contact MacArthur's headquarters in Manila to receive specific instructions. Advance units of his forces had to land in Japan to prepare for the Allied occupation. The various Allied Theater Commanders had to be notified concerning the units of the Japanese armed forces which would surrender to them and the areas they would occupy. The Army Corps assigned to the occupation had to be organized, transported, and landed in Japan. Allied prisoners of war in enemy territory had to be contacted and evacuated. Finally, overall policies for the guidance of the occupation had to be approved by the United States government.

While these preparations were proceeding on schedule, Japan was suffering from the initial shock of defeat. For the people, news of the acceptance of the Potsdam Declaration and of the cessation of hostilities came as a relief. After three and a half years of war, six months of which had been accompanied by intensive bombing, they were too dazed and shocked to understand the true significance of their surrender. Furthermore, no responsible official had given even a hint of what surrender would actually mean. When the Emperor had announced in mid-August that Japan had agreed to capitulate, he had not mentioned specifically the term "unconditional surrender." On the contrary, he had said that the acceptance of the Allied demands would pave the way for a lasting and glorious peace.

It is questionable whether even Premier Suzuki and those who agreed to capitulation really knew what to expect. Their decision had been forced upon them by their knowledge of their country's desperate straits. But in view of the fact that Japan had never before been defeated, they realized that they had failed and were in national disgrace. Under these circumstances, the least the Cabinet could do was to resign.

In order to preserve as much stability as possible in the interim period between the cessation of hostilities and formal surrender, the Emperor broke another precedent and selected the next Premier himself. He chose a blood relative, his uncle, Prince Higashikuni Naruhiko, a general with wide experience. The chief assignment of the new Cabinet, which was formed on August 17, 1945, was to maintain law and order throughout the nation and to surrender formally to the new Supreme Commander. Hence Higashikuni's Cabinet was composed of experienced and respected members of influential segments of society. For example, former Premier Konoye was made Vice-Premier; Shigemitsu Mamoru, a career diplomat, was Foreign Minister; Maeda Tamon, a moderate and an internationalist, was Minister of Education; Higashikuni temporarily assumed the post of Minister of War; and Admiral Yonai continued as Minister of Navy.

Many of the leading militarists seem to have been more aware than anyone else of the consequences, at least for themselves, of unconditional surrender. Together with many important government officials, they used the last two weeks in August, the period between the cessation of hostilities and the formal surrender, to destroy records which would incriminate them and to salvage such profits as they could from the catastrophe. For example, orders were issued by the Army and Navy to dispose of all of their war goods either at a nominal cost or without charge. It was estimated that goods worth 50 billion yen were involved in this gigantic liquidation. Furthermore, payments totaling 10 billion yen, a sum larger than any previous monthly military expenditure, were made for discharge allowances and pensions for senior officers, for canceled contracts, and for the settlement of manufacturers' accounts. When the occupation troops arrived, nothing was said about these questionable transactions.

By the end of August, 1945, the United States government and General MacArthur had completed their preliminary preparations for the surrender and occupation of Japan. General MacArthur and his troops had arrived in the Tokyo area for what he termed the greatest gamble in history. The specific documents for use at the time of surrender had been transmitted to the Supreme Commander for the Allied Powers. A general agreement had been reached on the basic policies under which the occupation was to operate.

The Surrender of Japan, September 2, 1945

On September 2, 1945, the stage was prepared for the final act of World War II. The U.S.S. "Missouri" was anchored in lower Tokyo Bay. The ceremony of signing the Instrument of Surrender took place on its deck. General Douglas MacArthur, Supreme Commander for the Allied Powers, accepted the surrender of Japan on behalf of the four major Allied Powers and "in the interest of the other United Nations at war with Japan." Foreign Minister Shigemitsu Mamoru and Chief of Staff Umezu Yoshijirō signed the document on behalf of Japan. The ceremony was concluded by a short speech from General MacArthur who was to direct the destinies of Japan for the next five and a half years. He set the tone of the occupation he was to command when he said:

> A great tragedy has ended. A great victory has been won. The skies no longer rain death—the seas bear only commerce—men everywhere walk upright in the sunlight.

The Instrument of Surrender ordered the immediate cessation of all hostilities and the unconditional surrender of all Japanese armed forces. All officials were commanded to obey all orders issued by the Supreme Commander and to perform their duties until relieved by him. Finally, the Japanese government undertook to carry out the provisions of the Potsdam Declaration and to take whatever action the Supreme Commander might require to implement it.

Another significant and interrelated part of the surrender of Japan was the proclamation issued by the Emperor on the same day. In order to assure the capitulation of all elements in the Japanese armed forces, particularly those in isolated overseas territories, and to guarantee the cooperation of Japanese officials and civilians with the occupation authorities, the United States government considered it advisable to prepare this proclamation for the Emperor. Thus, shortly after the Surrender Instrument was signed, the Emperor proclaimed that he had ordered his government and the Imperial Headquarters to sign the Instrument of Surrender on his behalf. He also commanded his people to lay down their arms and faithfully to carry out all of its provisions and all of the orders of the Imperial Government issued in connection with it. The entire Cabinet pledged its adherence to the surrender and to the proclamation by affixing their signatures to this Imperial Rescript. Thus all military and civil authority in Japan became subject to General MacArthur as Supreme Commander for the Allied Powers, referred to as SCAP.

But additional steps were necessary to effect the surrender of the Japanese armed forces overseas. Consequently, immediately after the completion of the ceremonies in which he accepted Japan's surrender, the Supreme Commander issued General Order No. 1 which contained detailed arrangements for the surrender of all of the Imperial armed forces. Each of the five Allied Commanders in the Far East was given an area over which he was ordered to continue to have jurisdiction. The Japanese forces were to surrender to the Allied Commander of the area in which they were located. Thus, those in China (excluding Manchuria), Formosa, and French Indochina north of 16° latitude surrendered to Generalissimo Chiang Kai-shek. Those in Manchuria, Korea north of 38° latitude, and Karafuto gave themselves up to the Commander of the Soviet Forces in the Far East. Those in the Pacific Islands capitulated to the Commander of the United States Fleet; those in Southeast Asia to Admiral Mountbatten or the Australian Commander. The Imperial General Headquarters and all Japanese armed forces in Japan proper and Korea south of the thirty-eighth parallel surrendered to General MacArthur.[18]

Finally, the basic policies for postwar Japan had been laid down by the United States in a document entitled, "The United States Initial Post-Surrender Policy for Japan." This overall policy statement, which was transmitted to General MacArthur at the end of August, 1945, was based on the general principles announced by the Allied leaders at Potsdam. It set forth the two basic objectives of the Allied Powers as the prevention of Japan from menacing the future peace of the world and the encouragement of the formation of a responsible government which would respect the rights of others.

This statement then outlined the means whereby these objectives would be achieved. These included:

1. The limitation of Japanese territory to the four main islands and to minor adjacent islands, as provided in the Cairo and Potsdam Declarations
2. The elimination of militarism in both political and economic life
3. The trial of war criminals by an Allied Tribunal
4. The establishment of guarantees for basic human rights
5. The exaction of reparations and the restitution of stolen goods
6. The development of democratic organizations in labor
7. The carrying out of basic reforms in agriculture and industry

The execution of these policies, as well as the general and specific operation of the occupation, was left to the discretion of General MacArthur as Supreme Commander. He was given wide freedom of action and powers broad enough to meet any exigencies that might develop. If the circumstances warranted it, he could even ignore the Japanese government as the agent for the execution of his orders and act directly. Consequently, the history of the occupation is, in many respects, that of the personal rule of General MacArthur. He conceived his mission to be the transformation of a militaristic state into a peace-loving democratic country. He provided the Japanese with the leadership and the hope they needed so desperately in their darkest hour of history.

Notes

1. Only the most crucial campaigns or battles in the Pacific are mentioned in this chapter. A helpful résumé, with excellent charts, is in United States Strategic Bombing Survey, *Summary Report (Pacific War)* (Washington: Government Printing Office, 1946). Donald MacIntyre, *The Battle for the Pacific* (New York: W. W. Norton & Co., Inc., 1966), contains detailed accounts of the most important naval battles. See also Samuel Eliot Morison, *History of United States Naval Operations* (Boston: Little, Brown & Co., 1948), and S. Woodburn Kirby, *et al., The War Against Japan* (4 vols.; London: Her Majesty's Stationery Office, 1959).

2. As the Pearl Harbor attack had not caught any American carriers in port, three carriers were available in the Pacific. In the Battle of the Coral Sea, one of these, the "Lexington," was sunk and the "Yorktown" was severely damaged. Japan had similar casualties. At the same time Japan was prevented from achieving its objective. At Midway, Admiral Nimitz had the advantage of knowing the plans of Admiral Nagumo as the Japanese code had been broken. The Japanese fleet was discovered by American planes which caught Admiral Nagumo off balance and forced him to withdraw. The "Yorktown" had been repaired in record time to enter the battle only to be lost. At the same time the Japanese occupied the western Aleutians. Professor Hayashi claims that Admiral Yamamoto, Commander of the Combined

Fleets, was so enraged by General Dolittle's air raid on Tokyo in April that the Midway attack was carried out in revenge, against the better judgment of earlier plans which excluded Midway from Japan's defense perimeter. See Hayashi Shigeru, *Taiheiyō Sensō* (Tokyo: Chuokoron, 1967), pp. 282 ff.

3. Aoki Kazuo (b. 1889) spent most of his adult life as a bureaucrat. After 1937 he became Vice-President of the Cabinet's Manchurian Affairs Board and later was Chairman of the Cabinet Planning Board. From 1940 to 1942 he acted as chief financial adviser to Wang Ching-wei's puppet regime in Nanking.

4. For a more detailed analysis of the lack of cooperation in the Axis partnership see F. C. Jones, *Japan's New Order in East Asia, Its Rise and Fall, 1937–1945* (New York: Oxford University Press, 1954).

5. This control was finally clarified and strengthened by the Extraordinary Wartime Administrative Authority to Act which became effective on March 18, 1944. By this law, Tōjō was given the power to decide all questions connected with its enforcement. For these and other changes in organization of the government resulting from the creation of the Munitions Ministry, see Hugh Borton, "The Administration and Structure of the Japanese Government," *Department of State Bulletin, XI* (December 24, 1944), pp. 817–33.

6. See Hayashi, *op. cit.*, pp. 421 ff.

7. Koiso Kuniaki (1880–1950) was a career army officer. His various posts put him in close touch with the Imperial Way Faction of the Army. He was Vice-Minister of War under General Araki, Chief of Staff of the Kwantung Army, and was Governor-General of Korea at the time of his appointment as Prime Minister. The most detailed account of the background of events during this period will be found in Robert J. C. Butow, *Japan's Decision to Surrender* (Stanford: Stanford University Press, 1954), pp. 30–58.

8. Konoye, Wakatsuki, Hiranuma, and Okada were the former Premiers who had been meeting secretly for several months. For details see Butow, *op. cit.*, pp. 14 ff. For a summary of the contents of Admiral Takagi's report and his connection with Admiral Yonai see United States Strategic Bombing Survey, *Japan's Struggle to End the War* (Washington: Government Printing Office, 1946), p. 3.

9. Considerable confusion has arisen over the question of whether Suzuki took the premiership with the explicit understanding that he was to end the war. Fortunately, Butow (*op. cit.*, p. 70), has correctly emphasized the fact that understandings are often reached in Japan without an explicit commitment (*haragei*). On the other hand, as a retired admiral, the thought of Japan's unconditional surrender to the Allies was more than Suzuki could stomach at this stage. For example, a few days before Germany's capitulation he boasted, "We finally believe that there will surely come in our grasp a golden chance." See also Hayashi, *op. cit.*, p. 440.

10. An exhaustive treatment of Japan's wartime economy will be found in Jerome B. Cohen, *Japan's Economy in War and Reconstruction* (Minneapolis: University of Minnesota Press, 1949). For a summary of the report of Sakomizu Hisamitsu see United States Strategic Bombing Survey, *Japan's Struggle to End the War, op. cit.*, pp. 6 and 16–17.

11. For a survey of these events see Strategic Bombing Survey, *ibid.*, pp. 6 ff.; Butow, *op. cit.*, pp. 112 ff. and Hayashi, *op. cit.*, pp. 447–52.

12. Dr. Leo Pasvolsky, Special Assistant to Secretary of State Cordell Hull, was primarily responsible for organizing the work of postwar planning within

the Department of State. Studies on postwar Japan were begun in the fall of 1942. Tentative conclusions on many of the questions raised by the War and Navy Departments had already been reached prior to February, 1944. They were confirmed in November, 1944, by the action of the State Department's Postwar Program Committee. See Hugh Borton, "Preparation for the Occupation of Japan," *Journal of Asian Studies,* XXV (February, 1966), pp. 203–6, and his *American Presurrender Planning for Postwar Japan* (New York: East Asian Institute, Columbia University, 1967), pp. 3–20.

13. In the narration of events connected with the formation of American postwar policies, the reader may note some divergencies with other accounts. In such places the author has relied on his personal experience. From 1942 to 1948, he was in the Department of State working on postwar policy for Japan. Toward the latter part of this period, he served as Chairman of the Subcommittee of the Far East. Complete documentation of the history of the formulation of American foreign policy during the war and postwar years will have to await the declassification of the documents of the State Department's Inter Divisional Area Committee and the Postwar Planning Committee (PWC) and of the minutes and documents of SWNCC and its subcommittees.

On the other hand, certain misconceptions about the process of the formulation of American postwar Japanese policy need immediate clarification. One of these concerns the growing belief that the so-called "China Crowd" was influential in determining American policy toward Japan. Harry Emerson Wildes claims that meetings between the "China Crowd" and the "Japan Crowd" developed in February, 1944, into SWNCC. While there may have been such groups and meetings held outside of the Department of State, the author can vouch from his own experience that the "China Crowd" had no determining influence on the final formulation of policies within the Department of State. Furthermore, SWNCC was not organized until the end of 1944. Neither SWNCC nor its Subcommittee on the Far East had as members or advisers any of Wildes' so-called "China Crowd." See Harry Emerson Wildes, *Typhoon in Tokyo* (New York: The Macmillan Co., 1954), p. 3.

It is equally mistaken to maintain, as some contemporary leftist groups in Tokyo are stating, that the Potsdam Declaration was basically a Soviet document. The original drafts of all of the basic postwar documents, including the Potsdam Declaration, were prepared in Washington. The record will show that drafts of the Potsdam Declaration; the Instrument of Surrender; the Imperial Rescript Announcing Surrender; the United States Initial Post-Surrender Policy for Japan of September 6, 1945; General MacArthur's General Order No. 1; and the Joint Chiefs of Staff Directive to him were considered by the Subcommittee of the Far East and transmitted to SWNCC for formal approval. The Cabinet decision approving the Potsdam Declaration was based on a new document prepared by Secretary of War Stimson which was based on the SWNCC draft. Although Mr. Stimson's document was new, the idea did not originate with him as inferred in his *Memoirs.* Such changes as were made in this document at Potsdam were largely at the request of Great Britain. Stalin was shown a copy of the Potsdam Declaration before it was issued but as the Soviet Union was not at war with Japan by July 26, 1945, he was not asked to approve it formally.

Fortunately, some of the documents are now available in Department of State, *U. S. Foreign Relations 1944* (Washington: Government Printing Office, 1968). I have tried to clarify the history of policy formation in my *American*

Presurrender Planning and "Preparation for the Occupation," noted above. See also H. L. Stimson and M. Bundy, *On Active Service in Peace and War* (New York: Harper & Row, 1948), pp. 366 ff. and 620, and James F. Byrnes, *Speaking Frankly* (New York: Harper & Row, 1947), p. 206.

14. There has been much discussion over what the Premier really meant by the term *mokusatsu* (to ignore by silence). See Butow, *op. cit.,* pp. 142 ff.; and Kazuo Kawai, "Mokusatsu, Japan's Response to the Potsdam Declaration," *Pacific Historical Review* (November, 1950).

15. For a detailed account based on exhaustive research and interviews with those connected with the decision to surrender, see Pacific War Research Society, *Japan's Longest Day* (Tokyo and Palo Alto, Calif.: Kodansha International Ltd., 1968); for details of the meetings on August 9 see pp. 23 ff. This book was published originally in 1965 as *Nihon no Ichiban Nagai Hi.*

16. For a detailed chronology of the U. S.–Japanese exchanges and texts of the notes see Department of State, *Occupation of Japan: Policy and Progress,* Department of State Publication 267, Far Eastern Series 17 (Washington: Government Printing Office, 1946), pp. 58 ff.

17. For vivid details of these and other events and the actions of the leading figures involved, see *Japan's Longest Day, op. cit.,* pp. 81 ff. and 327.

18. The text of General Order No. 1 will be found in SCAP, Government Section, *Political Reorientation of Japan, September 1945 to September 1948* (2 vols.; Washington: Government Printing Office, 1949), II, pp. 442 ff.

20

The Reorientation of Japan Under Occupation 1945–1952

The surrender and occupation of Japan were a gamble because so many variables were involved in the venture. There was no way of predicting with certainty how the nation would react to defeat and particularly to the occupation of its "sacred soil" by foreign troops. Heretofore, all of Japan's wars in modern times had been fought overseas and had been successful. When the Mongols had threatened to invade Japan in the thirteenth century, a divine wind (*Kami kaze*) had saved the Empire. Now that the gods had failed to save them, would the Japanese armed forces obey the Instrument of Surrender? Would the 3½ million Japanese troops overseas, particularly those under fanatical leadership, comply with their Emperor's plea to lay down their arms? Would the thousands of government employees continue to function in their respective positions in the Finance Ministry, in the railroads, in the post and telegraph offices, in the police system, in education, and in other government offices? If not, would the personnel of the occupation forces be capable of running Japan?

Finally, there was the overriding question as to whether the Allies would be able to make any progress toward achieving their basic objective of the demilitarization and democratization of Japan. Could a foreign military occupation hope to succeed in bringing about any fundamental change in the political outlook and habits of its erstwhile enemy? Could this "massive experiment in planned political change," as it has been called, possibly succeed?

Reaction to the Occupation

The answer to the more immediate and specific question as to how Japan would react to the occupation will become apparent from the account of the main events of this period of over six and a half years. It began officially on September 2, 1945, when Japan surrendered, and ended on April 24, 1952, when the San Francisco Peace Treaty went into effect. As for the larger question as to the acceptability and durability of the basic reforms inaugurated by SCAP, some would doubt whether the experiment was successful. On the other hand, in less than twenty-five years, ultranationalism, the widespread control of all aspects of society by a powerful military establishment, and the threat of Japan's dominance of Eastern Asia had been replaced by an essentially democratic, prosperous, energetic, and technologically advanced country. Its industrial capacity had surpassed all other nations except the Soviet Union and the United States. It had developed only a minimum arms industry and self-defense forces, but was allied with the United States.

It is impossible to assess accurately how many of these accomplishments are attributable to the occupation and how much they have been influenced by external forces. In the years between surrender and the Peace Treaty, the world had rapidly become polarized into two camps. In Germany, the eastern sector was as much a part of the communist world as West Germany was a part of the Western democracies. Chiang Kai-shek was driven from the Chinese mainland by the communists under Mao Tze-tung and his Chinese People's Republic. Korea was equally divided and in 1950 the North Korean communists, forced by the Soviet Union into believing they could conquer the south, crossed the thirty-eighth parallel. The United States and the Western democracies, recognizing a common danger in Europe and Asia, came to the rescue of the Republic of Korea in the south. General MacArthur, while continuing as SCAP in Japan, became the United Nations Commander in Korea. Before the treaty with Japan was concluded, the Chinese People's Republic had entered the Korean war. Thus Japan became inextricably enmeshed in the struggles of the free world against a united world communism.

To return to the immediate reactions of the Japanese to the occupation, even before formal surrender on September 2, 1945, there were indications that the Japanese would not resist. The first contingent of Allied troops which landed in Japan had not been molested. The occupation was orderly and devoid of incidents. Initial fear of individual Japanese toward the foreign soldiers quickly disappeared. When the GIs began to befriend the children, their mothers and sisters came out of hiding. Suspicion gave way to trust. SCAP's orders were followed as a matter of course by the armed forces and by civilians alike. Even the overseas contingents of the Army and Navy surrendered in routine fashion.

This docile submission of the military and civilian populace was caused by several factors. In the first place, the Japanese were accustomed to obeying their superiors. SCAP had complete and supreme authority. The Emperor told his people to obey this new authority and his subjects readily acquiesced. Secondly, the physical and psychological state of shock of most of the people made them receptive to the stark realities of their defeat. Civilian casualties had surpassed three-quarters of a million; over three million homes had been destroyed by raids or had been torn down for firebreaks. The average daily rations afforded about 1,680 calories; civilian goods were nonexistent. The will to resist and the physical means to support continued resistance were both exhausted.[1]

Moreover, the personality, attitude, and reputation of General MacArthur contributed to the success of the occupation. He instilled confidence and acted with benevolence. He exhibited a keen sense of timing in the implementation of the various policies which had already been determined in Washington and transmitted to him. In the early days of the occupation, he concentrated on military problems. After the demilitarization program was well under control, he shifted to nonmilitary matters. He then pressed for those reforms that would awaken a new political consciousness among the Japanese, such as the establishment of civil rights, the revision of the Constitution, and the elimination of ultranationalists by means of the purge. When progress had been achieved in these fields, he turned to economic problems. His task was made easier by two additional factors. Particularly during the early months of the occupation, when many of the reforms were carried out, he was able to operate in comparative isolation. No one could enter Japan without his explicit permission. Secondly, except for the Far Eastern Commission his power and authority were not shared with foreign collaborators.

Early Steps Toward Democratization

Since the foremost mission of the occupation was the elimination of militarism in Japan, SCAP first ordered the demobilization of the Imperial Army, Navy, and Air Force. Allied occupation forces were assigned to specific areas throughout the home islands to supervise this operation. It was completed in six weeks and shortly thereafter the Army and Navy Ministries were abolished. Simultaneously, Japanese troops stationed overseas were disarmed, brought home, and returned peacefully to civilian life. By the end of January, 1946, the demilitarization phase of the occupation had proceeded so smoothly that one of the two American Armies of Occupation was withdrawn.

In the meantime SCAP's nonmilitary activities increased in importance. General MacArthur perfected his organization and created a General Headquarters, Supreme Commander for the Allied Powers (GHQ, SCAP), with appropriate sections to supervise the various operations of the Japanese government. SCAP directives and orders were then issued to the Japanese Cabinet, which was held responsible for their execution. On some of the most important issues, however, such as the drafting of the new Constitution, while no formal directives were issued, SCAP played the decisive role.[2] (See page 463.)

On October 4, 1945, SCAP gave the first positive encouragement to new democratic tendencies in Japan. He issued a directive which came to be known as the "Japanese Bill of Rights." Its purpose was to remove the current restrictions on the freedoms of the people. It ordered the abrogation of legislation restricting basic human rights and the release of political prisoners. The Ministry of Home Affairs, center of centralized police control, was deprived of most of its powers. The police were forbidden to interfere with individual liberties.

The immediate effect of this directive was the resignation of Prime Minister Higashikuni. He insisted that he could not maintain peace and order without a Ministry of Home Affairs with strong police powers. Shidehara Kijūrō, who as Foreign Minister before the conquest of Manchuria in 1931 had advocated a friendly policy toward China, was selected as his successor. Shidehara's Cabinet was basically conservative and served as a willing tool of SCAP in an interim capacity until after the first postwar elections of April, 1946.

The conservative character of the Shidehara Cabinet and of the House of Representatives was more than counterbalanced, however, by the activities of SCAP in connection with the revision of the Constitution. If representative institutions were to prosper, if individual human freedoms were to be guaranteed, and if a new political reorientation was to be expected, basic revisions of the old Meiji Constitution were imperative. In the first place, during the first four months of the occupation, General MacArthur made it clear on several occasions that he believed a drastic change in the Constitution was necessary. He urged the Japanese to undertake this work themselves, under the guidance and general supervision of his headquarters. Vice-Premier Konoye was one of the first to take the initiative in this matter. Under the immediate protection of the Emperor, Konoye formed a constitutional drafting commission. His suicide on December 15, 1945, after he learned that he was to be arrested as a suspected war criminal, eliminated the possibility of his proposed constitutional changes being accepted.

In the meantime, General MacArthur had also told Prime Minister Shidehara orally that the reform of the Constitution was one of the most important tasks which his government should undertake. Consequently, the Cabinet formed its own committee under the chairmanship of Matsumoto Jōji, a noted professor of law. But all indications pointed to a concerted effort by the Cabinet to avoid making fundamental changes in the old Constitution. Matsumoto publicly talked about the weaknesses of a "government by the people." On February 1, 1946, the Cabinet finally submitted to SCAP its official draft which contained provisions contrary to the aims of the Potsdam Declaration and to fundamental principles which the United States government had agreed must be incorporated in a new Constitution. The Matsumoto draft paid little regard to the basic concept of "responsible government." The Emperor still remained the central political figure; the Privy Council continued as his chief advisory body. Basic human rights were not guaranteed.

Faced with this apparent disinterest of the Cabinet in basic constitutional reforms, SCAP took the initiative. In conferences on February 2–3, 1946, General Courtney Whitney, Chief of the Government Section, and General MacArthur decided on several basic principles to be followed in drafting a new constitution. The Emperor's powers were to be clearly restricted but he was to remain the head of the state. "War as a sovereign right of the nation" was to be abolished and was to be renounced "as an instrumentality for settling disputes." The peerage was not to extend beyond the present generation and the nobility was to be deprived of political power. Finally, the budget was to be modeled on the British system. The Government Section was then assigned the task of drafting a constitution based on these principles.[3]

A new draft was completed in little more than a week. It gave the Cabinet wide powers. Sovereignty, which was to reside in the people, was to be exercised by the executive, legislative, and judicial branches of the government. War was to be outlawed. Civil rights were to be guaranteed and the Cabinet was to be made collectively responsible to Parliament. If there was a vote of nonconfidence in Parliament, the Cabinet must resign or dissolve the Diet. General MacArthur gave his formal approval to this draft. General Whitney met with representatives from the Japanese Cabinet on February 13, 1946, and showed them the draft which his colleagues had prepared.

At this point, the accounts become confused as to what actually took place. The official SCAP account states that there was no compulsion used by SCAP toward the Japanese. On the other hand, it is reported that the latter were told that if the Cabinet did not act, "General MacArthur was prepared to lay the issue before the people." Two days of uninterrupted conferences between SCAP officials and Cabinet representatives followed. During these sessions, acceptable English and Japanese texts were adopted. On the next day, March 6, 1946, the text of the new draft of the Constitution was published in Japan with strong endorsements by both General MacArthur and the Emperor.

In the light of available evidence, this was clearly MacArthur's Constitution. An analysis of the official Japanese text indicates that the original text was in English rather than in Japanese. The limited time available for the Cabinet representatives to consider revisions denotes that they had little choice either on the content or on the form of the draft. General MacArthur's endorsement of the final draft on the day after the Cabinet representatives and SCAP officials had agreed on the English and Japanese texts clearly implies that these texts had already incorporated his wishes. The clearest evidence that this was basically a SCAP document, however, is found in its contents. The principles expounded by General MacArthur in early February were incorporated into the final text. But before it could become the basic law of the land, it would require Parliament's approval and the sanction of the Allied Powers.

Allied Participation in the Occupation

Up to this point, General MacArthur's actions had elicited only limited criticisms from the Allied Powers. They had willingly recognized the fact that the war in the Pacific had been almost exclusively an American campaign and that it was logical for the United States to play the paramount role in the occupation. They were not prepared, however, to relinquish their voice in the determination of basic policies for postwar Japan. When MacArthur published a new Constitution on his own initiative, they protested that he had gone too far.

These protests had some validity in view of the fact that eleven of the Allied nations were members of the Far Eastern Commission which had responsibility for formulating policies for Japan. Before surrender, the United States had taken steps to meet the desires of the Allies to participate in the control of postwar Japan. An American proposal was submitted to China, the Soviet Union, and the United Kingdom for the creation of a commission to advise General MacArthur. A Far Eastern Advisory Commission was formed but the Soviet Union refused to attend on the grounds that it did not give the Allies sufficient power. At the Council of Foreign Ministers in London in September, 1941, Soviet Foreign Minister Molotov recommended the establishment of a control council for Japan but this was unacceptable to the United States. When the Foreign Ministers met in December in Moscow, the problem of Allied participation in the control of Japan was high on their agenda. They wanted some arrangement whereby they could have more voice in the matter. On the other hand, the United States did not intend to forfeit its favored position in this control. General MacArthur, even though he was Supreme Commander for the Allied Powers, was an American general and was responsible to his government alone. Any other arrangement could not be seriously entertained. The Foreign Ministers reconciled their differences, however, by accepting the American proposal for the formation of an eleven-nation Far Eastern Commission in Washington with power to formulate policy and of a four-power advisory Allied Council for Japan to sit in Tokyo.[4]

The new Far Eastern Commission was responsible for formulating policies to govern postwar Japan; it could review directives issued by the Supreme Commander or his action on policy matters. On the other hand, it was forbidden to interfere with military matters or to discuss peace treaty problems. To meet the Soviet insistence on a veto, and also to protect General MacArthur, the approval of China, the Soviet Union, the United Kingdom, and the United States was required for all policy decisions.

On February 26, 1946, the Commission met for the first time in the Japanese Embassy building under the chairmanship of the United States Representative, Frank R. McCoy. This was precisely the time that the Japanese Cabinet was procrastinating on taking a stand on MacArthur's draft of the new Constitution. Just prior to a Commission meeting on March 6, 1946, reports reached Washington that the Tokyo press had published the text of the proposed Constitution and that it had received General MacArthur's personal approval. The next week, Commission members sought approval for a policy which would have required General MacArthur to postpone the elections which he had called for April, 1946, and to submit the Constitution to the Commission for approval.

After the American representative threatened to veto any such proposal, the Commission finally approved a more moderate policy. SCAP was asked to keep the Commission informed on the progress of the draft of the Constitution in the Japanese Parliament. Furthermore, he was requested to apprise the Japanese government of the fact that the Commission must be given an opportunity to approve the final draft. The Commission simultaneously requested SCAP's views on the advisability of postponing the elections. MacArthur's reply to this request was an unequivocal, "No." He and his Government Section became apprehensive lest the Commission interfere with the acceptance of the Constitution by Parliament.[5]

A New Political Atmosphere

Despite the apprehension of the Far Eastern Commission that an early election would favor the conservatives, SCAP had taken the initiative in pushing for political reforms. At the suggestion of the occupation authorities, the Diet had passed a new election law which gave women the right to vote and which reduced the age of the electorate to twenty years. Furthermore, in order to give the people greater freedom to select persons of their own choice for office, a SCAP directive abolished the terroristic and nationalistic societies and inaugurated a purge of the exponents of militant nationalism and aggression. Many of the original candidates for the first postwar election were made ineligible by this purge. Places were thus available for new political leaders.

The Bill of Rights Directive of October, 1945, which guaranteed political freedom, had also stimulated political activity. New parties were formed and the old ones were revived. For the first time, the Communists were permitted under the law to organize a party. Their leaders had been released from prison. Others, such as Nozaka Sanzō, returned home from exile, thoroughly indoctrinated with communist doctrine. Nozaka became president of the new party and proved to be one of the shrewdest and most capable postwar politicians. The Communist party sought widespread support by advocating popular causes, such as the alleviation of the food shortage, stricter controls on prices, higher wages, the nationalization of basic industries, and the termination of the occupation.[6]

The Social Democrats refused to join a united front with the Communists and formed a party of their own. Their membership came largely from the growing labor movement and the urban intellectuals. Their platform was far less radical than that of the Communists. Although their goal was the gradual nationalization of the banks and key industries, they concentrated their immediate attack on shortages, stricter controls, and higher wages.

The Liberal party and the Progressive party were the largest ones in Japan. They were fundamentally conservative and their members had, for the most part, belonged to the prewar Minseitō and Seiyūkai parties. The Liberal party, which, before the purge, had fifty members in the House of Representatives, advocated a *laissez-faire* economy, women suffrage, a lower voting age, a reorganization of the House of Peers and the Privy Council, but no major changes in the Constitution. Its chief leaders were Ashida Hitoshi and Yoshida Shigeru.

Premier Shidehara's Progressive party was the strongest in the Diet but its members were even more conservative than the Liberals. Its candidates supported a minimum of government interference in business and private life. It suffered most from the application of the purge directive which affected even some of the members of the Cabinet.[7]

The results of the election of April, 1946, the first with universal adult suffrage, were not startling. The election brought an end, however, to the control of the House of Representatives by members elected during wartime. Three-fourths of these members had been replaced by new persons with a more democratic outlook. The two leading conservative parties, the Progressives and the Liberals, obtained nearly half the seats in the House of Representatives, but their positions were reversed. The Liberals became the leading party. The Social Democrats elected only one less representative than the Progressives. The Communists were able to win only five seats. As a result of the poor showing of his party, Premier Shidehara was unable to keep his coalition Cabinet in office and resigned. (See Table 11.) He was succeeded by the President of the Liberal party, Yoshida Shigeru.

Consulate General of Japan, New York

YOSHIDA SHIGERU (1878–1967)

Though Premier Yoshida was a conservative, his earlier actions had not made him subject to the purge. He was a man of principle and was arrested when he urged an early end of the war.[8] Under his tutelage, the Diet strengthened its position as the sole legislative authority and the House of Representatives showed promise of becoming a genuine agency of popular government. In line with the new policy, which was officially defined as inspiring necessary reforms by suggestion and persuasion, SCAP informally presented proposals to the House of Representatives for improving its function. These proposals advocated the formation of permanent committees, the allotment of sufficient time for deliberations on important items such as the budget, the increase in salaries of the legislators, and the creation of a National Diet Library with a legislative reference service.

A New Constitution Is Adopted

In view of the approval which General MacArthur and the Yoshida Cabinet had already given to the draft of the Constitution, outright opposition to it had dwindled even before the draft was formally presented to Parliament in June, 1946. Only the Communists continued to favor postponement of a vote on its acceptance, but their opposition was not strong enough to cause a delay.

But the opposition in the Far Eastern Commission in Washington to the new draft and to its early adoption was a different matter. Many of the Commission members were convinced that the SCAP was pressing for immediate acceptance of the Constitution to forestall their interference. The Commission, which approved a document on basic principles for the new Constitution, insisted that two changes be made in the draft to make it consistent with these principles. The first change was that a majority of the Cabinet should be members of the Diet and that all the Cabinet members should be civilians. The Commission also insisted that the upper chamber should specifically be made inferior to the House of Representatives. All of these points were incorporated in the Constitution draft prior to its approval by the House of Peers in October, 1946. Shortly thereafter, the Far Eastern Commission cleared the way for final action in Japan. The Commission avoided a direct vote on the text of the Constitution and decided instead that a review should be made by the Diet during the second year of the operation of the Constitution. After approval by the Privy Council, the new Constitution was promulgated on November 3, 1946, to become effective May 3, 1947.[9]

The new Constitution had diametrically changed the basic political philosophy of Japan's government. (See Appendix II.) A limited constitutional monarchy had been superseded by a liberal one; the power and right to govern had been taken from the oligarchs and given to the people. A bicameral legislature, not the Emperor, was the highest organ of state. It was the sole legislative branch of the government. Its House of Representatives had superior budgetary and other powers over the new House of Councilors. Initiative for future amendments was vested in the Diet. The Emperor was deprived of all powers of government; he was now the symbol of the unity of the people. Contrary to the old Constitution, the responsibilities of the Cabinet were specifically enumerated. It was invested with all executive authority; it was collectively responsible for its acts to the Diet. The Premier was elected by Parliament; if he lost its confidence, he must resign or order a new general election to be held.

Another important innovation was the requirement that the judiciary be independent of the executive branch of the government. The new judges were not subject to Cabinet regulations. Their tenure in office must be approved by the electorate every ten years. The Supreme Court had full judicial powers, including that of judicial review. The fundamental human rights of the people were protected, for the first time, by the Constitution. All people were equal under the law, regardless of position, race, creed, or sex. Freedom of thought, religion, assembly, and speech were guaranteed and no longer subject to legal restrictions. Safeguards were provided against unwarranted arrests and against detention without adequate cause. The rights of workers to organize and bargain collectively were emphasized.

As for the elimination of militarism and aggressive tendencies, General MacArthur had taken personal interest in incorporating an article into the Constitution by which Japan renounced war and the use of force. (See page 463.) Article 9, which incorporated his views, stated that the Japanese people renounced war as a right of the nation, and the threat or use of force to settle international disputes. It also specified that land, sea, and air forces would "never be maintained." Ironically, this article on the renunciation of war was to plague the United States in less than five years when it sought to obtain support from Japan for a defense treaty against the Soviet Union.

In view of these and other provisions, this new basic charter of the nation created the legal framework within which "a peacefully inclined and responsible government," as provided by the Potsdam Declaration, could prosper. It remained for the future desires of the Japanese people, the operation of their new laws, and the extent of their adoption of these basic principles to determine whether democratic practices would expand and grow, or whether they would contract and wither.

Political Developments Under the New Constitution

In the months just before the new Constitution went into effect in May, 1947, there were significant developments which strengthened the liberal and democratic forces in Japan. The Government Section of SCAP insisted on a drastic extension of the purge to include officials in local government, leaders of the largest industrial and financial concerns, and influential persons in the various media of information. New ordinances, which the Japanese government must implement, ordered the removal and exclusion of "undesirable persons" (those who had supported militant nationalism and aggression) from public office in local assemblies and other city, prefectural, town, village and hamlet organizations. Even the heads of the block and neighborhood associations, which had controlled the people on the local level, were included. On paper, at least, extreme nationalists were to be eliminated from local politics.

The economic purge, which was directed at ultranationalists in business, affected a much larger number of persons than any of the other purges. The top executives, directors, and other influential officials of specially designated companies were subject to removal from office. These companies fell into three main categories: government-owned firms such as the Bank of Japan; companies engaged in business in occupied areas; and the family combines, or *zaibatsu* corporations. Nearly one-fourth of the persons screened under the economic program were adversely affected.

The third category of the revised purge included all those officials who had taken an active part in propaganda which supported expansionism, the war effort, or the exploitation of the occupied territories. Thus writers, leaders in the newspaper and radio world, and publicists could be excluded from public office or positions of importance in the media of information. As executed amid the enthusiasm for a "democratic reformation of Japan," these extended purges went far beyond the original intentions. They were designed by SCAP without the acquiescence of any significant segment of Japanese society. Their arbitrary classifications brought unjust treatment to many whose removal from responsible positions caused confusion and defeated the purpose of the program.[10] Even before the occupation ceased, many of those purged were taken off the list.

It was the rank and file of urban workers, particularly those in Tokyo, which gave Yoshida his greatest troubles and which presaged the emergence of a new political force. Since adverse economic conditions continued, labor disputes rose in importance. The Communists were in the forefront of what was described as a "labor offensive." Demands were made for a minimum wage, for larger tax exemptions for persons with low incomes, and for increases in monthly cash payments for wages. In late January, 1947, over 150,000 workers gathered in front of the Imperial Palace in Tokyo and demanded Yoshida's resignation. He stigmatized the leaders as rebellious and irresponsible persons, which only increased their animosity toward him. A general strike was called for February 1, 1947. It was avoided only at the last moment by the personal intervention of General MacArthur. Five days later, he announced that the momentous changes of the past year required a new election. In other words, he, too, had lost confidence in Yoshida.

While the Communists lost support in the labor movement because of the failure of their plans for a general strike, the Social Democrats gained in strength. The latter had refused to be drawn into the general strike. They had aptly criticized the efforts of the Yoshida Cabinet to check inflation as unrealistic and insincere. They found ready acceptance for their program of strict control over the coal, iron, steel, and fertilizer industries. They had profited from the extension of the purge which eliminated some of their most formidable conservative rivals.

The election for the House of Representatives, which the new Constitution had made the predominant chamber, was held on April 25, 1947. Yoshida and his party failed to obtain the largest number of seats in the House. Although no party won an absolute majority, the Socialists obtained the most seats. They increased their strength at the expense of the conservative parties. Katayama Tetsu, President of the Socialist party, formed a coalition Cabinet with some conservatives, but it was an uneasy partnership. As a Christian and an idealist, he enthusiastically supported the democratic institutions created and preserved by the new Constitution. As a politician and Prime Minister, his freedom of action was closely circumscribed because of his shaky political coalition. Practical economic conditions also hampered his program. He had inherited from the Yoshida Cabinet uncontrolled inflation and an economy which had not yet recovered sufficiently to supply essential consumers' goods. His inability to solve these problems, together with a new tendency toward polarization between the right and the left, brought his downfall in February, 1948.

Growth of Conservatism

Contrary to the phenomenal success of communism in China, the general tendency in Japan at this time was away from the leftists toward conservatism. When Katayama resigned, the Diet selected Ashida Hitoshi, president of the conservative Democratic party, as his successor. After eight months in office, he was ousted by the rival conservative party, the Liberals under the leadership of Yoshida Shigeru. In the next general election in January, 1949, Yoshida received an absolute majority and overwhelming support for his conservative policies. In June, 1950, when one-half of the members of the House of Councilors were up for election, his party increased its strength still further. Criticism of him was nullified by the markedly reduced scale of direct intervention of SCAP in internal affairs. In July, 1949, General MacArthur had announced that the Japanese government should "be permitted and encouraged to exercise the normal power of government in matters of domestic administration." He then proceeded to follow this policy.

While the Japanese electorate obviously preferred the conservatives, the successes of the Chinese communists had indirectly strengthened the

TABLE 11

POSTWAR ELECTIONS TO HOUSE OF REPRESENTATIVES[11]
(1946–1969)

	April 10, 1946	April 25, 1947	January 23, 1949	October 1, 1952	April 19, 1953	February 27, 1955	May 22, 1958	November 20, 1960	November 21, 1963	January 29, 1967	December 27, 1969
Liberals	139	132	264	238	202	112					
Hatoyama splinter					35						
Democrats						185 [a]					
Progressives	93	126	68	88	77						
Liberal Democrats							287 [b]	296	283	277	288
Socialists	92	143	49				166 [c]	145	144	140	90
Left-wing				56	72	89					
Right-wing				60	66	67					
Democratic Socialists								17	23	30	32
Communists	5	4	35	0	1	2	1	3	5	5	14
Kōmeitō										25	47
Others	135	61	51	25	14	12	13	5	12	9 [d]	15 [e]

[a] On November 24, 1954, Hatoyama formed the Democratic party which absorbed the Progressives.
[b] On November 15, 1955, all of the conservatives united to form the Liberal Democratic party.
[c] On October 13, 1955, the right- and left-wing Socialists united. In 1958 members of the former right wing split to form the Democratic Socialist party.
[d] Total seats in the House of Representatives increased in 1967 from 467 to 486.
[e] Includes 12 Liberal Democrats not officially sponsored by the party at the time of the election.

Japanese Communist party. It had an estimated membership of less than 100,000 yet it exerted an influence out of all proportion to its size. It kept the political and labor fronts in a state of continued agitation. In the election in January, 1949, it reached the zenith of its strength. It received 10 per cent of the total votes and sent 35 members to the House of Representatives. (See Table 11.)

The communists were faced, however, with a labor movement in which they were losing control. The National Congress of Industrial Unions had been dominated by left-wing elements but the collapse of the general strike in 1947 had been to the detriment of the radical leadership. The central government's direct interest in labor, with the SCAP's encouragement, blunted the communist labor offensive. New labor standards were adopted, which conformed to those set by the International Labor Office. A Labor Ministry was formed, and communist control was gradually eliminated from the most powerful executive bodies of the trade unions. In a few years, the Japanese Communist party also found itself suddenly attacked by its comrades abroad. Both the Soviet Union and the Chinese People's Republic criticized its revisionism.

Finally, with the United States convinced that communism was monolithic and hence should be contained wherever it appeared, SCAP moved to discredit the Japanese Communist party. In May, 1950, General MacArthur ordered the Japanese government to ban the twenty-four members of the Central Committee of the Communist party, and the seventeen leaders of the Communist daily newspaper, *Red Flag* (*Akahata*), from engaging in political activity, writing, speaking publicly, or working for the government. Rather than run the risk of arrest, the leaders of the party went underground. Although they were thus eliminated from the political scene, Marxist dogma and communist theory continued to have a strong appeal to the intellectuals.[12]

Premier Yoshida was firmly in control of the domestic political scene. He welcomed the new interest which the United States and SCAP were taking in the rehabilitation of Japan as a bulwark against communism in the western Pacific. He was sufficiently shrewd as a politician and experienced as a diplomat to appreciate that this new policy was a direct outcome of the rising tide of communism in Asia.

Police and Educational Reform and War Crimes Trials

The police in prewar Japan had formed a single force under the Home Minister and had stringently enforced controls over all aspects of Japanese life. During the first year of the occupation, therefore, SCAP had urged the decentralization of the police system and the abolition of the Home Ministry. By December, 1947, a new Police Law had been adopted which created local, municipal police forces and a national, rural police with limited powers. But this new decentralized system was never generally accepted, and the government constantly sought excuses to revert to the old system of a single national police force. However, there was strong opposition against giving the police too much power so that it was not until 1954 that the Diet authorized marked increases in their authority.

Since the prewar educational system had been consciously designed to produce persons who would willingly serve the state, it had contributed directly to the growth of ultrapatriotism and militant nationalism. If the objectives of the Allies, to foster individualism and abolish militarism, were to be achieved, therefore, basic reforms in education also were required and a radically different educational philosophy would have to be adopted. Shortly after surrender, schools were opened but military education and courses in ethics were stricken from the curriculum. Teachers with records as ultranationalists were removed from office. Revisions were begun on textbooks in history and geography. On January 1, 1946, the Emperor issued a rescript in which he denied his divinity and the superiority of the Japanese people.

In the spring of 1947, after prodding from SCAP, new education laws were passed by the Diet. They provided for individual initiative and inquiry, academic freedom, and equal educational opportunities. Administratively, schools were to be controlled by local elective school boards responsible to the local community. Despite this new approach, almost insuperable obstacles prevented a sudden change in the operation of the new educational system. Funds were not available to repair the large number of school buildings made unusuable by the war. There was a dearth of adequately trained teachers for the schools and especially for the newly created universities in each of the prefectures. Finally, the reforms initiated by the occupation authorities were not acceptable to the bureaucracy in the Ministry of Education. Hence, with the emergence of a nascent nationalism after the peace treaty, the natural tendency was to revert to a prewar pattern of centralized control over education.[13]

Another provision of the Potsdam Declaration designed to reduce Japan's future war potential called for the trial of war criminals. The war crimes trials were conceived in the belief that militarism and aggression could be discredited and discouraged by the punishment of those who committed war crimes. Military tribunals were held in those areas where persons had been victimized by Japanese military personnel. Furthermore, the International Military Tribunal for the Far East was formed to try those Japanese leaders who were accused of committing "crimes against peace, . . . conventional war crimes . . . and [crimes]

East–West

NEW EDUCATION AND OLD METHODS OF CALCULATION

against humanity." Composed of representatives from the eleven leading Allied Powers, the Tribunal began its deliberations in Tokyo in May, 1946. Twenty-eight persons were declared to be major war criminals. They included such prominent wartime leaders as former Lord Keeper of the Privy Seal Kido Kōichi; former Prime Ministers Tōjō, Koiso, and Hirota; militarists such as Araki, Itagaki, Doihara, and Hashimoto; and the ultranationalist and former Foreign Minister Matsuoka. In November, 1948, the Tribunal found all of the accused guilty of planning to secure Japan's domination over Asia by waging a war of aggression. Seven were condemned to death, sixteen to life imprisonment, one to twenty years, and one to seven years imprisonment.[14]

The International Tribunal for the Far East failed to accomplish its objective, in the sense that its activities and decisions failed to impress most Japanese. They had assumed from the start that the accused would be found guilty and would be condemned to death. They failed to understand or appreciate such concepts as due process, the right of the accused to have counsel and to be heard, and a person's innocence until proven guilty.

Economic Reform and Rehabilitation

Despite the main emphasis of SCAP during the first two or three years of the occupation on political and social reforms, economic problems were becoming increasingly acute and could not be ignored without threatening all aspects of Japanese life under the occupation. The period immediately following Japan's surrender had been one of acute scarcity. Such essentials as food, shelter, and clothing were in short supply and continued to be rationed. The whole economy was in such a state of collapse that industrial recovery was negligible. The average per-capita caloric intake for 1946 was estimated at 1,530 calories, well below the average for the war years. The quantity of rice collected for distribution for rationing had fallen by 50 per cent.

While General MacArthur was prohibited from actively rehabilitating the national economy, his Directive permitted him to take necessary action to prevent widespread disease and unrest which would endanger the occupying forces. Believing the situation to be critical, he ordered the Japanese government to improve its methods of food collection and distribution, and simultaneously forwarded to Washington specific requests for food imports.

Because of the worldwide shortage in grains, strict rationing was still practiced by many of the United Nations. Widespread starvation and undernourishment were prevalent in China, Southeast Asia, and India. MacArthur's request for food for Japan, a former enemy country, was bitterly criticized by members of the Far Eastern Commission representing those areas. But the first foods imported from the United States were released in April, 1946; their distribution during the next few months amounted to as much as one-fourth of the monthly rationed requirements.

The food shortage was only one aspect of the postwar economic stagnation and retrogression. Inflation was reaching dangerous proportions. The index figure for the cost of living for the average Tokyo wage earner had increased more than ten times from August, 1945, to January, 1946. Within the same period, the note issue had doubled and prices had risen to nearly three times their previous level. To meet this financial crisis, SCAP ordered the conversion of the currency, the freezing of bank deposits, and the elimination of war profits and indemnities. The results were immediate but not lasting. New inflationary trends appeared.

Perhaps the most immediate and basic economic reform advocated by SCAP was land reform. Too many people had been trying to eke out an existence for too long a time on too small amounts of land. Furthermore, the population continued to increase at a high rate and a small minority owned a disproportionately large amount of land. Nearly three-fourths of the farm population was dependent partially or wholly on rented land. They paid rents equal to half or more of their crops.

The land reform was designed, therefore, to give those who tilled the soil a chance to own it. A detailed reform program was prepared under SCAP's direction. By October, 1946, the Yoshida Cabinet had secured the passage in the Diet of implementing legislation. Under the new laws, absentee landowners were forced to sell all but a minimum amount of their land to the government. Noncultivators who lived on their land could retain 2.5 acres. Cultivators were restricted in most cases to farms of 7.5 acres. Tenant cultivators could buy the land they worked in thirty installments at moderate interest rates. Finally, rentals were not to exceed 25 per cent of the crop and written leases were required to be given by all landowners. Land reform was completed by 1950 with impressive results. It enabled three million cultivators to acquire five million acres of land. Along with the profits made by the farmers due to the high price of rice, this reform enabled them to eliminate their heavy rural indebtedness. Despite the objections from former landlords, the land reform program was too successful to be rescinded and greatly strengthened the stability of the rural economy.[15]

Two parallel developments, one external and the other internal, began to produce a marked change in Japan's postwar economic rehabilitation. The United States, and then other Western democracies, began to recognize that Japan, if encouraged, could become a valuable asset in the Cold War between the United States and the Soviet Union. As this antagonism increased in intensity and the Chinese communists took over more of the China mainland, Japan seemed much less of a future military threat than the communist world. Consequently, a policy of encouragement and assistance for Japan was introduced.

Both the effectiveness and urgency of such a policy was dictated by the continued deterioration of economic conditions. By July, 1947, expenditures of an average Tokyo family, three-fourths of which were spent in the black market, were greater than income. General economic instability was further exacerbated by heavy unfavorable trade balances and a shift in the composition of exports. Silk, the largest prewar export item, had been replaced by nylon. The inflation spiral continued and wages failed to keep up with it. Prior to December, 1948, no Japanese Cabinet, whether through unwillingness or inability, had undertaken a comprehensive program to achieve economic stability or maximize production. At that point SCAP ordered drastic steps to balance the budget, control prices and wages, and reform the tax structure. A new rate of exchange was established of 360 yen to the dollar. If Japan could find markets in the developing nations for its capital goods, as recommended by the Economic Commission for Asia and the Far East (ECAFE), its import surplus could be curtailed. In the interim, direct American aid continued to pour into Japan. By July, 1950, it had reached a total of $1.7 billion.[16]

One of the best illustrations of the shift or "reverse course" in American policy toward Japan is the treatment of the *zaibatsu* or family combines. The initial basic policy had called for the dissolution of the large banking and industrial combines as part of the demilitarization and democratization of Japan. In fact, in a report of an official American mission to Japan, the *zaibatsu* were described as "the greatest war potential in Japan. It was they who made possible all of Japan's conquests and aggressions." [17] Consequently, plans were developed for the deconcentration of economic power, and the dissolution of the five leading firms and their subsidiaries was begun.

But this whole policy toward the *zaibatsu* was being sharply criticized by American business circles. They argued that it was far better for the United States and Japan to permit the latter's economy to develop along traditional lines. This criticism coincided with the new proposals within the American government that Japan should be strengthened economically. The United States decided not to press for deconcentration of economic power. Although the Diet had passed a law to dissolve the huge corporations, the Cabinet, relieved of pressure from SCAP, permitted the law to lapse. The Japanese industrial firms rapidly reverted to prewar forms and industrial activity accelerated.

At almost the same time, attitudes were shifting on the matter of reparations. At Potsdam, the Allies had declared that postwar Japanese industries should be such as "to permit the exaction of just reparations in kind." Furthermore, those countries which had suffered most from Japanese invasion, such as China and the Philippines, demanded heavy reparations payments to them. The issue was argued long and hard in the Far Eastern Commission. As a result, in April, 1947, SCAP was authorized to make available as interim reparations 30 per cent of the surplus industrial capacity above the 1930–1934 average production level in certain specified industries. Though some transfers on this interim program began in 1948, the next year the United States insisted that the real problem was one of reviving Japan's peaceful industries.

By the outbreak of the Korean War in June, 1950, the program of encouragement of economic rehabilitation had produced encouraging results in Japan. It was to receive even more impetus from the war. The national budget had been kept in balance, the rate of notes issued by the Bank of Japan had greatly diminished. The manufacturing wage index had risen over 50 per cent. For the three years 1950–1952 the excess of receipts over payments in foreign exchange totaled nearly a billion dollars. Mining and manufacturing production indexes had risen from 100 in 1950 to 146.5 in 1952.[18]

Attempts at a Peace Treaty and the Korean War

Nothing signaled more dramatically the change in Allied policy toward Japan than the shifts in policies of the United States toward a peace treaty. By the spring of 1947 a draft of a peace treaty had been prepared by the Department of State. This draft was then shown to General MacArthur for his comments. Shortly thereafter, on March 19, 1947, he made an impromptu statement on the importance of an early peace treaty. He described the occupation as falling into three phases—military, political, and economic. He believed that necessary precautions had already been taken to ensure that Japan would not again menace world peace and that the military phase was over. The framework for political reconstruction had also been established. It was necessary only to watch and control. Finally, the main feature of the economic phase, a blockade, could be ended by signing a peace treaty and by the commencement of normal trade relations. He concluded that the treaty should place Japan under the general supervision of the United Nations for purposes of protective control.[19] In April, 1947, General MacArthur elaborated further on his desire for an early treaty. He was convinced that it would facilitate the settlement of differences in Europe over the German and Austrian treaties. He recommended that a conference be held that summer in Tokyo; six months after the treaty was signed, the occupation forces should begin an orderly withdrawal. The treaty should ensure peace;

it should not be punitive like the Versailles Treaty, which only produced another war within twenty-five years. The United States should persuade the other Allies of the advisability of this course of action and, if necessary, should sign a treaty without the Soviet Union. When General MacArthur's recommendations were conveyed to Secretary of State George Marshall, the latter agreed that a Japanese peace conference should be called in July, 1947.[20]

The United States invited the members of the Far Eastern Commission to a conference in August. To avoid the interminable wranglings on purely procedural problems which had characterized the meetings of the Council of Foreign Ministers, the United States proposed that a conference of deputies tackle problems of substance for the Japanese treaty. It also recommended that voting in such a conference be by a two-thirds majority; membership should be restricted to the states represented on the Far Eastern Commission. The reply from the Soviet Union to the American invitation concentrated on procedural questions. It accused the United States of unilateral action. It insisted that China, Great Britain, Russia, and the United States should first decide the treaty questions. The issue was further complicated by a Chinese proposal for a compromise voting procedure. During the next six months, the four powers failed to resolve their differences. Consequently the United States concluded that it was inadvisable to press the matter further at that time.

On the other hand, this failure to obtain agreement for an early peace conference highlighted the American conviction that positive steps should be taken to show Japan that it was considered as one of the free nations. In November 1948, the National Security Council adopted a general policy that Japan should be strengthened economically and politically to increase its stability and the chances of its opting for friendship with the United States. This new attitude toward Japan manifested itself in the new approaches to the Allies on a peace treaty. In the fall of 1949, Great Britain and the United States agreed that a liberal, nonpunitive treaty was essential to keep Japan on the side of the Western democracies. Furthermore, they indicated that American security arrangements against the USSR might best be developed through Japan permitting post-treaty American bases on its territory in exchange for American protection.[21]

The importance of Japan to the United States as a bastion against communism was underscored, of course, by the victories of the communists on the Chinese mainland, Chiang Kai-shek's flight to Formosa, and the growing military strength of the Korea People's Republic. To allay any fears that continued efforts for a peace treaty might mean withdrawal of American forces from Japan, Secretary of State Dean Acheson clarified the situation. In a statement in January, 1950, he placed Japan and Okinawa within the American defense perimeter in the western Pacific in which he promised that the United States would continue to maintain strong defensive forces. Shortly thereafter, the Sino-Soviet Treaty of Friendship, another important example of the growth of communism in East Asia, was signed. Its stated purpose was to prevent the rebirth of Japanese imperialism and acts of aggression by Japan or by any other state which would unite with it. The signatories also promised to strive for an early peace with Japan, which indicated clearly that Russia expected the Chinese People's Republic to be one of the signatories of the peace treaty.

On June 25, 1950, the North Korean Army suddenly thrust across the thirty-eighth parallel into South Korea. President Truman acted immediately to check this invasion which threatened the Republic of Korea, Japan, and the chief bastions of the American defense perimeter in the western Pacific. He placed the problem before the Security Council of the United Nations which demanded that the North Korean forces withdraw behind the thirty-eighth parallel and cease hostilities. President Truman requested General MacArthur to send aid to the Republic of Korea. Shortly thereafter the latter was appointed United Nations Commander.[22]

As General MacArthur became increasingly absorbed with the problem of checking the southern advance of the Korean communists, his interest in the business of the occupation of Japan decreased. Prime Minister Yoshida assumed greater responsibility for the operation of the government. Yet his position and that of his country was an anomalous one. Japan was still under occupation and was expected to accept without protest any demands which the Korean War might make upon it. At the same time, many Japanese considered the Korean War none of their concern and failed to accept the premise that a communist victory would be a threat to their own freedom and security. It seemed clear that Japan would take little responsibility for its security until it became independent and the occupation ceased.

Renewed Treaty Negotiations

During the first year of the Korean War, the United States pressed for a peace treaty with Japan. In mid-September, 1950, President Truman announced that he had appointed John Foster Dulles to begin negotiations with the Allies for a treaty. Mr. Dulles approached the problem from wide experience and with imagination. He started with three premises. The first premise was that it was to the military and political advantage of the Western democracies not to let Japan fall within the

Soviet orbit. Secondly, Japan could not be coerced to join the free-world orbit but would doubtless prefer to be an integral part of it rather than part of the communist world. Finally, it would be unrealistic to impose any military restrictions on Japan and a liberal attitude was called for. On the matter of procedure, Dulles carried on a series of preliminary bilateral negotiations with representatives of the members of the Far Eastern Commission. He also made several visits to Japan to conduct such discussions and negotiations as were necessary. It was suggested that the signatories should include all the countries at war with Japan who were willing to sign the treaty. If the Soviet Union was willing to sign the treaty, it should be permitted to do so.[23]

As for the territorial clauses, the American proposal noted that the terms of the Cairo and Potsdam Declarations had largely been carried out but that certain specific settlements must be clarified. In regard to the Ryūkyū Islands, the United States was prepared to assume a trusteeship over them at the appropriate time. In reference to the final disposition of Formosa and southern Sakhalin (Karafuto), it was recommended that the matter be settled by the four powers (Great Britain, Republic of China, Soviet Union, and the United States). On the all-important question of Japan's future security, it was proposed that Japan and the United States should continue a cooperative responsibility until the United Nations could assume it. Japan's commercial interests should be protected by a series of multilateral treaties until such time as new commercial arrangements could be made. Finally, the Allies should, in lieu of reparations, confiscate Japanese property within their own territory and their property in Japan should be restored to its rightful owners.

Bilateral negotiations were immediately begun on the basis of these principles. The territorial proposals concerning the Ryūkyū Islands were challenged by the Soviet Union, Communist China, the Chinese Nationalist government, and the Commonwealth nations. Furthermore, Australia, the Philippines, and the Soviet Union led the opposition to the proposal that no restrictions be placed on Japan's future rearmament.

In an *aide-mémoire,* the Soviet Union insisted that the treaty must first be approved by the four chief Allied Powers. Furthermore, China should be represented by the Chinese People's Republic, not by the government of Generalissimo Chiang Kai-shek. The Soviet Union also objected to the suggestion of the United States for a trusteeship for the Ryūkyū Islands. Furthermore, it indicated that continued controls were necessary both to prevent the future rearmament of Japan and to regulate its economy. A few days later, these views were parrotted by the Chinese Communist government. The American reply to the Soviet Union refused to concede, however, that "any single nation had the perpetual power to veto the conclusion by others of a peace with Japan."

It also rejected the suggestion that the Chinese Communists be included in the negotiations.

Dismissal of General MacArthur

In the spring of 1951 the military situation in Korea had a direct, if unexpected, effect on Japan. On April 3, 1951, the Chinese and Korean communist armies had been pushed back by the United Nations forces across the thirty-eighth parallel for the second time since the war began. This development set off a bitter debate on future policy for Korea both within the United States government and between the United States and other members of the United Nations participating in the war in Korea. One alternative, which was vigorously advocated by General MacArthur, argued that military necessity required an immediate push northward to roll the communists back across the Yalu River into Manchuria. The enemy should not have sanctuary in Manchuria so its supply bases and airfields should be subject to air attack and naval bombardment. It was assumed such attacks could be carried out without involving the United Nations in war with China.

The second alternative, which had widespread support from the United Nations and was official United States policy, was to hold the military line around the thirty-eighth parallel, refrain from bombing enemy territory outside of Korea, and negotiate for an armistice and peace. It was contended that to do otherwise would mean a war with China in which a decisive victory would be extremely difficult, if not impossible. In order to prevent further aggravation of the situation and to avoid greater international complications, President Truman advised General MacArthur to refrain from making public announcements on questions of policy unless they were first cleared in Washington. Nevertheless, on March 25, 1951, he announced on his own responsibility that "expansion of military operations to (the) coastal areas and interior bases would doom Red China to military collapse." President Truman decided that General MacArthur was no longer able "to give wholehearted support to the policies of the United States government and the United Nations." Consequently, on April 10, 1951, he ordered him relieved of his commands in the Far East. Lieutenant General Matthew B. Ridgway was appointed as his successor.[24]

The Japanese could not believe that the reports were true. They had come to consider General MacArthur as invincible. They had thought of him as the final authority on all things, whether these concerned the occupation of Japan or the war in Korea. Some saw in his dismissal a vivid illustration of the principle that in the United States the civil arm of the government was always stronger than the military. Others feared that his removal might signify a basic change and hardening in American policy, and more restricting proposals for the peace treaty. But their fears were allayed by Dulles being sent to Japan again to discuss further with the Japanese government a security arrangement whereby United States armed forces would remain in and near Japan on a provisional basis and the United States would continue to maintain a base on Okinawa.

Final Treaty Negotiations

After Dulles' return from Tokyo, a draft of a treaty was prepared and circulated to the fifteen governments already consulted. But there were still many disagreements among the nations concerned. The Soviet representative at the United Nations refused to discuss the matter with Dulles. The British regarded Formosa as an integral part of China; they favored including the Chinese People's Republic in the negotiations and advocated certain economic restrictions and controls. Several of the Allies in the Pacific rejected the concept of a Pacific Mutual Security Pact as the best safeguard against a resurgence of Japanese aggression. To solve the security problem Dulles suggested three separate parts: (1) a bilateral arrangement between the United States and Japan, (2) a triangular security pact among the United States, Australia, and New Zealand, and (3) a separate United States–Philippine agreement.

By July, 1951, most of the other objections, except those of the communist nations, had been ironed out, so the United Kingdom and the United States sent a joint invitation to fifty-five of the Allied Powers at war with Japan to attend a peace conference to be called at San Francisco on September 4, 1951. The invitation enclosed a draft of a peace treaty with Japan, with accompanying declarations and a protocol. It was explained orally to the recipients of the invitations that preparatory negotiations had been carried on for the past ten months among the powers principally concerned. Accordingly, the conference at San Francisco was for the purpose of signing the final text of the treaty. Changes were not expected to be considered at the Conference. Opportunity would be given to the participating governments, however, to make such statements as they considered necessary. Of the fifty-five governments invited to the conference, only three failed to accept the invitation.[25]

The Treaty of Peace With Japan

On September 4, 1951, at the opening ceremony of the Peace Conference at San Francisco, President Truman briefly outlined some of the accomplishments of the occupation of Japan. He then described the treaty as one which would work because it did not contain the seeds of another war but looked to the future. He also noted that as part of the development of regional arrangements for the defense of the Pacific, the United States had recently signed a Treaty of Mutual Defense with the Republic of the Philippines in which the two nations promised to come to each other's defense if attacked. Furthermore, a similar treaty had been signed by Australia, New Zealand, and the United States. He concluded that, in view of Japan's unarmed condition and of a request which it had made to the United States, those two countries would also enter into an agreement concerning Japan's security.

The proceedings of the conference were interrupted by the demand of the Soviet Delegate, A. A. Gromyko, that the Chinese People's Republic be invited to the conference. He maintained that the proposed draft treaty could not, in any measure, serve the purpose of a peace settlement with Japan or give any guarantees against the recurrence of Japanese aggression in the future. He claimed that the territorial provisions flagrantly violated the rights of both Communist China and the Soviet Union and that the economic clauses were designed to ensure foreign privileges which had been obtained during the occupation. As was expected, the Soviet bloc refused to sign the treaty.

The Treaty of Peace with Japan was signed on September 8, 1951, by forty-eight Allied nations and Japan. By its Preamble, Japan declared its intention to apply for membership in the United Nations, to conform to the principles of the Charter, and to adhere to the ideals of human rights and freedoms in its new Constitution. The Treaty ended the state of war with Japan and recognized the sovereignty of the Japanese people. Japan formally ratified the territorial clauses of the Potsdam Declaration. It recognized the independence of Korea; it renounced all rights, title, and claims to Formosa and the Pescadores, to the Kurile Islands, to Southern Sakhalin, and to the Mandated Islands in the Pacific. Finally, Japan promised to concur in an American proposal to place the Ryūkyū, Bōnin, and Volcano Islands under a United Nations trusteeship.

Another important section of the Treaty concerned problems connected with Japan's future security, including the termination of the occupation (Articles 5 and 6). While Japan accepted the obligations of the Charter of the United Nations to settle international disputes by peaceful means and to refrain from the threat or use of force, the Allied Powers recognized Japan's right of self-defense as a nation. The occupation forces were to be withdrawn within ninety days after the Treaty came into force. To avoid the creation of a military vacuum when the Treaty became effective, however, it was provided that foreign armed forces might be stationed or retained in Japanese territory under provisions of special international agreements.

In the political and economic clauses (Articles 7–13), Japan was not subjected to permanent disabilities, and no limitations were placed on its economy and trade. Pending the conclusions of treaties between Japan and the Allied Powers on commercial relations, on pelagic fishing, and on international air transport, each Allied Power would be entitled to most-favored-nation treatment on customs duties. The controversial reparation issue was dealt with in two stages. In the first place, the Treaty recognized the principle that Japan should pay reparations to the Allied Powers for damage and suffering caused by it during the war. On the other hand, the Powers recognized that, from a realistic point of view, Japan could not possibly pay the billions of dollars in damages. But the countries occupied by Japanese during the war still insisted on reparations payments. Consequently, certain Japanese surplus assets, such as excess of skilled workers and of industrial capacity, were made available in lieu of these payments. If these countries desired it, they could negotiate arrangements whereby Japan would process raw materials for them or supply them with expert technical assistance. By these clauses, countries such as the Philippines and Indonesia would be able to obtain reparations and at the same time speed their rehabilitation. The remaining clauses of the Treaty concerned claims, property, the settlement of disputes, and final clauses.

On the day the Peace Treaty with Japan was signed, the United States had taken advantage of the security clauses in the Treaty which provided that special bilateral agreements could be made for the continuance of foreign armed forces in Japan. The two nations had signed a separate United States–Japan Security Treaty. It gave the United States the right to station its land, sea, and air forces in and near Japan for the maintenance of the peace and security of the Far East and of Japan against external attack and large-scale internal disturbance instigated by an outside power. These special arrangements went into effect simultaneously with the Peace Treaty. The implementation of the Security Treaty was elaborated in an Administrative Agreement of February 28, 1952.

Technically the occupation was over and Japan had attained its autonomy and independence. In reality, because of its inability to provide for its own security, Japan continued to be dependent on the United States. The position of the Supreme Commander for the Allied Powers was dissolved and the occupation forces were changed to security forces, but from outward appearances there seemed to be no real change in the harsh fact that foreign armed forces remained in Japan under a foreign commander and they and their dependents enjoyed extraterritorial privileges. Consequently, as the months and years passed, the greatest strains on American–Japanese relations came from these special arrangements and the Security Treaties that followed. These strains increased as pressures arose within Japan for complete independence.

Notes

1. For a more detailed presentation of this subject, as well as other aspects of the first two years of the occupation, see Hugh Borton, "The Allied Occupation of Japan, 1945–47," in F. C. Jones, Hugh Borton, and B. R. Pearn, *The Far East, 1942–1946* (London: Oxford University Press, 1955), pp. 307–428. For two contrasting views on the degree of success of the occupation see Herbert Passin, *The Legacy of the Occupation* (New York: East Asian Institute, Columbia University, 1968), and Robert E. Ward, "Reflections on the Allied Occupation and Planned Political Change in Japan," in Robert E. Ward (ed.), *Political Development in Modern Japan* (Princeton: Princeton University Press, 1968), pp. 477–537.

2. This lack of directives on some of the vital issues is only one of the many problems which baffles the historian of the occupation of Japan. In view of SCAP's supreme authority and of the assumption by the Japanese government officials that even the lowest SCAP officer could veto an action taken by them, SCAP control was greater than appears on the record. Note, also, that SCAP henceforth came to be used to designate both General MacArthur as Supreme Commander and his headquarters. I have referred personally to General MacArthur in the text in those instances in which he was directly involved. For texts of most of the directives as well as a detailed and remarkably objective account of the occupation see SCAP, Government Section, *Political Reorientation of Japan, September 1945 to September 1948* (2 vols.; Washington: Government Printing Office, 1949.)

3. It was not simply fortuitous that the draft constitution as finally approved by General MacArthur contained the principles for a new constitution already adopted by the United States government as SWNCC 228, "The Reform of the Japanese Governmental System." The Joint Chiefs of Staff had already transmitted this document to him before work had begun in SCAP on constitutional reform. The principle of renouncing war was not in the SWNCC document and originated in Japan. It is difficult to determine the source of this idea. Professor Takayanagi, Chairman of the Commission on the Constitution, is convinced that the idea was first suggested to General MacArthur by Prime Minister Shidehara when they met on January 24, 1946, after which General MacArthur prepared a first draft of what later was to become Article 9. If such were the case, one is puzzled by the fact that no trace of this idea appeared in the draft prepared by the Cabinet's Committee and presented to SCAP on February 1. Presumably Shidehara would have asked his committee to include the idea. See Kenzo Takayanagi, "Some Reminiscences of Japan's Commission on the Constitution," in Dan Fenno Henderson (ed.), *The Constitution of Japan: Its First Twenty Years 1947–67* (Seattle: University of Washington Press, 1968), pp. 86–87. This book contains much valuable material on the Constitution and its operation.

There is an extensive bibliography on the new Constitution. Others of the best works are SCAP, *Political Reorientation . . . , op. cit.;* Borton, *op. cit.*, pp. 330 ff.; Theodore McNelly, "The Japanese Constitution, Child of the Cold War," *Political Science Quarterly*, LXXIV (June, 1959), pp. 176–95; Robert E. Ward, "The Commission on the Constitution and Prospects for Constitutional Change in Japan," *Journal of Asian Studies*, XXIV (May, 1965), pp. 401–29. SWNCC 228 is published in Theodore McNelly (ed.), *Sources in Modern East Asian History and Politics* (New York: Appleton-Century-Crofts, Inc., 1967), pp. 177–87. The best work in Japanese is Satō Tatsuo, *Nihon Koku Kempō Seiritsu Shi* (2 vols.; Tokyo: Yuhi Kaku, 1962–1964).

4. The initial members of the Far Eastern Commission were Australia, Canada, China, France, India, the Netherlands, New Zealand, the Philippines, the Soviet Union, the United Kingdom, and the United States. Burma and Pakistan joined after 1949. The Allied Council for Japan was limited to four members: China, the Soviet Union, the United States, and a member who represented the United Kingdom, Australia, New Zealand, and India. It had no power of control over, nor could it interfere with, SCAP's execution of policy. General MacArthur made its fortnightly meetings as perfunctory as possible. The Soviet delegate, Lieutenant General Derevyenko used the metings for propaganda purposes to embarrass SCAP. The Commonwealth member, Macmahon Ball, interpreted the Council's functions as being the eyes and ears of the Far Eastern Commission. For the latter's views see his *Japan, Enemy or Ally* (New York: John Day Co., 1949).

5. As the United States Representative on the Committee on Constitutional and Legal Reform, the writer well recalls the bitter attacks directed against SCAP's action. The atmosphere was charged with ill will because most of the representatives on that Committee had gone to Tokyo with the Advisory Commission. Prior to their return in January, 1946, they had been told by General Whitney that the problem of constitutional reform was a matter for the Japanese to consider and that no work was being undertaken by SCAP. Their charge that they had purposely been kept ignorant of what was transpiring was made all the more difficult to refute in view of the fact that the United States government had not been kept informed of the activities of the Government Section in February and March, 1946. There were no copies of the new draft Constitution available in Washington when it was published in Tokyo. For the text of the Commission's decisions of March 20, 1946, on the Constitution, see Far Eastern Commission, *Activities of the Far Eastern Commission's Report by the Secretary General, February 26, 1946—July 10, 1947* (Washington: Government Printing Office, 1947), Appendix 8, p. 63.

6. Nozaka had directed communist activities in Japan from Moscow from 1930 to 1940. During the war he had been with the communists in China. Other important communist leaders elected to Parliament in April, 1946, were: Tokuda Kyūichi, Secretary General of the party, and Shiga Yoshio, editor of the Communist daily, *Akahata*, and chief party theorist. For biographical details and an excellent, scholarly account of the communists in Japan, see Roger Swearinger and Paul Langer, *Red Flag in Japan: International Communism in Action, 1919–1951* (Cambridge: Harvard University Press, 1952); Robert A. Scalapino, *The Japanese Communist Movement 1920–1966* (Berkeley: University of California Press, 1967); and George M. Beckmann and Okubo Genji, *The Japanese Communist Party, 1922–1945* (Stanford: Stanford University Press, 1969).

7. The Progressive party had all but 27 of its 274 members purged. The Liberals lost 30 of their 50.

8. Before the war, Yoshida Shigeru (1878–1967) had been a career diplomat. His highest post was Ambassador to London. He was arrested in 1944 on orders from the War Minister during a roundup of those opposing continuation of the war. His first Cabinet was installed on May 22, 1946, with five Liberals and four Progressives. During the next eight years, he was Premier five times and for a total of nearly seven years. He was nominated Premier in April, 1946, by default. After the elections in April, 1946, the President of the Liberal party, Hatoyama Ichirō, was confident that he could form a Cabinet. His hopes were dashed when the press revealed that he had failed to include some damaging evidence in his purge questionnaire and SCAP found him ineligible for office. It is claimed that Yoshida, when he succeeded to the head of the party, promised Hatoyama the Presidency when his purge charges were cleared. When Yoshida failed to fulfill his promise in 1954, Hatoyama bolted the party and became the next Premier.

9. As mentioned above (note 3), SWNCC 228, "The Reforms of the Japanese Governmental System," was used as a guide by SCAP's Government Section in drafting the new Constitution. Likewise, it formed the basis of the Far Eastern Commission's "Basic Principle for the New Constitution" reducing to a minimum differences among the Commission, SCAP, and the Japanese Diet on the content of the Constitution. A more detailed account of the steps leading to the adoption of the Constitution is contained in Borton, *op. cit.*, pp. 348 ff. For the various stages of SWNCC 228, which the author drafted and later defended in the Far Eastern Commission, see Hugh Borton, "Preparation for the Occupation of Japan," *Journal of Asian Studies,* XXV (February, 1966), pp. 206 ff.

10. The overzealous SCAP officials who sponsored such an extensive purge failed to realize the transitory character of their efforts. Furthermore, strong jealousies existed between some of the sections of SCAP. When the Government Section started a comprehensive purge program, this action stimulated the Economic Section to do likewise. The total number of persons screened under the purges exceeded 700,000. Of these, about 115,000 military personnel and 87,000 civilians were purged. See Borton, "The Allied Occupation . . . ," *op. cit.*, p. 360.

11. See Borton, *ibid.*, pp. 336 and 369, and Hugh Borton, *et al., Japan Between East and West* (New York: Council on Foreign Relations, 1957), p. 11, and *Japan Report, 1955–1967*.

12. See Scalapino, *op. cit.*, especially chap. 2. For the role of the Communists in the labor movement see Swearinger and Langer, *op. cit.;* for the labor movement as a whole see Iwao Ayusawa, *A History of Labor in Modern Japan* (Honolulu: East–West Center, 1963).

13. Robert King Hall, *Education for a New Japan* (New Haven: Yale University Press, 1948).

14. Those sentenced to death were Doihara Kenji, Chief of the Kwantung Army Secret Service; Hirota Kōki, Premier and Foreign Minister; Itagaki Seishirō, Kwantung Army Staff and War Minister (1938–1939); Kimura Keitarō, Chief of Staff of Kwantung Army and Commander of Burmese Expeditionary Force; Matsui Iwane, Commander of Japanese Forces in China during the rape of Nanking; Muto Akira, Army Commander; and Tōjō Hideki, War Minister and wartime Prime Minister. During the trial two of the accused died and one went insane. The records of the trial are valuable

not only as a legal record but also as descriptive material of events in Japan from 1931 to the time of surrender.

15. The reader should not be shocked by the minimum acreage allowed an owner. An average farm equaled about 2.5 acres. For a concise account of the land reform program by one of its chief authors see W. J. Ladejinsky, "Agriculture," in Hugh Borton (ed.), *Japan* (Ithaca: Cornell University Press, 1952), pp. 46–64.

16. See Economic Commission for Asia and the Far East, Committee on Industry and Trade, *Problems and Prospects of Accelerated Economic Development in the ECAFE Region through Increased Trade with Japan* (Bangkok: ECAFE, May 9, 1950), E/CN; II/I & T/21, especially pp. 1, 2, 9, 12, and 14.

17. Edwin W. Pauley, *Report on Japanese Reparations to the President of the United States, November, 1945 to April, 1946* (Washington: Government Printing Office, 1946), p. 39.

18. Jerome B. Cohen, *Japan's Postwar Economy* (Bloomington: University of Indiana Press, 1958), pp. 100–1.

19. MacArthur's announcement about the need for an early treaty was directly connected with his having seen the draft prepared in the State Department. The author, who had been chairman of the State Department Committee to prepare such a draft, went to Tokyo on March 8, 1947, explicitly to obtain General MacArthur's views concerning the timing and contents of a treaty. General MacArthur was shown a copy of the treaty and subsequently thereto made his statement about an early treaty. As the statement was an impromptu one, there is no official text of it but the best source is SCAP, *Political Reorientation . . . , op. cit.*, II, pp. 765–66.

20. MacArthur's ideas on a treaty were conveyed personally to the author. His concept of a nonpunitive treaty, which John Foster Dulles championed after his appointment in 1950 as a special ambassador to negotiate a treaty, was counter to thinking about the treaty in 1947. The previous year, Secretary of State Byrnes had proposed to the Council of Foreign Ministers a twenty-five-year four-power disarmament and demilitarization treaty for Japan. This "control concept" was generally accepted as the best way to assure continued peace and was included in a modified form in the draft shown to General MacArthur.

Professor Dunn's study of the peacemaking is the best account on the whole subject and is highly recommended for those wanting further details. See Frederick S. Dunn, *Peace Making and the Settlement with Japan* (Princeton: Princeton University Press, 1963), pp. 53–77; Borton, "The Allied Occupation . . . ," *op. cit.*, pp. 421 ff.; and Bernard C. Cohen, *The Political Process and Foreign Policy: The Making of the Japanese Peace Settlement* (Princeton: Princeton University Press, 1957).

21. Dunn, *op. cit.*, pp. 77 ff.

22. President Truman sent this order on June 27, 1950, the same day that the Security Council took action. He also sent the U.S. Seventh Fleet to patrol the Formosa Straits to protect it from attack by Communist China and to prevent the Nationalists from attacking the mainland. Seoul fell before the Communists on June 29, and the next day United States ground forces entered the war. At the request of the Security Council, on July 7, 1950, President Truman appointed General MacArthur as United Nations Commander. The action of the Security Council was not vetoed by the Soviet

Union because its representative had not returned to the Council meetings since the walkout at the beginning of the year in protest to the refusal to admit Communist China.

23. This method of approach avoided another stalemate similar to that of 1947. The refusal of one of the major powers to agree to attend a conference could not prevent bilateral discussions with other powers. The new method also left open the question of participation of the Soviet Union in the conference. It enabled the United States to inform the Soviet Union, along with the other Allies, of its proposals for a treaty. If the Soviet Union refused to discuss these proposals, it must bear the onus for not doing so. This procedure also permitted sufficient agreement among the other powers before the peace conference convened to assure their signature at the conference. Dulles was ably assisted in his negotiations and in the preparation of the treaty by John M. Allison, a career Foreign Service Officer. The latter was rewarded for these services by appointment as U.S. Ambassador to Japan in 1953.

24. The Great Debate touched off by General MacArthur's dismissal was one of the bitterest in recent times in the United States. He returned home as a conquering hero and on April 19, 1951, addressed a joint session of Congress. At that time, he modified his views by saying that he felt military necessity required, among other things, "removal of restrictions on air reconnaissance of China's coastal area of Manchuria." The Senate hearings which followed did not result in his being accused of insubordination but all but a loyal few agreed that he had disregarded orders. It was an unfortunate ending to a career which would have remained unblemished if it could have ended before the Korean War began. U.S. Senate, 82d Congress, *Military Situation in the Far East. Hearings Before the Committee on Armed Forces and the Committee on Foreign Relations*, Part V (Washington: Government Printing Office, 1951), pp. 3179–80.

25. The problem of whether Nationalist China or Communist China or both should participate in the conference was avoided by not issuing an invitation to either the Republic of China on Formosa or the Chinese People's Republic at Peking. Burma, India, and Yugoslavia were the three states which did not accept the invitation. The Soviet Union accepted even though the Chinese People's Republic was not invited.

21

Seeking Autonomy in a Divided World 1952–1960

The history of the first decade and a half of Japan's new independence is one of tremendous vitality, growth, and transformations. To those involved, even though many had lived through the prewar years of military aggression, the horrors of defeat, and the loss of Empire, the successes of the present seemed to blot out the failures of the past. At the same time, for the leftists, for an increasing number of nationalists, and for the great majority of the younger generation born since the attack on Pearl Harbor, this new independence seemed to be compromised by the continuation of the close alliance of Japan with the United States.

For the conservative Liberal Democratic party, which has been in undisputed control since the amalgamation of the conservatives in 1955, political stability under a strong central government and continued alliance with America are considered to be the essential base for the nation's continued prosperity. For the opposition parties, for the leftist-oriented labor unions, including the National Federation of Teachers, and the radical *Zengakuren* (National Federation of Student Self-Governing Associations) and its anarchistic activist factions, the termination of ties with the United States is paramount to the achievement of real peace in the future. Although these opposition groups are deeply split over ideology and tactics and have increasingly begun to fight among themselves, they all agree that obstructionism, rather than a rationally conceived opposition, is the main course open to them.

From the point of view of political forces and rivalries and international developments, the period divides itself into two distinct parts, namely, before and after the Security Treaty crisis in the summer of 1960. As the crisis year of 1970 approached, when the United States–

Japan Security Treaty could be renounced by either side, the forces for polarization in Japanese society increased in intensity.

Post-Treaty Problems

While the Treaty of Peace with Japan formally ended the occupation and recognized the sovereignty of the Japanese people, it did not solve several essential problems. For one thing, the implementation of the new United States–Japan Security Treaty created innumerable points of friction. To comply with the new conditions created by these treaties, superficial changes were made in such matters as the name of the armed forces and the location of the headquarters of the American commander. But despite the treaty, anomalies continued which made the return of independence seem illusory to many Japanese and which resulted in increased antiforeign and especially anti-American sentiment. American air and naval bases, army posts, and housing developments for dependents of American military personnel occupied prominent parts of the countryside, the seacoast, or central areas in the cities. GIs from posts in Japan or on leave from the Korean front crowded the cities and resorts and lavishly spent their accumulated pay. Military personnel and their families were not subject to Japanese police control. Naturally they continued to assume a condescending if not haughty attitude toward their hosts. *In fine,* so long as foreign troops remained on Japanese soil, the change from occupation to autonomy under the Peace Treaty seemed to be only a technical matter. The Prime Minister was accused of being more pro-American than pro-Japanese.[1]

Only three days after the change from "occupation" to "independence," the latent animosities among both labor and university-student groups against the establishment, the Yoshida government, and American armed forces erupted in Tokyo. The Japanese Communist party and its sympathizers had obtained appreciable support for their plea that the American troops should be withdrawn from Japan. They had the backing of certain labor groups and of a large segment of the intellectuals and students in the Tokyo area. They controlled the executive body of the Student Federation (*Zengakuren*). The Federation had joined with labor in a united front in opposition to the government's proposed Antisubversive Activity Bill. Consequently, when the labor unions planned a big demonstration on May Day, 1952, thousands of students obeyed the posters of the Federation and appeared at the rally.

Tensions had been mounting in Tokyo for several weeks prior to May Day. There had been frequent student strikes at Tokyo University directed by the Federation in opposition to "restrictions on academic freedom." They objected, for example, to police interference in riots

East–West

May Day Riot in the Imperial Palace Plaza, 1952

on the campus. The organizers of the May Day celebration had been refused permission to hold their rally in the plaza in front of the Imperial Palace. When some 40,000 persons gathered at the rally on the other side of Tokyo, they were in a mood for excitement. When a small group of leftists began to chant "To the Imperial Palace," they broke up the organized meetings. The crowd picked up the chant. Vanguards broke away, marched across the city, and fought with the police in front of the Imperial Palace and the Allied military headquarters. There were several casualties on both sides. As an apparent afterthought, some elements in the crowd vented their anger in a momentary antiforeign demonstration. They destroyed some of the cars parked along the streets and owned by American military personnel.[2]

All respectable elements in society decried the outburst. The *Asahi* newspaper called it regrettable and demanded the trial of the leaders for sedition. It identified them as Communists. It predicted that the incident would be used by the Cabinet as demonstrating that more stringent antisubversive legislation was necessary. Other papers recommended that the Communist party be outlawed. Premier Yoshida quickly pressed for the passage of the Antisubversive Activity Law. Despite the strong opposition of organized labor, which insisted that the loose wording of the law would endanger normal, legitimate union activities, the May Day riots had strengthened support for the Bill. Consequently, it was approved by Parliament in July, 1952. It gave the Cabinet the power to ban activities which would lead to violence. In the hands of a Cabinet which had a high regard for human freedoms, it would not necessarily mean a loss of any of these newly acquired rights. In the hands of unscrupulous persons, it might lead to the serious curtailment of the basic human rights of important groups in society.

Rearmament and Mutual Defense

On the matter of rearmament, Prime Minister Yoshida was caught on the horns of a dilemma. He had signed a Treaty of Peace; yet Japan was far from being its own master. During the occupation, the nation had been completely disarmed physically. The Article on the Renunciation of War in the Constitution had psychologically disarmed the Japanese people. They believed themselves to be free from the horrors of future wars. As world tensions again mounted and the Western democracies were lined up against the Communist world, the conviction grew within Japan that if it refrained from rearming, involvement in war could be avoided. If the American armed forces were withdrawn then Japan would no longer be a target in any future American–Soviet war. The Communists and left-wing Socialists, many Christians, students, and intellectuals vehemently opposed rearmament and advocated neutralism and peaceful coexistence with the Communist world. They feared that if new armed forces were permitted in Japan a new military leadership and a possible dictatorship would emerge. They questioned their nation's economic capability to maintain a military establishment. They resented the United States using Japan as a buffer state against the Chinese People's Republic and against the Soviet Union. They maintained that rearmament was unconstitutional. If rearmament occurred without a constitutional amendment, people would lose respect for the Constitution.

At the other extreme, the conservative Progressives criticized Prime Minister Yoshida for not openly building up an Army as rapidly as possible. Furthermore, Yoshida had been pressed by Dulles to develop a security force capable of meeting any internal threat to peace and security. His Cabinet argued that the Constitution did not have to be revised to permit the formation of a defensive military force. The former Police Reserve was changed into a National Security Force and equipped with modern military equipment. In December, 1953, when visiting Japan, Vice-President Richard M. Nixon argued that the quicker Japan rearmed the better it would be. This policy was underscored in March, 1954, by the United States and Japan signing a Mutual Defense Assistance Agreement. This Agreement provided for military assistance from the United States in the form of goods, equipment and services, and the exchange of information. It bound both parties to keep a close curb on their trade with the Chinese People's Republic. Finally it required Japan to make a contribution, consistent with its political and economic stability, to the development and maintenance of its own defensive strength and the defensive strength of the free world.[3] By this treaty, Japan became closely bound militarily to the Western democracies.

Prime Minister Yoshida's long term as Prime Minister was rapidly coming to a close. After his success in the summer of 1952 with the passage of a new Antisubversive Activity Law, he also asked Parliament to grant him broader powers over the police. The Diet then refused to pass the annual budget until he withdrew his proposals for the police reform. Shortly thereafter he lost a vote of confidence. In the elections in April, 1953, he was partially vindicated. His party won the largest number of seats and the conservatives collectively still had a clear majority. (See Table 11.) But the split in the ranks of the conservatives indicated the growing dissatisfaction with his autocratic style. He was dubbed "One-Man Yoshida." He faced another crisis following the signing of the new Defense Agreement with the United States. His friends and colleagues were accused of bribery and corruption. He lost his temper and inadvertently swore at an opposition member of Parliament.

He insisted that the unpopular law to abolish the occupation reforms of the police system and to establish a new national police force should be passed. He also staked his political future on the adoption of laws which would fulfill Japan's obligations under the Mutual Defense Pact. In June, 1954, when these bills were pending, riots broke out in the House of Representatives when the Socialist members tried to force adjournment to prevent their passage. Their tactics failed and the new laws were passed. The question of the need to amend the Constitution was now an academic one; rearmament was a reality. Furthermore, the creation of centralized controls for the police was another sign of rejection of earlier reforms.

Yoshida's final downfall came in December, 1954. While he was on a trip around the world, dissident members of his party refused to obey his orders. Hatoyama Ichirō, who had always been jealous of Yoshida's long tenure of office, was ready to bolt the party. When Yoshida returned to Japan from his world trip, Hatoyama rallied his supporters, forced Yoshida out of office in December, 1954, and was elected Prime Minister. The public career of Yoshida Shigeru, the man who had guided his country during most of the past eight years, was over.

THE CONSERVATIVES CONSOLIDATE, 1954

Yoshida's downfall and the selection of his old political rival, Hatoyama, as his successor marked the end of the rule of Japan's most powerful postwar political figure. It also began a short period of intense jockeying for position by the leaders of various factions among the conservatives. Under these circumstances, political changes centered more on personalities than on policies. Hatoyama had become the new Prime Minister through winning support away from Yoshida, forming his own Democratic party, and then dissolving Parliament in January, 1955. In the ensuing election, his party stood for: (1) an adjustment of the nation's defense arrangements by improving the quality rather than the size of National Defense Forces; (2) the renovation of education; (3) expansion of normal trade relations to reduce reliance on United States procurements; and (4) reform and simplification of local administration. In the election, as his party won far more seats in the House of Representatives (185) than any other, he continued as Prime Minister. (See Table II.)

Shortly thereafter, with both moral and material support from the business community, a movement was started for an all-inclusive conservative party. But factional rivalries were not easily forgotten and merger negotiations continued for many months. Furthermore, the Socialists, who had gained in the election at the expense of the conservatives, had completed the formation of a single party from their right and left wings. Through persistence and skillful maneuvering, Kishi Nobusuke, the Secretary General of the Democratic party, finally obtained agreement among the key leaders for the formation of the Liberal Democratic party (*Jūminshūtō*). In so doing, he had assured his own selection as Prime Minister on February 25, 1957, which post he held until the Security Treaty crisis in June, 1960, caused his downfall.[4] Like the previous conservative parties, the platform of the Liberal Democratic party was vague. It proposed to stabilize the people's livelihood and to promote the public welfare at home. In foreign affairs, it pledged the restoration of independence and the adjustment of conditions to assure peace. It declared its foremost political principles to be the observance of democratic parliamentary government and opposition to all influences which sought to rule by violence, revolution, and dictatorship. The conservatism of the new party is further indicated by a brief description of Kishi's background.

During the 1930's, as a Bureau Chief in the Ministry of Commerce and Industry, Kishi began the rationalization program of industry. He also helped formulate the National Defense Plan. In 1935 he was transferred to Manchuria where he played a key role in its industrial development and came to admire General Tōjō Hideki. When the latter became Premier in October, 1941, Kishi became his Minister of Commerce and Industry. Arrested in December, 1948, as a war criminal, he was released without having been tried by the International Military Tribunal. As Prime Minister, his greatest efforts were directed toward strengthening Japan's defensive alliance with the United States.[5]

The Opposition Parties

As for the united Socialist party, it took issue with the Liberal Democrats on such subjects as Japan's nominal independence, neutralism, and rearmament. The Socialists maintained that Japan had failed to achieve independence after 1952 due to military and economic pressures from the United States and from the various agreements, especially the Mutual Defense Assistance Agreement of 1954. On the matter of Japan's rearmament, they opposed the current rearmament program and any amendments to Article IX of the Constitution. They advocated a neutral position in the Cold War, a treaty of peace with the Soviet Union, and resumption of full trade relations with the Chinese People's Republic. Finally, they held that a socialist society should be developed by legal, parliamentary means.

The Japanese Communist party, although considerably weaker politically than the Socialists, was a significant opposition force during this period, especially through the influence it exerted in organizations such as the Student Federation (*Zengakuren*) and the General Council of Trade Unions (*Sōhyō*). Its subsequent withdrawal from control of both of these organizations is indicative of the shifts in tactics dictated largely by developments such as the deaths of their own leader Tokuda and of Stalin. In 1955 the Japanese Communist party decided that it had followed too much ultraleftist adventurism, should give up its contention that revolution in Japan was imminent, and should seek national unification on the basis of struggle for independence and peace. This return to legalism and a united front enabled the Communist party to make common cause with the Socialists in opposing rearmament, closer ties with the United States, and constitutional revision.

The continued dominance of both Houses of Parliament by the conservatives through the Liberal Democratic party taught them to govern but did not necessarily assure their dedication to parliamentarianism. Conversely, the constant frustration of the Socialists and other opposition groups arising from their inability to win a majority taught them to oppose.

Attempts at Constitutional Revision

The unsuccessful attempt of the Liberal Democratic party to revise the Constitution was one of the most significant developments during the Hatoyama and Kishi Cabinets. It acted as a prologue to the grim drama of the violent confrontation between the conservatives and leftist opposition over the interlocked issues of the alliance with the United States and rearmament. Ever since the Peace Treaty had come into effect, conservatives had been urging that the government should face squarely the fact that the new Constitution was not drafted by the Japanese but was a product of the occupation. It was argued that Japan's independence would be complete only when basic revisions to the Constitution had been made to strengthen the status of the Emperor, clarify the locus of sovereignty, increase the authority of the Cabinet and the Prime Minister, and, above all, change drastically the provisions of Article IX which renounced war and prohibited the maintenance of land, sea, and air forces.

The problem soon developed into one of political strategy. Any constitutional amendment required initiation in the Diet and approval by two-thirds of the members of each of its Houses and by a majority vote in a national referendum. From the point of view of the opposition parties, therefore, if they could continue to hold at least one-third of the seats in either House, they could block any constitutional amendment. Hatoyama believed that the Constitution should be changed to remove any ambiguity about Japan's right to possess arms for self-defense. He insisted such a change would not mean revival of prewar militarism or a weakening of the Constitution's democratic features. As his party had a clear majority in the House of Representatives, he pressed for the passage of a bill establishing a special commission to consider the whole question of constitutional revision.[6] The Commission was to be advisory and to be composed of thirty members from the Diet and twenty lawyers and other professional leaders outside the government. Despite the obstructionist tactics of the Socialists, the bill establishing a commission was approved by the House of Representatives. When it faced strong opposition in the House of Councilors, further action on it was postponed until the next session of the Diet. In the meantime, the Liberal Democratic party publicly announced its detailed views on constitutional revision while public opinion polls indicated that more people opposed than favored revisions.

In 1956, the Socialists again tried to defeat legislation to establish a commission. They were unsuccessful in moving for a vote of nonconfidence against Hatoyama and in preventing the Diet from approving the Commission on the Constitution. They described it as a blatant and illegal attempt to prepare the way for constitutional revision and continued their obstructionism by refusing to serve on it.

When Professor Takayanagi Kenzō, a noted authority on constitutional law, was appointed Chairman of the Commission in 1957, he insisted that its formal recommendations should not necessarily reflect the official view of the Liberal Democratic party. In fact, the Commission and its staff were quite successful in carrying out an exhaustive and unprejudiced survey of the origin, writing, and adoption of the Constitution. While the conclusions of the Commission gave greater emphasis to the revisionists' arguments, its members were far from unanimous in their recommendations. There was basic agreement, however, on the following issues. First, Article IX prohibiting armed forces did not make it unconstitutional for Japan to develop its Self-Defense Force. Secondly, the Diet was the highest organ of the State and it would be dangerous for the future of democratic government in Japan if the Constitution were changed so as to allow a stronger relationship to develop between the legislative and executive branches. Furthermore, despite a contrary position taken by Chairman Takayanagi, a majority of the Commission concluded that the Constitution was not the result of a joint SCAP–Japanese effort but was, in fact, imposed on the Japanese government.[7]

In the seven years between the formation of the Commission on the Constitution and the publication of its final *Report* in 1964, the Government took no direct step to initiate any constitutional amendments. If it had done so, it would have been a futile move, for it could not have mustered the required two-thirds votes. It followed a policy of continued close alliance with the United States and quietly approved the buildup of its own Self-Defense Force. For their part, the Socialists, Communists, and other opponents of rearmament and the American alliance resorted to direct action leading to the crisis of 1960. For the moment, constitutional revision remained in abeyance.

Nationalism and Defense

The pervasiveness and virulence of prewar and wartime Japanese nationalism would make one assume that a considerable residue of this ultranationalism had survived the surrender. That such was not the case is clear from the complete lack of overt plans by the Japanese to sabotage the occupation or to assassinate any of the occupation personnel. Furthermore, it is also surprising that the government was unable to obtain support for at least minimum constitutional revisions. This complete disappearance of the most dangerous forms of prewar nationalism is attributable, of course, to many causes. They include: (1) the completeness of defeat; (2) the thoroughness of many of the reforms sponsored by the occupation, including the promulgation of a new Constitution; (3) the breakup of the prewar military forces and discrediting of their leaders; (4) the spiritual vacuum created by the disappearance of the magic and mystery surrounding the concept of *kokutai;* and (5) the inability of postwar nationalist groups to unite in a common cause or to obtain mass support.

At the same time, it would be a mistake to assume that the prevalent use by people at large of catch words such as "democracy," "freedom," "people's rights," and "peace" meant that they were fully aware of their meaning and significance. In fact, in 1950, Maruyama Masao, one of Japan's most perceptive political scientists, maintained that democracy was still an imported product and "had not become a positive symbol to regulate the Japanese way of life, completely displacing the old nationalism." Sometime later, he noted that postwar nationalism was primarily for home consumption, that it stressed the need to return to traditional ways of life and was essentially nonpolitical. Rather than the nationalists forcing the hands of the government by threats or direct action, postwar Cabinets were free to act on their own initiative.[8]

On the other hand, the government had to act cautiously on matters

Consulate General of Japan, New York

CHILDREN'S FESTIVAL, MEIJI SHRINE, TOKYO

which could be interpreted by the opposition as a reversion to prewar authoritarianism. For example, in 1958, Prime Minister Kishi sought revisions to the Police Duties Performance Law which would have enlarged the interrogation powers of the police and enabled them to search and detain those suspected of causing annoyance to the public. In this way it was hoped to control labor unrest and unruly demonstrations of any kind, including innocuous street snake dances so popular with labor and youth groups. The bill was violently opposed by the General Council of Trade Unions (*Sōhyō*) and the Socialist party. The latter's members in the House of Representatives adopted a familiar tactic. Knowing they would be defeated through normal parliamentary procedures because of their minority, for six weeks they physically blocked the entrances to the committee rooms and plenary session meetings in the House of Representatives, bringing its proceedings to a standstill. When the Vice-Speaker of the House declared a thirty-day extension, which the Socialists claimed illegal, the latter boycotted the sessions of the Diet. A compromise was finally reached between the Government and the Socialists whereby the extension of the Diet would be recognized as legal, the supplementary budget would be approved, and consideration of the Police Bill would be temporarily dropped.[9]

On the matter of strengthening Japan's defense forces, the Cabinet realized that it faced a predominantly antiwar and antimilitary attitude among the people as a whole. Consequently, it was forced to proceed cautiously. In 1952, with the coming into force of the Peace Treaty, the National Police Reserve was changed into a National Safety Force. In the summer of 1954, the Diet approved a Self-Defense Force Bill which established the Self-Defense Agency with Ground, Maritime, and Air Self-Defense Forces (*Jieitai*). Their purpose was to defend Japan's peace and independence, preserve its security, and defend it from direct and indirect aggression. The original bill provided for a Ground Force of 150,000 men and a budget of $241 million. By 1960, approval had been given for the formation of a National Defense Council and increases in the Self-Defense Forces to 231,000 men. Military expenditures for that year had risen 18 per cent since 1954 and equaled 8.9 per cent of the national budget but only one per cent of gross national product. This comparatively modest expenditure and the limited size of the Defense Forces were possible, of course, because of the Mutual Defense Assistance Agreement of 1954 whereby the United States contributed substantially to the rearmament and defense of Japan.

Another extremely important aspect of Japan's new defense establishment was the differences in control, personnel, and psychology of the Self-Defense Agency compared with the prewar Imperial Army, Navy, and Air Force. In the first place, the officers of the Self-Defense Forces were of an entirely different type from those in prewar days. No former officers above the rank of colonel had been recruited into the new forces. The new Constitution required that the Self-Defense Agency be headed by a civilian and contained no provisions which gave the military leaders special privileges. There was no provision for Supreme Command or direct access to the Emperor by the military leaders. The Self-Defense Forces were composed of volunteers and recruits and no politician dared suggest that conscription be reinstated. The ex-militarists were less influential with their own government than the American Military Assistance group. Some of the ex-militarists had formed their own patriotic organizations but these had no national importance. A few of them, such as ex-General Ugaki Kazushige and ex-Colonel Tsuji Masanobu were elected to the Diet. While the ex-militarists came to exert more influence as the war receded, it is clear that Professor Ivan Morris is correct in his conclusion that they played "a very small part in the scheme of things" in Japan in 1960.[10]

Business and Labor

While the ex-militarists have been of far less influence in postwar than prewar Japan, this situation is not true of the business world (*zaikai*). In view of the tremendous postwar national growth (an annual average of 9 per cent), this group is important in its own right. Furthermore, the business world has developed powerful organizations through which it influences and often controls the Liberal Democratic party. Particularly after 1952, the business world became active in national policy formation. Its goal was political stability under a strong and effective government. It has been an active participant in the management of national affairs, the establishment of sound monetary policies, the modernization and rationalization of industry, and the importation of new technology and foreign investments. It was the main source of financial support for the Liberal Democratic Party, and Prime Ministers such as Yoshida, Hatoyama, and Kishi needed to have support of the *zaikai* to remain in office.

The business world has exerted its greatest influence through four organizations. The Federation of Economic Organization (*Keidanren*) is composed of the most important national trade associations and 750 corporations, many of which receive contracts from the government and some of which are wholly state-owned corporations, such as the Japan National Railways, the Bank of Japan, and Japan Air Lines. Meetings of the Federation are attended by Cabinet Ministers. The Federation operates through committees on such vital problems as defense, finances, and production, and maintains an Economic Research Council. It is unquestionably the most influential business organization in Japan. Its quiet but effective Vice-President, Uemura Kogorō, who has guided its activities for many years, is more influential than many Cabinet ministers. Its committees have especially close relations with the Ministry of International Trade and Industry and the Ministry of Finance.

The Japan Committee for Economic Development (*Keizai Dōyūkai*) is nonprofit and nonpolitical. It was founded in 1946 by junior executives who were concerned with the responsibility of business for society and wanted to participate in making government policy which would aid recovery and speed national growth and economic independence. It concentrated on problems such as capital accumulation and the reentrance of Japan into world trade.

The third important group is the Japan Federation of Employers Association (*Nihon Keieisha Dantai Remmei*), formed in 1948, which is primarily concerned with industrial peace and greater productivity. The Employers Association, like the other two groups, has both public and private corporations as members. It acts as management's headquarters for labor policy, promotes labor legislation, and struggles with the demands of the labor unions. It maintains close liaison with the Ministry of Labor and Welfare. Finally, the Japan Chamber of Commerce and Industry, with its various trade associations, such as the powerful Iron and Steel Federation, is another of the most influential organizations of the business world.[11]

It is not known just how much these organizations have been responsible for Japan's postwar prosperity but it is obvious they have made a significant contribution to it. In the political field they constantly urged the conservative factions to submerge their differences, which resulted in the formation of the Liberal Democratic party. Representatives of the business world are appointed in increasing numbers as Cabinet Ministers of Finance, International Trade and Industry, Agriculture and Forestry, and Economic Planning. The ties between business and government are further strengthened by many politicians and bureaucrats seeking a second career in business. From the foregoing it is obvious that the business world and the Liberal Democratic party form a close partnership and are vitally interested in a prosperous economy and political stability. As for the latter, the continuance in power of any single individual is far less important than the party's remaining in control of the Diet. This was particularly true in 1960, when the dissident or opposition groups, composed of labor, the intellectuals, the Socialists, Communists, and Student Federation (*Zengakuren*) presented a formidable front against the Establishment on the issue of an alliance with the United States.

Before considering the Crisis of 1960, however, it is necessary to present background material on significant opposition groups in addition to the political parties. In particular, in contrast to the strong united front which management was able to present, organized labor was relatively weak and in disarray. For example, in 1960 the total number of unions had risen to 41,000 and membership had increased to 7.5 million. But, the portion of workers organized equaled only 33 per cent of the working force. Not only were the unions weak numerically, they did not produce anything like a revolution in the labor market because they were concentrated in modern industries so that collective bargaining took place only in the highest wage groups. Furthermore, unions continued to be based on enterprises rather than crafts so that the unions had little national impact on wages. To strengthen their organizations, they turned from economic to political action.

But ideological differences among the leaders of the strongest unions increased their rivalries and weakened the chances of a united front. The General Council of Trade Unions (*Sōhyō*), which was organized in 1950, was by far the strongest group with a membership ten years later of more than 3 million and with control over an equal number of additional persons. Two of its strongest affiliates were the Japan Teacher's Union (*Nikkyōsō*) and the National Railway Workers (*Kokurō*). During its early years, *Sōhyō* was under strong Communist leadership, which it eventually rejected and henceforth gave its support to the Socialist party. While it launched an annual wage increase offensive, it was highly politically conscious and strongly neutralist in terms of foreign policy. The next two largest federations were the General Federal of Labor (*Sodōmei*) and the All-Japan Trade Union Congress (*Zenrō*) which in 1962 combined to form the Japan United Congress of Labor (*Dōmei Kaigi*) with a membership of about 1.5 million. More moderate politically than *Sōhyō, Dōmei* supported the moderate Democratic-Socialist party. Although these unions were unable to form a united front politically and often called strikes to strengthen their respective positions, they were in agreement in their opposition to the proposed United States–Japan Security Treaty.[12]

Student Movement to 1960

Like organized labor, the student movement in Japan had always been politically conscious and involved in direct action. Many students were arrested in prewar days along with others accused of "dangerous thought." After 1948, the postwar student movement became an important force with the formation of the All-Japan Students' Self-Government Federation, known both at home and abroad by its abbreviated name of *Zengakuren.* From the date of its formation until the failure to prevent ratification of the United States–Japan Security Treaty in 1960, it was the undisputed leader of the student movement even though it was faced with a bitter internal struggle. After 1960, as will be noted later, fractionalization and violent factional differences resulted in the growth of semiautonomous, activist groups dogmatically maintaining the correctness of their particular interpretation of Marxism, Leninism, or Maoism and violently opposing the Japanese Communist party and its affiliated student group.

When first organized in 1948 with national headquarters at Tokyo University, *Zengakuren* was directly under communist control. The first Chairman of the Central Executive Committee, Takahashi Sasuke, the Vice-Chairman, and the Secretary were all communists. Two years later the Japanese Communist party broke with the *Zengakuren* leadership and withdrew its cell from the organization because of the prevalence of its "internationalism." By 1952, *Zengakuren* declared its objectives to be peace and independence for Japan, the economic improvement of student life, the protection of democratic rights, formation of a joint front with labor, and the denunciation of the proposed Anti-Subversive Activities Law. At that time its membership equaled about 55,000 students or 1.5 per cent of the total number of university students. During the riots of May, 1952, contrary to a previous decision of the controlling mainstream faction, members of the internationalist faction led the violent outbreaks against the police. Two years later, however, *Zengakuren* leadership at Tokyo University was favorably inclined toward the communists, though not under their control. A *Zengakuren* officer stated, "When we try to take advantage of freedom of speech to promote our vital interests we are oppressed. . . . It is the Japanese Communist Party which vigorously opposes unreasonable suppression of the basic freedoms . . . and stands by students when they are in trouble." [13] The radical tendencies of *Zengakuren* were recognized by the business organizations affiliated with the Federation of Employers Association, which agreed not to employ college graduates who were affiliated with it. Such an attitude, in the face of the fact that each year only about half of the annual group of college graduates find positions befitting their education and ambitions, stimulated the radicalization of the student movement. If a popular issue could be found around which support could be mustered, the ingredients were at hand for a confrontation with the authorities. Both the contents of the proposed new Security Treaty with the United States and the methods by which Prime Minister Kishi achieved his objective were just such issues.

United States–Japan Security Treaty, 1960

The Crisis of May, 1960, which has been described as the most significant internal upheaval in Japan since the Army uprising on February 26, 1936, threw the spotlight on the continuing weakness of Japan's democracy.[14] In view of the fact that many of the same opposition groups are constantly referring to a "Crisis of 1970," when the Security Treaty may be renounced by either signatory, an analysis of the issues and tactics used in 1960 by the government and by the opposition is pertinent. The objections to the treaty are partly explained by an increase in a new nationalism which resented the continued presence of American troops in Japan, regardless of their assignment. Every incident which involved a Japanese subject and an American soldier only inflamed feelings. Furthermore, as early as 1957, Prime Minister Kishi began negotiations with the United States for the withdrawal of its forces and also for a more specific guarantee and pledge from the United States that it would defend Japan from attack. In 1958 during the attacks on Quemoy Island off the China coast, Foreign Minister Fujiyama began talks in the United States on a defensive alliance. The business world also believed that Japan's economic recovery was linked with the successful conclusion of a bilateral security agreement.

By May, 1959, the leaders within the Liberal Democratic party had resolved their internal differences and agreed to let Kishi seek a new treaty with the understanding that he would then resign. The party also demanded that the treaty contain certain new restrictions which would give Japan a maximum of administrative control over its own destiny and a minimum of involvement in American strategy. Thus it was to insist that it have the right to veto the use overseas of American troops stationed in Japan. It also wished to eliminate the provision in the Treaty of 1952 that American troops could be used to quell Japanese internal disturbances.

On the other hand, in view of Kishi's previous record, there were those who were skeptical about his intentions. An increasingly larger number of people, in addition to the Socialists, Communists, and *Zengakuren,* were opposed to a new treaty on the grounds that it would involve Japan more deeply in American foreign policy, with which they did not agree, and would increase the chances of Japan's becoming an innocent victim in a future war. The Socialist and Communist parties and *Zengakuren* agreed to form a Council to oppose the treaty. In February, 1959, they issued a joint statement calling on the nation to join the united struggle against the treaty and demanding the restoration of relations with the Chinese People's Republic. The first major confrontation did not occur, however, until November 27. In the Diet, the Socialists had pressed for a nonconfidence vote against Kishi rather than approval of a Vietnam Reparations Bill. Chaos resulted and the Liberal Democrats rushed the Reparations Bill through the House of Representatives. On the same day, a massive but orderly demonstration had been organized to present a petition at the National Diet Building demanding the resignation of Kishi. Careful plans had been made to encircle the *Zengakuren* and union activists with moderate, orderly groups to prevent violence. But *Zengakuren* members and followers, totaling 12,000 persons, broke ranks and forced their way into the Diet Building compound. They were confronted by the guards and police and finally dispersed.

For the next seven months any move by the government stimulated a new confrontation. None of these countermoves by the opposition prevented Kishi from signing a new Security Treaty in Washington in January, 1960. When he returned to Tokyo, he ruled that the Diet could not amend the treaty but could only approve or reject it. He refused to dissolve the Diet so the opposition, which had only a minority of votes, decided to try to obstruct all Diet business so that it would adjourn without having approved the treaty. Their tactics failed on May 19, 1960, when they were ejected by the police from the chamber of the House of Representatives after which a plenary session, without the Socialist members present, approved an extension of the session and also the report of the committee sponsoring the new treaty. These tactics meant that the treaty ratification by the Diet would become automatic on June 18. In the interim, on June 10, James Hagerty, who had come to Japan to arrange for President Eisenhower's visit to ratify the treaty, and U.S. Ambassador Douglas MacArthur II were mobbed at Tokyo's airport. On June 15, a woman student was killed in a *Zengakuren*—police battle before the Diet Building.[15]

As for the Security Treaty, Kishi obtained many of the provisions he wanted. American troops in Japan were not to be used against internal disturbances, the treaty was to last for ten years after which either party could give notice to terminate it. Finally, each of the signatories, recognizing that an attack against either in the territories under the administration of Japan would be dangerous to the other's peace and safety, agreed to meet the common danger. (See Appendix III.) In the accompanying exchange of notes it was agreed that American troops in Japan could not be used overseas without Japan's consent. In other words, Kishi had obtained his defensive alliance. But the massive disorders and opposition directed against him caused his resignation the next week.

Other Foreign Relations

From the foregoing, it is obvious that Japan considered its foreign relations with the United States of paramount importance and that this fact determined, in large measure, its attitude toward other countries, especially those in the communist world. By 1960, Japan had become an active member of the United Nations and was serving on the Security Council. On basic issues it aligned itself with the United States. Nevertheless, as a result of unfinished business arising out of the war, such as the fact that neither the Soviet Union nor the Chinese People's Republic had signed a peace treaty and Southeast Asian nations were pressing their demands for exorbitant reparations, Japan faced many difficult problems with its Asian neighbors.

Japan's traditional animosity toward and fear of the Soviet Union was exacerbated by the continued insistence of the latter that the question of the return of the island of Habomai and Shikotan, was not negotiable. Japan had always treated them as part of the homeland rather than of the Kurile Islands, but the Soviet Union had occupied them as its own territory and continued to do so. Russia had refused to sign the San Francisco Peace Treaty but special arrangements on the repatriation of Japanese had been worked out. In 1956, the two nations signed a Peace Declaration and fishing and trade agreements. The latter was of only minor significance. In 1956, Japan's exports to the Soviet Union amounted to $1 million and imports to $3 million; in 1960 they had reached $60 million and $87 million respectively. The greatest problem for Japan in relation to the Soviet Union, over which it had little control, was whether an American–Soviet struggle would make Japan an unwilling participant.

As for the Chinese People's Republic there were few Japanese in 1960 who believed it to be as great a threat or problem as Washington considered it to be. This was partly the result of Japan's past associations with China, the similarity of the cultural background of the two peoples, and a naïve belief that China had no ulterior motives toward Japan. Consequently, when in 1952 Japan recognized the government of Chiang Kai-shek on Taiwan as "the government of China" it could not understand why Peking became so angry. Always hopeful that China would be a great potential source of trade, private negotiations were begun but Peking insisted that more formal relations would be possible only after Japan renounced its Security Treaty with the United States, recognized the Chinese People's Republic as *the* government of China, withdrew recognition from Taiwan, and followed a policy of neutralism. Limited but precarious trade arrangements were made. In 1954, exports equaled $16 million and imports $48 million. In 1958, China canceled the agreement because of an incident about its flag. In 1964, exports had reached $183 million and imports were $158 million. Prospects for future improvement of relations seemed dim.

Another set of problems centered around reparations. The peace treaty had not settled the issue. The various Southeast Asian nations occupied by Japan during the war were bitterly resentful of what they had suffered and demanded exorbitant reparations payments. For example, the Philippines' first demand was $8 billion. Negotiations on reparations were arduous and lengthy but were facilitated by the role played by leaders of the Japanese business world. Several of them acted as negotiators. They looked on reparations as a step toward the development of future trade in the area and insisted that payments should be made in capital goods and services which would contribute to the economic development of the region. As Table 12 indicates, reparations were supplemented by substantial government loans. In addition to agreements or reparations, in 1954 Burma signed a Peace Treaty and in 1960 the Philippines and Japan signed a Treaty of Amity

TABLE 12

Reparations Settlements with Southeast Asian Countries [16]
(In Millions of Dollars)

	Date Negotiations Started	Date Concluded	Reparations	Loans	Years To Pay
Burma:					
Original	1953	11/5/54	$200.0	$ 50.0	10
Supplement		3/29/63	140.0	30.0	12
Philippine Islands	1951	5/9/56	550.0	250.0	20
Indonesia	1951	1/20/58	223.8	400.0	12
South Vietnam		5/15/59	39.0	7.5	5

and Commerce. Much of the previous animosity and suspicion had given way to a willingness on the part of these developing nations to learn from and make use of Japan's advanced technological skills. Japan also took a more positive attitude toward Southeast Asia, looking on it as a future market for Japanese goods and services.

As for Japanese–Korean relations, these continued to be strained with neither side willing nor able to understand the other. For example, President Syngman Rhee arrogantly decreed that all Koreans in Japan, whether from the north or south, must become citizens of the Republic of Korea. He made fantastic financial claims against Japan. Japanese fishermen were forbidden to operate within sixty miles of the Korean coast. Talks were begun between the two nations in an attempt to settle some of the issues, only to be interrupted. The same procedure was repeated three times more without success prior to Rhee's demise in 1960. The previous year, relations had been strained to the breaking point by Prime Minister Kishi's approval, over Rhee's vehement objection, for the repatriation to North Korea of 80,000 Koreans resident in Japan.[17] Basically, each side mistrusted the other; each believed it could get along without the other.

Despite many unsolved problems, both external and internal, Japan had made considerable progress toward a new independence. At the same time, the defensive alliance with the United States which Kishi had won at the expense of his own political future was a mixed blessing. It gave Japan security but also made it vulnerable to the threat of war resulting from international crises in which the United States was involved.

Notes

1. From personal observation, the author can testify to the fact that the changes which occurred in the spring of 1952 in reference to American troops in Japan were almost imperceptible. Some of the steps which were taken

to indicate a change were ludicrous. Signs in English with the marking GHQ were painted out or changed but many Japanese didn't know the exact meaning of the signs anyway. U.S. Army cars were painted black but they were easily distinguishable by their licenses or by their occupants. The luxurious exclusive compounds, separate schools, and tax-exempt exchanges for all American military personnel and their dependents were obvious indications that "the Welfare State" still existed for the "occupation personnel." Few Japanese excused this situation on the grounds that much of the time and effort of the United Nations military personnel were taken up with the war in Korea.

2. The mob was composed of a large proportion of young people. The campus at Tokyo University was completely deserted that day. There were practically no incidents of attacks on foreigners, not even on those who were in the center of the scuffle. It was basically a fight between the police and the leaders of the vanguard who had come armed with homemade weapons for a fight. The author, who was fortuitously on the fringe of one of the groups in another part of the city, noted no anti-American attitude or activity.

3. For the text of the Mutual Defense Assistance Agreement, signed March 9, 1954, see U.S. Department of State, *Bulletin,* April 5, 1954.

4. In November, 1954, Hatoyama Ichirō had split off from the Liberal party, formed the Democratic party, and ran on that ticket in the elections early the next year. He was Prime Minister from December 10, 1954, until December 23, 1956, when he lost support of the majority of the new Liberal Democratic party. Ishibashi Tanzan was selected as Prime Minister on December 23, 1956. He served for two months. On February 25, 1957, Kishi Nobusuke became the new party President and Premier. For a provocative analysis of postwar politics see Robert A. Scalapino and Junnosuke Masumi, *Parties and Politics in Contemporary Japan* (Berkeley: University of California Press, 1964), pp. 52 ff.

5. Kishi, the older brother of Satō Eisaku who became Premier in 1964, was born in 1896 and later adopted into the Kishi family. In 1954 he was expelled from the party by Yoshida but later was a key force in forming the Liberal Democratic party. For a sympathetic biography of Kishi see Dan Kurzman, *Kishi and Japan* (New York: Ivan Obolensky, 1960).

6. It should be borne in mind that constitutional revision was an issue on which the Socialists, the Social Democrats, and the Communists united so that the Liberal Democratic party at no time could secure a two-thirds majority in the House of Representatives. (See Table 11.)

7. An excellent analysis of the extent of the work of the Commission, its significance and conclusions, has been made by Robert E. Ward, "The Commission on the Constitution and Prospects for Constitutional Change in Japan," *Journal of Asian Studies,* XXIV (May, 1965), pp. 401–29; and Dan Fenno Henderson (ed.), *The Constitution of Japan: Its First Twenty Years, 1947–1967* (Seattle: University of Washington Press, 1968).

8. See Ivan I. Morris, *Nationalism and the Right Wing in Japan: A Study of Postwar Trends* (London: Oxford University Press, 1960), pp. 21 and 102 ff.

9. There were several variations of these tactics by the opposition and the government. In 1954, and on subsequent occasions, the police were called into the chamber of the House of Representatives and then ejected the Socialists. Facing continued frustration as a minority party, the Socialists tried

to obstruct parliamentary procedure and thus prevent action being taken on legislation they opposed. If they had been able to continue this obstruction until the statutory date for adjournment of the Diet arrived, they would have defeated the legislation, at least temporarily, by preventing its passage. For details of the 1958 crisis see Lawrence A. Olson, *Dimensions of Japan* (New York: American University Field Staff, Inc., 1963), pp. 189 ff.

10. Morris, *op. cit.*, pp. 207 ff. A concise summary, with pertinent statistics on the Self-Defense Forces from 1950–1963, is given in James W. Morley, *Japan and Korea: America's Allies in the Pacific* (New York: Walker and Co., 1965), pp. 110–12.

11. As those familiar with the work will realize, in this section I have relied heavily on the extremely careful and valuable study of Chitoshi Yanaga, *Big Business and Japanese Politics* (New Haven: Yale University Press, 1968).

12. Morley, *op. cit.*, pp. 85–86; and Solomon Levine, "Labor Markets and Collective Bargaining in Japan," in William W. Lockwood (ed.), *The State and Economic Enterprise in Japan* (Princeton: Princeton University Press, 1965), pp. 653 ff.

13. Lawrence H. Battistini, *The Postwar Student Struggle in Japan* (Rutland, Vt.: C. E. Tuttle Co., 1956), p. 35.

14. Scalapino and Masumi, *op. cit.*, p. 3.

15. Hagerty was President Eisenhower's press officer. For further details and an excellent report on the whole subject see George B. Packard III, *Protest in Tokyo: The Security Treaty Crisis of 1960* (Princeton: Princeton University Press, 1966).

16. Adapted with permission of the publisher from Yanaga, *op. cit.*, p. 206; for details of the reparations settlements see pp. 202–29.

17. See Richard Hawks Mitchell, *The Korean Minority in Japan* (Berkeley: University of California Press, 1967).

22

Japan in the 1960's

Conservative Supremacy Continues

Before Kishi was forced to resign in June, 1960, the leaders of the business world had already decided that the next Prime Minister should be Ikeda Hayato (1899–1964). Having served as a bureaucrat in the Finance Ministry before his election to the House of Representatives in 1949, as Secretary General of the Liberal Democratic party, Finance Minister in Yoshida's third Cabinet and as Minister of International Trade and Industry under Kishi, Ikeda was a natural choice to become president of the Liberal Democratic party and Premier.[1] His style and personality were far less flamboyant than that of Kishi so his premiership was characterized by comparative political tranquillity, a less belligerent attitude toward the Socialists, and a recognition of the force of public opinion on such matters as the revision of the Constitution. He also launched a campaign to double the nation's income in a decade, turning interest away from political problems toward improvement in economic conditions. In foreign affairs, he supported close relations with the United States and increased aid to Southeast Asia but was not yet ready to negotiate a settlement with the Republic of Korea. In the elections in November, 1960, his party increased its strength in the House of Representatives to its postwar peak at the expense of the Socialists, but it could not achieve a two-thirds majority. The Japan Socialist party showed surprising strength, despite the assassination of its chairman in October, 1960, but the right-wing Democratic Socialists made a poor showing. In the election three years later, Ikeda lost some support but not nearly enough to threaten his majority.

When he suddenly announced, in 1964, his intention to resign because of illness, after consultation with the business leaders to whom he owed much of his success, he established a precedent by selecting his own successor. His choice fell upon Satō Eisaku (1901–   ), who, throughout the remainder of the 1960's, successfully overcame strong opposition to his policies and kept himself and the Liberal Democratic party in power.

In order to understand the complexity of this task, we must first turn to a brief description of how the Liberal Democratic party operates. Like almost all organizations in Japan, it is composed of innumerable factions whose leaders command unfailing loyalty of their followers through the time-honored hierarchical relationship of "boss to protégé" (*oyabun kobun*). Such a relationship usually develops from the boss having performed a certain favor for his protégé as Yoshida did when he appointed Ikeda Vice-Minister of Finance. At the death of a faction leader, new alignments will occur unless the successor is strong enough to rally support for loyalty solely to him.

Factions serve several important functions in Japanese politics. In the first place, they provide an important psychological need of members of the Diet to have close personal relationships with a group small enough for its members to know each other. Faction leaders choose the party leaders and make recommendations for appointments. A successful party president is one who can maintain an equilibrium among them. Many a Prime Minister will reshuffle a Cabinet to win support from dissident faction leaders by increasing their representation in the government. Factions also are important for raising funds for election campaigns and distributing funds to their members. They are extremely important during party presidential elections.

On the other hand, a strong national party organization and factions are mutually antagonistic but they cannot exist without each other. There is always the danger, however, that the leader of a large faction will become disenchanted with the party and bolt it to form his own. At this stage of Japan's political history, however, it would seem most unlikely that this would happen in the Liberal Democratic party. The pressure from the business world for a single conservative party has a tremendous centripetal force on party leaders. If this were not the case, the Liberal Democratic party would not be strong enough to hold together. As an organization it is extremely weak. In 1966, it was reported to have had only 300,000 dues-paying members.[2]

When Satō Eisaku became Prime Minister on November 9, 1964, he was thoroughly familiar with the inner workings of his party. He had become a bureaucrat forty years earlier, had been a loyal party worker, and served as Finance Minister in the Kishi Cabinet.[3] He also had the support of twenty powerful business groups and his party had a large majority in the Diet. His Foreign Minister and Finance Minister were his college associates at Tokyo University. The entire Cabinet was highly educated and capable with a high respect for harmony and decorum in their personal relations and an insatiable desire to advance Japan's technology and build the national economy so that it would be accepted as a world power on the basis of equality, inferior to none.

Consulate General of Japan, New York

SATŌ EISAKU (1901–)

To them "responsible government" meant that ambitious political leaders, the bureaucracy, and business would work closely together to achieve this end. How well they succeeded can be judged from what follows.

In the first place, Satō's political control was sufficiently complete for him to wait for more than two years after his appointment before calling an election in January, 1967, for the House of Representatives. His party members ran for election on the basis of the record of his Cabinet. Though the Liberal Democratic party lost five seats and received only 48 per cent of the total vote compared to 60 per cent in the previous election, it still commanded a strong majority with 277 seats. The Socialists also lost four seats and their percentage of the total vote declined. The losses of both parties were largely due to the appearance of a new party on the scene, the *Kōmeitō*, the political arm of the popular Value Creating Society (*Sōka Gakkai*). (See Table 11, page 472.)

Postwar Economic Growth

As previously indicated, Japan's political stability and postwar development were enhanced and even made possible by its economic prosperity. Without question, Japan's phenomenal continued postwar economic growth has been the most significant characteristic of its very recent history. As indicated in the previous chapter, the perilous state of the economy in the early years of the occupation had improved as time passed, under the combined impact of more stringent government controls and the shift in American policy to encourage Japan's industrial recovery. By 1950, American aid had totaled $1.7 billion. The outbreak of the Korean War that summer and the resultant special procurements by the United States gave added impulse to an economy which has shown a continued 9 per cent annual average increase in gross national product. This has meant a tripling of production every twelve years and has led to Japan's becoming the third greatest industrial power in the world. Having geared its future to the continuance of a growth economy, though perhaps at a reduced rate, it is in order to consider briefly the chief features of Japan's contemporary economy.

Postwar economic problems differ drastically from the prewar ones. Military expenditures have been kept to a minimum. Whereas in 1944 they amounted to 68 per cent of national income, in 1968 they were a mere .9 per cent. The average annual rice production increased by 36 per cent from 1933–1937 to 1963–1967. While population growth continues, the rate of increase has declined. Thus the per-capita production of rice for these thirty years fell by only 4.8 per cent. (See Table 3, page 300.) During a decade of mechanization in agriculture, employment in farming fell off by about one-third, making more labor available for higher productivity trades. The concentration of industrial development on heavy industries, petrochemicals, and electronics has allowed Japan to compete successfully in world markets. Shipbuilding, in which Japan is the undisputed world leader, is the most outstanding example of this new phenomenon. The readiness with which the Ministry of International Trade and Industry granted the exemption of specific industries from the Anti-Monopoly Law encouraged new combines to form.

The pattern of foreign trade has shifted dramatically. China no longer plays a central role. In 1968, trade was carried on in roughly equal amounts with Asia (mainland China accounted for only 2 per cent), North America, and the widely separated areas of Europe, South America, Africa, and Oceania. (See Table 15, page 522.) The international milieu has been favorable to Japan's reintegration into the world

Consulate General of Japan, New York

RUSH HOUR CROWDS IN TOKYO

TABLE 13

JAPAN'S POSTWAR ECONOMIC GROWTH[5]
(Annual Averages; Index Numbers: 1934 = 100)

	1934–1936	1951–1953	1954–1956	1957–1959	1960–1962	1963–1965	1966–1968
1. Population (in millions)	68.6	85.8	89.2	91.8	94.3	97.2	99.6
2. Real total national income	100	116	142	182	262	437	585
3. Percentage annual gain	4.1%	8.5%	8.0%	9.5%	12.0%	14.3%	16.8%
4. Per capita	100	93	109	136	190	275	378
5. Production, agriculture, forestry, and fishing	100	112	127	141	154	163	179
6. Manufacturing	100	116	168	247	408	609	730
7. Volume of exports	100	38	71	104	150	305	379
8. Family consumption level	100	95	115	130	152	240	261
9. Gross savings in percentage of national product	19.0%	28.6%	26.9%	31.3%	39.3%		

economy. It has remained at peace. It has shared in the general postwar recovery. It quickly learned and improved on technological advances. Finally, the close alliance of the business world with the bureaucracy and the conservative Liberal Democratic party, which has continued in power since 1955, has allowed for efficient economic planning.[4]

This rapid growth has taken place in all aspects of the economy and has even exceeded the long-range predictions of the Economic Planning Agency established in 1955. As noted in Table 13, in the decade after the Peace Treaty was signed both total national income and per-capita income more than doubled. In the next six years (1960–1962 to 1966–1968), the national income had doubled again while per-capita income nearly doubled. Manufacturing production had risen three and one-half times in the decade from 1952 and an additional 80 per cent in the next six years. Agricultural production, which had risen only 37.5 per cent and 16 per cent respectively during the same periods, was at a rate much greater than that of the population increase. In terms of gross national product, the average annual increase for the decade 1952 to 1961 was 9.6 per cent despite the fact that there were slight depressions in both 1954 and 1958. For the next seven years the annual average increase was 13.7 per cent. (See Table 14.)

TABLE 14

POSTWAR GROWTH RATE (GNP)[6]
(Adjusted for 1934–1936 Average Price;
Index Number: 1934–1936 = 100)

Fiscal Year	Index	Percentage Increase Over Previous Year
1946	65.0	—
1947	71.5	10.0%
1948	83.2	16.4
1949	86.5	3.9
1950	97.0	12.2
1951	110.1	13.5
1952	121.7	10.5
1953	129.9	6.7
1954	134.2	3.3
1955	148.0	10.3
1956	161.3	9.0
1957	174.0	7.9
1958	179.6	3.2
1959	211.7	17.9
1960	239.6	13.2
1961	273.1	14.0
1962	284.6	4.2
1963	322.4	13.3
1964	378.4	17.6
1965	416.2	10.0
1966	480.1	15.4
1967 *	563.6	17.4
1968 *	666.7	18.3

* Calculated on basis of nominal increases.

One of the most phenomenal achievements has been in shipbuilding. For example, in 1966, Japan launched 6.7 million gross tons, by far the largest of any country and 47 per cent of the world's new tonnage. This was nearly a fourfold increase in Japanese shipbuilding in five years. In the same quinquennium Japan became the world's third largest automobile manufacturerer, steel producer, and petroleum refiner, and had built one of the world's safest fully automated, high-speed train services between its two largest cities, Osaka and Tokyo.

FOREIGN TRADE

If there is any single aspect of Japan's economy which is vulnerable, it is foreign trade. Since the whole economy is posited on the assumption that raw materials will be imported, processed, and then exported at a profit, the whole economy would immediately be adversely affected

Consulate General of Japan, New York

THE WORLD'S LEADER IN SHIPBUILDING

if a war or other international complication were to cause this trade to be interdicted. But the postwar structure of Japan's trade is such as to reduce to a minimum any such eventuality.

China is no longer important to Japan either as a source for raw materials or as a market for finished goods. In 1964 it accounted for only 2 per cent of exports and imports. In the protracted Sino-Japanese trade negotiations that have taken place in subsequent years, the total agreed trade has decreased notably until it will probably not exceed $100 million each way in 1969 or about one per cent of the total. At the same time, China has indicated that further trade will depend on whether Japan renounces the Security Treaty with the United States.

Japan's exports and imports are widely diversified throughout the world. Asia accounts for nearly one-third of total trade and Japan's activities, especially in south and southeast Asia, are likely to increase. Another important aspect is the continued increase in Japanese–American trade. In 1954, the United States purchased 17 per cent in value of Japan's exports and supplied 25 per cent of its imports. In 1968,

TABLE 15

POSTWAR OVERSEAS TRADE OF JAPAN[7]

	Exports					Imports				
	1934–1936	1954	1964	1967	1968	1934–1936	1954	1964	1967	1968
Total value (in millions)	$928	$1,629	$6,673	$10,442	$12,972	$980	$2,399	$7,938	$11,663	$12,987
Quantum of trade (index)	100	55	237	120*	149*	100	86	328	147*	161*
	Distribution by Regions, in Percentages									
Total	100	100	100	100	100	100	100	100	100	100
Asia	64	49	33	34	34	53	31	30	31	31
Mainland China	(18)	(1)	(2)	(2.8)	(2.5)	(10)	(2)	(2)	(3)	(2)
South and Southeast Asia	(18)	(32)	(21)			(16)	(19)	(13)		
North America	17	21	34	35	37	25	46	38	36	35
United States	(16)	(17)	(28)	(29)	(32)	(24)	(25)	(30)	(28)	(27)
Canada	—	(1)	(2)	(3)	(3)	(1)	(5)	(5)	(5)	(5)
Europe	8	9	16	16	15	10	8	13	15	15
United Kingdom	(4)	(3)	(3)	(3)	(3)	(2)	(2)	(2)	(2)	(2)
EEC	(3)	(4)	(5)	(5)	(6)	(4)	(4)	(6)	(5)	(6)
South America	2	10	3	3	3	2	7	5	5	5
Africa	6	8	9	9	7	3	2	5	6	6
Oceania	3	3	5	5	4	7	6	9	8	9
Australia	(2)	(2)	(4)	(4)	(3)	(6)	(5)	(7)	(7)	(7)

* 1965 = 100.

these figures had risen to 32 per cent and 27 per cent respectively. While imports from the United States have remained constant, from Japan's point of view, it is extremely important that exports to the United States have increased by so much. This factor has contributed greatly to the improvement of Japan's overall trade balance and its balance of payments. At the end of 1968, there was a surplus balance of $1.1 billion. Increases in trade in recent years with Europe and members of the European Economic Community and with Australia are significant new developments and may lessen Japan's heavy dependence on the United States. (See Table 15.)

There are additional characteristics of Japan's economy which could relieve it of future strain. The industrialization of Japan has taken place with fewer changes in the social organizations and social relations that existed in preindustrial Japan than was the case in Western models. Many small industries still operate with nonunion workers and with a management that is personally interested in its employees for whom it

Consulate General of Japan, New York

EXCELLENCE IN ELECTRON MICROSCOPES

takes a lifelong responsibility. Workers make a commitment for life to a company, large or small, and expect the employer to do the same. In contrast to industry in the West, interpersonal relations in Japanese industry are still considered more important than efficiency. The system of recruitment, employment, and incentives is, within the Japanese context, self-consistent. It allows for considerably more flexibility than the highly impersonal, mechanized system in the West.[8]

The establishment in 1966 of the Asian Development Bank and the election of Watanabe Takeshi as its President will do much toward strengthening Japan's economic relations with the rest of Asia. Its primary purpose is to facilitate the supply of funds and techniques necessary for the development of Asian nations. The initial contributions of $200 million each by Japan and the United States indicate the value they both place on its future. In the important field of crude oil, nearly all of which is imported to meet Japan's needs, Japan is breaking away from dependence on foreign companies for supplying crude oil and for capital development of refineries. Japanese-owned independent companies have obtained important Near Eastern concessions which supply over one-fourth of oil imports. Another important development has been that of atomic energy in the power field. After the formation of an Atomic Energy Commission in 1956, with the Chairman a member of the Cabinet, Japan rapidly overcame its nuclear trauma and in 1965 the first atomic electric power plant began commercial operations. Thus, barring some unexpected development, the essentials for Japan's continued economic growth were available.

Political Opposition Groups

In the decade of the 1960's, while Japan's continued economic prosperity boded well for the future and enhanced the strength of both the business world and the Liberal Democratic party, opposition groups became increasingly frustrated. As a result, in the Diet the Socialists continued their obstructionist tactics, and throughout the country the frequency, intensity, and seriousness of demonstrations and riots increased. In the elections for the House of Representatives in November, 1963, January, 1967, and December, 1969, and for the House of Councilors in July, 1968, the Socialists had hoped the electorate would swing to their support. In each case, the number of their representatives declined. Those of the more conservative Democratic Socialists increased while the Japanese Communist party's strength remained practically the same.[9] What is the explanation, therefore, for this apparent paradox of the strongest opposition party losing in the elections and yet the Satō Cabinet being faced with the increasing harassment?

The answer is to be found in the expanded support which the opposition has received and the increased violence of some of the groups, especially the new extremist, anti-Communist factions of the student movement. After their defeat in their attempt to stop the ratification of the Security Treaty in 1960, both the Socialist party and the General Council of Trade Unions (*Sōhyō*) turned to political realism. The latter agreed that the struggle against "American Imperialism" should not be the center of their activities. Nevertheless, as the United States expanded its military commitment in South Vietnam, began bombing North Vietnam, and showed few signs of relinquishing control over Okinawa, the United States again became the center of attack. *Sōhyō's* new leaders were young men who came from the labor bureaucracy of skilled laborers. The rank and file were both white- and blue-collar workers. They espoused a neutralism which leaned toward racial sensitivity and pacifism, with a commitment to international cooperation. They continued to refuse to form a united front with the politically unpopular Communists.[10]

As for the so-called crisis of 1970, the Socialist Party advocated a joint front with the Democratic Socialist party and the Kōmeitō in favoring neutrality, disarmament, and the renunciation of the Security Treaty. With *Sōhyō's* support, the Socialists urged a dissolution of the Diet prior to 1970 in the hope of strengthening their position in a new election.

The history of the Japanese Communist party during the decade of the 1960's is complicated and reflects the increasing animosity between the Soviet Union and the Chinese People's Republic. In a word, the Japanese Communists attempted, without any real success, to remain aloof from the Moscow–Peking controversy. In the spring of 1961, Nosaka and other members of his mainstream faction of the party exerted the predominant influence and urged rejection of illegal activities. There followed a decided swing toward support of Peking. The Soviet Union was severely criticized for its nuclear tests, its *rapprochement* with Yugoslavia, and its decision to withdraw missiles from Cuba. In 1963, though the Japanese Communist party tried to prevent it, the Sino-Soviet dispute broke into the open at the Conference on the Council Against the Atomic and Hydrogen Bombs (*Gensuikyō*), at Hiroshima. The Chinese delegate called the Test Ban Treaty, which the Soviet Union had already signed, "an utter fraud to the people of the world." The Soviet representative vehemently attacked the Chinese position and his delegation literally turned their backs on the Chinese speakers. Later the Japanese Communist party stated it could not support the treaty and expelled Shiga for agreeing with Moscow. In October, 1964, the party's preference was clear from its praise of China's successful nuclear test. Since then, this tendency to befriend Peking has wavered in view of the irritation caused by the latter's attempt, following the Cultural Revolution, to win support for Maoism by circumventing the Japanese Communist party and contacting directly radical groups in the labor and student movement. Neutralism toward both Moscow and Peking is the pronounced policy. While the party's strength has waned within the Japanese labor movement, through its Democratic Youth League and the *Minsei* faction of the student movement it has created a potentially powerful organization for the future.

Another important group, whose future influence as an opposition force may become important if its present growth rate continues, is the *Sōka Gakkai* (Value Creating Society) and its political arm, the *Kōmeitō*. This society was founded in 1946. It considers Nichiren, the ardent nationalist Buddhist priest of the thirteenth century, to be the ultimate Buddha, and salvation to come through faith in him and repetition of the incantation, "Praise to the Lotus Sutra." *Sōka Gakkai* offers to its believers a simple explanation of the world. Its objective is immediate personal happiness for its members through the convergence of secular and sacred law. It claims that true democracy will come about only when everyone participates in politics; it formed its own political party, the *Kōmeitō,* for this purpose. Its political program advocates clean government, more responsibility for youth, world peace through brotherhood, no revision of the Constitution, and a reduction of the Self-Defense Forces. With these popular objectives, a mere attestation of faith in the Lotus Sutra as a prerequisite for membership, and an actively supported evangelism directed toward the middle and lower classes, *Sōka Gakkai* has had a phenomenal growth. By 1969, membership in terms of households reportedly numbered 7 million, with total individual membership over 15 million. In the House of Councilors' election of 1965 the Kōmeitō received 5 million votes and won 20 seats. In the 1969 election for the House of Representatives, it increased its membership from 25 to 47. Its future influence is unpredictable if for no other reason than that Kōmeitō Diet members have had little political experience.[11]

The Student Movement and Riots

Opposition to many of the basic policies of the Liberal Democratic cabinets of the 1960's, especially their foreign relations, the close alliance with the United States, the visits of the American naval ships and nuclear submarines, and the reluctance to resolve the Okinawa problem have all been popular themes championed by the leaders of the student movement. But other more significant and subtle factors have changed the

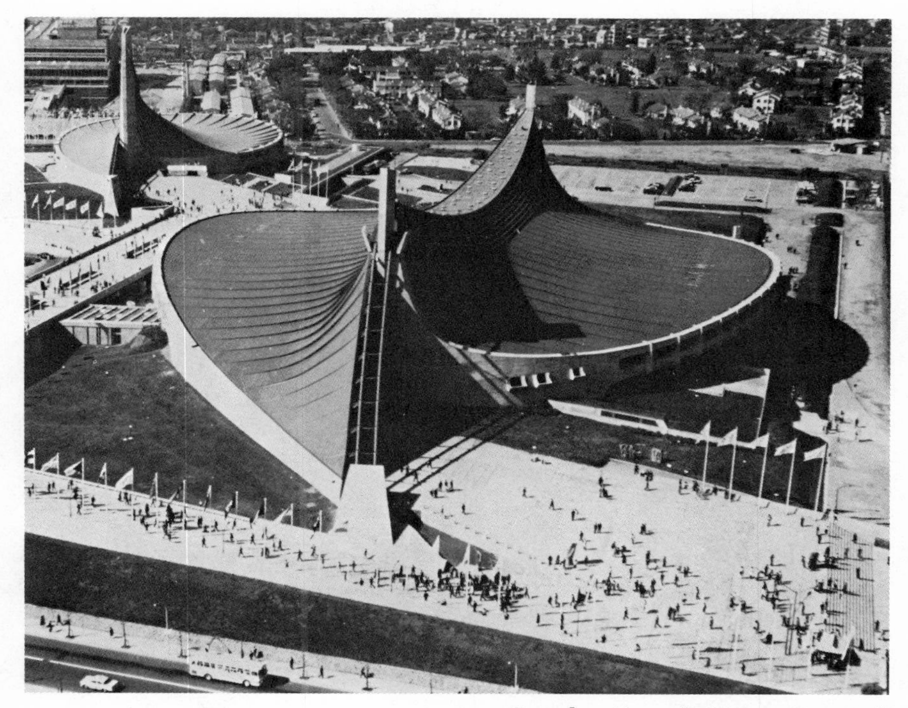

Consulate General of Japan, New York

NATIONAL INDOOR GYMNASIUMS DESIGNED BY TANGE KENZO FOR TOKYO'S 1964 OLYMPIAD

basic character of Japanese student protests during the decade following the ratification of the United States–Japan Security Treaty in 1960.

The highly politicized character of the movement has led to unbelievably intense internal rivalries for power resulting in vicious demonstrations and riots. As a result, the university campuses have become the scenes of pitched battles between contending student factions. To outline an extremely complicated situation, by the middle of the decade, a coalition of three activist, ultraleftist factions had wrested control of *Zengakuren* from the mainstream group which favored orderly nonviolent demonstrations. This coalition group has been known as the *Sampa Rengō,* and on many occasions its factions have fought each other. For example, the most violent antagonism exists between the extreme leftist *Sampa Rengō* factions and the *Minsei* or *Yoyogi* faction, which is controlled by the Communist party. In view of these deep ideological cleavages, the drive of one faction or group of factions to obtain prestige, power, and eventual control over another and over the student movement has led to promotion of popular causes and to the escalation of violence. Crash helmets with plastic shields, staves, and iron pipes have replaced school caps, armbands, and banners. The police have developed special riot squads and trucks with water cannon to control the rioters. As they have become more disruptive, unprecedented numbers of arrests have been made. The leaders have been charged with violation of the Anti-Riot Law and the courts have begun to apply its severe penalties.

Furthermore, the leaders of the radical activists have recognized that the legal, nonviolent movement of the previous decade failed to stop the government from ratifying the Security Treaty of 1960. They also have realized that the opposition parties were against the continuation of the Security Treaty, which could be nullified or changed after 1970. They hoped that if they took a strong position against the Treaty, they would gain support from the minority political parties. As noted later, the reversion of Okinawa was another popular cause which they vehemently championed.

At the same time, the radical students are stating an obvious fact when they claim that the Establishment has failed to grapple seriously with overdue reforms in society at large, in the economic system, and in the education system, especially in the universities. They are convinced of the necessity of a revolution. Herein lies their passionate urge to obstruct the government's moves for continuance of the American alliance and to destroy any and all institutions of higher learning. They assume that if they can bring this about, the entire Establishment will crumble.

As for the riots directed against the larger political or international issues, in October, 1967, they took on a more ominous form. Under the radical *Sampa Rengō,* 2,500 students clashed with police at or near Tokyo's airport in an attempt to halt Prime Minister Satō's departure for South Vietnam. An ultraradical student from Kyōto University was killed and 600 persons were wounded. The next month, the students again rioted in a vain attempt to keep the Prime Minister from leaving for the United States. During the next four months, several demonstrations of varying size resulted in confrontations with the special riot police. These included protests against the visit to Japan of the U.S.S. "Enterprise" which had just left the Vietnam war zone, and against the construction of an American Army field hospital on the edge of Tokyo.

On October 21, 1968, dubbed International Anti-War Day, a massive demonstration was held against the Japan National Railway for allegedly transporting American oil for use in Vietnam. The students streamed into Shinjuku Station, Tokyo's main transfer center for commuters. The rioters spilled onto the railroad tracks, disrupted traffic, and used the rock ballast to fight the police. Over 300 demonstrators were arrested for violation of the Anti-Riot Law. On the same day a year later, when the demonstrations were called to demand the immediate reversion of Okinawa, most of the extremist student factions joined forces, adopted guerrilla tactics, and extensively disrupted Tokyo's normal life. The riot police kept damage to a minimum and made hundreds of arrests. These activities of the extremists, and the fact that the radical elements were estimated to comprise less than 10 per cent of the student population, alienated the Socialists and labor groups, the press, and the people at large.

Student demonstrations and activities against the universities are best illustrated by the tragic example of Tokyo University. The student strike at Japan's most prestigious university began in early 1968 when internes at the School of Medicine demanded improved working conditions. The resulting impasse between the internes and the administration closed the Medical School. The strike soon took on a political nature. It caused the cancellation of commencement. After students had occupied and held the main Medical School building, University President Ōkochi Kazuo requested the police to eject them. In the summer, the activities of student factions and of the Joint Struggle Committee created constant turmoil causing the closing of the entire university.

In November, 1968, a bloody tragedy was avoided when 6,000 students from the communist-supported *Minsei* faction and 7,000 anti-communist members of *Sampa Rengō* held separate parts of the main campus and threatened to attack each other. They were kept from doing so by the police. Two months later, after 370 ultraradical students refused to leave the main administration building in which they were entrenched, the Acting President called in the riot police. After two days' siege, the occupants were overcome and arrested but the University's landmark, Yasuda Hall, was severely damaged. Ironically, the radical faction which had occupied the building had played into the hands of their archenemies, the *Minsei* faction. The *Minsei* members were well disciplined and followed the current policy of their parent, the Japanese Communist party, of orderly, lawful demonstrations. In line with this policy, when the police were called in to clear Yasuda Hall, the *Minsei* members withdrew from their section of the campus before the police arrived. By so doing the *Minsei* seemed to have gained control of the University's Self-Government Association. Negotiations with the University's administration finally resulted in its opening in the summer of 1969. As for the country as a whole, the *Minsei* apparently had the upper hand, controlling perhaps 65 per cent of the Self-Government Associations in the nation and able to muster 35,000 supporters.[12]

In the face of ever increasing protests and riots by extremist students and the closing of numerous universities, in August, 1969, the Satō government forced through the Diet a University Normalization Law. It provides that any university which is closed because of students' demands shall, with the assistance of a special mediation commission, have a year's time to resolve its difficulties. If these have not been settled during this period, the Minister of Education may close permanently any public university and may request the trustees of any private university to do likewise. During the latter part of 1969, the new University Law was apparently having an effect in quieting campus disorders. Several universities which had been closed by students were opened by the authorities, usually with the help of the police in ejecting the recalcitrant students.

Okinawa (the Ryūkyū Islands) and the Security Treaty

In the 1960's, the future of Okinawa was the most difficult issue facing Japan and the United States. Since the American forces captured the Ryūkyū Islands in April, 1945, they have been under continuous American military control. Okinawa, the largest and most important of these islands, soon expanded into an important military base. Under the terms of the Peace Treaty with Japan, the United States acquired the authority to exercise administrative rights over the Ryūkyūs. It did not acquire the sovereignty of the islands. In 1953, the United States announced that it would remain in the islands for the foreseeable future and formally recognized Japan's residual sovereignty of them. By 1959 it had leased for use as military bases over 10 per cent of the arable land on the islands and 20 per cent on Okinawa island. This situation, along with the questionable methods of payment for use of the land and the general dislocation of the people, contributed to the considerable ill-will which the inhabitants of the islands felt toward the United States. The Okinawans, who total more than 900,000 persons, had been part, though the poorest part, of the Japanese Empire. Now their main objective was to revert to Japan.

While the American installations were a source of employment for many Okinawans and provided a substantial part of their income, it was far from enough to sustain the economy of the islands. Japanese politicians, notably the Socialist party, took up the cause of the reversion of Okinawa to Japan. The American military authorities insisted that it was crucial as a military base. Part of its advantage, from the point of view of the American military, was that it was outside the restrictions of the Security Treaty. In other words, the United States was not required to consult with Japan prior to moving troops, ships, or nuclear weapons into or out of the area. In 1961, during the Ikeda–Kennedy talks, the former requested that more self-government and economic assistance be given to Okinawa. President Kennedy agreed to appoint a civilian as Civil Administrator of the islands and to double American aid to $12 million yearly. All the islands were now referred to as Okinawa.

Constant points of friction continued, however, between the American authorities and the Okinawans. For example, a communist was elected mayor of the main city of Naha, which the U. S. Civil Administration decided was intolerable. The Mayor was not allowed to take office. When American B-52 bombers flew from Guam to Okinawa and then proceeded with a full load of bombs to Vietnam, the Japanese were highly offended. In 1967, the reversion issue was in everyone's mind; the return of the Ryūkyūs to full Japanese sovereignty and control became the symbol of Japan's true independence. The United States, on the other hand, still claimed that Okinawa was as important a base as before and would not agree to specifying a date when it was to return to Japan. In November, 1967, when Premier Satō met President Johnson in Washington, the issue still was not resolved. The most they could agree on was that a solution should be reached promptly on the question of a date when the administrative rights of the Ryūkyūs should revert to Japan and that an advisory commission be established whereby both governments would keep the matter under review. As a palliative for the failure to agree on a reversion date, the United States consented to the immediate return of the Bonin Islands to Japan.

Furthermore, the U. S. High Commissioner authorized the election by the Okinawans of a Chief Executive to take on many of the responsibilities of local government. In November, 1968, the election of Yara Chōbyō to the new position reflected the yearning of the Okinawans to return to Japan. Yara had been president of the Teacher's Union and leader of the reversion movement. He ran on a reformist ticket. His opponent, the candidate of the Liberal Democratic party, advocated the integration of Okinawa with Japan through gradual economic and social welfare. Both before and after the election, Okinawans protested the continued use of the base for American bombers going to Vietnam.

In Japan proper, Prime Minister Satō was being pressed from all sides to insist on a commitment from the United States, before June, 1970, as to the exact date when Okinawa would be returned to Japan with the understanding that the same restrictions which apply to American bases in the rest of Japan would apply to Okinawa. In other words, the permission of the Japanese government would have to be obtained for nuclear weapons on the base or for the departure overseas of American forces from the base. This view was also receiving the support of many Americans outside government, such as Edwin O. Reischauer, former U. S. Ambassador to Japan.

The question of the reversion of Okinawa also had important security implications for Japan and was inextricably tied into the question of the continuation of the United States–Japan Security Treaty. Although the opposition groups, especially the radical students, constantly referred to the "Crisis of 1970" in relation to the Treaty, the legal and parliamentary situation was far different from that of a decade earlier. It will be recalled that in 1960 Prime Minister Kishi signed the Treaty in Washington, and ruled that the Diet could not amend it but could only approve or reject it. His task, therefore, was one of strategy to get the Diet's approval. After June, 1970, however, Japan's approval was necessary only if changes were to be made in the original agreement. If neither Japan nor the United States took any action, the Treaty would automatically continue in force indefinitely. So long as this situation existed, Japan could expect that United States forces would remain in the Pacific and thus contribute to security in the Far East. In the meantime, Japan might well be expected to develop defense forces of sufficient strength to defend itself.

Self-Defense Forces

These factors, plus the possibility that the United States, for either political or economic reasons, might decide at some point that it could no longer carry the heavy burden of paying for the defense of Japan, underline the importance of Japan's Self-Defense Forces. As noted earlier, these had started at a strength of about 150,000 and built up to over 200,000 in four years. By 1967, they had reached an actual strength of 231,400. During the same period, United States armed forces in Japan had decreased from 210,000 to 36,400. Although some politicians hinted at the possibility of nuclear armament, the populace as a whole abhorred the thought of being involved in nuclear warfare. For example, in February, 1968, Agriculture and Forestry Minister Kuraishi stated that he considered the Constitution to be "silly," that Japan must defend itself and must have a military force of 300,000 men and "one atom bomb to ensure the safety of the next generation." This indiscretion was pounced upon by the Socialists who refused to participate in the Diet's proceedings until Kuraishi resigned two weeks later to avoid further embarrassment to Satō's Cabinet. The Prime Minister felt compelled to reiterate once more his party's three basic principles in reference to nuclear weapons: the prohibition against their introduction, storage, or use by Japan. While the nation complacently relaxed under the American nuclear umbrella, anyone who advocated Japan's becoming a nuclear power was liable to harsh criticism.

The main effort in rearmament, therefore, was directed toward the improvement and modernization of the Self-Defense Forces with conventional weapons. These included heavy artillery, type-61 tanks, and F-104 jet fighters for the Air Force. The Maritime Force relied on small, fast ships, including 40 destroyers and escorts. The 1969 budget allowed for an appropriation of $1,344 million, which equaled 7.2 per cent of the total budget. A fair share of this went toward domestic contracts for the manufacture, on a license basis with General Electric, of 34 Phantom jet fighters. The Maritime Forces placed orders for eight new 2,000-ton patrol ships.[13]

Foreign Relations with Asia

Japan's contemporary attitude toward China is an enigma to the foreign observer, for it takes the form of an apparently naïve belief that neither the defeat of Japan in World War II nor the success of the Chinese People's Republic has made any appreciable difference in the relationship of the two countries. Japan seems to assume that it could handle China were it not for the American attitude toward Formosa and Peking. When China exploded its first nuclear device, few Japanese objected despite their trauma about nuclear weapons, and the Communist party applauded. The Japanese considered the matter more political than military and saw little danger from China's potential nuclear capabilities.

Furthermore, Prime Minister Satō has insisted that politics and economics can be separated in dealing with the People's Republic of China and that trade can therefore be carried on without any formal diplomatic arrangement. However, Japan's delegates to Peking, who negotiated a trade agreement for 1969, were forced to sign a political statement as part of the trade agreement. By so doing the Japanese admitted that the United States–Japan Security Treaty was a threat to the peoples of China and Asia. They also agreed to promote the normalization of Sino-Japanese relations, "to oppose any plots to create two Chinas," and to recognize that Peking was the only legitimate Chinese government. The statement concluded that relations should be based on the following three basic principles: (1) Japan would not take a hostile attitude toward Peking; (2) Japan would correct the policy of the separation of economics and politics; and (3) the liberation of Taiwan was a purely internal Chinese problem. To make matters worse, the total amount of trade allowed under the agreement was far less than in previous years. There seemed nothing but a hardening of China's position and in Japan a continuing of a nostalgia for an old order which would never return.

As for Japanese–Korean relations, the ingrained mutual animosity between the two nations and peoples was reflected in the prolonged unwillingness of both sides to come to an agreement. Prejudices have been strong, and it is difficult for the Japanese to overcome their feeling of superiority over all Koreans. Even after Syngman Rhee was ousted as President in 1960, there was little Korea had which Japan needed. Consequently, it took five more years before the two nations could come to an agreement on formal recognition of each other's position on fisheries, economic cooperation, the legal status of Koreans in Japan, and property claims. Property claims were finally settled on the basis of Japan granting Korea $300 million in aid, $200 million in loans, and $300 million on a private credit basis. In view of Korea's complete absorption in her own plans for industrial development and the continued antipathy between the two nations, it is unlikely that their future relationship will be much more than formal.

Finally, Japan's future with South and Southeast Asia appears somewhat unpredictable. As already noted, it has shown interest in the Asian Development Bank. Trade opportunities are arising as a consequence of conditions resulting from the reparations agreements. Many Asians are receiving technical training in Japan and numerous Japanese specialists, such as agronomists and engineers, are serving in the area. India has been an important source of iron ore. But the trade statistics show that the greatest attraction for Japanese products and Japan's greatest needs both come from the industrially advanced nations. On the other hand, with Japan's willingness to increase its aid to the developing nations, new types of relationships with them may develop which will be far more beneficial to all concerned than now seems probable.[14]

Satō–Nixon Agreement—November, 1969

Such was the general situation in the fall of 1969 when Prime Minister Satō made plans to visit President Nixon in Washington to reach an agreement on the various outstanding issues between their two nations, especially the reversion of Okinawa and the future of the United States–Japan Security Treaty. For their part, the militant students and other antigovernment groups vowed that they would stage a mass demonstration to prevent Satō's departure. They were frustrated, however, by elaborate precautionary measures taken by the police. Despite numerous confrontations, the rioters were kept well away from the Tokyo airport. Some predicted that student riots had reached their high water mark.

The Satō–Nixon meetings covered most of the problems of mutual concern to Japan and the United States. Their conclusions were announced on November 21, 1969. On the matter of the Security Treaty, they agreed that existing conditions in the Far East required the continuance of the Treaty and of the presence of American forces in the Far East. They approved of the reversion of Okinawa to Japan during 1972 with the United States retaining a base there but with Japan assuming the defense of the islands. The details for such an arrangement were to be worked out through bilateral consultations. In recognition of the tensions in the Korean Peninsula, Premier Satō, indicating an extension of Japan's security responsibilities, stated that the security of the Republic of Korea was essential to Japan's own security. On economic matters, he promised that Japan would move toward a general liberalization of economic restraints against other nations such as import quotas and the restriction on foreign capital investment. As a result of this conference, Satō insisted that a new era in Japan's postwar independence had begun. While the implementation of these points of agreement might cause real difficulties as a result of different interpretations given to them by Japan and the United States, the most explosive issue between them—the reversion of Okinawa—had been settled.[15]

Upon his return to Tokyo, Satō was pleased to receive a warm welcome. Many Japanese seemed surprised that he had been able to persuade the United States to agree to Okinawa's reversion. He decided to seek the support of the electorate for his basic policies. These he outlined as: (1) the support of the no-war provision of the Constitution, (2) the development of a Self-Defense Force adequate to defend Japanese territory, (3) the continuance of the Japan–United States Security Treaty for a considerable time, (4) the reliance on the United States' nuclear arsenal for the general defense of the Far East. The returns of the general election of December 27, 1969, for the House of Representatives substantiated Satō's contention that his policy of continued close alliance with the United States met with general approval. The Liberal Democrats won a clear majority with 288 seats. The Socialists declined to 90, the Democratic Socialists remained about the same with 32, while the Kōmeitō nearly doubled from 25 to 47. The Communists' representation increased to 14. (See Table 11, page 472.) The support for the Liberal Democratic party was greater than predicted and its immediate future was secure. Prime Minister Satō's reorganization of his Cabinet reflected shifts in power among the factions within the party.[16]

Japan Today and Tomorrow

One of the first impressions of the sojourner in Japan in 1970 is the crowds of people everywhere. This is not a new phenomenon but has been intensified. In the streets of the cities, in the subways and buses, the department stores and markets, the deluxe superexpress trains and the locals, the country lanes and the superhighways, the schools and the universities, and in urban apartment houses and thatched-roofed farmhouses, people are everywhere. Yet nowhere are the crowds more circumspect nor have people learned better how to live with their crowded conditions.

As the standard of living has improved, with the average salary comparable to that of Italy, a revolution has taken place in the purchase of consumers' goods. Private automobiles, which before the war were practically nonexistent, are now owned by over 11 per cent of the population. Cars, color television, and air conditioners are the three most important status symbols of the new "salary man." But these modern luxuries or conveniences are not all blessings. Like all large metropolitan areas, Tokyo, the world's largest city with a population in 1969 of about 11 million, is replete with the contrasting and contradictory facets of modern urban society. The wealthy and poor live cheek to jowl. Tokyo boasts the world's most spectacular observation tower yet the city is so plagued with air pollution that the upper half of the tower is often encased in smog. There is a new system of express highways throughout the city yet it is harassed with unbelievably massive traffic jams. A new four-lane express highway connects it with the cities of Kyōto and Ōsaka, running through the most populated part of the nation, but the world's highest traffic accident rate takes away much of the pleasure of driving.

In preparation for the 1964 Olympic Games, Tokyo's subway system was extended and improved, yet its rush hour makes that of New York seem tame. The nation is justly proud of Tange Kenzo's most imaginative and graceful gymnasium built for the Olympics. At the same time increasing numbers of postwar Japanese are returning to make obeisance before their great national shrines built in traditional style such as that of the Emperor Meiji.

High incomes for more people have also brought greater demands for both domestic and foreign products, and more leisure time for travel, recreation, music, the theater, and sports. While foreigners will be visiting Ōsaka to see Expo '70, Japanese office workers, both men and women, will be taking vacation cruises to Hong Kong or Hawaii and middle-class newlyweds will be enjoying their honeymoon in Taiwan or the United States. Even the farmers, who for centuries have been the "foundation of Japanese society" and whose entire families have toiled from dawn to dusk to exact the most from tiny plots, have come into their own. Their incomes have improved at a faster rate than those of the urban workers, and three-fourths of them own mechanical equipment which lightens their labor and increases their productivity.

Although there are many external changes in postwar Japan, the industriousness of the people, their facility to grasp innovations, and their

Consulate General of Japan, New York

Tokyo's Ginza at Night, 1970

dexterity and willingness to carry out their assignments are some of the chief ingredients for Japan's success. Their belief in the importance of education has increased their capabilities to deal with a highly technological society. It is little wonder that Japan has gone so far so quickly.

In the century prior to World War II, Japan was transformed, almost exclusively by its own efforts, from an isolated feudal state to an aggressive Empire willing to challenge the United States or any other nation for the supremacy of Asia. In the quarter-century since its defeat in

1945, it has again exhibited a unique resilience in its recovery from devastation to become the world's third industrial power. During this last effort, though it initially received limited assistance from the United States, in the past fifteen years its initiative, managerial ability, technological advancement, and physical energy have come from within the nation. It is understandable, therefore, why there is a constant search for ways of expressing a new independence and a yearning to be free from dependence on the United States for security.

But as the noted Japanese writer, Hasegawa Nyozekan has expressed it, "Japan's genius is essentially practical, not theoretical. . . . It owes its strength to practical men, not saints and savants." If the practical men continue to rule Japan, and this has certainly been the case in recent years, they will favor close collaboration with the United States, including continuation of the defensive alliance through the Security Treaty, so long as it is to Japan's advantage to do so. They will increasingly deal with the United Nations, Peking or Taiwan, Moscow or Paris, Manila or New Delhi from the point of view of their own self-interest rather than America's interest. By the same token, the highly practical leaders of the Liberal Democratic party and of the business world will take measures to see that no one threatens their position, especially the extremists of either the right or the left. They have too much respect for democratic principles and processes and too vivid memories of what the militarists brought upon their country during World War II to countenance a military–rightist alliance. They also cherish sufficiently their own position of power to be willing to use that power to prevent the radical left from threatening them. But two imponderables remain. Can this power be kept from corrupting, and can justice be meted out with mercy?

Notes

1. Ikeda Hayato (1899–1965) was born in Kyūshū, graduated from the Fifth Higher School in Kumamoto and Kyōto University. Some of his most faithful supporters in later years were those who had been his classmates in these two institutions. He started in the Finance Ministry and in 1940 attracted the attention of a close friend and adviser of Yoshida Shigeru. Subsequently, Yoshida appointed Ikeda as Vice-Minister of Finance after which his career as a politican was assured. In 1960, business leaders spent large sums to assure his victory as Kishi's successor. He would doubtless have remained in office much longer if he had not died of cancer in 1964. See Chitoshi Yanaga, *Big Business and Japanese Politics* (New Haven: Yale University Press, 1968), pp. 141 ff.

2. For an illuminating study on how the conservatives operate and stay in power, see Nathaniel B. Thayer, *How the Conservatives Rule Japan* (Princeton: Princeton University Press, 1969). Further explanation of the

operation of factions with supporting data will be found in Robert A. Scalapino and Junnosuke Masumi, *Parties and Politics in Contemporary Japan* (Berkeley: University of California Press, 1964), pp. 54 ff. and appendices.

3. Satō Eisaku (1901–) is a bureaucrat turned politician. Upon graduation from Tokyo University in 1924 he entered the Ministry of Transportation. In 1934 he went to the United States to study for three years on a government scholarship. He returned to the Transportation Ministry and in 1941 became a bureau chief and in 1947 Vice-Minister. The next year, Yoshida persuaded him to enter politics and he was soon appointed Chief Cabinet Secretary. In 1949 he was elected to the House of Representatives and became Secretary General of the Party in 1950. In 1957 he was appointed Finance Minister in the Cabinet of his older brother, Kishi Nobusuke.

4. There are several valuable and useful works on Japan's recent economy. These include: Jerome B. Cohen, *Japan's Postwar Economy* (Bloomington: University of Indiana Press, 1958), which includes data to 1956; William W. Lockwood, "Japan's 'New Capitalism,'" Martin Bronfenbrenner, "Economic Miracles and Japan's Income-Doubling Plan," and Hugh T. Patrick, "Cyclical Instability and Fiscal–Monetary Policy in Postwar Japan," in William W. Lockwood (ed.), *The State and Economic Enterprise in Japan* (Princeton: Princeton University Press, 1965), pp. 447–619; Warren S. Hunsberger, *Japan and the United States in World Trade* (New York: Council on Foreign Relations, 1964).

5. Statistics for this table were taken or adapted from the following sources:

a. Items 1–4, 6, 8, and 9 for the years 1934–1936 and 1951 through 1962 from William W. Lockwood, "Political Economy" in Herbert Passin (ed.), *The United States and Japan.* Copyright © 1966 by The American Assembly, Columbia University, New York, N. Y. Reprinted by permission of Prentice-Hall, Inc., Englewood Cliffs, N. J., p. 101. Sources for the above are as follows: Basic annual series, before adjustment to consistent index base, are from Japan. Economic Planning Agency, *Showa 31-nendo no kokumin shotoku* (National Income), *1956* (Tokyo: 1958), pp. 120–21, and *Japanese Economic Statistics, passim;* Bureau of Statistics, *Japan Statistical Yearbook, passim;* and Bank of Japan, *Economic Statistics Monthly, passim.* Figures are three-year averages, except for two years, 1963 and 1964. For national income (except 1934–1936) and family consumption these are fiscal years beginning April 1; other data are averages for calendar years.

b. Items 5 and 7 for the years 1934–1936 and 1951 through 1962 from William W. Lockwood, "Japan's New Capitalism," in William W. Lockwood (ed.), *The State and Economic Enterprise in Japan* (Princeton: Princeton University Press, 1965). Copyright © 1965 by Princeton University Press; No. 2 in the Series of Studies in the Modernization of Japan. Table on p. 449 with permission of the publisher.

c. All statistics from 1963 through 1968 from Bank of Japan, *Monthly Statistics;* Cabinet Bureau of Statistics, *Nihon Tōkei Nenkan, 1966* (Japanese Statistical Yearbook, 1966; Tokyo: 1967) *passim* and *Nihon Tōkei Geppō* (Monthly Statistics), March, 1969, *passim.*

6. Cabinet Bureau of Statistics, *Nihon Tōkei Nenkan, 1966* (Statistical Yearbook; Tokyo: 1967); Bank of Japan, *Monthly Statistics,* February, 1966; and *Nihon Tōkei Geppō,* March, 1969. The indices and annual increases for 1967 and 1968 are calculated from the new computations of the Economic Planning Agency which use 1965 as a base year. Thus the rate of increase

will probably be modified when the Bureau of Statistics releases its figures for these years.

7. Lockwood, "Political Economy," *op. cit.*, p. 111; and Bank of Japan, *Economic Statistics,* January and March, 1969, and Cabinet Bureau of Statistics, *Nihon Tōkei Nenkan, 1966* (Japan Statistical Yearbook; Tokyo: 1967).

8. James C. Abegglen, *The Japanese Factory: Aspects of its Social Organization* (New York: Asia Publishing House, 1959).

9. As will be seen from Table 11, in the House of Representatives, the Socialists declined from 145 to 144, 140, and 90. The Democratic Socialists rose from 17 to 23, 30, and 32. The Communists rose from 3 to 5, and 14. In the House of Councilors, in comparison to those elected in 1965, the Socialists declined from 36 to 28 while the Democratic Socialists and the Communists rose from 3 to 7 and 3 to 4 respectively.

10. Robert A. Scalapino, "Labor and Politics in Postwar Japan," in Lockwood (ed.), *op. cit.*, pp. 669 ff.

11. The first writings on the Value-Creating Principle appeared in 1930. In 1937, Toda Josei (d. 1958), the second President of *Sōka Gakkai,* was imprisoned during the war because of his opposition to State Shintō. During his presidency, the movement attracted national attention. Ikeda Daisaku (1928–) became the third President in 1960 and the society has flourished under his militant leadership. Its official publication is Sōka gakkai, *The Nichiren Shoshu Soka gakkai* (Tokyo: Seikyo Press, 1966).

12. Only three months prior to the crisis with the Medical School, President Ōkochi had been re-elected by the faculty for a second term. Presidents of the National Universities such as Tokyo are selected by the faculty from their membership. In an interview in November, 1967, in his office in Yasuda Hall, which was later occupied by students, he told the author of his hope to restrict the size of the undergraduate body of 12,000 and to enlarge the graduate departments. He deplored the fact that the university regulations in Japan permitted students to take four years to pass the first two years of college and four more years to pass the next two, thus allowing them ample time for political action.

For more detailed material on the factions in the student movement see Junnō Fukushiri, "The Student Movement," *Japan Quarterly* (April–June, 1969), pp. 148 ff.

13. Figures for the Self-Defense Forces were kindly provided by Dr. Martin E. Weinstein. See his "Japan's Postwar Defense Policy," Ph.D. thesis, Columbia University, 1969.

14. This whole problem is treated by Lawrence Olson, in *Japan in Postwar Asia* to be published for the Council on Foreign Relations, by Frederick A. Praeger, Inc., in 1970.

15. The matter of prior consultation with the Japanese government over the use overseas of American forces stationed at Okinawa and the storage of nuclear weapons was not completely settled by the Communique. These issues will become acute if the Vietnam War is not settled prior to the date set for final reversion. For a complete text of the Communique see *The New York Times,* November 21, 1969.

16. Satō formed his fourth Cabinet on January 14, 1970. Some of his most important appointments were: Foreign Minister, Aichi Kiichi; Finance Minister, Fukuda Takeo; Minister of International Trade and Industry, Miyazawa Kiichi; Minister of Education, Sakata Michita; and Director of Defense Agency, Nakasone Yasuhiro.

Bibliographical Note

In view of the availability of both comprehensive and selective bibliographies of material in Japanese and European languages, the following notes are not meant to be exhaustive. They are prepared for the reader who does not have access to these references and who may wish to read further in some of the more important subjects covered in this book. For the sake of convenience, the notes are arranged under the five periods covered by the Parts of the book. More works are listed in European languages than in Japanese on the assumption that those readers who read Japanese will also be familiar with or have access to the extensive Japanese bibliographies.

If the reader is interested in more detailed bibliographical information, the most helpful guide in European languages is *A Selected List of Books and Articles on Japan in English, French, and German* (Cambridge: Harvard-Yenching Institute, revised and enlarged, 1954), compiled by Hugh Borton, Serge Elisséeff, William W. Lockwood, and John C. Pelzel. This annotated bibliography lists over 1,700 titles, arranged topically. Both comprehensive and special bibliographies are listed in the first section. For current listings of publications on Japan, the most comprehensive coverage is in the annual *Bibliography of Asian Studies* published by the Association for Asian Studies in its *Journal of Asian Studies.* Prior to 1956, this bibliography was published as the *Far Eastern Bibliography.* A select number of both Japanese and Western language references, arranged both topically and according to historical periods, is given in the *American Historical Association's Guide to Historical Literature* (New York: The Macmillan Co., 1961), Section P, "Japan," pp. 296–318.

As for annotated bibliographies in Japanese, the Bibliographical Series of the Center for Japanese Studies of the University of Michigan are the most useful. The following volumes in this series are especially pertinent to the subjects covered by this book: John W. Hall, *Japanese History: A Guide to Japanese References and Research Materials* (Ann Arbor: University of Michigan, Center for Japanese Studies, Bibliographical Series No. 4, 1954); and Robert E. Ward, *A Guide to Japanese Reference and Research Materials in the Field of Political Science* (Ann Arbor: University of Michigan, Center for Japanese Studies, Bibliographical Series No. 1, 1950). Students and librarians will find much valuable bibliographical and other information in Herschel Webb with Marleigh Ryan, *Research in Japanese Sources: A Guide* (New York: Columbia University Press, 1965).

Sir George B. Sansom has written two excellent companion volumes on the cultural background of Japan. They are *Japan, A Short Cultural History* (New York: Appleton-Century-Crofts, Inc., 1944) and *The Western World and Japan* (New York: Alfred A. Knopf, Inc., 1950). The former covers the period from earliest antiquity through the eighteenth century; the latter describes the impact of European civilization on Japan and its historical development down to about 1894. For a more detailed excellent history from its origins to 1867 see his three volumes: *A History of Japan to 1334; A History of Japan 1334–1615;* and *A History of Japan 1615–1867* (Stanford: Stanford University Press, 1958, 1961, and 1963).

A most readable yet condensed history is *Japan Past and Present,* revised and enlarged edition (New York: Alfred A. Knopf, Inc., 1964), by the outstanding scholar and former United States Ambassador to Japan, Professor Edwin O. Reischauer. His more interpretive study, *The United States and Japan,* 3rd ed. (Cambridge: Harvard University Press, 1965), is provocative and is especially illuminating for understanding contemporary problems.

Other volumes which cover this same general period include Professor Chitoshi Yanaga's *Japan Since Perry* (Hamden, Conn.: Archon Books, 1966). Particularly useful as a reference, this single volume contains a vast amount of detailed material. It also includes an extensive bibliography of Japanese and English works. Originally published in 1949, it has not been brought up to date. Another work, with far less detail, is that of William G. Beasley, *The Modern History of Japan* (New York: Frederick A. Praeger, Inc., 1963). The same period, in both China and Japan, is ably presented in John King Fairbank, Edwin O. Reischauer, and Albert M. Craig, *East Asia: The Modern Transformation* (Boston: Houghton Mifflin Co., 1965).

Since the end of World War II, scholarly works on modern Japan have been on the increase in the United States and other English-speaking countries. This phenomenon reflects both the enlarged interest in Japan resulting from the war and the maturation of Japanese studies in America. Furthermore, thanks to the leadership of Professor John W. Hall and other scholars, the formation of a Conference on Modern Japan sponsored by the Association for Asian Studies has done much to increase our understanding of many aspects of Japan's modern development. As a result of a series of six seminars, to which a total of over seventy Japanese and American scholars contributed papers, four of the valuable Studies in the Modernization of Japan have already been published by the Princeton University Press with two others scheduled for publication in 1970. Together, these volumes, which cover a wide range of subjects by many of the best scholars in the field, have deepened our knowledge of modern Japan. Each volume concentrates on a general subject, with articles on various historical periods from before the Meiji Restoration to recent times. Their titles, in order of their appearance, are: Marius B. Jansen (ed.), *Changing Japanese Attitudes Toward Modernization* (Princeton: Princeton University Press, 1965); William W. Lockwood (ed.), *The State and Economic Enterprise in Japan: Essays in the Political Economy of Growth* (Princeton: Princeton University Press, 1965); R. P. Dore (ed.), *Aspects of Social Change in Modern Japan* (Princeton: Princeton University Press, 1967); and Robert E. Ward (ed.), *Political Development in Modern Japan* (Princeton: Princeton University Press, 1968). James W. Morley (ed.), *Dilemmas of Growth in Prewar Japan* (Princeton: Princeton University Press), and Donald Shivley (ed.), *Tradition and Modernization in Japanese Culture* (Princeton: Princeton University Press), are scheduled for publication in 1970.

PART I: 1850–1868

Several important works have appeared recently on the opening of Japan. One of these is a comprehensive and thoroughly enjoyable biography of Commodore Perry: Samuel Eliot Morison, *"Old Bruin" Commodore Matthew C. Perry, 1794–1858* (Boston: Little, Brown and Co., 1967). The best primary sources are: Roger Pineau (ed.), *The Japanese Expedition 1852–1854. The Personal Journal of Commodore Matthew C. Perry* (Washington: Smithsonian Institution, 1969), and the official account of the expedition, Francis L. Hawks (ed.), *Narrative of the Expedition of an American Squadron . . . Under Commodore M. C. Perry* (3 vols.; Washington: Nicholson, 1856). An interesting summary of the expedition has been made by Arthur Walworth in *Black Ships off Japan* (New York: Archon Books, 1966). Both Hawks and Walworth contain texts of the Kanagawa Treaty. *The Complete Journal of Townsend Harris,* edited by M. E. Cosenza (Rutland, Vt.: Charles Tuttle Co., revised ed., 1959), is fascinating and instructive. It also contains texts of the conventions which Harris signed with the Japanese government and of the United States–Japanese Commercial Treaty of 1858. The journal of his secretary, Henry C. J. Heusken, which adds further interesting comments on their difficulties, has been edited by Jeannette C.

Van der Corput and Robert C. Wilson as *Japan Journal 1855–1861* (New Brunswick, N. J.: Rutgers University Press, 1964). For Russia's early relations with Japan, a valuable work based on both Japanese and Russian sources is George A. Lensen, *The Russian Push toward Japan: Russo-Japanese Relations 1697–1875* (Princeton: Princeton University Press, 1959). Reaction of the Japanese to the innumerable problems raised by the demands of the Western powers are ably presented in W. G. Beasley, translator and editor, *Select Documents on Japanese Foreign Policy 1853–1868* (London: Oxford University Press, 1955). Britain's part in opening Japan is covered by his *Great Britain and the Opening of Japan* (London: Oxford University Press, 1951). For a thorough, exhaustive, and fascinating account of Britain's early contacts with Japan written from primary sources, see Grace Fox, *Britain and Japan 1858–1883* (Oxford: Clarendon Press, 1969).

Two significant studies have made available much new material on the complicated events in the last few years of the Tokugawa dictatorship. The first of these, by Professor Albert M. Craig of Harvard, *Chōshū in the Meiji Restoration* (Cambridge: Harvard University Press, 1961), describes both the political forces operating within that feudal domain and its role in the restoration to power of the Emperor. The second, by Professor Marius B. Jansen of Princeton University, *Sakamoto Ryōma and the Meiji Restoration* (Princeton: Princeton University Press, 1961), uses the life of Sakamoto, a warrior of the domain of Tosa, to clarify further events leading to the Meiji Restoration. An earlier and broader study, which devotes considerable space to the collapse of the Tokugawa dictatorship is E. Herbert Norman, *Japan's Emergence as a Modern State* (New York: American Institute of Pacific Relations, Inc., 1940). The author of this pioneer work has been accused of making an oversimplified Marxist analysis of Japan's economic development. Nonetheless, the author did much to stimulate further analysis by others of the modernization process.

Another important monograph that concentrates on agrarian Japan prior to the Meiji Restoration is Thomas C. Smith, *The Agrarian Origins of Modern Japan* (Stanford: Stanford University Press, 1959). The prewar lectures of one of Japan's outstanding economic historians, which contain additional background material, have appeared as Eijirō Honjō, *Economic Theory and History of Japan in the Tokugawa Period* (New York: Russell and Russell, 1965).

Several additional special studies should be mentioned. Professor R. D. Dore in *Education in Tokugawa Japan* (Berkeley: University of California Press, 1965) has concluded that education was much more widespread than heretofore believed. For an analysis of political thought, especially that of the ultrapatriot Yoshida Shōin, see David M. Earl,

Emperor and Nation in Japan (Seattle: University of Washington Press, 1964). Professor Herschel Webb of Columbia University has written a perceptive analysis of a new kind of monarchic government in *The Japanese Imperial Institution in the Tokugawa Period* (New York: Columbia University Press, 1968).

There is a vast amount of source material in Japanese on the opening of the country by the Western powers. The most exhaustive primary sources are *Dai Nihon Komonjo Bakumatsu Gaikoku Kankei* (Japanese Historical Documents, Foreign Relations at the end of the Tokugawa Period), edited and published by the Shiryō Hensan Jo of Tokyo University. The same office has also published much valuable material in *Ishin Shi* (History of the Restoration), in six volumes, edited by Ishin Shiryō Hensan Jimu Kyoku (Tokyo: Meiji Shoin, 1939–1943). More recently, the bureau has been publishing *Dai Nihon Ishin Shiryō* (Historical Documents on the Restoration Period), in eight sections. Still far from complete, the series covers the period from 1846–1871. The first two volumes, dealing with the periods from 1846–1853 and 1854–1857, are particularly pertinent to this section.

Among the innumerable histories of the Tokugawa Period in Japanese, the most outstanding is Kurita Mototsugu, *Edo Jidai, I* (The Tokugawa Period, Part I), in *Sōgō Nihon Shi Taikei, IX* (Tokyo: Naigai Shoseki Kabushiki Kaisha, 1929). For economic history, see Honjō Eijirō,* *Meiji Ishin Keizai Shi Kenkyū* (Studies in Economic History of the Meiji Restoration; Tokyo: Kaizōsha, 1930); and Tsuchiya Takao, *Zoku Nihon Keizai Shi Gaiyō* (Outline of Japanese Economic History: Continued; Tokyo: Iwanami, 1941). One of the most detailed and unbiased accounts of political events of the Meiji Restoration is Osatake Takeki, *Meiji Ishin* (The Meiji Restoration; 4 vols.; Tokyo: Hakuyōsha, 1942–1949).

Two important analytical studies of modern Japan have recently appeared. They are Oka Yoshitake, *Kindai Nihon no Keisei* (The Formation of Modern Japan; Tokyo: Kōbun-dō, 1952), and Yanaihara Tadao (ed.), *Gendai Nihon Shōshi* (A Short History of Present-Day Japan; 3 vols.; Tokyo: Misuzu-shobo, 1961–1962). Professor Inobe Shigeo was one of the first scholars to concentrate on the international and political developments of the period in his *Ishin Zenshi no Kenkyū* (Studies of the Early History of the Restoration; Tokyo: Chūbun-kan, 1935). Tsuji Zennosuke's *Kaigai Kōtsū Shiwa* (Historical Essays on Foreign Relations; Tokyo: Naigai Shoseki Kabushiki Kaisha, 1930) is also important. A more recent work by a scholar who is a specialist on the period prior

* To be consistent with common usage, in this "Bibliographical Note" the names of authors of books in Japanese are given with the family name preceding the given name.

to the restoration is Konishi Jirō, *Kaikoku to Jōi* (The Opening of Japan and the Expulsion of the Western Powers) which is volume 14 in *Nihon no Rekishi* (History of Japan; Tokyo: Chūō Kōron, Tokyo, 1966). The most representative work by one of the leftist writers is Tōyama Shigeki's *Meiji Ishin* (The Meiji Restoration; Tokyo: Iwanami, 1951).

Part II: 1868–1890

There are numerous works which cover all or part of this period. In political history, see W. W. McLaren, *A Political History of Japan During the Meiji Era, 1867–1912* (London: Charles Scribner's Sons, 1916). Significant documents and primary sources for the Restoration and the Constitution have been published in his "Japanese Government Documents," *Transactions of the Asiatic Society of Japan,* XLII, part I (1914). It contains the official translations of the Constitution and of the basic laws which accompanied its promulgation. Another important volume on the Constitution is Hirobumi Itō, *Commentaries on the Constitution of the Empire of Japan,* translated by Myoji Itō (Tokyo: Chūō Daigaku, 1931). This concise volume, which has been published in various editions, gives Itō's views on the meanings of the various articles. It came to be considered almost as sacrosanct as the Constitution.

Several important books have appeared recently which add new information and interpretation to the formation of the Meiji Constitution and the government which it established. These include George M. Beckmann's *The Making of the Meiji Constitution* (Lawrence: Kansas University Press, 1957), which is particularly valuable for its translation of ten key documents. In George Akita, *Foundations of Constitutional Government in Modern Japan 1868–1900* (Cambridge: Harvard University Press, 1967), the author stresses the unexpected difficulties which confronted the oligarchs after Parliament was formed and the skillful manner in which they resolved these problems. Two studies which stress the German political philosophy behind the Constitution and its interpretation are Joseph Pittau, *Political Thought in Early Meiji Japan 1868–1889* (Cambridge: Harvard University Press, 1967), and Johannes Siemes, *Hermann Roesler and the Making of the Meiji Constitution* (Tokyo: Sophia University Press, 1966). In reference to biographical material, Masakazu Iwata has included much helpful material in his *Ōkubo Toshimichi, the Bismarck of Japan* (Berkeley: University of California Press, 1964).

A study of the Japanese government by Harold S. Quigley, *Japanese Government and Politics: An Introductory Study* (New York: Century, 1932), was long the standard work. A more interpretive and provocative summary, with emphasis on the role of the oligarchy, is Robert K.

Reischauer, *Japan, Government and Politics* (New York: Thomas Nelson & Sons, 1939). Robert A. Scalapino, *Democracy and the Party Movement in Prewar Japan* (Berkeley: University of California Press, 1953), largely supersedes these two studies. It is particularly valuable for its analysis of the social origins of the early parties.

In reference to economic materials, a vast amount of new work is being done in developing the most reliable statistics possible in order to enhance studies of economic growth. The Economic Research Center of Hitotsubashi University, under the general supervision of Professor Kazuski Ohkawa, has begun publication of a series of volumes on Japan's Estimates of Long-Term Economic Statistics, entitled *Chōki Keizai Tōkei* (Tokyo: Tōyō Keizaishi Shimpōsha, 1966–). As of 1969, of the projected 13 volumes, the following six have appeared: *Shihon Suttoku* (Capital Stock), vol. 3; *Kojin Shōhi Shishutsu* (Per Capita Receipts and Expenditures), vol. 6; *Zaisei Shishutsu* (Financial Transactions), vol. 7; *Bukka* (Commodity Prices), vol. 8; *Nōrin Gyō* (Agriculture, Forestry and Fisheries), vol. 9; and *Tetsudō to Denryoku* (Railroads and Electric Power), vol. 12. Headings and entries are in both Japanese and English. This series is considered the standard source by present-day economists. A more concise source of general statistics is that compiled by the Statistics Bureau of the Bank of Japan entitled *Iko Hompō Shūyō Keizai Tōkei* (One Hundred Years' Economic Statistics of Japan; Tokyo: Nihon Ginkō, 1966), with three English supplements containing translations of the explanatory notes.

Professor Ohkawa and Henry Rosovsky have published a summary of a forthcoming study on Japan's economic growth in Lockwood, *State and Economic Enterprise, op. cit.*, in an essay entitled "A Century of Japanese Economic Growth." An earlier work, which has stood up well despite the fact that limited reliable economic statistics were available when it was written, is William W. Lockwood's *The Economic Development of Japan: Growth and Structural Change 1868–1938* (Princeton: Princeton University Press, expanded edition, 1968). Originally published in 1954, the expanded new edition contains a chapter on "Japan's New Capitalism" which covers material to 1963. Professor James Nakamura has raised serious doubts concerning the high rate of Japan's agricultural production in his *Agricultural Production and the Economic Development of Japan 1873–1922* (Princeton: Princeton University Press, for the East Asian Institute of Columbia University, 1966). Two special studies which concentrate on this period are Johannes Hirschmeier, *The Origin of Entrepreneurship in Meiji Japan* (Cambridge: Harvard University Press, 1964) and Thomas C. Smith, *Political Change and Industrial Development in Japan: Government Enterprise, 1868–1880* (Stanford: Stanford University Press, 1955).

In the field of foreign relations, those with China were paramount during this period. A thorough study of early Chinese–Japanese relations based on Chinese sources, which throws much light on the Ryūkyū controversy and also on the struggle to control Korea, is T. F. Tsiang's "Sino-Japanese Diplomatic Relations, 1870–94," *Chinese Social and Political Science Review*, 1933. Other important, detailed material on the Korean question is contained in Frederick Nelson, *Korea and the Old Order in Eastern Asia* (Baton Rouge: University of Louisiana Press, 1946). Well over half of Grace Fox's study, *Britain and Japan 1858–1883, op. cit.*, on Britain's relations with and influence on Japan is devoted to this period.

The task of selecting representative and significant writings on society and culture in Japan in 1890 is exceedingly difficult. Numerous histories, reminiscences, autobiographies, and interpretive works have been compiled by those who lived in Japan during the Meiji Period. For some of these the reader is referred to Hugh Borton *et al.*, *A Selected List of Books and Articles on Japan, op. cit.* Some works which should receive special mention include Inazo Nitobe's *Japanese Traits and Foreign Influences* (London: Kegan Paul, Trench, Trubner & Co., Ltd., 1927); Ryusaku Tsunoda, William T. de Bary, and Donald Keene, *Sources of Japanese Tradition* (New York: Columbia University Press, 1958), pp. 591–718, containing translations of selected contemporary material; Carmen Blacker, *The Japanese Enlightenment, a Study of the Writings of Fukuzawa Yukichi* (Cambridge: Cambridge University Press, 1964), a lucid synthesis of the ideas of an outstanding intellectual of the time, and the revised translation of his autobiography by Eiichi Kiyooka entitled *The Autobiography of Fukuzawa Yukichi* (New York: Columbia University Press, 1966).

For an expression of the contemporary official view of Japanese education, see Dairoku Kikuchi, *Japanese Education* (London: John Murray, 1909). This work should be supplemented by the perceptive analysis of the outstanding sociologist and authority on Japan, Herbert Passin, *Society and Education in Japan* (New York: East Asian Institute, Columbia University, 1965). In literature, a representative example is Marleigh Ryan's *Japan's First Modern Novel: Ukigumo of Futabatei Shimei* (New York: Columbia University Press, 1967). A series of interesting articles on late nineteenth-century religion appears in Hideo Kishimoto (compiler), *Japanese Religion in the Meiji Era,* translated by John F. Howes (Tokyo: Obunsha, 1956).

Studies and sources in Japanese are extensive. As for the previous period, one of the most helpful general surveys is Yanaihara Tadao (ed.), *Gendai Nihon Shōshi, op. cit.* General collections of contemporary material are too numerous to mention. A few of the most valuable include:

Itō Hirobumi (ed.), *Hisho Ruisan* (Confidential Materials; 27 vols.; Tokyo: Ruisan Kankōkai, 1933–1936). This collection contains documents, laws, ordinances, treaties, and other pertinent material on the various phases of history from 1868 to about 1890. Hashimoto Hiroshi, *Ishin Nisshi* (Diaries of the Restoration; Series I, 10 vols.; Series II, 10 vols.; Tokyo: Shizuoka Kyōdo Kenkyūkai, 1932–1935), contains a diary of the Council of State, records of Shogun's headquarters, the Emperor's trips from Kyōto to Tokyo, journals of the chief participants in the events of the period, financial reports, and a roster of officials. Yoshino Sakuzō (ed.), *Meiji Bunka Zenshū* (Collected Works on Meiji Culture; 24 vols.; Tokyo: Nihon Hyōronsha, reprint edition, 1955–), is an excellent collection of documents and contemporary essays and writings on various aspects of the Meiji Period. The material is arranged topically in separate volumes under subjects such as history, government, foreign relations, finance, literature, etc. Another extensive work (96 vols.) is projected by Hara Shobo entitled *Meiji Hyakunen Shi Sōsho* (Collection of a Hundred Years of Meiji History) to be completed in 1971. Contemporary newspaper material has been reissued by Nakayama Yasumasa in *Shimbun Shūsei Meiji Hennen Shi* (A Chronicle of Meiji History from Newspaper Collections; 15 vols.; Tokyo: Zaisei Keizai Gakkai, 1935–1940).

For a general cultural history the reader is referred to *Gendai Nihon Bummei Shi* (A Cultural History of Recent Japan; 18 vols.; Tokyo: Tōyō Keizai Shimpōsha, 1940–1944). Foremost among Japanese works on constitutional history is Ōtsu Junichirō, *Dai Nihon Kensei Shi* (A Constitutional History of Japan; 10 vols.; Tokyo: Hōbun-kan, 1927–1928). Another standard work, though much more condensed, is that of Osatake Takeki, *Nihon Kensei Shi Taikō* (An Outline of Japanese Constitutional History; 2 vols.; Tokyo: Nihon Hyōronsha, 1938). A recent careful study of the Meiji Constitution is Inada Masatsugu, *Meiji Kempō Seiritsu Shi* (2 vols.; Tokyo: Yūhikaku, 1960–1962). The studies of Suzuki Yasuzō, especially those written before he emphasized the Marxist interpretation of history, such as *Nihon Kempō Shi Gaisetsu* (A General Outline of the History of the Japanese Constitution; Tokyo: Chūō Kōron, 1941), are valuable for the light they throw on the contribution of Prussian political scientists to the framing of the Constitution. For an excellent collection of essays on political problems of the period see Watanabe Ikujirō, *Meiji Shi Kenkyū* (Studies in Meiji History; Tokyo: Rakuro Shoin, 1944).

On economic problems, the material is also abundant. A valuable collection of economic and financial material has been edited by Professors Ōuchi Hyōe and Tsuchiya Takao and published as *Meiji Zenki Zaisei Keizai Shiryō* (Historical Material on Economics and Finance of the Early Meiji Period; 21 vols.; Tokyo: Kaizōsha, 1931–1936). The *Kōbushō Enkaku Hōkoku* (Official History of the Ministry of Industry), frequently referred to in Part II of this book, is in volume 17. Two valuable single volumes are Tsuchiya Takao, *Zoku Nihon Keizaishi Gaiyō, op. cit.;* and Takahashi Kamekichi, *Meiji Taishō Sangyō Hattatsu Shi* (History of the Expansion of Industry during Meiji and Taishō; Tokyo: Kaizōsha, 1927). One of the best analyses of the relationship of landlord-entrepreneur groups with the early parties and with government-sponsored industries is Horie Yasuzō, *Nihon Shihon Shūgi no Seiritsu* (Establishment of Japanese Capitalism; Ōsaka: Daidō Shoin, 1938). As noted above, the best basic statistical material is in Ohkawa Kazushi (ed.), *Chōki Keizai Tōkei* (Estimates of Long-Range Economic Statistics) and the Bank of Japan's *Iko Hompō Shūyō Keizai Tōkei* (One Hundred Years' Economic Statistics), *op. cit.*

Concerning foreign relations, the two most important collections are those published by the Foreign Office. Its *Dai Nihon Gaikō Bunsho* (Collected Documents on Japanese Diplomacy; 45 vols.; Tokyo: Nihon Kokusai Kyōkai, 1936–1963) contains basic documents, arranged chronologically, on foreign relations from 1868 to 1912. The Taishō section begins with 1913. By 1969 there were 19 volumes covering to 1918. The Treaty Division Office has published a collection of treaties in Gaimushō Jōyaku Kyoku (ed.), *Jōyaku Isan* (Collection of Treaties; 9 vols.; Tokyo; Gaimushō Jōyaku Kyoku, 1926–1929). A relatively objective study by Kiyosawa Kiyoshi, entitled *Nihon Gaikō Shi* (A Diplomatic History of Japan; Tokyo: Tōyō Keizai Shimpōsha, 1941), covers the period from 1868–1931. An important new series is *Nihon Gaikō Shi Kenkyū, Meiji Jidai* (Studies in the History of Japanese Foreign Relations: The Meiji Period; Tokyo: Nihon Kokusai Seiji Gakkai, 1957).

An interesting and enlightening publication for social aspects of the Meiji Period is *Gahō Kindai Hyakunen Shi* (An Illustrated History of the Past Century; Tokyo: Kokusai Bunka Jōhōsha, 1951). This chronological, illustrated history of Japan during the past century is a convenient reference. Arranged in small volumes, each of which covers 5–10 years, it has photographs or drawings of the main events or individuals for each period. For a standard literary history see Homma Hisao, *Meiji Bungaku Shi* (A Literary History of the Meiji Period; 3 vols.; Tokyo: Tokyo Dō, 1935–1943).

Part III: 1890–1915

For a general account of political developments during this period, the reader is referred to William W. McLaren, *A Political History of Japan, op cit.* Political events are also given in some detail in Robert

A. Scalapino, *Democracy and the Party Movement, op. cit.* The role of the oligarchs in the early constitutional government is emphasized in Robert K. Reischauer, *Japan, Government and Politics, op. cit.* Two recent monographs, based on extensive use of Japanese sources, present important detailed information on the period each covers. For the formative years of Japan under the Constitution see George Akita, *Foundations of Constitutional Government in Modern Japan, 1868–1900, op. cit.* The rise to power of the Seiyūkai party and of its proponent, Hara Kei, is ably presented in Tetsuo Najita, *Hara Kei in the Politics of Compromise 1905–1915* (Cambridge: Harvard University Press, 1967).

In view of the importance to Europe of the Sino-Japanese War of 1894–1895 and of the interest of the powers in China, Japan's international relations in this period have received extensive treatment in European languages. William H. Langer devotes a large section of his *The Diplomacy of Imperialism, 1890–1902* (2 vols.; Alfred A. Knopf, Inc., 1951), to events in the Far East, to the problem of concessions in China, and to the Anglo-Japanese Alliance. The same is true of H. B. Morse, *The International Relations of the Chinese Empire* (3 vols.; London: Longmans, Green, and Co., Inc., 1918). A thorough study based on Chinese sources of the causes of the Sino-Japanese War is T. F. Tsiang, "Sino-Japanese Diplomatic Relations, 1870–1894," *op. cit.* For the role of Korea and Japan's relations with it see Hilary Conroy, *The Japanese Seizure of Korea: 1868–1910* (Philadelphia: University of Pennsylvania Press, 1960), and C. I. Eugene Kim and Han-kyo Kim, *Korea and the Politics of Imperialism, 1876–1910* (Berkeley: University of California Press, 1967). Professor Conroy has been accused of bias in favor of Japan but presents much new and important material. It should be checked with the Kims' study. For a perceptive interpretation of America's position toward the Open Door and China's territorial integrity see Akira Iriye, *Across the Pacific: An Inner History of American–East Asian Relations* (New York: Harcourt, Brace and World, Inc., 1967). In some respects, Iriye's study, which uses Japanese, Chinese, and Western sources, corrects the isolationist interpretation contained in the work that long remained the standard one on this subject. It is A. Whitney Griswold's *The Far Eastern Policy of the United States* (New York: Harcourt, Brace and Co., 1938; paperback edition, New Haven: Yale University Press, 1962).

Documentary material on American–Japanese relations, taken from United States archives, is contained in Payson J. Treat, *Diplomatic Relations Between the United States and Japan, 1853–1895* (2 vols.; Stanford: Stanford University Press, 1932); and *Diplomatic Relations . . . , 1895–1905* (Stanford: Stanford University Press, 1938). Two significant diaries by Japanese diplomats of this era are A. M. Pooley (ed.), *The*

Secret Memoirs of Count Tadasu Hayashi, 1850–1913 (New York: Nash, 1915); and Kikujiro Ishii, *Diplomatic Commentaries,* translated by William R. Langdon (Baltimore: Johns Hopkins University Press, 1936). For details on how decisions were made by the Japanese government, see S. T. Takeuchi, *War and Diplomacy in the Japanese Empire* (New York: Doubleday, Doran & Co., 1935).

Several special books on foreign relations of this period should be noted. Russia's expansion into the Far East, especially in Siberia and Manchuria, and the clash of its policy with China and Japan are thoroughly covered in Andrew Malozenoff, *Russian Far Eastern Policy 1881–1904* (Berkeley: University of California Press, 1958). Details of the Boxer Uprising are treated in Chester C. Tan, *The Boxer Catastrophe* (New York: Columbia University Press, 1955). For an excellent study on the first and second Anglo-Japanese Alliances, based on extensive Japanese and European archival and published sources, see Ian Nish, *The Anglo-Japanese Alliance: The Diplomacy of Two Island Empires 1894–1907* (London: University of London Athlone Press, 1966).

The standard work on President Theodore Roosevelt's role in the Portsmouth Conference, Tyler Dennet's *Roosevelt and the Russo-Japanese War* (New York: Doubleday and Co., Inc., 1925) has been largely superseded by Raymond A. Esthus, *Theodore Roosevelt and Japan* (Seattle: University of Washington Press, 1966). For the "War Crisis" resulting from the anti-Japanese activities on the West Coast and the movement to exclude Japanese laborers from the United States, see Charles E. Neu, *An Uncertain Friendship: Theodore Roosevelt and Japan 1906–1909* (Cambridge: Harvard University Press, 1967). A perceptive analysis of how the decisions connected with the Russo-Japanese War were made and who made them will be found in Shumpei Okamoto, *The Japanese Oligarchy and the Russo-Japanese War* (New York: Columbia University Press, 1970).

As for general economic studies, William W. Lockwood covers this period in its entirety in his *The Economic Development of Japan, op. cit.* A concise narrative of Japan's development presented more chronologically than in Lockwood is George C. Allen, *A Short Economic History of Modern Japan, 1867–1937* (with a supplementary chapter on economic recovery and expansion, 1945–1960) (New York: Frederick A. Praeger, Inc., 2nd revised edition, 1963). For special subjects see Lockwood's *State and Economic Enterprise, op. cit.,* and James Nakamura, *Agricultural Production, op. cit.* Lawrence Klein and Kazushi Ohkawa have edited the papers for a conference on Japan's economic growth in *Economic Growth: The Japanese Experience Since the Meiji Era* (Homewood, Ill.: The Dorsey Press, 1968). Professors Ohkawa and Henry Rosovsky have in preparation a volume entitled *A Century of*

Economic Growth. See also the latter's *Capital Formation in Japan, 1868–1940* (New York: The Free Press of Glencoe, Inc., 1961). The results of one group of scholars working on population problems have been published by Ernest F. Penrose in his *Food Supply and Raw Materials in Japan . . . , 1894–1927* (Chicago: University of Chicago Press, 1930).

As for material in Japanese, two reference works are particularly useful for the modern period. The first of these is an historical dictionary on recent Japanese history compiled by the Historical Studies Bureau of Kyōto University entitled *Nihon Kindai Shi Jiten* (Tokyo: Tōyō Keizai Shimpōsha, 1959). The first part contains entries on important events and people and the remainder of the book is devoted to charts, statistical tables, chronologies, etc., covering the period from mid-nineteenth century to World War II. The second invaluable reference for the period 1889–1947, in which the tables are easier to use than in the previous entry, is Tōyama Shigeki and Adachi Yoshiko, *Kindai Nihon Seijishi Hikkei* (Indispensable Information on Recent Political History of Japan; Tokyo: Iwanami, 1961).

Many of the series listed in the previous section also cover the period 1890–1915. For example, see Yoshino, *Meiji Bunka Zenshū, op. cit.,* and Nakayama, *Shimbun Shūsei, op. cit.,* and the collection of treaties published by the Foreign Office in *Jōyaku Isan, op. cit.* Typical of various collections of special studies of Japan's recent history is *Nihon Gendai Shi Taikei* (11 vols.; Tokyo: Tōyō Keizai Shimpōsha, 1960–). Some of its best volumes are those on technology, military history, philosophy, arts and crafts, finance, and history of agriculture. Basic source material and documents on political history will be found in the collection published by the Imperial Diet entitled *Gikai Seidō Shichijūnen Shi* (History of Seventy Years of the Diet System; 12 vols.; Tokyo: Ōkurashō Insatsukyoku, 1960–). Edited by the Upper and Lower Houses, by 1969 volumes 1–6, 8, and 10 had appeared. The first five volumes cover the history of the Constitution and the Diet. The remainder will include political parties, chronology of the Diet, and glossary of members and chief events.

There are various general histories which are largely devoted to the quarter century after the promulgation of the Constitution. Pertinent material on the growth of nationalism will be found in Watanabe Ikujirō, *Meiji Jidai Shi* (History of the Meiji Period; Tokyo: Waseda Daigaku Shuppambu, 1916). While the volumes vary in quality, much factual material can be found in the six-volume collection published by the Asahi Shimbun as *Meiji Taishō Shi* (History of the Meiji and Taishō Periods; 6 vols.; Tokyo: Asahi Shimbunsha, 1930–1931). Perhaps the most valuable single source of information on political events from about

1900 to 1921 is Hara Kei, *Hara Kei Nikki* (The Diary of Hara Kei; 13 vols.; Tokyo: Kangen Sha, 1950–1951).

A word of warning is necessary in reference to many of the political and economic studies on Japan's recent history. Several excellent scholars, such as Hayashi Shigeru, Inouye Kiyoshi, Masumi Junnosuke, Mitani Taiichirō, Oka Yoshitake, Rōyama Masamichi, Ōkubo Toshiaki, and Tsuchiya Takao, who have concentrated on political and economic aspects of recent history, have maintained an objective point of view. Ōkubo Toshiaki, *Kindai Shi III* (Recent History, III), in *Nihon Zenshi* (vol. 10; Tokyo: Tokyo Daigaku Shuppan Kai, 1964), is one of the best single volumes. Another outstanding example is Inouye Kiyoshi and Suzuki Masashi, *Nihon Kindai Shi* (2 vols.; Tokyo: Godo Shuppan, 1956). Professor Masumi Junnosuke covers in detail, with profuse quotes from primary sources, political history from the Constitution to Hara's death in 1921 in *Nihon Seitō Shi Ron* (Historical Studies of Japan's Political Parties; 4 vols.; Tokyo: Tokyo Daigaku Shuppan Kai, 1965–1968). One of the best single volumes on the formation of party cabinets is Mitani Taiichirō, *Nihon Seitō Seiji Keisei* (Formation of Party Governments in Japan; Tokyo: Tokyo Daigaku Shuppan Kai, 1967). On the other hand, some scholars interested in Japan's history after 1890 approach the problem from the Marxist viewpoint. Thus, in using a work such as Shinobu Seisaburō, *Meiji Seiji Shi* (Political History of the Meiji Period; Tokyo: Kenshinsha, 1951), which contains much valuable material, the reader should realize that the author writes from a Marxist viewpoint.

In reference to economic material in Japanese, as indicated in the section on works in Western languages, the various departments of the government have issued annual statistical reports, but by far the most significant information is contained in Ohkawa Kazushi (ed.), *Chōki Keizai Tōkei* and Nihon Ginkō, *Shūyō Keizai Tōkei.* (See page 547.) Other earlier collections of important economic data are Takimoto Seiichi (ed.), *Nihon Sangyō Shiryō Taikei* (Collection of Historical Material on Japanese Industry; 15 vols.; Tokyo: Chūgai Shōgyō, 1926) and Meiji Zaisei Hensankai, *Meiji Zaisei Shi* (Meiji Financial History; 15 vols.; Tokyo: Meiji Zaisei Hensankai, 1905). Another valuable collection is that of Ōuchi Tsutomi *et al., Nihon ni okeru Shihon Shugi no Hattatsu* (The Development of Japanese Capitalism; 11 vols.; Tokyo: Tokyo Daigaku Shuppan Kai, 1955–).

Part IV: 1915–1941

The first part of this quarter century of Japan's recent history, especially prior to the Manchurian Incident of 1931, has been largely neglected by both Japanese and Western historians. Thus, there is no single volume in a European language which covers these years, though the colorful account written by a British newspaper editor who lived in Kōbe, A. Morgan Young, overlaps most of it. His *Japan in Recent Times, 1912–1926* (New York: William Morrow & Co., Inc., 1929) recounts the events as he saw and experienced them. The development of political parties during approximately the same period, as seen from contemporary source material, is described by Peter Duus in his *Party Rivalry and Political Change in Taishō Japan* (Cambridge: Harvard University Press, 1968). Scalapino, in his *Democracy and the Party Movement, op. cit.*, has a concise description of the chief political events. A. Morgan Young's second book, *Imperial Japan, 1926–1938* (New York: William Morrow & Co., Inc., 1938), supplements his work for the earlier years.

As for World War I, James W. Morley, in *The Japanese Thrust into Siberia, 1918* (New York: Columbia University Press, 1957), has skillfully analyzed the steps followed by the military leaders in achieving their objectives. Two monographs deal especially with American–Japanese relations and the Paris Peace Conference. They are Russell H. Fifield, *Woodrow Wilson and the Far East: The Diplomacy of the Shantung Question* (New York: Thomas Y. Crowell Co., 1952), and Burton F. Beers, *Vain Endeavor: Robert Lansing's Attempt to End American–Japanese Rivalry* (Durham, N. C.: Duke University Press, 1962).

The last decade of this period (1931–1941) has attracted much more attention, particularly after World War II, when new materials were available on the forces and events leading up to the war. For a general survey of the prewar decade, based on materials available before the war, see Hugh Borton, *Japan Since 1931—Its Political and Social Development* (New York: American Institute of Pacific Relations, Inc., 1940). For studies on the growth of militarism and nationalism, John M. Maki's *Japanese Militarism—Its Cause and Cure* (New York: Alfred A. Knopf, Inc., 1945) is especially useful, as is Daniel C. Holtom's *National Faith of Japan: A Study of Modern Shinto* (London: Kegan, Paul, Trench, Trubner & Co., Ltd., 1938).

For events leading to the occupation of Manchuria by Japan in 1931 see Sadako N. Ogata, *Defiance in Manchuria: The Making of Japanese Foreign Policy 1931–1932* (Berkeley: University of California Press, 1964). In S. R. Smith, *The Manchurian Crisis, 1931–1932* (New York: Columbia University Press, 1948), special emphasis is given to the relationship of the Manchurian Incident to the League of Nations. The best analysis of the growth of nationalism and militarism and its relation to Japan's foreign policy in the decade prior to World War II is James B. Crowley's *Japan's Quest for Autonomy: National Security and Foreign*

Policy 1930–1938 (Princeton: Princeton University Press, 1966). It is supplemented by Richard Storry, *The Double Patriots* (Boston: Houghton Mifflin Co., 1957), with its detailed analysis of the membership and interrelationship of the nationalist societies. The significance of civilian nationalists and the role of one of them, Kita Ikki, is ably set forth by George M. Wilson in his *Radical Nationalist in Japan* (Cambridge: Harvard University Press, 1969). The deleterious effect of this nationalism on the leading liberals is vividly illustrated by Frank O. Miller's monograph entitled *Minobe Tatsukichi, Interpreter of Constitutionalism in Japan* (Berkeley: University of California Press, 1965). For a translation of an important school textbook which expounded the basis of ultranationalism see Robert K. Hall (ed.), *Kokutai no Hongi* (Cardinal Principles of the National Entity of Japan), translated by John O. Gauntlett (Cambridge: Harvard University Press, 1949). Four important books on the growth of the social democratic and communist movements are George O. Totten III, *The Social Democratic Movement in Prewar Japan* (New Haven: Yale University Press, 1966); George M. Beckmann and Okubo Genji, *The Japanese Communist Party 1922–1945* (Stanford: Stanford University Press, 1969), Roger Swearingen and Paul Langer, *Red Flag in Japan: International Communism in Action, 1919–1951* (Cambridge: Harvard University Press, 1952), and Robert A. Scalapino, *The Japanese Communist Movement 1920–1966* (Berkeley: University of California Press, 1967).

For an excellent account of American Far Eastern policy, including that toward Japan, see Dorothy Borg, *The United States and the Far Eastern Crisis of 1933–1938* (Cambridge: Harvard University Press, 1964). A complementary study for the later years of international events in Asia has been made by F. C. Jones in *Japan's New Order in East Asia, Its Rise and Fall, 1937–45* (New York: Oxford University Press, 1954). The outstanding study of events leading to the outbreak of the war in the Pacific is Herbert Feis, *The Road to Pearl Harbor; the Coming of the War between the United States and Japan* (Princeton: Princeton University Press, 1950). The basic documents on the negotiations between the two countries have been published by the U. S. Department of State as *Foreign Relations of the United States, Japan, 1931–1941* (2 vols.; Washington: Government Printing Office, 1943).

For the role of General Tōjō Hideki in leading Japan to war see the thorough study of Robert J. Butow, *Tojo and the Coming of the War* (Princeton: Princeton University Press, 1961). Translations of records of the Liaison and Imperial Conferences leading to a decision for war appear in Nobutake Ike (ed. and trans.), *Japan's Decision for War* (Stanford: Stanford University Press, 1967).

In reference to economic materials, the entries mentioned in the previous section are also applicable for this period. (See page 552.) In addition, other studies include the biennial *Problems of the Pacific* of the American Institute of Pacific Relations, Inc., which first appeared in 1928; Harold G. Moulton, *Japan, an Economic and Financial Appraisal* (Washington: Brookings Institution, 1931); and John E. Orchard, *Japan's Economic Position, the Progress of Industrialization* (New York: Whittlesey House, 1930). A later appraisal, which is especially valuable on developments prior to 1936, is E. B. Schumpeter (ed.), *The Industrialization of Japan and Manchukuo, 1930–1940* (New York: The Macmillan Co., 1940). For the background of the legal status of Manchuria see C. Walter Young, *Japan's Jurisdiction and Legal Position in Manchuria* (3 vols.; Baltimore: Johns Hopkins University Press, 1931). The best history of the labor movement in English is that of Iwao Ayusawa, *A History of Labor in Modern Japan* (Honolulu: East–West Center Press, 1966).

Finally, a few monographs which concern special aspects of Japanese society prior to World War II should be mentioned. One of the first field studies to be carried out by a cultural anthropologist was a village study in Kyūshū by Professor John F. Embree. His findings appeared as *Suye Mura, a Japanese Village* (Chicago: University of Chicago Press, 1939). A useful and informative survey of various phases of Japanese culture will be found in John W. Hall and Richard K. Beardsley, *Twelve Doors to Japan* (New York: McGraw-Hill Book Co., 1965). The outstanding contribution on the question of Japanese in Hawaii and on the American continent has been made by Bradford Smith in his *Americans from Japan* (Philadelphia: J. B. Lippincott Co., 1949).

Because of the vast amount of Japanese material on this period published since the war, the following entries are illustrative of what is available. For general survey histories, Ōkubo's *Kindai III, op. cit.*, Inouye and Suzuki's *Nihon Kindai Shi, op. cit.*, and Yanaihara's *Gendai Nihon Shōshi, op. cit.*, will be found most useful. An extremely valuable collection of primary source material from about 1920 to World War II is *Gendai Shi Shiryō* (Source Materials on Recent History; Tokyo: Misuzu Shobō, 1962–). By 1969, a total of 30 volumes had appeared, edited by well known scholars, on subjects such as nationalism, Manchuria (2 vols.), the Chinese War (5 vols.), the Socialist Movement (11 vols.), Korea, and the Staff of the Imperial Headquarters. Material collected from newspapers from 1911 to the present is being published as *Shimbun Shūsei Taishō Shōwa Hennen Shi* (A Chronology of Taishō and Shōwa History from Newspaper Collections; Tokyo: Taishō Shōwa Hennenshikai, 1955–).

Among the numerous diaries and memoirs written by key officials during the interbellum years, one of the most valuable is that of Premier Hara

Kei entitled, *Hara Kei Nikki, op. cit.* Another important memoir is the diary of Harada Kumao, Secretary to the last of the Elder Statesmen, Saionji. This work is entitled *Saionji Kō to Seikyoku* (Diary of Prince Saionji; 8 vols.; Tokyo: Iwanami, 1952). Shigemitsu Mamoru, who was an important diplomat during this period, has written of the turmoil and strains in his *Shōwa no Dōran* (The Upheavals of the Shōwa Period; 2 vols.; Tokyo: Chūō Kōronsha, 1952).

For a general political history of this period see Rōyama Masamichi, *Seiji Shi* (Political History) in *Gendai Nihon Bummei Shi* (Tokyo: Tōyō Keizai Shimpōsha, 1940), II. Another detailed political history is Kudō Takeshige, *Taishō Kensei Shi* (A Political History of the Taishō Period; 2 vols.; Tokyo: Okano Shogakkai, 1930). The last volume of Masumi's *Nihon Seitō Shi Ron, op. cit.,* deals with the earlier years. The most detailed account, though it must be used with caution because of the leftist bias of the author, is Shinobu Seisaburō, *Taishō Seiji Shi* (Political History of the Taishō Period; 4 vols.; Tokyo: Kawada Shobō, 1950–1952). For a chronological descriptive reference to political events after 1926 see Ikeda Takeshi, *Shōwa Seiji Keizai Shi* (Political and Economic History of the Shōwa Period; Tokyo: Kokumin Kyōiku Tosho, 1947). Another, more recent study is that of Kurihara Ken, *Shōwa Shi no Oboegaki* (Reflections on Shōwa History; Tokyo: Yushindo, 1955).

Many Japanese scholars have devoted themselves to an analysis of the growth of prewar fascism and other causes of World War II. Among those works dealing with fascism, the following are particularly perceptive: Hata Ikuhito, *Gun Fuashizumu Undō Shi* (History of the Military Fascist Movement; Tokyo: Kawada Shobō Shinsha, 1962); Kinoshita Hanji, *Nihon Fuashizumu Shi* (History of Japanese Fascism; 2 vols.; Tokyo: Iwazaki, 1949). As for background material on World War II, one of the best summaries of the material presented at the International Military Tribunal for the Far East is Aoki Tokuzō, *Taiheiyō Sensō Zenshi* (History of the Years prior to the Pacific War; 3 vols.; Tokyo: Gakujutsu Bunka Fukyūkai, 1953). The most exhaustive account is that edited by Tsunoda Jun entitled *Taiheiyō Sensō e no Michi* (The Road to the Pacific War; 8 vols.; Tokyo: Nihon Kokusai Seiji Gakkai, 1963). About half of this material is being translated for publication in English under the editorship of Professor James W. Morley of Columbia University.

Also under the editorship of Professor Tsunoda, ten authorities on international relations are preparing separate volumes for *Kindai Nihon Gaikō Shi* (History of Japan's Recent Diplomacy; 10 vols.; Tokyo: Hara Shobō, 1968–). The series covers subjects such as Japan's relations with Russia, World War I, Manchuria, the Washington Conference, the United States, and the New Order in East Asia. The last three volumes have already appeared. For a general prewar survey see Watanabe Ikujirō, *Nihon Kinsei Gaikō Shi* (History of Japanese Diplomacy in Recent Times; Tokyo: Chigura Shobō, 1938). Two significant postwar studies are Hosoya Chihiro, *Shaberia Shuppei no Shiteki Kenkyū* (Historical Study of the Siberian Expedition; Tokyo: Yūhikaku, 1955), and Hata Ikuhito, *Nitchū Sensō Shi* (History of the Sino-Japanese War 1937–1941; Tokyo: Kawada Shobō Shinsha, 1961).

As for economic material, there are innumerable official publications. For a general economic survey see Ōuchi Hyōe, "Keizai" (Economics) in Yanaihara Tadao, *Gendai Nihon Shōshi, op. cit.* For a study of the growth of capitalism in Japan the reader is referred to the compilation of Professor Ōuchi and others entitled *Nihon Shihon Shugi no Kenkyū* (Studies of Japanese Capitalism; 2 vols.; Tokyo: Kōdōsha, 1948), and to the comprehensive series of studies of special aspects of capitalism edited by Kajinishi Mitsuhaya and others under the general title *Nihon ni okeru Shihon Shugi no Hattatsu* (Development of Japanese Capitalism; Tokyo: Tokyo Daigaku Shuppankai, 1956–), I–XI. The Research Bureau of the Bank of Japan has written a financial history of Japan since 1931 as follows: Nihon Ginkō Chōsa Kyoku, *Manshū Jihen Igo no Zaisei Kinyū Shi* (Financial and Monetary History from the Manchurian Incident; Tokyo: Nihon Ginkō, 1948). A discussion of public finance during the thirties will also be found in Hijikata Seibi, *Zaisei Shi* (History of Finance) in *Gendai Nihon Bummei Shi* (vol. 6; Tokyo: Tōyō Keizai Shimpōsha, 1940).

Part V: 1941–1970

The selection of representative studies for the war and postwar years is complicated by many factors. Foremost is the quantity of material available. For example, during the occupation, a vast amount of special reports and studies on all phases of postwar life was produced by the various sections of the General Headquarters of SCAP. In using this material, it should be remembered that it was often carefully edited to present the occupation in a favorable light. Some of it was translated from uncritical Japanese reports. In recent years, many Westerners who received their Japanese language training as a result of the Pacific War, or who comprise a new postwar generation with extensive language competence, are beginning to publish important monographs or special studies on this period. In this connection, the reader is referred to the volumes of the Conference of Modern Japan. (See page 543.)

Extremely useful summaries of the various phases of the Pacific War, with helpful maps, will be found in the United States Strategic Bombing Survey, *The Campaigns of the Pacific War* (Washington: USSBS, Naval

Analysis Division, 1946). For a single volume see Donald MacIntyre, *The Battle for the Pacific* (New York: W. W. Norton & Co., Inc., 1966). An official British account is S. Woodburn Kirby, *et al., The War Against Japan* (4 vols.; London: Her Majesty's Stationery Office, 1959).

There are several studies on the struggle within Japan on the question of whether to surrender. One of the first was that of Robert J. C. Butow, *Japan's Decision to Surrender* (Stanford: Stanford University Press, 1954). A more recent work is Lester Brooks's *Behind Japan's Surrender: The Secret Struggle that Ended an Empire* (New York: McGraw-Hill Book Co., 1968). A detailed account based on exhaustive research by the Pacific War Research Society entitled *Nihon no Ichiban Nagai Hi* has been translated as *Japan's Longest Day* (Tokyo: Kodansha International, Ltd., 1968). The decision to use the atomic bomb and its effect on the end of the war is ably presented by Herbert Feis in *Japan Subdued: The Atomic Bomb and the End of the War in the Pacific* (Princeton: Princeton University Press, 1961).

A convenient, official summary of the various international decisions and policies concerning Japan will be found in U.S. Department of State, *Occupation of Japan: Policy and Progress,* Department of State Publication 2671 (Washington: Government Printing Office, 1946). Official documents on United States policies are beginning to be published in the Department of State's *Foreign Relations of the United States, Diplomatic Papers, 1944. Near East, South Asia and Africa, Far East* (Washington: Government Printing Office, 1965). For a summary of postwar planning, by one who was personally involved in it, see Hugh Borton, *American Presurrender Planning for Postwar Japan* (New York: East Asian Institute, Columbia University, 1967).

The best single source for data on the occupation is the monthly reports of SCAP which first appeared in October, 1945, and stopped with the issue of September, 1948: Supreme Commander for the Allied Powers, *Summation of Non-Military Activities in Japan* (Tokyo: GHQ, Supreme Commander for the Allied Powers, 1945–1948). SCAP, in a thoroughly objective account of the occupation, also published most of the pertinent documents connected with constitutional reform and political movements in Supreme Commander for the Allied Powers, Government Section, *Political Reorientation of Japan, September 1945 to September 1948* (2 vols.; Washington: Government Printing Office, 1949). The basic study of the role of the Far Eastern Commission is George H. Blakeslee, *A History of the Far Eastern Commission* (Washington: Government Printing Office, 1953).

For three authoritative reviews of the occupation written by State Department officials, see Edwin M. Martin, *The Allied Occupation of Japan* (Stanford: Stanford University Press, 1948); Robert A. Fearey, *The Occupation of Japan, Second Phase: 1948–50* (New York: The Macmillan Co., 1950), and Hugh Borton, "The Allied Occupation of Japan, 1945–47," in F. C. Jones, Hugh Borton, and B. R. Pearn, *The Far East, 1942–1946* (London: Oxford University Press, 1955), pp. 307–428. Two divergent views on the success of the Allied occupation are given in Herbert Passin, *The Legacy of the Occupation* (New York: East Asian Institute, Columbia University, 1968), and Robert E. Ward, "Reflections on the Allied Occupation and Planned Political Change in Japan," in Ward, *Political Development . . . , op. cit.*

For the San Francisco Peace Conference, see U. S. Department of State, *Record of Proceedings of the Conference for the Conclusion and Signature of the Treaty of Peace with Japan* (Washington: Government Printing Office, 1951). The history of the peace settlement is quite fully covered in Frederick C. Dunn, *Peace Making and the Settlement with Japan* (Princeton: Princeton University Press, 1963), and Bernard C. Cohen, *The Political Process and Foreign Policy: The Making of the Japanese Peace Settlement* (Princeton: Princeton University Press, 1957).

It remains to mention a few studies on certain aspects of post-treaty Japan. For a general analysis of the political scene see Robert A. Scalapino and Junnosuke Masumi, *Parties and Politics in Contemporary Japan* (Berkeley: University of California Press, 1964). The importance of the business world in all phases of contemporary Japanese life is well presented by Professor Chitoshi Yanaga in *Big Business and Japanese Politics* (New Haven: Yale University Press, 1968). A helpful analysis of the ruling Liberal Democratic party has been made by Nathaniel B. Thayer in *How the Conservatives Rule Japan* (Princeton: Princeton University Press, 1969). Other valuable studies on the political scene are Ivan I. Morris, *Nationalism and the Right Wing in Japan: A Study of Postwar Trends* (London: Oxford University Press, 1960), and Robert A. Scalapino, *The Japanese Communist Movement 1920–1966, op. cit.*

The most important political problem in postwar Japan has been the new Constitution and the question of its revision. In 1964, the Commission on the Constitution, after seven years' work, published a voluminous report. An invaluable résumé and evaluation of this material was made by Robert E. Ward in "The Commission on the Constitution and Prospects for Constitutional Change in Japan," *Journal of Asian Studies,* XXIV (May, 1965), pp. 401–29. A bibliographical analysis of the work of the Commission by John Maki and reminiscences of the Commission Chairman are among the valuable papers edited by Dan Fenno Henderson and published in *The Constitution of Japan: Its First Twenty Years, 1947–1967* (Seattle: University of Washington Press, 1969).

A collection of perceptive articles on various phases of contemporary Japan by a resident observer, Lawrence A. Olson, has appeared in *Dimensions of Japan* (New York: American University Field Staff, Inc.,

1963). As for Japan's world position in relation to Asia see the provocative book by Professor Edwin O. Reischauer, first published before he was American Ambassador in Tokyo, *Wanted: An Asian Policy* (New York: Alfred A. Knopf, Inc., 1955). Excellent résumés of current problems presented at a recent American Assembly have been edited by Herbert Passin in *The United States and Japan* (Englewood Cliffs, N. J.: Prentice-Hall, Inc., 1966). An important study on America's role in defending Japan is that of George B. Packard III, *Protest in Tokyo: The Security Treaty Crisis of 1960* (Princeton: Princeton University Press, 1966).

Other significant works on contemporary Japanese life are: Lawrence H. Battistini, *The Postwar Student Struggle in Japan* (Rutland, Vt.: C. E. Tuttle Co., 1956); Herbert Passin, *Society and Education in Japan* (New York: Teachers' College, Columbia University, 1965); Ronald P. Dore, *City Life in Japan* (Berkeley: University of California Press, 1958); John B. Cornell and Robert J. Smith, *Two Japanese Villages: Matsunaga, a Japanese Mountain Community; Kurusu, a Japanese Agriculture Community* (Ann Arbor: Center for Japanese Studies, University of Michigan, 1956), and James C. Abegglen, *The Japanese Factory: Aspects of its Social Organization* (New York: Asia Publishing House, 1959).

In the field of economics, an important study is that of Jerome B. Cohen, *Japan's Economy in War and Reconstruction* (Minneapolis: University of Minnesota Press, 1949). He has also brought the problems up to date to the Peace Treaty in his *Economic Problems of Free Japan* (Princeton: Center of International Studies, Princeton University Press, 1952). For the later years, several chapters in Lockwood, *State and Economic Enterprise, op. cit.*, are valuable. The standard work on trade is that of Warren S. Hunsberger, *Japan and the United States in World Trade* (New York: Council on Foreign Relations, 1964). Valuable research on Japan's economic role in Asia is being carried on by the Economic Commission for Asia and the Far East, such as *Problems and Prospects of Accelerated Economic Development in the ECAFE Region through Trade with Japan* (Lake Success: United Nations, Economic and Social Council, 1950). Various Japanese government agencies, such as the Ministry of International Trade and Industry, the Prime Minister's Office, and the Bank of Japan issue regular reports. The latest official statistics will be found in Cabinet Bureau of Statistics, *Nihon Tōkei Nenkan* (Japan Statistical Yearbook), and Nihon Ginkō, *Monthly Statistics* and *Nihon Tōkei Geppō* (Japan Statistical Monthly).

As for Japanese material on the Pacific War and the postwar years, new material is appearing constantly so that the current *Shuppan Nenkan* (Publication Annual) should be consulted for the latest works. Reference to the bibliographies in the works already cited in this section will also be helpful. As new volumes of *Shimbun Shūsei Shōwa Hennen Shi, op. cit.,* appear, this set will become increasingly valuable. The same can be said for *Nihon Seiji Gakkai Nempō, Seijigaku* (Annals of the Japan Political Science Association, Political Science; Tokyo: Iwanami Shoten, 1950–); and the annual yearbooks such as *Asahi Nenkan* (Tokyo: Asahi Shimbunsha, 1969). Another series covering politics, economics, law, etc., which is in the process of publication, is *Shiryō Sengo Nijūnen Shi* (Historical Documents on Postwar Twenty-Year History; 6 vols.; Tokyo: Hyōronsha, 1965–1967).

A carefully compiled history of the Pacific War is that of the Historical Studies Research Society: *Taiheiyō Sensō Shi* (History of the Pacific War; 5 vols.; Tokyo: Rekishigaku Kenkyūkai, 1953–1954). For a single volume on the Pacific War see Hayashi Shigeru, *Dai Heiyō Sensō* (The Pacific War), in *Nihon Rekishi* (Tokyo: Chūō Kōron, 1966), XXV. For a concise account of the postwar years, Yanaihara Tadao has written *Sengo Nihon Shōshi* (A Short Postwar History of Japan; Tokyo: Tokyo Daigaku Shuppansha, 1958). On the new Constitution, see Satō, *Nihon Koku Kempō, op. cit.* Two significant works on the last months of the war include Konoye Fumimaro, *Heiwa e no Doryoku* (Efforts Toward Peace; Tokyo: Nihon Dempō, 1946), an attempt by Konoye to justify his peace efforts; and the invaluable collection of Foreign Office documents on the end of the war edited by Kurihara Ken for the Foreign Office as Gaimushō, *Shūsen Shiroku* (Documentary History of the End of the War; Tokyo: Shimbun Gekkansha, 1952).

In addition to the various statistical data and official reports published by the Japanese government, the volumes of Professor Ohkawa's *Chōki Keizai Tōkei* (Long-Range Economic Statistics), *op. cit.,* will be found invaluable. The same is true for Nihon Ginkō, *Iko Hompō Shūyō Keizai Tōkei* (One Hundred Years' Statistics), *op. cit.,* its *Geppō Tōkei* (Monthly Statistics) and *Nihon Tōkei Geppō* (Japan Monthly Statistics). General works on postwar economic conditions include the study by Inouye Seimaru and Usami Seijirō, *Kokka Dokusen Shihon Shugi Ron* (Views on State Monopolistic Capitalism; Tokyo: Chōryūsha, 1950). Inaba Hidezō has written a two-volume work on the actual state of the nation's economy called *Nihon Keizai no Genjitsu* (Real Conditions of Japan's Economy; 2 vols.; Tokyo: Jiji Tsushinsha, 1949 and 1950). The economic research office of the Mitsubishi interests published a general survey of economic production, Mitsubishi Keizai Kenkyūjo, *Nihon Sangyō Keizai Sōran* (Survey of Japanese Economic Production; Tokyo: Mitsubishi, 1949). Professor Ōuchi Hyōe has also written on the probable trend of postwar finances in his *Sengo Nihon Zaisei no Ayunda Michi* (The Probable Direction of Postwar Japanese Finances; Tokyo: Jiji Tsushinsha, 1950).

APPENDIXES

APPENDIX I

The Potsdam Proclamation

PROCLAMATION DEFINING TERMS FOR JAPANESE SURRENDER

July 26, 1945

(1) WE—THE PRESIDENT of the United States, the President of the National Government of the Republic of China, and the Prime Minister of Great Britain, representing the hundreds of millions of our countrymen, have conferred and agree that Japan shall be given an opportunity to end this war.

(2) The prodigious land, sea and air forces of the United States, the British Empire and of China, many times reinforced by their armies and air fleets from the west, are poised to strike the final blows upon Japan. This military power is sustained and inspired by the determination of all the Allied Nations to prosecute the war against Japan until she ceases to resist.

(3) The result of the futile and senseless German resistance to the might of the aroused free peoples of the world stands forth in awful clarity as an example to the people of Japan. The might that now converges on Japan is immeasurably greater than that which, when applied to the resisting Nazis, necessarily laid waste to the lands, the industry and the method of life of the whole German people. The full application of our military power, backed by our resolve, *will* mean the inevitable and complete destruction of the Japanese armed forces and just as inevitably the utter devastation of the Japanese homeland.

(4) The time has come for Japan to decide whether she will continue to be controlled by those self-willed militaristic advisers whose unintelligent calculations have brought the Empire of Japan to the threshold of annihilation, or whether she will follow the path of reason.

(5) Following are our terms. We will not deviate from them. There are no alternatives. We shall brook no delay.

(6) There must be eliminated for all time the authority and influence of those who have deceived and misled the people of Japan into embarking on world conquest, for we insist that a new order of peace, security and justice will be impossible until irresponsible militarism is driven from the world.

(7) Until such a new order is established *and* until there is convincing proof that Japan's war-making power is destroyed, points in Japanese territory to be designated by the Allies shall be occupied to secure the achievement of the basic objectives we are here setting forth.

(8) The terms of the Cairo Declaration shall be carried out and Japanese sovereignty shall be limited to the islands of Honshu, Hokkaido, Kyushu, Shikoku and such minor islands as we determine.

(9) The Japanese military forces, after being completely disarmed, shall be permitted to return to their homes with the opportunity to lead peaceful and productive lives.

(10) We do not intend that the Japanese shall be enslaved as a race or destroyed as a nation, but stern justice shall be meted out to all war criminals, including those who have visited cruelties upon our prisoners. The Japanese Government shall re-

move all obstacles to the revival and strengthening of democratic tendencies among the Japanese people. Freedom of speech, of religion, and of thought, as well as respect for the fundamental human rights shall be established.

(11) Japan shall be permitted to maintain such industries as will sustain her economy and permit the exaction of just reparations in kind, but not those which would enable her to re-arm for war. To this end, access to, as distinguished from control of, raw materials shall be permitted. Eventual Japanese participation in world trade relations shall be permitted.

(12) The occupying forces of the Allies shall be withdrawn from Japan as soon as these objectives have been accomplished and there has been established in accordance with the freely expressed will of the Japanese people a peacefully inclined and responsible government.

(13) We call upon the government of Japan to proclaim now the unconditional surrender of all Japanese armed forces, and to provide proper and adequate assurances of their good faith in such action. The alternative for Japan is prompt and utter destruction.

APPENDIX II

Text of Japan's Two Constitutions*

1889

The Constitution of the Empire of Japan (Meiji Constitution, 1889)

Preamble

Having, by virtue of the glories of Our Ancestors, ascended the Throne of a lineal succession unbroken for ages eternal; desiring to promote the welfare of, and to give development to the moral and intellectual faculties of Our beloved subjects, the very same that have been favoured with the benevolent care and affectionate vigilance of Our Ancestors; and hoping to maintain the prosperity of the State, in concert with Our people and with their support, We hereby promulgate, in pursuance of Our Imperial Rescript of the 12th day of the 10th month of the 14th year of Meiji, a fundamental law of State, to exhibit the principles, by which We are to be guided in Our conduct, and to point out to what Our descendants and Our subjects and their descendants are forever to conform.

The rights of sovereignty of the State, We have inherited from Our Ancestors, and We shall bequeath them to Our descendants. Neither We nor they shall in future fail to wield them, in accordance with the provisions of the Constitution hereby granted.

1946

The Constitution of Japan

We, the Japanese people, acting through our duly elected representatives in the National Diet, determined that we shall secure for ourselves and our posterity the fruits of peaceful cooperation with all nations and the blessings of liberty throughout this land, and resolved that never again shall we be visited with the horrors of war through the action of government, do proclaim that sovereign power resides with the people and do firmly establish this Constitution. Government is a sacred trust of the people, the authority for which is derived from the people, the powers of which are exercised by the representatives of the people, and the benefits of which are enjoyed by the people. This is a universal principle of mankind upon which this Constitution is founded. We reject and revoke all constitutions, laws, ordinances, and rescripts in conflict herewith.

We, the Japanese people, desire peace for all time are are deeply conscious of the high ideals controlling human relationship, and we have determined to preserve our security and existence, trusting in the justice and faith of the peace-loving peoples of the world. We desire to occupy an honored place in an inter-

* For ease in comparing the two documents, the articles of the Meiji Constitution are arranged not in sequence but topically to correspond with the articles of the 1946 Constitution, which are presented *seriatim*. The Meiji Constitution is, nevertheless, complete.

We now declare to respect and protect the security of the rights and of the property of Our people, and to secure to them the complete enjoyment of the same, within the extent of the provisions of the present Constitution and of the law.

The Imperial Diet shall first be convoked for the 23rd year of Meiji and the time of its opening shall be the date when the present Constitution comes into force.

When in the future it may become necessary to amend any of the provisions of the present Constitution, We or Our successors shall assume the initiative right, and submit a project for the same to the Imperial Diet. The Imperial Diet shall pass its vote upon it, according to the conditions imposed by the present Constitution, and in no otherwise shall Our descendants or Our subjects be permitted to attempt any alteration thereof.

Our Ministers of State, on Our behalf, shall be held responsible for the carrying out of the present Constitution, and Our present and future subjects shall forever assume the duty of allegiance to the present Constitution.

national society striving for the preservation of peace, and the banishment of tyranny and slavery, oppression and intolerance for all time from the earth. We recognize that all peoples of the world have the right to live in peace, free from fear and want.

We believe that no nation is responsible to itself alone, but that laws of political morality are universal; and that obedience to such laws is incumbent upon all nations who would sustain their own sovereignty and justify their sovereign relationship with other nations.

We, the Japanese people, pledge our national honor to accomplish these high ideals and purposes with all our resources.

Chapter I. The Emperor

Article IV. The Emperor being the Head of the Empire the rights of sovereignty are invested in him, and he exercises them in accordance with the provisions of the present Constitution.

Article I. The Empire of Japan shall be ruled over by Emperors of the dynasty, which has reigned in an unbroken line of descent for ages past.

Article II. The succession to the throne shall devolve upon male descendants of the Imperial House, according to the provisions of the Imperial House Law.

Article III. The person of the Emperor is sacred and inviolable.

Article V. The Emperor exercises the legislative power with the consent of the Imperial Diet.

Chapter I. The Emperor

Article 1. The Emperor shall be the symbol of the State and of the unity of the people, deriving his position from the will of the people with whom resides sovereign power.

Article 2. The Imperial Throne shall be dynastic and succeeded to in accordance with the Imperial House Law passed by the Diet.

Article 3. The advice and approval of the Cabinet shall be required for all acts of the Emperor in matters of state, and the Cabinet shall be responsible therefor.

Article XVII. The institution of a Regency shall take place in conformity with the provisions of the Imperial House Law.

The Regent shall exercise the supreme powers which belong to the Emperor in his name.

Article X. The Emperor determines the organisation of the different branches of the Administration; he fixes the salaries of all civil and military officers, and appoints and dismisses the same. Exceptions specially provided for in the present Constitution or in other laws shall be in accordance with the respective provisions bearing thereon.

Article VIII. In case of urgent necessity, when the Imperial Diet is not sitting, the Emperor, in order to maintain the public safety or to avert a public danger, has the power to issue Imperial Ordinances, which shall take the place of laws. Such Imperial Ordinances shall, however, be laid before the Imperial Diet at its next session, and should the Diet disapprove of the said Ordinances, the Government shall declare them to be henceforth invalid.

Article IX. The Emperor issues, or causes to be issued, the ordinances necessary for the carrying out of the laws, or for the maintenance of public peace and order, and for the promotion of the welfare of his subjects. But no Ordinance shall in any way alter any of the existing laws.

Article XI. The Emperor has the supreme command of the army and navy.

Article XII. The Emperor determines the organisation and peace standing of the army and navy.

Article XIII. The Emperor declares war, makes peace, and concludes treaties.

Article VI. The Emperor gives sanction to laws, and orders them to be promulgated and put into force.

Article VII. The Emperor convokes the Imperial Diet, opens, closes, and

Article 4. The Emperor shall perform only such acts in matters of state as are provided for in this Constitution and he shall not have powers related to government.

The Emperor may delegate the performance of his acts in matters of state as may be provided by law.

Article 5. When, in accordance with the Imperial House Law, a Regency is established, the Regent shall perform his acts in matters of state in the Emperor's name. In this case, paragraph one of the preceding article will be applicable.

Article 6. The Emperor shall appoint the Prime Minister as designated by the Diet.

The Emperor shall appoint the Chief Judge of the Supreme Court as designated by the Cabinet.

Article 7. The Emperor, with the advice and approval of the Cabinet, shall perform the following acts in matters of state on behalf of the people:

Promulgation of amendments of the constitution, laws, cabinet orders and treaties.

Convocation of the Diet.

prorogues it, and dissolves the House of Representatives.

Article XIV. The Emperor proclaims the law of siege. The conditions and operation of the law of siege shall be determined by law.

Article XVI. The Emperor orders amnesty, pardon, commutation of punishments, and rehabilitation.

Article XV. The Emperor confers titles of nobility, rank, orders, and other marks of honour.

Dissolution of the House of Representatives.

Proclamation of general election of members of the Diet.

Attestation of the appointment and dismissal of Ministers of State and other officials as provided for by law, and of full powers and credentials of Ambassadors and Ministers.

Attestation of general and special amnesty, commutation of punishment, reprieve, and restoration of rights.

Awarding of honors.

Attestation of instruments of ratification and other diplomatic documents as provided for by law.

Receiving foreign ambassadors and ministers.

Performance of ceremonial functions.

Article 8. No property can be given to, or received by, the Imperial House, nor can any gifts be made therefrom, without the authorization of the Diet.

Chapter II. Renunciation of War

Article 9. Aspiring sincerely to an international peace based on justice and order, the Japanese people forever renounce war as a sovereign right of the nation and the threat or use of force as means of settling international disputes.

In order to accomplish the aim of the preceding paragraph, land, sea, and air forces, as well as other war potential, will never be maintained. The right of belligerency of the state will not be recognized.

Chapter II. Rights and Duties of Subjects

Article XVIII. The conditions necessary for being a Japanese subject shall be determined by law.

Chapter III. Rights and Duties of the People

Article 10. The conditions necessary for being a Japanese national shall be determined by law.

Article 11. The people shall not be prevented from enjoying any of the fundamental human rights. These fundamental human rights guaranteed to the people by this Constitution shall be conferred upon the people of this and future generations as eternal and inviolate rights.

Article 12. The freedoms and rights guaranteed to the people by this Constitution shall be maintained by the constant endeavor of the people, who shall refrain from any abuse of these freedoms and rights and shall always be responsible for utilizing them for the public welfare.

Article 13. All of the people shall be respected as individuals. Their right to life, liberty, and the pursuit of happiness shall, to the extent that it does not interfere with the public welfare, be the supreme consideration in legislation and in other governmental affairs.

Article 14. All of the people are equal under the law and there shall be no discrimination in political, economic or social relations, because of race, creed, sex, social status or family origin.

Peers and peerage shall not be recognized.

No privilege shall accompany any award of honor, decoration or any distinction, nor shall any such award be valid beyond the lifetime of the individual who now holds or hereafter may receive it.

Article 15. The people have the inalienable right to choose their public officials and to dismiss them.

All public officials are servants of the whole community and not of any group thereof.

Universal adult suffrage is guaranteed with regard to the election of public officials.

In all elections, secrecy of the ballot shall not be violated. A voter shall not be answerable, publicly or privately, for the choice he has made.

Article XXX. Japanese subjects may present petitions, provided that they observe the proper form of respect, and comply with the rules specially provided for such matters.

Article 16. Every person shall have the right of peaceful petition for the redress of damage, for the removal of public officials, for the enactment, repeal or amendment of laws, ordinances or regulations and for other matters; nor shall any person be in any way discriminated against for sponsoring such a petition.

Article 17. Every person may *sue* for redress as provided by law from the State or a public entity, in case he has suffered damage through illegal act of any public official.

Article 18. No person shall be held in bondage of any kind. Involuntary servitude, except as punishment for crime, is prohibited.

Article XIX. Japanese subjects shall all equally be eligible for civil and military appointments, and any other public offices, subject only to the conditions prescribed and Laws and Ordinances.

Article XX. Japanese subjects are amenable to service in the army or navy, according to the provisions of law.

Article XXVIII. Japanese subjects shall, within limits not prejudicial to peace and order, and not antagonistic to their duties as subjects, enjoy freedom of religious belief.

Article 19. Freedom of thought and conscience shall not be violated.

Article 20. Freedom of religion is guaranteed to all. No religious organization shall receive any privileges from the State, nor exercise any political authority.

No person shall be compelled to take part in any religious act, celebration, rite or practice.

The State and its organs shall refrain from religious education or any other religious activity.

Article XXIX. Japanese subjects shall, within the limits of the law, enjoy liberty in regard to speech, writing, publication, public meetings, and associations.

Article 21. Freedom of assembly and association as well as speech, press and all other forms of expression are guaranteed.

No censorship shall be maintained, nor shall the secrecy of any means of communication be violated.

Article XXII. Subject to the limitations imposed by law, Japanese subjects shall enjoy full liberty in regard to residence and change of abode.

Article 22. Every person shall have freedom to choose and change his residence and to choose his occupation to the extent that it does not interfere with the public welfare.

Freedom of all persons to move to a foreign country and to divest themselves of their nationality shall be inviolate.

Article 23. Academic freedom is guaranteed.

Article 24. Marriage shall be based only on the mutual consent of both sexes and it shall be maintained through mutual cooperation with the equal rights of husband and wife as a basis.

With regard to choice of spouse, property rights, inheritance, choice of domicile, divorce and other matters pertaining to marriage and the family, laws shall be enacted from the standpoint of individual dignity and the essential equality of the sexes.

Article 25. All people have the right to maintain the minimum standards of wholesome and cultured living.

In all spheres of life, the State shall use its endeavors for the promotion and extension of social welfare and security, and of public health.

Article 26. All people shall have the right to receive an equal education correspondent to their ability, as provided by law.

All people shall be obligated to have all boys and girls under their protection receive ordinary education as provided for by law. Such compulsory education shall be free.

Article 27. All people shall have the right and the obligation to work.

Standards for wages, hours, rest and other working conditions shall be fixed by law.

Children shall not be exploited.

Article 28. The right of workers to organize and to bargain and act collectively is guaranteed.

Article XXVII. The rights of property of Japanese subjects shall not be violated. Such measures, however, as may be rendered necessary in the interests of the public welfare shall be taken in accordance with the provisions of the law.

Article 29. The right to own or to hold property is inviolable.

Property rights shall be defined by law, in conformity with the public welfare.

Private property may be taken for public use upon just compensation therefor.

Article XXI. Japanese subjects are amenable to the duty of paying taxes, according to the provisions of law.

Article 30. The people shall be liable to taxation as provided by law.

Article XXIII. No Japanese subject shall be arrested, detained, tried or punished, except according to law.

Article 31. No person shall be deprived of life or liberty, nor shall any other criminal penalty be imposed, except according to procedure established by law.

Article XXIV. No Japanese subject shall be deprived of his right of being tried by judges determined by law.

Article 32. No person shall be denied the right of access to the courts.

Article 33. No person shall be apprehended except upon warrant issued by a competent judicial officer which specifies the offense with which the person is charged, unless he is apprehended, the offense being committed.

Article 34. No person shall be arrested or detained without being at once informed of the charges against him or without the immediate privilege of counsel; nor shall he be detained without adequate cause; and upon demand of any person such cause must be imme-

Article XXV. Except in the cases provided for in the law, the house of no Japanese subject shall be entered or searched without his permission.

Article XXVI. Except in cases provided for in the law, the secrecy of the letters of Japanese subjects shall not be violated.

Article XXXI. The provisions contained in the present chapter shall not interfere with the exercise, in times of war or in case of national emergency, of the supreme powers which belong to the Emperor.

Article XXXII. Each and every one of the provisions contained in the preceding articles of the present chapter

diately shown in open court in his presence and the presence of his counsel.

Article 35. The right of all persons to be secure in their homes, papers and effects against entries, searches and seizures shall not be impaired except upon warrant issued for adequate cause and particularly describing the place to be searched and things to be seized, or except as provided by Article 33.

Each search or seizure shall be made upon separate warrant issued by a competent judicial officer.

Article 36. The infliction of torture by any public officer and cruel punishments are absolutely forbidden.

Article 37. In all criminal cases the accused shall enjoy the right to a speedy and public trial by an impartial tribunal.

He shall be permitted full opportunity to examine all witnesses, and he shall have the right of compulsory process for obtaining witnesses on his behalf at public expense.

At all times the accused shall have the assistance of competent counsel who shall, if the accused is unable to secure the same by his own efforts, be assigned to his use by the State.

Article 38. No person shall be compelled to testify against himself.

Confession made under compulsion, torture or threat, or after prolonged arrest or detention shall not be admitted in evidence.

No person shall be convicted or punished in cases where the only proof against him is his own confession.

Article 39. No person shall be held criminally liable for an act which was lawful at the time it was committed, or of which he has been acquitted, nor shall he be placed in double jeopardy.

Article 40. Any person, in case he is acquitted after he has been arrested or detained, may *sue* the State for redress as provided by law.

shall, in so far as they do not conflict with the laws or the rules and discipline of the army and navy, apply to the officers and men of the army and of the navy.

Chapter III. The Imperial Diet

Article XXXIII. The Imperial Diet shall consist of two Houses: the House of Peers and the House of Representatives.

Article XXXIV. The House of Peers shall, in accordance with the Ordinance concerning the House of Peers, be composed of members of the Imperial Family, of Nobles, and of Deputies who have been nominated by the Emperor.

Article XXXV. The House of Representatives shall be composed of members elected by the people, according to the provisions of the Law of Election.

Article XXXVI. No one can at one and the same time be a member of both Houses.

Article LIII. The Members of both Houses shall, during the session, be free from arrest, unless with the consent of the House, except in cases of flagrant delicts, or of offenses connected with a state of internal commotion or with a foreign trouble.

Chapter IV. The Diet

Article 41. The Diet shall be the highest organ of state power, and shall be the sole law-making organ of the State.

Article 42. The Diet shall consist of two Houses, namely the House of Representatives and the House of Councillors.

Article 43. Both Houses shall consist of elected members, representative of all the people.

The number of the members of each House shall be fixed by law.

Article 44. The qualifications of members of both Houses and their electors shall be fixed by law. However, there shall be no discrimination because of race, creed, sex, social status, family origin, education, property or income.

Article 45. The term of office of members of the House of Representatives shall be four years. However, the term shall be terminated before the full term is up in case the House of Representatives is dissolved.

Article 46. The term of office of members of the House of Councillors shall be six years, and the election of half the members shall take place every three years.

Article 47. Electoral districts, method of voting and other matters pertaining to the method of election of members of both Houses shall be fixed by law.

Article 48. No person shall be permitted to be a member of both Houses simultaneously.

Article 49. Members of both Houses shall receive appropriate annual payment from the national treasury in accordance with law.

Article 50. Except in cases provided by law, members of both Houses shall be exempt from apprehension while the Diet is in session, and any members apprehended before the opening of the session shall be freed during the term of the session upon demand of the House.

Article LII. No Member of either House shall be held responsible outside the respective Houses, for any opinion uttered or for any vote given in the House. When, however, a Member himself has given publicity to his opinions by public speech, by documents in print or in writing, or by any other similar means, he shall, in the matter, be amenable to the general law.

Article 51. Members of both Houses shall not be held liable outside the House for speeches, debates or votes cast inside the House.

Article XLI. The Imperial Diet shall be convoked every year.

Article XLII. A session of the Imperial Diet shall last during three months. In case of necessity, the duration of a session may be prolonged by Imperial Order.

Article 52. An ordinary session of the Diet shall be convoked once per year.

Article XLIII. When urgent necessity arises, an extraordinary session may be convoked, in addition to the ordinary one.

The duration of an extraordinary session shall be determined by Imperial Order.

Article 53. The Cabinet may determine to convoke extraordinary sessions of the Diet. When a quarter or more of the total members of either House makes the demand, the Cabinet must determine on such convocation.

Article XLIV. The opening, closing, prolongation of session and prorogation of the Imperial Diet, shall be effected simultaneously for both Houses.

In case the House of Representatives has been ordered to dissolve, the House of Peers shall at the same time be prorogued.

Article XLV. When the House of Representatives has been ordered to dissolve, Members shall be caused by Imperial Order to be newly elected, and the new House shall be convoked within five months from the day of dissolution.

Article 54. When the House of Representatives is dissolved, there must be a general election of members of the House of Representatives within forty (40) days from the date of dissolution, and the Diet must be convoked within thirty (30) days from the date of the election.

When the House of Representatives is dissolved, the House of Councillors is closed at the same time. However, the Cabinet may in time of national emergency convoke the House of Councillors in emergency session.

Measures taken at such session as mentioned in the proviso of the preceding paragraph shall be provisional and shall become null and void unless agreed to by the House of Representatives within a period of ten (10) days after the opening of the next session of the Diet.

Article LI. Both Houses may enact, besides what is provided for in the present Constitution and in the Law of the Houses, rules necessary for the management of their internal affairs.

Article 55. Each House shall judge disputes related to qualifications of its members. However, in order to deny a seat to any member, it is necessary to pass a resolution by a majority of two-thirds or more of the members present.

Article XLVI. No debate can be opened and no vote can be taken in either House of the Imperial Diet, unless not less than one third of the whole

Article 56. Business cannot be transacted in either House unless one-third or more of total membership is present.

number of the Members thereof is present.

Article XLVII. Votes shall be taken in both Houses by absolute majority. In the case of a tie vote, the President shall have the casting vote.

Article XLVIII. The deliberations of both Houses shall be held in public. The deliberations may, however, upon demand of the Government or by resolution of the House, be held in secret sitting.

[Cf. Article LI.]

Article XXXVII. Every law requires the consent of the Imperial Diet.

Article XXXVIII. Both Houses shall vote upon projects of law submitted to it by the Government, and may respectively initiate projects of law.

Article XXXIX. A Bill, which has been rejected by either the one or the other of the two Houses, shall not be again brought in during the same session.

Article XL. Both Houses can make representations to the Government, as to laws or upon any other subject. When, however, such representations are not accepted, they cannot be made a second time during the same session.

All matters shall be decided, in each House, by a majority of those present, except as elsewhere provided in the Constitution, and in case of a tie, the presiding officer shall decide the issue.

Article 57. Deliberation in each House shall be public. However, a secret meeting may be held where a majority of two-thirds or more of those members present passes a resolution therefor.

Article 58. Each House shall select its own president and other officials.

Each House shall establish its rules pertaining to meetings, proceedings and internal discipline, and may punish members for disorderly conduct. However, in order to expel a member, a majority of two-thirds or more of those members present must pass a resolution.

Article 59. A bill becomes a law on passage by both Houses, except as otherwise provided by the Constitution.

A bill which is passed by the House of Representatives, and upon which the House of Councillors makes a decision different from that of the House of Representatives, becomes a law when passed a second time by the House of Representatives by a majority of two-thirds or more of the members present.

The provision of the preceding paragraph does not preclude the House of Representatives from calling for the meeting of a joint committee of both Houses, provided for by law.

Failure by the House of Councillors to take final action within sixty (60) days after receipt of a bill passed by the House of Representatives, time in recess excepted, may be determined by the House of Representatives to constitute a rejection of the said bill by the House of Councillors.

Article 60. The budget must first be submitted to the House of Representatives.

Upon consideration of the budget, when the House of Councillors makes a decision different from that of the House of Representatives, and when no agreement can be reached even through a joint committee of both Houses, provided for by law, or in the case of failure by the

Article LIV. The Ministers of State and the Delegates of the Government may, at any time, take seats and speak in either House.

Article XLIX. Both Houses of the Imperial Diet may respectively present addresses to the Emperor.

Article L. Both Houses may receive petitions presented by subjects.

Chapter IV. The Ministers of State and the Privy Council

Article LV. The respective Ministers of State shall give their advice to the Emperor, and be responsible for it.

All laws, public ordinances, and imperial rescripts, of whatever kind, that relate to the affairs of state require the counter-signature of the Minister of State.

Article LVI. The Privy Council shall, in accordance with the provisions for the organization of the Privy Council, deliberate upon the important matters of State, when they have been consulted by the Emperor.

House of Councillors to take final action within thirty (30) days, the period of recess excluded, after the receipt of the budget passed by the House of Representatives, the decision of the House of Representatives shall be the decision of the Diet.

Article 61. The second paragraph of the preceding article applies also to the Diet approval required for the conclusion of treaties.

Article 62. Each House may conduct investigations in relation to government, and may demand the presence and testimony of witnesses, and the production of records.

Article 63. The Prime Minister and other Ministers of State may, at any time, appear in either House for the purpose of speaking on bills, regardless of whether they are members of the House or not. They must appear when their presence is required in order to give answers or explanations.

Article 64. The Diet shall set up an impeachment court from among the members of both Houses for the purpose of trying those judges against whom removal proceedings have been instituted.

Matters relating to impeachment shall be provided by law.

Chapter V. The Cabinet

Article 65. Executive power shall be vested in the Cabinet.

Article 66. The Cabinet shall consist of the Prime Minister, who shall be its head, and other Ministers of State, as provided for by law.

The Prime Minister and other Ministers of State must be civilians.

The Cabinet, in the exercise of executive power, shall be collectively responsible to the Diet.

Article 67. The Prime Minister shall be designated from among the members of the Diet by a resolution of the Diet. This designation shall precede all other business.

If the House of Representatives and the House of Councillors disagree and if no agreement can be reached even through a joint committee of both Houses, provided for by law, or the House of Councillors fails to make designation within ten (10) days, exclusive of the period of recess, after the House of Representatives has made designation, the decision of the House of Representatives shall be the decision of the Diet.

Article 68. The Prime Minister shall appoint the Ministers of State. However a majority of their number must be chosen from among the members of the Diet.

The Prime Minister may remove the Ministers of State as he chooses.

Article 69. If the House of Representatives passes a non-confidence resolution, or rejects a confidence resolution, the Cabinet shall resign en masse, unless the House of Representatives is dissolved within ten (10) days.

Article 70. When there is a vacancy in the post of Prime Minister, or upon the first convocation of the Diet after a general election of members of the House of Representatives, the Cabinet shall resign en masse.

Article 71. In the cases mentioned in the two preceding articles, the Cabinet shall continue its functions until the time when a new Prime Minister is appointed.

Article 72. The Prime Minister, representing the Cabinet, submits bills, reports on general national affairs and foreign relations to the Diet and exercises control and supervision over various administrative branches.

Article 73. The Cabinet, in addition to other general administrative functions, shall perform the following functions:

Administer the law faithfully; conduct affairs of state.

Manage foreign affairs.

Conclude treaties. However, it shall obtain prior or, depending on circumstances, subsequent approval of the Diet.

Administer the civil service, in accordance with standards established by law.

Prepare the budget, and present it to the Diet.

Enact cabinet orders in order to execute the provisions of this Constitution and of the law. However, it cannot include penal provisions in such cabinet orders unless authorized by such law.

Decide on general amnesty, special amnesty, commutation of punishment, reprieve, and restoration of rights.

Article 74. All laws and cabinet orders shall be signed by the competent Minister of State and countersigned by the Prime Minister.

Article 75. The Ministers of State, during their tenure of office, shall not be subject to legal action without the consent of the Prime Minister. However, the right to take that action is not impaired hereby.

Chapter V. The Judicature

Article LVII. The Judicature shall be exercised by the Courts of Law according to law, in the name of the Emperor.

The organization of the Courts of Law shall be determined by law.

Article LX. All matters that fall within the competency of a special Court shall be specially provided for by law.

Article LVIII. The judges shall be appointed from among those who possess proper qualifications according to law.

No judge shall be deprived of his position, unless by way of criminal sentence or disciplinary punishment.

Rules for disciplinary punishment shall be determined by law.

Chapter VI. Judiciary

Article 76. The whole judicial power is vested in a Supreme Court and in such inferior courts as are established by law.

No extraordinary tribunal shall be established, nor shall any organ or agency of the Executive be given final judicial power.

All judges shall be independent in the exercise of their conscience and shall be bound only by this Constitution and the laws.

Article 77. The Supreme Court is vested with the rule-making power under which it determines the rules of procedure and of practice, and of matters relating to attorneys, the internal discipline of the courts and the administration of judicial affairs.

Public procurators shall be subject to the rule-making power of the Supreme Court.

The Supreme Court may delegate the power to make rules for inferior courts to such courts.

Article 78. Judges shall not be removed except by public impeachment unless judicially declared mentally or physically incompetent to perform official duties. No disciplinary action against judges shall be administered by any executive organ or agency.

Article 79. The Supreme Court shall consist of a Chief Judge and such number of judges as may be determined by law; all such judges excepting the Chief Judge shall be appointed by the Cabinet.

The appointment of the judges of the Supreme Court shall be reviewed by the people at the first general election of members of the House of Representatives following their appointment, and shall be reviewed again at the first general election of members of the House of Representatives after a lapse of ten (10) years, and in the same manner thereafter.

In cases mentioned in the foregoing paragraph, when the majority of the voters favors the dismissal of a judge, he shall be dismissed.

Matters pertaining to review shall be prescribed by law.

The judges of the Supreme Court shall be retired upon the attainment of the age as fixed by law.

All such judges shall receive, at regular stated intervals, adequate compensation which shall not be decreased during their terms of office.

Article 80. The judges of the inferior courts shall be appointed by the Cabinet from a list of persons nominated by the Supreme Court. All such judges shall hold office for a term of ten (10) years with privilege of reappointment, provided that they shall be retired upon the attainment of the age as fixed by law.

The judges of the inferior courts shall receive, at regular stated intervals, adequate compensation which shall not be decreased during their terms of office.

Article 81. The Supreme Court is the court of last resort with power to determine the constitutionality of any law, order, regulation or official act.

Article LIX. Trials and judgments of a Court shall be conducted publicly. When, however, there exists any fear that such publicity may be prejudicial to peace and order, or to the maintenance of public morality, the public trial may be suspended by provision of law or by the decision of the Court of Law.

Article 82. Trials shall be conducted and judgment declared publicly.

Where a court unanimously determines publicity to be dangerous to public order or morals, a trial may be conducted privately, but trials of political offenses, offenses involving the press or cases wherein the rights of people as guaranteed in Chap. III of this Constitution are in question shall always be conducted publicly.

Article LXI. No suit at law, which relates to rights alleged to have been infringed by the illegal measures of the administrative authorities, and which shall come within the competency of the Court of Administrative Litigation specially established by law, shall be taken cognizance of by a Court of Law.

CHAPTER VI. FINANCE

Article LXII. The imposition of a new tax or the modification of the rates (of an existing one) shall be determined by law.

However, all such administrative fees or other revenue as are in the nature of compensation for services rendered shall not fall within the category of the above clause.

The raising of national loans and the contracting of other liabilities to the charge of the National Treasury, except those that are provided in the Budget, shall require the consent of the Imperial Diet.

Article LXIII. Existing taxes shall, in so far as they are not altered by new laws, continue to be collected as heretofore.

Article LXIV. The annual expenditure and revenue of the State shall, in the form of an annual Budget, receive the consent of the Imperial Diet. Any expenditure which exceeds the appropriations set forth under the various heads of the Budget, or those not provided for in the Budget, shall be referred subsequently to the Imperial Diet for its approval.

Article LXV. The Budget shall be first laid before the House of Representatives.

Article LXIX. In order to supply unavoidable deficits in the Budget, and to meet requirements unprovided for in the same, a reserve fund shall be established.

Article LXVI. The expenditure in respect of the Imperial House shall be

CHAPTER VII. FINANCE

Article 83. The power to administer national finances shall be exercised as the Diet shall determine.

Article 84. No new taxes shall be imposed or existing ones modified except by law or under such conditions as law may prescribe.

Article 85. No money shall be expended, nor shall the State obligate itself, except as authorized by the Diet.

Article 86. The Cabinet shall prepare and submit to the Diet for its consideration and decision a budget for each fiscal year.

Article 87. In order to provide for unforeseen deficiencies in the budget, a reserve fund may be authorized by the Diet to be expended upon the responsibility of the Cabinet.

The Cabinet must get subsequent approval of the Diet for all payments from the reserve fund.

Article 88. All property of the Imperial Household shall belong to the defrayed every year out of the National Treasury, according to the present fixed amount for the same, and shall not hereafter require the consent thereto of the Imperial Diet, except in case an increase thereof is found necessary.

Article LXVIII. In order to meet special requirements the Government may ask the consent of the Imperial Diet to a certain amount as a continuing expenditure fund, for a previously fixed number of years.

State. All expenses of the Imperial Household shall be appropriated by the Diet in the budget.

Article 89. No public money or other property shall be expended or appropriated for the use, benefit or maintenance of any religious institution or association, or for any charitable, educational or benevolent enterprises not under the control of public authority.

Article LXXII. The final account of the expenditure and revenue of the State shall be verified and confirmed by the Board of Audit, and it shall be submitted by the Government to the Imperial Diet, together with the report of verification of the said Board.

The organisation and competency of the Board of Audit shall be determined by law separately.

Article 90. Final accounts of the expenditures and revenues of the State shall be audited annually by a Board of Audit and submitted by the Cabinet to the Diet, together with the statement of audit, during the fiscal year immediately following the period covered.

The organization and competency of the Board of Audit shall be determined by law.

Article 91. At regular intervals and at least annually the Cabinet shall report to the Diet and the people on the state of national finances.

Article LXVII. The fixed expenditure based upon the supreme powers of the Emperor and set forth in this Constitution, and such expenditure as may have arisen by the effect of law, or as appertains to the legal obligations of the Government, shall be neither rejected nor reduced by the Imperial Diet, without the concurrence of the Government.

Article LXX. When there is urgent need for the adoption of measures for the maintenance of the public safety, and when in consequence of the state either of the domestic affairs or of the foreign relations, the Imperial Diet cannot be convoked, the necessary financial measures may be taken by means of an Imperial Ordinance. In such cases as those mentioned in the preceding clause the matter shall be submitted to the Imperial Diet at its next session for its approval.

Article LXXI. When the Imperial Diet has not voted on the Budget, or when the Budget has not been brought into actual existence, the Government shall carry out the Budget of the preceding year.

Chapter VIII. Local Self-Government

Article 92. Regulations concerning organization and operations of local public entities shall be fixed by law in accordance with the principle of local autonomy.

Article 93. The local public entities shall establish assemblies as their deliberative organs, in accordance with law.

The chief executive officers of all local public entities, the members of their assemblies, and such other local officials as may be determined by law shall be elected by direct popular vote within their several communities.

Article 94. Local public entities shall have the right to manage their property, affairs and administration and to enact their own regulations within law.

Article 95. A special law, applicable only to one local public entity, cannot be enacted by the Diet without the consent of the majority of the voters of the local public entity concerned, obtained in accordance with law.

Article LXXIII. When it has become necessary in future to amend the provisions of the present Constitution, a project to the effect shall be submitted to the Imperial Diet by Imperial Order.

In the above case, neither House can open the debate, unless not less than two-thirds of the whole number of Members are present, and no amendment can be passed, unless a majority of not less than two-thirds of the Members is obtained.

Chapter IX. Amendments

Article 96. Amendments to this Constitution shall be initiated by the Diet, through a concurring vote of two-thirds or more of all the members of each House and shall thereupon be submitted to the people for ratification, which shall require the affirmative vote of a majority of all votes cast thereon, at a special referendum or at such election as the Diet shall specify.

Amendments when so ratified shall immediately be promulgated by the Emperor in the name of the people, as an integral part of this Constitution.

Chapter X. Supreme Law

Article 97. The fundamental human rights by this Constitution guaranteed to the people of Japan are fruits of the

Article LXXIV. No modification of the Imperial House Law shall be required to be submitted to the deliberation of the Imperial Diet.

No provision of the present Constitution can be modified by the Imperial House Law.

age-old struggle of man to be free; they have survived the many exacting tests for durability and are conferred upon this and future generations in trust, to be held for all time inviolate.

Article 98. This Constitution shall be the supreme law of the nation and no law, ordinance, imperial rescript or other act of government, or part thereof, contrary to the provisions hereof, shall have legal force or validity.

The treaties concluded by Japan and established laws of nations shall be faithfully observed.

Article 99. The Emperor or the Regent as well as Ministers of State, members of the Diet, judges, and all other public officials have the obligation to respect and uphold this Constitution.

Chapter XI. Supplementary Provisions

Article 100. This Constitution shall be enforced as from the day when the period of six months will have elapsed counting from the day of its promulgation.

The enactment of laws necessary for the enforcement of this Constitution, the election of members of the House of Councillors and the procedure for the convocation of the Diet and other preparatory procedures necessary for the enforcement of this Constitution may be executed before the day prescribed in the preceding paragraph.

Article 101. If the House of Councillors is not constituted before the effective date of this Constitution, the House of Representatives shall function as the Diet until such time as the House of Councillors shall be constituted.

Article 102. The term of office for half the members of the House of Councillors serving in the first term under this Constitution shall be three years. Members falling under this category shall be determined in accordance with law.

Article 103. The Ministers of State, members of the House of Representatives and judges in office on the effective date of this Constitution, and all other public officials who occupy positions corresponding to such positions as are recognized by this Constitution shall not forfeit their positions automatically on account of the enforcement of this Constitution unless otherwise specified by law. When, however, successors are elected or appointed under the provisions of this Constitution, they shall forfeit their positions as a matter of course.

Chapter VII. Supplementary Rules

[Article LXXIII.]

[Article LXXIV.]

Article LXXV. No modification can be introduced into the Constitution, or into the Imperial House Law, during the time of a Regency.

Article LXXVI. Existing legal enactments, such as laws, regulations, Ordinances, or by whatever names they may be called, shall, so far as they do not conflict with the present Constitution, continue in force.

All existing contracts or orders, that entail obligations upon the Government, and that are connected with expenditure, shall come within the scope of Article LXVII.

APPENDIX III

Security Treaty of 1960

TREATY OF MUTUAL COOPERATION AND SECURITY BETWEEN JAPAN AND THE UNITED STATES OF AMERICA

Japan and the United States of America,

Desiring to strengthen the bonds of peace and friendship traditionally existing between them, and to uphold the principles of democracy, individual liberty, and the rule of law,

Desiring further to encourage closer economic cooperation between them and to promote conditions of economic stability and well being in their countries,

Reaffirming their faith in the purposes and principles of the Charter of the United Nations, and their desire to live in peace with all peoples and all governments,

Recognizing that they have the inherent right of individual or collective self-defense as affirmed in the Charter of the United Nations.

Considering that they have a common concern in the maintenance of international peace and security in the Far East,

Having resolved to conclude a treaty of mutual cooperation and security,

Therefore agree as follows:

ARTICLE I

The Parties undertake, as set forth in the Charter of the United Nations, to settle any international disputes in which they may be involved by peaceful means in such a manner that international peace and security and justice are not endangered and to refrain in their international relations from the threat or use of force against the territorial integrity or political independence of any state, or in any other manner inconsistent with the purposes of the United Nations.

The Parties will endeavor in concert with other peace-loving countries to strengthen the United Nations so that its mission of maintaining international peace and security may be discharged more effectively.

ARTICLE II

The Parties will contribute toward the further development of peaceful and friendly international relations by strengthening their free institutions, by bringing about a better understanding of the principles upon which these institutions are founded, and by promoting conditions of stability and well being. They will seek to eliminate conflict in their international economic policies and will encourage economic collaboration between them.

ARTICLE III

The Parties, individually and in cooperation with each other, by means of continuous and effective self-help and mutual aid will maintain and develop, subject to their constitutional provisions, their capacities to resist armed attack.

ARTICLE IV

The Parties will consult together from time to time regarding the implementation of this Treaty, and, at the request of either Party, whenever the security of Japan or international peace and security in the Far East is threatened.

Article V

Each Party recognizes that an armed attack against either Party in the territories under the administration of Japan would be dangerous to its own peace and safety and declares that it would act to meet the common danger in accordance with its constitutional provisions and processes.

Any such armed attack and all measures taken as a result thereof shall be immediately reported to the Security Council of the United Nations in accordance with the provisions of Article 51 of the Charter. Such measures shall be terminated when the Security Council has taken the measures necessary to restore and maintain international peace and security.

Article VI

For the purpose of contributing to the security of Japan and the maintenance of international peace and security in the Far East, the United States of America is granted the use by its land, air and naval forces of facilities and areas in Japan.

The use of these facilities and areas as well as the status of United States armed forces in Japan shall be governed by a separate agreement, replacing the Administrative Agreement under Article III of the Security Treaty between Japan and the United States of America, signed at Tokyo on February 28, 1952, as amended, and by such other arrangements as may be agreed upon.

Article VII

This treaty does not affect and shall not be interpreted as affecting in any way the rights and obligations of the Parties under the Charter of the United Nations or the responsibility of the United Nations for the maintenance of international peace and security.

Article VIII

This Treaty shall be ratified by Japan and the United States of America in accordance with their respective constitutional processes and will enter into force on the date on which the instruments of ratification thereof have been exchanged by them in Tokyo.

Article IX

The Security Treaty between Japan and the United States of America signed at the city of San Francisco on September 8, 1951 shall expire upon the entering into force of this Treaty.

Article X

This Treaty shall remain in force until in the opinion of the Governments of Japan and the United States of America there shall have come into force such United Nations arrangements as will satisfactorily provide for the maintenance of international peace and security in the Japan area.

However, after the Treaty has been in force for ten years, either Party may give notice to the other Party of its intention to terminate the Treaty, in which case the Treaty shall terminate one year after such notice has been given.

In Witness Whereof the undersigned Plenipotentiaries have signed this Treaty.

Done in duplicate at Washington in the Japanese and English languages, both equally authentic, this nineteenth day of January, 1960.

For Japan:

Nobusuke Kishi
Aiichiro Fujiyama
Mitsujiro Ishii
Tadashi Adachi
Koichiro Asakai

For the United States of America:

Christian A. Herter
Douglas MacArthur II
J. Graham Parsons

Index